The Japanese Seizure of Korea: 1868-1910

A Study of Realism and Idealism in International Relations

by Hilary Conroy

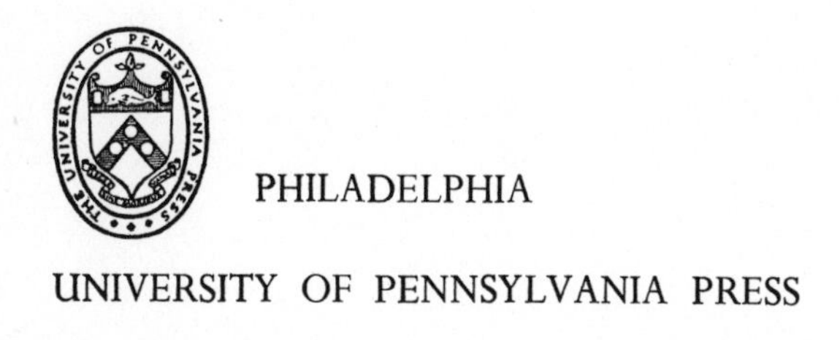

PHILADELPHIA

UNIVERSITY OF PENNSYLVANIA PRESS

PUBLISHED IN GREAT BRITAIN, INDIA, AND PAKISTAN
BY THE OXFORD UNIVERSITY PRESS
LONDON, BOMBAY, AND KARACHI

LIBRARY OF CONGRESS CATALOG CARD NUMBER: 60-6936

PRINTED IN GREAT BRITAIN
BY W. & J. MACKAY & CO LTD, CHATHAM

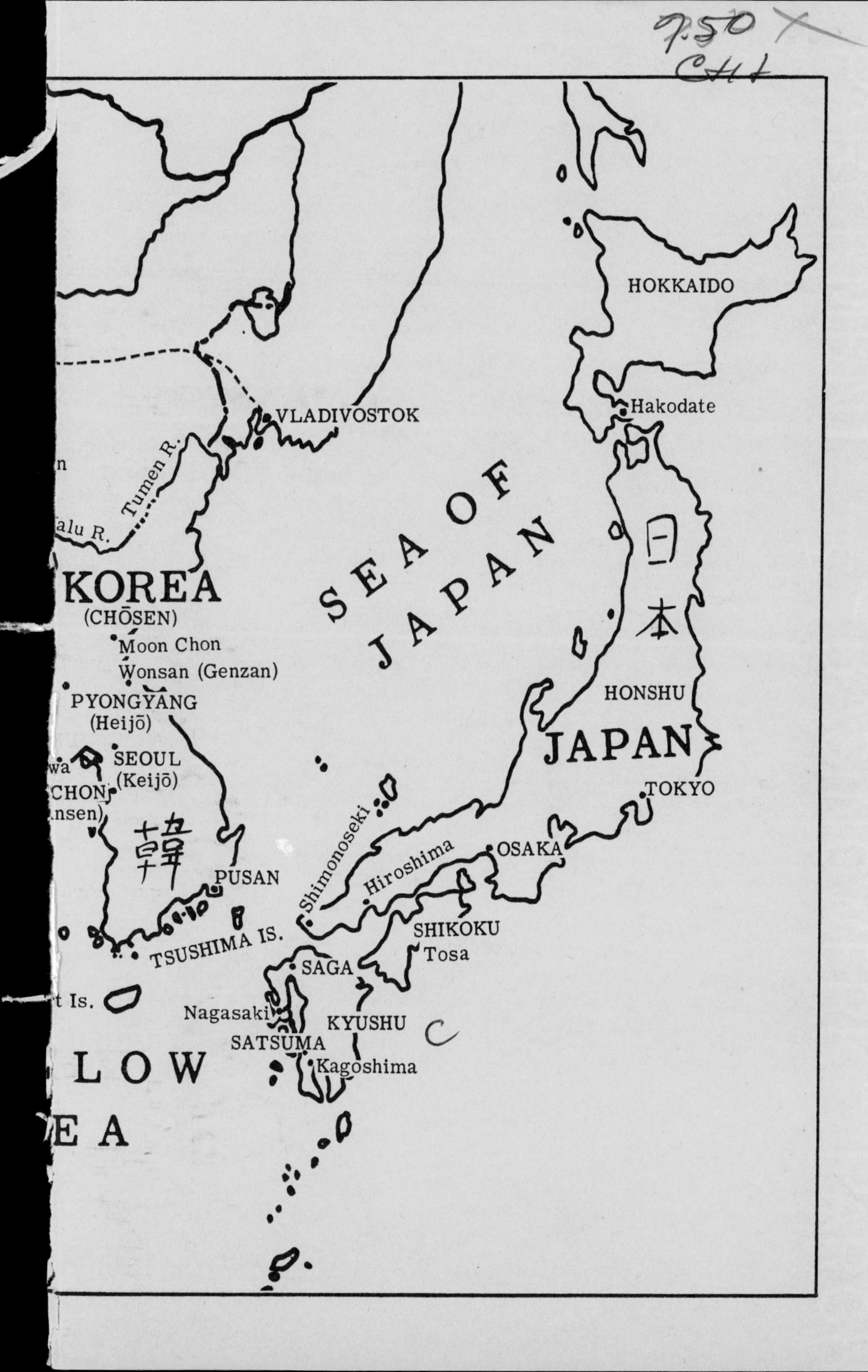

7.50 X
CH+
HOKKAIDO
Hakodate
VLADIVOSTOK
Tumen R.
alu R.
SEA OF
JAPAN
日
本
KOREA
(CHŌSEN)
Moon Chon
Wonsan (Genzan)
PYONGYANG
(Heijō)
SEOUL
(Keijō)
韓
HONSHU
JAPAN
TOKYO
Shimonoseki
Hiroshima
OSAKA
PUSAN
TSUSHIMA IS.
SHIKOKU
Tosa
SAGA
Nagasaki
KYUSHU
SATSUMA
Kagoshima
LOW
EA

The Japanese Seizure of Korea : 1868-1910

second instance to those scholars with whom he has argued along the pages of this book. In that regard he wishes to emphasize that it is the very excellence of their ideas and interpretations which has stimulated him to criticize them.

In addition, specific acknowledgments are due the following Japanese scholars and friends, who helped him find his way through Japanese archives and whose interest and help in this study were invaluable: Professor Yoshitake Oka of Tokyo University, Messrs. Yoshiyuki Sakurai and Tokue Shibata of Tokyo Metropolitan University, Nobutoshi Hagihara and Taketoshi Nishida of Tokyo University, Masaru Masaki and Kenji Kita. Also a special thanks to Mrs. Evelyn B. McCune for the loan of her late husband's document collection. My wife was chief typist, ably assisted at various crises by Miss Joan Betson. But none of these is responsible for errors of fact and interpretation, which discredits the author reserves to himself.

University of Pennsylvania
September, 1959

HILARY CONROY

Japanese terms used frequently in text

Chōsen. Japanese name for Korea.

Chōsen Mondai. The Korean Problem. Japanese documents and newspapers frequently used this term to denote the whole complex of Japanese-Korean relationships.

Gappō. Korean "merger" with Japan. Meaning annexation.

Jiyū Minken. People's rights. The many sided movement for freedom, progress, etc. which swept Japan in the 1880's and early 1890's.

Jōi. Expel the Barbarians (i.e., foreigners, especially Westerners). Part of the slogan of the Imperial restoration movement which defeated and ousted the Tokugawa shogunate in 1868. The term was later used by reactionary societies. See also Sonnō jōi.

Kunrentai. Training troops (Korean, trained by Japanese officers).

Mankan Kōkan. Exchanging Korea for Manchuria. Name attached to Japanese proposal to Russia, before Russo-Japanese war.

Seikan. Conquer Korea, as advocated by some Japanese in the early 1870's.

Seikan Ron. The argument over whether to conquer Korea (1873).

Sonnō Jōi. Revere the Emperor and expel the Barbarians (Westerners). Slogan of the Imperial restoration movement of the 1860's and later of the reactionary societies.

Abbreviations used in footnotes

Archives Japanese Ministry of Foreign Affairs Archives on Library of Congress microfilm.

NGB *Nihon Gaikō Bunsho* (or *Dai Nihon Gaikō Bunsho*). Japanese foreign affairs documents series, published by the Japanese Foreign Office, Tokyo.

Contents

List of Illustrations

(Prints by courtesy of Mr. Yoshiyuki Sakurai, from his collection)

The illustrations follow page 352

The Japanese Seizure of Korea : 1868-1910

I

Seikan Ron: Insult, Revenge and a Long Shadow

The Meiji Restoration (1868) was for Japan a momentous event. The forces for political, social, economic, and cultural change which it unleashed transformed an archaic feudal society into a modern state at a pace which still leaves historians breathless. There is a glory of achievement about it which is apt, however, to blind those who study it to the fact that, along with the political power and prestige which it brought to its leaders, it also brought shame. For, with their decision to modernize Japan and do business with the Western world, the samurai architects of the Restoration violated their honor and their tradition, not only in the immediate short-range sense but to an historical depth of more than 200 years. This they did in a land where honor and tradition had long been accounted first virtues, insisted upon as such by the very warrior class from which these leaders emerged. Indeed, the presumption that they had superior honor and tradition was the principal justification of samurai rule in Japan. And the traditions of the political and social order which they had erected proclaimed their devotion to a Confucianist isolationism (*sakoku*), whose chief tenet was that Westerners, being barbarians possessed of a subversive ideology, must be kept out of Japan.

These Restoration leaders in their own generation, having branded the Tokugawa shogunate as weak and traitorous for truckling to foreigners, had risen to fame and power on the solemn principle of *Sonnō Jōi*, exhalt the Emperor, expelling his and their barbarian enemies. But for practical reasons, best epitomized in the bombardments of Kagoshima (1863) and Shimonoseki (1864) by the Westerners, they abandoned half their principle and more of their tradition, accepted the humiliating unequal treaties the Tokugawa had made with the West and the sight of Westerners strolling the streets of their greatest cities, and prepared to re-pattern their country after models they had formerly scorned or despised. This was the practical, intelligent choice, and they charted the new course with determination to see it through. And yet, though their minds were sure, their feelings were not. Deep feelings, sincerity (*seijitsu*), for which the Japanese have always had great respect even though the object of the sincerity may be false, argued no. In their hearts, if a historian may use the term, they were sorely troubled that the old ways were inadequate to meet the exigencies of the new situation, and they were ashamed that they with samurai swords and bushidō spirit, could not hold back the Western wave.

This is why the Korean refusal to recognize or even to accept the documents of the new Restoration government made its leaders so angry. For the Koreans, in suggesting that they were betraying the old traditions, said what sincerity also said and, as with the man who curses his wife for reminding him of something of which he himself is ashamed, the wrath that consumed Japan's Great Council of State over the Korean issue was fierce beyond all proportion to the question at hand.

Seikan Ron is an expression which occurs again and again in Japanese documents and newspapers of the 1870's. With its Confucian overtones it means "the argument [*Ron*] over whether Japan should inflict righteous punishment [for the insult] by conquering Korea [*Seikan*]," though "Conquer Korea Argument" is a good enough translation for practical purposes. The argument reached its climax in Tokyo in October, 1873. One scholar has used the term "great divide"[1] to define its place in Meiji political history, and certainly one can call to mind evidence in plenty to support that idea. The argument split the Restoration leadership, which had hitherto operated as a closely knit group, squarely down the middle. It resulted in assassinations, riots, and rebellions, including a full-scale civil war (the so-called Satsuma Rebellion). It resulted in the death of several of the leading protagonists, including both the loser of the argument (Saigō Takamori) and the winner (Ōkubo Toshimichi). Indeed, at its height, the pressure of the quarrel reached such intensity that worry over it ruptured a blood vessel in the brain of the Prime Minister, Sanjō Sanetomi, who had desperately tried to find a compromise.

The story is so full of emotional power and samurai spirit that Japanese historians seem to write of it with a particular relish, and it has in fact inspired a three-act drama by Yamamoto Yuzō,[2] a drama, which, with no embellishment of history, has the grip of a psychological-mystery thriller. It has everything but humor, which fact may also be important in our historical appraisal.

"Great Divide" it was in splitting the leaders of the Meiji government into irreconcilable factions. These have been called by various names: anti and pro conquest, or peace party and war party, or domestic affairs faction and overseas expansion faction, or capitalistic group and feudalistic group. And after the affair was over, with the victory and control of the government going to the anti-conquest group, we may speak of "Government" versus "anti-Government" or simply "ins" against "outs." But in accepting the term Great Divide, we must be careful in using it. We must not accent the division too strongly, even though it was a division to the death of the two leading protagonists. Regardless of the division, all parties to the dispute had a great deal in common. They were all of samurai heritage, all participants in the work of the Restoration,

[1] Nobutaka Ike, *The Beginnings of Political Democracy in Japan* (Baltimore: Johns Hopkins University Press, 1950), p. 53.

[2] Yamamoto Yuzō, *Saigō to Ōkubo* (Saigō and Ōkubo) (Tokyo: Kadokawa Bunko, ed., 1954).

and even on the subject of conquering Korea, many writers have argued, it was to become not so much a question of *whether* but of *when*, a *jiki no mondai* as the Japanese say, a question of timing. At any rate if we look closely at the attitudes of the key participants early in the dispute, before the final crystallization into pro-conquest and anti-conquest camps, we see that many of them, especially of the latter group, were indefinite or unclear in their attitude. Ōkuma Shigenobu, who was at first pro-conquest, then neutral, then anti-conquest, is described as completely "impossible" in his attitude by Mutsu Munemitsu, a pro-conquest man.[3] Kido Kōin, anti-conquest in the October climax, did not even attend crucial earlier meetings to argue against the Seikan (Conquer Korea) idea. Ōkubo, who emerged as leader of the anti-conquest party, had to be persuaded away from his original determination not to enter the quarrel at all. And he was ever suspicious that Iwakura Tomomi, who had assumed the role of chief persuader, would in fact desert the anti-conquest cause before the dispute was over. So suspicious was he that he extracted a signed testament of support from Iwakura (and also from Sanjō) before entering the arena.[4]

Among the pro-conquest group, a similar indefiniteness of attitude becomes clear after the event. Saigō retired to Satsuma to lick his wounds and defy the government, but there is no indication that he seriously kept at the Korean problem. What he seems to have wanted was a last, peaceful staying place (*anju no chi*),[5] and in fact such expressions as we have of Saigō indicate that two years later at the time of the Kanghwa Incident, when Koreans fired on

[3] Watanabe Ikujirō, *Meijishi Kenkyū* (Study of Meiji History) (Tokyo: Kyōritsu Shuppan, 1944; rev. ed.), p. 111. Watanabe's study is the author's chief source for this and other intimate details of the inner cabinet argument over Seikan. Though somewhat old fashioned it is still the best source for such details because Professor Watanabe had access to many materials, including court documents, to which other scholars have not had access.

[4] *Ibid.*, pp. 87, 112-16. These matters will be discussed in more detail subsequently in this chapter.

[5] Tōyama Shigeki, *Meiji Ishin* (The Meiji Restoration) (Tokyo: Iwanami Shōten, 1951), p. 332.

a Japanese surveying party, he was opposed to strong Japanese retaliation.[6] Saigō died still in opposition to the triumphant anti-conquest party, but other advocates of Seikan were not so steadfast. Many lived on to participate in Japanese political life and even in the government. The aforementioned Mutsu was later to be foreign minister at some of the most critical stages in the development of the Meiji government's long-range Korean policy. And when one remembers that Itō Hirobumi, right-hand man to Ōkubo and Iwakura in 1873, was Mutsu's prime minister, one can see that the ultimate course of the Conquer Korea Argument, if one follows it beyond the fierce October days of 1873, was toward compromise, not division. It is interesting to read the reminiscing comments of surviving participants in the great political struggle over Korea, published in leading Japanese newspapers to commemorate Korean Annexation Day, August 22, 1910.[7] Clearly, a sense of mellowed satisfaction had come over them all. The time was all right, the solution good enough. Forty years of worrying and quarreling over what the Japanese by then called the Korean Problem (*Chōsen Mondai*) was at an end and a sort of prideful rosiness hung about, epitomizing the fact that, despite bitterness and political feuding along the way, the direction of Japanese opinion and policy was toward compromise, toward general national agreement on Korea.

But before proceeding further into the long-range implications of the great argument of 1873, it is necessary to consider in some detail the embitterment of Japanese-Korean relations which accompanied the establishment of the Restoration government in Japan and the policy argument which emerged therefrom among Japanese leaders. Japanese-Korean relations had been quiescent, if not friendly, since the advent of the Tokugawa to power in Japan in 1600. Koreans had not forgotten Hideyoshi's adventurous

[6] Tōyama Shigeki, "Seikan Ron, Jiyūminken Ron, Hōken Ron" (The Conquer Korea, People's Rights and Feudalism Arguments), *Rekishigaku Kenkyū*, No. 143 (Jan. 1950), p. 5.

[7] See below, chap. viii, pp. 389–392.

invasion of their country in the 1590's, but the Tokugawa had made a clean reversal of his expansionist policy. During Tokugawa times Korea and Japan reached a standoffish sort of *modus vivendi*, whereby congratulatory missions were exchanged and a limited trade conducted through the intermediation of the Japanese lord of Tsushima island, located midway between Japan and Korea. These were further facilitated by the maintenance of a small Japanese settlement at Pusan, carefully circumscribed and watched by Korean officials in order to keep personal contact between Japanese and Korean subjects at a minimum.[8] Actually, the chief interest in the whole arrangement lay with Tsushima, for that island's economy benefited considerably from exchange with the Koreans and it stood to lose a great deal if Korean relationships were further curtailed or ruptured. Indeed, the leaders of the Restoration party in Japan quickly grasped this fact and clearly distrusted Tsushima as a representative of the Japanese national interest in Korean negotiations. Nevertheless, it was through the Daimyō of Tsushima that both the last messages of the Tokugawa government and the first messages of the new Restoration government were delivered to Korea.

Rumors were flying fast in the closing months of 1867 and early 1868 as the four-clan coalition (Satsuma, Chōshū, Tosa, Hizen) defied the Tokugawa and in the name of the emperor began to move forces against them. Korean officials had been watchful and wary of developments in Japan for some time and the extent to which they were worried about the direction of affairs there may be surmised from a series of inquiries which they addressed to the Tokugawa government through Lord Sō of Tsushima. They were troubled, they said, about strange Western ships off the Korean

[8] George M. McCune, "The Exchange of Envoys between Korea and Japan during the Tokugawa Period," *Far Eastern Quarterly*, V (1946), 308-25; "The Japanese Trading Post at Pusan," *Korean Review*, I, (1) (1948), 11-15; "Korean Relations with China and Japan, 1800-1864" (Ph.D. diss., University of California, Berkeley, 1941). Carl F. Bartz, Jr., "The Korean Seclusion Policy, 1860-1876" (Unpub. Ph.D. diss., University of California, Berkeley, 1952), pp. 30-34.

coast; they had heard that Nakahama Manjirō (who had visited America) was negotiating on behalf of the shogunate with a certain Chinese at Edo for the construction of some eighty ships at Shanghai—to what purpose not being clear. The Tokugawa government responded with reassurances. The eighty-ship rumor was false; Japan was building its strength, but was friendly with foreigners; she regretted Korea's trouble with Westerners, and she planned to send envoys to Korea to explain the world situation to the Koreans. Lord Sō received the reply from Edo but, being aware of the decline in Tokugawa fortunes, decided against sending the reply directly to Korea. Instead, under the date of November 20, 1867, he forwarded the whole correspondence to Iwakura of the pro-Imperial party at Kyoto.[9]

During the spring of 1868, as the imperial armies moved victoriously against the Tokugawa, the Restoration government, still in process of organization, instructed Lord Sō that "transactions with Korea should be based on the orders of the imperial government"[10] and that he should be careful "not to blemish our national authority" in dealing with Korea.[11] Sō promised to obey.[12] In June, 1868, however, he was instructed that "from now on all diplomatic relations must be through the Foreign Office in Osaka. This applies to relations with Korea."[13] Then on August 10, Sō was instructed to "inform Korea that the Tokugawa Shogunate has been abolished and the new government is now established." As for diplomatic formalities with Korea, "these will be decided after domestic affairs [in Japan] are settled."[14] In conformance with this instruction the Lord of Tsushima notified the Korean government as follows: "It is a privilege for me to inform you that our

[9] Gaimushō (Japanese Foreign Office), *Dai Nihon Gaikō Bunsho* or *Nihon Gaikō Bunsho* (Japanese Foreign Affairs Documents) (Tokyo: 1936-present, continuing series), I: 1, pp. 69-80. This series hereafter referred to as NGB.

[10] *Ibid.*, p. 573.

[11] *Ibid.*, p. 574.

[12] *Ibid.*, pp. 657-59.

[13] *Ibid.*, p. 791.

[14] *Ibid.*, p. 931.

government has changed back into the Emperor's hands, and we are glad to have good relations with your country. I was authorized to contact your government by the Emperor's government. We hope to maintain good relations with you forever." Sō, in a separate document, explained something of the emperor's 2000-year-old authority and the fact that now, after a period in which the governing power had rested with the Tokugawa, the emperor wished to reassume control of the government, including foreign relations.[15]

During the winter and spring of 1868–69 there were many conferences between Tsushima representatives and Korean officials at Pusan, to whom these documents were delivered, but the Koreans refused to accept them on the grounds that they were improperly written, particularly because they referred to a Japanese imperial line and emperor and asked for some new type of "official" relations. By June, 1869, Lord Sō was convinced that an impasse had been reached when he notified the Japanese foreign office as follows: "Korea does not accept our notification of the establishment of the new government. This is because they wish to avoid intercourse with the Imperial government. There is no other recourse than to negotiate with the Korean King face to face in his capital. This they may resist with force. Therefore you must decide whether to adopt a strong policy."[16]

Meanwhile, among high Japanese officials, at least one had anticipated the impasse, and had laid down his recommendation on the matter of Korea. On March 13, 1869, Councilor Kido, who as leader of the Chōshū element of the Restoration coalition had great influence, addressed a memorandum to Sanjō and Iwakura in which he stated that he did not believe the Korean matter could be resolved "without recourse to arms and weapons" and that the establishment of order inside Japan being of utmost importance "it is not reasonable to resort to arms at once. . . Our national

[15] NGB, I: 2, pp. 690, 692-93.
[16] NGB, II: 2, p. 217; II:3, pp. 410-12.

strength is not sufficient."[17] As a result of this and as a result of Lord Sō's official notification of the breakdown of negotiations, there was considerable discussion of the Korean matter amongst high government officials, and a fact-finding mission under Sada Hakubō was sent out by the Foreign Office to Tsushima and Pusan. A number of interesting points regarding relations with Korea were uncovered. The anomalous position of Tsushima was for the first time fully realized. It was found that Tsushima had not only received annual stipends of rice (some 30,000 *koku*) and money from the Tokugawa, but had accepted a dependent-country (*zokkoku*) relationship with Korea, out of which it received rice, beans, and money from Korea. Also, the trade at Pusan had been conducted in such a way as to underscore Japanese inferiority. Tsushima had used a half seal provided by the Koreans to identify its trading ships and every year had sent a tribute ship to Korea which brought back documents (i.e., instructions) from Korea. About three hundred Tsushima Japanese were living in a prescribed area at Pusan, the gate to which was closely watched by Korean officials who forbade the Japanese either entry or exit from the area after dark. Tsushima, however, had needed the Korean trade badly because it was a "poor and lonely island."[18]

Thus there was a forgiving note in the investigators' report, but it was emphasized that this state of affairs could not be allowed to continue. The Foreign office concurred that relations with Korea should be taken out of Tsushima's hands.[19] During the course of the investigation Lord Sō urged upon the imperial government that he should have a higher title, that of prefectural governor, thus to enhance his bargaining position in relations with Korea. That this was stamped "Disapproved" may be taken to imply some measure of criticism of Tsushima's past handling of the Korean relationship.[20]

[17] NGB, II:1, pp. 205-8.
[18] Sada Inquiry, May 15, 1870: NGB, III, 131-38.
[19] Foreign Office to Council of State, May 15, 1870: NGB, III, 138-43.
[20] Jan. 8, 1870: NGB, II:3, 473-74.

The fact-finders had also looked into the matter of Korea's relationship with China. "Korea," it was observed, "is subordinate to China and sends tribute to China every year . . . but it has the power to rule itself. . . . Orders from China are not necessarily accepted. Korea liked the Ming, but not the Ch'ing and therefore preserves Ming ceremonies. Even with regard to foreign relations Korea decides for itself, but if there is difficulty they refer the matter to Peking. Up to this time we have heard nothing about Korea's reporting to China about Japan. But Korea is very cunning. . . ." The matter of trade was also considered and an interesting observation made: "The price of goods in Japan is high, in Korea low, so Japanese selling goods in Korea cannot expect to profit. . . . Therefore the method of trading should be changed. As other countries do in Japan with Western money as the medium of exchange, so Japan should force the value of Korean money down. . . . Even if we open three harbors in Korea, if we do not circulate our money we cannot expect much profit. . . ."[21]

After submitting their fact-finding report, the investigating team proposed to the Foreign Office that "now is a good time to send an envoy to Korea," noting that China was deeply involved in the Tientsin Incident (1870) in which some Frenchmen had been murdered.[22] Imperial Councilor Kido, who had evidently been rethinking his position on Korea (he was tentatively appointed imperial envoy to Korea in January, 1870, but had made no move to activate this) now reversed his opposition to the idea of strong action and in a statement to his fellow councilors dated July 24, 1870, he supported the idea that Japan should make an attempt to open intercourse with Korea. "I do not think China will oppose Korean-Japanese intercourse, and in anticipation of Korea's not accepting our proposal we should prepare military forces, warships, munitions, and machines. I think the Imperial Conference has set the basic policy, but I should like to have a clarification as to what

[21] Sada Inquiry, *op. cit.*
[22] NGB, III, 147.

is to be done if the worst happens [hostilities] while I am envoy to Korea."[23] Kido's shift in position at this stage is difficult to explain. Tabohashi suggests that it was due to the influence upon him of one Ōshima Masatomo, a Tsushima official and personal friend of Kido who hoped to regain for Tsushima a preferred position in a larger Korean relationship.[24] Indeed, Kido's subsequent return to a more cautious approach may be taken as evidence that some such passing influence was at work.

It is clear also that the Foreign Office (*Gaimushō*), where Ōkuma Shigenobu was rising, was not eager to have either Tsushima or Kido become directly involved in Korean negotiations, and they submitted a proposal that Foreign Office representatives now be dispatched to Korea to negotiate directly with Korean officials prior to the dispatch of an imperial envoy. This was approved by the Council of State (*Dajōkan*), and one Yoshioka Kōki of the Foreign Office was appointed to head a mission to Pusan to negotiate with Korean officials and through them to contact the Korean court at Seoul. Moriyama Shigeru, who had earlier been a member of the fact-finding commission, became a member of this delegation also; others were Sagara Masaki and Hirotsu Koshin. They went first to Tsushima where they obtained an interpreter, Urase, and then went on to Pusan to contact the district Korean government office, called by the Japanese *Toraifu*.[25] However, it is interesting to note, in view of the Ōshima-Kido Foreign Office rivalry noted above, that just prior to the arrival of the Foreign Office team in Tsushima Ōshima had dispatched this same Urase to Pusan on a hasty mission to make one final effort to bolster Tsushima's fading prospect of handling the negotiations. Urase pleaded with the Korean reception officer that he might lose his

[23] Council of State to For. Off., Jan. 4, 1870: NGB, II:3, 437. Kido to Council of State, July 24, 1870: NGB, III, 145-47.

[24] Tabohashi Kiyoshi, *Kindai Nissen Kankei no Kenkyū* (A Study of Modern Japanese-Korean Relations) (Seoul: Chōsen Sōtokufu Chūsūin, 1940), I, 300. This work hereafter cited as Tabohashi (1940).

[25] NGB, III, 148-49, 170-71.

position if the negotiations did not give some evidence of success. The Korean admitted that "this would not be good," but went on to say that Korea was a "dependent country" to China and was accustomed to calling China the "High Country" and her ruler "Emperor," whereas the Japanese ruler had been called "Great King." "Korea cannot change and call Japan by the same title as China. That is the reason your communications have been refused."[26] Thus Urase's unofficial effort failed and he returned to Tsushima to become official interpreter for Yoshioka's mission. Shortly thereafter, Lord Sō addressed an official communication to "higher authority" asking to be relieved of his duties with regard to Korean intercourse inasmuch as "the Emperor is now carrying this on through the Foreign Office." One senses that he was piqued, for he appended a reminder that "of course, our interpreters are well versed on Korea, but they can be hired by the Foreign Office."[27]

The Yoshioka mission then entered upon a year of very frustrating negotiations, which they began with a recommendation, that was to win the hearty approval of the Foreign Office, to the effect that all relations with Korea, including the right of trade, be taken over from Tsushima.[28] They decided that the Japanese of the Pusan agency, as manned by Tsushima people, had in some cases been "impolite, savage, and cruel, having exploited Koreans for money," and, to insure that Korean officials would have no further grounds for complaint, they "cleaned up" the Pusan agency, sending many of the people back to Tsushima. Korea being a "stagnant, stubborn, and shrewd country," it would be necessary to use "sometimes strong words and sometimes sweet words," but in the end "if we keep patience they will understand us step by step."[29]

[26] Memo of conversation, Sept. 14, 1870: NGB, III, 150-54.

[27] Jan. 9, 1871: NGB, III, 173-74.

[28] Sawa, etc., to Ōkuma, May 25, 1871: *Ōkuma Kenkyū Shitsu* (Ōkuma document collection at Waseda University), Doc. No. K679.

[29] Yoshioka to Foreign Minister, Feb. 24 (2 letters), 26, 1872 and to Pusan agency, Feb. 24, 26, 1872: NGB, V, 304-8.

This proved an overly optimistic estimate. Even though the Japanese envoys tried to use the idea of closing down the Japanese agency at Pusan as a threat implying hostile action, the Toraifu did nothing but stall. They had to refer every question to Seoul, and, whenever the Japanese envoys pressed for an answer, a new delegation of Koreans would appear with whom it was necessary to start the procedure all over again. Answers again and again were promised "sometime later," and, although in earlier stages of the negotiations this was intimated to mean twenty-five or thirty days, a Korean official finally admitted that this might mean "six or seven or ten years." "Our envoy said, 'just write it down,' got a memo, and returned to Japan."[30] After Yoshioka gave up, another Foreign Office official, Hanabusa Yoshimoto, who was also aided by Moriyama and Hirotsu, tried his hand at Korean diplomacy, beginning in the late summer of 1872. He, like the others, made no progress. Korea would not even acknowledge the existence of the new Japanese government. And during the later stages of the efforts at negotiation, insulting inscriptions appeared on the walls of the Japanese compound at Pusan and some Japanese were subjected to bodily attack by Korean youths, actions which, the Japanese could point out, had "had no counterpart in the previous 200 years of peaceful Japanese-Korean relations."[31]

Meanwhile Seikan Ron was "boiling up"[32] in Japan. A preview of the intensity the argument was to assume is provided by two incidents which occurred during the course of the negotiations just described. In July, 1871, a Kagoshima samurai, who feared that the impending effort to open official relations with Korea would result in war, committed *harakiri* at the gate of the Imperial Council Building, while, as was characteristic of such political suicides in

[30] For. Min. Soejima to Prime Minister, Sept. 12, 1872: NGB, V, 341-42. Also For. Min. to Pr. Min., June 12, 1872: NGB, V, 317 *et seq.*

[31] Tabohashi (1940), I, 293-94; also see II, 891-93.

[32] Itō Hirobumi used this expression in a contemporary memorandum, No. 141: *Kensei Shiryō Shitsu* (archive of materials relating to the history of constitutional government, Diet Building, Tokyo).

Japan, clutching a last explanatory letter to his bosom. He said that the Japanese people were poor, had little to eat; Japan had many problems. There was "no time to condemn the impoliteness of Korea." There was no assurance that war with Korea would result in a quick victory. It was very dangerous to regard Korea as merely a small country. See the example of Hideyoshi! "If I die my superiors may hear my voice."[33] The caliber of this man, who thus took his own life in the hope that by so doing he might impede the development of the Conquer Korea idea, may perhaps be estimated from the fact that his younger brother, Mori Arinori (Yūrei), as first Japanese minister to the United States and then minister of education, was the principal architect of Japan's universal education system and would certainly rank among the ablest and most enlightened of the Meiji leaders.

On the other hand pro-conquest sentiment had an almost equally spectacular first manifestation. In March, 1872, a Foreign Office official, Maruyama Sakuraku, was abruptly dismissed from his post and arrested for private plotting. He had become dissatisfied with the government's "cautious" approach in the conduct of the Korean negotiations, and, finding his superiors at the Foreign Office unreceptive to bolder ideas, he began to organize a Conquer Korea party and to collect and borrow money for the purpose of outfitting a private warship for attack on Korea.[34] The scheme was foiled when news of it leaked to unsympathetic government officials. But despite its failure a war party was beginning to make strong headway in Japan.

Saigō Takamori of Satsuma, who had been commander of the Satsuma forces in the imperial coalition against the Tokugawa and whose subsequent elevation to the rank of field marshall made him the highest military officer of the new government, gradually

[33] Nakayama Yasumasa (comp.), *Shimbun Shūsei Meiji Hennenshi* (Newspaper Collection, Meiji Period) (Tokyo: Zaisei Keizai Gakkai, 1934-36), I, 338-39. This collection hereafter cited as *Meiji Hennenshi*. Cf. Tabohashi (1940), I, 309-10. Ōkubo Toshiaki, *Mori Arinori* (Tokyo: Bunkyō Shoin, 1944), 8-9.

[34] Tabohashi (1940), I, 309-10.

emerged as the leader of this group. Saigō's role in the Conquer Korea (Seikan) movement may be described simply and emphatically as pro-war, pro-conquest, pro-expansion. In fact, his leader ship of the Seikan cause was so dynamic and so spectacular that his name has been idolized by Japanese ultra-nationalist-expansionist societies ever since. Yet it has curious psychological overtones. It is not the leadership of a conqueror, who, like Hideyoshi, is dreaming of empire with himself at the head of it. There is rather an air of defeatism, of futility in Saigō's attitude, which is underscored by a detail which all Japanese accounts emphasize: Saigō insisted that he should go to Korea first, before any troops went, to incite the Koreans to kill him, thus creating a clear *casus belli.*[35]

The dramatist Yamamoto in his historical play dealing with these events has Ōkubo analyse Saigō's attitude as follows: "I think Saigō wanted to find a place to die. He wanted Korea to be that place. He is continually seeking a place to die. He is a very lonely person and perhaps only I understand him. He would like to sacrifice his own life [and thereby] let young soldiers render distinguished service."[36] Historically Saigō played out the death theme in 1877 four years after the climax of the Seikan argument. This was in leading the desperate but futile rebellion of Satsuma samurai against the Meiji government which he had helped to create. Why such melancholia in this man of might and fury?

To understand Saigō better it is helpful to recall Toynbee's concept of the alternatives facing the members of a dying civilization, what he so picturesquely calls Herodianism (accommodation)

[35] *Ibid.*, I, 328. Watanabe, *op. cit.*, 95-96. Tōyama, "Seikan Ron . . .", 4. Kiyozawa Kiyoshi, *Gaiseika to shite no Ōkubo Toshimichi* (Ōkubo Toshimichi as a Statesman) (Tokyo: Chūō Kōron Sha, 1942), 11. Tanaka Sōgorō, *Seikan Ron Seinan Sensō* (The Conquer Korea Argument and the War of the Southwest) (Tokyo: Hakuyōsha, 1939), 63. Smimasa Idditti, *The Life of Marquis Shigenobu Ōkuma* (Tokyo: Hokuseido, 1940). 155.

Three letters of Saigō, recently published in translation, clearly express his wish to die in Korea. See Wm. Theodore deBary (ed.), *Sources of Japanese Tradition* (New York: Columbia University Press, 1958), 655-56.

[36] Yamamoto, *op. cit.*, 84-85. Cf. Idditti, *op. cit.*, 153; "weary of this world".

and Zealotism (die-hard resistance). In this frame of reference Saigō might best be described as a Herodian who tried to turn back, and yet knew that Zealotism could promise nothing, except death. Saigō knew as well as his fellow architects of the Meiji Restoration that the old order had to be amended, that Confucianist-isolationism and a feudal society were inadequate for a Japan which had to compete in the modern world. He played a leading role in the establishing of the new government, 1868–69, then returned to Satsuma to see to local problems, but in 1871 he returned to the central government to lend his great weight to pushing through the final steps in the abolition of feudalism. For the first five years of the Meiji (Enlightened) era, he co-operated in the far-reaching changes which the times demanded. He trod the road of accommodation; he wore a Western suit. It is interesting to see him literally wearing a Western suit in a portrait printed in Sir George Sansom's *The Western World and Japan.*[37] Does he look uncomfortable in it? Saigō tried to keep pace with the new era. But its demands were unrelenting.

The old order was dying and each new returnee from a European inspection tour had a new idea to hasten its demise. Even in Saigō's own special preserve, the military, a young Chōshū clansman, Yamagata Aritomo, who returned from such a tour in 1870, was pushing ideas of universal military service which, though difficult to refute in terms of efficiency and national power, would further wreck old order traditions and ideals. The crux here was the position of the samurai class, specifically those samurai of southwestern Japan who had followed Saigō in the War of the Restoration. They had expected to be the principal beneficiaries of the governmental reordering which took place after the defeat of the Tokugawa. The new leadership being of them, by them, and for them, a neo-shogunate of the southwest had seemed in store. But having assumed the reins of power the "neo-shogunate" found itself facing a startling reality. *Jōi* had failed; the Western barbarians had not

[37] (New York: Alfred A. Knopf, 1950), 331. Cf. Idditti, *op. cit.*, 138-39.

been driven from Japan. In fact, they were pressing now politely but relentlessly into Japan as they had into China. Unless the new leaders could co-ordinate the resources of the empire more effectively than was possible under the feudal system, they would soon be taking orders from Westerners.

They abolished feudalism, but this inevitably made the social and economic position of the samurai class insecure. The Restoration government as a whole was by no means insensitive to this. It went as far as it could, given the circumstances, to maintain the privileged position of the samurai, giving them a new honorific designation, *shizoku* (gentry), and almost bankrupting itself in efforts to pay them off for their land contracts with pensions, bonds, and opportunities to buy in cheaply on government-developed business enterprises.[38] These policies were designed to give the samurai a head start in the new non-feudal Japan, and they accomplished this in many individual cases. But they required on the part of the samurai an attuning toward business, and a considerable swallowing of pride. The samurai could no longer count on his two swords and his hereditary feudal privileges; if he managed his financial affairs poorly, there was nothing to prevent his slipping into impoverishment. Numerous samurai were unwilling or unable to make the adjustment. Scornful of business activities, they merely squandered their money settlements, and they became an embittered and complaining element in Meiji society.

Saigō, of all the members of the Restoration government, was the most responsive to their dissatisfaction. He was a man of great "sincerity." Less adaptable than others, he remained truer to tradition, albeit to the outdated tradition of military feudalism. He was one of those embarrassing people who in a time of broadening horizons and new challenges become over indulgent to those very

[38] Thomas C. Smith calls attention to the role of Iwakura and Ōkubo in this in his *Political Change and Industrial Development in Japan: Government Enterprise, 1868-1880* (Stanford: Stanford University Press, 1955), 33-34.

institutions of the old order which are least supportable from the viewpoint of rational analysis. Saigō is described by a Japanese writer as a man of "stomach" (*hara*), possessed of the courage and vigor to lead a million troops, but to be contrasted with men of "mind."[39] "Stomach" told him that the prestige and traditional values of the samurai must be revitalized. Their profession was the honorable one of arms, not the petty affairs of trade. An expedition to Korea to avenge insults would provide honorable employment for dislocated samurai. However, the fact that this was second-rate Jōi was not lost on Saigō. What the Koreans said was essentially true. Japan had abandoned the old order, had taken up barbarian ways. He had himself been a party to the process, and he was ashamed. He would expiate his failures in Korea with death, and his beloved samurai would have a final moment of glory before a new world of modernization closed in on them, a new world which he could not face.

Thus the disillusioned Herodian view of Saigō goes far to explain his vigorous yet curiously fatalistic championing of the Conquer Korea idea, and also the aura of tragic grandeur with which subsequent generations of Japanese have cloaked his memory. In a sense, all Japanese since 1868 have been caught up in the machinery of modernization and most have at some time or other felt an urge to turn back.[40]

The war party began to take definite shape during 1872. During that year Saigō discussed the possibility of a Korean expedition with other government leaders, and he found several of them congenial to the idea, notably Itagaki Taisuke and Gotō Shōjirō of Tosa, Etō Shimpei of Hizen, and Soejima Taneomi, also of Hizen, who had become the dominant figure at the Foreign Office when

[39] Matono Hansuke, *Etō Nampaku* (Biography of Etō Shimpei) (Tokyo: Nampaku Kenshokai, 1928), I, Foreword, 4.

[40] On the *Jōi* idea as related to Korea see Watanabe, *op. cit.*, p. 69 and Tanaka, *op. cit.*, 61. A recent study of Saigō estimates him to be a small and unintelligent man. unworthy of his subsequent fame. But this does not alter the fact that he has had it. See Tsuda Saōkichi, "Saigō Takamori Ron" (The Argument about Saigō Takamori), *Chūō Kōron* (Oct. 1957), 280-87. Also note 73 below.

Ōkuma turned his principal attention to finance. Japanese accounts of the formation of this Seikan party generally make a commendable but not very successful effort to classify its respective elements into subgroups, assigning variant motives to each.[41] The results are in some ways more confusing than helpful, and it may be sufficient to say that their outlook, like Saigō's, was conditioned by home-grown class and sectional prejudices—except for Soejima who began with these but who absorbed in addition some sophisticated (?) Western imperialist advice. This will be discussed shortly, but in general it should be emphasized that the Conquer Korea advocates exhibited a narrowness of outlook which contrasts sharply with the broader nation-world view which other members of the governing circle were developing.

The opportunity for the advancement of an expansionist policy in 1872 was in fact largely the result of the absence from the country of those members of the inner government circle who would be most likely to oppose it. These were Iwakura Tomomi, court aristocrat and vice-president of the Imperial Council beneath Sanjō, who was actually a much stronger personality than Sanjō (Iwakura was also minister of foreign affairs, but Soejima became head of the Foreign office in his absence); Kido Kōin, of Chōshū, who was increasingly resentful of Saigō's growing power in state affairs; Itō Hirobumi, also of Chōshū, Kido's protégé; Ōkubo Toshimichi, of Satsuma, long-time friend of Saigō, but unlike him in personality, a man of craft and caution. They left Japan in December, 1871, bound on a round-the-world tour to attempt to secure treaty revision for Japan, and, except for a hurried return trip from the United States by Ōkubo and Itō in the spring of 1872 to obtain certain credentials, these men were largely out of touch with events in Japan and the Far East until their respective individual returnings in the spring, summer, and early autumn of

[41] E.g. Tabohashi (1940), I, 323-25; Tanaka, *op. cit.*, 3, 8, 60-61; Kokuryūkai (ed.), *Seinan Kiden* (Records of the Southwest, i.e., Satsuma Rebellion) (Tokyo: Kokuryūkai Hombu, 1908-12), I: 2, 648-49, lists some ten subdivisions.

1873. It cannot be said that these members of the Iwakura mission were *ipso facto* opposed to a strong Korean policy. Kido's earlier leaning toward Seikan has already been alluded to, and it may be said of them in general that they had not to this point arrived at a decision or a policy on Korea, either singly or as a group. They were all as irritated as Saigō at Korean intransigence, and the only point they had urged upon their colleagues who remained at home was that nothing drastic should be done in their absence, not alone on Korea but on anything.[42]

The first concrete result of the informal discussions of 1872 among the stay-at-homes was the dispatch of two of Saigō's personal followers, Kitamura and Beppu, on an intelligence gathering mission to Korea in August of that year. Shortly thereafter others were sent to China to gain an estimate of Chinese military strength and the likelihood of Chinese interference in Korean affairs.[43]

Meanwhile, a related problem provided the opportunity for taking soundings at Peking and contributed to the consolidation of the Seikan sentiment. This was the Liu-ch'iu (Ryūkyū) Formosan dispute, which had had its beginnings in November, 1871, when sixty-nine Liu-ch'iu islanders were shipwrecked off Formosa. They were attacked by the savage Botan tribe of south Formosa and some fifty-four were killed. The matter was brought to the attention of the Japanese government by Kirino Toshiaki, commander of Satsuma's Kumamoto garrison and a close friend of Saigō. This was deemed a matter of interest to Japan because of Satsuma's long-standing relationship with Liu-ch'iu, which in Satsuma eyes amounted to consideration of these islanders as Satsuma subjects. This was despite the even longer standing

[42] Idditti, *op. cit.*, 143, says there was a signed agreement to this effect. I could not find it.

[43] Kuzū Yoshihisa (ed.), *Nisshi Kōshō Gaishi* (History of Sino-Japanese Negotiations) (Tokyo: Kokuryūkai, 1938-39), I, 69-70. Kuzū Yoshihisa (ed.), *Tōa Senkaku Shishi Kiden* (Records of Pioneer East Asia Adventurers) (Tokyo: Kokuryūkai, 1933-36), I, 38. Marius Jansen, *The Japanese and Sun Yat-sen* (Cambridge: Harvard University Press, 1954), 24.

tributary relationship between the Liu-ch'iu king and the Chinese court. Saigō urged a punitive expedition against the Formosans. A division of opinion developed, however, whereby Inoue Kaoru, the finance minister, a Chōsū clansman and close friend of the absent Itō and Kido, opposed the venture as likely to upset the finances of the government. Imperial councilor Ōkuma also urged caution, arguing that the Liu-ch'iu relationship with China must be clarified before any undertaking might be considered.

Soejima supported Saigō, and was in turn able to offer in support of their contention the advice of a newly appointed Foreign Office adviser, Charles W. LeGendre. LeGendre, a Frenchman by birth, had married an American woman, immigrated to the United States, become an American citizen, and risen to the rank of major-general in the American Civil War. Later as American consul at Amoy he had become involved in Formosan affairs as early as 1867, when an American ship, the *Rover*, off course because of a storm, put in there, only to meet hostile natives who massacred the whole ship's company, including the captain and his wife. After that, LeGendre had gone to Formosa in company with Chinese officers, sought out the chief of the aborigines, and obtained an agreement that there would be no further attacks on Americans or Europeans who happened to land there. And after the attack on the Liu-ch'iuans in 1871, LeGendre urged the Chinese to punish the Formosans for violation of this agreement. However, this time the Chinese would not co-operate, taking the view that LeGendre was an intruder into affairs that were none of his business. Mr. Low, the United States minister at Peking, seems to have concurred in this opinion. Shortly thereafter, LeGendre was recalled by President Grant to be minister to Argentina. Enroute home in the late summer of 1872, he stopped in Tokyo. There the United States minister to Japan, Charles E. DeLong, who was inclined to be rather adventurous in the conduct of his office, was in close touch with Soejima and introduced LeGendre to the Japanese Foreign minister as a "Formosan expert." Soejima offered LeGendre a post as adviser to the Foreign Office and he accepted. Regarding Formosa he gave Soejima reassuring advice. The Chinese, he said, though they claimed the island, had never exercised effective jurisdiction over it; therefore it should be regarded as unoccupied and would become the property of whatever country effectively occupied it. And he predicted that America would not oppose its being taken by a friendly country (like Japan).[44]

LeGendre continued to advise the Foreign Office through the critical months of 1873 as the Korea argument and the subordinate but related Formosa argument were coming into focus. There remains no day by day or month by month record of these advices, the original documents having been lost in the Tokyo earthquake of 1923 before scholars made any use of them. But their general tenor may be judged from one document which survived and which was studied by Hori Makoto. It shows that LeGendre favored an aristocratic type of government for Japan, arguing that the position of the *kazoku* (noble) and *shizoku* (military) class must be protected by giving them "public land" and "the leadership of public enterprises." "If you give equal rights to all the people you will have something like the Paris Commune." On foreign policy he said that Korea "by itself is nothing to worry about," but because of its location it constituted "a first step toward Japan." And he urged that Japan seek an alliance with Russia against Britain, develop Hokkaido, and "either control Korea or make Korea strong enough to defend itself." Then Japan could "with Russian acquiescence," advance into "confused China."[45] Another LeGendre document,

[44] NGB, VII, 5-6. See also Yoshino Sakuzō, "Nihon Gaikō no Onjin Shōgun LeGendre" (LeGendre, Benefactor of Japanese Diplomacy), *Meiji Bunka Kenkyū* (July, August 1927). Edward H. House, *The Japanese Expedition to Formosa* (Tokyo, 1875), 5 and Appendix. Kokuryūkai, *Nisshi . . .*, I, 48; *Seinan . . .*, I: 2, 551. Payson J. Treat, *Diplomatic Relations Between the United States and Japan* (Stanford: Stanford University Press, 1932), I, 474-83, notes that U.S. Minister DeLong recommended LeGendre for the Foreign Office post and was reprimanded for it by the State Department. Treat calls him "L.P." LeGendre, which underscores the fact that many things about him are obscure, even his first name, though "Charles W." seems most frequently used.

[45] Hori Makoto, "Beijin LeGendre Kengensho ni tsuite" (Concerning the Proposals of the American LeGendre), *Kokka Gakkai Zasshi*, LI, 5 (May 1937), 114-17, 123-28.

written after he left the Foreign Office advisership, possibly in 1876, has been recently discovered in German archives materials, deposited there by the German representative in Tokyo in 1887. It warns of possible German penetration of the Far East and urges Japan to take Formosa and Korea for the sake of Japanese "security."[46]

Also LeGendre set forth some *ex post facto* judgments on the Conquer-Korea argument in a book called *Progressive Japan: A Study of the Political and Social Needs of the Empire*, which was published in 1878. Here he compares the Japanese temperament to the French:

> It would be most absurd to imagine that modern liberty is necessarily based upon the sovereignty of the people represented by a central assembly. It was upon this erroneous idea that the French, at the end of the eighteenth century, first abolished royalty and the nobility, then all distinctions between classes and individuals, and finally, in 1792, adopted a republican form of government. The state founded upon such a basis, not being suited to the temperament of the people, instead of fostering public freedom . . . absorbed it. . . . So true is it, that a nation, born like an individual, with certain tendencies and dispositions, will always return to them, whatever obstacle may stand in the way.
>
> Japan's civilization has been the work of an aristocracy—the work of a few, who originally imposed their rule by force. The conservation of the civilization must also be the work of an aristocracy.

On Soejima and the Korean question he has the following to say:

> . . . it would require very little ingenuity to make her [Japan] strong. This he [Soejima] proposed to do by opening a new field to the military classes both in Corea and aboriginal Formosa, two countries with which Japan had accounts of long standing to settle. Besides the possession of these two strategical points to any would-be conqueror of either Japan or China had not escaped his penetration; and he felt that, in

[46] Ernest L. Presseisen, "Roots of Japanese Imperialism: A Memorandum of General LeGendre," *Journal of Modern History*, XXIX, 2 (June 1957), 108-11.

presence of the culpable indifference of China regarding these countries, which in their condition were but abandoned grounds, inviting occupation by any power that would think fit to possess their territory, Japan had a right, if not to annex both Corea and aboriginal Formosa, at least to place them under her protecting arm. . . .

The main argument against this plan was that it was to be apprehended that a new field for distinction and glory, once having been given to the samurai, possibly, afterwards, nothing could ever stop them in their ambitious pretentions. This, it is reported, Mr. Soyeshima thought, was not to be feared; for by the side of the war-like samurai he would place a free people militarily organized on the North German plan and by which after their labors in both aboriginal Formosa and Corea had been completed, they would be restrained in their duty pending the time in the natural order when they would be absorbed by it. And besides, from patriotism, the very source of the motion in which he proposed to keep all the native elements of reorganization, he expected to produce the equilibrium of their powers, the security of the nation and the regeneration of Asia. . . . This was the manner in which he, a consummate Chinese scholar and a skeptic at heart, but a Shintoist both by the force of custom and duty, wished to put to use even the superstitious aspirations of the fanatical sects of the old school, and make them fulfill the prophecy of the past ages. . . . And, thus, Mr. Soyeshima had shown himself a true reformer. Although he did not hesitate to advise doing away with anything of the past that had outgrown its national usefulness still he never exhibited of the wreckless [*sic*] disposition for changes of foreign growth, which Mr. Shimadzu so justly ascribed to some of the members of the present government. . . .[47]

LeGendre's advice was adventurous, if not sound, and though we cannot be sure how much, it certainly contributed something to the advancement of expansionist sentiment in the Japanese government.

In the same month that LeGendre began tendering his advice to the Japanese Foreign Office, though he seems to have had no prior

[47] "General" LeGendre, *Progressive Japan: A Study of the Political and Social Needs of the Empire* (New York and Yokohama: C. Levy, 1878), 7-9, 25, 97-99.

connection with arrangements for this, the Meiji government took its first clear-cut step toward expansion. On September 14, 1872, an imperial edict was issued, proclaiming the kingdom of Liu-ch'iu abolished and establishing in its place a Ryūkyū Han (fief). Its king became a Japanese peer, and the foreign relations of the islands were taken over by the Japanese Foreign Office.

Thus retroactively, at least, the Japanese government could call the Liu-ch'iu shipwrecks Japanese subjects, and, if it were to launch a punitive expedition against Formosa, something of a legal foundation could be claimed. Bold spirits in Japan were beginning to see the Liu-ch'ius, Formosa, and Korea as overseas activity grounds for restless samurai; Soejima was carefully setting the diplomatic stage. He next sought to forestall possible Chinese interference against Japanese action in any one of these areas. In November, 1872, Soejima petitioned the emperor for appointment as envoy extraordinary and minister plenipotentiary to the Chinese court. The official job at hand was to exchange ratifications of a treaty of friendship and commerce with China negotiated the preceding year. But in his petition he referred to himself as "the one person who can force the Chinese to recognize our expedition to Formosa." He received the appointment in March, 1873 and, accompanied by LeGendre and Yanagihara Zenko, he proceeded to Peking shortly thereafter. Yanagihara, in conversations with the Tsungli Yamen, called attention to Japanese claims to Liu-ch'iu and suggested the idea of a Japanese expedition to punish those Formosans who had committed outrages against the "Liu-ch'iuan subjects of Japan." The Chinese refused, though there was a vagueness in their answers which was later used advantageously by the Japanese; however the subject was temporarily dropped. Then Yanagihara alluded to Korea, climaxing his remarks with a rhetorical question: "Then concerning peace or war for Korea your country has no authority." Chinese reply, "That is correct." Soejima interpreted this broadly, as evidenced in his report to the Imperial Council on his return to Japan, July 26. "I asked the

Chinese government the relationship between China and Korea. They told me that they permitted complete freedom of internal and external policy for Korea so they had no responsibility for Korea's arrogant attitude." This he called a "guarantee" that China would not interfere with Japan's dispatching either envoys or military power to Korea.[48]

By the time of Soejima's return, Saigō and Itagaki had brought the Council of State (*Dajōkan*) to the brink of a commitment to Seikan. In June, Moriyama reported intensification of difficulties at Pusan and the subject was discussed at a Council meeting that same month. At this meeting Itagaki suggested that a military expedition should be dispatched to Pusan to protect Japanese residents there and at the same time an envoy should be sent to open direct negotiations with the Korean government. Saigō then made his dramatic proposal that before any troops were sent he himself should go ahead as envoy. Itagaki then supported Saigō's idea, and, though no one at the meeting voiced opposition to it, Council President Sanjō ruled that action should be deferred. There the matter rested until the return of Soejima from China, but, just one week after that, on August 3, Saigō addressed a letter to Sanjō in which he recalled that the Korean problem had been in abeyance some five or six years. "If we cannot obtain our objective it will be a matter of shame to posterity. Now is the time to dispatch a special envoy who will make clear their [the Koreans'] incorrectness. I suppose the reason that you have endured this situation until now is that you have been waiting for this opportunity. Therefore I urge you to send me to Korea. I can promise that I will not bring humiliation to Japan. Please decide this as soon as possible." About the same time he wrote to Itagaki, "I do not

[48] Tabohashi (1940), I, 317-18, 321. Watanabe, *op. cit.*, 86. Hyman Kublin, "The Attitude of China during the Liu-ch'iu Controversy, 1871–1881," *Pacific Historical Review*, XVIII, 2 (May 1949), 217-19. Yoshino Sakuzō (ed.), *Meiji Bunka Zenshū* (Collected materials on Meiji Culture) (Tokyo: Nihon Hyōronsha, 1928-30), V, 65. Kokuryūkai, *Nisshi* . . ., I, 57-60. Treat, *op. cit.*, I, 450-83. Alfred Stead (ed.), *Japan by the Japanese* (New York: Dodd, Mead & Co., 1904), 158-59.

pretend to be able to achieve such a diplomatic feat as Mr. Soejima would do, but I am confident that I can accomplish such a thing as getting assassinated." It seems that Saigō's determination to have this appointment was stimulated by a worry that Soejima, newly returned from successful feats of diplomacy in China, might seek the Korea appointment, and he was therefore at pains to argue that a person inexperienced at diplomacy (himself) would bring a clearer definition of issues in Korea than could a seasoned diplomat, who might conceivably neglect honor.

On August 17 another full-dress conference was held at which Saigō's proposal was approved and he was designated to be envoy to Korea. Sanjō himself agreed to it, but, the next day following a conference between himself and the emperor, he told the councilors that the emperor wished to be told of the appointment of Saigō *after* the return of Iwakura. It should be observed that neither Kido, who had returned from the world tour on July 26, nor Ōkubo, who had returned on May 26, participated in these decisions. Kido, who was an imperial councilor, should have attended the August 17 meeting but he deliberately stayed away. Ōkubo, who was a cabinet minister (finance), was not technically an imperial councilor and therefore his absence from the deliberations might, on the surface, be explained by this. At any rate, neither lifted a finger against the proposition before the return of Iwakura, who arrived with Itō and other members of the mission in September. Iwakura immediately moved to have Ōkubo appointed to the Imperial Council. This was an extremely strategic move, for Ōkubo, a Satsuma man and a long-time friend of Saigō, could, if he would, neutralize or even undermine Saigō's dominance of the council. Ōkubo at first refused. He knew that to accept would be to invite a situation wherein he would be the direct antagonist of Saigō. However, Iwakura, with Itō acting as go-between, undertook to persuade him that he would have the full support of himself, Kido, and also Sanjō. Finally on October 10 Ōkubo accepted, with misgivings, for he wrote to Iwakura and Sanjō, "I accept . . . at the risk of my life." At the same time he wrote to his son: "Since there is no one but me to take this responsibility, I take it with the risk of death. Even if I die it will be to my honor. After my death please carry out your father's spirit of patriotism, become a useful person to our country, and work hard."

At the same time Soejima was officially made a councilor also. This would seem to balance out Ōkubo's appointment, but actually Soejima as foreign minister had been in the midst of things all along so that his appointment merely verified a status he had already reached.

With Ōkubo's acceptance an anti-war coalition had been formed, but its strategy had not yet been settled. Sanjō, despite assurances to Ōkubo that he was with the coalition, sought a compromise. On the twelfth he advised Iwakura as follows: "The matter of sending the envoy has already been decided so we cannot change that. But we should postpone the time." On the thirteenth they visited Ōkubo to discuss this idea, but found him angry. Having made up his mind to take up the struggle, he advocated a direct challenge to the war party, and, accusing his partners of weakness, he reminded them of the critical meeting scheduled for the following day. October 14 brought the first of a series of tumultuous Council sessions where the two sides faced each other directly and openly. This was no ordinary conference; whether mentally aware of it or not the participants were emotionally aware of the fact that they had reached a great divide. All present were members of a bankrupt civilization. The issue before them in its broadest ramification was whether to go forward with accommodation to the needs and pressures of the time or to try to turn back. And this was to be decided in an arena of personal relationships wherein the old samurai ethical codes and traditions were still predominant. A heavy sense of honor and betrayal hung over this and the subsequent discussions of the Korean issue.

Saigō won the first round. He bluntly demanded the appointment, as already decided at the August meeting. Iwakura and

Ōkubo spoke in opposition, the latter stressing his concern over domestic problems. Ōki and Ōkuma supported them. (This seems to be Ōkuma's first clear statement of his position. Before Iwakura's return he made no move to oppose the Conquer-Korea idea, and, on October 9, when pressed for an opinion, he said that he did not approve it specifically, but he would not take a stand; he would observe the government's decision without being a part of it.) After some discussion Sanjō admitted that the matter of Saigo's appointment had already been decided and could not be altered. Ōkubo threatened to resign. Ōkuma asked to be excused from the meeting. Saigō demanded to know where he was going, and Ōkuma replied lamely that he had an appointment in Yokohama to attend an evening party with a foreigner. Saigō asked him if he were a minister or not and called it "shameful" that he would think of withdrawing from such a meeting on account of a foreigner's invitation. Ōkuma resumed his seat.

The meeting ended in disagreement, but with no evident weakening in Saigō's position. That night Sanjō sent a letter to Iwakura explaining the difficulties of his position. He suggested that, though Saigō's appointment must stand, he (Sanjō) might be appointed commander of the army and navy, that he might be in a position to curtail the operation.

On October 15 another meeting was held. Saigō did not attend; instead he simply restated his position in a letter to Sanjō. At the meeting Sanjō again upheld Saigō's appointment because "the decision has already been made." On the morning of the seventeenth Iwakura, Ōkubo, and Kido sent their resignations to Sanjō and the third meeting in the series scheduled for that day convened without them. Whether these resignations constituted a stratagem to put pressure on Sanjō is not clear, but this is likely, for Iwakura had written to Itō and Ōkuma on the night of the fifteenth saying that he had not yet given up and summoning them to a strategy conference on the sixteenth. Whether planned as strategy or not the resignations produced that effect in a sudden and dramatic way. Council President Sanjō, who had desperately sought to satisfy both sides, collapsed in the early morning hours of October 18, out of his mind. According to one Dr. Hoffman, the cause was a broken blood vessel in his brain.

With Sanjō incapacitated, Iwakura, as vice-president of the Council, took charge of his own, Ōkubo's and Kido's letters of resignation and assumed the acting presidency of the Council. On October 22 Saigō, Itagaki, Etō, and Gotō visited Iwakura to demand that the "decision of the conference" be put into effect. Iwakura refused saying, "Until my eyes are black [dead] I will not allow you to carry out your idea." The last climactic Council meeting was held on October 23. Iwakura said that he would see the emperor the following day and advise him to reverse the decision earlier presented by Sanjō. Etō admonished him that as acting council president for Sanjō he must represent Sanjō's opinion. "To present two divergent opinions is disloyal to the Emperor." Iwakura replied, "I shall present my opinion alongside the opinion of the former minister; I think my opinion is the best policy." At this point Kirino threatened Iwakura with his sword but Iwakura would not be moved, "until my eyes are black. . . ."

Saigō and the other pro-war councilors then submitted their resignations. Iwakura went immediately to the emperor, to whom he presented a résumé of the conferences and emphasized that the primary task was to strengthen the country internally. On the twenty-fourth the imperial decision was announced. Conquering Korea was indefinitely postponed; the resignations of Saigō, Itagaki, Etō, Gotō and Soejima were accepted. Even before the imperial decision was announced Saigō had left Tokyo for Kagoshima. On the twenty-fifth the victorious anti-war members gathered at Ōkuma's house and reached agreement on future policy. Terashima Taneomi was appointed minister of foreign affairs to replace Soejima; Itō became minister of industry, Ōkuma of finance, and Katsu Awa, minister of the navy. All were to be members of the Council of State along with Iwakura, Ōkubo, and Kido.[49]

In the course of the great debate, Ōkubo had summed up the anti-war position most eloquently in a seven-point document which perhaps more than the often quoted Charter Oath of 1868 or even the Meiji Constitution of 1889 deserves to be called the foundation document of Meiji Japan. It is dated October, 1873 (no day, no addressee).

In order to govern the country and protect the people it is necessary to have a flexible policy and to watch the world situation; always watching the situation we go forward or retreat. If the situation is bad we simply stop. The reasons why I say that it is too early to send a mission to Korea are as follows: (1) . . . the basis of our government is not yet firmly established. We have made remarkable progress in abolishing the clans, etc., and if we look at the central part of Japan, everything seems accomplished, but if we look at the countryside, many people who oppose this will be seen. We have established a fortress and have good military equipment, so they dare not rise up against us. But if we reveal some weak point, they will be quick to take advantage. There is no special problem now, but we must look to the future. With the restoration many new laws have been promulgated, but people are not yet at ease and they fear our government. In the last two years there have been many misunderstandings and these led to uprisings. It is a truly difficult situation. This is one reason why I am opposed to making war on Korea.

(2) Today government expenditures are tremendous, and income is below expense. Thus if we open fire and send several tens of thousands of men abroad we will incur enormous expense. This will require heavy

[49] My account of these meetings follows mainly Watanabe, *op. cit.*, 85-91, 95, 109-21, 127-28. (See note 3 above for evaluation of Watanabe.) It also draws on Tabohashi (1940), I, 319-27; Idditti, *op. cit.*, 152, 155; Nobutaka Ike, "Triumph of the Peace Party in Japan in 1873", *Far Eastern Quarterly*, II, 3 (May 1943), 293-94; Sanematsu Takamori (adapted by Moriaki Sakamoto), *Great Saigō: The Life of Saigō Takamori* (Tokyo: Kaitakusha, 1942), 348, 364; Sidney D. Brown, "Kido Takayoshi (1833–1877): Meiji Japan's Cautious Revolutionary", *Pacific Historical Review*, XXV, 2 (May 1956), 154-55. These sources add a few details but do not contradict Watanabe's account.

taxes or foreign loans or the issuance of paper notes and will lead to higher prices, social unrest and uprisings. Already we have 5,000,000 in foreign loans; even this is difficult to pay.

(3) Our government has started to stimulate industries, but it will be several years before we get results. . . . If we now begin an unnecessary war, spend a huge amount of money, shed blood, and worsen the daily life of the people, all these government works will break like a bubble and lose several decades of time. We will regret it.

(4) Regarding the foreign trade situation. Each year there is a one million yen deficit . . . and our gold reserve decreases. Thus our international credit worsens, leading to inflation and our people's livelihood becoming hard. Also the export of our products faces difficulties. If we open fire without thinking of our economic and military power, our soldiers will have a bad time and their parents will be in difficulty; they will cease to work well and our national product will decrease. Such things as weapons must be purchased from foreign countries; our foreign trade deficit will become worse and worse.

(5) In regard to the diplomatic situation, the most important countries for us are Russia and Britain. . . . Relations with them are uncertain. I fear that Russia will interfere unless we secure our independence. If we open fire on Korea, Russia will fish out both the clam and the bird and get a fisherman's profit. Thus we should not begin a war in Korea now.

(6) In regard to the Asian situation, Britain is especially powerful, watching with a tiger's eye. Our foreign loans depend on Britain. If there is trouble and we become poor, Britain will surely interfere in our internal affairs on that pretext. Look at India . . . observe carefully the process by which India became a colony. We must build our industry, our exports, etc. It is our most urgent business.

(7) The Japanese treaties with Europe and America are not equal. This is harmful for our independence. Therefore we must do our best to revise them, or England and France will send armies on the pretext of an insecure internal situation. . . . The first thing is to revise the treaties, the Korean business after that.

Conclusion. As I have said above we must not hurry to begin war. Of course, we cannot overlook the arrogant attitude of Korea, but we have no clear reason to attack Korea. Now it is argued, send the envoy and depending on his reception open fire or not. But we may be sure from experience that his reception will be cold, so this automatically means open fire. Thus we must decide about sending an army before we send the envoy. If there is war we must have more than 100,000 soldiers, laborers, ships, etc. It will cost many times 10,000 yen. Even though we are victorious, the expense will be far beyond the profit. Also after the victory there will be uprisings over there. Even though we get all kinds of goods in Korea, they will amount to less than the expense. Also it is said that neither China nor Russia will intervene, but there is no proof. It is said that we cannot endure Korean arrogance, but this is an insufficient reason and it would be very bad to open fire without thinking of our security and our people's welfare. Therefore I oppose. . . .[50]

The logic of Ōkubo and the astute political management of Iwakura had won the great October fray. From some quarters came compliments on their victory. For example, the governor of Ishikawa prefecture hastened to reassure Iwakura that "though you are often criticized" and "though it is natural for the Japanese people to be angry [at Korea's attitude] nevertheless it has taken fifteen or so years to end the feudal regime; this has finally been accomplished, but if we send an army to Korea . . . other countries will laugh at us." He urged Iwakura to stay at the helm.[51] The most influential newspapers of the time, the *Tōkyō Nichi Nichi* and the *Yubin Hochi*, both supported the anti-war position, the latter in spite of the fact that it was very sympathetic to the samurai class's feelings of dissatisfaction. It advocated the idea that *shizoku* (samurai) should lead the politics of the country as "the bearers of the people's rights." But it held that, if there were a victory in Korea, the dissatisfied would be even more dissatisfied. Therefore war was no solution to samurai troubles. *Nichi Nichi* argued that

[50] Ōkubo Toshikazu (ed.), *Ōkubo Toshimichi Bunsho* (Ōkubo Toshimichi Documents) (Tokyo: Nihon Shiseki Kyōkai, 1927–31), V, No. 708, 53-63. Ike, "Triumph . . .", gives a slightly different version of this document, p. 294; and there is another in deBary, *Sources* . . ., 658-62. It seems to me that Sidney Brown, "Kido . . .," may overestimate Kido's and underestimate Ōkubo's role in the victory of the "peace party," 151, 154-55.

[51] *Iwakura Tomomi Kankei Bunsho* (Documents relating to Iwakura Tomomi), V, 390-92.

the self-conscious samurai, as "relics of the feudal past," could not be relied on. And as for conquering Korea, all "high class intelligent people," it said, were opposed to the idea. This was the "correct opinion."[52]

At the Foreign Office, now under the new management of Terashima Munenori, formerly governor of Yokohama, there was a reconsideration of the whole problem. Korean specialist Moriyama submitted a new recommendation on January 11, 1874, in which he emphasized that the basic reason for Korea's refusal to open relations with Japan was not so much that Korea feared Japan, but that recent incidents in Korea involving the French and Americans had led them to place Japan in the same category. Therefore, "it is necessary for Japan to alleviate this fear of Korea. Lord Sō [of Tsushima] has long experience; entrust to him the task of easing Korea's fear." This evidently represented the considered opinion of the Foreign Office under their new outlook, for Terashima recommended to Sanjō that negotiations between Japan and Korea should again be entrusted to Sō "in accordance with the old custom." Moriyama was sent to Pusan again in the spring of 1874 to prepare the way for negotiations by Sō. Actually he began to negotiate without waiting for Sō's arrival. But an expense list which he submitted to the Foreign Office, referring to gifts of books, swords, and screens for Korean officials, is an interesting indication of his re-emphasis on old style friendship with Korea as the order of the day, while the reconstituted Japanese government rethought the Korean problem.[53]

Ōkubo's anti-war statement represents the ideological basis of this rethinking. It has been defined as the internal construction principle. It brings to mind immediately adjectives like realistic, rational, careful, cautious. These are indeed descriptive of the

[52] Tōyama, "Seikan Ron . . .," 2. Cf. *Yubin Hochi* (Newspaper), Oct. 22, 1875 and *Tōkyō Nichi Nichi*, Oct. 19, 1875.

[53] Recommendation of Moriyama Shigeru, Jan. 11, 1874, No. A695; Terashima to Sanjō, Jan. 10, 1874, No. A694; Moriyama report, Oct. 2, 1874, No. A698;For. Off. Korea desk to Terashima, Dec. 25, 1874, No. A699: Ōkuma Kenkyū Shitsu.

ingredients of government policy generally, as well as toward Korea through the rest of the Meiji era. But they are not quite sufficient, for they do not consider the darker side of this Ōkubo approach to policy formulation. To see this darker side, it is necessary to observe certain events of 1874, which add elements of cynicism and callousness. These events were the Saga insurrection and the Formosa expedition. They developed from the fact that although "high class intelligent people" might be satisfied with the victory of the Ōkubo-Iwakura faction, the restless samurai elements which Saigō, Itagaki, and Etō had championed were by no means ready to subside. One Nishimura Teiyo, a fifth-rank official of the Hokkaido Colonization Office (*Kaitakushi*), warned prophetically in a communication addressed to Sanjō and Iwakura that the government should conquer Korea in order to solve the problem of disaffected samurai. "If there is war with Korea, they will become officers and devote their lives to the cause of the country. . . . But if the government is anti-Seikan, fails to see the internal situation, and merely tries to suppress the samurai, one cannot tell what kind of trouble will arise. . . . The samurai then will not consider the security of the nation."[54]

Iwakura did not read Nishimura's proposal, at least not immediately, for even as it was being drafted he himself became the first victim of the sort of trouble predicted therein. On the night of January 14, as he left the imperial palace grounds, he was met by a disorderly crowd, from which several ruffians emerged, attacked, and wounded him. Later the culprits were apprehended, identified as disaffected Conquer-Korea advocates, and executed.[55] Iwakura recovered, but meanwhile Ōkubo, who now as home minister was responsible for the maintenance of internal security, was soon faced with Seikan uprisings in Saga prefecture (the former Hizen feudatory in northwestern Kyushu), which threatened to become a

[54] Nishimura Teiyo to Sanjō and Iwakura, Jan. 20, 1874, No. A695: Ōkuma Kenkyū Shitsu.

[55] *Meiji Hennenshi*, II, 109, 180.

full-scale rebellion. Reports of disturbances in Fukuoka, Nagasaki, and through Saga prefecture generally reached Tokyo in early February, 1874. *Tōkyō Nichi Nichi* on February 12 reported that some 2500 samurai rebels were defying government authority there. The movement had got its start in mid-January when one of a number of small groups, under the leadership of one Takaki Tarō, quarrelled with a prefectural official over the question of a meeting place to discuss the Korean issue. This, combined with the "unexpected return home [to Saga]" of resigned Councillor Etō Shimpei, provided the sparks necessary to ignite smoldering discontent. Etō himself took over the leadership of a "United Conquer-Korea party," which was composed of several factions, and proclaimed open rebellion. Evidently he expected Itagaki to follow his lead, for he had joined Itagaki in a samurai manifesto demanding an elected assembly which was issued on January 17—perhaps also Saigō, for he sought out Saigō at a hot spring on March 1 and urged him to join the rebellion. In this he was disappointed, for neither Itagaki nor Saigō lifted a hand, though Saigō was "very melancholy" about the matter.

Ōkubo, on the contrary, moved with dispatch to suppress the rebels. Taking command of the government forces in person, he left Yokohama on February 14 for Saga aboard the steamer *Hokkai Maru*. Two navy ships with seven cannons between them followed the next day. Two regiments were ordered out of Osaka to Saga, and other troops were ordered into the fray from garrisons at Kumamoto and Yokoshima. A Council of State order dated February 19 officially commanded government leaders of all prefectures and metropolitan areas that Saga rebels were to be subjugated. Government forces were quickly victorious. They entered Saga under Ōkubo's command on February 22, won a succession of victories, and entered Saga castle on March 1, which all but ended the campaign. Etō was rumored hiding in Kagoshima by mid-March. That he was not receiving the protection of Saigō there, however, is underscored by the fact that Saigō and his former feudal lord, Shimazu Hisamitsu, arrived in Yokohama to pay a visit to the capital on March 17. A government order, reported in the press on March 18, deprived Etō of his honors and court rank, and thereafter he was hunted down relentlessly. He was reported in Tosa on April 2, where four of his rebel collaborators were captured and where by April 4 there was "no doubt that he would be captured any day." He was taken on April 13; and the Tokyo newspaper *Nichi Nichi* on April 28 made a lead story of his demise: "Distinguished Meiji Retainers Beheaded, Heads Exposed: Etō Shimpei, Shima Yoshitake, and followers punished . . ." Seikan Ron was over, and Etō's head would serve as grim warning to any who tried to raise the issue again. Two days after the news of Etō's execution, a report that "Koreans Slaughter Crew of Japanese Drifting Ship" raised scarcely a ripple. No one was now looking for a Korean *casus belli.*[56]

Casualties in the Saga affair had not been heavy, thanks perhaps to the speed with which Ōkubo acted. A report dated March 25 listed government losses at 337, killed and wounded. But it is clear that Ōkubo was alarmed by the specter of samurai discontent when he saw it in riotous action. In his argument against a Korean war he had said that "we have a fortress and have good military equipment, so they dare not rise against us." But the Saga samurai had dared, and, lest the obituaries of their leaders prove an insufficient deterrent to future revolt, Ōkubo decided to put in motion the Formosa chastisement expedition, which would at least partially satisfy samurai hotheads and yet promised to be neither so dangerous nor so expensive as conquering Korea.

The Formosa expedition idea, as explained above, had been advanced by Soejima and LeGendre as a sort of little sister accompaniment to Seikan. It lay dormant through the great October crisis and the subsequent reconstitution of the Council of State,

[56] The course of the rebellion may be traced in contemporary newspapers. *Meiji Hennenshi,* II, 117, 122, 124, 127-29, 134, 136, 140-41, 145, 146, 151, 157. See also Sanematsu, *op. cit.*, p. 377.

but subsequent events indicate that Ōkubo was fully aware of its possibilities as a diversionary enterprise for restless samurai spirits. He, with Ōkuma's assistance, made a thorough investigation of the whole matter in January, 1874, and set down certain basic points. There was, they noted, a legal basis for such an expedition stemming from the fact that the murdered Ryūkyū islanders were under Japanese imperial protection and that the Chinese themselves had given Japan reason to believe that Formosa, at least the "savage part," was unoccupied territory. It was anticipated that further negotiations with the Chinese would be necessary to "eliminate Chinese protests" but that protracted negotiations would gain time while the object of the expedition might be achieved.[57] Kido, who had not played nearly so active a role as Ōkubo in defeating Seikan, however, pronounced himself completely in opposition to such a Formosan undertaking, and in a memorial published March 9 in *Tōkyō Nichi Nichi* he employed some of Ōkubo's own arguments, to wit: the first objective must be to build up the country internally. Only later may soldiers be employed outside; and he made special reference to the Formosa issue. In May Kido temporarily left the government.[58]

Nevertheless Ōkubo, even amidst his vigorous repression of the Saga revolt, was looking ahead to healing the breach with the south-western samurai by arranging a Formosa expedition. It may well be that the aforementioned journey of Saigō and Shimazu to the capital in March was occasioned by negotiations on this score. At any rate, expedition plans began to take definite shape in April, with Saigō's younger brother, Saigō Tsugumichi, appointed to organize and command a Formosa expeditionary force, and Ōkuma designated as chief of an "office of affairs for the savage area of Formosa." But clearly Ōkubo was handling the strategy. He made a special effort to associate Westerners, particularly Americans, with the expedition. LeGendre was to advise and

[57] NGB, VII, 1-2.
[58] *Meiji, Hennenshi*, II, 138, 164.

accompany the expedition, and Lt. Commander Douglas Cassel, U.S.N. and former Lt. James R. Wasson of the U.S. Army Engineers were engaged as staff officers to Saigō. An American steamer, the *New York*, was engaged as a troop carrier. A number of ships, including the *New York*, a British ship the *Yorkshire*, a French vessel, and various Japanese owned ships sailed from Shinagawa (Tokyo) on April 6, bound for Nagasaki where troops and supplies were to be loaded.

The American participation might have proceeded as planned had LeGendre's friend, DeLong, still been in the post of American minister to Japan. However, he had been replaced by Judge John A. Bingham, a man of cautious temperament who gave meticulous attention to his duties. Bingham protested the employment of Americans and an American ship in the affair in a note to Foreign Minister Terashima dated April 18 and the story of the "American Minister's Criticism of the Formosa Expedition" made sensational news in the Japanese press. This disturbed Ōkubo greatly, and he dispatched a messenger post haste to Nagasaki to order Saigō Tsugumichi to delay preparations and await further orders. Tsugumichi, however, in the spirit if not on the advice of the elder Saigō, refused to comply. His 3600 soldiers were ready in full samurai fervor, and he argued that he had a commission directly from the emperor, with which even the prime minister could not interfere; if foreign complaints embarrassed the government, it might answer that he was a pirate! And in outright defiance of the order from Tokyo he dispatched one ship on April 27 and four more on May 2. Ōkubo probably anticipated such action, for he was himself enroute to Nagasaki, arriving there on May 3, just too late to prevent the latter departure. He and Ōkuma thrashed out the matter with Saigō. They approved the expedition as such but required Saigō to agree in writing that the Americans, Cassel and Wasson, who had already left for Formosa, would be detached from the expedition and sent back to Japan; General LeGendre, who was still in Nagasaki, would be sent back to Tokyo; and most important of all, the expedition would be limited: once the savages had been punished, the greater part of the expedition would be withdrawn from Formosa, leaving only a small security force. Saigō left for Formosa, and Ōkubo and Ōkuma returned to Tokyo. The Council of State officially proclaimed the Formosa expedition on May 19.

Meanwhile the British minister to Japan, Sir Harry Parkes, had informed his counterpart in Peking, Mr. Thomas Wade, of the impending expedition, and Wade had questioned the Chinese government as to whether the Formosan area in question was claimed by them and whether the Japanese had consulted with them and obtained permission to punish the savages. The Tsungli Yamen replied that Formosa was indeed Chinese territory, that they had given no such permission, and urged him so to inform Minister Parkes. As Ōkubo had anticipated, Japan had a diplomatic problem on its hands, though not, as it proved, an insoluble one. The subsequent negotiations were tedious and drawn out, but their culmination, handled by Ōkubo himself, was a complete success for Japan. There were three stages to the negotiations, Formosa, early Peking, and late Peking. In Formosa, Saigō was true to his agreement. He sent back the Americans and conducted a limited campaign. His forces occupied only southern Formosa, where they forced the surrender of almost all the native tribes, but they did not venture into the north where they would have become entangled with the Chinese. During the course of the campaign, which lasted from June 1 to June 25, the Fukien viceroy, Pan Wi, came to Formosa and negotiated a preliminary settlement with Saigō. This anticipated that China would pay Japan for the cost of the expedition, and would prevent further outrages by the savage tribes; Japanese forces would remain stationary until final agreement had been reached, whereupon they would withdraw.[59]

[59] See Treat, *op. cit.*, I, 543-53. U.S. Department of State, *Papers Relating to the Foreign Relations of the United States* (1874), 676-77. House, *op. cit.*, 160-70. NGB, VII, 38-40. Kokuryūkai, *Nisshi* . . ., I, 82-85. *Meiji Hennenshi*, II, 156, 164-65.

At Peking Yanagihara, who had been Soejima's voice the year before, was now Ōkubo's. He handled the first stage of the negotiations, arriving on July 31 and remaining the chief negotiator until Ōkubo himself arrived on September 10. Yanagihara was instructed that the settlement of the dispute by negotiation was most desirable and he was to avoid unnecessary delay. His chief objective was to obtain compensation and to try to get the Chinese first to suggest the amount. Saigō's troops would be withdrawn after the agreement had been signed, but he had no authority to promise a specific date for complete withdrawal. Yanagihara got nowhere in his efforts to obtain agreement to these terms, but the fact that he expressed them set the stage for Ōkubo's coming and the latter's administering of the diplomatic coup. When Ōkubo arrived, he immediately took a stronger position. He reminded the Chinese that "under international law" they had no claim to southern Formosa as their territory since they exercised no effective jurisdiction over it, and he cited the Rover case as an earlier example. The Chinese responded that international law was something "recently created by Western nations" and China had no need to observe it. The affair should be settled on the basis of "truth".

Nevertheless the Tsungli Yamen gradually came around to accepting the principle of compensation. But they would not agree to put it into writing until Ōkubo, after a dramatic threat to end the negotiations and leave for home on October 25, subtly invited the mediation of British Minister Wade. Wade at the last moment obtained a definite offer from the Tsungli Yamen. Ōkubo dropped his plans to depart, resumed negotiations, and quickly concluded an agreement, accepting the Chinese offer of 500,000 taels compensation and obtaining a statement from China admitting the right purpose of the expedition. Papers were signed on October 31, with Wade countersigning the contract guaranteeing payment of the money by China. Ōkubo immediately departed for Formosa, where he informed Saigō of the settlement and made arrangements for the departure of the troops, then returned triumphantly to Tokyo on November 27. Saigō brought the entire expedition home from Formosa in early December, except for the few who had been killed in the fighting and the several hundred who died of disease.[60]

The outcome of the Saga revolt and the Formosan expedition was an immense personal triumph for Ōkubo. His prediction that he would be left almost alone to beat down the advocates of Seikan had proven accurate, as Iwakura by accident and Kido by choice left the field of decision making almost exclusively to him at the critical stage. The result was the emergence of that part of the Meiji period (1874–78) which a Japanese historian has called "the absolutism of Ōkubo."[61] This may be an overstatement, but the stamp of Ōkubo was indelibly impressed upon Japanese government thinking in these years, and it is important for the understanding of future developments to estimate just what the Ōkubo imprint was. Perhaps the best way to describe this is to employ the Japanese word, *jūjutsu*. Ōkubo put a jūjutsu quality into the management of political-diplomatic affairs, the sudden thrust, the diversionary feint, the back-step, the use of one opponent's weight against another. And in the Saga-Formosa affair, he gave a remarkable demonstration of the efficacy of such tactics. Here Ōkubo had many opponents, Etō and his Saga rioters, the Saigōites, Itagaki and his followers, Western diplomats, the Chinese. The quick thrust took Etō's head and gave pause to Saigō and Itagaki; the diversionary feint to Formosa then distracted the Saigōites and tied up some of their energies in a limited and "legally defensible" activity; the gymnastics about the participation of Westerners in the affair, coupled with the Peking negotiations, served to emphasize the international respectability of the expedition and Japan's earnestness to be right with the Western powers.

[60] See NGB, VII, 225, 306. *Meiji Hennenshi,* II, 238, 245. Kokuryūkai, *Nisshi . . .,* I, 103-16. Treat, *op. cit.,* I, 553-56. House, *op. cit.,* 195.

[61] Tōyama, *Meiji Ishin,* 320.

The Japanese historian, Kiyozawa Kiyoshi, in his study of Ōkubo as a politician-diplomat stresses Ōkubo's skill in gearing together internal politics and external diplomacy. The Seikan argument, says Kiyozawa, reveals his policy stand, but the Formosa affair reveals his diplomatic finesse.[62] One may summarize Ōkubo's object lessons of the year 1874 as follows: the first problem is the internal construction of Japan, but since this requires great sacrifices it will stir strenuous opposition in Japan. Therefore (1) a well-timed, carefully calculated, and judiciously limited foreign adventure, which is capable of justification in Western international formulae, is not unduly risky and can render domestic affairs more manageable; (2) the practical problems of carrying out such a venture are sufficiently complicated to require leadership at once nimble enough to back-step obsequiously in the event of serious Western opposition and ruthless enough not to flinch at exterminating old friends in Japan. Here is the darker side, the cynicism and callousness contained in the policies of Ōkubo and his supporters, but in justice to them one should not forget the pressure under which they worked.

The government oligarchy having now, under Ōkubo's leadership, demonstrated a success formula, it sought to broaden its base of support. Efforts in that direction were primarily the work of Itō and Inoue, Chōshū clansmen who despite the defection of Kido, had supported the government through the Formosa affair. Kido's feeling that indulgence in the expedition had been an unwarranted and dangerous compromise of the internal construction principle was no doubt assuaged by the fact that the southwestern samurai had after all been kept in hand. At any rate he agreed to meet Ōkubo in conference. Itagaki, somewhat mollified that a stronger foreign policy seemed in the making and hopeful that he might be able to further the fortunes of a political movement, the *Risshisha* (Realize Ambitions Society), through which Tosa samurai were attempting to force the government to accept a deliberative assembly, also

[62] Kiyozawa, *op. cit.*, 1, 5-6.

agreed to participate. The elder Saigō remained aloof, and busied himself with a private school for teaching Confucian principles and samurai ethics in Kagoshima. The conference met at Osaka in February, 1875, with the result that both Kido and Itagaki rejoined the government. Kido again became an integral part of the oligarchy, but Itagaki was obviously giving it a trial run, and as we shall see, he soon quit once more. Saigō's school and Itagaki's party should be remembered, for they are indicators of the future of Seikan advocacy and of a divergence of approach among the advocates. Saigō's school was the direct antecedent of the reactionary society, the Genyōsha, which made a speciality of the Korean problem; and the Risshisha was the direct antecedent of the Liberal party, the Jiyūtō, which also made something of a specialty of the Korean problem. In the long run these outcrops of 1873 were to have a large effect on Japan's Korean policy, but as of autumn, 1875, Ōkubo, Iwakura, Kido, Itō, and their supporters were moving toward the solution of the Korean problem in their own cautious, methodical way.

Moriyama, it will be recalled, was in Pusan and Torai during much of 1874, trying to rebuild a friendly relationship with Korean officials on the anticipation that Sō of Tsushima would then carry on. He had rather good success, obtaining an agreement with local Korean negotiators that "though we have had relations for 300 years, it is now necessary to make revisions." The new stipulations were that there should be a Japanese consul and subordinates at Pusan to look after Japanese people there and to negotiate with Korean officials; there should be foreign trade, except in certain restricted items; and provision should be made for settlements regarding "drifting" ships. These could be "with or without China's approval." Upon receiving this report the Japanese government decided not to send Sō after all, but to have Moriyama return (January, 1875) to push the negotiations further. This time he displayed less sensibility to Korean feelings, and the Korean negotiators were soon complaining of a "lack of sincerity" on

Moriyama's part, evidenced by the fact that he again was insisting on using the character *dai* (great) to refer to Japan, the word *kōjō* (imperial) to refer to the Japanese emperor. And even worse, perhaps, he had come on a steamship and approached them in Western clothes.[63] Negotiations were soon deadlocked again.

However, this seems to have been part of a deliberate plan to increase the pressure on Korea. While in Japan, Moriyama and his Foreign Office colleagues, Hirotsu and Sada, had proposed to Foreign Minister Terashima that a warship might be dispatched to Korean waters on the excuse of surveying. Terashima was receptive to the idea and took it up with Iwakura and Sanjō who approved the dispatch of three ships, the *Kasuga*, the *Unyo*, and the *Teiu*, on condition of great secrecy. "Only a very few even among the ministers knew of it."[64] Presumably Itagaki was not in on the planning since the primary object of the secrecy was to prevent the excitement of Conquer-Korea advocates. However, the Tokyo newspaper *Choya* reported soundings being taken, hopes for a treaty, and rumors of war with Korea all in one issue, July 17, 1875.[65] The ships maneuvred near Pusan and Torai, and then in mid-September moved up the coast to Jinsen (Inchon). There a small boat from the *Unyo* was sent ashore to secure drinking water. On September 19, its crew was fired on by Koreans on shore, but they were able to put out to sea again and were picked up by the *Unyo*. The Japanese then sent another boat under flag of truce to inquire into the matter; this too was fired upon. Whereupon, on September 21, the Japanese opened fire, silenced the shore battery, killed some thirty Koreans, took the weapons away from the rest, and obtained their drinking water.[66]

This *Unyo*, or Kanghwa, incident, for it occurred near the island

[63] Tabohashi (1940), I, 350-52, 363-66. Japanese Ministry of Foreign Affairs, Archives (Library of Congress Microfilm), "Confidential Instructions," SP 5, 10, This collection hereafter cited as Archives.

[64] Tabohashi (1940), I, 396-97.

[65] *Meiji Hennenshi*, II, 362-63.

[66] Treat, *op. cit.*, I, 591. Tabohashi (1940), I, 398-400.

of Kanghwa, like the affair of the Formosa aborigines, was right for the exercise of the Ōkubo formula. The Conquer-Korea advocates were again in opposition, Itagaki resigning from the government on the grounds that its action was not vigorous enough and Saigō criticizing government action as too strong for its moral foundations because "the real situation regarding the Kanghwa incident is not so clear"—as in the case of the earlier insult. But this disjointing of the opposition only serves to indicate that Ōkubo and the other anti-war leaders were moving deftly toward their sort of solution to the Korean problem, one which, while further undermining the stand of samurai war-hawks in Japan, would avoid costly military involvement, and would be justifiable in terms of Western international practice. During October, November, and December, 1875, Ōkubo, Iwakura, Kido, and Sanjō met frequently to work out a firm yet peaceful approach. At first, it was decided that Kido should go to Korea as chief negotiator, but his health was not good and this idea was abandoned. Finally Lt. General Kuroda Kiyotaka and Inoue Kaoru were appointed envoy extraordinary and vice-envoy respectively to carry out negotiations in Seoul, and the aforementioned Mori Arinori (Yūrei), whose brother had committed suicide in opposition to Seikan, was appointed envoy to Peking to bring up the matter there. Before dispatching either of these, Foreign Minister Terashima called American Minister Bingham into conference and explained to him that it was Japan's intention to send a commissioner to Korea to insist on the negotiation of a treaty of commerce and friendship. He solicited Bingham's advice and also, apparently, a copy of *The Narrative* of Perry's expedition, which, of course, served to emphasize that Japan, while expecting to be diplomatically correct in the matter, might employ the threat of force. Bingham urged avoidance of war but admitted that "by some means Korea should be made amenable to reason and justice." In considering specific matters connected with the project he advised that, though the commissioner might go aboard a man of war, it should ride outside the harbor while he went ashore in a small boat; and the use of foreign nationals and ships (reminiscent of the Formosa affair) should be avoided. Terashima also consulted the British Chargé Plunkett the same day.[67]

The Kuroda-Inoue mission was ominous in physical aspect when in January, 1876, it departed for Korea. It consisted of two men-of-war and four transports containing several thousand soldiers. But the government's instructions to the envoys emphasized peaceful intent and methods.

The Koreans have refused our envoys and letters, but we expect to get good results by peaceful methods. . . . The Korean government has not yet spoken words to break off friendship and our people in Pusan have been treated as heretofore. Whether the attack [on the *Unyo*] was made at the order of the [Korean] government or with its implicit approval or whether it was initiated by local officials is not certain and should be ascertained; our government does not consider that friendship between us has wholly discontinued. . . . Therefore our envoys shall concentrate on peaceful agreement. If the Korean government accepts friendly relations and foreign trade, this might be considered as an alternative to compensation [for the *Unyo* incident]. . . . If peaceful relations are established, we should not be bound by the Tokugawa example, but should go one step further as follows: there should be an agreement of perpetual friendship and exchange of diplomatic compliments on the same level. Subjects of both countries should be able to trade in designated places, both people being able to conduct commerce freely in Pusan and Japanese residence and trade should be allowed at Kanghwa city. The Korean government should facilitate Japanese coming and going at Pusan, Seoul, and other places. Japanese ships should be able to take soundings and measurements in Korean seas. Shipwrecked peoples should be mutually returned. Ministers should reside in capitals of both countries. Diplomatic officials should be on the same level. Consulates should be established in trading places to

[67] See Treat, *op. cit.*, I, 592-93. Tabohashi (1940), I, 416, 417, 421. Tōyama, "Seikan Ron . . .," 5. Robert A. Scalapino, *Democracy and the Party Movement in Prewar Japan* (Berkeley: University of California Press, 1953), 60-61.

control traders. If it is expedient, some of the above items may be set aside.[68]

Confidential instructions as to tactics were as follows:

If the Koreans do not accede to our request, it is probable that they will resort to one of these three methods of behavior. (a) They will treat our representatives with violence. (b) Our representatives will not be received and our messages will be ignored though the representatives will not be attacked. Or (c) they will say when asked for a new agreement that they cannot answer without an order from China, or they will employ other delaying tactics.

If the Koreans resort to (a) you should retreat to Tsushima, send a full report, and await further orders. If (b) you should lodge a letter of protest, send a report to Tokyo, and await further orders. If (c) you should argue thusly. Japanese-Korean relations were never before mediated by China. Last year the Korean negotiator Pak promised Moriyama that he would accept a message from the Japanese foreign minister with or without China's approval. But this year the bombardment was made. Was it with Chinese approval? If it was done without Chinese approval, then there should be compensation paid and a new agreement made directly by the Korean government, not through China. If Korea wishes to withhold reply until she has an answer from China, then, while waiting for the answer, Japanese soldiers should be stationed in Seoul, should be supplied there, and we should occupy Kanghwa castle . . . .

You [our envoy] may revise the course to meet the situation, sacrificing some of our demands. But the following are absolute: trade at Pusan and Kanghwa, freedom of navigation in Korean waters (starting date subject to negotiation), apology for Kanghwa incident. If the Koreans continue to boast and refuse these basic Japanese requests, then even though they do not resort to violence, you may break off relations, saying that peaceful relations are now impossible, return to Japan, and await further orders, preserving the face [dignity] of the mission.[69]

[68] Archives, SP 5, 7-9.
[69] *Ibid.*, 10-12.

The Kuroda-Inoue mission sailed from Shinagawa on January 6, 1876, made a leisurely voyage to Inchon, disembarked, and began negotiations with Korean officials on February 10. They reminded the Koreans of the impolite treatment Japanese envoys had received in Korea ever since the Meiji Restoration, protested the bombardment of the *Unyo*, and offered to accept a treaty of friendship in settlement of these matters. Negotiations, they insisted, must be accomplished within ten days. Events then moved swiftly. Substantial agreement *was* reached within ten days, and a treaty was concluded on February 26. This Kanghwa Treaty provided for the inauguration of diplomatic relations between Korea and Japan, promised Japan three open ports in Korea and the right to conduct surveys in Korean waters, and referred to Korea as an "independent" (English text) or "self governing" (Chinese text) country enjoying "the same sovereign rights as Japan." To the Japanese this constituted an "open expression" that Korea was an "independent nation."[70]

The smoothness and ease with which the treaty was concluded was, of course, not merely the product of the negotiations at Seoul. By February 10, when these negotiations were begun, there lay in the background almost a month of discussions in China on the subject of Sino-Japanese-Korean relations. These were at first between Japanese envoy Mori and various officials of the Tsungli Yamen at Peking, and then between Mori and Li Hung-chang at Paoting-fu. The previous negotiations by Ōkubo at Peking on the Formosa question provided a clear precedent for such discussions, but the specific proposal that an envoy be sent to China came from Kido. Mori, at this time a Foreign Office official, had made a study of the Korean affair in co-operation with E. Peshine Smith, Foreign Office legal adviser, and after presenting his views to the cabinet had been accepted as envoy on November 14. He emphasized that

[70] *Ibid.*, 13. Cf. Bartz, *op. cit.*, 177-82. Negotiations at Seoul were made easier by the fact that the anti-foreign Taewongun had "retired" in 1873 (Bartz, 125). That the Japanese were well aware of this is indicated by a discussion of the subject in "Conditions in Korea," Feb. 11, 1876, No. A715: Ōkuma Kenkyū Shitsu.

stress should be put on peace in the negotiations concerning Korea. The last paragraph of his instructions said that he was to explain that because Japan and China were neighbors Japan would not conceal matters, but had sent him to explain the Korean affair openly. Mori arrived in Peking on January 5 and was soon engrossed in debate with the Tsungli Yamen over the nature of the relations between China and Korea. Korea, they said was a "dependent country" of China. When queried on the meaning of dependent, they explained that "though Korea is a dependent country of China it is not a territorial possession; hence in its domestic and foreign affairs it is independent [self governing]." Mori replied that then indeed the "dependency" of Korea was an "empty name". Since it was free in both its foreign and domestic affairs, it was actually an "independent state." The Tsungli Yamen replied that there is "no man who does not know that Korea is a dependent state even though it manages its internal and foreign affairs."

This impasse over how to define Korea's international position was not resolved, but Mori argued that China nevertheless should urge Korea to receive the Japanese envoys. On this the Tsungli Yamen turned to Li Hung-chang for advice. Li advised that since Japan had come "ostensibly for peace and not war" China should take her words "at their face value," and advise Korea to receive the envoys and to send her envoy to Japan to explain the *Unyo* incident. As for a trade treaty, that would be up to Korea, but if there were war, Korea, "poor and weak," would be no match for Japan. In fact, she would in all probability "follow the precedent of the Ming dynasty and ask help from us [China]." This would result in a "predicament." On February 5 the Chinese advice was passed to Korea that it should negotiate with the Japanese.

The intricate question of what actually was the international status of Korea at this time depends, as Nelson has so aptly pointed out, on whether one applies Confucian or Western concepts, and this need not be a principal concern of this study. However, it should be noted that Mori developed his arguments from Western rules of international law, which he held to be basic.[71]

The Treaty of Kanghwa constituted the solution to the Korean problem as devised by the anti-war party, which emerged from the crisis of 1873 as the government of Japan. And it constituted an instruction in the handling of politics and diplomacy which Ōkubo, Iwakura, and Kido passed on to Itō, their younger collaborator who in a real sense was their collective heir. In addition, the point should be emphasized that this Kanghwa solution to Seikan Ron was in no sense a compromise. It was the fulfillment of the victory of the anti-Seikan forces in the argument of 1873, the translation of a negative determination *not* to allow the nation to embark on a foolish and dangerous war of conquest into a positive answer to the extremists. It indicated precisely how a carefully balanced and cautiously pursued program of action diplomacy could achieve the limited objective of recognition, trade, and an apology[72] without losing sight of the larger one, the forward march through "internal construction" to full and powerful nationhood for Japan—and for bonus gain some credits in the West for helping Korea to define her "independence" and opening her to the currents of "civilization."

However, the course of Chōsen Mondai (The Korean Problem) had not been run. The Kanghwa solution was in fact only a first, temporary solution. The Seikan advocates had been defeated, and the Korean insult redressed in a manner far more astute and intelligent than the emotional campaign they had urged. But the fact that they did not subside, but rather remained in bitter opposition to the government, suggests that there were far deeper issues involved than the Korean "insult" and its resolution per se. It has been said early in this chapter that the direction of Japanese opinion

[71] M. Frederick Nelson, *Korea and the Old Orders in Eastern Asia* (Baton Rouge: Louisiana State University Press, 1946), 126-34. Archives, SP 5, 13-16. Tabohashi (1940), I, 515-19, 529-43. Bartz, *op. cit.*, 160-64. T. C. Lin, "Li Hung-chang: His Korea Policies, 1870–1885," *Chinese Social and Political Science Review*, XIX, 2 (July 1935), 214-17. T. F. Tsiang, "Sino-Japanese Diplomatic Relations, 1870–1894," *Chinese Social and Political Science Review*, XVII (1933–34), 56-57.

[72] The "apologizing" mission came in May, 1876. Archives, SP 5, 23.

and policy was toward compromise, toward general national agreement on Korea. The ultimate solution, annexation, was quite different from the Kanghwa solution; in fact, on the surface, at least, it would seem to resemble what the Conquer-Korea party wanted in 1873—accomplished thirty-seven years later, very quietly. How is that a compromise?

This may be a good place to anticipate somewhat and suggest that during those thirty-seven years a Great Compromise on Korea was worked among the political forces of Japan, a compromise which involved, or required, the compromising (in the bad sense) in Japan of the best promise of the Meiji (enlightened) era. To say it over-simply and perhaps over-dramatically—the price paid for Korea was political freedom in Japan, and beyond that the possibility of Japan's playing a wholesome role in leading other Asian peoples to freedom and self-respect. This was because, curiously perhaps, the Seikan tradition amidst all its chauvinism held within it an expression, albeit an imperfect one, of the aspirations of Japanese and other Asian peoples for such freedom and self-respect. We shall see this cropping to the surface repeatedly as we discuss the further unfolding of Japan's relations with Korea—signs of noble aims and attitudes which, however, are lost as surely as Korea is gained.

Such considerations as these lead into the deeply laid political, social, and moral consequences of the Korean problem for Japan. They should and will be referred to recurrently in the course of this study, but they can be properly evaluated only as part of its conclusion. However, at this point, to return again to Seikan Ron, they may help us to understand a little better the nature of the Great Divide of 1873. It is interesting to note that, although there can be no question that the victorious anti-conquest group constituted a veritable personification of realistic intelligence, and their subsequent record of leadership in Meiji Japan was nothing less than brilliant, they have elicited little enthusiasm from the Japanese people. It has been rather the foolish, impulsive, perhaps stupid,

Conquer-Korea advocates who have been heroes to subsequent generations. To be sure Ōkubo, Iwakura, Kido, and their protégés, Itō and Yamagata, have been regarded with respect, or awe, but with a certain coldness attached, even hostility. However, with Saigō and Itagaki there is real warmth. Theirs are the names which have evoked popular enthusiasm.[73] Why has this been so? One reason, it would seem, is that the former, victorious group as the subsequent Meiji government represented authority, which the populace realized more and more was above them, not of them, an aristocratic absolutism, however intelligent, which considered them, the people, important merely as cogs in the machinery of national power. Saigō and Itagaki represented defiance of this authority, and hence, perhaps undeservedly, they became symbolically leaders of the people against the government. This is quite clear as far as Itagaki (and Gotō), who became the nucleus of the Liberal party, are concerned, but with Saigō the point is clouded by the fact that Saigō was, as described by post-1945 Japanese as well as Western historians, "a very reactionary figure,"[74] the type who would have founded, had he lived, the very sort of ultranationalist societies which later idolized his memory.

Warrior feudalist, Saigō was to the core, and yet to dismiss him

[73] One day at lunch in 1956 the author casually asked a Japanese student to compare Ōkubo and Saigō. He thought a moment, then replied, "To say it very simply Ōkubo was a great man up there, but Saigō was a great man down here, with us." One finds ample demonstration of Ōkubo's keen intellect in his "Memorial on Moving the Capital to Osaka," which is quoted in John R. Black, *Young Japan: Yokohama and Yedo* (London: Trubner & Co., 1881), II, 184-87. Also in letters to Saigō, Konoe, and Shimazu, translated by W. G. Beasley in *Select Documents on Japanese Foreign Policy, 1853–1868* (London: Oxford University Press, 1955), 301-3, 311-13. These show his mind at work in pre-Restoration days. Yet on a questionnaire put to young Japanese in the early 1950's asking them to name the ten famous Japanese they most respected, Saigō ranks high (near atomic physicist Yukawa), but Ōkubo is not to be found, nor are Iwakura, Kido, Itō, Yamagata—none of the Meiji oligarchs. With Saigō are Fukuzawa Yukichi and Ozaki Yukio, who may be considered followers of Itagaki's liberal tradition or improvers of it, though Itagaki himself is absent. See Jean Stoetzel, *Without the Chrysanthemum and the Sword: A Study of the Attitudes of Youth in Postwar Japan* (New York: Columbia University Press, 1955), 235.

[74] E. Herbert Norman, "The Genyosha: A study in the Origins of Japanese Imperialism," *Pacific Affairs*, XVII, 3 (Sept. 1944), 265.

and the Saigō inspired ultra-nationalist societies of the future as merely reactionary is to overlook a very important fact. They, like Itagaki's liberals, had a popular, anti-government base, and, in their own narrow, reactionary way, they too cried out popular grievances against the enlightened but absolutist Meiji oligarchy. The Japanese historian Tōyama Shigeki from a post-World War II vantage point says that the Ōkubo group returned from the European tour (1872) as *zettaishugi seijika* (absolutist politicians) and he makes the astonishing suggestion that if Saigō instead of Ōkubo had been heading the government constitutionalism might have been realized in Japan about Meiji year 10 (1877).[75] It would seem to be going much too far to call Saigō a constitutionalist, but perhaps we can understand Saigō better by likening his brand of independence to that of the American states-rightist, southern planter who, owning hundreds of slaves, shouts for freedom (against federal interference), or the Texas cattle baron, almost feudalistic in social and economic behavior, who nevertheless proclaims a fight to the death for Texan rights. Whether for Saigō's Satsuma or Calhoun's South Carolina[76] this becomes, of course, a perversion of the meaning of freedom and independence for the individual, and yet in an imperfect world even unenlightened sectionalism may play a role in blocking the creation of a greater tyranny, the centralized efficiently geared police state. Perhaps it is an instinctive realization of this which brings ordinary people to look upon the sectionalist who calls for liberty (of his section) as a spokesman in their behalf. (Or it could be semantical confusion.) At any rate, Saigō had this sort of appeal, and, it should be emphasized, the liberal leaders who advocated Seikan, Itagaki and Gotō of Tosa and Etō of Saga, had it too. In particular, a generous portion of the liberalism

[75] Tōyama, *Meiji Ishin*, 319; "Seikan Ron . . .," 8. It is also noteworthy that Fukuzawa Yukichi, perhaps the greatest of the Meiji liberals, though he did not agree with Saigō, could not refrain from paying tribute to Saigō's "spirit of resistance to autocracy" in an article published just before his death. Ishikawa, *Fukuzawa Yukichi Den*, II, 508-23.

[76] Satsuma, like South Carolina, was unusually proficient, and pathetically stagnant, in maintaining tradition. See Robt. Sakai, "Feudal Society . . . in Satsuma," *Journal of Asian Studies*, XVI, 3 (May 1957), pp. 365-73.

of the extremely class-conscious Itagaki should be attributed to Tosa sectionalism. This, of course, again emphasizes the fact that the Saigō tradition and the Itagaki tradition were not nearly so far apart as their respective appellations, reactionary and liberal, would imply.

Thus, at least, a part of the popular affection for the Conquer-Korea leaders was due to their identification with liberty (of some brand or other) as against government authoritarianism. And this half way explains the nature of the Great Divide.

To get at the other half of the explanation, let us attempt to characterize the overall policy approach of the anti-war, the government, group. As applied to Korea, it is clear that no love for the Koreans, no inhibitions about conquest, no heartfelt respect for an imperial decision already made stayed their hand in 1873. Their policy toward Korea over the years seems remarkably inconsistent—weak in 1873, quite strong in 1875–76, weak in 1882, weaker yet in 1884–85, strong in 1894–95, weaker in 1896, gradually growing stronger to 1910. Yet it was consistent in the light of one concept, *Realpolitik*. In fact, not only their Korean policy, but their whole generalship of the Meiji government was pervaded with Realpolitik. The most careful consideration of all factors, the domestic economy, the internal political situation, and particularly international power relationships, preceded their every move. If Realpolitik seems too harsh a word for this, perhaps realism will do, but the meaning of this should be inquired into further.

In recent years, out of sensitivity to the chaos wrought by the twentieth-century's two world wars and the imminent danger of a third, has come a new respect for this sort of Realpolitik, or realism, which is usually associated with the nineteenth century. Scholars, and some statesmen, seeking to make the processes of international relations intelligible and their conduct intelligent, have set forth an indictment of idealism, and the deleterious effects of its injection into international politics, so damning that the formerly prominent idealist school, which along with Woodrow Wilson failed to find a way to "make the world safe for democracy," is in retreat or even in rout. The realist argument, which may hark back to Machiavellian roots and an early scientific formulation as "raison d'état" by Friedrich Meinecke, has been given a precise theoretical structure and abundant illustrations by Hans Morgenthau. In particular, he presents the concept of national interest "defined in terms of power" as "the main signpost" of international politics. So impressive has been the work of Morgenthau and others[77] who have helped to bring the realist argument into focus that Kenneth W. Thompson in a recent nonpartisan analysis of "theories and problems of foreign policy," while attributing the "revival" of this realist approach to only "a handful of analysts and scholars," dignifies it with the appellation "analytical," in contrast to a now "discredited" "ideological" approach by which "the policies of states vis-à-vis the rest of the world are merely expressions of prevailing political, social and religious beliefs."[78]

Of all its proponents, perhaps George Kennan, the author successively of "containment" and "disengagement," has argued most brilliantly the case for an intelligent realism in international politics. In his writings and speeches the rather ponderous theories of Morgenthau become vivid and meaningful in terms of specific problems of international relations viewed both historically and contemporarily. And he is particularly sensitive to a phenomenon which is clearly applicable to the Japanese case, one he remarks on, as do others of the realist school, with a sense of distress. This is that, although the most congenial atmosphere for the conduct of realistic diplomacy is one of privacy, or secrecy, wherein skilled

[77] Hans J. Morgenthau, *Politics Among Nations* (New York: Alfred A. Knopf, 1948; 2nd ed.: 1954), see esp. chap. 1, 5. Friedrich Meinecke, "Das Wesen der Staatsrason," in *Die Ideeder Staatsrason in der neueren Geschichte* (2nd ed.: Munich and Berlin: Verlag von R. Oldenbourg, 1925). Cf. Edward H. Carr, *The Twenty Year Crisis, 1919–1939* (London: Macmillan, 1951); George F. Kennan, *American Diplomacy, 1900–1950* (Chicago: University of Chicago Press, 1951).

[78] Kenneth W. Thompson, "Theories and Problems of Foreign Policy," in Roy C. Macridis (ed.), *Foreign Policy in World Politics* (Englewood Cliffs, New Jersey, Prentice-Hall, 1958), esp. 351-52.

diplomatists, insulated from popular pressures, can carry on hard and often distasteful bargainings in pursuit of the national interest, democracy makes no provision for such diplomacy, indeed is hostile to it. Such elements as the people, the press, and public opinion have been congenital troublemakers for realistic diplomacy. Kennan's realist plea is for more insulation, more privacy so that experts in diplomacy and military affairs can do what is necessary to erect defences and construct power balances without public outcry or interference. Otherwise national rivalries become involved in "legalistic-moralistic" illusions, are blown up to gigantic scale, and result in bloody and senseless crusades after one ideal or another.[79]

His reasoning is compelling, and yet a sensitive person may feel a certain uneasiness about his argument. He will wonder whether in the last analysis a gifted and elite diplomatic corps (even American) could really be trusted to pay heed to ordinary people's interests in international affairs. Might they not become so enamoured of the chesslike character of international politics that they would soon be behaving like all such elites in history, certainly including Japan's Meiji oligarchy, and come to consider the people in whose interest they presumably work as merely pawns in the game. Then he may also ask himself whether, after all, even the most astute custodianship of the national interest (meaning enlightened national interest, insofar as national interest is capable of being enlightened), whether even this, with its necessary little wars, pressures here and there to fill power vacuums, and deals with odious regimes can in any sense satisfy a human race which has known the inspiration of Christ and Buddha and Gandhi, and read the words of Jefferson and Lincoln. Here we may be close to the reason why realistic diplomacy suffers from the light of publicity and the heat of popular feeling. We have observed the elements of cynicism and callousness in Ōkubo's realistic handling of the Korea-Formosa issues, and it is perhaps not too much to say that that sort of cold calculation, a setting aside of feelings and ideals,

[79] Kennan, *op. cit.*, chaps. 4 and 6.

even honesty and honor, in the interest of proper timing and tactical advantage, is a necessary concomitant of the realistic approach. Then should not the tendency for people at large to denounce such machinations when they have the means of expression be applauded rather than deplored?

But again, before we call what the realists offer a shoddy betrayal of the best that is in us, we must take into account the miserable historical record of bloody crusades conducted in the name of mankind's highest ideals. And we must be prepared to admit that, granted every group's propensity to identify right with itself, the alternative to their uninspiring formula for balance and uneasy peace in an evil or incompetent world may be unceasing international strife on an ever ascending scale. Must mankind therefore forget its aspirations and accept realism to avoid disaster?

A shelf full of books might not settle this question, but the question in itself is sufficient for our present purpose of understanding better the nature of the Great Divide of Seikan Ron. We have seen that the victorious anti-Seikan, the peace party became Authority, the government, whereas the Conquer-Korea, the war party became Liberty, the opposition. And we have suggested that the policy of Authority, the government, in the broadest sense was Realpolitik (or realism). The policy of the opposition was not exactly unrealism but, as we shall see in observing its activities in the course of this study, it was often close to that. But to see it in its best light let us call it idealism, with certain reservations. For just as the "liberty" of the Seikan party was full of sectionalism (and unenlightened sectionalism at that), so its idealism had many impurities.

The chief ingredients of this idealism at the time of the Seikan breach were the narrow, traditional samurai values, a chivalry bounded by class and clan, coupled with generousness to inferiors. This, however, was the best idealism feudal Japan had known. With Saigō, the concept of samurai chivalry is displayed at its best. Not only did he receive loyal support from his followers, but he gave *them* his all. The most touching part of Saigō's story to succeeding generations of Japanese is that he thought his own followers wrong or foolish for wishing to rise in rebellion against the victorious government, but he nevertheless rose with them in 1877 when he found he could no longer dissuade them, giving his life for loyalty to his followers and in protest that the government was compromising the virtues of the traditional samurai society.[80] Saigō in the best samurai tradition was always ready, willing, and eager—so it seems—to die for loyalty or honor or a cause, even though the cause involved might seem unwise even to him. Later Genyōsha (Black Ocean Society) and Kokuryūkai (Black Dragon Society), admirers of Saigō, put great stress on the same sort of heroics.

Though this loyalty-unto-death is not so clear in the Itagaki liberal element of the Conquer-Korea party, it is nevertheless present there also. Etō Shimpei did die in rebellion against the government; Itagaki himself won lasting fame for his words, "Itagaki may die, but not liberty," as he received a would-be assassin's wound. And the later role of the liberals, like the reactionaries, as critics, schemers, plotters, and activists against government policies brought them into frequent clashes with government authority and hence to court and jail.

Itagaki, himself, lived too long and compromised too much with the government to be as fully accredited as Saigō, as one who would not bow to political expediency. But some of Saigō's supporters, including his younger brother and Mutsu, later did the same, and the Genyōsha–Kokurūykai ultra-nationalist societies founded in his honor did not refrain from taking government money whenever they could get it.

In short, the idealism of the Seikan advocates was as tarnished as their liberty, but, in the heat of political argument and in the role of opposition to authority, they and their successors could pass

[80] *Iwakura Kō Jikki* (Authentic Records of Prince Iwakura) (Tokyo: Iwakura Kō Kyūseki Hozonkai, 1927), III 407. This is the official report on the activities of Saigō's men at Kagoshima by Yanagihara Zenko, who was sent there by the Tokyo government to investigate.

in the dark as idealists, defenders of principle, fearless advocates of honor and liberty; this in contrast to the government, which stood for authority, oppression, politicking for tactical advantage, Realpolitik.

Here is the real division of Seikan Ron. And we may sum it up by returning to our earlier equation—mind versus sincerity, that sincerity which is rooted in intimate past relationships and associated with what is euphemistically called a "way of life." Of course, all the Meiji leaders were equipped with both. But as a group they had put aside sincerity to undertake the reforms necessary to the modernization process. They had undertaken these not because they liked them, not because they had real enthusiasm for them, but rather because a realistic appraisal of the circumstances of the day clearly indicated that they were necessary if Japan was to be saved from colonial status and anything at all of the old order preserved.

Until 1873, mind stood up over sincerity, but then the not so very important question of how to deal with the Korean insult provided a spark which ignited the smoldering fuse of emotion among the Meiji leaders. All of them felt it, but some of them, the more realistic (and the more false?), put sincerity behind them again, and with cold logic shattered Seikan Ron as an argument. And they went ahead with vigor and determination to do whatever was necessary, whether driving their own people or bowing to foreigners, not for an ideal but for a realistic goal, namely, the refashioning of Japan into a powerful nation state. But the Conquer-Korea advocates could not be dissuaded by logic. Less realistic (and less false?) than their opponents, they reacted against the continuous, galling, mortifying demands of Realpolitik. They stood up for sincerity, lost the debate of 1873, and their place in the government. But their influence lived on to plague the practitioners of Realpolitik with exhortations to right and honor. At first, these stood merely for old-fashioned samurai virtues, but gradually the Itagaki element became imperfect exponents of a newly learned concept of liberty for common men, and the Saigō element became even more imperfect exponents of self-respect for Asians. One might expect this idealism to have a salutary effect on the course of modern Japan, and yet idealism can be remarkable for working in reverse, especially when it loses its direction in its fervor and starts out from false or narrow premises. Seikan Ron gave it that false start and therefrom cast a long shadow over the whole Meiji era, and indeed beyond.

II

Realism Established: A "Safe and Sane" Korea Policy

Ōkubo Toshimichi, victor in Seikan Ron, architect of the first, the Kanghwa, solution to the Korean problem, and "absolutist politician" par excellence was assassinated on May 14, 1878, while on his way to his office in a jinricksha. His assassins, seven in number, immediately proceeded to a police station where they surrendered and presented a letter of explanation of the deed. In this letter they protested the "crimes" of the government leaders. The "worst people" were Ōkubo, Iwakura, and Kido (Kido "fortunately" already being dead of illness). The next worst were Itō, Kuroda, Ōkuma, Sanjō, and Kawaji. The "crimes" of these government leaders consisted of "stopping public discussion, suppressing peoples' rights, issuing arbitrary decrees, beginning unnecessary enterprises and spending wealth for unnecessary things, ousting loyal people from the government and planting the seeds of civil war, making mistakes in diplomatic intercourse and allowing the national honor to fall down. . . When Saigō, Kirino and the others were active in the government such things could not be done." Therefore "for the prosperity of the people" they would "kill Ōkubo first hoping that the deed will encourage the Japanese people and that others will kill Iwakura and the rest."[1]

[1] Document signed by Shimada Ichirō and six others, *Iwakura Kō Jikki*, III, 536-41. Kawaji was a police official who, according to Saigō partisans, tried to arrange the

The assassination of Ōkubo and this letter of complaints mark the end of the Seikan era. Though brief, the letter illustrates in a terse way some of those further reaching aspects of the argument over Korea which have been discussed in the latter part of Chapter I. However, Korea is not specifically mentioned in the bill of particulars against Ōkubo, nor was it ballyhooed as a grievance for the Satsuma Rebellion of the previous year, which had culminated in Saigō's death.[2] Seikan was the fountainhead from which both the rebellion and the assassination derived, but the fact that it was not raised as a principal issue in these climactic events indicates clearly that with the Kanghwa settlement its force as an argument had been spent to the degree that temporarily, at least, the Korean problem was clearly in anti-Seikan, government hands. The Conquer-Korea dissidents were directing their activities elsewhere, with the result that for a few years the government had an opportunity to work in the realist tradition of Ōkubo to establish a solid and settled relationship. As a matter of fact, considering that Itō took the helm in the 1880's and continued to be the most powerful single personage in the government to his death in 1909, and considering that during that long period of leadership he gave his personal attention to the Korean problem at every critical point, one is tempted to say that an Ōkubo-Itō "safe and sane" approach ruled Korean relations all the way from Kanghwa to annexation. However, to say this is to open up immediately a very large area of controversy, for it would seem to follow this assumption *ipso facto* that, since the course from Kanghwa to annexation was deliberate and careful, then without any reference to the irresponsible schemes of the Conquer-Korea party, the responsible anti-Seikan managers

assassination of Saigō in January, 1877, under secret government instructions. This "rumour" was a factor in setting off the Satsuma Rebellion: see Yanaghihara's "Report on Kagoshima," *Iwakura Kō Jikki*, III, 404-11. But a detailed, though not very scholarly, study dismisses it as a rumor without foundation; see Hidaka Setsu, *Meiji Hisshi: Saigō Takamori Ansatsu Jiken* (The Saigō Assassination Incident) (Tokyo: Shōyōsha, 1938).

[2] Yanagihara, *op. cit.*

of the Meiji government were guilty of a calculated and villainous plot to seize Korea. Is this true? Or is the converse more likely, that, as a contemporary student of the problem concluded, "It was the policy of the [Japanese] imperial government, whose objectives were commercial and not territorial, to secure the perfect independence of the Hermit Kingdom, and to lead it into the light of modern civilization."[3]

On this issue, Western language studies of the subject, scholarly as well as popular, have been divided, to put it crudely, into pro and anti Japanese interpretations. Of course, the above pro-Japanese quotation, coming from the dissertation of a Japanese student at Columbia University, might be dismissed as a young man's apologetic for his homeland. But the thesis was accepted by John Bassett Moore; and further, the same interpretation was echoed by many Americans. W. E. Griffis, "speaking from forty five years of experience with and study of the Japanese" said that "Japan attempted to redeem Cho-sen [Korea] from medievalism . . ., to coax her into modern national life." G. Trumbull Ladd entitled an article in the *Yale Review*, "The Annexation of Korea: an Essay in Benevolent Assimilation." These were short-range evaluations, written in 1910 and 1912 respectively. But from long range, after a thorough search of Western documents and a painstaking analysis of Japanese policies in the Meiji period, Payson J. Treat concluded in the 1930's that "irrespective of what individual Japanese might have thought or said, Japan wanted Korea to be independent and progressive." These examples are aside from official Japanese government publications which, of course, played the progress and civilization theme ad nauseum.[4]

[3] Seiji G. Hishida, *The International Position of Japan as a Great Power* (New York: Columbia University Press, 1905), 164.

[4] W. E. Griffis, "Japan's Absorption of Korea," *North American Review*, CXCII (Oct. 1910), 516, 525-26. G. Trumbull Ladd, "The Annexation of Korea: An Essay in Benevolent Assimilation." *Yale Review*, N.S. I (July 1912), 639-59. Payson J. Treat, "China and Korea, 1885–1895," *Political Science Quarterly*, XLIX (1934), 514, 542–43; see also Treat's *Diplomatic Relations . . ., 1853–1895*, chaps. 28, 40 and his *Diplomatic Relations . . ., 1895–1905*, 275-77. Residency General, *Annual Report for 1907 on Reforms*

However, the picture of Japan as a scheming aggressor, painted at first by friends of Korea like Homer Hulbert and Fred Dolph, and then, when they obtained the means of self-expression, by expatriate Koreans, began to find a large measure of acceptance in scholarly work of the 1930's and early 1940's until, at World War II's end, M. Frederick Nelson in his brilliant study of *Korea and the Old Orders in Eastern Asia* could conclude that "Korea, as the first major step in Japanese expansion, was the stepping stone to the 'incident' in China, which, in turn, was later broadened into a plan for a 'new order' for the entire Pacific. . . . The Japanese-proposed new East Asiatic order lacked, however, the ethical basis which the former Chinese system possessed."[5]

Considered over the whole first half of the twentieth century the two views probably found about equal support, though the calculated plot view gained such popularity in the World War II era that those who had followed the progress and civilization theme were talked about as pro-Japanese. It is instructive, however, that Paul Eckel, who among postwar textbook writers has made the greatest effort to fathom the Korean dilemma, can only point to

---

and Progress in Korea (Seoul, 1908), *Second Annual Report on Reforms and Progress in Korea, 1908–1909* (Seoul, 1909). Government General, *Annual Report on Reforms and Progress in Chosen (Korea), 1910–1911* (Seoul, 1911).

[5] Nelson, *Korea and the Old Orders . . .*, 296. See also Homer Hulbert, *The Passing of Korea* (New York: Doubleday, Page & Co., 1906); Fred A. Dolph, "Briefs for Korea" (presented to U.S. House and Senate Committees on Foreign Affairs, 1919); *Japanese Stewardship of Korea, Economic and Financial* (Washington, 1920); "Statement," *Congressional Record*, 66th Cong., 1st Sess., Sept. 19, 1919.

Sunoo Hag-wo'n, ". . . Development and Technique of Japanese Imperialism in Korea, 1904–1910," *Korean Review*, I, 1 (June 1948), 27-51. F. A. McKenzie, *Korea's Fight for Freedom* (New York: Fleming H. Revell Co., 1920): Younghill Kang, The Grass Roof (New York: Scribner's, 1932). Henry Chung, *The Case of Korea* (New York: Revell, 1921). Lin, "Li Hung-chang . . ."; Tsiang, "Sino-Japanese Diplomatic Relations . . ."; Andrew J. Grajdanzev, *Modern Korea* (New York: Institute of Pacific Relations, 1944). Robert T. Oliver, *Korea: Forgotten Nation* (Washington: Public Affairs Press, 1944).

These works helped to build the refutation to the idea that Japan came to Korea as the bearer of "progress and civilization."

the difficulties one encounters in trying to make an interpretative analysis, and refrains from doing so.[6] Prewar Japanese scholarship, when it tried to be objective, for understandable reasons, merely recorded events and avoided probing the problem in an interpretative way.[7] Postwar Japanese scholarship has been uninhibited by political considerations, unafraid to probe the matter to the depths, but—and perhaps this is a measure of the difficulty—it has not fully resolved the issue either. Perhaps the best summary statement is from Hatada, as follows: "The whole country seethed with the conquer Korea argument. But there was disagreement regarding the time and the leadership of Korean conquest and, with the Saigō party's being defeated, it did not come to fruition (1873). But the government, which restrained the Saigō party, was not against the subjugation of Korea, and it aimed for the opportunity by which it could effect this through its own strength." This, in particular the use of the word "aim" (*nerau*), would seem to give credence to the plot idea, although Hatada thereafter pays considerable attention to Japanese economic penetration which "bound Korea as a market place for Japanese capitalism"—without saying whether the government "aimed" at that or not.[8]

All this becomes involved in the question of motives, and it might be argued by some that there is no point in trying to establish what the Japanese government "aimed" to do with regard to Korea. It is what they *did* that counts, and further what they did may be

[6] Paul Eckel, *The Far East Since 1500* (New York: Harcourt, Brace & Co., 1948), 270-71. Frank Williston points to a need for American re-examination of the Korean question in his "Reflections on American-Korean Relations," *Korean Review*, I, 1 (June 1948), 3-10.

[7] Tabohashi, whose work was referred to in the last chapter and will be used much more during the course of this study, is an example of this prewar tendency to factual reporting with a minimum of interpretation. Even so, Tabohashi's "strictly truthful way of writing" got him into some trouble. See the Preface to his postwar work, *Nisshin Seneki Gaikōshi no Kenkyū* (A Study of the Diplomatic History of the Sino-Japanese War) (Tokyo: Toko Shoin, 1951), hereafter cited as, Tabohashi (1951). Another example is Takeuchi ,Tatsuji's, *War and Diplomacy in the Japanese Empire* (Chicago: University of Chicago Press, 1935).

[8] Hatada Takeshi, *Chōsen Shi* (History of Korea) (Tokyo: Iwanami Shōten, 1951), 166, 168.

taken as the best indication of what they aimed to do. But premeditated murder and accidental death are very different things in courts of law, though the difference may be academic to the dead man. And it would seem to be of some consequence in working toward an understanding of the motive forces in international relations, as well as toward a fair appraisal of the Meiji government, to know whether they schemed the seizure of Korea, or were pushed into it by forces beyond their control, or fell into it through lack of foresight; whether honorable intentions turned dishonorable through ineptness, or whether they were dishonorable to begin with. And by what standard do we measure them?

For a standard of measurement we might take American Far Eastern policy, which, while considered by some (Kennan, etc.) to have been inept, is not generally adjudged to have been villainous, even though it included two annexations (Hawaii and the Philippines). Indeed, Theodore Roosevelt seems to have been quite willing to equate this American interest in the Philippines with the Japanese interest in Korea, at least to trade diplomatically on that basis. How far is such a comparison justified? Or to ask it another way, how far was the Japanese "opening" of Korea like the American "opening" of Japan? Completely different—for the Japanese "aimed" to take Korea and the United States had no such aim as regards Japan. However, a skillful anti-Americanist might build a great plot theory from Perry to MacArthur to show that the ultimate American aim all along was control of Japan. Such a theory might be facile, though it would be false. And yet, the very possibility of contriving such a theory should make us careful of an easy acceptance of a plot theory in the Japan-Korea case, even though we dislike what the Japanese did to Korea. This matter of assessment of motives, not only those of the Japanese government, but also of the non-government or anti-government groups which addressed themselves to the Korean problem, is complicated. But the details which unfold with the years should reveal keys and clues to its resolution.

The relations between Japan and Korea between 1877 and 1882 are indeed reminiscent of American efforts through Townsend Harris to translate Perry's Treaty of Kanagawa into a working relationship. They are complicated by a larger number of "drifting ship" problems, but these, of course, can be explained by geographical proximity. There is even a long-suffering (but understanding) Townsend Harris-like character, the first Japanese minister to Korea, Hanabusa Yoshimoto. The trials and tribulations he underwent in getting established at Seoul, with apparently no Korean Okichi-san to give him solace, make it difficult to picture him other than sympathetically. Other problems of this period concerned Japanese efforts to conduct surveys along the Korean coast, and the opening of three ports to Japanese commerce. All of these were allowable under the treaty,[9] but getting the details settled was another matter. All in all it can be said, however, that the Japanese acted with great patience and circumspection, in order, so it would seem, to turn the Kanghwa settlement into an active working relationship, and there seems to be no sign at this stage of a great plot in operation.

For example, with regard to the drifting ship problem, there is considerable correspondence, much of it involving Ōkubo himself in the last year of his life, and Foreign Minister Terashima. The problem was one of Korean ships drifting to Japan; and the governors of Nagasaki and Yamaguchi and other coastal areas opposite Korea wanted to know what to do about them. The matter was complicated by the fact that these ships were frequently in a damaged condition and their captains had no money to repair them. Or members of the crew might be ill or would die. "What do we do with them?" asked the Japanese governors. If a Korean crew member dies shall we put up a memorial stone; how large a one? Apparently the problem had been building up for many years. The Nagasaki governor posed it this way. "The Korean people are very shrewd. Especially after a famine in Korea many extra

[9] Articles 2, 4, and 7.

people set themselves adrift on the sea and come in here. We put them to work in industry but they are very idle. Also they are very happy to have their ships repaired at our expense."[10]

The problem was passed back and forth between the home and foreign ministries with the main gist of opinion being as follows: We should try to do as nearly as possible what the Koreans wish. However, with regard to repairing ships, if we repair them, we should be guaranteed repayment by the Koreans, and if we cannot be sure of this we should send the captain back to get the money before the repairs are made. Or the ship should be sold and the money therefrom given to the captain. If the ship is badly damaged and there is no buyer, we should burn it. This may seem bad but a damaged ship is no good. If they refuse to allow it to be burned, it means they refuse our protection. Of course, there is no way to force them, but there is no need for us to pay for it. So just do nothing. It is terribly expensive to bring a damaged ship back to Pusan, but if stupid, stubborn Koreans refuse to burn, we need not care. With regard to destitute Koreans, if they have no clothes at all we should give them clothes, but we should not replace merely reserve clothing which they have lost. If there is a death, we should send the corpse back to Korea if the Koreans will pay for shipment, but if there is no money, we should bury it here and put up a memorial stone. However, the memorial stone should be no more than minimum size (4 *sun* by 1 *shaku*, approximately 5 inches by 12 inches) with only essential information carved on it.[11]

During the course of the intramural discussions in the Japanese government, the foreign minister instructed the Japanese agent

[10] Senior Sec. Home Min. to Senior Sec. For. Min., June 26, 1877: NGB, X, 206-7.

[11] The following documents are all in NGB, X: Home Min. Ōkubo to For. Min. Terashima, Feb 13, 1877, No. 93, 199-200; Terashima to Dep. Home Min., Mar. 2. 1877, No. 94, 201; Dep. Home Min. to Terashima, Mar 15, 1877, No. 95, 201-2; Terashima to Dep. Home Min., Mar. 19, 1877, No. 96, 202-3; Senior Sec. Home Min. to Senior Sec. For. Min., Apr. 14, 1877, No. 98, 204; Senior Sec. For. Min. to Jap. Agent in Pusan, Kondo, May 25, 1877, No. 99, p. 206; Kondo to Sen. Sec. For. Min., June 21, 1877, No. 100, 206; Sen. Sec. Home Min. to Sen. Sec. For. Min., June 26, 1877, No. 101, 206-7; Sen. Sec. For. Min. to Sen. Sec. Home Min., July 2, 1877,

at Pusan, Kondo, to take up the matter with the Korean authorities there. He did, and reached an agreement with them whereby they accepted in general the Japanese thoughts on the problem.[12] Perhaps the most interesting thing about this settlement of the drifting ship problem is that the Japanese government did not try to bring the treaty into force and undertake direct negotiations at Seoul. Rather they did it semiofficially through the traditional pattern of negotiations at Pusan. Seemingly, they did not wish to complicate the problem of "opening" Korea by bringing up minor issues at Seoul at this time.

Surveying the Korean coast was a necessary prelude to the selection of the two harbors which in addition to Pusan were to be open ports. The Japanese government did not proceed very rapidly on this either. They did not press it during 1876, and early in 1877, as the Foreign Office was becoming anxious that the surveys be undertaken lest a long lapse between treaty and selection of the harbors lead the Koreans to assume that nothing would be done, the Satsuma Rebellion complicated matters. Foreign Minister Terashima, during the spring of 1877, tried to get the navy to supply a ship, but by May 4 he was complaining to Iwakura that the navy was using the southwest (Satsuma) rebellion as an "excuse" not to do so.[13] In September, however, the navy promised a ship, at first the *Tsukuba*, but shortly the *Takōmaru* was substituted. Terashima instructed the Foreign Office representative, Deputy Minister Hanabusa, to accompany the expedition, consulting

---

No. 102, 207-8; Kondo to Sen. Sec. For. Min., July 9, 1877, No. 105, 210-11; Dep. Home Min. to For. Min., July 17, 1877, No. 103, 208-9; For. Min. to Dep. Home Min., July 20, 1877, No. 104, 210; Terashima to Pr. Min. Sanjō, Aug. 27, 1877, No. 106, 211.

And the following are in NGB, XI: Ōkubo to Terashima, Mar. 14, 1878, No. 129, 273-76; Nagasaki Governor to For. Min. and Home Min., Mar. 30, 1878, No. 131, 276-77; For. Min. to Pusan Agent, Apr. 17, 1878, No. 132, 277-79.

[12] See above, note 11, doc. Nos. 99, 100, 105.

[13] Terashima to Iwakura, May 4, 1877, No. 107: NGB, X, 214-15.

directly with the ship's captain on the choice of harbors to determine which harbors would be "fit for our use, one on the east coast (Kankyo district) and the other near Moppo or Yoko or in the Keikido." After deciding on the harbors he was to discuss the matter with the Korean government, but the date of opening, which according to the treaty was to be twenty months after signing, therefore October 27, 1877, might be "postponed somewhat."[14]

On the matter of the establishment of a permanent Japanese representation in Seoul, some groundwork, though it proved to be mainly in quicksand, had been laid in the summer of 1876 by Miyamoto Koichi, a Foreign Office official who came to Seoul to negotiate a supplement to the Treaty of 1876, clarifying certain matters referred to therein. He was mainly concerned with trade and currency regulations, which had been settled only in a general way in Article XI of the treaty, which article also provided for the coming of a Japanese commissioner such as himself to negotiate with a Korean commissioner on these matters. He succeeded in negotiating an eleven-article "supplementary treaty"[15] which may have clarified a few points on trade regulations in the open ports to be, but which was not much more precise than the original treaty had been and which in some aspects was merely repetitive.

Miyamoto had his troubles. It was hot and rainy in Seoul during July and August as the discussions were being held. He himself was ill most of the time and had to conduct negotiations "from a sick bed in a small Korean house." One of his entourage died. Thus the supplementary treaty itself was not very successful from the Japanese point of view, but Miyamoto came out worst of all when he tried to discuss matters connected with stationing a permanent Japanese representative at Seoul, his rights to have his family there,

[14] Memo to Hanabusa, enclosure in Terashima to Dep. Navy Min., Sept. 12, 1877, No. 113: NGB, X, 219. See also Dep. Navy Min. to Terashima, Sept. 10, 20, 1877, Nos. 112, 116: NGB, X, 219, 221-22. The districts according to Korean names were respectively Hamyong (northeast), Cholla (southwest), and Kyonggido (west central).

[15] Henry Chung (comp.), *Treaties and Conventions between Corea and other Powers* (New York: H. S. Nichols, Inc., 1919), 209-12.

having a "playing and walking area" in which they could move freely, and having free access to travel on whatever roads they pleased. The Kanghwa Treaty specified that the "Government of Japan at any time within fifteen months from the date of the signature of this Treaty, shall have the right to send an Envoy to the capital of Korea, where he shall be admitted to confer with the Minister of Ceremonies on matters of a diplomatic nature. He may either reside at the capital or return to his country on the completion of his mission. The Government of Chosen in like manner shall have the right to send an Envoy to Tokyo, Japan. . . . He may either reside at Tokyo or return home on the completion of his mission."[16]

Miyamoto tried to develop the argument around the question of *size* of the playing and walking area and proclaimed his willingness to reduce it from ten *ri* to four *ri*. But the Koreans refused to give any clear statement that a Japanese representative should be stationed at Seoul at all. They switched the playing and walking business to Pusan, where there were already Japanese residents, of course, and magnanimously allowed ten *ri* there, which was incorporated in the supplementary treaty.[17] In return they got Miyamoto to sign a statement on the envoy's stationing, so ambiguous and even negative that it promised to be an additional obstacle to the envoy when he came. It said, "The dispatch of an envoy to Korea being merely for purposes of [friendly] relations and trade, the duties do not require the stationing of an envoy in Korea. And in regard to Japanese envoys' coming and going, it should be limited to certain roads." Though Miyamoto signed this, he reserved the right of further negotiation on the matter to the Japanese government, and in conversation he got the Koreans to say that a future Japanese envoy might "stay a long time" and "show his national flag in Seoul." At one point in the negotiations the Koreans brought up the Japanese pirate (*Wakō*) raids on Korea

[16] Kanghwa Treaty, Article 2.
[17] Supplementary Treaty, Article 4.

of the fifteenth century. Perhaps Miyamoto was ashamed. Anyway, he "gave in beyond his instructions."[18]

So Hanabusa came. His final instructions were to present the Korean foreign minister a letter from Foreign Minister Terashima, to "discuss and decide" which ports should be opened to the Japanese, to insist on the necessity of a Japanese representative's being stationed in Seoul with freedom to travel on roads of his own choosing. If the Koreans tried to argue that a representative at Seoul was unnecessary, he was to "cite the example of other countries and persuade them that to reject this is to violate the Treaty." However, "although the place where the Minister stays must, of course, be Seoul, the Korean people may not understand, and if there is difficulty, you may establish the site temporarily between Kanghwa and Jinsen; but the road must be open to Seoul so that the Minister can go there any time." Hanabusa, in accepting these instructions, suggested to Terashima that he should "argue for two months, then if there is no result, return calmly and try again next spring," which suggestion Terashima approved.[19]

Hanabusa kept a diary of his experiences and his arguing, from September 9, 1877, when he was told of his assignment by the Council of State, until January 11, 1878, when he reported his results at Akasaka Palace to the emperor and his ministers. The document deserves a few paragraphs of résumé and quotation, not because important agreements are discussed therein, but because it gives an intimate view of the tortuous process of negotiation which, projected over several years, resulted in the implementation of the Treaty of Kanghwa. Hanabusa came to Korea, as has been said, aboard the *Takōmaru*, which was to take surveys of various potential open port areas before depositing the envoy at Inchon for his journey overland to Seoul. However, not even the first leg of the journey went smoothly. Under his entry of October 4, Hanabusa

[18] Tabohashi (1940), I, 613-19, 637. Terashima sent a letter of thanks to the Korean foreign minister for the hospitality shown Miyamoto, June, no day, 1877, No. 134: NGB, X, 310.

[19] Terashima to Hanabusa, Sept. 24, 1877, No. 117 and encl. 1: NGB, X, 222-26.

reports that cholera had broken out aboard the ship, and that he and the others of his party had to land at Pusan by small boat, the crew of the *Takōmaru* being prohibited from landing and "the dead bodies burned" to prevent spread of the disease. (Apparently diplomats were regarded as exempt from contagion.)[20] The *Takōmaru* then returned to Nagasaki to be cleaned, and Hanabusa remained at Pusan, where the head of the Japanese compound, Kondo, put him in touch with Korean district officials at Torai. On October 8 some Korean officials came to Pusan to see him, but the entertainment he provided failed because the Koreans did not like the meat and wine. On the ninth he and Kondo and others went to Torai. Kondo had a "Japanese horse," but Hanabusa and the others in their party tried to ride "Korean horses" and were "much troubled." Returning, some "crazy farmers" obstructed them.

On October 30 the *Takōmaru* returned from Nagasaki, and on November 3 "after bowing to the Emperor's photograph" Hanabusa left Pusan aboard her to undertake the surveying. On November 9, somewhere along the coast, he and the ship's officers entertained Korean local officials. After exchanging gifts they talked about the past year's drought. "The Koreans said it was terrible and is equally bad this year." Hanabusa asked if they would like to get some Japanese rice. If both the Japanese and Korean governments would help, he suggested, it might be obtained. The rural officers' reply was "not clear." The captain of the *Takōmaru* asked about the geography of the area. They said they knew nothing, which Hanabusa thought was "strange." When shown the ship's engines, they said, "Never in our whole lives have we seen such machines."

On November 24 Hanabusa and his party were landed at Kimpo where they took a hotel for the night, met a district officer, and arranged to go on to Seoul the following day. En route to

[20] Not so in Hawaii, where Inoue Kaoru's adopted son, arriving at Honolulu in 1885 aboard a smallpox-infested immigrant ship, had to stay aboard for seventeen days. Hilary Conroy, *The Japanese Frontier in Hawaii, 1868–1898* (Berkeley: University of California Press, 1953), 72-73.

Seoul there were "noisy crowds of natives," and "guards and musicians" were numerous. At Seoul they were met by an "official host" with whom they began conversations on November 26. Hanabusa steered the conversation to the subject of rice shortage and famine. "If you need help we will be glad to help. Please send this message to your government. . . . Since coming into your country we have been entertained with many dishes by your government officials, and I thank you very much. But when I think of hungry people even this sweet food will not go into my stomach. . . ."

The official host answered, "I am ashamed . . . but there is a special situation. . . . If my country received your rice, then my country would have the responsibility of giving rice to your country if there is a famine there. But my country is too small to take that responsibility."

Hanabusa answered: "Why didn't you say so earlier? My country already has foreign relations with other countries. Even if there is famine, there is no need for your help. Therefore your 'special situation' is not valid."

Touché for Hanabusa, but in most of his conversations he did not score so well. On November 27 he paid his first call at the office of the Korean foreign minister (minister of ceremony). There was some question as to whether he should be allowed to see the minister at all because "a final communication from the Japanese government" on the subject of his visit "had not been received." However, an interview was arranged at which Hanabusa presented Terashima's letter and announced the matters he had come to discuss. The minister objected that all these things were not mentioned in the letter, but a certain conviviality was established over chicken, soup, boiled fish, rice, persimmons, sake, chestnuts, and entertainment by dancing boys. On the twenty-eighth Hanabusa sent a letter asking the foreign minister to begin talks on the matter of ports. The same day, "hearing a noise outside the gate, I [Hanabusa] went out and saw a Korean official beating a Korean who was lying on the ground. The officer explained that this was one of the guards assigned to our party, that he had managed matters badly, and was being punished."

On November 29 the foreign minister sent a reply that the matter of opening ports was not his business, so he could not discuss it. Rather, he said, it should be discussed with the official host. Hanabusa protested that this attitude was inconsistent with Article II of the treaty, but he was told by a lower official that "even though we understand it is improper we cannot push the matter. The people in Seoul are noisy and impolite; popular feeling is bad and bad ones stir it up. We cannot tell what will happen." Gradually, being unable to get to the foreign minister, Hanabusa fell into discussing the port problem with his official host and other lesser officials, on the assumption, presumably, that the talks would be faithfully reported to higher echelons. He suggested Moon Chŏn as a possibly satisfactory place, but was told that it was close to a burial ground and therefore consultation about it was impossible. "Then," said Hanabusa, "my government wants provisionally to open Jinsen or Kanghwa, though I can postpone this." The Korean said, "Very good [postpone it]". Hanabusa said, "Then let us talk favorably about Moon Chŏn."

Korean official: That is very difficult.

Hanabusa: If it is difficult, let us discuss it carefully. . . . Our government has already mapped Korea, but we found no good place north of Moon Chˇn. Therefore we cannot accept your sacred tomb objection.

Korean official: I don't know the custom in your country, but here we do not do anything in a sacred tomb area. . . .

Hanabusa: Even if a Japanese representative goes there we will give no inconvenience to the people. Therefore there is no reason to object.

Korean official: Truly it is troublesome. . . .

Hanabusa: If we wished to possess these places, of course there would be trouble, but we only wish trade. Therefore there will be no trouble. . . .

Korean official: Having your envoy come to Seoul is very troublesome and expensive. Therefore next year in talking about the port situation, please do it by letter. The result will be the same and I will keep my face.

Hanabusa: I am sorry it is so expensive, but a representative must come. We can discuss economizing. . . . What kind of cost is necessary?

Korean official: I will ask my government.

Hanabusa: On every trivial matter you must ask your government. I will accept what you say as representative of your government, but you act like a messenger boy. . . .

Korean official: According to your representatives last year it is customary in your country to decide things in a hurry, but here we discuss matters thoroughly and then the King must decide.

Hanabusa: Do you know about the problem that time when an American named Jenkins recruited bad people in Shanghai, came to Kanghwa, and violated the tombs?

Korean official: I know the problem.

Hanabusa: The reason is that someone in your country told Jenkins that there were treasures in those tombs, treasures so much respected by Koreans that they would pay anything for their return if they were taken for ransom. The fundamental reason for such a problem is that you have no open harbor and no knowledge of foreigners. If you had a [foreign] settlement near the sacred tomb, this would protect [guarantee] it. The reason this Jenkins was not punished by the American government is that Jenkins told the lie that the Korean government had invited him, then Koreans treated him badly. This was believed. But if your government made formal objection to the American government, he would be punished.

These conversations came to a semi-climax on December 7 when Hanabusa's Korean host brought him a document from his government stating simply and directly, "We cannot open sacred places. Therefore please select others." Another round of argument began. Hanabusa warned that a war might soon break out between Russia and England . . .

Our government cannot overlook the future.

Korean official: If something happens, *then* we'll ask your help. . . .

Hanabusa: I must report to my country and I cannot report nothing. I came to make a peaceful friendship . . . but you tell me this is impossible and say not to come again. . . . You will regret it if other countries occupy [your ports]. . . . Therefore reconsider or you will have trouble for a hundred years. . . . We have close relations with Russia. We know well about the Russo-Turkish war. . . .

Korean official: Your country knows the world situation so well; we are at ease.

Hanabusa: Your country is like a mud snail, at ease with its head in its shell; but if you look out you will see bad fishes swimming by. Therefore be careful.

Korean official: When you return to Japan, please help us.

Hanabusa: Yes, but to do so you must first accept our offer. . . .

Thereafter for several days the talks were concerned with the issue of playing and walking around Seoul by some members of the Japanese diplomatic party and sailors from the *Takōmaru.* A Japanese second lieutenant, who insisted on going through the inner city gate to see some tombs, found himself unable to get back one night. He had to sleep outside the gate, though he was allowed to receive a cushion to sleep on, sent by the Japanese. (No doubt, the Japanese played and walked a little deliberately to pose the issue in a preliminary way.)

Meanwhile negotiations moved along somewhat from the impasse over Moon Chŏn. Talk turned to the possibility of a Japanese coaling station somewhere else along Moon Chôn Bay. After Hanabusa gave assurances that this would not mean that houses would be built and guards stationed in the area, he was told that coal might be deposited there after six months.

With this very small area of agreement opened, Hanabusa announced his impending departure. At this there were feasts and exchanges of gifts, but one final cloud arose. When Hanabusa's party departed Seoul on December 21, they left behind six Japanese to pack up heavy items of baggage with instructions to leave these in the care of Koreans "until our return next time." Hanabusa was dismayed, though he should not have been astonished, when the Koreans in a masterful expression of their hope that there would be no next time carted the baggage post haste all the way to Kimpo, and handed it back to him just as he was preparing to embark. Touché for the Koreans. The irritated envoy could only dispatch a letter to Seoul calling it "unthinkable that you cannot handle a few packages, when we would pay the bill." We are not told what happened to this baggage, but, from his description of all the difficulties his party had in the next few days in getting their goods aboard ship amidst cold and ice, it seems that Hanabusa had to take everything back with him.[21]

These, of course, represented only the first stage of the negotiations which eventually settled Hanabusa in Seoul as Japanese minister and opened three ports to Japanese commerce and residence. For over a year after this the Japanese registered no progress at all, except that within their own counsels they arrived at a definite decision to press for the opening of the ports of Genzan (Wonsan) and Jinsen and not to accept less desirable places.[22]

But Hanabusa, though accredited as permanent Japanese representative at Seoul, was not able to settle there, being required to trek back with all his furnishings each time he came. In fact, some ground was lost as the scene of argument shifted back to Pusan when Korean officials in that district began to levy "illegal" duties on Japanese goods. At Pusan, where the tradition of the

[21] This résumé of Hanabusa's mission is based on his diary, which appears as "attached document No. 1" in Hanabusa to Korean Foreign Minister, Dec. 18, 1877, No. 132: NGB, X, 239-88. See also Hanabusa to Terashima, Nov. 28, 1877, No. 130: NGB, X, 236-37. In this document Hanabusa reports that the surveys taken up the coast from Pusan had revealed that most of the small villages had poor harbors and "therefore we have decided to discuss only Eiko (Yong-heung)." However, the diary indicates that he could not get the Koreans to discuss this place at all.

[22] Actually, Genzan was not their first choice on the east coast, but the Koreans, refusing other places, implied they might talk about it, which prompted the Japanese to make it a principal target of their efforts. Regarding the survey of 1878, see Terashima to Sanjō, Feb. 20, 1878, No. 139: NGB, XI, 284-86; Terashima to Senior Naval Officer, Apr. 16, 1878, No. 148: NGB, XI, 286-87; Dep. Navy Min. to For. Min., Oct. 5, 1878, No. 148: NGB, XI, 295.

old-fashioned Tsushima trade remained, Japanese traders had continued to be active, following generally the old formalities while looking forward to the implementation of the Kanghwa Treaty to improve their situation. In December, 1878, Hanabusa was in Pusan, with the Japanese warship *Hiei* at his back, demanding that the Koreans rescind these duties. At first they refused. But, after consultation between Hanabusa and the captain of the *Hiei*, two squads of Japanese marines landed from the ship, marched to a mountain side near the offending customs station, and held a drill there "with empty rifles." Also, the ship's guns were fired. At this the Korean officials "were afraid" and repealed the duties "on their own initiative." Subsequent instructions from Seoul confirmed their action.

The Japanese realized well enough that this sort of squabbling at Pusan was distracting them from their larger objective of gaining Korean acquiescence to the opening of ports and the establishment of a permanent Japanese legation at Seoul, but they turned it to usefulness. In the spring of 1879 Hanabusa was ordered back to Seoul to bring up the matter of "compensation" for the trade loss the Japanese had suffered at Pusan, but "in lieu of which" various other matters might be settled. Foreign Minister Terashima stressed as "very important" the opening of Genzan and Jinsen, especially Genzan which had a great "strategic" importance to Japan and Korea "vis à vis a neighbouring country [Russia.]"[23]

Hanabusa began his new series of discussions in Seoul in June, promising his best efforts to open Genzan and prepared to "keep on insisting and staying." Persistence finally had its reward, for he could report on August 9 to the Foreign Office that the Korean government had finally agreed to the opening of Genzan. Regarding Jinsen, "we talked nine times, but they refuse on the excuse that the people would oppose it. I said then we will open it in twenty

[23] Archives, SP 5, 26-30. Hanabusa to Terashima, Jan., no day, 1879, No. 190: NGB, XI, 304-6. Terashima to Sanjō, Feb. 27, 1879, No. 120: NGB, XII, 211-13. Tabohashi (1940), I, 698-700.

months and meanwhile you can persuade the people. But they refused." Hanabusa left Seoul on September 3 and returned again via the *Takōmaru* to Japan. "Almost half the crew had beriberi."[24]

However, Hanabusa was truly indefatigable. After many subsequent stops and starts in the negotiations he finally got a Korean offer in January, 1881, to open Jinsen if the Japanese envoy would live there and go to Seoul only for business. Two weeks after that Hanabusa had an offer to open Jinsen in twenty months (i.e., September, 1882) with no mention of the requirement that the envoy live there.[25]

By the summer of 1882, as the time for the opening of Jinsen drew near, it seemed that Hanabusa's long and patient persuadings had been crowned with success. He had been accepted as minister at Seoul, not merely informally, but formally, having been allowed finally to present his credentials and an imperial letter in an audience with the Korean king. Hanabusa's request to do this had set the Korean court in an uproar, but finally, after he agreed to bow six times in the ceremony, it had been arranged. The Japanese legation was set up just outside the west gate of Seoul. The port opening problem seemed to be solved. Indeed, the long shunned envoy seemed to be achieving popularity of a sort. Koreans in fair numbers were becoming interested in visiting Japan, and were coming to the Japanese legation for advice and arrangements. In February, 1881, a Korean official dropped the hint to him that "soon some Koreans may secretly go to Japan." Hanabusa tried to quiz his informant, but he would say no more "because my superior officer might be coming." Later Hanabusa learned that even the king was favourably inclined toward the idea. He writes:

Another Korean official visited me and said in a small voice, "as yet the Korean government will not permit us to go to Japan, but soon

[24] Terashima to Sanjō and encl., Mar. 31, 1879, No. 122: NGB, XII, 216. Encl. in Inoue, For. Min., to Sanjō, Sept. 11, 1879, No. 123: NGB, XII, 217. Encl. in Inoue to Sanjō, Oct. 4, 1879, No. 124: NGB, XII, 220-21.

[25] Hanabusa to For. Min. Inoue, Feb. 2, 1881, No. 141 and Feb. 28, 1881, No. 146: NGB, XIV, 331-42, 352-54. Tabohashi (1940), I, 729-30. Archives, SP 5, 34.

some of our high class young men will go secretly. But I fear your government and people will despise them." "No," I said, "we shall be very happy. Even though they come secretly, if you will tell me in advance, we will arrange it all carefully." . . . ten days later a Foreign Office official came and said Yi Tong-in would come and visit me. Two days later Yi came and said . . . he would soon go to Japan, and Korea would buy Japanese ships. I was happy, but I asked, "Are you authorized by the Korean government?" He said, "Yes, please approve the plan." I said, "I approve, but I hope the Korean government will officially tell me about it." He said, "It must be a secret for we fear a leak."

This secrecy is to be explained by the fact that some groups at the officially seclusionist Korean court were becoming less devoted to the creed, especially when it served their factional interest.

Hanabusa learned later that some thirty-five Koreans had "very secretly" left for Pusan. He thought Yi was with them but "suddenly today he appeared with six *kamme* of silver and twenty tiger skins to ask me to send them to Japan on a Japanese ship. He said the others had already left, but he had trouble carrying these. He wanted to mint the silver in Osaka. . . . He said he would catch the others. . . ." It was May before the group, including some fifty persons, got to Japan. Hanabusa had urged that they be shown around "museums, Hibya Park military parade, flower viewing" and Japanese government officials tried to keep track of them, but they "found it troublesome" to stay in the navy hotel the government had designated for them, and they "spread out over various private hotels." "So," said Foreign Minister Inoue, "there was no special way to protect them, but I notified the chief of Tokyo police." Several smaller groups went also in 1881 and early 1882 to study "the regulation of customs duties," "copper and leather manufacturing," to buy machines for mining, steel, and leather production, to get military training, and many other things.

In Seoul a Korean military leader "who is trusted by the King" many times visited Hanabusa's military attaché, a young second lieutenant named Horimoto Reizo. They arranged for Horimoto to train some Koreans, but many Korean spectators "gathered about and laughed." So it was decided to get a special training ground (with a fence), and Horimoto got approval to train a "special technical force" of Korean guardsmen. In May, 1882, at the time of the marriage of the Korean crown prince, Hanabusa joined in the festivities, was received by the king, and presented him with a small steamboat and two guns, symbols of progress.[26]

But perhaps the surest sign that Korea was responding was a governmental reorganization undertaken by the Koreans themselves in 1881. The new chart of offices was rather complicated, but the change was in the direction of a larger emphasis on foreign relations. To the chart which was passed up from Hanabusa through the Foreign Office to Japan's Council of State was appended the comment: "Probably the new age of Korea begins with this reform."[27]

All this is certainly reminiscent of the American effort to open Japan to the currents of "civilization and progress" in the years after Perry's visits, even to "secret" trips abroad by young Japanese. A firm yet patient handling of a backward country was bringing hopeful signs that some elements among its people were awakening. It might be said, no, this is not a fair equation, for the Japanese had more sinister designs. Were they not merely laying a subtle groundwork for their seizure of Korea?

On this it should be possible to find a clue in their attitude to competition. Of course, it would not necessarily prove that they were scheming annexation if they did not help competitors establish

[26] From the following letters, all of which are in NGB, XIV: Hanabusa to For. Min. Inoue, Feb. 10, 1881, No. 123, 290-303; same to same, Apr. 15, 1881, No. 125, p. 303; Ueno, F.O., to Prince Arisugawa, Apr. 28, 1881, No. 126 and May 8, 1881, No. 127, 204-5; Inoue to Sanjō, Pr. Min., June 2, 1881, No. 128, 306; Ueno to Sanjō, July 23, 1881, No. 129 and June 8, 1881, No. 153, 307-8, 365-69; Kondo, Pusan, to Inoue, Sept. 2, 1881, No. 130, 308; Inoue to Fukuda, Seoul, Dec. 16, 1881, No. 137, 313-14.

See also Archives, SP 5, 33-36; Tabohashi (1940), I, 748, 751; Bartz, "Korean Seclusion . . .," 186. On the Korean court background, see Bartz, *ibid.*, 125-35, 183-84.

[27] Ueno, Vice For. Min., to Sanjō, Apr. 14, 1881, No. 152, with encl. (Hanabusa report): NGB, XIV, 362-64. Same to same, Mar. 28, 1881, No. 151: *ibid.*, pp. 360-61.

themselves in Korea. But did they try to keep other nations out? There has been strong suspicion that they did, evidenced by the fact that the first request of Commodore Shufeldt, representing the United States, for a treaty with Korea was forwarded through the Japanese to Seoul and the answer came back negative. The Koreans complained that Shufeldt's request was improperly addressed and further that Korea's foreign relations were restricted to the "neighboring" country of Japan. Shufeldt later obtained his treaty (the United States-Korea Treaty signed in May, 1882) through the aid of Li Hung-chang. Nelson discusses this episode, emphasizing Li's role and Korea's dependent state relationship to China, which made Li's influence effective, and he leaves the impression that Japan tried to block Shufeldt's efforts.[28] However, Treat's careful recounting of the affair from original documents, which he cites, gives no such definite impression; rather his tendency is the other way, toward Minister to Japan Bingham's opinion that the Japanese acted in good faith.[29] Also the Japanese Foreign Office record of the matter (preserved as confidential in their files) shows very clearly that Inoue, then foreign minister, advised the Korean government, "The American motive is nothing but friendly foreign trade. Your persistence in isolation is bad. It will invite unexpected harm. Therefore accept the American offer." And it describes the Korean refusal to entertain Shufeldt's request as "extremely against our [Japan's] advice." Later when a Korean delegation came to Tokyo to discuss the matter, Inoue advised a "swift opening of relations with the United States, England, and France and a plan for self defense."[30] The evidence would seem to add up to Japan's having made a genuine effort to help the American effort to obtain a treaty. That she did not do more may have been due to a point noted by Tsiang, namely, Japan had promised Korea not to transmit letters of other nations to her officials.[31] All told, it seems clear

[28] Nelson, *op. cit.*, 139-40.

[29] Treat, *Diplomatic Relations . . ., 1853-1895*, II, 122-26, 138-39.

[30] Archives, SP 5, pp. 31-32.

[31] Tsiang, *op. cit.*, p. 64.

that the Japanese were pursuing no great plot versus Korea as far as the midpoint of 1882.

However, on July 23, 1882, Japanese cautious implementation of the Kanghwa solution was rudely interrupted by an anti-Japanese riot in Seoul. Does this presage a change?

The *èmeute* of 1882 was in part a Korean reaction against the implementation of the Treaty of Kanghwa and the prospect of the admission of other foreigners to the country, and partly a struggle for supremacy in court circles between the Taewongun, the father of the king and former regent, and the queen, Min, whose faction had become predominate since the king had reached his majority in 1873. The Taewongun, who as regent was noted for his vigorous enforcement of the seclusion policy, persecution of Christians, and the killing or driving off of foreigners who landed on Korean soil, had been in retirement since 1873 and had watched the Min family gain power at court while pursuing a foreign policy less drastically exclusionist than he would have had it. The prospect of a reform in the Korean military, of which Horimoto was an advance signpost, especially disquieted those military men who had a vested interest in the old system, and plots emanating from them were soon asking leadership of the Taewongun. The signing of the American treaty in May had been followed by drought and crop failures, which tied the foreign intrusion to natural disasters in the whispers which circulated about, and were enlarged by the leaders of the plot. On the evening of July 23 a mob riot broke out in Seoul, and a number of the king's chief ministers, who were of the Min faction, were "sought out in their homes and hacked to bits." "The King escaped as though by a miracle, and the mob gazed on what they thought was the dead body of the Queen. Everyone knew that she was to have been poisoned by the Regent's order, but she had heard of what was coming and had prepared. A female attendant was poisoned in her place, she slipped out of her rooms . . . to safety."[32]

[32] F. A. McKenzie, *The Tragedy of Korea* (New York: E. P. Dutton & Co., n.d.),

An attack on the Japanese legation followed, which according to Tabohashi's account, was planned and led by the eldest adopted son of the Taewongun, who hoped by this spectacular feat to gain an important position. Hanabusa and his legation employees tried to hold off the attackers from the veranda, and they shot fifty or sixty of them, but the crowd set fire to the legation building and the situation was soon hopeless. The Japanese tried to get to the palace but could not, and then with Hanabusa leading twenty-eight others the band beat an inglorious retreat in darkness to Inchon, a number of them being killed along the way. But finally the survivors, including Hanabusa, got off into a small boat, from which, by great good fortune, they were picked up by the British surveying ship, *Flying Fish.* Meanwhile in Seoul, the rioters also attacked the barracks housing the Korean troops which Lieutenant Horimoto was training Japanese style. The barracks was destroyed and Horimoto was killed. Several other Japanese, away from the legation or barracks, were hunted down and slain.[33]

Hanabusa was deposited at Nagasaki, from whence he speedily contacted Tokyo for instructions. His telegram reporting the incident reached Tokyo on July 30. Foreign Minister Inoue, after consulting Lieutenant General Yamagata Aritomo, called an emergency cabinet meeting to discuss the matter. It was decided that an apology and damages "to the full extent of international law" should be demanded of Korea. However, it was also decided that "this kind of affair is typical of the time of opening up diplomacy in Eastern countries, so the incident should be given sympathetic consideration." Hanabusa should return to Korea imme-

---

16-17. "Report" by Ensign George C. Foulk, encl. in U.S. Min., Lucius Foote, to Sec. State, Dec. 17, 1884, No. 128: U.S. Diplomatic Despatches, Seoul. This report is printed in George M. McCune and John A. Harrison (eds.), *Korean-American Relations* (Berkeley: University of California Press, 1951), I, 101-13, see esp. p. 103.

[33] Archives, SP 5, pp. 36-37. Tabohashi (1940), I, 759-84. Hatada, *op. cit.*, pp. 170-71. Contemporary accounts in *Yubin Hochi* (newspaper), July 31, 1882; *Tōkyō Nichi Nichi*, July 31, 1882; *Jiji Shimpō* (newspaper), Aug. 10, 1882. See *Meiji Hennenshi*, V, 117-18, 128-30.

diately as envoy extraordinary minister plenipotentiary to make the demands, and he should be accompanied by a strong guard of army-navy troops; "as an emergency measure" warships should be dispatched to Pusan and Genzan to protect Japanese residents. These decisions having been made, Foreign Minister Inoue and the Foreign Office Korea specialist Miyamoto went to Shimonoseki to meet Hanabusa and instruct him precisely on how to handle matters on his return to Seoul. They told him of the decision to send warships to Pusan and Genzan, and instructed him to send Kondō, the Pusan consul, ahead to Inchon to set the stage for his own arrival. He should follow immediately aboard a warship with a battalion of soldiers as guard. It was emphasized, however, that the dispatch of navy ships and soldiers was "only to protect residents and not to open fire." Even "troublesome Koreans" should not be attacked. "If you think there is need to open fire, request instructions."

Upon his arrival back in Korea Hanabusa found no reason to "open fire," but the diplomatic situation was more complicated than had been anticipated in Japan. In fact, on August 10, two days before he arrived at Inchon, a pair of Chinese investigators arrived, Ma Chien-chung and Admiral Ting Ju-ch'ang. Hanabusa disregarded them and pushed on to Seoul, where he arrived on August 16. There he refused to discuss affairs with anyone but the king, to whom he presented Japan's demands on August 20. However, political affairs in Seoul were very unsettled and the position of the king insecure. After three days, Hanabusa saw he was getting nowhere and left Seoul for Inchon, making clear that he was violently angry and intended to depart for Japan. Korean negotiators, however, came after him there, discussions were held aboard his ship, and an agreement was reached speedily.[34]

But behind this was more than Hanabusa's show of anger.

[34] Hanabusa to For. Min. Inoue, telegram, Nagasaki, July 30, 1882, No. 116: NGB, XV, 215. Same to same, letter, July 30, 1882, No. 118: *ibid.*, 216-21, enclosing report of Kondo, Pusan, July 27 and letter of Hanabusa to Korean king, July 26, 1882, cf. Tabohashi (1940), I, 788-90. Kokuryūkai, *Nisshi* . . ., I, 169-78.

Actually it was the Chinese who took command of the situation and cleared the way for a settlement. Probably the most detailed description of how they came to intervene is provided by Ensign George C. Foulk, U.S.N., who, as assistant to the first American minister to Korea, compiled a background report on events in Korea prior to December, 1884, which was sent to the Department of State by the minister at that time. On the matter he says,

> The Chinese consul at Nagasaki telegraphed to China that the Japanese were sending a force to seize Korea; this at least was the substance of what was told three Corean nobles, then at Tientsin in China, by the Chinese authorities there. These Corean nobles were, in order of rank, Cho Yong Ha, Kim Yun Sik, and O-Yun Chung.
>
> Cho was a noted Chinese scholar and a strong Confucianist. Min Yong Ik [nephew of the queen] has represented to me that Cho and his companions at Tien-Tsin held powers plenipotentiary; however, this is denied emphatically by So Kwang Pom and the progressive party, who say that such powers were simply assumed, such deliberate assumption of the King's powers being no unusual thing for members of the Min faction. Knowing that Korea was helpless after the revolt of the soldiers to resist an invasion of the Japanese, Cho applied to the deputy viceroy at Tien-Tsin (Li Hung-chang then being absent, in mourning for his mother) for the use of Chinese troops which he might take to Corea. His first appeal was refused, but on the second, made by him as holding powers plenipotentiary, the use of soldiers was granted him; Cho and his companions came to Chemulpo with the soldiers on board Chinese vessels of war.[35]

Whether a Korean appeal occurred in this way or not, intervention at Seoul was soon a matter of Chinese policy. Three to four thousand troops poured in. They speedily re-established order in Seoul. On August 25 Ma took the Taewongun into custody, and, within a matter of hours, had him shipped to China. He then instructed the Koreans to negotiate with the Japanese. The timing is so close here that it is difficult to know whether the Korean nego-

[35] "Report," by Foulk, *op. cit.*

tiators who sought out Hanabusa at Inchon did so in pursuance of these instructions from Ma or in advance of them, possibly due to the fact that the Japanese demands registered at Seoul were less than had been anticipated. At any rate Ma urged the Koreans to negotiate and then himself offered to mediate the dispute. This Hanabusa's delegation rejected, making the point clear that they regarded Korea as an independent nation capable of settling its diplomatic affairs itself. Terms of the settlement, signed by Korean and Japanese representatives on September 3, were as follows: Korea promised to arrest and punish parties guilty of the assault on the Japanese within fifteen days; the Japanese dead (twelve according to Japanese account, thirteen according to others) were to be accorded a proper funeral; Korea would pay 50,000 yen for the families of the dead and injured Japanese and 500,000 yen in ten yearly instalments for damage done the legation and to defray the cost of dispatching the Japanese expedition; Japanese soldiers (one battalion) could now be stationed (for five years) around the Japanese legation to protect it; Korea would send an "important" mission to Japan to proffer an official apology for the incident; Japanese envoys, consuls, and their followers henceforth would be allowed unrestricted travel in Korea (having obtained passes from the Korean Foreign Office), Japanese residents of open port areas should be allowed greater freedom. One additional port would be opened.

During the three days of conferences which preceded the signing of this Treaty of Chemulpo, certain other matters were discussed as well, especially the general attitude toward foreigners which the Taewongun had fostered and publicized with memorial stones set up about the country urging the people to "guard right, expel wrong." Hanabusa proposed that these should be destroyed, for they were bad for Japanese and bad for Koreans too. After the signing, Hanabusa and his party remained to witness the "proper funeral" for the Japanese dead and the execution of three of the "villains" who had been "convicted" of killing Japanese. On

September 18 he left Seoul for Japan in the company of Pak Young-hyo, brother-in-law of the Korean king, who had received appointment as envoy extraordinary to bear the message of apology to Japan. Thus the incident of 1882 was settled.[36]

However, three further matters connected with it should be introduced here. First, the Japanese government, after receiving two instalments of 50,000 yen each (for 1883 and 1884) on the 500,000 yen indemnity, "taking account of the position of Korea—poor and weak," decided to cancel the full remaining amount due. This was announced to Korea in a letter to the king brought to Seoul on November 2, 1884. Secondly, Minister Hanabusa did not return to Korea. He was replaced as minister resident by Takezoe Shinichirō, who presented his credentials in Seoul on January 7, 1883. Thirdly, the Chinese, as the Japanese-Korean settlement was being effected, made a "trade agreement" with Korea which changed markedly the whole future outlook.[37]

The significance of these three happenings requires some explanation, which will be given in subsequent pages as part of an attempt to evaluate Japanese policy during the years 1882–84. As to Japan's handling of the 1882 incident in the immediate sense, American Minister Bingham in Tokyo was impressed with its moderation while Minister Young in Peking felt that the imposition of the indemnity was too harsh.[38] Perhaps Bingham and Young were influenced respectively by the environment in which they worked. However, in terms of the frame of reference earlier set forth in this chapter, that of the American opening of Japan and subsequent developments as the treaties were being put into effect, it would seem that there is much ground for comparison. Thus the murder of Heusken, coupled with the Namamugi incident and other anti-foreign outbreaks, the punitive expedition to western Japan and the Shimonoseki settlement of 1864, and the terms of

[36] Archives, SP 5, 37-40. Tabohashi (1940), I, 788-820. Tsiang, *op. cit.*, 73-76.

[37] Archives, SP 5, 41, 45-46; text of "trade agreement" in *Papers Rel. to For. Rel. of U.S.* (1883), 173-76.

[38] Treat, *op. cit.*, II, 165.

that settlement, which required opening of the Straits, payment of an indemnity for expedition costs, and an apology,[39] just about match what happened in Korea in 1882. And it is a most interesting parallel that Japan's forgiving the Korean indemnity in 1884 followed an American precedent. For the United States had returned its share of the Shimonoseki indemnity to Japan in 1883. The comparison should not be pushed too far, of course, for by 1883 the United States, following Minister Bingham's sympathetic approach, was cautiously encouraging and helping Japan toward a treaty revision program to free her from the inequalities of the treaty system which had opened her doors.[40] The United States was doing this despite the unsympathetic attitude of Britain and other treaty powers, though by no means in any headstrong idealism which might impair American commercial or other interests. However, the question of whether in Korea Japan did not play something of the same role, versus China, in the later 1880's should be examined.

Though this was not made explicit at the time of the 1882 incident, the fact was that China was by no means prepared to accept the idea that Korea was an "independent sovereign state." This meant in effect that regardless of how mild and patient and understanding an attitude the Japanese government and the governments of other treaty powers might take with regard to the opening of Korea, there were to be complications from China, whose leaders did not accept Western assumptions about sovereignty and trade and the desirability of "progress" in general. Indeed, within a very short time after the 1882 affair they were to reveal themselves as most determined to maintain and then to strengthen the traditional Confucian hold of China on Korea. Nelson has explored this Sino-Korean, father-son relationship with great sensitivity, probing its historical roots, observing its operation in

[39] Frank E. Ross, "The American Naval Attack on Shimonoseki in 1863," *Chinese Social and Political Science Review*, XVIII (1934–35), 146-55.

[40] Treat, *op. cit.*, II, 167 *et seq.*

specific instances, and concluding that it was, all told, an honorable rather than an oppressive type of big country-little neighbor association. He shows that it had strong ethical overtones, and in practical terms had given Korea a certain security under China's paternal wing. Oversimplifying, one might sum up his study as showing how stupid Westerners, by their inability to see beyond their preconceived notions of international relations, aided and abetted a scheming Japan, which knew the angles from both sides, to destroy a rather lovely old system.[41]

Nelson's study is a marvelous correction for myopia among those legionnaires who think of the nation-state system as the end-all and the be-all of international relations. Yet does it not, after all, give the Confucian international system too favorable a press? For, if we grant Nelson's positive evaluation of the Chinese system, must we not, considering the chaos which has accompanied its breakdown in the Far East, conclude that the world would be much better off if it had been left intact? Perhaps those who see the course of the twentieth century in terms of world-wide conflict and degradation would say so. (Kennan applies a similar argument when he suggests that the kaiser's Germany might best have been let alone.)[42] But would any but the utterly disenchanted be willing to consider the presumptions on which the Chinese system was built as supportable in our time—the bowing and scraping, the class distinctions, the relegation of exchange of goods and ideas to the rank of suspect activity, the resultant cultural and intellectual stultification? Is this not, after all, best described as feudal or medieval or by some term that emphasizes its inadequacy for the modern era. T. C. Lin, writing in 1935, called the old Sino-Korean relationship "fundamentally similar to that of the British Self-governing

[41] Nelson, *Korea and the Old Orders . . .*, entire. Mary C. Wright, in a recent article, emphasizes that post-1860 Chinese diplomacy was surprisingly adaptable, yet could not escape its Confucian foundations, especially as regards Korea—"The Adaptability of Ch'ing Diplomacy: The Case of Korea," *Journal of Asian Studies*, XVII, 3 (May 1958), 363-81.

[42] Kennan, *American Diplomacy*, 55-56.

Dominions to the British Crown at present . . . with Korea recognizing the overlordship of China, but singularly free in her internal administration and external relations."[43] This is giving the old Chinese system a good press too. But can it really be called "fundamentally similar" to the dominion system, when there were no parliaments, no representative bodies, no appreciation of the dignity of the ordinary man, even Chinese, let alone Korean? No. But would it not have been better, considering what has happened since, if the old system, left intact in its forms, could have been liberalized within, thus avoiding a power scramble and the tragedies that have befallen Korea and indeed every nation involved in the Far East in the last three-quarters of a century? To this one must say "of course," if a breath of fresh air could really have been pumped into the old order. Thus a legitimate question for our study to attempt to answer, becomes why was such not accomplished, where does the main responsibility lie? In particular, does the responsibility lie with Japan, and if so, with whom in Japan?

The Japanese had, of course, been aware that Korea was considered a "dependent State" by the Chinese at the time they undertook to obtain a formal treaty with her in 1876, as Mori's visit to Peking testifies. And from this, their very effort to obtain a treaty, any treaty at all, could be interpreted as a scheme to fool the Chinese and undermine the relationship. However, to interpret it that way is hardly fair in view of the fact that under the Ōkubo-Iwakura-Kido leadership Japan was moving into Western-style in many fields, and it would not necessarily be presumptive of aggressive designs on Korea that her new Gaimushō (Foreign Office) should seek to make treaties (Western-style) with Far Eastern as well as Western countries. In fact, Japan had already negotiated such a treaty with China herself in 1871, a treaty based on the recognition of the two nations' respective equality and sovereignty. And in the very year of the Korean treaty, 1876, China stationed a diplomatic representative in Tokyo. It would

[43] Lin, *op. cit.*, 203.

not have been an unreasonable assumption for Mori to think that China too was coming around to the new style in diplomatic affairs, and that the explanations about the dependency of Korea which officials of the Tsungli Yamen and Li Hung-chang gave him were merely windy echoes of the past, meant perhaps for the ears of tradition-minded members of the Board of Rites but no longer descriptive of actual relationships, and certainly of no import for the future.[44] He listened politely so that there would be no unnecessary antagonisms over the matter, and knew when Li approved the prospective treaty that he had honored the past but was going along with the future. Then during the six years after the signing of the Kanghwa Treaty, up until the incident of 1882, Japan's emissaries had proceeded to work out the details of the new style Japan-Korea relationship with Korea directly, which required patience and circumspection. They did not seek to invoke any special Chinese influence to get things done—officially, at least, forgetting that there might be such a thing. And when Hanabusa returned to Korea after the incident with his 800-man escort, he did not know about or expect Chinese help in settling the affair.

The representatives of Western powers, which sought treaty relations with Korea, were, as Nelson shows so well, honestly mystified at the paradoxical Chinese description of Korea's status as that of a dependent state of China, yet free and responsible in the management of both its domestic and foreign affairs. But Shufeldt like Mori listened politely as Li Hung-chang explained the dependency of Korea at great length, then went ahead to sign an American-Korean treaty based on presumptions of sovereign competence on either side. He simply ignored the fact that Li and his Chinese subordinates literally negotiated the treaty for Korea in Tientsin and set up the signing ceremony at Inchon. The American

[44] The evidence presented by Mary Wright, *op. cit.*, showing that the Tsungli Yamen was indeed trying to modernize Chinese diplomacy, indicates that Mori had good grounds for this assumption.

State Department in receiving the treaty took the position that Korea was "de facto independent" and that the aid which Shufeldt had from China in the making of the treaty was "in no sense a recognition of China's suzerain power." And it considered as of no consequence the letter to the president which the king of Korea sent along with the signed treaty explaining that "Korea is a dependency of China, but the management of her government affairs, home and foreign, has always been vested in the sovereign."[45]

Thus, in general, until the incident of 1882, Japanese and American official attitudes toward Chinese claims of suzerainty over Korea had been much the same; listen to them politely, but ignore them, for they are the voice of the past and have no present validity or future importance. After that incident, however, as the Chinese began to move to give substance to their claim, there was a divergence perhaps best described as, for the Japanese Foreign Office, "worried," for the American State Department, "continued unworried." This is, of course, partly explained by difference in distance and hence degree of interest in Korea, but not entirely, for the American State Department was well informed on the problem by its ministers in China and Japan and had a particular interest at the time because ratification of the Korean treaty was pending in the Senate.[46] Actually, the two governments put a different evaluation on China's likelihood of doing much to upset the developing treaty relationships with Korea.

Japanese Foreign Minister Inoue undertook a review of the whole question of Korean dependency on China. In this, he particularly sought the opinions of Iwakura and Itō, who, since the passing of Ōkubo and Kido, had become the leading men of the

[45] Nelson, *op. cit.*, 109-63, esp. 144-45, 157. Cf. Freylinghuysen to Young, Aug. 4, 1882, No. 30: U.S. State Dept., Instructions, China.

[46] Also Lucius Foote, when he arrived in Seoul as first American minister to Korea, made a quick but fairly accurate appraisal of Sino-Korea relations looking back to 1636, which he forwarded to the secretary of state. Foote to Sec. State, Aug 21, 1883, Dipl. Despatches, Seoul. Nelson attributes the U.S. attitude to failure to understand the Chinese international system, but I would say that the State Department had rather good information on it.

oligarchy. Their opinions were somewhat different. Iwakura said that "it is not quite clear whether Korea is a sovereign country or a belonging country to China. At the time of our concluding the treaty with Korea, Korea said it was an independent country, but now Korea says it is a dependent country to China. So it is necessary to make sure, asking Korea. It is a good idea not to argue directly with China; and we should seek the opinion of America, England, France, Germany, and others."[47]

Itō expressed the contrary view that it was "very urgent" that Korea be "independent," declare it "publicly," and send representatives abroad. "We should," he said, "give them [Koreans] some help and make them feel some obligation. They have no power and no resources, and that is why they have no alternative but to depend on China. Therefore to help them declare their independence and remove the declaration by the King that Korea depends on China should be our policy."[48] However, Itō was voicing his sentiments from afar, being in Europe, and when Inoue analysed the situation with both of these opinions in mind he came to the conclusion that "though there might be much desire among Koreans for help from Japan in making secure their independence, if you go inside the matter only Kim Ok-kiun, Pak Young-hyo, and Pak Young-kyo are really dedicated in this." Therefore it was "too early" to act on the assumption that this was also the desire of the Korean court. Inoue decided to avoid giving aid to the Korean independence party, and he did not give any encouragement to Pak Young-hyo when the latter came to Japan as the bearer of Korea's apology for the incident. Instead, he adopted what Tabohashi calls a "paradoxical policy," seeking to maintain a co-operative attitude toward China, while at the same time encouraging Korea to make treaties with other countries, in the hope that they, like the United States, would regard Korea as an

[47] *Iwakura Kō Jikki*, III, 897-99. Cf. Tabohashi (1940), I, 902-3.

[48] Inoue to Itō, Nov. 17, 1882, in Itō Hirobumi (ed.), *Chōsen Kōshō Shiryō* (Materials on Negotiations with Korea) (Tokyo: Hisho Ruisan Kankokai, 1936), I, 251-53. Tabohashi (1940), I, 904-5.

independent country and that through their influence Korean independence would "gradually be realized."[49]

It was especially with an eye to smoothing relations with China that Inoue changed ministers at Seoul. The new appointee, Takezoe, was of an old Kumamoto samurai family. He was a close student of China, and was well versed in Chinese poetry and literature. Since 1880 he had been Japanese consul at Tientsin, and he had a broad personal acquaintanceship with many important people in China. In fact, he was a friend of Ma Chien-chung, who presumably, since he had been the head man of the Chinese investigating team after the incident, would continue to be a directing influence in any further Chinese moves in Korea. Takezoe had been present at the negotiations at Inchon, and, while Hanabusa was off to Seoul, had talked informally with Ma about some of the problems involved, assuring Ma that Japan had no hidden idea of invading Korean territory or interfering in Korean domestic affairs. He explained the Japanese demands relative to settling the incident, Ma agreeing that they were comparatively light "from the viewpoint of international law" but urging that Korea was very poor and that the military expense reparation demand should be cut down.[50]

At any rate it may fairly be stated that a principal reason for Inoue's putting Takezoe in Seoul was to keep relations with the Chinese on as smooth a keel as possible. This interpretation is at variance with that of Tsiang and Nelson. Tsiang says "the Japanese government appointed Takezoe, a Chinese scholar of some repute, Minister in Korea to support the reformers." This would seem in itself a curious paradox, a Chinese scholar to support the anti-Chinese exponents of a new order. But it is basic to a further presumption, which many studies have held, namely that Takezoe and therefore the Japanese government were behind the famous and bloody revolutionary attempt by the Independence (pro-Japanese)

[49] Inoue to Itō, Nov. 17, 1882, in *Chōsen Kōshō Shiryō*. Tabohashi (1940), I, 905-7.
[50] Tabohashi (1940), I, 841-43, 907. Cf. Tsiang, *op. cit.*, 75.

party in Seoul which occurred on December 4, 1884.[51] Whether such is a correct appraisal of that situation or not we shall consider shortly, but first it is necessary to consider the relationship of Takezoe's appointment to the total situation as it was developing in Korea. Even granting that Takezoe would try very hard to maintain smooth relations with the Chinese and their representatives in Korea, this was not to be easy, unless Japan were prepared to give up entirely the idea of maintaining direct relations with Korea as a sovereign state and to see her small but budding trade there jeopardized; in other words to see the Kanghwa solution, which had been so painstakingly developed, broken down. In the first place, Ma did not long remain the first Chinese representative in Korea. Due seemingly to a rivalry at home between his followers and those of General Wu Ch'ang–ch'ing, the commander of the Chinese troops which had come to Korea in September and which remained in force in Seoul, Ma was recalled. Takezoe, nevertheless, established a "friendship" with Wu and it is noteworthy that, until Wu left Korea in 1884, there were no clashes between his forces and the Japanese legation battalion. Tabohashi attributes this to the "friendship."[52]

But regardless of personalities, a new Chinese policy of strong interference was replacing the traditional benign attitude that Korea, though dependent, should manage its own affairs. The network of Chinese influence in Korea was rather difficult to fathom, but it was most effective. There was General Wu with his

[51] Tsiang (*op. cit.*, 84-85) says: "Legally Takezoe was the representative of his government, which must accept the responsibility for what he did, unless disavowing him, which it never did . . . but Takezoe's zeal outran the intentions of his government." Nelson does not make this fine distinction, but merely blames the Japanese—*Korea and the Old Orders* . . ., 170-71.

[52] Tabohashi (1940), I, 910-11, 919. For trade, see Shikata Hiroshi, "Chōsen ni okeru Kindai Shihonshugi no Seiritsu Katei" (The Process of Formation of Modern Capitalism in Korea), in *Chōsen Shakai, Keizai Shi Kenkyū* (Studies in Korean Economic and Social History) (Tokyo: Tōkōshoin, 1933), 162-64. Nihon Nōshōmushō (Japan Ministry of Agriculture and Commerce) (trans.), *Rokoku Ōkurashō Kankoku Shi* (The Russian Finance Ministry's Situation in Korea)(Tokyo: Nōshōmushō, 1905), Japan-Korea import-export trade tables, 114-15. For fuller discussion see below, chap. IX.

troops, assisted by Yüan Shih-k'ai (the man of the future). But the main political and commercial influence was now exerted by Li Hung-chang himself through P. G. von Möllendorff, a German who had formerly been in the Chinese customs service (and who later went to work for Russia), and Chen Shu-tang, former Chinese consul at San Francisco. Von Möllendorff became inspector general of Korean customs and adviser to the Korean Foreign Office, and, as the newly appointed American minister, Lucius H. Foote, pointed out in one of his early dispatches, "he [von Möllendorff] seemed to feel that there should be no intercourse with the [Korean] Government except through his intervention." Chen, as "Commissioner for China to manage the Commerce of Korea," posted "Commercial and Trade Regulations for the Subjects of Korea and China," which stated that Korea "having been from ancient times a tributary [dependent] state of China . . . [these] regulations are to be considered so many concessions on the part of China to her tributary [dependent] state and are not within the scope of the 'Favored Nation Rule' existing between the several Treaty Powers and China." As it turned out, these attitudes and acts were only preliminary to the installation of Yüan Shih-k'ai as resident of Korea in 1885, which made him effective ruler of the country, but they constituted a clear indication that Chinese policy was to tighten up the old order, no longer to watch passively as the "opening" process unfolded.[53]

Though the question is not directly relevant to our analysis of Japanese policy-making on Korea, it is natural here to ask why

[53] Foote (Seoul) to Sec. State, Oct. 23, 1883, No. 34; Nov. 8, 1883, No. 39 and encl. 1; Nov. 10, 1883, confidential, unnumbered: Dipl. Desp., Korea. This last (Nov. 10) dispatch included a translation of a letter from Li Hung-chang to the Korean king describing the new trade arrangements as follows: "Therefore I desire to inform you from my heart that all matters which relate to Commerce you ought to have the liberty to arrange as you deem proper, but you must not permit any precipitate discussion with these [foreign] plenipotentiaries, which shall modify the purport of your former notice that Chosen is a dependency of China, dated Tientsin, Sept. 24." The king, adds Foote, "manifests great indignation and says that never before has China attempted, so directly, to interfere in the affairs of his Kingdom." See also Young (Peking) to Sec. State, Dec. 26, 1882, No. 85; Dipl. Desp., China.

did China begin this tightening up process. Was it not, after all, fear of Japanese designs on Korea that caused her to do so? Perhaps it was. Mary Wright has shown that the Tsungli Yamen "recognized the potential threat from Japan" as early as 1867 and kept it very much in mind during the 1870's and early 1880's.[54] Another scholar asked the author whether China's policy of interference might not have been a sort of "belated reaction to Seikan Ron." Again, perhaps it was. But we should not assume that, because China acted on the premise that she was protecting Korea from aggressive Japanese designs, Japan necessarily had such designs, at least in any specific sense in 1883. If, for example, Japan was only trying to open Korea, not seize it, in the same sense that the United States had tried to open Japan, then the Chinese decision to intervene actively might be said to have been based on a false premise and to have been extremely ill-omened, not only in Korea, for refurbishing dependence and stagnation, but also in China, for helping to harden the Confucian mold around the advocates of a more adaptable diplomacy. We do not wish to prejudge this question, we only wish to keep it open, because, although there assuredly had been Conquer-Korea advocacy in Japan, one of the more significant aspects of that argument was that it had been defeated, at great personal and political cost, by the Japanese themselves.

At any rate, in the face of China's tightening up of her relations with Korea, which began with the institution of the trade regulations of 1883, how did the Japanese react? Foreign Minister Inoue decided to steer a cautious, middle course. His appointment of Takezoe and his cold, realistic assessment of the shallow depth of reform sentiment in Korea are indicative of his willingness to back-step somewhat on the progress Japan had made in opening Korea. This did not mean that he was willing to give it all up. However, he now placed his hope for the further development of the opening process, not in Japanese unilateral action, nor in

[54] Wright, *op. cit.*, 380-81.

support of Korean progressives, but in collective pressure to be exerted by Japan and other treaty powers, especially the United States. This was the other part of his "paradoxical" policy, and it could be construed as a continuation of his aforementioned efforts in behalf of an American treaty. In fact, as early as August 16, 1882, as Hanabusa was settling in Seoul to begin negotiations concerning the incident, Inoue's assistant, Deputy Foreign Minister Yoshida, entered into conversations with U.S. Minister Bingham in Tokyo to put forth a proposal that, before the United States ratified its treaty with Korea, it would be well for the United States, Britain, and Japan to seek an understanding with China on the matter of the Sino-Korean relationship. Bingham reported the suggestion to Washington, but he did not endorse it. Since, as has been shown, American officials had not been inclined to take the Chinese claim of suzerainty over Korea very seriously anyway, and this could be interpreted as foreign meddling in an American treaty, it is not surprising that the State Department took no cognizance of the suggestion. However, although Bingham did not appreciate this, it is clear that Yoshida's proposal derived from an anticipation of just such Chinese interference in Korea as actually developed. Yoshida's fears had been aroused by a note from the Chinese minister in Tokyo, who having been informed, as were the ministers of other legations there, of Hanabusa's return to exact a settlement and apology, replied that "Japan is one of our treaty states and it keeps an embassy in one of our dependent states. Therefore we will protect them [the Japanese embassy] ourselves."[55]

Although the United States had not responded to Yoshida's suggestion, Inoue renewed the joint understanding idea in December (1882) after the trade regulations had made the Chinese intentions clearer. It was brought up in Peking by the new Japanese minister, Admiral Enomoto, in conversations with American Minister Young. Enomoto first alluded to a rumor that China was

[55] *Re* Bingham see Treat, *op. cit.*, II, 163. Chinese note quoted in Archives, SP 5, 39.

planning to "resume sovereignty over Siam" as well as Korea, which rumour Young had heard also, and to which he gave some credence, though the Tsungli Yamen had denied it. This was no doubt Enomoto's way of urging that the problem was broader than merely the Korean case. But "a day or two" later he specifically broached the Korean situation. Young reported the conversation in detail.

> He [Enomoto] said that his government would never consent to see Corea a Chinese province, and capable at any time of becoming a base of attack upon Japan. . . . The Admiral disclaimed any purpose on the part of his Government of occupying Corea. He said quite frankly that if his own views had been adopted years ago Japan could have made herself secure. I understood the Admiral to mean that he belonged to that party in Japan which would settle the Corean question by annexing Corea. But the Government was not of that mind . . . [and it was] the firm policy of his Government to maintain Corean independence. . . . [He said] there had been suggested the idea of a Congress to be composed of representatives of England, Germany, Russia, France, the United States, and Japan to hold its sessions in Tokyo and take up the whole Corean business. Japan would propose that the Powers should guarantee the independence of Corea and its neutrality . . . like Belgium. . . . He said he would like to see Corea politically another Belgium.

Having explained this and added that he had talked to Sir Harry Parkes about the matter and gained the impression that Parkes was favorable to the idea, Enomoto then asked Young directly what would be the United States' attitude. Young said he could give no answer on that. Enomoto then asked Young for his personal opinion. Young said that was of "no value." Enomoto then said that "Japan had great confidence in America, that we had opened her doors to Western Civilization, and it was natural for Japan to come to America for advice, especially in a case as critical as the present. . . ." Young then advised that Japan should make a direct request through its representative in Washington to the State Department, but warned that "high international considerations" were involved. He explained that the United States had declined to enter into such conferences on European questions, but that she had done so with respect to the South American republics. He also warned that Russia might bring up boundary questions, to which Enomoto replied that "Russia had been treating Japan very well."

Young summed up the conversation as "curious and interesting" but he suggested to the secretary of state that one reason Japan wanted such a congress was so that "she would act and deliberate with Western Powers as an equal." He also noted that Enomoto had said nothing about inviting China to the congress.[56]

Minister Young also received, about this time, a letter from Inoue himself, rather elaborately thanking the United States for the presence and courtesy of the *U.S.S. Monocacy*, which had been in Korean waters at the time of the incident, and enclosing a copy of the Japanese-Korean settlement of the incident.[57]

However, Young formed his conclusions on the issue of Chinese interference in Korea independently of the Japanese suggestions. He had received a detailed analysis of the situation posed by the issuance of the trade regulations from Mr. Chester Holcombe on December 19. In this Holcombe showed himself very much aware of what the Chinese were trying to do. He noted that there was no indication in the regulations of the independence of the Korean king. They served, he said, "to unmask the strategic movements [of] the past year, of which Corea has been the subject and H.E. Li the principal organizer." These were to get the United States, England, and Germany to make treaties "to effectively secure the autonomy of the Corean King against any attempt upon it by Russia or Japan," then with the trade regulations "to render nugatory" any advantages the Western powers fancied they had gained. Thus we "pull their chesnuts out of the fire" and "they eat them."

[56] Young to Sec. State, Dec. 28, 1882, No. 87, confidential; same to same, Dec. 27, 1882, No. 86: Dipl. Desp., China.

[57] Young to Sec. State, Jan. 2, 1883, No. 92: Dipl. Desp., China. Inoue's letter is dated Dec. 4, 1882. Inoue also wrote a letter of thanks to the captain of the *Monocacy*.

But, he advised that the United States go right ahead and ratify its Korean treaty anyway, for it was a "mistaken idea" on the part of the Chinese to think that they could prevent the application of the "Favored Nation Rule." The United States could claim the same rights, and with Britain and Germany doing so also they would be successful in obtaining them. Also Japan, "exasperated . . . by recent events in Corea," might make harsh demands and back them by force. The pushing of the most favored nation claims would restrain any hostile intentions, and obtain the desired end by peaceful means. So argued Mr. Holcombe.[58]

Young seconded Holcombe's urging that treaties with Korea should "be ratified by the Powers as they can claim by the most favored nation clause all that China gets." And he added, rather condescendingly, "I think that the disposition for Asiatic nations to enter into treaty relations with each other should be encouraged. . . . The Japanese treaty with Corea last summer and even this extraordinary [Sino-Korean] treaty are steps toward Western ways and Western laws and in that have value."[59] While Young reached this unworried conclusion after considerable analysis, Bingham in Japan was not even concerned enough to probe the situation. He interpreted the trade regulations as a convention which did not affect the powers' relation to Korea as an independent state.[60].

United States policy on Korea, as it crystallized in the spring and early summer of 1883, sought to treat Japan and China with "perfect impartiality," a favorite phrase of Secretary of State Freylinghuysen, and had "no immediate interest" in the relations between Korea and China. It recognized that the trade regulations gave Chinese merchants an "enormous advantage", but this could be corrected eventually by the application of the most favored nation principle. The instructions to Mr. Foote, the new minister

[58] Chester Holcombe Commentary on Trade Regulations, Dec. 19, 1882, encl. 2 in Young to Sec. State, Dec. 26, 1882, No. 85: Dipl. Desp., China.

[59] Young to Sec. State, Dec. 26, 1882, No. 85: Dipl. Desp., China.

[60] Treat, *op. cit.*, II, 179.

to Korea, were rather verbose in telling him how to deal with the Sino-Korean relationship, but put into a capsule summary they were "to report fully as to the relations of Corea, China, and Japan that appropriate steps may be taken to secure for our citizens the privileges granted to the Chinese in the Commercial Regulations."[61] The United States viewed Korea as an independent sovereign state but saw no need to go beyond safeguarding its own treaty rights in asserting it. Minister Foote re-echoed this sentiment in the fall of 1884 when he predicted, "fortified as Corea is, by the Treaties lately concluded here, it has seemed to me that China would, in time, voluntarily relinquish her claim to suzerainty; that this is the earnest desire of the King and his people there is no doubt."[62]

However, looking back from the present at the tragic record of wars fought in and over Korea, one must ask whether a golden opportunity was not missed in the American failure to pick up the Japanese proposal that Korea be pronounced independent and neutral by as many countries as could be brought to do so. If the proposal had been merely a Japanese scheme or trick, Enomoto's lamentations on his government's reversal of his own policy predilection would not make sense—nor would a Japanese Foreign Office self-analysis of its policy as of the time when Minister Foote was taking up his duties in Korea. "The United States regards Korea as independent; she wants no annexation of Korea and seeks peace in the Far East; she feels that Korea needs enlightenment. This coincides with ideas long held by the Japanese government."[63]

In December, 1883, by which time the dust had settled on the 1882 incident, Takezoe returned to Tokyo for an extended stay. By that time the Japanese government had settled into a somewhat less than satisfactory, in terms of the promise of the Kanghwa

[61] Freylinghuysen, Sec. State, to Foote, Mar. 17, 1883, No. 3: Dipl. Desp., Korea. Freylinghuysen to Young, Mar. 16, Apr. 11, May 26, 1883, Nos. 94, 107, 124: Dipl. Desp., China.

[62] Foote to Sec. State, Seoul, Sept. 4, 1884, No. 104, confidential: Dipl. Desp., Korea.

[63] Archives, SP 5, 44.

settlement, but realistic solution to the Korean problem. Far better in the eyes of the world and far more sensible in terms of their own resources than conquering Korea, they had proceeded in the anti-Seikan tradition of cautious, unemotional intelligence to open Korea to the fresh air of modernization and to gain a few commercial benefits therefrom. For this, progressive nations could only thank them, especially in view of the fact that they were evidently welcome, as far as the Japanese were concerned, to participate also. Until the incident of 1882 it had all been very satisfactory and promising indeed. After that the Chinese interposed difficulties, had tried to turn the clock back. But the Japanese government had not allowed itself to become excited and irrational, though it was worried, for, as Enomoto's conversation with Young reveals, the anticipation that conditions in Korea were involved—beyond questions of insult, trade, and modernization—with Japanese national security was beginning to impress the minds of Japanese government leaders. It was not yet clear how this question of security would develop, for China, though capable of exerting sufficient pressure in Korea to render Japanese influence slight, could hardly be considered a menace to Japan itself. Thus, in the absence of a clear and pressing security threat, Inoue's policy was grounded in worry rather than fear, and inclined toward cautious rather than desperate measures. With careful logic he picked his way through the alternatives, deciding to back-step somewhat to conciliate China while relying on the collective relationship of the treaty powers with Korea to keep things moving there in the "right" direction envisioned in the Kanghwa settlement. Essentially, this policy was much like that of the United States, except Inoue, being less confident that the trend of the treaties and the times would defeat the Chinese intervention, sought a specific international congress to make sure. And he may have been taking a longer look ahead to the implications for Japanese security of unsettled conditions and international rivalries in Korea versus a settled international guarantee of Korean independence.

From 1876 through 1883 the cool realism of anti-Seikan governed Japan's Korea policy. This policy was progressive in the sense that it aimed to bring the fresh currents of the modern era into Korea and that it was not exclusivist toward other nations which sought to establish treaty relations with Korea. But, as a realistic policy, its ultimate frame of reference was Japan, not Korea. It could therefore compromise many things where Korea was concerned, but ultimately nothing where Japanese security was concerned. Yet within that frame of reference it was cautious and enlightened, at least through 1883, with the government oligarchy solidly in control of policy formulation and execution. However, the year 1884 found other forces in the Japanese political scene beginning to challenge this "safe and sane" Korean policy. Their influence must now be considered.

III

Enter Idealism : Liberal Aspirations Challenge Government Caution

The first Koreans to become enamoured of ideas of progress and freedom were those who had a chance to go outside Korea to visit "progressive" countries. One is tempted to describe them as "inspired" rather than "enamoured," considering that many who took up the cause paid sooner or later in imprisonment, torture, or death, and still the survivors carried on. Syngman Rhee, though a younger contemporary of those whom the inspiration of new horizons first touched, may be taken as a prime example of the strength of the impact upon them. Still "dedicated" at eighty. And yet the case of Rhee argues that, viewed across the years, the vision of progress and freedom for Koreans has been something of a rainbow, so much pie in the sky for so long that even those who, like Rhee, dedicated their lives to its attainment have tended to lose their perspective. The frustrations, disillusionments, and viciousness which they encountered and countered along the way were so overpowering that the early liberalism vanished in suspicion and bitterness. Had some of them been able to read the future in those late nineteenth-century days of inspiration, they might themselves have described their condition cynically as "enamoured" rather than "inspired." Also, "enamoured" makes room for the bizarre, for the misconceptions about progress and freedom and the human foibles which entered into particular situations. One thinks of

Pak Chung-yang, the first Korean minister to the United States, who, coming to meet the president in 1888, smuggled in a few cases of Manila cigars and got a young Korean student to sell them for him.[1]

Whether enamoured or inspired, there existed by 1883 a doughty band of Koreans who had sniffed the heady wine of the new world outside Korea and were mightily interested in tasting it. They are variously called the Independence party, the Progressive party, the Reform party, or the pro-Japanese party, though the latter name implies a narrower breadth than was actually the case.[2] However, their first contact point with the new world was Japan, and indeed for many years they found there a haven of retreat, sustenance, and hope. Their leadership came from the membership of those early missions to Japan, the ratification mission for the treaty of 1876, the cultural mission of 1881, the apologizing mission of 1882, some members of which remained longer than the missions per se to observe and study progress unfolding. The above-mentioned Pak Chung-yang, who was a member of the cultural mission of 1881, was by no means the liveliest or most perceptive of these missioners to Japan, even though he later became minister to the United States and prime minister of Korea. He is described by Horace N. Allen (who guided him into both jobs) as "a weak imbecile of a fellow."[3] The ablest proved to be Hong Yong-sik, founder of the Independence party, who was killed in 1884; Pak Young-hyo, brother-in-law of the king and by virtue of his princely rank the first in prestige among the reformers; So Kwang-pom; and Kim Ok-kiun, who was perhaps the most vivacious and audacious of all. All were members of the Korean nobility. Others prominent in the group were two relatives of So,

[1] Fred Harvey Harrington, *God, Mammon and the Japanese* (Madison: University of Wisconsin Press, 1944), 240-41.

[2] U.S. Minister Foote in an early dispatch describes Korea as "stagnant and impoverished" but adds, "there are many well intentioned men. . . . They compose the party of progress and are opposed to seclusion." Foote to Sec. State, June 26, 1883, No. 9: Dipl. Desp., Korea.

[3] Harrington, *op. cit.*, 228.

So Che-pil and Han Kin-chik, Pyon Su, and Pak Young-kyo, also killed in 1884. All of these had, by 1883, been to Japan, some of them for extended stays, and several of them, Hong, So Kwang-pom, and Pyon were members of the first Korean mission to the United States, which visited this country in September, 1883.[4]

When Hong returned from the United States he described his experience as having been in "a light so bright as to dazzle" him. Perhaps the United States was so dazzling as to be a little unreal, but Japan was a close-by, real, and accessible place where things were being done which pointed clearly in the direction of those accomplishments observed in the United States: the New York Hospital, the Western Union Telegraph Office, the New York Fire Department, Havermyer's Sugar Refinery, and the Brooklyn Navy Yard.[5] Japan's accomplishments might not be so spectacular as these but she was doing remarkable things for a country only thirty years out of seclusion; here indeed was something to be studied. The institutional and technical advances which the Korean visitors observed were, of course, largely the result of the policies and efforts of the Japanese government in their determined march forward on the Ōkubo principle of "internal construction." However, the leaders of this, from Ōkubo himself to Inoue Kaoru, who, as foreign minister in the early 1880's was the official host of these missions, were cold and oligarchic gentlemen. As has been shown, though their policy was progressive, they did not allow emotion or enthusiasm to get the better of their realistic judgment. In short, they were not inclined to see their "internal construction" program in Japan jeopardized by involvement in Korean reform any more than in the Korean conquest (Seikan) which they had squelched so effectively. Probably the Korean progressives-to-be did not analyse this out at that early stage, but they must have felt a

[4] Foote to Sec. State, July 13, 1883, No. 14; Dec. 17, 1884, No. 128 and encl. and Freylinghuysen to Foote, Oct. 16, 1883, No. 27, Instructions: Dipl. Desp., Korea. Cf. McCune and Harrison, *Korean-American Relations*, I, 32-34, 105-6, 112-13. Bartz, "Korean Seclusion . . .," 186.

[5] Foote, No. 128 (encl.) and Freylinghuysen, No. 27, *op. cit.*

contrast of atmosphere in the somewhat chilly formality of Japanese officials as against a delightful warmth they found when they escaped their official guides, "spread out over various private hotels," and met those spirited critics of the oligarchs, the incautious and enthusiastic Japanese liberals.

Japanese liberals and liberalism have been discussed in many places and from many angles, especially as related to the development of political parties and parliamentary government in Japan, and it is not necessary here to attempt a thorough analysis of their complexities. However, as related to Korea, it should be observed that the Japanese liberals who took up the Korean problem in the early 1880's were either Liberal party followers of Itagaki and Gotō or members of Fukuzawa Yukichi's Keio school group. Since these groups were coparticipants in the *Jiyū minken* (freedom and popular rights) movement and strong advocates of parliamentary government and Western style liberalism in general, it would not be necessary to separate them except for the fact that they had come to liberalism by somewhat different routes. Itagaki and Gotō had come to liberalism by way of Seikan Ron. It was as advocates of Conquer Korea that they had first broken with the cautious conservatives, and their early party organizations had advocated Seikan in equal voice with Jiyū minken. However, the Kanghwa settlement had punctured the Conquer Korea balloon and by 1880, when the Jiyūtō (Liberal party) laid down its planks for the future, the emphasis was on fighting the oligarchy for constitutional government, civil rights, equality, and "national advance and prosperity."[6] "National advance and prosperity" could possibly be interpreted to mean expansion overseas, but this was by no means clear, and if the other three planks were applied to peoples outside Japan such an interpretation could hardly hold at all. Conquer Korea was nowhere to be found. And as a Liberal party Korea

[6] Scalapino, *Democracy and the Party Movement* . . ., 66. It could even be argued that "Itagaki's main purpose [in 1873] was not to attack Korea but to make a good constitution." Kokuryūkai, *Seinan* . . ., I: 2, 650.

policy began to take shape in the eighties, it was built around a theme of Help Korea—toward progress and freedom, rather than around the avenging insults thesis of Seikan. However, Seikan was in the heritage of the Liberal party; whether it would ultimately affect the efforts of Japanese liberals on behalf of Korea remained to be seen.

Fukuzawa came to liberalism without benefit of Seikan. In fact at the time of the Kanghwa Incident, when there seemed to be a flurry of renewal of Conquer Korea sentiment, to which Itagaki and other people's rights advocates were responding, the Keio group warned that "the People's Rights and Conquer Korea arguments should not stand together." This was because, explains Japanese historian Tōyama Shigeki, the Fukuzawa group came from a lower class [than Itagaki etc.] and thus were able to point out the weakness of the "*shizoku* [samurai] consciousness" which was appealed to by the Conquer Korea idea.[7] In other words, Fukuzawa was able, at this stage anyway, to see that liberty and people's rights should be disconnected from conquering Korea, lest perhaps they be ruined by it. This is an interesting and almost prophetic idea, which, unfortunately, Fukuzawa himself did not remember long enough. But it suggests that a very high evaluation should be placed on Fukuzawa's liberalism. It is possible to take a rather condescending view of "liberalism" as espoused by Itagaki and his Liberal party by emphasizing its inability to extract itself from nationalism, its confusion of individual rights with national rights, its Seikan roots, and its inclinations toward chauvinism. Certainly such a view has much to support it, and we have noted already in this study the tarnished nature of Liberal party liberalism. However, this line of thinking should not be pushed too far for two reasons. First, it comes very easily to the implication that this tarnished liberalism is the Japanese variety, in contrast to a purer form, untainted by nationalism, in Western countries, at least in

[7] Tōyama, *Meiji Ishin,* p. 329. Tōyama cites *Yubin Hochi* of Jan 6, 1876. *Hyōron Shimbun,* and other newspapers, *ibid.*, p. 339.

some Western countries. Purer form there may be, if one underscores the comparative and admits that the difference is only in degree, and perhaps in very slight degree at that. How far can a liberal candidate get in any democratic country without a considerable appeal to nationalism? Would a fair answer be, not very far anytime, and nowhere in a time of external crisis? Secondly, as specifically concerns the Korean problem, this line of thinking comes easily to the presumption that the only reason Japanese liberals took an interest in Korean progressives was to use them as pawns in a Japanese nationalist scheme to gobble up Korea. Befriending Korean progressives becomes then merely an extension of Seikan Ron. The details to be presented will, I think, indicate otherwise, even in the case of the Seikan-based Liberal party. But the very large influence of Fukuzawa and the Keio school group in the relationship between Japanese liberals and Korean progressives would seem to point all the more clearly in that other direction.

Fukuzawa, despite his many other activities, devoted a great deal of time and energy to the Korean problem. And since he towers above most of the other Japanese liberals in intellect and perceptivity, the direction and impact of his thought and action should be given special consideration. How high Fukuzawa towered is difficult to say, but this writer is inclined to rate him far above the easy definition that pictures him as a nineteenth-century liberal-nationalist, who, alas, let nationalism get the better of him. Fukuzawa does not categorize so easily. His thought is by no means confined by national or class boundaries. In his activities we can see an example of a philosophically well-grounded liberalism at work on the international problem with which we are specifically concerned.

Fukuzawa was born in 1835, into a lower samurai family in Kyushu, and it seems likely that his earliest perception of injustice and inequality stemmed from his observation of the "material impoverishment and psychological frustration" of his own lower samurai class. That he felt this deeply is shown by his effort to teach a lesson on feudal discriminations by describing conditions in his own "old feudal clan,"[8] However, Fukuzawa did not seek relief from his sense of injustice merely in bitterness against the upper samurai or some other scapegoat. He was stimulated by Perry's coming to learn Dutch, and then English, and by the dawn of the Meiji era he had managed two trips to the United States and one to Europe. By that time he had discovered that education was the key to improvement and he conducted his classes imperturbably through the War of Restoration, convinced that the spirit of independence and self-respect he was cultivating was more important than which side won the civil war. And through his career he refused to align himself permanently with a group or party, though he took a vital interest in the issues of the day and never hesitated to level scathing criticism at whomever, according to his sense of values, seemed to deserve it.

Fukuzawa's sense of values has been probed by one of the most brilliant young historians of postwar Japan, Maruyama Masao. Maruyama seeks to explain the basis of the many seeming contradictions in Fukuzawa. (The Korean problem reveals some of these, though Maruyama stresses those connected with his advocacy, yet criticism, of the *minken* (popular rights) movement.) At the root of his philosophy Fukuzawa held to a "relative" principle, which meant essentially that one group is not always right, and that any single idea, whether progressive or reactionary, if pushed too far, becomes "the enemy of civilization." (I remember the remark of a colleague of mine, who perhaps said this even more succinctly: "Push any idea to its logical conclusion and you'll be sorry.") Without this "relative" principle one comes to the phenomenon of "indulgence," for which Fukuzawa reserves his most scathing criticism. Indulgence means the use of a panacea to approach problems. And this is "idleness of the human spirit." The formulist and the opportunist possess different versions of this same attitude.

[8] Carmen Blacker (trans.), "Kyūhanjō (Conditions in an Old Feudal Clan) by Fukuzawa Yukichi," *Monumenta Nipponica*, IX, 1-2 (1953), 304-29.

They are both guilty of "idleness of the human spirit." We can find the phenomenon of indulgence in a political situation when that which was created as a means becomes an end in itself. Feudal society is an example of this, with its sharp distinctions between high and low and its emphasis on tradition. The supernatural authority of rulers is an example of this. And also the popular rights movement, when it becomes guilty of "ultrapoliticalism" and makes a fetish of devoting all its energy to overthrowing the government and acquiring political power, exemplifies this. In all of these the means has become the end.

The opposite of indulgence, says Fukuzawa, is "the spirit of independence." Progress means the "complication of things" and the "dispersion of value." There are many roads to the development of value; therefore tolerance is necessary. Freedom cannot be imposed. The fundamental task of the Meiji Restoration is "through the dispersion of value to make dynamic the spirit of the people." The phenomenon of indulgence is most prevalent in a closed society. The more dynamic the society the more the "spirit of independence."

The modern civilization of Europe he regarded as an indispensable instrument for the independence of Japan. But European civilization is not an end in itself. Civilization in Europe is only the present stage of civilization in general. And even the independence of a country is merely conditional in character. (Thus, says Maruyama, it is not correct to regard Fukuzawa either as a mere Europeanist [Westernist] or a mere nationalist.)

Maruyama puts Fukuzawa's philosophy into a chart as follows:

I. MIND

Bad qualities	*Ideal qualities*
Indulgence in things	Independence of the thing (subject)
Inflexibility of perspective	Mobility of perspective
Making judgments absolute	Making judgments relative

Bad qualities	*Ideal qualities*
Extremism based on one value	Tolerance based on a multiplicity of values
Respect for customs or mores	Respect for intelligence
Reproduction of the same past behavior	Ceaseless advance by trial and error

II. SOCIETY

Fixation and simplification of social relations	Complication of social relations
Concentration of values to central authority (the state)	Dispersion of values to various social forces (civil society)
Ostentatious character of institutions (where institutions become the end in themselves)	Practical character of institutions (where institutions are instruments)
Reign of one ideology	Coexistence of various ideologies
Uniform control	Unification (agreement) through opposition (compromise)

Lastly, Fukuzawa leavened his philosophy with the "*ujimushi* principle." The characters *uji* and *mushi*, which are combined in the word *ujimushi*, mean respectively worms and bugs. In combination, however, ujimushi is a sort of slang term meaning children, like small fry. Hence, ujimushi is the worms and bugs or the small fry principle. After all, Fukuzawa told an audience of Keio students, "life is like the play of children." If people take life too seriously, they fall into indulgence. Yet we are here. We have appeared upon this world, so there must be some purpose. Therefore we should realize that life is like the play of children, yet we should not treat it as lightly as that; we should work at it as though it were not play.[9]

[9] Maruyama Masao, "Fukuzawa Yukichi no Tetsugaku" (The Philosophy of Fukuzawa Yukichi), *Kokka Gakkai Zasshi*, LXI, 3 (1947), pp. 129-63. See also Miyakawa Tōru, "Fukuzawa Yukichi ni okeru 'Keimō Seishin' no Kōzō" (The Structure of the "Spirit of Enlightenment" in Fukuzawa Yukichi), *Tōyō Bunka Kenkyūjo Kiyō*, VI (Nov. 1954), 241-64 and John W. Morrison, "Japan and the West: The Career of Fukuzawa Yukichi," *The Western Humanities Review*, VII, 3 (1953) 233-44, for discussion of Fukuzawa's career and ideas.

This should be enough to indicate that, whatever the shortcomings of Japanese liberals as a whole, they had among them a man of outstanding intellect and perceptivity, who was not merely appreciative of liberal thought as he found it in the West or as it might contribute to the national development in Japan, but who had an eye on ultimate meaning and universal truth. Of course, we should not make Fukuzawa better than he was. His philosophy must be pieced together, as Maruyama has done it, from his vast array of speeches and writings, which are mainly action pieces relating to a particular situation or occasion. Probably he himself could not have set down their meaning in so coherent a pattern. And furthermore, he shows himself at times in the course of his career, like his liberal friends who emerged from Seikan beginnings, to be susceptible to the use of non-liberal instruments—like soldiers and gunpowder—to accomplish liberal ends, which was also true of Lincoln, Wilson and Franklin Roosevelt. But he had most of the ingredients of the best in the liberal tradition, and this should be remembered in our effort to assess the role Japanese liberals played in relation to the Korean problem.

Japanese liberals involved themselves in the Korean problem partly out of sympathy for the nascent progressive movement in Korea and its Korean leaders and partly in the hope that by contributing to it they would contribute to the achievement of liberal goals in Japan. The first theme is illustrated by Fukuzawa's statement in 1881 to the effect that the two young Koreans he was putting up in his own house reminded him of himself, as he had been earlier as a student in the United States.[10] The second is illustrated by the argument of Sugita Teiichi, a Liberal Party member, who urged that if reform could be achieved on the continent (Korea, China) the reform of Japan would be "automatic."[11] At any rate, to the Japanese liberals, whichever way one

[10] Ishikawa Mikiakira, *Fukuzawa Yukichi Den* (Life of Fukuzawa Yukichi) (Tokyo: Iwanami Shōten, 1933), III, 289.
[11] Oka Yoshitake, lecture at Tokyo University, May 28, 1954.

looked at the matter, the aid and encouragement of Korean reformers promised good results for the cause of people's rights.

Fukuzawa and other Japanese liberals began to be in close touch with potential Korean reformers about 1881. From that time, the tempo of their activity on the Korean problem increased rapidly until it arrived at a sort of crescendo with the Seoul Uprising, which broke in December, 1884, and the Osaka Incident, which reached its climax in the fall of 1885. Then there was a tapering off of activity, though not of interest and sympathy, as the participants in these affairs were harassed, surveilled, or jailed by Japanese authorities, until the murder of Kim Ok-kiun in April, 1894, set off a new wave of active campaigning in behalf of Korean "reform and independence." This period from 1881 to 1894 is, of course, the period during which the liberal forces in Japan waged an intense struggle to wrest control of the government from the Itō-led oligarchy. The oligarchy sought to keep them in check with the promise of a constitution made in March, 1882, but the liberals knew this for what it was, a stalling for time while the oligarchs, minus Ōkuma, who had been ousted for developing liberal proclivities, could design a way to safeguard autocratic controls even within a constitutional framework. The liberals were in bitter and even violent opposition to the government during the years in which their interest in the Korean problem was developing.[12]

Nevertheless, on the Korean issue there was, for a time, no clear cleavage with the government, for its policy too, following Kanghwa and the opening, was to urge the Korean government toward reform and the assertion of Korean independence. Yet the Japanese government, as a conservative oligarchy, was most assuredly not interested in these as an extension into practice of liberal principles. It saw them as an antidote to backward, unsettled, unfriendly, and unpredictable conditions in Korea, wherein might lurk serious

[12] Scalapino, *op. cit.*, 103-8. See also George M. Beckmann, *The Making of the Meiji Constitution: The Oligarchs and the Constitutional Development of Japan, 1868–1891* (Lawrence: University of Kansas Press, 1957), 53-95.

danger to Japanese security, and to that end sought their realization. But a precise threat to Japanese security had not yet taken shape, and so there was no reason to push them to a point of serious international complication for Japan. Furthermore, it should be remembered that what the Japanese Foreign Office called the Great Principle of Japan's foreign policy in the 1880's was neither the conquest of Korea, nor the reform and independence of Korea. Indeed it had nothing to do with Korea or any other area of Japanese expansion. It was treaty revision, revision of the unequal treaties with Western countries, which bound Japanese sovereignty.[13] Everything, foreign and domestic, had to be considered in the light of that, and Minister Young, in his observations that a congress of the powers to declare the independence of Korea would give Japan an opportunity "to act and deliberate with Western Powers as an equal,"[14] was very much on the mark. The Japanese Foreign Office was pleased to underwrite Korean reform and independence in a way that would contribute to the Great Principle, but its enthusiasm for them did not go beyond bounds set by caution and prudence. Thus, after the Incident of 1882, as Foreign Minister Inoue showed his readiness to trim the sails of progress in deference to the reality of Chinese intervention in Korea, the liberals were becoming alienated on Korean policy too. The Seoul Uprising of December 4–8, 1884, in which the Korean Independence party of Kim Ok-kiun and Pak Young-hyo tried to take over the government, brought the cleavage into sharp relief.

"Fukuzawa wrote the plot and trained the actors,"[15] said Inoue Kakugorō, in reference to this uprising. Inoue Kakugorō, to be distinguished from the foreign minister, Inoue Kaoru, whom he detested, was a young non-samurai of Hiroshima prefecture, who came to Tokyo to study at Fukuzawa's school, lived at Fukuzawa's house, and acted as tutor to Fukuzawa's son. A favorite with his

[13] Gaimushō, *Jōyaku Kaisei Keika Gaiyō* (Outline of Progress toward Treaty Revision) (Tokyo, 1950), Preface, p. 3. Cf. Conroy, *Japanese Frontier* . . ., 52-53.

[14] See above chap. II, n. 55.

[15] Ishikawa, *op. cit.*, III, 340.

teacher, he became the most active of the Keio group on Korean affairs and contact man with Gotō Shōjirō and other members of the Liberal party. Also, it seems that he handled secret correspondence between Fukuzawa, Kim Ok-kiun, and Pak Young-hyo by means of a telegraphic code they devised. In a sense Kakugorō was Fukuzawa in action on the Korean problem, although his propensity toward exuberance, indiscretion, and violence made him perhaps more of a caricature than a faithful reflection. Fukuzawa himself once spoke of him as a "monomaniac on politics" and as being "lacking in sense."[16] One might describe him as a bright but blundering boy who tried to take Fukuzawa's ideas out of the classroom and put them into practice—too energetically. But one cannot doubt the sincerity of his efforts on behalf of his teacher and the cause. (He went to jail for them.) And one should not dismiss his personal ideas too lightly. After considerable time and travel in Korea he made up a sort of what's wrong-with-Korea summary, which he presented to the Korean king. The following is a summary of its main points.

The people of Korea are in general very poor. In food, clothing, housing, and income they are much worse off than the Japanese. They have almost no savings. Much of the population is idle. People stroll the streets with long pipes in their mouths. In the country one sees men trying to cultivate the land while wearing ceremonial hats and slippers. This is because the upper class takes all the profit, so the people have no incentive to work. Transportation is very bad. Goods cannot easily be exchanged between rich districts and poor ones. Korea is rich in hides, lumber, beans, minerals, but the natural resources are disregarded. The population is decreasing and morality is deteriorating. According to the government survey the population is 10,500,000, but according to my estimate it must be 26,500,000. However, the population and the number of homes are diminishing. There are many degrading

[16] *Ibid.*, 369. Kondō Yoshio (ed.), *Inoue Kakugorō Sensei Den* (Life of Teacher Inoue Kakugorō) (Tokyo: Denki Hensankai, 1943), 1-31, 135-42. Cf. Ishikawa, *op. cit.*, III, 341, 367.

customs: pilferage, sex, lying, low type religion. Taxes are too heavy. Bribery is prevalent among local officials.

He recommended reform in these matters, relying on foreign funds.[17]

Kakugorō apparently knew Kim and Pak from the time of their earliest visits with Fukuzawa, but he became very active on Korean affairs as a result of discussions between Fukuzawa and these Korean visitors at the time of the apologizing mission of 1882. On that occasion the Koreans came to Fukuzawa for advice and he recommended such things as sending greater numbers of Korean young men to Japan to study, the reform of the Korean system of writing by mixing *on-mun* (native Korean) letters with Chinese characters, and the establishment of a newspaper in Seoul. They accepted all these ideas and to get the newspaper started they hired three of Fukuzawa's students, Ushiba Takuzo, Takahashi Masanobu, and Inoue Kakugorō.[18] As events proved, Kakugorō was the dynamo of the group. Fukuzawa's parting advice was "do not forget you are Inoue Kakugorō and do not forget you are a Japanese."[19] One could interpret this as an indication of Japanese nationalism in the venture, but in view of Kakugorō's impetuous nature, it might have been merely straight advice, lest this eager young man of twenty-three jump headlong into a Korean cauldron. Years later Kakugorō recalled his setting-out on this first mission to Korea: "The purpose of my going to Korea was in a word to make Korea move toward civilization. The reason I had that purpose was because I had stayed for three years in Fukuzawa's house and was much influenced by his discussions. . . . On the eve

[17] Kakugorō presented this to the king just before he left Korea for the last time in 1886, telling the king that, unless such reforms were undertaken, he could "do nothing more" and would return to Japan. Inoue Kakugorō, *Kanjo no Zammu* (Memory of Seoul) (Tokyo: Shunyōdō, 1891), 104-6. This booklet was reprinted under the same title in the journal *Fūzoku Gahō* (illustrated Report on Manners and Customs) (Jan. 1895), entire issue.

[18] Ishikawa, *op. cit.*, III, 297-98. Kondō, *op. cit.*, 31-34. Tabohashi (1940), I, 910.

[19] Kondō, *op. cit.*, 35.

of departure he [Fukuzawa] told my wife, 'Inoue may be killed in Korea, so make a number one delicious breakfast tomorrow.' "[20]

Fukuzawa also gave Kim and Pak some lessons in theoretical politics, the main point of these being that "all civilized nations in the world, including Japan, have sovereignty, but Korea with a culture 2000 years old still belongs to big old China. For the first time Kim and Pak realized the true significance of independence."[21] Fukuzawa's ideas on how to bring about the great general objective of progress and independence for Korea do not form a very consistent pattern, particularly as concerns the use of force. In one editorial he noted the similarity between the opening of Japan by the United States and that of Korea by Japan. This gave Japan a rank of "first friendly nation" to Korea and a special concern for the progress of her civilization. "We should be prepared to spend money on it," he said. And further, he warned that Japanese residents in Korea must expect and should be prepared for the sort of anti-foreign attacks by isolationist groups that foreigners in Japan had encountered at the end of the Tokugawa period. "We should show our military dignity in Korea to impress them. To assist and improve the civilization of our neighbor with our military forces is nothing but friendly relations and we should do it." Yet on another occasion he wrote, "It is natural that many Japanese who see Chinese interference in Korea want to use physical force against China, but I rely on another principle—modern civilized philosophy. . . . Political and military devices are nothing without learning. I urge the extension of the civil power of learning (*gakumon no bunken*) beyond Japan."[22]

Probably Fukuzawa felt, in fleeting moments at least, some misgivings about the contradiction involved in spreading "civilization" by force, but he did not allow this to dampen the enthusiasm of

[20] *Jiji Shimpō* (newspaper), Aug. 27, 1910.
[21] Tabohashi (1940), I, 909.
[22] Ishikawa, *op. cit.*, III, 277-78, 295-97.

Kim, Pak, and Kakugorō even when their prospectus for progress in Korea came to include a revolutionary plot, complete with assassination targets. It seems doubtful that Fukuzawa was in on all the final gory details, but certainly he knew the general outline of what his pupils and advisees were scheming. To that extent he did "write the plot and train the actors."

The plot which culminated in the uprising of December, 1884, developed only slowly, and, in a sense, it was as much the result of frustration as active planning. At the time of Kakugorō's arrival in Seoul, January, 1883, he and the Korean reformers expected help from the Japanese legation. Pak, at the time of the apologizing mission, had seemingly had very cordial relations with Foreign Minister Inoue, who had arranged for him to obtain a loan at the Yokohama Specie Bank. This loan was in the first instance to provide the money for the indemnity payment which Korea owed Japan as a result of the settlement of the 1882 Incident. In addition, Pak apparently received extra money which he used as a political fund. Perhaps he used some of this money to hire Kakugorō and the other students. However, there is conflicting evidence on the matter of the extra money. Kakugorō says Pak was promised it but never got it.[23] Historian Tabohashi says he got 120,000 yen, and then tried to get more, going to various banks and finally to Shibusawa, head of the Dai Ichi Bank. Shibusawa told him that "if you get Foreign Minister Inoue to guarantee it, you can borrow 100,000 to 200,000 yen . . . but Inoue refused."[24] Anyway, by the summer of 1883 the reformers felt that the Japanese Foreign Office was conciliating China and slighting them. Kakugorō complains, "I was disappointed to find that the Japanese government, having changed its policy frequently, had no definite policy on Korea. Once they supported Kim and Pak, accusing China when the

[23] Inoue Kakugorō, *op. cit.*, 15-16.

[24] Tabohashi (1940), I, 912-14. Documents regarding a loan of 170,000 yen appear in NGB, XV, 283-89, but they are inconclusive. Archives, SP, 5, 73, speaks of Korea's having a 170,000 yen credit.

Incident [1882] occurred in Seoul, but now they were forgetting their previous policy and disregarding Kim and Pak."[25] Kim visited Foreign Minister Inoue in the summer of 1883 and found that Inoue "was not glad to see him."[26] Takezoe in Seoul was "intimate" with General Wu and "disregarded" the reformers, though they had expected him to give them guidance. This seriously undermined the "cultural policy" (*bunka seisaku*) which had been outlined for the reformers by Fukuzawa, and though Pak had planned to develop reform through "culture building," in Korea the results were "disappointing"; Ushiba and Takahashi returned to Japan.[27]

Inoue Kakugorō, however, though disappointed, persisted. He did not get his newspaper started as soon as expected, but after establishing contacts in the Korean Foreign Office, and in fact getting a post as an adviser there, he launched the newspaper, the first in Korea, in November (1883). It was called *Kanjō Jumpō* (Seoul Trimonthly). He was soon in trouble with the Chinese, who distributed a "Kill Inoue" pamphlet. In February, 1884, his tenth issue, Inoue wrote an article entitled "The Savagery of the Chinese." In it he told of such things as the case of a Chinese soldier going into a Korean shop to buy vegetables—with no money. When the Korean shopkeeper refused to let him have the vegetables, the Chinese soldier shot him. This evoked a statement from Yüan Shih-k'ai, who was then a deputy commander of the Chinese troops in Seoul, that this incident had been done by a non-Chinese wearing a Chinese uniform. The Chinese also protested to the Korean government and demanded that the newspaper be suspended. Two months later Li Hung-chang himself sent a letter to the Korean government complaining that the article in question and the newspaper generally were "very impolite" to China. Shortly thereafter Kakugorō "resigned" his position as Foreign Office adviser and as

[25] Inoue Kakugorō, *op. cit.*, 21.
[26] Ishikawa, *op. cit.*, III, 300.
[27] Tabohashi (1940), I, 916-17.

editor of the newspaper, and returned to Japan (May, 1884).[28]

Despite his ouster under Chinese pressure, Kakugorō was not dispirited when he returned to Japan. In fact, the prospects for the Independence party seemed to him rather good. He had had some conversations on this score at the Japanese legation in Seoul after Minister Takezoe's departure for Tokyo the preceding December and found the attaché left in charge, Shimamura, more sympathetic to his views than Takezoe had been. The Sino-French embroilment over Annam seemed to promise a chance to undermine Chinese influence in Korea and they had talked about that.[29] Also the return of the members of the Korean mission to the United States increased the prestige and influence of the reformers. Hong Yong-sik, vice chief of the mission, had returned during the winter, begun a connection (somewhat hesitantly) with the reformers, and received an appointment as postmaster general from the king. In May the *U.S.S. Trenton* arrived at Inchon with the chief of the mission and nephew of the Queen, Min Yong-ik, So Kwang-pom, and Pyon Su. All received elevations in rank and position, Min becoming a vice-president of the Foreign Office. The number of Chinese troops in Seoul was reduced to 1500 in June, Chinese instructors of Korean troops were dismissed by the king, von Mollendorff resigned from the Foreign Office, a number of Japanese coming under contracts made with Kim Ok-kiun arrived from Japan to begin teaching the use of machinery for paper manufacture, pottery-making, etc. In July, fourteen Korean military students returned from Japan. They were exercised before the king and "gave great satisfaction." The king had American Minister Foote send a wire to Admiral Shufeldt asking him to come as adviser in foreign affairs and military matters. As Foote wrote later, "The arrival of a military officer from the United States to organize and instruct Corean Troops is anxiously hoped for. Fourteen young Coreans educated at the military school at Tokio

[28] Kondō, *op. cit.*, 41-46.
[29] Tabohashi (1940), I, 919, 923.

are waiting to assist him and four thousand stand at Arms—Breechloading Rifles—purchased in the United States, by order of His Majesty, undistributed until he shall arrive."[30]

Truly, reform was on the move in Seoul. And in Japan also, though the government remained "cool," Kim, Fukuzawa, and friends had a large project on the fire. Kim, with an introduction from Fukuzawa, had gone to see Gotō Shōjirō of the Liberal party the preceding autumn to ask him for financial aid and armed support for the liberal cause in Korea. Gotō had expressed great interest in the idea, and in fact began talking in terms of one million yen which he said he could supply, and "samurai comrades" which he said he could send to Korea to help. He said, however, that to be sure that there would "never be any duplicity", he wished to have a letter from the Korean king regarding this. "Without such a letter some small person might interfere with this large thing." After much talk, but apparently with no letter from the king and definitely no money from Gotō, they hit upon the idea of seeking money from the French legation in Tokyo. Kobayashi Kuzuo, secretary of the Liberal party, knew French and had friends there, and it now being the spring of 1884, France and China were at odds over Annam. The French might be well pleased to see some diversionary activity at Seoul to trouble China, and out of it could come Korean independence. With Kobayashi interpreting they had an interview with the French minister, Adam Sienkiewiscz, at which they explained the whole idea. They needed ships, or a ship, and money. Could France supply a ship from her Asiatic squadron and could the minister obtain a million yen fund for them to draw on? Sienkiewiscz' reply was "not definite," but he seemed agreeable to the idea, and promised to give it careful thought, and said that he would invite contributions of money. Negotiations continued into the summer, with Sienkiewiscz becoming more and more en-

[30] Foote to Sec. State, Sept. 3, 1884, No. 105 and Dec. 17, 1884, No. 128 (encl.): Dipl. Desp., Korea. Cf. Foote to Sec. State, Oct. 19, 1883, No. 32, *ibid.* and McCune and Harrison, *op. cit.*, I, 53-55, 106-9.

couraging. He did not think he could get the money "officially" from France, but he had a friend in the Bank of Paris . . . and "if the opportunity comes, there will be a fund of one million yen and a warship to meet the need."[31]

Thus, while Inoue Kakugorō was in Tokyo during the late spring and summer of 1884, he and Kim and Fukuzawa had many things to talk about. Between the prospering prospects of the Independence party in Seoul and the Liberal party-French legation scheme in Tokyo, they could well be encouraged. Kakugorō told Kim that chances for a move in Seoul were excellent; the Annam affair between France and China was weakening the Chinese hold there. Kim said he would gather those Koreans who were in Japan, and Kakugorō undertook visits to Foreign Minister Inoue Kaoru and Takezoe, who was still in Tokyo, to persuade them to help out the cause. With prospects so good even the cautious might be emboldened. Kakugorō found them more friendly than he had expected, and in fact he seems to have received a promise from them of financial support for his newspaper in Seoul. Kakugorō, however, did not know of high-level policy conferences which had been going on between Takezoe, Foreign Minister Inoue, Deputy Minister Yoshida, and Itō himself. Itō had heard about the Gotō-Kobayashi-Sienkiewiscz negotiations, apparently from Gotō himself, who, being both loquacious and boastful, might accidentally have divulged the scheme; or he might have told Itō deliberately to sound out the possibility of government support. Anyway Itō, hearing the plan, pretended to be sympathetic, but immediately consulted with Foreign Minister Inoue as to how to thwart its execution. They decided that they had not been paying enough attention to the activities of the Korean independence party and its Japanese friends, that they should keep a closer watch on them, and at the same time woo them away from the idea of French-Liberal

[31] Tabohashi (1951), 3-4. Ishikawa Ryoichi (ed.), *Jiyūtō Ōsaka Jiken* (The Liberal Party's Osaka Incident) (Tokyo: Jiyūtō Ōsaka Jiken Shuppankyoku, 1933), 12-23. Itagaki Taisuke, *Jiyūtō Shi* (History of the Liberal Party) (Tokyo, 1913), II, 346-47. Kondō, *op. cit.*, 50.

party co-operation. This may explain the offer of money to Kakugorō for his newspaper. In terms of large policy Inoue thought that the idea that the Franco-Chinese conflict presented an opportunity to sweep Chinese influence out of Korea should be seriously considered, but he stressed again the conclusion he had reached earlier, that the Independence party was a dubious factor, neither strong nor important. Takezoe agreed with Inoue. Itō and Yoshida emphasized that any conflict with China must be avoided. It was decided to proceed, as before, with a policy of promoting Korean independence, but within the definite limits imposed by avoiding conflict with China. As for the Independence party, Takezoe could handle it in whatever way seemed best to him. With these ideas in mind Takezoe returned to Korea in October, arriving in Seoul on October 30.[32]

Meanwhile in Seoul, dark clouds had come on to the horizon of the Independence party. In the first place, Admiral Shufeldt had not appeared, so the young Tokyo-trained cadets were leaderless. He had written, "leaving the question of his coming to Korea somewhat in doubt" and urging "the question of expense etc." Minister Foote wrote the State Department in September, stressing the importance of the matter and remarking on the "anxiety of the King." He expressed the hope that "there will be no delay in sending forward some Military Officer who can organize the Corean troops, and if Admiral Shufeldt does not come, that some capable man may be designated to act as advisor to the Corean Government." By November when he learned for certain that Shufeldt would not come, he could only report that "the truth is that the King's patience is exhausted with the long delay and in the meantime those persons are not wanting who have intimated to him that, had he asked Great Britain or Germany, to perform a like service, it would have been done at once."[33]

[32] Tabohashi (1940), I, 923-24. Kondō, *op. cit.*, 49-50.

[33] Foote to Sec. State, Sept. 17, 1884, No. 110 and Nov. 15, 1884, No. 124: Dipl. Desp., Korea. McCune and Harrison, *op. cit.*, I, 56.

In the second place, Min Yong-ik, erstwhile chief of the mission to the United States, was showing unmistakable signs that his exposure to progress and civilization had not taken. Ensign George C. Foulk, Minister Foote's aide at the American legation, who spoke Korean and who was very friendly with Korean progressives, especially So Kwang-pom and Pyon Su, observed the increasing evidence of this as did the progressives themselves. After his return on the *Trenton* Min had seemed sincere, for a time, in expressions of progressive intention, but as early as June 2 So told Foulk that "Min-Yong-Ik, in spite of all that had been done for him, and however good his intentions had been while abroad, might be turned directly to the opposite of what might be expected from him; that what he had learned and seen through his Confucian training and the hereditary instincts of his family, might be employed, after the manner of the Chinese, against Western progress." So's fears were soon borne out. Min began plans for a trip to China, which, however, he postponed. Then he originated a plan for "changing the national dress in certain details" which seemed to Foulk like "an approach to the Chinese custom." Then he cooperated with the Chinese commissioner, Chen, in arguments concerning a possible substitute for Admiral Shufeldt as adviser. Also he resigned his Foreign Office position and took up a command as general of the Right Palace Guard Battalion, in which capacity he brought in five Chinese military instructors. He blocked appointments of the young Korean army officers who had returned from Japan and the employment of the Japanese who had made contracts with Kim Ok-kiun. Foulk says, "By September of 1884, Min-Yong-Ik was entirely clear of the progressive party. His associates were Chinese . . .; he did not receive visits from Westerners in the daytime, and on several occasions showed contemptuous insolence in their presence. . . . During the autumn the number of Chinese in Seoul increased rapidly . . . [and] they began to extend their homes and trading places into the countryside; they came and went as they pleased without passports. . . ."

Min-Yong-ik's defection from the progressive ranks, as Foulk realized, meant more than merely an individual's change of mind. It meant that the whole inner core of the Korean government, the Min family, headed by the queen herself was turning to the Chinese. This would have the direst of implications for the reformers. Foulk's report continues:

> In October one of the progressive party leaders told me that unless foreign intervention prevented, Corea would soon be irreclaimably in the hands of the Chinese, and with great bitterness went on to say that his small party had not only lost power to proceed further and had been receding, but they were in actual danger of execution; that this might follow any charge against them by the Chinese faction. He also stated that part of the King's revenue meant to be used by the King through them to fulfill all progressive contracts had been cut off from him by the Mins (notably through Min-Thai-Ho [father of Min Yong-ik], who controlled the chief revenues). . . . On October 25 one of the progressive party leaders called upon me, and at once began to speak passionately of the unfortunate situation of the King and his party. Later, with deliberation, he stated that for the sake of Corea, Min-Thai-Ho, Cho-Yong-Cha, the four generals and four other lower officials possibly, would have to be killed. Though the officer was passionate in his manner, he was one whom I had always found positive and correct in his statements to me; his words, therefore, did not seem empty to me, and I became indignant that he should communicate such an idea to me. A few sharp words passed between us and he then quieted down.[34]

Such was the desperation some of the progressives were feeling at the time Takezoe returned to Seoul. Their hopes, so high in the early summer, seemed about to be dashed against a Chinese wall, and perhaps their heads with them.

Takezoe was soon in the center of a political maelstrom. Inoue Kakugorō, who had returned to Seoul in August, was in close

[34] "Report" by Foulk, encl. in Foote to Sec. State, Dec. 17, 1884, No. 128: Dipl. Desp., Korea. McCune and Harrison, *op. cit.*, 106-11.

touch with Shimamura, Takezoe's assistant at the legation, on the one hand and with Kim, Pak, and friends on the other. Kakugorō and Shimamura discussed matters with Takezoe on November 1, and, according to Kakugorō, Takezoe assured them that "our government is going to attack China this time." And then, calling in Kim Ok-kiun, had asked whether the Independence party had the "determination to carry out a reformation with the help of Japan." Such statements would indeed, if Takezoe made them, seem to constitute an open invitation by the Japanese government to the Independence party to stage a rebellion. However, historian Tabohashi, in commenting on these statements, is quite right in making certain reservations. He notes that for Takezoe such statements sound surprisingly irresponsible and that the information that he made them comes from Kakurogō and the Korean progressives.[35] Certainly Kakugorō, Kim, Pak, et al, and very possibly Shimamura *wanted* him to make them. They were there to persuade him to make them, and it could be that their own wishful thinking crept into their accounting of the episode. But Takezoe would be quite out of character with his past caution and the caution of his superiors in Tokyo if he did make them, especially in view of the fact that he had just returned to Seoul after some eleven months away from his post. He could not have had any full sense of the situation in Seoul; he knew that his foreign minister had little confidence in the Independence party.

The Japanese Foreign Office version of Takezoe's role is rather different. It says that

> the pro-Chinese party had become strong enough to try to send into exile the pro-Japanese ministers, Kim Ok-kiun and Pak Young-hyo. Reflecting on how to escape injury themselves Pak, etc. first wished to try to kill the members of the treacherous party, and this was repeated to our minister [Takezoe]. Our minister strongly warned against this rash attempt. But observing that their minds were made up and anxious about future policy, he drew up two plans, A and B, which he submitted

[35] Tabohashi (1940), I, 924, 928. Ishikawa, *Fukuzawa . . . Den,* III, 316, 327.

to the Japanese government. Plan A. Since it is extremely difficult to maintain the dual position of Japan and China in Korea, instead of this, if it can be based on a request of the King, shall we help them [the Independence party] in an uprising and attack the Chinese as enemies, thus stopping their empty pride? Or Plan B. Shall we make it our chief concern to preserve the peace in Eastern Asia, while admitting as far as possible the necessity of protecting the pro-Japanese party from grievous injury? Our government chose plan B and so instructed him by telegram on November 28. This instruction, however, did not reach him until after the Uprising.[36]

Fukuzawa, who was, of course, not present, but who apparently got his information from Kim, says that "Kim visited Takezoe [soon after Takezoe's return] and Takezoe said, 'What is your problem?' Kim said, 'I cannot explain it to people I do not trust completely.' But Kim felt Takezoe was more friendly. . . . [Then] on November 25 or 26 Kim visited the Japanese legation and explained the problem to Takezoe for the first time . . . [and] Takezoe agreed. . . . The Koreans judged that the attitude of the Japanese government had changed."[37]

In exploring the possibility of Takezoe's complicity, Tabohashi takes note of his bringing to the king the information that Japan was cancelling the remainder of the 500,000 yen indemnity, and says that on this occasion he had a private conversation with the king in which he advised the king that if he were ever in danger he could take refuge in the Japanese legation and even go to Japan; he also refers to a speech by one Asayama, a Korean-speaking

[36] Archives, SP 5, 47-48. Takezoe to Itō and Inoue Kaoru, Nov. 12, 1884 in Itō, *Chōsen Kōshō Shiryō*, I, 266-67 and Itō to Takezoe, Nov. 28, 1884, *ibid.*, 295. In this reply to Takezoe Itō said: "Plan A is not moderate. Plan B is good. Our government does not want to support one Korean party against another or interfere publicly. The best way is to let the Japanese party enlighten Korea through moderate efforts. Be careful regarding this."

[37] *Jiji Shimpō* (newspaper), Sept. 1, 2, 1910. This from a posthumously published article of Fukuzawa, billed by *Jiji Shimpō* (Aug. 27, 1910) as "not known during Fukuzawa's lifetime" but dealing with "many secret matters." Cf. Kuzū Yoshihisa, *Nisshi* . . ., I, 183.

subordinate of Takezoe at the Japanese legation, who at a dinner party celebrating the birthday of the Emperor Meiji (November 3) at which foreigners were present, spoke in a very derogatory fashion of the Chinese. "Though his Korean was not completely understandable, such a thing was unprecedented."[38]

Tabohashi summarizes as follows:

> There is still doubt as to what extent Takezoe agreed with the action plan of the Independence Party. It might be true that the Independence party told him of the details of its plan, or did it through Shimamura or Asayama, and judging from the results it cannot be denied that Takezoe was shown a list of the names of the persons marked to be killed and agreed to it, and also he agreed to protect the Korean King with legation guard troops. Foreign Minister Inoue denied Takezoe's co-action in the incident, but it seems that the Korean Foreign Office claim is closer to the facts. There are surely grounds for considering Takezoe responsible. And the last and most important thing is that while Takezoe had asked instructions of the Japanese government, he did not wait for the instructions, but got into the direct action. It is true that the Independence Party-Min relations were worsening day by day, but there was no fear that the Min would take direct action from their side, because inside the Min were many diverse opinions and they could not take united action. Also for them to attack the Independence Party would set them into conflict with Japanese troops, which was contrary to Yüan Shih-kai's advice. Until October 30, when Takezoe returned to his post, there was no evidence that the Independence Party would attack the Min, but after this . . . there were many visits by Kim, Pak, etc. to the Japanese legation. . . . According to Kim, direct action was decided on November 30 and the time set for about December 3 or 4 . . . Kim strongly persuaded Takezoe and as a result Takezoe, before getting the approval of the Japanese Foreign Office, decided on his own authority on direct action—so I [Tabohashi] believe.[39]

Tabohashi's judgment on the relationship of the Japanese minister to the plot of the Independence party deserves profound

[38] Tabohashi (1940), I, 924-26.
[39] *Ibid.*, 937-41.

respect. All of Tabohashi's voluminous work on Sino-Korean-Japanese relations is in the highest scholarly tradition. He always shows the most scrupulous regard for the facts, to tell them truthfully being his single overriding objective; he searched the vast array of pertinent Chinese, Japanese, and Korean sources as no Westerner can ever hope to do, and probably no Far Easterner can or will ever do again. In addition, on the matter of Takezoe's relationship to the 1884 Uprising, he is especially careful to make his conclusion clear. In most cases he is content to let the facts speak for themselves, but in this, which he obviously regards as a vital issue, he tries to draw a final conclusion on Takezoe's and hence the Japanese government's responsibility (and duplicity). And his conclusion, considering the time and the climate of the 1930's in which he worked, is heroic. Knowing full well that a conclusion unfavorable to Japan might ruin his chances for publication of that and future works and his own reputation as a Japanese, he brands Takezoe with a large measure of responsibility and holds the interpretation of the Korean government to be closer to the facts than that of the Japanese foreign minister.

It may be, however, that Tabohashi, as a Japanese historian determined to be fair and truthful, sets his standards of conduct for the Japanese minister and the Japanese government too high. If it were a true and universally accepted precept of international law that sympathy or support for a revolutionary attempt against the government of a state by an official of a presumably friendly nation is illegal and morally reprehensible, then the Japanese government would stand condemned. But so would every other government. And in the particular case at hand, leaving aside the whole complex question of whether Korea was being helped toward "independence and civilization" by those foreigners, Japanese and other, who gave advice and succour to the Independence party, the fact that the Japanese minister was responding to very ardent persuasions of idealists who put "civilization" first and diplomatic technicalities second is important. In this connection Tabohashi may give Takezoe and the Japanese government worse than their due when he says that "until October 30 . . . there was no evidence that the Independence Party would attack the Min . . . but after this . . . there were many visits by Kim, Pak, etc. to the Japanese legation. . . ." This clearly implies that Takezoe helped stir up the reformers. However, from Ensign Foulk's testimony, which Tabohashi did not know, we have seen that some of the leaders of the reform party (he does not name them) paid similar visits to him before October 30 and gave evidence both of violent intention and fear that they (the progressives) were "in actual danger of execution." In addition to the information from Foulk already cited, the following is also pertinent to this:

On October 26, during a call on Min Yong Ik, I [Foulk] learned that the separation of the two parties was so wide as to prevent any discussion of public affairs in which officers of the two parties might be brought together; this convinced me that a crisis was near at hand and one which would probably result in bloodshedding and violence not confined to the official classes of Coreans. . . .

On October 28 I told him [Minister Foote] every detail of what I had heard, and expressed firmly the opinion that these were sufficient to forewarn some serious outbreak in Seoul. On October 31 I called upon Ensign Bernadon and Mr. W. D. Townsend, the two other Americans in Seoul, and told them what I believed to be the situation. On this day Hong-Yong-Sik called upon me, and I received notes from two other members of the progressive party requesting interviews; these I was forced to refuse, and on the following day I set out from Seoul to make a second journey into the interior of Corea in accordance with my instructions from the Navy Department.[40]

Thus Independence party members, contrary to Tabohashi's estimate, *were* thinking of desperate measures before Takezoe arrived, and it requires no great imagination to see that Foulk, had he not literally got out of town at the critical moment, might also have become involved in the plot, to the discredit of the American

[40] "Report" by Foulk, *op. cit.*

legation. It is interesting, though, that something made Foulk become "indignant" at the idea of an assassination plot, despite his great sympathy for the reformers and the fact that he was a military man. Perhaps there is a stage-of-civilization question involved here whereby an American tradition that placed assassinating the political opposition simply beyond the pale was working on Foulk, in contrast to Korean, Japanese, and Chinese traditions which as yet worked no such inhibition, even in progressive circles. Or it may be that the American political scene has never produced issues so bitter as those posed in Seoul in the fall of 1884. It is an interesting question, where does a man stop in supporting a cause he believes in?

Another point which Tabohashi does not sufficiently consider is the effect of the Kim-Fukuzawa-Gotō overture to the French legation. In the work quoted above, in which he sets forth his specific judgement on the complicity of Takezoe, Tabohashi gives some information on the relationship between Kim and the Japanese liberals, but he does not consider the French loan scheme. In another work, published eleven years later, he does discuss this subject in good detail, despite the fact that this later book is specifically concerned with the Sino-Japanese War, 1894–95, and only incidentally with the 1880's. Such a discussion really belongs in the earlier work, which describes in minute detail the course of Japanese-Korean relations from the 1870's to 1894 and gives over several chapters to the events of 1883–84. It seems as if he were putting into the later volume some information which belonged in the earlier one, but which he had not known at that time of writing. However, the French loan scheme should have some considerable weight in the evaluation of the Japanese government's relationship to the Seoul Uprising, for, taken in the context of the treaty revision objectives and the general air of caution in which the Foreign Office operated, it is clear that this sort of thing would be very disturbing to the official mind. Anti-government liberals in undercover collaboration with the representative of a European power, indeed the European power which had produced the most violent revolution in history, portended trouble, whatever the reason for collaboration. Discovery of it would build a sense of urgency in government circles that the intriguers, whom they had been ignoring, must now be weaned away from their French connections and kept under surveillance. Hence the greater interest in the Independence party and its Japanese friends which Takezoe displayed on his return to Seoul might have begun in caution, rather than in bold design.

At any rate if one adds to, or subtracts from, Tabohashi's judgment these two items which he did not consider, namely Foulk's testimony and the French loan scheme, a picture emerges in which the role of the Japanese liberals is enlarged and that of the Japanese government, including the minister at Seoul, reduced. This does not relieve Takezoe of responsibility, for when he saw the plot developing he did not get out of town as Foulk had done, but he seems to have been pulled and prodded by Kim, Pak, Kakugorō, and friends into affording such aid and comfort for the plotters as he gave, rather than to have led them. As the incident unfolded he and the Japanese government turned their backs on the reformers so obdurately as to win their undying enmity.

According to a memoir which Fukuzawa compiled from remarks of Kim Ok-kiun, the final plot was hatched at the home of Pak Young-hyo, where some twenty young Koreans, all graduates of the Tōyama Gakkō, a Japanese military training school in Tokyo, were present. They decided to kill seven government ministers and set December 4, or "if rain December 5," as the date of the coup. Kakugorō seems also to have attended the meeting and he sent a report on it to Fukuzawa, which, however, did not reach Fukuzawa until December 10, by which time the uprising was over. The reason for the selection of the December 4 date seems partly to have been that a dinner party was being given that night by the postmaster general, Hong, one of the reformers, at which some of the targets of the plot would be present. But probably more important was the anticipation that Takezoe, who had been temporarily persuaded to favor the plot, and whose legation troops would be needed at the crucial moment, had informed Tokyo of what was impending and would receive explicit orders to prevent it. Specifically a Japanese steamer, the *Chitose Maru*, was due at Inchon on December 7. Since it might carry such instructions, the plotters thought it necessary to strike first.[41]

The uprising began at the postmaster general's party. United States Minister Foote, who was present, reported as follows the following day:

> There were present Pak Young Hio, brother-in-law to the King; Kim Hong Chip, president of the Corean foreign office; Kim Ok Kinn [Ok-kiun], vice-president; Von Mollendorf, superintendent of customs, myself, my secretary and interpreters; W. G. Aston, Esq., Her Britannic Majesty's consul-general; Chen Sher Tang, Chinese commissioner; the Japanese secretary of Legation and several other minor officials. As the dinner drew to a close an alarm of fire was given, and nearly all the guests withdrew from the table and went out of doors to view the fire, which seemed near at hand. Perceiving no immediate danger, I returned, with the President of the Corean Foreign Office and several others, to the table. A moment thereafter Min Yong Ik entered the room, his face and clothing covered with blood, which was streaming from seven or eight ghastly wounds. The utmost consternation ensued; The Corean officials divesting themselves of their robes as they ran, rushed to the courtyard which was already half filled with soldiers and servants. At this moment a shot was fired, and the entire crowd precipitated themselves over the rear walls and disappeared. . . .[42]

Foote's next report, dated December 17, was a detailed summary of the events of the next several days and included as an enclosure the background report by Foulk, which has already been cited. Foote says,

[41] Ishikawa, *Fukuzawa . . . Den*, III, 324-25, 344. Kondō, *Inoue . . . Den*, 54-55.
[42] Foote to Sec. State, Dec. 5, 1884, No. 127: Dipl. Desp., Korea. McCune and Harrison, *op. cit.*, I, 96.

It seems that the entire movement is an attempted revolution, concocted by a few ill advised young men, under the leadership of Kim Ok Kinn [Ok-kiun], vice-president of the Corean foreign office, Hong Heng Shik, postmaster-general, and Pak Young Hio, brother-in-law of the King.

Ostensibly dissatisfied with the non-progressive spirit manifested by the leading officials, they determined to seize the government, obtain control of the person of the King, and to administer public affairs for their own purposes. Their first move in the plot was the attempted assassination of Min Yong Ik, and during the excitement occasioned thereby, they rushed to the palace, informed the King that he was in great danger, and persuaded him to move to a smaller place. The King, fearing perhaps some great public commotion taking place, sent messengers to the Japanese legation asking the Minister to come to the palace with a guard of soldiers. After three messages of this kind the minister consented, and went to the palace, the Japanese soldiers, two hundred in number being stationed at the gates. In the meantime five of the leading officials of the government were called to the palace, ostensibly by the direction of the King, and while there put to death. . . .

On the morning of the 4th . . . I went to a small palace occupied by the King. We found crowds of excited people in the streets. Corean soldiers were massed around the entrance, outside; within, Japanese soldiers were guarding the gateways. In the palace I saw the leading revolutionists, who had been installed in the positions made vacant by the death of the high officials. I also met the Japanese minister and his secretary of legation. The King had little to say. . . .

As before stated, I had arranged with the assistance of Ensign Bernadon, U.S.N., as complete a system of defense as possible. By the kindness of the Japanese Minister, four Japanese soldiers had been sent to the legation. I had also asked for, and obtained, a Corean guard, upon whom I placed but little reliance. Early in the morning of the 6th the populace commenced to commit outrages upon Japanese subjects residing in various parts of the city. The cry was "Death to the Japanese!" During the day numbers were killed and their property destroyed. Several came to the legation for refuge, and I gave directions that all who came should be admitted. Between 3 and 4 o'clock P.M. we heard firing in the direction of the palace, and shortly thereafter the Japanese guard, one hundred and eighty in number, evacuated the palace grounds and marched to their legation. Along the line of march they were attacked by the people with stones and occasional shots. After they reached their legation great numbers of angry people gathered in the vicinity making threats and occasional shots were fired. Between 4 and 5 o'clock P.M. on the 7th the Japanese soldiers and civilians left their legation grounds and marched out of the city on their way to Chemulpo. Two cannon shots were fired at them as they passed, and an occasional volley of musketry, which they returned.

The wildest excitement now prevailed. As night came on we noticed that the Japanese legation buildings were in flames. . . .

During the 6th and 7th a number of public and private buildings were burned. On the morning of the 8th I was asked to have an audience with His Majesty, who had temporarily taken up his residence at the Chinese camp. In company with other representatives, I waited upon His Majesty. At this audience we were asked if we could consistently go to Chemulpo and have an interview with the Japanese Minister, conveying to him the earnest desire of His Majesty to maintain friendly relations with Japan. . . .

Referring to the events of the 6th instant, I would say that the conflict with the Japanese troops was brought about by an attempt of the Chinese troops to force their way into the palace grounds, ostensibly to protect the King. In this attack Corean troops joined forces with the Chinese. During the engagement the King determined to seek a place of greater safety. "Learning this fact," as Mr. Takezoye, the Japanese minister says in a note to me, "I took my leave of His Majesty and withdrew with the Japanese guard."[43]

Foulk reported the aftermath to the uprising on January 31.

The torture and trials of twelve persons implicated in the conspiracy were concluded on the 27th instant, and they were sentenced to death; six were executed a few hundred yards from this legation, and five on the main street of the city on the 28th and 29th instant. These persons were placed face down in the streets and decapitated by from six to ten blows of a dull instrument, while a rope secured to their queues served

[43] Foote to Sec. State, Dec. 17, 1884, No. 128: Dipl. Desp., Korea. McCune and Harrison, *op. cit.*, I, 97-101.

to open the wounds. The bodies were all dismembered and distributed about the streets for exposure for three or four days. . . .[44]

These American sources give a sufficiently detailed report of the course of events during the hectic days of the uprising and its aftermath, but their authors were not fully acquainted with the inside workings of the rebel group, particularly its Japanese associations. From Japanese sources we learn that aside from the legation guards, certain Japanese *sōshi* (adventurers) participated in the fray. Kim Ok-kiun, it is said, desired the participation of young Japanese because "Koreans are not suitable for bold and swift direct action." However, most of the Japanese residents in Seoul were merely traders so "it was difficult to get suitable people." Kim knew he could get people from Japan, but there was not time, and in the end he could get only four such men. Tabohashi was able to find the name of only one of these, one Sōshima Wasaku of Nagasaki prefecture, who was killed in the fighting.[45]

Inoue Kakugorō was, of course, in the inner circle which plotted the uprising, but exactly what he did as it unfolded is difficult to say. Presumably he was close to Kim and Pak Young-hyo throughout, as they were his special friends. He remonstrated with Takezoe not to give up the Japanese legation, arguing that with the 200 soldiers and 100 or so other Japanese at hand it could be defended. Told that food was short, "I urged there was some rice in the warehouse . . . but no one would take my word."[46] However, he went to Inchon with the Japanese party, accompanied by Kim, Pak, and four others of the Korean rebels. Hong Yong-sik (Hong Heng Shik), the postmaster general and probably the third man in the rebel leadership, had become prime minister as a result of the coup. He refused to flee and, remaining in Seoul, was killed. By the time they reached Inchon, Kakugorō knew that the same fate

[44] Foulk to Sec. State, Jan. 11, 1885, No. 146: Dipl. Desp., Korea. McCune and Harrison, *op. cit.*, I, 116-17.
[45] Tabohashi (1940), I, 948.
[46] Inoue, *Kanjo no Zammu*, 69.

awaited Kim and Pak if they stayed in Korea. His object therefore was to get them out. The Japanese ship, *Chitose Maru*, had arrived at Inchon, but Minister Takezoe, now thoroughly disillusioned with the reformists, refused to allow the Koreans to go on board. Kakugorō, however, went out to the ship and persuaded the captain to take them secretly. When the *Chitose Maru* left Inchon for Nagasaki on December 11, Inoue Kakugorō and six Koreans, including Kim and Pak, were aboard. From this time Kakugorō had a place in his heart for the *Chitose Maru*. Years later in 1905 he sought out her hulk, then a wreck in Aomori Bay, and wrote a memorial for her. By that time, he commented sadly, of the six Koreans who had escaped aboard her, three had been assassinated, two had gone to America, and one, Pak, was somewhere in Japan "wandering and seeking."[47]

Upon his arrival at Nagasaki, Kakugorō sent telegrams reporting the uprising to Fukuzawa Yukichi and to Foreign Minister Inoue Kaoru. Through Fukuzawa the news was first broken to the press in Japan,[48] but the Foreign Office had already got the news. The first intimation of the affair reached the Japanese government through the Chinese legation in Tokyo. Word came to it from Peking and the news was told to the Japanese foreign minister on December 11. The Foreign Office immediately telegraphed Hara Kei, in Tientsin, for a report. Then at last, on December 13, came Takezoe's report from Inchon. He had had no time to report earlier. Prime Minister Itō Hirobumi, Foreign Minister Inoue, Itō's secretary, Itō Miyoji, and Yamagata were the principal formulators of policy decision, though they got advice from many others in the government. There was some consideration of whether Takezoe and his connection with the uprising should be disavowed and Takezoe punished, but, the precise extent of his involvement not being known, it was decided not to do this. Inoue held that Takezoe had not been well versed in the situation in Korea and had been taken advantage of by the Independence party, other Japanese, and his

[47] Kondō, *op. cit.*, 65, 67. Ishikawa, *Fukuzawa . . . Den*, III, 344.
[48] Kondō, *op. cit.*, 65.

own subordinates who were in sympathy with the Independence party. It was decided that Inoue, accompanied by a battalion of soldiers, should go to Korea with an "accusing letter" to the Korean king, demand the punishment of those responsible for injury to Japanese, reparations, and an apology. He was also to investigate the part China had played in the incident, to negotiate with a Chinese representative who had plenipotentiary powers, and to try to obtain a promise that Chinese troops would also evacuate. "Based on past relationships we cannot fail to recognize Korea's independence." But, Itō emphasized in summarizing the cabinet decision for Inoue, "We want to avoid hostilities with China. . . . We cannot yet decide whether to risk war with China for Korean independence in the future. But for now we must avoid it."[49]

Concerning negotiation of a settlement with Korea, the position of the Japanese government was very like that assumed after the 1882 incident, except that it was not so severe. When Inoue arrived at Inchon at the end of December, he sent a note to the American minister, requesting an interview before he went to Seoul. Foote saw him on January 2, at which interview he asked Foote's opinion on many points. Foote told him that "any adjustment which involved the disintegration of any portion of Corean territory would, in my opinion, be most unwise." and, to his "satisfaction," Foote could report that Inoue "agreed with me on this point . . . He said that his government desired an amicable adjustment, that questions between Japan and Corea, and those between Japan and China must be treated separately, that he should exact first, from the Corean Gov't, an apology, and, secondly, a money indemnity, that the amount of the indemnity would not exceed one hundred and fifty Thousand dollars. I came from the interview with the full conviction that, as far as Japan was concerned, there would be a wise, prudent and liberal policy pursued."[50]

[49] Itō to Inoue, Dec. 26, 1884 in Itō, *Chōsen Kōshō Shiryō*, I, 336-37. Archives, SP 5, 48-49. Tabohashi (1940), I, 1015-18, 1043.

[50] Foote to Sec. State, Dec. 31, 1884, No. 136 and Jan. 2, 1885, No. 138, (confidential): Dipl. Desp., Korea. McCune and Harrison, *op. cit.*, I, 114-16.

Inoue's negotiations were approximately in that vein. On two things he was adamant. He would not allow a Chinese to be present while he was negotiating with the Korean representative (Kim Hong-chip) and he would not guarantee to turn over to the Korean government those members of the Independence party who had escaped to Japan. On the first point a crisis occurred on January 8, when in the course of discussions between Inoue and Kim a Chinese ambassador, Wu Ta-chin, "intruded into the room." Inoue stood up, shook hands, and said: "Today I am negotiating with a Korean official. It is not convenient for you to be present today." Wu wrote out a note to Inoue saying that "naturally" he was entitled to be present, and they exchanged several notes in writing. Inoue insisted that matters concerning Korea should be negotiated with Koreans, things regarding China with Chinese, and the two not intermingled. He asked Wu if he had credentials permitting him to negotiate for China, and Wu said no. Thus Inoue "checked Wu's intention" and Wu left. On the matter of the delivery of Kim Ok-kiun and the other insurrectionists to Korea, which was at one point demanded by the Korean negotiator, Inoue explained that these were "political criminals." He said that the practice of international law was such that they could not be returned forcibly; and anyway Japan and Korea had no treaty calling for the extradition of criminals.[51]

These episodes, as well as Inoue's pre-conference talk with Minister Foote, indicate rather neatly the Japanese government's emphasis on conducting diplomacy in the Western-style modern way, on standing with progressive nations in a "wise, prudent, and liberal policy." Shaking hands with a fellow oriental, which must have seemed extraordinary to Wu, the emphasis on international law, and the explanation of such complicated matters as the rights of political refugees and the nature of extradition treaties built into the conferences the same air of firm yet patient teaching of back-

[51] Archives, SP 5, 50-51, 53. Tabohashi (1940), I, 1059-60.

ward people which had characterized the Japanese handling of Korea since 1876.

The specific terms of settlement called for an apology from Korea, punishment of those who had killed or injured Japanese subjects, damages totalling $110,000 to those Japanese who suffered, and restitution of Japanese buildings. Takezoe was recalled, though this was not part of the agreement. Inoue was back in Tokyo within thirty days, having made an agreement which could only be praised in terms of progressive international practice. Mr. Foote made this clear in commenting on the settlement to American Minister Bingham in Japan: "The difficulties growing out of the late troubles have been successfully adjusted upon terms most creditable to Japan and most liberal to Corea. The fortunate settlement is due largely to the wisdom and firmness of His Imperial Japanese Majesty's Ambassador, Count Inouye."[52]

Following Inoue's negotiations at Seoul, Itō himself went to China to seek a basic settlement which would reduce the probability of future Sino-Japanese clashes in Korea. This will be discussed in the following chapter. But enough has been said to indicate the general tenor of Japanese government policy after the 1884 Seoul Uprising. It was as it had been a year before; safe and sane, with cool realism tempering any urge to promote the independence and progress of Korea, and no sign of aggressive intent. Takezoe had allowed himself temporarily to be swayed beyond the dictates of prudence by hot-headed and impatient advocates of progress, but the Japanese government showed itself determined not to allow a situation to develop wherein the burden of upholding a reformist government in Korea would fall on its shoulders alone. In fact, Foulk reported that the new Japanese representative in Seoul had informed him that "as his countrymen are regarded with so much distrust by Coreans and Chinese in Corea, he should discourage attempts by the Corean government to obtain instructors

[52] Treat, *Diplomatic Relations* . . ., II, 215. Foote to Sec. State, Jan. 9, 1885, No. 140 (and encl.). Archives, SP 5, 50-51, 53.

of all kinds from Japan and advise the employment of Americans."[53] The Japanese government, fingers slightly burned by the 1884 affair, was content to let the United States take the lead in any further effort to promote "civilization" in Korea.

However, to Inoue Kakugorō and other Japanese liberals such indifference was sheer betrayal. Kakugorō had an open break with Foreign Minister Inoue in March, 1885, when he called on him, denounced him for weakness, and said that he would "never see him again." Fukuzawa on this occasion was more tolerant. He chided Kakugorō for being so angry at the foreign minister, explaining that he merely wished to avoid war with China.[54] Kakugorō returned to Seoul to salvage what he could of "civilization," where, however, he was soon being sought by Japanese authorities on charges of complicity in the famous and fantastic Osaka Incident.

The Osaka Incident was the Japanese liberals' answer to their government's refusal to help Korea. The government might make a cowardly retreat from principle, but they were prepared to "kill ourselves for righteousness." They would organize an expedition to Korea to put the Independence party back in power. The originators of the scheme were the aforementioned Liberal party secretary, Kobayashi Kuzuo, and perhaps the most dynamic exponent of liberty and equality in the entire Japanese liberal movement, Ōi Kentaro. Kobayashi and Ōi were ex-samurai who had become advocates of Western learning and who had a special area of common interest in French studies. Ōi was noted as an expert in French law from the fact that he had translated the French Code into Japanese while assisting the then minister of justice, Etō Shimpei, in 1873. He had left the government service in 1876, and had become a leading advocate of the Jiyū minken (people's

[53] Foulk to Sec. State, Mar. 12, 1885, No. 153: Dipl. Desp., Korea.

[54] Kondō, *Inoue . . . Den*, 78-79. Ishikawa, *Fukuzawa . . . Den*, III, 344-45. The Japanese legation at Seoul reported to For. Min. Inoue that Kakugorō had left Korea "suddenly," "against our advice."—Dep. Min. Kondō, Seoul, to For. Min. Inoue, Mar. 12, 1885, No. 129: NGB, XVIII, 207-8.

rights) movement, being especially active during the period 1881–84 when rural unrest reached almost revolutionary proportions. He was outspokenly sympathetic with lower class aspirations, criticizing the more conservative members of his own Liberal party, as well as the government. He and his followers advocated free and universal suffrage, demanded reduced taxes, and opposed conscription. As a lawyer he was much concerned with civil rights, and he defended many persons who were jailed by the authorities for anti-government activities. He worked hard for the introduction of Western culture to Japan, and was in the vanguard of those who demanded a Diet and representative government.[55]

Ōi was the oldest member of the group, being 43 in 1885; Kobayashi was 30. Information on others of the inner circle, which numbered perhaps thirty to forty people, is scant, but some of them were as follows: Isoyama Seibei, age 34, from Hitachi in northern Honshu, of a wealthy family of sake manufacturers, very frank in nature, liked sake and conversation, became a popular rights advocate, first choice of Ōi to be leader of the "action" band which was to go to Korea; Arai Shogo, age 30, well-to-do farmer from Shimotsukenokuni near Tokyo, as a youth studied Chinese and English, his wife was a niece of Etō Shimpei, he became interested in the argument for a parliament when that idea was in its infancy, carried "people's opinions" to the Council of State (Dajōkan) and the Senate (Genrōin), but since they paid no attention he resorted to speaking and writing, jailed several times for contempt of officials, succeeded Isoyama as leader of the action band; Tashiro Tsuekichi, born in Fukushima prefecture, by trade a blacksmith, but became a swordsmith, jailed for counterfeiting money to aid the people's rights movement, arrested a second time for participation in the Fukushima Affair (1883) when the governor of Fukushima arrested many Jiyūtō members on charges of sedition,

[55] Scalapino, *op. cit.*, 103-8. Marius Jansen, "Ōi Kentarō; Radicalism and Chauvinism," *Far Eastern Quarterly*, XI, 3 (1952), 307-8. Hirano Yoshitarō (ed.), *Bajō Ōi Kentarō Den* (Biography of Ōi Kentarō) (Tokyo: Ōi Bajō Den Hensanbu, 1938), chaps. 1-4.

released after 100 days, went to Tokyo where he met Isoyama and others; Inagaki Ryūnosuke, age 37, had studied in Tosa under Kataoka Kenkichi as a youth, then went to Tokyo, good at fencing; Ochia Toraichi, from Saitama near Tokyo, had been involved in an "incident" there and gone into hiding, worked in a copper mine for ten months, went to Tokyo and met Ōi; Kageyama Hideko, age 21 (or 19), the only girl in the band, from Okayama, studied from girlhood, was skilled in English and English literature, became a teacher in a primary school, advocate of "women's liberation," later established a women's night school in Tokyo and a women's magazine *Sekai Fujin* (Woman's World).[56]

Kobayashi and Ōi, à la Française, regarded themselves as latter-day Lafayettes, helping Korea toward independence and progress as Lafayette had helped America. They drew up a proclamation of Korean independence in Japanese, English and French, and, so Koreans could read it, had one Yamamoto Ken, who had a school of Chinese learning in Osaka, render it into Chinese. The proclamation stated that, "Right and courageous Japanese people hereby proclaim to the world that Korea has been independent since its establishment by the Yi [dynasty]. . . . There should be no interference by other countries, but the Chinese came with military forces and made the country subordinate to them, destroyed its national authority and its freedom. . . . Now Korea is going to reform its basic policies. . . . On behalf of Heaven we shall assist this reformation. This was originally the will of the Korean King and the Korean people, and this is the principle of freedom. . . . The great principle of freedom cannot fail [as testified by] the beautiful story of thirteen states [American] with the French assisting against England. . . . We will kill ourselves for righteousness."[57]

The plan was to send a party of stalwarts under Isoyama's

[56] Biographical information on these and a few others in Ishikawa, *Jiyutō Ōsaka* . . ., 35, 37, 41, 43-51, 78, 151-54. On Miss Kageyama see also *Kaizō Shimbun*, Dec. 2, 1885, and *Meiji Hennenshi*, VI, 200. Here her age is given as 19, whereas Ishikawa gives 21.

[57] Hirano, *Bajō Ōi* . . ., 92-94.

leadership to Korea to set the stage for a return of Kim, Pak, and the Independence party, and it was anticipated that once they "opened fire for Korean independence" many European and American revolutionary groups would help them.[58] But there were difficulties. The first problem was, of course, to raise money and collect weapons. Money was especially hard to come by as it was a depression period, and some of the band resorted to thievery. One night seven of them visited a lonely monastery near Nara, determined to get 1000 yen. They encountered an old monk, who informed them that he had "only yesterday deposited the monastery's money in a bank in Nara," but he gave them a one-yen note. Naturally they were dissatisfied with this and they undertook forcibly to search the place while the monks frantically clanged the temple bell. The money raisers made off with 320 yen. A great tragedy struck in late October when Isoyama, "becoming discouraged at the money problem," absconded with what funds there were. This called for a council of war at Osaka between Ōi and Kobayashi, at which they officially ousted Isoyama from command of the group and installed Arai in his place, with Ōi somehow obtaining a new supply of money. Arai, Inagaki, and several others left Osaka "with bombs" on November 20 for Nagasaki, which was to be the port of embarkation for Korea. However, Inagaki would not take orders from Arai, and this caused more difficulty. Meanwhile police were investigating "an unusual number of robberies" in the Osaka area, and on November 23 they surprised Ōi and Kobayashi at their hotel and arrested them. A roundup of the rest of the partisans followed speedily in both the Osaka and Nagasaki areas, Arai being caught in November 26, Isoyama on December 6. The number arrested is difficult to determine, estimates running from 63 to 130, but as the nature of the plot came to light the authorities cracked down hard. They charged Ōi and friends with possessing bombs, inciting riots, etc. Some thirty-one were

[58] Report of Tokyo Dep. Chief of Police to For. Min. Inoue, Dec. 15, 1885, NGB, XIX, 518-19.

convicted, with Ōi, Kobayashi, and Isoyama receiving six-year sentences and Arai five.[59]

Immediately after the arrest of the band at Osaka and Nagasaki the Japanese government dispatched a Foreign Office official, Kurino, and policemen to Seoul to arrest Inoue Kakugorō and other "suspicious characters."[60] Here, however, they encountered an interesting turn of the tables. Kakugorō begged protection from the Korean Foreign Office, and the Korean foreign minister, reminding Kurino of what international law had to say on sanctuary for political criminals, refused to allow his arrest. Kurino then tried to negotiate an extradition treaty to allow search and arrest, but after a month he gave up and left Korea. Inoue Kakugorō remained in Seoul, publishing his newspaper, though the authorities would have their measure later when he returned to Japan.[61]

These efforts of the liberals to translate their ideals into action might be dismissed as merely ridiculous. Certainly Fukuzawa's ujimushi (worms and bugs) principle could be applied to the

[59] Ishikawa, *Jiyūtō Ōsaka* . . ., 65-80. Many of the sources on the Osaka Incident, as well as on the French loan scheme, are, as Tabohashi (1951, 4-5) says, "defective as to accuracy," with "not a few contradictions." But, as he emphasizes, "not such that they must be thrown out as fabrications." Certainly this is true of Ishikawa's *Jiyūtō Ōsaka Jiken*, which apparently Tabohashi did not use, but which is probably the most detailed report of the affair. It is poorly organized, repeats itself, and yet clearly its editor had inside information of a detailed variety. Other principal sources are Itagaki's *Jiyūtō Shi*, Hiranō's *Bajō* . . ., and Ishikawa's *Fukuzawa* . . . *Den*. These have been used by Tabohashi and Jansen ("Ōi . . ."). They all tend to bias in favor of the schemers, although Tabohashi and Jansen are careful not to reflect this bias. A good cross-check on details of the affair is provided by Japanese government investigation reports. Except for considering Ōi, Kobayashi, and their friends as "criminals" rather than heroes, these are in substantial agreement with the sources mentioned above.

See Osaka Acting Governor to Home Min., Nov. 3, Dec. 23, 1885; Tokyo Dep. Chief of Police to For. Min. Inoue, Dec. 15, 1885, Inoue to Takahira (Seoul), Dec. ?, 1885—these appear as attached documents to Takahira (Seoul) to For. Min. Inoue, Jan. 3, 1886: NGB, XIX, 513-20. Takahira's letter includes information he got in Seoul from an "informer". For contemporary press accounts see *Kaizō Shimbun*, Nov. 25, 1885; *Tokyo Nichi Nichi*, Dec. 2, 1885; *Meiji Hennenshi*, VI, 192, 196-97. These are detailed and informed accounts.

[60] A Japanese Foreign Office index lists Kakugorō under the category, "Dangerous Thoughts, 1885," Seen by author at Gaimushō, Tokyo.

[61] Kurino to For. Min. Inoue, Jan. 4, 1886: NGB, XIX, 524-25. Kondō, *Inoue* . . . *Den*, 95-96, 101-2, 133. Foulk to Sec. State, June 3, 1886, No. 267: Dipl. Desp., Korea,

Osaka affair with devastating effect: a bunch of dirty-faced schoolboys playing cops and robbers. However, the Boston Tea Party had a similar look. The ideals espoused by the dirty faces should not be dismissed too lightly. Ōi, speaking in defense of his actions at his trial, made a brilliant and searching inquiry into the whole pattern of activity of the Meiji government. He found Japan still a tyranny, with the government in the hands of a selfish minority. He attacked favoritism, class distinction; he demanded that the differentiation between "noble people" and "lower people" should be broken down, not bolstered as the government was doing with its new peerage. "We are aiming," he said, "to reform society, basing it on freedom and equality. Thus not only is reform needed in politics, but also in education and religion." He called the traditional philosophies of Confucianism, Buddhism, and Shintoism unprogressive. He connected all this to the Korean problem by emphasizing that freedom and equality did not stand alone in one country. "We do not wish to accuse Koreans of impoliteness or invade them. We wish merely to sympathize with them and to help them from difficulties . . . to give back political authority to the Independence party and bring safety and happiness to the Korean people. . . . People say this is impossible because it is a different land, but if you look at the teachers of religion, they regard people of all nations as brothers. . . . There are vicious customs in Korea. They punish crimes to three generations. So we who know liberalism cannot stand aside doing nothing . . .." Ōi admitted to being afraid no one would believe him, but, "I want to clarify this all over the world and for the future."[62]

The efforts of Japanese liberals to promote the establishment of a progressive regime in Korea in 1884-85 were abortive and somewhat ridiculous. But there is no need to disparage the motives of the people who involved themselves in these episodes merely because they had the idea that freedom and progress were for

[62] Ishikawa, *Jiyūtō Ōsaka Jiken*, 145-46. Hirano, *Bajō* . . ., 148-66. Jansen, "Ōi . . .," 310-11.

export as well as home consumption. The shortcomings of isolationist liberalism, if not fully appreciated in the world of the nineteenth century, have been amply demonstrated since. That freedom is indivisible and knows no national boundaries is perhaps the final truth of the liberal creed. But one of the saddest facts liberals have had to learn (or should surely be learning) is that in exporting freedom in a nation state system it is incredibly easy to spoil the product and, worse, to ruin the very ground in which it grows. In specific terms, the principal importance of the affairs of 1884–85 for Japan was the association of Jiyū minken (people's rights) and Korean "independence" in the minds of Japanese liberals and all those other ordinary Japanese who were chafing under various government oppressions. We have observed already the beginning stage of this formulation in the rather vague and illogical association of Seikan and liberty. Conquer Korea and Liberty. That formula made no sense, as Fukuzawa and his Keio students had been quick to see. But even there the words Korea and liberty were linked. The effect of the 1884–85 episodes was merely to change a verb in a slogan, "conquer" to "free." Free Korea and Liberty. This made sense. With it the liberals had a foreign policy and a domestic program, both ringing with idealism and capable of exciting immense enthusiasm. Beside this the government's caution abroad-oppression at home was pale indeed.

IV

Realism Resumed

On February 27, 1885, the Japanese government issued a confidential "Imperial instruction" to all prefectural governors:

> In regard to negotiations with China, Councillor Itō has been ordered to China as Envoy Extraordinary Minister Plenipotentiary to decide everything. Negotiations with foreign countries are very important, and in consideration of the future . . . the nation's eternal great accounting interests should not be misled. Relations with neighboring countries should not be impaired and a good outcome should be achieved in a conciliatory manner. This is the Imperial consideration. Therefore you prefectural governors should be well versed in this Imperial instruction.[1]

This communication is revealing of the tone of the Japanese government's Korea policy for the next eight years, 1885–1893. It was to continue to seek the "good outcome" of the independence of Korea and progressive measures within that country, but only within the framework of conciliation, namely, conciliation of the big brother in the background, China. And prefectural governors were to see that no headstrong Help Korea advocates upset the apple-cart of conciliation.

Foreign Minister Inoue had hoped to make an agreement with the Chinese while he was in Korea in January, 1885, and he was

[1] Archives, SP 5, 56.

accredited to do so, if he could organize negotiations with their representatives. However, although two Chinese representatives were there, the above-mentioned Wu and another, they were not accredited to settle issues between China and Japan, nor would the Chinese government send a representative so accredited to Korea.[2] However, there were some 600 Japanese troops in Seoul, facing probably 2000 Chinese, some of whom had already clashed during the uprising of December.[3] If the probability of an outbreak of further hostilities was to be removed, a settlement of some kind was necessary, and Itō dispatched himself to China to obtain one.

He and Inoue were determined to try for an immediate settlement despite the fact that there was sure to be popular opposition in Japan. A student demonstration in Tokyo in January, demanding strong measures against China, gave them a sample of this. Government orders were issued to teachers to control their students.[4] Then the imperial order of February 27 put prefectural officials on the alert to control popular "foaming";[5] and lastly a rigid censorship of the press was exercised to prevent an outcry against the terms of the treaty which Itō proceeded to negotiate at Tientsin. The hand of censorship is clear from a study of Japanese newspapers of late April, May, and June, 1885. The treaty was signed on April 18 and Itō left Tientsin on the nineteenth. By the twenty-first, Tokyo newspapers were speculating on what the treaty might contain and "hoping to read its contents in the near future."[6] On May 12 *Yubin Hochi* complained: "We wish the Tientsin Treaty to be

[2] Tabohashi (1940), I, 1023. Treat, *Diplomatic Relations* . . ., II, 216, citing Young (Peking) to Sec. State Freylinghuysen, Apr. 2, 1885.

[3] Foulk says specifically that there were 600 Japanese—Foulk to Sec. State, Mar. 9, 1885, No. 152, confidential: Dipl. Desp., Korea; figures on the Chinese are not so specific but 2000 seems a fair estimate, for they were definitely superior in number to the Japanese force.

[4] Tabohashi, *op. cit.*, p. 1066.

[5] The Japanese Foreign Office description uses this term—Archives, SP 5, 56.

[6] *Yubin Hochi*, Apr. 21, 1885; *Jiji Shimpō*, Apr. 22, 1885; *Tōkyō-Yokohama Mainichi*, Apr. 21, 1885.

published. . . . Many days have passed since Ambassador Itō returned to Japan, but why does not the government issue the terms of the Treaty. . . ."[7] The treaty was finally published by the Council of State on May 27, without comment, and the terms were printed immediately thereafter by the several newspapers. However, not one of them carried editorial comment. They merely repeated woodenly the official government announcement. Considering the very large coverage given the Seoul Uprising and Inoue's settlement earlier, the high pitch of public excitement over Itō's going to China, and the fact that at least three of the newspapers, Fukuzawa's *Jiji Shimpō*, the *Tōkyō-Yokohama Mainichi*, and *Yubin Hochi*, were run by liberals who were strong critics of the government, the only explanation is censorship.[8]

While the government utilized censorship to hold down public clamor in Japan, Itō carried out his mission with great circumspection. Before going to China he visited American Minister Bingham in Tokyo for advice, just as Inoue had visited Minister Foote in Korea before seeing Korean negotiators. Bingham urged that "a peaceful settlement could be reached if China and Japan would agree to withdraw their military forces from Corea, and recognize the rightful and exclusive autonomy of the Government of Corea within its territorial domain." Itō told Bingham that he concurred in these views and that he would seek a settlement with China on that basis. Itō negotiated in gingerly fashion in China, but definitely within the framework of Bingham's advice. This was despite the fact that he arrived in China at a time when the diplomatic trumps

[7] The files of this and all other major Japanese newspapers of the Meiji era, and many minor ones, are housed in Tokyo University's Meiji Shimbun Bunko, where the author studied them. Many articles from these are reproduced in the *Meiji Hennenshi* collection (very carefully and accurately as the author can attest from numerous cross-checks) but, where that collection is not cited for a newspaper reference, the original was used.

[8] *Yubin Hochi*, May 28, 1885 *et seq.*; *Jiji Shimpō*, May 27, 1885, *et seq.*; *Tōkyō-Yokohama Mainichi*, May 28, 1885, *et. seq.* *Yubin Hochi* reflected Ōkuma-Kaishintō (Progressive party) opinion as did *Tōkyō-Yokohama Mainichi*, whose editor, Numa Morikazu, was a Kaishintō leader. Cf. *Tōkyō Nichi Nichi*, May 28, 1885 and *Meiji Hennenshi*, VI, 91. This was generally the government mouthpiece.

were all in his hand. The Chinese government was engaged in rather desperate negotiations with France in an effort to settle the Sino-French hostilities over Annam. Itō, had he chosen to call at the French legation in Tokyo instead of at the American, or had he got in touch with French representatives in China, might easily have arranged a Franco-Japanese diplomatic front to put maximum pressure on China.[9] However, the background of Liberal party soundings at the French legation in Tokyo notwithstanding, he did not do this, and the fact that he did not may be taken as additional evidence that his principal objective was to find a peaceful settlement, not diplomatic advantage. This is not to say that he was straightforward to the point of abandoning all efforts at diplomatic finesse. He had in his entourage, which consisted of twenty-one persons, Saigō Tsugumichi, then minister of commerce and industry in the Tokyo government and lieutenant general of the army, who, of course, like his elder brother, was known as a strong policy advocate. There was perhaps a subtle suggestion of alternatives here, negotiate with Itō the gentleman or with Saigō the militarist. However, his presence on the mission may also have been to confuse Itō's critics in Japan. Anyway, Saigō was a very cowed militarist on this occasion, for Itō permitted him no part in the negotiations.

The Japanese mission went first to Peking, where it presented its credentials to the Tsungli Yamen and requested an audience with the emperor. (This was a bit of diplomatic finesse, for the Chinese had told them to stop at Tientsin and negotiate with Li Hung-chang.) Chinese court officials refused the imperial audience, saying that the emperor was too young. Itō accepted this, but then asked to be shown evidence that Li Hung-chang had plenipotentiary power to negotiate a settlement. After some argument he was shown a paper attesting Li's plenipotentiary power. Finally, on April 3, after he had been in China over a month, Itō settled down to negotiations with Li at Tientsin. He stressed immediately that

[9] Treat, *op. cit.*, II, 216-18.

Japan's objective was peaceful friendly relations, and he suggested that the talks be divided into two sections, (1) about the past and (2) about the future. "Let us talk first about the future. . . . The reason we have soldiers in Korea is due to the violence of the Korean people, but we do not expect to continue this forever. . . . It is likely that in the future if there are Japanese and Chinese soldiers in Korea, there will be trouble between them. This is as logical as for a fire to burn. Therefore if we want friendly relations these forces should be withdrawn."

An argument developed about who was to blame for the armed clash that had occurred in Seoul. Itō held that the Japanese had gone to the king at his request, and that the Chinese had attacked them. "If your general had taken time to negotiate, it might have been possible to avoid difficulties. Anyway the Japanese were inside and the Chinese outside, so it is clear that the Chinese did the attacking." He demanded punishment of the Chinese general responsible for this and indemnification for injured Japanese subjects. After many arguments and a couple of seeming deadlocks agreement was reached along these general terms, though without any specific admission of guilt on the part of the Chinese. Both countries were to withdraw their troops from Korea within four months. Neither Chinese nor Japanese instructors were to train Korean soldiers, rather a recommendation was to be made to the Korean king that he train his own army. And in the case of disorders in Korea so severe as to require the dispatch of troops by either China or Japan, written notice of such intention to dispatch troops would be sent by the one to the other. In an addendum to the treaty Li stated that the soldiers of Japan and China had entered into hostilities in Korea and "I regret it. The Chinese fault was in not being cautious enough and they deserve to be disciplined. A Mrs. Honda says her home was entered and Japanese people killed. There is no proof from our side but I shall send investigators and if it is definitely proved that Chinese soldiers killed Japanese subjects, they will be penalized severely by Chinese Law. I wish you to investigate your facts too." To which Itō appended the reply, "They should be investigated."[10]

Itō had hoped also to get some mention of the sovereignty or at least the autonomy of Korea written into the agreement. He did not succeed, though it may be considered that the merely equal right of China with Japan to dispatch troops was an implication to that effect. Also he held that Japanese legation guards who were there under the 1882 Japanese-Korean agreement should not fall under the ban on troops. However, the Japanese did evacuate these guards along with their other troops in July, which was within the four-month deadline. Mr. Takahira, Japanese chargé at Seoul, informed the Korean government on this occasion that Japan was evacuating the guards, but that she did not give up the right to have them if needed, under the terms of the 1882 settlement.[11]

Having made the Tientsin Treaty, otherwise known as the Li-Itō Convention of 1885, the Japanese government undertook precautionary measures to see that Korean refugees and Japanese liberals in Japan did not upset it. At first, other than the orders to teachers and prefectural governors and the censorship already mentioned, they did nothing more drastic than apply a cold shoulder to the Korean progressives who had fled to Japan on the *Chitose Maru.* When these arrived at Nagasaki, no government officials offered to help them, and they made their way to Fukuzawa, who took them in. However, in May, three of them, Pak Young-hyo, So Kwang-pom, and So Che-pil (Philip Jaisohn), left Japan for America. Tabohashi suggests the possibility, though there are no documents on it, that the Japanese government passed expense money to them via Fukuzawa to get them out of the country. Kim Ok-kiun refused to go, and remained in Japan.[12]

Then with the coming to light of the Osaka Incident in late November, Japanese officialdom began to crack down hard. As

[10] Archives, SP 5, 57-61. *Tōkyō Nichi Nichi,* May 28, 1885, gives Council of State treaty release. *Meiji Hennenshi,* VI, 91-92. See also Tabohashi (1940), I, 1079-1122.

[11] Archives, SP 5, 63.

[12] Tabohashi (1951), 8-9.

might be expected, the incident made sensational news in Korea, where it was reported that Kim Ok-kiun "had sailed for Korea with renegade Japanese in eight Japanese junks." About the same time the rumor spread in Seoul that Pak, So Kwang-pom, and So Che-pil were conspiring in America, that they had threatened Queen Min, and that the United States would supply their fellow conspirators in Japan with dynamite. "Missionaries in San Francisco" were, according to the rumours, helping the plotters there.[13] The Japanese government, as already related, made clear that it was stopping not sponsoring the scheme by arresting Ōi and his fellow conspirators, bringing them to trial, and sentencing them.[14] According to the recollection of the trial judge years later "even ministers from Tokyo came to hear the judgment, and the government brought strong pressure for conviction without asking whether the charges were true or not."[15] The judgment was handed down on September 19, 1886, but thereafter the defendants appealed for a new trial. In March, 1888, the original judgment was thrown out and a new trial called for Nagoya. Its verdict was by no means favorable to the defendants, as the originally imposed six-year sentences were upped to nine years. However, the culprits were released in February, 1889, by the amnesty proclamation which accompanied the promulgation of the constitution.[16]

Inoue Kakugorō also had his troubles with the authorities. He left Korea in December, 1886, despairing of hope for "progress" there,[17] and went to the United States to look into the possibility of organizing a Japanese immigration experiment. He arrived in San Francisco in June, 1887, visited one "chief of the immigration

[13] Foulk to Sec. State Bayard, Dec. 12, 1885, No. 262 and Dec. 29, 1885, No. 265 (both confidential): Dipl. Desp., Korea. Takahira (Seoul) to For. Min. Inoue, Jan. 3, 1886, No. 209: NGB, XIX, 513-14.

[14] Under date of Jan. 20, 1886, For. Min. Inoue instructed Takahira in Seoul to report officially to the Korean government that Ōi, etc., had concocted a plot, but were already under arrest—No. 212: NGB, XIX, 544.

[15] Hirano, *Bajō . . .*, 174.

[16] Tabohashi (1951), 7-8.

[17] Inoue, *Kanjo no Zammu*, 106.

bureau," and later bought fifty acres of land in Callaberos County. Judging that Japanese settlers could do well there, he then returned to Japan to report to Fukuzawa and discuss the possibility of developing a broad enterprise for Japanese farmers in the San Joaquin Valley. However, trouble awaited him in Japan. He was seized by Tokyo police on charges relating to activities in connection with the Seoul Uprising and the Osaka Incident. His arrest, said Kakugorō, was at the instruction of Inoue Kaoru. At his trial the authorities produced code sheets he had used to correspond in cipher with Kim and Pak (Kakugorō had torn these up and given them to a hotel maid to burn, but apparently she had not done so). Also used against him was a memorandum on Korean affairs he had sent to the Council of State in 1885. This criticized the Korean policy of Inoue Kaoru and the Tientsin Treaty. The prosecutor immediately connected Fukuzawa with Kakugorō's activities and said that perhaps Fukuzawa had inspired the Seoul Incident, and the judge asked whether the real author of the memorandum in question was not Fukuzawa. Kakugorō rejoined that he alone had written the memorandum, that he alone had used the code book, and that he alone had been involved in the Seoul Uprising. Fukuzawa had nothing to do with any of them. He added that in fact it was Foreign Minister Inoue, himself, who had "inspired" him in his Korean ventures in 1885. Fukuzawa was called to court as a witness, though he was not formally accused. Kakugorō, however, was convicted of having "insulted" Foreign Minister Inoue and Prime Minister Itō, of having told lies to the Korean foreign minister and others, and of having published lying articles. He was sentenced to up to a year in jail, where he spent about a year. He too was released on constitution day, February 11, 1889.[18]

While thus harassing his Japanese friends, Japan's officialdom became increasingly unhappy about the continued presence of Kim Ok-kiun in Japan. They had refused to turn him back to Korea, but it is clear that they were not pleased to have him in

[18] Kondō, *Inoue . . . Den*, 108, 128-45. Ishikawa, *Fukuzawa . . . Den*, III, 363-69.

Japan. Kim did not actually take part in the Osaka Incident. He seems to have been advised by Fukuzawa to lie low after his return to Japan following the Seoul fiasco and to have rejected the invitations of Ōi and Kobayashi to participate actively.[19] But he began to win notoriety as the *object*, now, of assassination plots. The Min family, which had resumed political authority in Korea after the failure of the 1884 coup, began, apparently as early as the summer of 1885, to engineer plots to bring about Kim's demise in Japan. One Sō Jō-shun (Japanese name Noda Heijiro) and another Korean named Cho, who seems to have had secret instructions from the Seoul court, sought out Kim in Japan, bearing a message from a cousin of the king, who claimed to be "regretful for the failure of the coup the year before" and to have inside information that the king's "confidence" in Kim was "unchanged." Kim talked to them openly about the possibility of gathering together some 1000 "descendants of Koreans living in Japan," going with them to Korea, and ousting the Min—all of which was duly reported back to the Min. A confusion of this may have given rise to the rumours of Kim's coming with the Osaka adventurers. Sō and Cho did not make an assassination attempt, however, perhaps because some of Kim's friends became suspicious of them.[20] But another agent came from Korea a few months later, and Kim became alarmed. In May, 1886, he sent a letter to Foreign Minister Inoue telling him there was an agent of the Korean king in Japan to kill him. The Tokyo Metropolitan Police explored the situation and the Foreign Office wired Chargé Takahira at the Japanese legation in Seoul on June 7 telling him to investigate a rumor that the Korean government had sent an agent to assassinate Kim. It added that Kim was threatening to produce a letter written to the would-be assassin as proof, so that he could ask protection from a Japanese court. "Therefore," continued the Foreign Office instruction, "the

[19] Tabohashi (1951), 6, 8. Tokyo Dep. Chief of Police to For. Min. Inoue, Dec. 15, 1885: NGB, XIX, 518.
[20] Tabohashi (1951), 9-10.

Japanese government, in order to preserve friendly relations with Korea and internal security in Japan, is going to order Kim to leave Japan, and at the same time recommends that the Korean government call back the assassin."[21]

Foreign Minister Inoue explained the situation to Home Minister Yamagata, who would have to originate the ousting order, as follows: "As you know after the Seoul uprising Kim came to Tokyo and has lived here. But we want him to leave Japan, so please instruct the police chief and the provincial governor to this effect. The reason is that as long as Kim stays in Japan there will always be diplomatic trouble with Korea and China. . . . We have heard of an assassination plan and have advised the Korean government to call back the assassin."[22]

On June 12, Kim was handed an order by the governor of Kanagawa prefecture to leave the country, but he delayed because "no foreign ship would accept him." Inoue then advised Yamagata to send him to the Bonin Islands, on the grounds that he and his four followers were "persons adrift." This would "solve our problems," both as to "Sino-Korean relations" and "domestic peace and security." Yamagata complied and Takahira subsequently reported that the Korean government agreed to this. The governor of Kanagawa ordered the would-be assassin "escorted" back to Korea.[23] Subsequently Kim was moved to Sapporo, in Hokkaido, where "he suffered from the severe climate and often presented petitions to the government to be transferred [to Tokyo]." In 1889 he was allowed to return to Tokyo because of illness.[24]

The conduct of Japanese diplomacy in Korea after the signing of the Tientsin Treaty likewise shows the Japanese government to

[21] Archives, SP 5, 64.

[22] For. Min. Inoue to Home Min. Yamagata, June 9, 1886, No. 238: NGB, XIX, 573, 74.

[23] Archives, SP 5, p. 64. Inoue to Yamagata, Aug. 2, 1886, No. 247 and Yamagata to Inoue, Aug. 4, 1886, No. 248 and enclosures: NGB, XIX, 582-83. The Deputy home minister (encl. 3) reported that he had tried to send Kim to the United States, but failed and so sent him to the Bonins.

[24] Archives, SP 5, p. 75. Cf. Kokuryūkai, *Nisshi* . . ., I, 218.

be avoiding controversies and complications. In August, 1885, Foulk, who had become chargé of the United States legation with the departure of Minister Foote the preceding February, summarized the Japanese attitude as follows: "While Japan was formerly highly active in using her influence in the affairs of Korea, since the treaty of last April with China, she has been apparently little more than a passive observer. The new Japanese legation, now being built, is small and insignificant. The representative is a Charge d'affair ad. interim. There is much to indicate that Japan has greatly altered her policy in regard to Korea, yielding much to the Chinese claim of suzerainty."[25]

This description of the situation by Foulk is interesting, especially in view of later American evaluations of post-1885 Japanese policy objectives. Our newest (and best) textbook on modern Japan, Hugh Borton's *Japan's Modern Century* published in 1955, says the following:

> This agreement [Tientsin Treaty] settled the crisis temporarily. Japan was not yet strong enough to force the Korean issue and China was confident that propinquity and historical precedent gave it an advantage. As the American Minister in Japan described it: "Japan's policy was to allow Korea to be recognised as belonging to China in order to forestall the designs of any other country. . . . When Japan should fight China, Korea could be taken without fear of protest from European powers."[26]

Surely here is evidence that the Japanese government was developing a scheme to seize Korea, at least from the moment the Tientsin Treaty was signed. Borton has always been scrupulously careful, even amidst the bitterness of World War II, not to be unfair to Japan in his evaluations, and his acceptance of this one must be taken as an expression of obligation to follow the evidence, with no hint of malice toward Japan. Yet, as with Tabohashi on the Seoul Incident, he is in this case scrupulous to a fault, for the

[25] Foulk to Sec. State, Aug. 16, 1885. No. 214: Dipl. Desp., Korea. McCune and Harrison, *Korean-American Relations*, I, 126.

[26] Hugh Borton, *Japan's Modern Century* (New York: Ronald Press Co., 1955), 167.

evidence is not so solid as it seems. Borton refers to Nelson[27] (*Korea and the Old Orders in Eastern Asia*) as his source for the American minister's quotation, which is the nub of his paragraph. But if we go beyond this to Nelson's citation, we sense vaguely that something is amiss. Nelson's footnote refers to a diplomatic dispatch from "Heard to Gresham" (Gresham being secretary of state), dated July 29, 1893.[28] This is curious. First, the date, 1893, would seem to indicate that this might be only a latter-day evaluation of Japanese policy after 1885. Actually it is not even that. If we examine the original dispatch, we find that it refers to a recent (1893) policy "change" which "general opinion" was attributing to Japanese fear of Russia but which "to my mind" had an "ulterior purpose." Thus, according to the dispatch itself, any Japanese scheme to seize Korea was linked in time, if not in motive, with a Russian scare of 1893. Its author's speculations concern the then and there not the previous.

Secondly, Nelson, in the text of his work, attributes the dispatch to "the American representative in Japan," which leads Borton to assume that this was "the American Minister in Japan." But, according to Nelson's footnote, this was "Heard," who would seem to be Augustine Heard, who in 1893 was United States minister to *Korea*. Checking further, we find confusion confounded. The name on the dispatch itself is not Heard, but Herod.[29] Herod was Joseph Rogers Herod of Indiana who was actually *a* United States representative in Japan, but of very recent origin. He was appointed second secretary of the legation in Tokyo on January 4, 1893 and he entered upon his duties there on March 4. On May 29 he crossed over to Seoul to act as chargé of the American legation at Seoul during the absence of Minister Heard and Secretary Horace N. Allen, returning to Tokyo on September 15.[30] Thus "to my mind"

[27] *Ibid.*, note 13, p. 169.

[28] Nelson, *Korea and the Old Orders* . . ., 205-6 and note 42, 206.

[29] Herod to Gresham, July 29, 1893, No. 428 (confidential): Dipl. Desp., Korea.

[30] Treat, *op. cit.*, II, 394. U.S. Dept. of State, *Register* (corrected to Jan. 1, 1895) (Washington: Government Printing Office, 1895), p. 17.

is to the mind of a neophyte second secretary from Tokyo on a short visit to Seoul, at a time when neither of the responsible representatives of that legation was present.

This description of the Heard-Herod scholar's quagmire may seem to be too much ado about a quotation. It is necessary therefore to be as clear as possible about the reasons for introducing it here. It is not the author's purpose merely to pick a flaw in two excellent books on Far Eastern history,[31] nor would he say that Herod's dispatch proves nothing as concerns Japanese policy in 1893. Indeed there is evidence that the American ministers themselves, Heard at Seoul and Dun at Tokyo, were concerned about certain vagaries of Japanese policy in that year. Whether they meant a "change" in the direction suggested by Herod will be discussed shortly. However, the image of the Japanese as a two-faced people and of Japanese foreign policy as being continuously devious from the Meiji era to Pearl Harbor is a very strong one in the Western world. Of course, no thoughtful person puts this in absolute terms, but the image is damaging enough that it would seem to be desirable that those who study the Japanese record in international affairs try to estimate whether they find deviousness and dishonesty sufficiently worse than the norm of international conduct to warrant special comment; or if they do not find the Japanese record especially odious in this regard, to try to explain why such an image has developed. The present study, limited as it is to the Meiji era and the Korean episode, cannot provide a conclusive answer, but, since the record of the process of Japanese assumption of control over Korea has given a strong impetus to the development of the image, a close look at that process should contribute to our understanding of how far the image is true, how far distorted. The above discussion of the Herod dispatch is a small case in point.

[31] I discovered the Heard-Herod mix-up by the merest chance, and my own comment on the dispatch, made at the time I read it at the National Archives several years ago before I had any notion of what use might be made of it, indicates that it impressed me also: "This letter long and windy and speculative but very interesting."

At any rate, the reader who has come along with this study thus far will have observed that it would be stretching much too much to say that before 1885 the Japanese government had a plan in operation to seize Korea. The evidence is quite the contrary. Whether the Tientsin Treaty of that year should be regarded as a beginning point for the development of such a plan is our present question. We have examined a specific example of the sort of evidence on which such a presumption is based, but find it unconvincing. In fact, that whole argument which holds the Tientsin Treaty to be a step in the direction of Japanese control over Korea has a look of "damned if you do and damned if you don't" about it. Up to the time of that treaty the evidence that Japan was planning to take Korea is adduced from her effort to *gain* influence in the peninsula and conversely to cut down Chinese influence. But then after Tientsin the same end is adduced from her apparent willingness to see Japanese influence *diminish* and the Chinese hold tighten (so that "when Japan should fight China, Korea could be taken without fear of protest from the European powers"). Could the Japanese Foreign Office have been that adept at calculated villainy?

The question might be resolved by looking at it from another side. Does the Tientsin Treaty and its aftermath really indicate a change in Japanese policy, from active to passive, from challenging Chinese influence to acquiescing in it? We have already observed that beginning with the Kanghwa Treaty of 1876 Japanese official policy advocated the principle of Korean independence and reform but pushed the realization of these in practice only as far as a cautious handling of everyday vicissitudes would allow. It also showed a marked tendency to follow American advice and precedents. In 1882, when Chinese intervention began to raise a clear obstacle, it sought American aid in getting an international agreement to oppose this. When such was not forthcoming, Japanese policy trimmed itself further to the situation, without, however, abandoning the principle. 1884 found the liberals concocting a do-or-die-for-principle campaign which almost caught policy makers off guard, but they reacted at Seoul and Tientsin true to form, making conciliatory agreements. With realistic caution they gave ground to the vicissitudes. This is completely in character with previous policy, but we should ask, was the conciliation at Tientsin and after so great that it must be interpreted as a change in policy, whereby Japan came to a new principle, namely *support* of the pretensions of China (possibly for the ulterior end suggested by Herod, Nelson, and Borton)? Actually Foulk's dispatch, already cited, in which he remarks on the small size of the new Japanese legation and the lower diplomatic grade of Chargé Takahira might be used more effectively than Herod's to back a contention that Japan had changed her policy. To repeat Foulk's summary, "There is much to indicate that Japan has greatly altered her policy in regard to Korea, yielding much to the Chinese claim of suzerainty."[32] He does not say why Japan changed her policy, but one looking for a plot could say a change is always suspicious. However, there are other interesting circumstances to consider.

Under date of July 14, 1884, American Secretary of State Freylinghuysen had informed Lucius H. Foote as follows: "The diplomatic and consular appropriation act for the current fiscal year, approved July 7, 1884, reduces the grade of your office from that of Envoy Extraordinary and Minister Plenipotentiary to that of Minister Resident and Consul General, without change of salary." As a result of this demotion Foote sent in his resignation in September.[33] When he left his post in February, George Foulk took over the American legation as acting chargé d'affairs, at which post he labored for two years, but not in very commodious circumstances. This he explained in a letter to the secretary of state dated February 18, 1886, in which he asked to be relieved of the post.

[32] Foulk to Sec. State, Aug. 16, 1885, No. 214: Dipl. Desp., Korea.

[33] Freylinghuysen to Foote, July 14, 1884, No. 58, Instructions and Foote to Sec. State, Sept. 17, 1884, No. 112: Dipl. Desp., Korea. McCune and Harrison, *op. cit.*, I, 36-38.

"It is simply impossible for one person to execute for any length of time, without clerical assistance, the work called for at this legation. The pay of Chargé d'Affairs ad interim is wholly insufficient to meet the necessary expenses of such an officer living here in charge of the legation, yet I have been unable to secure even this for a period of six months. . . . legation household establishment unprovided with many of the barest necessities for living in it . . . embarrassingly in debt personally . . . have suffered constant humiliation."[34] Foulk was relieved by one William H. Parker, who was dispatched to Seoul as minister resident and consul general in charge of the American legation. However, far from improving the situation, this made it worse. The State Department frantically recalled Foulk to Seoul the following September where he found that "the Minister has been intoxicated during a considerable part of his residence here. Korean and Foreign officials ceased to visit him . . . Americans came to the American legation for advice and found the minister drunk."[35]

Thus, curiously enough, Foulk's own circumstances defeat the possibility of using his "size of legation-rank of representative" testimony as proof that Japan had changed her policy and begun to bolster Chinese claims. Was this true also of the United States? For a similar ulterior motive? No, it was not. When Yüan Shih-k'ai, calling himself His Imperial Chinese Majesty's Resident in Korea, made himself "the biggest man in town" in Seoul during the years 1885–93, Americans there (except the hard-drinking Parker) were much incensed at his high-handed tactics and tried to "parry his thrusts" to assert Chinese hegemony over Korea. But they were unable to do much. For their efforts they received only "scolding" from their superiors in Washington, whose attitude was well summarized by Secretary of State Gresham: "With few exceptions the record of our diplomatic history shows no departure from the wise

[34] Foulk to Sec. State, Feb. 18, 1886, No. 279: Dipl. Desp., Korea. McCune and Harrison, pp. 40-41.

[35] Foulk to Sec. State, Sept. 7, 1886, No. 2; Dipl. Desp., Korea. McCune and Harrison, 42-44.

policy of avoiding foreign alliances and embarrassing participation in guaranteeing the independence of distant states."[36]

Professor F. H. Harrington, from whose work the above quotations were taken, discusses all this in detail, with candor and good humor. His portrayal of the American role in Korean affairs from 1885 to 1893 boils down to something of the following. American representatives in Seoul, like Foulk, Allen, Dinsmore, Rockhill, and Heard, were trying to help the progress of Korean independence and reform as best they could without overstepping their instructions. But they could do little in the face of Yüan's sometimes adroit, sometimes heavy handed assertion of Chinese hegemony, particularly in view of State Department caution. Adjectives like ineffective, inconsistent, or even blundering might be applied to this, but certainly it was well intentioned, not scheming or vicious.

However, immediately upon turning from American policy to Japanese, with Harrington also, as with Borton and Nelson, things take on a sinister look. And he says: "After backing out in 1885, the islanders had effected 'complete indifference' as to the fate of Korea. No longer did they fight the Manchu suzerain claims. Instead they pushed them to keep Russia back. And, by so doing, to save Chosen for Japan when the time was propitious for driving the Chinese out." For this he cites an imposing list of secondary works but then comes down to Herod, whose comments he finds "most revealing."[37]

We are aware, of course, that Japan did fight China in 1894 and oust Chinese influence from Korea, and that this, even without Herod's speculations, could be taken as evidence presumptive that the Japanese government was planning the coup de grâce many years before. But unfortunately for the theory, though perhaps fortunately for our faith in the human race (to 1893), it is not supported by evidence *minutus*; the pattern of Japanese activity in

[36] Harrington, *God, Mammon* . . ., 205-46, esp. 223, 245, 246.

[37] *Ibid.*, 247-48. Harrington cites specifically Herod's dispatch of Aug. 21, 1893, which reiterates his theory, but in not quite such strong terminology as the July 29 dispatch.

Korea during these eight years is much too inconsistent and, yes, blundering to be part of an evil plan. Indeed, if one must seek a classification for it, the general category would probably be Americanus. Let us test this with some specific Japanese actions and reactions.

When General Yüan Shih-k'ai returned to Korea in the fall of 1885, he came as the Chinese commissioner "in Charge of Diplomatic and Commercial Intercourse" for Korea, which, according to his card bearing an English translation, meant "H.I.C.M. Resident, Seoul." This worried Foulk, and others also apparently, for Foulk reports that on November 20, "Mr. Baber, Consul General for England, and Mr. Takahira Kogoro, chargé d'affairs ad interim for Japan, called upon me to discuss the title and rank of Mr. Yuen [sic], the new Chinese representative. The latter officer [Takahira] showed much interest and some anxiety."[38] This was only the beginning of the Chinese assumption of authority over Korean affairs. The return of the Taewongun from Tientsin,[39] long stays by Min Yong-ik in China,[40] and a purge by Yüan of royal favorites who might oppose Chinese influence in August, 1886,[41] were some of the means by which the traditional, but dormant, Chinese Confucian authority over Korea was made more active than it had been since the Yüan dynasty ruled Korea directly in the thirteenth century. As these developments unfolded, Japanese representatives on the spot in Korea were inclined to be quite exercised, but from Tokyo counsels of caution prevailed. In the summer and fall of 1886 Foulk reported the attitude of the Japanese legation as follows: "Mr. Takahira expressed to me

[38] Foulk to Sec. State, Nov. 25, 1885, No. 255 (confidential): Dipl. Desp., Korea. McCune and Harrison, 138.

[39] Foulk to Sec. State, Oct. 14, 1885, No. 237; Oct. 15, 1885, No. 240; Oct. 20, 1885, No. 243: Dipl. Desp., Korea. Nos. 240 and 243 are reproduced in McCune and Harrison, 135-37, No. 237 is not.

[40] Foulk, No. 255; Dipl. Desp., Korea. Parker to Bayard, July 20, 1886, unnumbered and Aug. 26, 1886, No. 26: Dipl. Desp., Korea. No. 26 in McCune and Harrison, 144.

[41] Foulk to Sec. State, Sept. 8, 1886, No. 3: Dipl. Desp., Korea. McCune and Harrison, 148-54. Harrington, *God, Mammon . . .*, 215-16.

clearly that the attitude of China has reached a point at which the understanding arrived at between Japan and China in the convention at Tientsin in regard to Korea has been departed from and the interference of his government would seem to be imperatively necessary. He intimated that he would like . . . to return to Japan to lay the situation in Korea before his government."[42] However, the Japanese Foreign Office did not register any official protest, and in 1887 the chargé ad interim was reposted to Shanghai as consul, and Kondō, from a background of long experience at Pusan, became chargé at Seoul. It is interesting that American Chargé Foulk, who seems to have had good times talking over Chinese villainies with his Japanese counterpart, was also recalled in 1887. The publication in *Foreign Relations* of his description of events leading up to the attempted coup of December, 1884, produced the accusation from Yüan that he had known of the plot in advance and "sat quietly and saw our nobles butchered." Yüan demanded his recall, and Washington complied, though Minister Dinsmore described this as "against my desire and against the earnest desire of His Majesty the King of Korea and all his people." There is no reason to presume that Takahira's departure was in any way connected with Foulk's or the result of pressure from Yüan, for he had in his last months in Seoul come to regard Chinese encroachments with "apparent indifference."[43]

However, Kondō almost went beyond the dictates of caution

[42] Foulk to Sec. State, June 2, 1886, No. 206 (confidential) and Oct. 14, 1886, No. 13 (confidential): Dipl. Desp., Korea. No. 13 also in McCune and Harrison, 154-56.

[43] Dinsmore (Seoul) to Sec. State, May 27, 1887, No. 20 and Oct. 14, 1887, No. 62: Dipl. Desp., Korea. There are some signs that Takahira's "indifference" was not quite steadfast enough to suit the cautious-minded Tokyo government. E.g., he had been trying to obtain a mining concession concerning which Prime Minister Itō instructed his successor: "We must avoid future friction. Therefore stop the official negotiations, . . . Of course, it is all right for you to recommend a private party once in awhile." Itō to Kondō, Nov. 22, 1877, unnumbered: NGB, XX, 269-70, same volume, summary. 31-33.

Regarding Foulk's ouster see Dinsmore to Sec. State, May 3, 1887, No. 14 (confidential); May 9, 1887, No. 16; June 20, 1887, No. 29; Dipl. Desp., Korea. Foulk "Report" in *Foreign Relations*, 1885, p. 335 *et seq.*

immediately after taking up his duties in Seoul. Dinsmore and Allen, even as Foulk was being ousted, worked out another plan to cut into Chinese influence—a new Korean mission to the United States. The King appointed Pak Chung-yang as EEMP to head the mission in August, 1887, and Allen prepared to accompany them. They were to establish a Korean legation in Washington. But by October great trouble had developed—Yüan's doing. He was preventing the mission's departure, reminding the Korean king of his dependent status, and insisting that any Korean legation which might be established in Washington should be subject to the Chinese legation there. Kondō was sympathetic to the American effort. He told Dinsmore that Japan "could not regard China's conduct with indifference, as it strikes at the relations between Korea and Japan as well as the other treaty powers." And he furnished Dinsmore "confidentially" a copy of a telegram from Li Hung-chang to Yüan Shih-k'ai which said that Korean representatives abroad must first present themselves to the Chinese minister and be introduced by him to the foreign office in question.[44] However, when Kondō sought instructions from the Japanese Foreign Office as to what course he should take, he was told to "refrain from becoming entangled in this case; but if Japanese treaty rights or merchants are in danger you should inquire for further instructions."[45] The Japanese Foreign Office, like the American State Department, was avoiding diplomatic embroilment in Korea.

Yet despite its cautious policy the Japanese government did become involved in a major controversy with Korea. This began to build up in 1888. It was on the issue of the export of foodstuffs from Korea to Japan, sometimes called the "bean export controversy." According to Japanese-Korean treaty arrangements, trade in foodstuffs should be unimpeded unless the Korean government "shall

[44] Dinsmore to Sec. State, Sept. 30, No. 53; Oct. 3, No. 60; Oct. 15, No. 63; Nov. 17, unnumbered (confidential), 1887: Dipl. Desp., Korea. See also Harrington, *God, Mammon . . .*, pp. 228-41.

[45] Archives, SP 5, pp. 65-66.

have reason to apprehend a scarcity of food within the limits of the Kingdom," whereupon they might institute prohibition of export, having given Japanese consuls one month's notice. In January, 1888, Korean officials at Pusan, claiming famine conditions, prohibited the export of rice at that port. The Japanese consul at Pusan reported that the famine claim was untrue, that there was "no reason for the Korean government to prohibit the export of rice," in response to which the Foreign Office instructed Kondō at Seoul to protest to the Korean government that "only in case of famine could there be such export prohibition."[46]

However, the following year, even though, according to the Japanese, "there was a bumper crop and Korean farmers were happy," the governor of the Genzan (Wonsan) district ordered the farmers not to sell. Kondō again protested, and the Korean government's answer was "vague." Finally in April, 1890, the ban was lifted, but "Japanese merchants had suffered losses for eight months." They demanded an indemnity of 140,626 yen, 95 sen, 7 rin (evidently having figured the loss down to the last grain of rice). Kondō asked his Foreign Office for instructions, as a delegation of Japanese merchants went to Tokyo to demand action. After an investigation of the claims the Foreign Office pared down the demand to 91,789 yen, 74 sen, 6 rin (also precise), plus interest, which, however, brought the total up to a round 141,000 yen. In February, 1891, a new representative, Mr. Kawakita, who would bear added weight as minister resident, was sent to replace Kondō and take over the negotiations. However, he caught pneumonia waiting three hours in zero weather to present his credentials to the king, and died on March 8. Nevertheless, in September the Japanese government through a new "deputy minister," Kajiyama, demanded that Korea pay the 141,000 yen. The Korean government, according to the Japanese interpretation, "by excuses tried

[46] Den, Consul at Pusan, to Dep. For. Min., Jan. 14, 1888, No. 98: NGB, XX, 270-76; cf. No. 100, p. 277. Kondō (Seoul) to For. Min., Jan. 16, 1888, No. 99: NGB, XX, 276-77; For. Min. to Kondō, Mar. 6, 1888, No. 101: NGB, XX, 278-79; cf. Nos. 102, 103, 104, 105, pp. 279 *et seq.*

to evade the responsibility" and negotiations became prolonged and bitter. In July, 1892, the Koreans offered to pay 62,400 yen, but this was not satisfactory to the Japanese. At the end of 1892, as Seoul awaited the coming of a new Japanese full minister, Ōishi Masami, who, according to Heard, was believed by Koreans to be a friend of Kim Ok-kiun and likely to be more antagonistic to the Korean government than his predecessors, the issue was far from resolved.[47]

Another controversy which was coming to a head at this time involved Japanese fishing rights off the Korean coast. This also waxed large in 1888. Up to that time the Japanese had been gradually obtaining fishing rights in various areas by agreements with the Korean government. One in fact was made for the Inchon area in the summer of 1888.[48] But in December Consul Den at Pusan reported Korean protests against Japanese fishing in the Pusan coastal area. The Foreign Office instructed Kondō at Seoul to "insist" on Japanese fishing privileges in Korean coastal waters.[49] The main argument developed about fishing privileges in the vicinity of Quelpart Island, about which, the Koreans said, the Japanese must cease all fishing activity. Particular attention was called to this area by a fracas over "drinking water" in which a Japanese killed a Korean. Also there were questions of taxes set by the Korean government, fish drying places, and other details. The Japanese government charged that this was the beginning of an effort to break down the whole system of fishing rights secured under their treaties with Korea. It sent one Hayashi to investigate specific problems but he was "drowned."[50]

[47] Archives, SP 5, pp. 70-73. Heard to Sec. State Blaine, Mar. 16, 1891, No. 135 and Heard to Sec. State Foster, Dec. 18, 1892, No. 345 (confidential): Dipl. Desp., Korea.

[48] Kondō to For. Min., July 12, No. 121 and July 13, No. 122, 1888: NGB, XXI, 358-64.

[49] Den (Pusan) to Dep. For. Min., Dec. 11, 1888, No. 123 and For. Min. to Kondō (Seoul,) Dec. 24, 1888, No. 124: NGB, XXI, 364-69.

[50] Archives, SP 5, pp. 67-70. NGB, XX, summary, p. 34. Heard to Blaine, Apr. 28, 1892, No. 267: Dipl. Desp., Korea.

These arguments were between Japan and Korea and did not, up to 1893, involve China directly, although there can be little doubt that Chinese advice and influence contributed to Korean refusals to give ground. There were also controversies which involved the Chinese more directly. One of these, which had the distinction of being settled, involved telegraph rates. Until 1888 the only telegraphic lines to Seoul were from Inchon and thence by cable to Tientsin or from the Yalu River, where a connection was made to a Chinese line to Mukden and Peking. The Japanese had laid a cable from Nagasaki to Pusan, but it was not yet connected by telegraph with Seoul. Thus the Japanese, like other foreigners, were dependent upon a Chinese controlled telegraph. This could conveniently cease operating at times, as when Yüan was trying to solidify his power in Seoul, in August, 1886. Or it could be insecure, as the Japanese Foreign Office presumed it to be when, after the Osaka Incident, they resorted to contacting their representatives in Seoul by getting the Hawaiian chargé in Tokyo, an American named Robert Irwin, to wire Foulk in Seoul to transmit a message to their legation. Foulk handed over the first such telegram to the Japanese legation but refused thereafter "to take the smallest part" in such transmissions.[51]

Thus the Japanese Foreign Office was extremely anxious to open up a Pusan to Seoul telegraph line. It put strong pressure on the Korean government, arguing that the Chinese monopoly violated previously made Japan-Korea cable agreements, and the Korean government finally assented, promising at one time that the line would be completed by April 20, 1887. But a Korean plea of famine delayed the start of construction a month. Then Yüan Shih-k'ai insisted on being the guarantor of the contract for materials, which was made with a German firm. Arranging this

[51] Foulk to Sec. State, Dec. 29, 1885, No. 265 (confidential) and, regarding telegraphs, see also Foulk to Sec. State, Sept. 2, No. 1, Sept. 7, No. 2, 1886, Sept. 25, 1885, No. 231: Dipl. Desp., Korea. McCune and Harrison, pp. 41-44, 131-33, 141-44. Harrington, *God, Mammon . . .*, p. 215.

took four months more. In the face of these delays the schedule had to be revised, but the Japanese insisted that the line absolutely had to be finished before winter set in, 1887. At one point their representative threatened to "just sit here" at the Korean Foreign Office until the work was started. However, the ship from Germany with the wire aboard was wrecked in the Red Sea, so the date for completion was moved up to June 9, 1888. The line was actually completed by that time, but then the rate controversy developed. The Korean government said that China had to be consulted on determination of message rates. The Japanese held that rates should be decided by direct Korea-Japan negotiation. After several more months of argument, the Japanese seemingly won their point and a rate agreement was signed without consulting the Chinese.[52]

Another controversy, which incidentally reveals that the Japanese had not given up all effort to sponsor "reform" in Korea, concerned the coinage. In 1887 the Korean mint office was having difficulty getting materials and at one point offered to make a contract with Japanese advisers who might help them, but there were no suitable persons in Korea at the opportune moment and, by the time the Japanese had arranged a contract, Yüan interfered and stopped the proceedings. However, in 1891 a Mr. Ōmiya Chōbei of Osaka was given a contract by the Korean government to come to Korea, become chief of the Korean Mint, and effect a reform of the coinage. To help the project the Yokohama Specie Bank, which had earlier set aside a credit of 170,000 yen for the Korean government, and added to this 20,700 yen in accrued interest, now decided to turn the remaining balance over to Korea to improve the financial stability of the country and get the project off to a good start. However, difficulties soon developed. Ōmiya quarreled with a Japanese metal exporter, Masuda Nobuyuki, certain Koreans "sought advantage," and, most serious of all, the Chinese govern-

[52] NGB, XX (1887), summary, pp. 33-35. Kondō to For. Min., June 12, July 2, 16, Aug. 5 thru Dec. 17, 1888, Nos. 73-75, 80-87: NGB, XXI, 201-24. Dinsmore to Sec. State Bayard, July 18, 1888: Dipl. Desp., Korea.

ment protested that the Chinese year title had been omitted on the face of the coins. (It had been decided to date the first coins Year 501 of the Yi dynasty, which had its inception in 1392.) Also the Chinese objected to the use of the character Dai (Great) in Dai Chōsen (Great Korea), which was also to appear on the coins. This, the Chinese said, was inconsistent with Korea's position as a dependent state. Minting operations were in suspension and controversy in full bloom in 1893.[53]

Another matter in which Japan and China were at odds during the comparative calm of the Tientsin Treaty period concerned the trade situation at the open ports, specifically Inchon (Jinsen) and Wonsan (Genzan). Foreign trade at Pusan remained almost completely in Japanese hands, but at the other two ports, which the Kanghwa Treaty settlement had opened to the Japanese, the aforementioned trade regulations of 1882 plus the general Chinese political ascendancy after 1885, began to take its toll. In March, 1888, the Japanese consul in Inchon warned the Foreign Office that a newly opened Chinese steamship line to Shanghai would injure the Japanese position. From Shanghai Takahira sent a translation of a letter purportedly from Yüan to Li Hung-chang explaining Yüan's thinking on the matter: "After 1884 the Japanese were badly off in Korea, so they sent shrewd people like Takahira and Kondō who have pushed economic activities and stayed away from politics . . . now all rely on Japanese ships. Many Chinese asked me to open a Chinese line to obstruct the Japanese monopoly . . . so I did." That summer the Japanese Foreign Office, hearing that Yüan was prohibiting Chinese merchants from loading cargo in Japanese ships, ordered but then recalled a protest to the Chinese government. And at the same time, in response to various reports on commercial prospects, Deputy Foreign Minister Aoki instructed Japanese consuls in Pusan, Seoul, Inchon, and Wonsan to stimulate economic activities "in order to compete with China." In August Japanese Consul Watanabe was reporting

[53] Archives, SP 5, pp. 73-74. NGB, XX (1887), summary, pp. 31-32.

ideas on "how to push Chinese out of the Japanese settlement in Wonsan."[54]

The crisis resulted in the Japanese undertaking a searching analysis of the nature of their trade with Korea, in which they found that a very large percentage of the Japanese goods imported by Korea came under the classification "calico" (cotton goods from Europe), which was processed through Japanese merchants at Nagasaki, but which could just as easily go through Chinese merchants in Chinese ports, thus eliminating the Japanese entirely. Japanese freight rates compared unfavorably with those of the China Merchant Steamship Company. Suggestions for improving the situation emphasized such things as special effort to increase trade in native Japanese products, especially silk; better organization of Japanese merchants to eliminate "inner struggle", and opening local markets in Korea. But as Deputy Foreign Minister Aoki commented, "we cannot force Japanese merchants to do these things." The outlook was "pessimistic."[55] Indeed, despite their studies and their efforts, the Japanese were not able to recover the initiative in trade competition with the Chinese, as the following figures on imports at the three open ports testify.[56] [See next page.]

In export trade from these ports Japanese merchants maintained a lead of over nine to one versus Chinese competitors through the whole period, 1885 to 1893. But in that last year, although the percentage remained the same, there was a drop in volume of

[54] Suzuki (Inchon) to Dep. For. Min., Mar. 18, Apr. 4, June 1, 1888, Nos. 107, 108, 91: NGB, XXI, 311-13, 230-46. Takahira (Shanghai) to Dep. For. Min., Mar. 17, 1888, No. 109: NGB, XXI, 313-17. Dep. For. Min. to Consuls in Pusan, Inchon, and Wonsan, June 1, 1888, No. 92: NGB, XXI, 246-51. Watanabe (Wonsan) to For. Min., Aug. 22, 1888, No. 115: NGB, XXI, 326-42. For. Min. to Shioda (Peking), July 5, 1888, No. 113 and Shioda to For. Min., Aug. 3, 1888, No. 114: NGB, XXI, 324-26.

[55] Dep. For. Min. to Consuls, No. 92, *op. cit.* Table comparing Japan's NYK line and China Merchant Steamship Co., see attached Doc. No. 112: NGB, XXI, 323. Chart of Japan-Korea trade in NGB, XX, (1887) summary, p. 28 and discussion pp. 28-29.

[56] The following tables taken from Shiokawa Ichitarō, *Chōsen Tsūshō Jijō* (The Condition of Korean Commerce) (Tokyo: Yao Shōten, 1895), pp. 56, 61, 63. An estimate of this work will be given in chap IX.

THE TOTAL AMOUNT OF IMPORTS

Import port: Jinsen

Year	*From China*	*From Japan*	*China*	*Japan*
1885	$ 242,680	$726,760	25 per cent	75 per cent
1886	406,856	941,550	30 "	70 "
1887	641,340	827,113	44 "	56 "
1888	636,092	1,049,486	38 "	62 "
1889	729,037	1,113,647	40 "	60 "
1890	1,312,614	1,259,218	51 "	49 "
1891	1,738,044	1,426,463	57 "	43 "
1892	1,716,231	1,323,588	56 "	44 "

Import port: Genzan

Year	*From China*	*From Japan*	*China*	*Japan*
1885	$ 70,662	$314,843	18 per cent	82 per cent
1886	31,057	905,910	4 "	96 "
1887	101,321	591,783	15 "	85 "
1888	224,236	504,390	31 "	69 "
1889	321,982	429,522	43 "	57 "
1890	343,352	392,266	47 "	53 "
1891	266,885	260,836	51 "	49 "
1892	310,382	234,790	54 "	43 "

Import port: Pusan

Year	*From China*	*From Japan*	*China*	*Japan*
1885	$ 0	$335,789	0 per cent	100 per cent
1886	17,102	416,893	4 "	96 "
1887	0	661,891	0 "	100 "
1888	0	642,239	0 "	100 "
1889	50,565	755,949	6 "	94 "
1890	3,576	1,436,413	0 "	100 "
1891	43,365	1,439,169	0·3 "	99·7 "
1892	28,940	997,297	0·3 "	99·7 "

THE TOTAL SUM OF THREE PORTS

Year	*From China*	*From Japan*	*China*	*Japan*
1885	$ 313,342	$1,377,392	19 per cent	81 per cent
1886	455,015	2,064,353	17 "	83 "
1887	742,661	2,080,787	26 "	74 "
1888	860,328	2,196,115	28 "	72 "
1889	1,101,585	2,299,118	32 "	68 "
1890	1,660,075	3,086,897	32 "	68 "
1891	2,148,294	3,226,486	40 "	60 "
1892	2,055,555	2,555,675	45 "	55 "

exports to Japan from $3,219,887 to $2,271,928.[57] At any rate, behind the "bean export controversy" lay a several-years effort by Japan to devise means to maintain Japanese trade in Korea against mounting Chinese competition.

One other matter might be mentioned before we attempt to draw a conclusion concerning these several areas of controversy between Japan, Korea, and China. It will be recalled that P. G. von Mollendorff was urged upon Korea as inspector general of customs and adviser to the Korean Foreign Office by Li Hung-chang in 1883. Mollendorff was cordially detested by the Japanese, as well as by American and other foreign representatives in Seoul. In 1885 he was ousted amidst disclosures that he was secretly making agreements with Russia.[58] Li then sent O. N. Denny, formerly American consul at Tientsin, to take the Foreign Office advisory post. His appointment, according to Denny, was the result of the Tientsin Treaty talks at which Japan stipulated that an American should be named adviser to the Korean government. T. F. Tsiang, from Chinese documents, locates the Japanese urging of an American adviser in June, just after the Tientsin settlement. It was included as one of several points of a memorandum from Inoue

[57] Shiokawa, *op. cit.*, p. 64.

[58] Foulk to Sec. State, July 5, 1885, No. 192 (confidential) and Aug. 4, 1885, No. 211: Dipl. Desp., Korea. McCune and Harrison, pp. 81-83, 120-23.

to Li Hung-chang, which was presented by Japan's minister to Peking, Enomoto. While calling for the appointment of an American, Inoue also urged that Li exert pressure on the Korean king to have capable ministers in office at court and appoint a new Chinese agent to Seoul who, together with the American adviser, would consult with him (Inoue) in Tokyo before taking up their posts. Li instead sent Yüan Shih-k'ai and the Taewongun directly to Seoul, with no reference to Inoue. But then a few months later, though Yüan said no American would come, he sent Denny, again without reference to Inoue.[59]

Denny, though thought to be a friend of China, became antagonistic to Yüan as the latter increased his power in Seoul, and, in 1887 when the "Resident" moved to block the sending of the missions to the United States, an open break occurred. Denny went to Tientsin expecting to persuade Li to recall Yüan. But Li would not. Denny was furious at this, and the following February he published a thirty-page pamphlet entitled *China and Korea* in which he bitterly denounced Chinese policies in Korea in general and Yüan Shih-k'ai in particular.[60] This ended his career as adviser. Denny's successor was another American, a most interesting one—none other than the famous General LeGendre, adviser to the Japanese Foreign Office in the heady days of Seikan Ron and certainly of friendly disposition to Japan. Just how the Japanese could have engineered his appointment at a time when Yüan was riding high is not clear, but U.S. Minister Heard, in reflecting on his appointment, had no doubt that it was through "influences mainly Japanese." LeGendre, like Denny before him, soon ran afoul Yüan, and Heard expected his ouster in 1890. However, somehow he held on, perhaps in part because Heard supported him,

[59] Foulk to Sec. State, No. 25, 1885, No. 255; Apr. 23, 1886, No. 297; June 2, 1886, No. 306: Dipl. Desp., Korea. All three are "confidential." Nos. 255 and 297 reproduced in McCune and Harrison, pp. 137-40, 147-49.

[60] Dinsmore (Seoul) to Sec. State, Nov. 11, 1887 (confidential) and Aug. 24, 1888: Dipl. Desp., Korea. Neither dispatch is numbered; the second contains Denny's pamphlet, dated Feb. 3, 1888, as an enclosure.

and in 1892 he was sent to Japan by the Korean government to try to negotiate a settlement of the fishing dispute and perhaps other issues. Heard urged the American minister in Tokyo to "give him a lift," for failure might mean his ouster and a further weakening of American influence in Korea.[61]

Having observed these several sources of controversy in the Japan-Sino-Korean relationship from 1885 to the beginning of 1893, is it possible to draw any conclusion as to what the Japanese government was trying to do? And specifically is there any evidence that it was aiming to clear Western influence out of Korea and solidify Chinese control there in the anticipation that Japan could then fight China and seize the peninsula? Perhaps the best way to approach a conclusion on this is to note first the projection into the critical years, 1893–94, of the several problems presented. As has been said, on the telegraph Japan gained her objective of officially settling issues directly with Korea, though Allen reported in 1891 that the Chinese actually were obtaining control again.[62] On the fisheries LeGendre arranged a compromise which the Japanese government was willing to accept, and which Heard endorsed, but acceptance was delayed at Seoul when the British representative entered objections and the Chinese were not pleased.[63] The coinage project was abandoned and Mr. Ōmiya returned to Japan.[64] On the foodstuff export indemnity issue a real crisis developed. Ōishi the new Japanese minister, upon his arrival in Seoul in January, 1893, jumped into this with both feet, bringing it up at inappropriate times, demanding Korean agreement to pay the indemnity, and finally in May, serving an ultimatum that diplomatic relations would be severed if Korea did not come to terms within fourteen

[61] Heard to Sec. State, June 3, 1890, No. 12 and Apr. 28, 1892, No. 267: Dipl. Desp., Korea. See also Treat, *Dipl. Rel. . . .*, II, 392, citing Coombs (Tokyo) to Sec. State, Dec. 19, 1892, No. 63 and Heard to Coombs, Nov. 4, 1892.

[62] Allen (Seoul) to Sec. State Blaine, June 16, 1891, No. 174 (enclosing Sino-Japanese telegraph agreement): Dipl. Desp., Korea.

[63] Heard to Sec. State, Jan. 17, 1893, No. 358 (confidential): Dipl. Desp., Korea. Cf. Treat, II, 392.

[64] Archives, SP 5, p. 75.

days. It seems clear that Ōishi had been given a free hand by his Foreign Office to push these negotiations to the limit, and that he had been ordered to leave Korea if the ultimatum did not produce results; but the long ultimatum interval may be taken as an indication that a negotiated settlement was still anticipated. American Minister Coombs in Japan learned that the good offices of the United States would be acceptable there. Before they were arranged, however, Itō requested the help of Li Hung-chang in settling the dispute; Li informed Yüan, who applied pressure to the Korean Foreign Office, and an offer of 110,000 yen was made. Japan accepted.[65] Thus the particular dispute was settled, but a new export ban was shortly announced, which Allen reported to be the result of Yüan's order and a "matter of life and death to Japanese trade. . . . The result will be the failure of Japanese banks and merchants here. . . . Under guise of prohibition of the export of rice officials are levying such taxes on all produce as to practically suppress trade . . . a violation of treaty rights . . . Japanese chiefly interested but one American firm Morse-Townsend and Co. greatly affected."[66] Meanwhile Ōishi was recalled and Ōtori Keisuke was sent as minister to Seoul and also accredited to Peking.

Japan's accrediting of Ōtori to Peking as well as Seoul was the particular act which set off the wave of speculations from which Herod derived his "ulterior purpose" theory. Herod's superior in Tokyo, Minister Dun, also did some speculating, but he rebuffed Herod's more extreme views. He informed Herod it was "very possible" that Japan and China might reach some understanding to oppose the encroachment of any other power in Korea, and that Japan did recognize the "overshadowing influence of China"

[65] Heard to Sec. State, Mar. 27, Apr. 6, May 6, May 20, 1893: Dipl. Desp., Korea. Cf. Treat, II, 412-14. Funaoka Seigo, *Japan im Sternbild Ostasiens* (Tokyo: Tōhō Shoten, 1942), II, 568. Tsiang, "Sino-Japanese Diplomatic . . .," p. 105. Tsiang quotes a telegram from Itō to Li: "Korea refused to pay indemnity on grain losses. Please ask Yuan to persuade Korea to pay the principal without interest. Otherwise Japan will withdraw her representative and break relations with Korea."

[66] Allen to Sec. State, Nov. 7, Nov. 28, Dec. 20, 1893, Nos. 481, 490, 504: Dipl. Desp., Korea.

there. But he did not think Japan recognized the sovereignty of China over Korea "either tacitly or otherwise," and he attached "no special significance" to the accrediting of Ōtori both to Seoul and Peking, "further than the fact that Mr. Ōtori's long residence in China and knowledge of the complicated political relationships between the government of Korea and Japan fit him peculiarly to represent Japan at this time in Korea."[67] Actually Minister Heard had reported what may have been the principal source of these speculations as the crisis was building up in February. He speaks of a visit from Mr. Dmitrevsky, the Russian representative at Seoul, who informed him that his (Russian) colleague in Peking had been told "semi-officially" that "Japan had solicited the Chinese government to unite with them to drive all Western foreigners out of Korea and keep it for themselves. China refused, and informed Russia." Mr. Dmitrevsky added his own opinion, "They [the Japanese] and more particularly Mr. Oishi are mad with dread and hatred of Russia. . . ."[68]

This is a very interesting point, but we shall defer discussion of the Russian question for a few pages so as not to lose sight of our immediate objective of reaching a conclusion on the condition of Japan's Korean policy vis â vis China as of 1893. Perhaps that condition is best described as nervous. At least, from our review of developments of the several preceding years, this would seem to be much closer to accuracy than to imply that a well thought out plan was approaching climax in that year. Japanese policy makers, led by Itō and Inoue, had begun the Tientsin Treaty era on the presumption that the chief ingredient of a realistic policy on Korea was caution, that "a good outcome" *could* be achieved in a "conciliatory manner." In terms of goals they continued to define a good outcome as Korean reform and independence, reform being the introduction of modern techniques and institutions, independence the movement away from dependence on China toward sovereignty.

[67] Herod to Sec. State, Aug. 21, 1893, No. 436: Dipl. Desp., Korea, quoting Dun.
[68] Heard to Sec. State, Feb. 10, 1893, No. 364 (confidential): Dipl. Desp., Korea.

They sought these, not for "freedom's" sake or "to kill ourselves for righteousness" but because with their achievement an unsettled and unfriendly Korea would become settled and reasonably friendly to Japan. There was no great hurry. In practice these objectives could be realized only gradually. Japanese policy makers had learned by 1885 that they had to take into consideration not only Korean intransigence, which they had been winning over, 1876–82, but Chinese intransigence as well.

Thus trade and the sponsorship of mild reform programs by Japan and other progressive nations, rather than direct political and diplomatic pressure, would supply a slower but surer (and safer) impetus. This was particularly in line with American policy, from which again and again they took their cue. Thus they tried to break the Chinese telegraph monopoly by pressing construction of the Pusan-Seoul line, the monopoly of Chinese advisers at court by supporting Americans Denny and LeGendre. (Also they helped in the making of an Austrian -Korean treaty, which was signed at Tokyo, June 23, 1892.) They sought to counter Chinese influence by stimulating Japanese trade. They tried to encourage progress in ways that were not overtly political, for example, coinage, but they avoided direct diplomatic challenges which would be sure to bring down the wrath of the Chinese: hence the decision not to become involved in the American mission case. Concerning this, it should be observed that, although Japanese nonsupport of the project might be considered evidence of undercutting American efforts to counter the Chinese, the case is not so clear-cut as that. American representatives in Seoul, especially Allen, who was the principal sponsor of the project, were inclined to go considerably further in bolstering Korean independence than the State Department,[69] and, had the department anticipated the complications

[69] E.g., Bayard (to Dinsmore, Feb. 9, 1888, No. 64, Instructions) advises Dinsmore and notes similar advice to Minister Denby at Peking that agitation by U.S. representatives in behalf of Korea's complete independence is unwise, that the U.S. is interested only in the observance of treaty obligations.

which developed, it is not improbable that Allen too would have been ordered to desist. Since Japanese Chargé Kondō did show sympathy for the project in its earlier stages and the Japanese Foreign Office did not quash this until the complications were apparent, it would seem that caution rather than plot was behind their order to Kondō to stay clear of involvement.

When we observe the Japanese moves of 1893 against this background they do not fit into a neat scheme at all. The furious antics of Ōishi to force satisfaction at Seoul seemed to serve notice that Japan was changing to what Minister Heard called "an independent, pushing policy."[70] But then suddenly, the appeal to Li Hung-chang, the recall of Ōishi, who promptly resigned from the diplomatic service, and the appointment of Ōtori to Peking as well as Seoul—all were signs of conciliation compounded, unparalleled by anything done before. Ōtori was so conciliatory that, by November, 1600 Japanese residents in Korea had signed a petition to the Diet demanding his removal as minister to Korea.[71] Truly Japan's Korea policy came into the year 1893 like a lion and went out like a lamb. Why? Did the Japanese Foreign Office, even if it had not been developing the plan all along, suddenly, at midyear perhaps, embark on a brilliant though devious scheme to conciliate China, aid her in ousting Westerners from Korea, thus clearing the way for the coup de grâce, a well-planned Sino-Japanese war out of which Japan would seize Korea? We have already observed that many, if not most, of our best books on the subject are inclined to this interpretation. However, this author would suggest that such an appraisal presumes a much higher degree of cold calculation than Japanese policy makers could possibly have applied to the Korean question in 1893. The Ōishi-Ōtori story reveals policy contradiction, and, while it is possible to be contradictory according to plan, it is much more likely for contradiction to result from indecision, conflict of opinion, and

[70] Heard to Sec. State, Dec. 18, 1892, No. 345 (confidential): Dipl. Desp., Korea.
[71] Allen to Sec. State, Nov. 20, 1893, No. 483 (confidential): Dipl., Desp. Korea.

nervousness. It may well be that the reason for the meandering of 1893 was not nearly as devious as Mr. Herod surmised. It was simply that from the Japanese point of view Korea policy was a failure; it had become evident that "a good outcome" was not being achieved by conciliation, and an agonizing reappraisal was in process. What are the indications that this was the case?

First, the evidence of failure. The Chinese influence in Korea was proving stronger than any of the treaty powers, including Japan, had thought possible. In the treaty-making stage the Japanese had taken the dependent state relationship somewhat more seriously than had other foreigners, for instance the Americans, and they had been quite concerned at the Chinese show of force in Seoul in 1882. But, after all, progress was on the move; a relationship that had always been tenuous and was now outdated could hardly be maintained, unless perhaps by force. And with the Tientsin Treaty requiring the withdrawal of Chinese as well as Japanese troops, there could be no force. Time and tide were on the side of progress (and Japan). But the incredible happened. After 1885, by other means than military force, the Chinese were able to assert their influence over Korea until it was quite clear to all foreigners in the country that they were running things—whatever things they pleased, from selection of the king's ministers to trade in the Japanese port settlements.

How they did this is not exactly an oriental mystery since Nelson's explorations into the historical-philosophical foundations of Chinese elder brotherhood to Korea, but the specific techniques which Yüan Shih-k'ai employed are still somewhat obscure. American observers of the process, while bitterly resenting Chinese pretensions, [72] at times showed a certain awed respect for the way they handled affairs. Heard once sent to Washington an article entitled "Suzerainty" which sought to explain the Chinese system, remarking, "They make policy accomplish the purposes of marching

[72] See Allen to Sec. State, Nov. 4, 1893, No. 479 (confidential): Dipl. Desp., Korea. Yuan rode to the king's palace in a chair; everyone else walked in the mud, etc.

armies."[73] He also evaluated Chinese versus Japanese relations with Koreans as follows: "The Japanese are more and more insolent toward Koreans and the Koreans hate them. The Chinese treat the Koreans with good humor, if with condescension, playing the role of elder brother. The Koreans look up to them with confiding affection. Yet there is no recognition of vassalage as understood by us. All Koreans say they believe in the independence of this country."[74] Heard also reported a conversation on the subject of the Sino-Korean relationship which he had with Li Hung-chang in Tientsin, while he was there once on vacation: "Li said he had favored treaties for Korea . . . riches and prosperity, but he never contemplated any change in the relative position of the two countries [China and Korea] . . . he was quite willing that Foreign Powers should treat her [Korea] as if she were independent, but if the King were to attempt to emancipate himself and to assert his independence, China would interfere. . . . He was very emphatic on this point . . . I said little."[75]

The course of events after 1885 shows clearly that the Chinese were indeed masters of the philosophy and technique of elder brotherhood and could apply it most effectively in Korea. And there is much to be said on the far-reaching implications for international relations of "policy that can accomplish the purposes of marching armies." Sovereign states constantly at war with one another had then and have now a great deal to learn from an appraisal of Confucian international ideas. The Confucian system, at its best, was a sophisticated and benevolent type of regional organization, involving sponsorship and guidance by China of smaller countries which, by adherence to it, could derive economic benefits and a certain degree of security, without losing their political identity. But the meaning of this late nineteenth-century period of Chinese ascendancy in Korea must also be assessed in

[73] Heard to Sec. State, Feb. 23, 1891, No. 125 and encl.: Dipl. Desp., Korea.
[74] *Ibid.*, Dec. 18, 1892, No. 345 (confidential).
[75] *Ibid.*, June 22, 1891, No. 175.

specific terms, as it related to conditions in Korea and in turn to Japanese policy formulation. In Korea, contemporary observers are agreed, it did not bring the "riches and prosperity" which Li professed to be his desire. Foulk wrote in 1886: "There can be no question as to the desire for and capability of improvement on the part of Korea; also there can be no question as to the policy being pursued by China to . . . bind Korea to her own civilization of paganism and stagnation."[76] Dinsmore in 1887 found, "The spirit of resistance seems almost to have died out of the Koreans. Yuan dictates . . . under a system of intimidation mixed with an affectation of disinterested kindness. The King . . . sickly acquiescence."[77] In 1892 Allen laid before the State Department the words of a Korean official, Cho, who had resigned in disgust: "Public affairs are in such a condition that our country scarcely deserves the name of country . . . sale of offices, constant interference and conflict of orders, money in a debased state and forced on people . . ."[78] Heard called Cho's comments "not overdrawn. The King is totally unable to institute reforms. . . . I am not sure that a revolution would not put better men in control." And in another dispatch he described the condition of Seoul as "filth, the result of ignorance and negligence."[79]

This added up to a conclusion which Heard was almost voicing in his double negatived hint that a revolution might be in order, namely, that reform would not come by cautious means. Thus all those, including Itō and Inoue, who had presumed that the march of time plus a cautious nudge here and there was all that was really needed to insure the triumph of progress over tradition in Korea, were in confusion by 1893. The Chinese had nudged tradition with such deftness that 2000 years of history were arrayed in an ideo-

[76] Foulk to Sec. State, Nov. 1, 1886, No. 15: Dipl. Desp., Korea.

[77] Dinsmore to Sec. State, May 27 1887, No. 20; Dipl. Desp., Korea. Cf. Harrington, *God, Mammon* . . ., p. 226.

[78] Allen to Sec. State, Aug. 12, 1892, No. 294 and encl.: Dipl. Desp., Korea.

[79] Heard to Sec. State, Nov. 10, 1892, No. 327 and Mar. 1, 1893, No. 368: Dipl. Desp., Korea.

logical battle line to halt progress in its tracks. And the Japanese saw the promise of their Kanghwa settlement, which in the early 1880's had led bright young Koreans to look to Japan for inspiration, turn to acid in their mouths, as by the early nineties Japanese were more and more detested in Korea. Those Koreans who had shown friendship for Japan were called traitors. An excellent commentary on the Japanese position was a celebration held at the king's palace in December, 1893, to celebrate the three hundred-year anniversary of the driving out of the Japanese (Hideyoshi's invasion in 1593). The Japanese minister did not attend.[80]

Perhaps China would incorporate Korea as a province, perhaps not, but either way the "new age of Korea," which the Japanese government had anticipated in 1881, was not coming to pass. The result of Japanese realization of this was the appearance in 1893 of the first serious cleavage on Korea policy in policy making circles since Seikan Ron. Men like Enomoto, and especially Mutsu, now foreign minister in 1893, had sympathized with the Conquer Korea advocates in the 1870's. Mutsu, in fact, had been jailed for plotting armed uprising in connection with the Satsuma Rebellion of Saigō. But they, like Saigō's brother, Tsugumichi, and many others, had rejoined the government afterwards, and, as illustrated by Enomoto's conversation with Minister Young and Saigō's support of Itō at Tientsin, acquiesced in the cautious policy toward Korea. Actually they did more than acquiesce, for as responsible members of the governing oligarchy they worked so long within the policy framework set by Itō and Inoue that it could almost be said Seikan was dead in them.[81] Otherwise Itō would have ousted them from the oligarchic team, for he dominated every phase of its activity from the death of Iwakura in 1883 until the Sino-Japanese

[80] Allen to Sec. State, Dec. 13, 1893, No. 503 and Dec. 20, 1893, No. 504 (confidential): Dipl. Desp., Korea.

[81] Perhaps the last of Mutsu's *Seikan* rough edges was polished off during his assignment as minister to the United States during the late 1880's. Admiral Enomoto was foreign minister from 1891 to August, 1892, during which time Japanese policy was notably quiescent.

War. However, by 1893 the evidence that conciliation was working a bad outcome in Korea was becoming so strong that the question which had been answered affirmatively in the 1870's posed itself again. Was caution really realistic?

While awaiting the arrival of Ōishi in Seoul, Minister Heard suggested that there had "always been two parties in Japan, one in favor of peace with China, as represented by the Li-Itō convention, which has been the policy hitherto pursued by the government, and one opposed to it in favor of an independent, pushing policy. The latter has been gaining ground, and it is said that the newly appointed minister, Mr Ōishi, is sent to represent it."[82] That Ōishi was a pusher is rightly said, but there was not as much cleavage within Japan's policy-making circle as Heard implies. It should be noted that Mutsu, with Itō standing behind him, appointed *both* Ōishi, the pushingest, and Ōtori, the givingest representative Japan had placed in Korea in a decade, in quick succession. Within diplomacy's inner circle in Japan Mutsu, who had become foreign minister in August, 1892, and Enomoto, who had spent a quiet year and a half in that post before Mutsu took the helm, would seem from their backgrounds to be inclined to bolder policy, while Itō and Inoue were well-established paragons of caution. Perhaps Mutsu was more favorable to giving Ōishi a free rein than Itō, but they were not fighting Seikan Ron over again. They were all realists by 1893. They were none of them rash, none of them anxious to spend money or men in reckless enterprises. They would do only what seemed necessary in terms of Japan's "eternal great accounting interests."

Dissatisfied with the way things were going in Korea, the oligarchs were in a mood to experiment, yet they could not afford a Korean crisis. Their main business of treaty revision was coming to a head, with vital conferences scheduled for the near future, and, from long experience in pursuit of the treaty revision objective, dating back to the Iwakura mission of 1872, they knew that the

[82] Heard to Sec. State, Dec. 18, 1892, No. 345 (confidential): Dipl. Desp., Korea.

powers, especially Britain, with whom the forthcoming talks were scheduled, were quick to seize on evidence of Japanese irresponsibility as a reason, or an excuse, to defer negotiations. Hence, experimentally, they tried threats with Ōishi, but became so nervous during the fourteen days during which the Koreans and Chinese were supposed to be getting nervous, that they could not even wait for American good offices. Instead they backstepped more obsequiously than ever before by asking Li Hung-chang to help them off the hook.

However, beyond the fact of Chinese supremacy in Korea, there were reasons why waiting out the Korean problem began to seem unrealistic to Japan's leaders. If Chinese supremacy had been all, Ōtori, as minister to Seoul *and* Peking, could probably have kept friction over small matters at a minimum, so long as he made no serious attempt to promote a reform program or otherwise give affront to Chinese suzerainty in Korea. But by 1893 two other matters, large ones, disturbed the Japanese official mind. The first was Russia, which, from the point of view of Japanese policy makers, was beginning to pose a security problem of the first magnitude. Herod, before proceeding to "my own mind" on the subject, noted that "general opinion" counted Japanese fear of Russia heavily in the moves of 1893. It is likely that general opinion was in some degree correct. Yamagata, the military chief of the oligarchy, as might be expected, was the one to call specific attention to Russia as a menace to Japan. He memorialized the emperor in 1892 to warn that the completion of the Trans-Siberian Railroad would bring on a crisis in the Far East for which Japan must be ready. Russia, he said, was blocked in the Balkans, but the successful completion of her railroad, which would be seen within ten years, would enable her easily to penetrate Mongolia, Manchuria, and take Peking itself.[83] In October, 1893, he entered vigorously

[83] Kuroda Kashihiko, *Gensui Terauchi Hakushaku Den* (Life of Field Marshall Count Terauchi) (Tokyo: Gensui Terauchi Hakushaku Denki Hensho, 1920), Part 1, chap. 8, pp. 183-84.

into the argument regarding military appropriations being engaged in by the Diet, warning that "though the majority of politicians and Diet members favor cutting taxes, the nation is in danger; this is no time to reduce the budget. . . ."[84]

For background to this concern about Russian advances one could point to the great fear and hatred which was felt in Tokugawa Japan for "Giant Red Hairs" who came down occasionally from Kamchatka. This had prompted writers like Hayashi (Rin) Shihei, Honda Toshiaki (Rimei), Satō Shinen, and others to adopt an anti-seclusionist position long before Perry's arrival and demand Japanese expansion northward to set up bulwarks against Russia. There was a high degree of emotional exaggeration in these writers, but it is interesting to note that the very calculating Iwakura in his opposition to Seikan Ron in 1873 sought to turn the attention of the Conquer Korea councillors away from their project by "turning their eyes" to Russian relations and the Sakhalin question. Saigō had responded, "When you take up the Sakhalin problem I might become envoy to Russia, but today I wish to focus on Korea."[85] That this was merely strategy for the occasion by Iwakura, however, is clearly indicated in the fact that the Japanese government undertook negotiations in St. Petersburg the following year, and, pursuing a most friendly and conciliatory approach, reached agreement with Russia on outstanding northern boundary questions in a treaty signed in 1875. Admiral Enomoto handled these negotiations and thus his aforementioned comment to U.S. Minister Young in Peking in 1882 that "Russia had been treating Japan very well"[86] had some authority behind it.

To that point Russia and the Korean problem had not been linked up, and, when Russia undertook treaty relations with Korea in 1884, Japan had no objection. The bizarre activity of von Mollendorff the following year, when on his own authority he

[84] Shinobu Seizaburō, *Mutsu Gaikō* (Mutsu's Diplomacy) (Tokyo: Sōbunkaku, 1935), p. 158. *Dai Nihon Teikoku Gikai Shi* (History of the Japanese Imperial Diet), I, 1409.

[85] Watanabe, *Meijishi Kenkyū*, p. 188.

[86] See above, chap. II, note 55.

contracted for Russian advisers for Korea through the secretary of the Russian legation in Tokyo, Alexis de Speyer, astonished the whole diplomatic colony in Seoul and embarrassed both the Korean and Russian governments. However, this was settled by von Mollendorff's removal and overshadowed by the concurrent Port Hamilton-Port Lazareff affair. Here, the British occupied certain south Korean islets in a sort of beat-them-to-it retaliation for Russia's intended taking up of a leasehold at Wonsan, which von Mollendorff evidently had promised. Yet, even this latter affair did not unduly excite Japanese fear of Russia for it was more an expression of the Asia wide Anglo-Russian rivalry than a specific design on Korean territorial integrity, and, although the Japanese government was concerned about it, the concern was perhaps directed more at the British, who did occupy, than the Russians, who merely intended; anyway, the affair was finished by the withdrawal of the British force in 1887.[87]

The Japanese evaluation of Russian influence in Korea as of 1888 may be brought out by reference to several dispatches concerning a proposition to extend telegraphic connections from Seoul to Vladivostok by a land cable. Denny brought the idea to Kondō at Seoul and asked if the Japanese government would help. Kondō did not know what to say. He felt that it might "help Korean independence" by cutting down dependence on China, but he thought that if the idea was Russian inspired and the financing were to be Russian it was "bad." He thought perhaps Japan should supply some capital for the project and try to have Japanese employees on the line. Foreign Minister Ōkuma instructed him "not to worry." To erect such a land cable, Ōkuma said, would violate already existing Japan-Korean cable agreements and he did not think the Russian government would interfere to push it.[88]

[87] Foulk observed and reported these events closely. Foulk to Sec. State, May 19, July 5, Oct. 14, 1885, Nos. 179, 192, 258; Dipl. Desp., Korea. McCune and Harrison, pp. 73-75, 81-83, 85-86.

[88] Kondō (Seoul) to For. Min., Mar. 18, 1888, No. 72 and July 16, 1888, No. 76: NGB, XXI, 200-1, 208-9. For. Min. to Kondō, Aug. 11, 1888, No. 78: *ibid.*, pp. 209-10.

Though the Japanese probably had no specific knowledge of it, a high level Russian conference on Korea held in April the same year indicates that the "don't worry" approach of the foreign minister rather accurately appraised the real tone of Russian policy at the time. The conference decided that the

acquisition of Korea would not only not give us any advantage, but would not fail to entail very unfavorable consequences. . . . Since that time [Tientsin Treaty], the Government of the Mikado [Japan], believing it unwise to expose itself to the danger of a collision with China, not only gave up its aspirations as to Korea, but for a time showed a complete indifference to the future of the latter country. But recently this Government began to show some anxiety about the means of securing Korea from being seized by the Chinese. Such a direction of Japanese policy is in perfect agreement with our point of view, and we must do our best to support Tokyo in this direction. . . . Should China's tutelage of Korea be confined to the preservation of the existing traditional connections between the two countries, we would not . . . oppose such an order of things. . . . Unfortunately, the Chinese Government does not limit itself to the preservation of relations which till recently have existed, but under the influence of apprehension inspired by our supposed designs as well as due to its self-confidence awakened during recent years, now seemingly aspires to submit to its control even the internal policy of Korea—of course, with the view to turn this country in future into a Chinese province. In case this design should be realized at some later time, our position in South Ussuri will become extremely dangerous, for instead of a weak and inoffensive neighbor on our flank there will appear China which has various and considerable material means at her disposal. . . . England . . . encourages the self-confidence and ambition of Chinese statesmen.[89]

Yamagata's warning on the crisis he anticipated was thus not merely a revival of an old bugaboo about Giant Red Hairs, nor a short-term scare derived from von Mollendorff's maneuverings in

[89] Proceedings of the Meeting of the Special Committee held May 8 (April 26), 1888: Krasny Archiv, "First Steps in Russian Imperialism in Far East," *Chinese Social and Political Science Review,* XVIII (1934-35), 236-44.

Korea. The oligarchs were too realistic for that, nor were they "mad with dread and hatred of Russia," as Dmitrevsky estimated Japanese in general and Ōishi in particular to be. Yamagata's warning simply served strong notice on the inner circle of the Japanese government that a new factor had now to be considered in the Far East international picture, namely one Russian railroad, which would so greatly increase Russian power in the area that Russians would be able within a few years, if they wished, to occupy Manchuria by force of arms (as indeed they did in 1899), and perhaps north China. Yamagata was taking what military men call a long cold look ahead and he was demanding what they always demand when they see possible trouble impending, more preparedness. The corollary on Korea was obvious: the pursuit of a good outcome was becoming a more urgent matter than it had been in 1885; something more than caution might be needed if Korea policy were to remain realistic.

The other matter which disturbed the Japanese official mind and made government realists willing to consider a revision of the cautious policy toward Korea was the state of Japanese politics. The first Diet had opened in 1890, and, despite the careful hedgings to its power set by Itō and his fellow constitution makers, the political opponents of the oligarchy were making the most of whatever opportunity they had, forcing the oligarchs to reshuffle cabinets and obstructing them in every possible way. The liberal parties (Jiyūtō and Kaishintō) led the fight, and most of the Japanese press was with them against the oligarchs. The issue at stake was, in the last analysis, whether Japan would really have parliamentary government or not, whether the cabinet and hence the whole executive apparatus of the government should be responsible to the elected representatives of the people. To establish its supremacy the Diet fought with every weapon at its command; and one of its weapons, unfortunately for the future of liberalism in Japan, was foreign policy.[90]

[90] U.S. Minister to Tokyo Coombs discussed the Diet situation at length in a dispatch to the Sec. of State, Feb. 3, 1893, No. 89: Dipl. Desp., Japan. He referred to Ōkuma's

The liberals found that they could embarrass the oligarchs by calling them cowardly in foreign affairs.

We have already observed the way in which liberal groups headed by Fukuzawa and Ōi had plunged into the Korean problem in the early 1880's, and had been squelched. But they were back in action by 1890. After his release from jail Inoue Kakugorō was elected to the first Diet as a member of the Jiyūtō and the Daidō Club, an organization whose special province was opposition to government "weakness" on treaty revision.[91] Ōi was not elected until 1894, being unable at first to meet property qualifications, but he nevertheless engaged in political activity with great gusto. He established a newspaper called the *Azuma Shimbun* which conducted its own straw vote election on August 25, 1891. Ōi was "elected" foreign minister, won fourth place on the list of prime ministers and second place for army minister. In 1892 he launched a new political party, the Tōyō Jiyūtō (Oriental Liberal Party). This represented actually the left wing of the Jiyūtō, which under Ōi's leadership was in conflict with the right wing under Hoshi Tōru. The Tōyō Jiyūtō demanded universal suffrage, a broad social program for laborers and farmers, revision of the treaties, and an active continental policy, all to be based on a constitutional representative system and popular opinion.[92]

In attacking the oligarchy on foreign policy Ōi, Kakugorō, and the other advocates of parliamentary government, including Fukuzawa, were moving on to quicksand. This was because even though their demand for a more active continental policy was rooted philosophically in the desire to extend the blessings of

---

argument that the cabinet must be formed out of the Diet, noting that "all the enterprises of the Government have been rejected by the Diet. Among them are some which are most important and require immediate attention. . . . But when the reasons for their rejection are enquired into there is one answer . . . the people's representatives have no confidence in the Cabinet."

[91] Kondō, *Inoue . . . Den*, pp. 169-72 and Appendix, p. 3.
[92] Hirano, *Bajō . . .*, pp. 273-76, 278, 283, 291, 300. Jansen, "Ōi . . .," pp. 313-14.

liberty and equality—for which they were leading advocates at home—to others on the continent, the sharp political infighting tended to over-simplify the issue to weak policy (oligarchs) versus strong policy (liberals) or even peace (oligarchs) versus war (liberals). That the liberals did not think this through to its bitter conclusion is indicated by their inconsistency in trying to block government budgets for larger military appropriations at the same time that they were demanding stronger policy. For a time in 1893, probably for political advantage rather than reasons of principle, Hoshi Tōru and his section of the Jiyūtō showed signs of responding to government persuasions to work with Foreign Minister Mutsu on a cautious foreign policy, but late that year Hoshi was ousted from the Diet on charges of corruption brought by strong policy advocates. And in the spring of 1894, Ozaki Yukio, who was to stand as the most sterling exponent of parliamentary government for the next half-century, may have contributed to its ruin in advance when he succeeded in welding together six political groups in the Diet to attack the Itō-led cabinet for "compromising and expedient diplomacy."[93]

The main antagonists of the oligarchs during the four hectic years, 1890–94, were the liberal parties and their friends, intellectuals, particularly journalists, discontented businessmen, discontented farmers, and others seeking a voice in the government through political processes which were Western in origin. Their leaders were mainly men who had a wide acquaintance with and admiration for Western institutions and ideas, especially those of the most progressive, most liberal variety. They found their models

[93] Oka Yoshitake, "Jiyūtō Saha to Nashiyonarizumu: Ōi Kentarō no Baai" (The Left Wing of the Liberal Party and Nationalism: Case of Oi Kentaro), *Shakai Gaku Hyōron* (May 1951), pp. 9-14. Oka, Lecture at Tokyo University, May 28, 1954.

Ozaki Yukio, *Gakudō Kaikoroku* (Memoirs of Ozaki) (Tokyo: Yūkeisha, 1951), I, 214-16, admits that he and his friends favored a strong policy. Scalapino, *Democracy and the Party Movement . . .*, pp. 158-67, reviews the first six Diet sessions, to June 1, 1894. For a long-range evaluation of Ozaki see Douglas H. Mendel, Jr., "Ozaki Yukio: Political Conscience of Modern Japan," *Far Eastern Quarterly*, XV, 3 (May 1956), pp. 343-56.

in the United States, in England, or in France (this in contrast to the oligarchs who found their model in Prussia). However, another set of antagonists to the oligarchs were beginning to make their presence felt by the early 1890's and to march at times in step with the liberals. These, for want of a better term, we may call reactionaries, although later in this study we shall discuss them more fully and attempt a more precise definition. However, they should be introduced here. Unlike the liberals they were not interested in or enamoured of Western-style institutions; rather they were bitterly anti-western. They stemmed directly from the heritage of Jōi (Expel the Western Barbarian), Saigō Takamori, and the Satsuma Rebellion. Defeated and scattered after that episode, a few of them had reorganized in 1881 as the Genyōsha (Black Ocean Society), whose name was a reference to the strait of "black" water between Japan and Korea. Their leaders were Kyushu-ites, first Hiraoka Kōtarō and then Tōyama Mitsuru. Ideologically, they were the voice of the past, the Old Eastern World, the Confucian heritage, samurai ethics. They would have turned back if they could, but the past was dying and Western-style progress was on the march in Japan. They could not revolt; even Saigō had failed. They would not participate in Western-style politics, so they took refuge in emotion, moralizing over the lost samurai virtues of courage and loyalty, sentimentalizing about Asia, its countries and peoples, who in their view were being washed over by tidal waves from the West and sold out by their own governments.

Actually samurai ethics and Asia were out of fashion even as ideals in a Meiji (enlightened politics) era, and yet there was a way, and the reactionaries found it, to cloak them in respectability and to turn them into a powerful emotional lever, capable of stirring the conscience of the whole Japanese nation, a nation so recently emerged from the old Asiatic past that even the leaders of the march forward had moments of uncertainty. By presenting their ideals as essential ingredients of the imperial honor, the reactionaries were able to turn to advantage the fundamental contradiction of New Japan. For the throne was "the banner of the new age";[94] it had been made so by realist oligarchs who, determined to have modernization in a hurry, made practical use of it whenever necessary to stifle opposition. Even the liberals, despite their enthusiasm for Western political ideas, and despite the fact that they were repeatedly victims of the oligarchy's manipulation of the throne, could not bring themselves to attack it. Yet the implications inherent in the imperial institution ran ultimately in the opposite direction from modernization and progress. In the last analysis the throne, with its "god-emperor," its age-old traditions, and its mysterious workings, was more congenial to the spirit and purposes of the reactionaries than to those of either realists or liberals, especially inasmuch as only the reactionaries could claim to be 100 per cent against the Western barbarian disturbers of His Majesty's peace of mind. Out of government, never exposing themselves to the reality (and shame) of bargaining with Westerners across the conference table, they could speak as purists on imperial honor.

The reactionaries were only beginning to find their potential effectiveness in the early 1890's; they were literally *rōnin* (masterless warriors), left leaderless by Saigō's death, without a really coherent program and inclined, like their prototypes of Tokugawa times, more to personal vengeance taking than to organized political action. But government "weakness" on treaty revision gave them an excellent target at which to fire anti-Western and anti-government sentiments. Japan should boldly declare an end to Western privileges and throw any objectors out of the country. "From of old," said Tōyama, "our principle is *Sonnō jōi*" (Revere the Emperor; Expel the Barbarians).[95] We have observed that liberals Kakugorō and Ōi also went on record for ending "weakness" on

[94] Masaharu Anesaki, *History of Japanese Religion* (London: Kegan Paul, 1930), p. 329.
[95] Jansen, *The Japanese and Sun Yat-sen*, p. 40.

treaty revision. Thereby hangs a tale of how liberals combined with reactionaries to make common cause against the oligarchy on this issue. This proved to be an unholy alliance for liberalism, contributing much to its loss of focus, to its substitution of nationalist for liberalist aims as treaty revision blended into the Korean problem to become a blurred demand for "strong policy," without making clear exactly why.

Actually the government had made a fair amount of progress toward treaty revision during the 1880's. And when dissatisfaction began to well up, Itō and Inoue had offered Ōkuma, since 1881 a party leader and outstanding government critic, the post of foreign minister in 1888, to try to bring the matter to a successful conclusion. Liberals would have done well to have supported his efforts. Far from being unfriendly to the West they were the most ardent advocates of a Western-style legal and political structure, the institution of which the treaty powers held to be sine qua non for treaty equality. Of course, this being almost accomplished, the desire for full-scale recognition was in the heart of every sensitive Japanese, the more so if he were a fighter in the cause of freedom and equality. Teach a backward people, yes. But once taught, as the Japanese had been, freedom and equality became their birthright. So it was set forth in Western books. The treaty powers should have recognized this and given ground much more quickly than they did. It would have been a magnificent triumph for Ōkuma, and a good send-off for parliamentary government in Japan if full treaty revision had been granted in 1889. But unfortunately it was 1894 before even an American minister, despite Bingham's earlier sympathy for Japanese aspirations, fully appreciated the problem. Then Minister Dun said what should have been said at least five years before: "The day has passed when anything short of Japan's standing on an equal footing with the other powers of the world will be tolerated by them. . . . An indefinite continuance of present conditions can only lead to a feeling of irritation throughout the country that in time may result in a spirit of animosity disastrous alike to the welfare of the people of Japan and of foreign interests here."[96]

The treaty powers undoubtedly deserve a large share of blame for the loss of focus that came to Japanese liberalism. But the liberals themselves were guilty of some of the indulgence Fukuzawa had warned against. They might have exercised some degree of patience, especially while Ōkuma was making his try, but instead they played to harass the government and wreck the negotiations. The leading harassers were the aforementioned Daidō Club, which Gotō Shōjirō and Liberal party friends, like Kakugorō, organized especially to build up the treaty revision issue. Ōi, too, was a member and a most ardent spokesman against compromise treaty revision.[97] The fact that Ōkuma was a rival party leader, who had sold his soul, if only temporarily, to the government, doubtlessly added to the incentive for indulgence and the denunciation was vehement.

Meanwhile, as liberals were whipping up anti-Ōkuma sentiment, reactionaries plotted to "help" them in the sort of way that contributed a large push to turning errant liberalism into crass chauvinism. The Genyōsha hatched a plot on Ōkuma's life. This was by no means a new approach to the problem of treaty revision for them. Earlier when Inoue Kaoru was foreign minister, they had planned to assassinate him in Fukuoka for his "appeasing" approach to treaty revision, but somehow the plot had not been brought to fruition. Now Ōkuma was sullying the imperial honor in an unbearable way by talking treaty revision with Westerners in other than the most belligerent tones. One Kurushima Tsuneyoshi was delegated to do the job. At first he intended to use a sword, but, finding the guard around Ōkuma strict, he changed his mind to favor a bomb. Since good bombs were apparently hard to come by, even for assassins, he asked his chief Tōyama Mitsuru to obtain

[96] Treat, *Dipl. Rel.* . . ., II, 422-23. Treat says Minister Swift had been negative on this in the period 1889-91.

[97] Hirano, *Bajō* . . ., p. 227. Jansen, "Ōi . . .," p. 312.

one for him. Tōyama went to Ōi Kentaro, where, one may presume, after some mutual denunciation of Ōkuma and treaty revision, he obtained a bomb. (Perhaps the bomb was one left over from the Osaka affair.) In addition Takano Rinzo, editor in chief of Ōi's newspaper, seems to have discussed the plot with Kurushima. On October 18, 1889, Kurushima threw the bomb, which did not kill Ōkuma though it cost him a leg, then committed suicide at the gate of the imperial palace.[98] The resulting outcry was more against Ōkuma than against the assassin, whose patriotic motive was well publicized, and the negotiations for treaty revision were broken off. Subsequently Aoki and then Enomoto, each of whom held a brief tenure as foreign minister following Ōkuma, tried to reinstitute negotiations in those brief periods of relative calm when the Diet was between sessions; but it was December, 1893, before Mutsu could again take up negotiations in earnest.[99] By then Ōkuma's party, the Kaishintō, as well as Gotō-ites, Ōi-ites, and others, almost the whole liberal front, had joined the reactionaries to decry government weakness on treaty revision, and they were broadening the issue into a general demand for a stronger foreign policy.

In sum, it is clear that Japanese policy makers needed no great plot to bring them around to a re-evaluation of Korea policy in 1893. The following considerations posed it: (1) Caution and conciliation had resulted in Chinese ascendancy and chaotic political conditions in Korea; there was no sign that either was abating. (2) Greatly augmented Russian power in the Far East was forecast for the near future. (3) Political parties were making a desperate bid to break the power of the oligarchy in Japan; in this struggle they were joining reactionary groups to make stronger foreign

[98] *Tōkyō Nichi Nichi*, Oct. 19; *Jiji Shimpō*, Oct. 20; *Meiji Hennenshi*, VII, 326-28. Hirano, *Bajō* . . ., p. 230. Kuzū, *Tōa Senkaku* . . ., II, 432-36, 721-22. Jansen, "Ōi . . .," pp. 312-13.

It is strange that the police did not trace the bomb to Ōi. Does this indicate that he was not so close to the plot as the "patriotic" sources say? Or perhaps the Home Ministry was glad to see Ōkuma mauled? In addition to the attacks on Inoue and Ōkuma was another which took the life of Mori Yūrei in April, 1889.

[99] Treat, *Dipl. Rel.* . . ., II, 430: also pp. 311, 314, 365, 371.

policy into a popular demand, one which Japanese friends of Korea, Japanese residents in Korea, nearly everyone interested in Korea supported. Thus, past experience, future prognosis, and present pressures seemed to demand a bold move in, around, or for Korea. Yet the oligarchs hesitated. What was the realistic thing to do? No decision was made in 1893, but 1894 brought what Foreign Minister Mutsu called "various unexpected happenings."[100]

[100] Mutsu to Itō, Aug. 16, 1894: Archives, MT 1.6.1.5, pp. 539-40.

V

"Various Unexpected Happenings"

Japanese policy makers came into the year 1894 in a mood of dissatisfaction with the drift of affairs in Korea and on the defensive in the face of demands from the Diet for a bolder foreign policy. Within the inner group of the oligarchy itself there was division of opinion, with Yamagata and military men generally exerting a pressure for greater audacity, while Itō and his foreign minister, Mutsu, held the line for caution. Between Itō and Mutsu there was some slight disagreement. This has been described by Shinobu Seizaburō, author of the standard study of Mutsu's diplomacy in this period, in the following way. "Both Itō and Mutsu agreed on the basic objective of peace. . . . but there was a minor difference. Itō's idea was 'insofar as possible without breaking the peace, we shall maintain the nation's honor.' Mutsu said, 'Within the limitation of not impairing the nation's honor, we shall to the utmost seek peaceful means to settle the situation.' " In other words Mutsu in the hour of crisis would be less adamant as a hold-out for caution than Itō. But, as Shinobu also points out, Mutsu felt himself to be on the horns of a diplomatic dilemma, wherein the successful negotiation of treaty revision precluded "positive action" in Korea, yet a solution to the Korean problem was "absolutely necessary."[1]

Mutsu's first attention in 1894 was to treaty revision. He under-

[1] Shinobu, *Mutsu Gaikō*, pp. 134, 141-42.

took negotiations directly and exclusively with Great Britain, which had long stood as the principal obstacle to the progress of Japanese aspirations for treaty equality. These negotiations promised to be of the most delicate sort, with the British, fully aware that they were doing Japan a great favor, ready to delay the proceedings at the slightest provocation. Thus Mutsu had to spend most of the month of February reassuring the British government that Japan had in mind no such drastic measure as unilateral denunciation of the treaties, which implication had seemed, to the British chargé, to be contained in a sentence in an article in the *Tōkyō Nichi Nichi* newspaper.[2] The late spring and early summer of 1894 were the critical months for these negotiations, and it is difficult to conceive of the Japanese government as deliberately fomenting a Korean crisis at this time. However, two spectacular events, the murder of Kim Ok-kiun in Shanghai on March 28 and the dispatch of Chinese troops to Korea to suppress the Tonghak rebellion on June 6, brought on a crisis situation as a result of which Japan embarked on war with China and a single-handed effort to force "reform" in Korea. Such drastic actions would seem to imply bold and willful contrivance; but when one watches the process of policy decision unfold step by step one is struck by the extent to which improvisation rather than calculation underlay the moves of Japanese policy makers. Hesitant, nervous, flustered, and, ultimately, frustrated are adjectives which might be applied to the oligarchs as they tried to solve the Korean problem by bold, swift action in 1894–95. Foreign Minister Mutsu in a memorandum to Itō, dated August 16, 1894, urging the cabinet to decide on a "fundamental policy toward Korea," used words which ring back again and again as one observes the trend of Japanese policy through these years and beyond—toward the eventual conclusion that only by annexation could the Korean problem be solved. He said: "The Korean situation as anticipated and prepared for at the time Ōtori was sent to Korea developed and changed unexpectedly; various unexpected

[2] Treat, *Dipl. Rel. . . .*, II, 418-21.

happenings have led step by step into the present situation."[3]

The assassination of Kim Ok-kiun, and a bizarre sideplay of attempted assassination with Pak Young-hyo as the object, had the effect of focusing on Korea the growing popular feeling in Japan that the "weak" foreign policy of the government should be amended. The liberal press leaped with alacrity to proclaim Kim a martyr in the cause of civilization and to condemn the Chinese and Korean governments which had welcomed (or plotted) his death, and the Japanese oligarchs who had treated him so shabbily. And reactionaries from Genyōsha circles joined in to weep (crocodile?) tears for Kim, and proclaim the imperial honor offended.

Kim was lured to his death by two Koreans, Yi and Hong, who succeeded in winning his confidence and then tempting him with a proposition that Li Hung-chang was dissatisfied with the direction of affairs by the Min family in Korea and would provide help for his return to activity there. Apparently they promised him money from a Shanghai bank, if he would go to Shanghai to get it. Hong accompanied him to "help him get the money," and shortly after their arrival at Shanghai, as Kim lay resting at a Japanese hotel in the International Settlement, shot him dead. Settlement police arrested the assassin, but, on the demand of Chinese officials and the acquiescence of the British consul general, turned him and the body of Kim over to Chinese authorities, who in turn placed both body and assassin aboard a Chinese gunboat and returned them to Korea. There the Korean government, to the horror of the diplomatic community, showered the assassin with rewards and honors and had the body of Kim cut into segments and displayed about the country.

Meanwhile Yi, after seeing Kim and his assassin off to Shanghai, set in motion a plot to kill Pak Young-hyo, who had recently returned to Japan from America. He and two other Koreans (brothers) and a Japanese named Kawakubo made elaborate arrangements to lure Pak to the Enraikan Hotel in Tokyo. There they collected

[3] For. Min. Mutsu to Pr. Min. Itō, Aug. 16, 1894: Archives, MT 1.6.1.5, pp. 539-40.

four trunks (for portions of the body?) and blankets to catch the blood. But Pak was warned by friends, refused to go to the hotel, and took refuge in a private school. The ringleader, Yi, apparently in desperation to conclude the assassination before the news broke on the Kim affair, decided to try to kill Pak at the school on March 28. Kawakubo now refused to help, and it seems that the brothers stayed away also. Yi went to the school where *he* was captured and tied up by Pak's friends, and forced to confess the whole plot, including the forthcoming assassination of Kim. Pak sent a message to Fukuzawa Yukichi regarding the peril to Kim, but it is not clear whether Fukuzawa took any action at that late moment to try to save him. Possibly Fukuzawa notified Japanese police of the fracas involving Pak. At any rate the police descended on the schoolhouse and arrested Yi, Kawakubo, Pak, and several of Pak's friends, without making any precise distinction between villain and victim. They were brought into Tokyo district court on March 31. However, the two brothers of Yi's assassinating band made for the Korean legation, where, at first, the Korean minister gave them asylum. This brought the Japanese Foreign Office into the picture.

In general, the Foreign Office's approach to this latest Kim-Pak complex was to prevent its becoming blown up into a serious diplomatic embroilment with China and Korea, though at first Foreign Minister Mutsu probably felt a strong temptation, to which some of his own Foreign Office underlings contributed, to make an issue of the disposal of the body of Kim. But very quickly, as he and Itō saw the heights to which Japanese domestic political passions were being fanned, they adopted an approach of "calm and routine" diplomacy, refused in the end to admit any right or responsibility of the Japanese government to interfere in the Kim case, and tried by police measures to silence those Japanese who demanded such interference.

The Foreign Office began by taking note of Kim's departure from Kobe on March 23. This event was reported to Mutsu who cabled Ōtori in Seoul on the twenty-fifth, advising him to inform the Korean government of Kim's departure from Japan. Ōtori did so. Then, after Kim's death, that news was relayed to Ōtori from Tokyo as soon as it was received from the Japanese consul at Shanghai. Ōtori immediately conveyed this information to the Korean government and also to Yüan Shih-k'ai. Whether they knew it already or not, the Korean king and the Min family sent a message thanking Ōtori for the information, and expressing concern for the safety of the assassin. Ōtori told them that the assassin had seemingly been arrested in Shanghai, but said that he would inform the Japanese government of their concern. Mutsu, however, already feeling the sting of popular disapproval in Japan, responded by siding with the corpse rather than the assassin, and instructed Ōtori to make representation to the Korean government, in co-operation with representatives of the other treaty powers at Seoul if possible, to the effect that the body of Kim should not be mutilated. Ōtori did so when the body arrived at Inchon on April 9, but alone, for the other representatives decided not to meddle in the matter beyond explaining unofficially to the Korean Foreign Office how such acts were regarded abroad. Mutsu also had Ōtori remonstrate with the Korean government that, assassination "being a notorious crime against humanity," they should not honor the assassin. To do so would "impair the reputation of Korea before the world." Ōtori received an answer thanking him for his advice, but explaining that Eastern nations differed from Western nations in legal system and popular sentiment and, having cited the *Spring and Autumn Annals* for justification, saying that the assassin would be rewarded. With this Mutsu let the matter drop, the reasons for which are to be seen in domestic developments in Japan.[4]

Immediately after the news of Kim's assassination reached Japan, Ōi Kentaro, Inoue Kakugorō, and others organized a Society of the Friends of Mr. Kim, opened an office on the Ginza,

[4] These events are described in Tabohashi (1951), pp. 30-36, and contemporary accounts, Allen to Sec. State, Apr. 6, 1894, No. 551 and Apr. 17, 1894, No. 554: Dipl. Desp., Korea and *Jiji Shimpō*, May 2, 1894, support his findings.

and took up as their immediate objective the obtaining of Kim's body so that it could be given an honorable funeral. Active in the organization of this society was one Okamoto Ryunosuke, who was to make a considerable impression on the course of Japan's Korea policy during 1894–95. His importance lies in the fact that, unlike Ōi and Kakugorō, he was not *persona non grata* in government circles; he seems to have had a minor post in the Foreign Office, and to have had some acquaintanceship with Mutsu, and in the flurry of excitement set off by Kim's assassination he was probably the principal agency by which the Kim society got a hearing in Foreign Office circles. At any rate, amidst a rising clamor stimulated by the society that Japan should demand the body of Kim, in which even Prime Minister Itō was badgered with inquiries as to "the prospects of obtaining the body," Okamoto obtained an authorization to go to Shanghai along with one Saito Shinichiro to "investigate conditions." Saito seems to have been a bona fide investigator, but Okamoto was mainly anxious to "get the body." Needless to say, he failed for it was already shipped to Korea. But his effort sharply defined the body of Kim as a political issue in Japan, and no doubt encouraged Mutsu to instruct Ōtori to make the protestations as to its treatment discussed above.[5]

Meanwhile Fukuzawa paid touching tribute to Kim in an editorial in his *Jiji Shimpō* on March 30, and led by *Jiji* various Tokyo newspapers launched a fund drive in memory of Kim, partly on the presumption that his body would be obtained. The money was to be used for a suitable funeral, a memorial stone, and as a fund to help Korean refugees in Japan. At the end of April a series of Kim Ok-kiun meetings were held in Tokyo. Omakoto seems not to have participated in these, perhaps for fear of losing his Foreign Office connection, for by that time the Japanese government was taking a very dim view of these proceedings. The meetings, which attracted eight hundred to a thousand people, were mainly devoted

[5] Tabohashi (1951), p. 38. Itō memo, undated, No. 101: Kensei Shiryō Shitsu (Itō collection).

to a denunciation of the government's policies and its betrayal of Kim, whose corpse had by this time been quartered in Seoul. Batteries of speakers vented their criticisms under such lecture titles as "An Outline of the Meiji Government's Diplomacy" (Shiga Jūko), "The Present Cabinet's Korea Policy" (Ōi Kentaro), "Our Duty to Neighboring People" (Komuro Shigehiro), "On the Kim Ok-kiun Affair" (Itakura Chu). The government's response was to send police to "keep order," which consisted of stopping speaker after speaker as he warmed up to vehemence. For example, "The speaker said, 'The Korean and the Chinese governments have humiliated us. . . .' At this he was ordered to stop." There were plenty of speakers, however, and the criticism of the government was "severe." Ōi Kentaro received "huge applause."[6]

Early in May a rumor circulated in Tokyo that the head of Mr. Kim had been or would be received there,[7] and elaborate plans were made for a memorial service. Meanwhile the sixth Diet opened session on May 12, and the Kim affair came up for attention. On May 18 one Representative Moriya, claiming to represent the sentiment of the Japanese people, said that Kim had bought a return ticket to Japan before his departure for Shanghai, had stayed in a Japanese hotel in Shanghai, and had "wanted to stand under Japanese protection to the last." But he was shot, and his body given over to China and Korea. Mutsu replied to this in a written communication to the Diet in which he finally stated the government's position with firmness and clarity. He said that "as for the corpse of a Korean subject named Kim. . . . The incident having occurred in Chinese territory the matter of the Chinese government's delivery of the corpse lies outside our authority." Nevertheless, on May 20 the Friends of Mr. Kim and their friends,

[6] *Jiji Shimpō*, Mar. 30, Apr. 5 *et seq.* (memorial fund); *ibid.*, Apr. 21, 22, 23, 1894. *Tōkyō Nichi Nichi*, Apr. 22, 1894 (regarding meetings).

[7] *Kokumin Shimbun* (newspaper), May 6, 1894, voiced the "rumor" that a certain Japanese had received a box, one *shaku* by eight or nine *sun* in size, containing the head of Kim. It had come from Korea via Nagasaki and Kobe to Shimbashi Station in Tokyo. *Meiji Hennenshi*, IX, 62.

who included many Diet members, held a grand ritual in his honor at Aoyama Cemetery. They had no body, not even a head, but they reverently buried what was said to be a lock of his hair. The following day one Matono Hansuke audaciously called on Mutsu and demanded that Japan go to war to avenge Kim's death. Mutsu, probably not unmindful of the fates of other government leaders at the hands of patriotic assassins, seems to have equivocated somewhat, refusing to entertain such an idea, but referring the gentlemen to General Kawakami "if he wished to talk about war." On the twenty-second *Jiji* newspaper carried a headline story about the numerous supporters of a non-confidence move against the Itō cabinet in which Inoue Kakugorō and other Kim sympathizers figured prominently. A non-confidence motion succeeded on June 1, to which Itō responded by dissolving the Diet.[8]

Of course, the Kim case was only one source of fuel for the many-sided Diet attack on the oligarchs, which led up to the dissolution of the sixth Diet. And in fact, interest in Kim seems to have faded rapidly after the ceremony of May 20, with the government-hushing operation, which had begun in mid-April, contributing to this.

Similarly, the Pak affair in Tokyo, which was clearly within the area of Japanese authority, produced a few moments of tension, but was not allowed to develop into a casus belli. When Mutsu learned that two of the would-be assassins of Pak were being sheltered at the Korean legation, he sent the Korean deputy minister a sharp demand that they be turned out. After some hesitation the minister complied on April 3, but then filed a protest against the pressure the Japanese had exerted, packed his bags, and left Tokyo on April 5. Since he designated no one to take charge of his legation, this had the look of breaking relations. Mutsu immediately instructed Ōtori to ask the Korean government whether it intended to evacuate the Korean legation in Tokyo. The

[8] Tabohashi (1951), pp. 39-41. Shinobu, *op. cit.*, p. 162. *Jiji Shimpō*, May 23 and June 3, 1894.

Korean government responded by ordering a temporary minister to take over the legation, and the affair was smoothed over, though there was some hubbub about it in the Japanese press. Pak and friends and enemies were brought to trial in June. The cases against Pak, Yi, and Kawakubo were dismissed for lack of evidence, but several of Pak's followers were given a month in jail and two-yen fines for beating up Yi. Yi and the brothers were ordered deported back to Korea as undesirable aliens.[9]

Thus, the Kim assassination and the related attempt on the life of Pak cannot be said to have been planned by the Japanese government to afford it a casus belli, as is sometimes alleged. Rather, it reacted to the tension which these cases created by refusing to make a serious issue of them. Their chief importance was probably as a dramatic re-emphasis of the idea that people's rights in Japan would be served somehow by strong action in Korea. The oligarchs refused to make Kim or Pak an excuse for such strong action, but, if they chose to do so on another ground, people's rights advocates could hardly do more than cheer them on.

The Tonghak Rebellion was the Korean version of the Satsuma Rebellion of Japan, the Boxer Movement in China, the Wahabi in Arabia, and perhaps the Mau Mau in Kenya. It was a rising against the government for reactionary rather than progressive reasons. In Toynbee terminology it was Zealotism, a desperate, though unrealistic, effort to reassert tradition in the face of change.

Led by disaffected Confucianists and fallen nobles, and supported by farmers who found the mercantile activity of the port cities penetrating the countryside and menacing their way of life, the Tonghak (Eastern Learning Society) proclaimed itself the defender of old Eastern virtues against foreigner and foreign-poisoned government alike. Very possibly the Taewongun, who

[9] Archives, SP 5, pp. 75-76. Tabohashi (1951), pp. 38-47. Ishikawa, *Fukuzawa . . . Den*, III, 386. Stead, *Japan by the Japanese*, pp. 201-2. Kokuryūkai, *Nisshi . . .*, I, 219-20. *Jiji Shimpō*, Mar. 30, Apr. 18, Apr. 24 and *Tōkyō Nichi Nichi*, Mar. 30, Apr. 18, 1894. *Meiji Hennenshi*, IX, 46-47, 53-54, 57. Allen to Sec. State, Apr. 6, No. 551 and Apr. 17, No. 554, 1894: Dipl. Desp., Korea.

was tradition minded and anti-foreign in his own sentiments, was in contact with its leaders. For, despite the fact that the Chinese had returned him to Korea, he had not been able to rebuild his power and prestige against the Min, who beneath the Chinese aegis had the run of things at court.

The Tonghaks expressed real grievances of a social and economic nature, as well as the more spectacular demand for expulsion of foreigners, Japanese and Western, as betrayers of Eastern learning, customs, and ceremonies. Exactly what their attitude to the Chinese was is not clear, though Yüan Shih-k'ai had a contemptuous view of *them*, once telling the British representative at Seoul that they were all cowards: "cut off a couple of heads and that will be the end of them."[10] Actually the Tonghaks tried very hard to avoid rebellion, which may have prompted Yüan's remark. Philosophically they advocated passive measures to secure the redress of grievances. Several times during the 1880's and as late as 1893 they petitioned the king for various things, including recognition of the society as a legal body. But they were outlawed, and, after considerable riotous activity in 1893, they came into full-scale rebellion through a wide belt in south Korea in the spring of 1894.[11]

The most interesting aspect of the Tonghak Rebellion for our study is the Japanese relationship to it. Just as Kim and Pak and the reform-independence group they headed were the ideological counterparts of Japanese liberals and their friends and fellow conspirators in the cause of liberty and freedom in the Orient, so Tonghak rebels were the ideological counterparts of Japanese reactionaries. Alike advocates of Confucian virtue, opposed to

[10] Heard to Sec. State Gresham, Apr. 6, 1893, No. 383 (confidential): Dipl. Desp., Korea.

[11] Clarence N. Weems, Jr., "The Korean Reform and Independence Movement, 1881–1898" (Unpub. Ph.D. diss., Columbia University, 1954; University Microfilms, Ann Arbor, "Doctoral Diss. Series," No. 8859), abstract, pp. 85-100. Hatada, *Chōsen Shi*, pp. 180-84. William E. Griffis, *Corea, The Hermit Nation* (New York: Scribners, 1907), pp. 473-75. Benjamin B. Weems, "Grass Roots Nationalism in Nineteenth Century Korea: The Tonghak Movement, 1860-1905," Paper presented at Far Eastern Assoc. Meeting, Philadelphia, April, 1956.

modernization and progress along Western models, and angry at government—whether Japanese, Korean, or Chinese—for compromising old traditions, they were natural friends and fellow conspirators in the cause of Oriental tradition. It is not surprising that Genyōsha circles made contact with the Tonghaks, and in the spring of 1894 Uchida Ryōhei, nephew of Hiraoka Kotarō and protege of Tōyama Mitsuru, crossed to Korea, sought out the Tonghak leaders, and offered his services and those of fellow adventurers he could muster. These Japanese entered the Tonghak ranks as the Ten Yu Kyō (Saving Chivalry under Heaven) contingent.[12] Out of this, friendships were formed and connections established which were to continue for many years and have a considerable influence on the course of Japanese policy toward Korea.

While Uchida and his friends could find common ground with the Tonghaks as traditionalists, other Japanese in Korea, the diplomatic and trading communities, were the object of bitter enmity by the Tonghaks as betrayers of that tradition. In April, 1893, the Japanese legation at Seoul temporarily evacuated Japanese families to Inchon for safety when Tonghak notices appeared in Seoul and were posted on the gates of the legation itself. The notices said that "Japanese and foreign rebels and thieves are now introduced into the bowels of our land and anarchy has reached its zenith. . . ." They spoke of the "disgrace" of the year 1876 (the Japanese treaty year) and called for patriotism and filial piety. The Japanese evacuation alarmed American and British representatives at Seoul, who to that time had not thought the movement to be menacing enough to require such a drastic measure, and Minister Heard questioned the Japanese legation secretary, Sugimura, on the extent of the danger. Sugimura replied

[12] Kuzū Yoshihisa, *Nikkan Gappō Hishi* (Secret History of the Merger of Japan and Korea) (Tokyo: Kokuryūkai, 1936), I, 9. Kokuryūkai, *Nisshi* . . ., I, 220. Shinobu, *op. cit.*, p. 164 and many other Japanese sources mention this. C. N. Weems, *op. cit.*, pp. 83, 101, expresses some doubts about Japanese participation in the Tonghak movement as early as 1894, but he did not use these Japanese sources. This question will be discussed subsequently, see below chap. VIII.

that the action had been taken on the basis of rumors and as a preventive measure. He did not explain to Heard what, Tabohashi says, was also in his mind: that the Japanese were more particularly the object of Tonghak hatred than the other foreigners. Tonghak posters, which specified Japanese (*Wa*) separately from other foreigners (*Yō*), may be evidence of this. The result of the scare was that British, American, German, Chinese, and Japanese ships assembled at Jinsen prepared for an emergency, which, however, did not develop immediately.[13] But the disaffection slowly festered. Russian reports from Korea early in 1894 referred to the flight of local officials and Japanese residents from an area taken over by the rebels and noted that "the excitement of spirits that has prevailed for some time is assuming larger and larger proportions."[14]

Thus we have the phenomenon of an anti-Japanese movement being participated in by Japanese. Harrington explains this:

> Perhaps Japan went further to create the crisis of 1894. The Tong Hak rebellion reached its peak at a time convenient for Nippon, and that was not quite accidental, for the Japanese appear to have poured funds into the movement. . . . Step One, the Tong Hak rising, was thus tied up with Tokyo. So was Step Two, the calling of troops from China. Allen was acquainted with the background there. He knew that Sugimura, Japanese legation secretary in Seoul, had urged the measure on Yüan Shih-k'ai. Allen and the other Occidental diplomats made light of the Tong Hak, asserting that it represented purely local troubles. The Japanese by contrast magnified the danger, insisted that Chosen could not handle the insurgents. Wherefore, Sugimura said, China should accept suzerain responsibility. So it was to be . . . Manchu troops. . . . And this brought on Step Three, the intervention of Japan.

Harrington goes on to say, however, that there was no monopoly of blame. "If the Japanese were splashed with war guilt, so was

[13] Tabohashi (1940), II, 224-26, 251. Heard to Sec. State, Apr. 4, 6, 20, 1893, Nos. 381, 383 (confidential), 391: Dipl. Desp., Korea. Treat, *Dipl. Rel.* . . ., II, 445-46.

[14] Cassini, Russian Min. at Peking to Russ. Min. For. Affairs, Mar. 10, 1894, No. 9: Krasny Archiv, "Russian Documents relating to the Sino-Japanese War, 1894–1895," *Chinese Social and Political Science Review*, XVII (1933–34), 481.

China. [China did send troops.] Nor was Korea guiltless. The utter impotence, the hideous corruption of her government. . . ."[15]

Though it may not seem so at first reading, this is, after all, a very harsh judgment on the Japanese. It assigns part of the war guilt to China and even a little to Korea, but does it not put the Japanese guilt on an entirely different plane? China was blundering and stubborn, Korea frightened and stupid; but Japan, stirring up a rebellion in Korea with anti-Japanese overtones to make it look natural, then inveigling the Chinese into sending troops to put it down, all to the purpose of creating a setting for Japanese military intervention, war with China, and seizure of Korea—this would come under the heading of diabolical international criminality. Is the case really clear enough to warrant that conclusion or implication? One cannot say for certain, but the following pieces of evidence would seem to favor a less harsh judgment.

First are certain observations contained in communications of the Russian minister in Tokyo, Hitrovo. In February, 1894, Hitrovo wrote to his counterpart in Seoul, Waeber:

I am secretly informed through a private source that it seems a serious insurrection is being fomented in Korea, the father of the King [Taewongun] acting at the head of the plot; that the insurrection will break out the coming summer, in any case not later than autumn; that agents of the conspirators are purchasing arms in Japan and China; that four thousand rifles purchased are already concealed in a certain store-house at Kanagawa; that three steamers have been bought, one of which is said to have come from Japan; that some Japanese are participating in it and conniving at it; that nothing of this plot is known to the Japanese Government. . . .

He added that the money for all this was being supplied by the Taewongun, some from China, and that the plotters hoped to get money from a Mr. Walker, a Yokohama banker.[16]

[15] Harrington, *God, Mammon . . .*, pp. 250-52.
[16] Hitrovo to Waeber, Feb. 21, 1894, No. 50: Krasny Archiv, *op. cit.*, pp. 480-81.

In early June, as Chinese troops moved into Korea to suppress the uprising and Japan announced her intention to send troops also, Hitrovo had an extended conference with Foreign Minister Mutsu, which he reported to his minister of foreign affairs in detail. Toward the close of his report he made the following comments concerning the state of popular opinion:

> Only very recently the age-old hatred of the Japanese people towards the Chinese and Korean Governments was inflamed by the murder in Shanghai of Mr. Kim Ok-kiun, a Korean emigrant, and by the attempt on another emigrant in Tokyo, Mr. Yung-siu [Pak Young-hyo]. Mr. Kim, who during his life already enjoyed considerable popularity in Japan, is at present growing into a legendary hero. According to rumors his relatives and especially his younger brother are playing a prominent role in the Tonghak insurrection. More than this, in Korea as well as among the common people in Japan, a legend has already formed that the spirit of the murdered Kim appears to the insurgents and commands their up-to-now invincible hosts.[17]

Harrington used these letters, but he makes no differentiation between the Japanese government and those Japanese involved with the Tonghaks and with Kim. Of course, his book is only incidentally concerned with the inner workings of Japanese politics. However, it may be that failure to give sufficient attention to these inner workings has led to over-simplification of the Japanese diplomatic process, especially with regard to the Korean problem. Is it conceivable that, as Hitrovo says in the first of these two dispatches, "nothing of this plot is known to the Japanese Government"? Of course we cannot be sure, but the author has found nothing to indicate that the Foreign Office was sponsoring the movement. It should probably be presumed that they knew or suspected that Japanese were getting into the fray before the rebellion reached its peak in May; but this was clearly the sort of adventure which Itō and the Foreign Office had guarded against

[17] Hitrovo to Min. For. Affairs, June 8, 1894, No. 31: Krasny Archiv, *op. cit.*, pp. 489-90.

since the great Seikan policy dispute. It was an effort by their critics to lead or force them into decisive action, regardless of consequences. Tōyama and Uchida cannot be considered to have been beginning a career as mere government hirelings. Here was their first bold stroke in the shaping of a messianic-mystic pan-Asianism into which course they hoped to and eventually did (in the 1930's) drag reluctant oligarchs. Here too in the exaltation of the ghost of Kim (a Western-style reformer safely dead) they were beginning a pattern of co-operation with Japanese liberals, who were one with them in opposition to the oligarchs and who were, not unnaturally, losing their focus as they found the Western liberalism they had expounded tainted by Western imperialism. This was a time of subtle ideological shift which saw the liberals, worn out by a losing struggle for cabinet responsibility to the Diet, merging with reactionaries on the Korean issue, a merger which was eventually to end in the bankruptcy of Japanese liberalism while breathing new fire into the inheritors of Saigō's tradition. This is the road trod by opponents of the government, post-1895. We shall discuss it more fully in subsequent chapters.

But the main point for our attention here is that those Japanese who loved the Tonghaks, like those who loved Kim, were the opponents, the hecklers, the enemies of the oligarchs, ever needling, prodding, trying to rock the ship of state off the course of realism into uncharted and dangerous seas. This was a thing the oligarchs were determined to avoid. They were playing the game of diplomacy according to the style Western States had taught them, practically, carefully, realistically. By this they had brought Japan to the very edge of success in the great undertaking: treaty revision, a place in the sun for Japan, recognition as a full-fledged, Western-style modern state. Crusades and causes, whether liberal or reactionary, were anathema to them. There was not the slightest inclination in policy making circles to move in behind the Tonghaks and save Korea for Confucian virtue, in the manner of Ten Yu Kyō, Tōyama, and Uchida, or free the Korean masses from their oppressive government, as recommended by Japanese liberals.[18]

Helping Tonghaks was thus not a Japanese government proposition. However, what of the proposition that they pointed with alarm to the rebellion to entice the Chinese to intervene? Ōtori, having been in Tokyo for consultation in the period preceding the dispatch of Chinese troops, this comes down to the activities of Seoul legation secretary, Sugimura, who was left in charge. Allen's opinion that Sugimura set a trap for Yüan by urging him to call for Chinese troops[19] seems to be supported by Chinese sources. Shinobu says that according to Chinese sources Sugimura visited Yüan on June 3 and told him that he expected China to dispatch troops and that there was no objection to this from the Japanese side. Shinobu supposes that he might have done this to seek out "the real intention" of the Chinese, though Sugimura does not mention this in his diary.[20]

Sugimura's diary is an amazingly full, frank, and revealing record of the doings of the Japanese legation in Seoul from May, 1894, through the Queen Min murder episode in 1895. His discussion of the Tonghak affair and the Chinese dispatch of troops is pertinent here.

> On May 4, 1894, Minister Ōtori left Seoul for Japan and from that day I took charge of the legation business as deputy minister. At that time the Tonghak were spreading in the south and west in the Cholla Do area and General Hong was appointed to suppress it. This general had assisted the Queen during the riots of 1882, and so the King and Queen favored him. He took 800 soldiers and left the capital on the 5th. Min Yong-ik argued in favor of sending troops to crush the Tonghak, but

[18] *Tokyo Mainichi* (newspaper) which represented Kaishintō party opinion expressed the liberal argument as follows: "The Tong Hak revolted against the bad policies of the Korean government. . . . If the Chinese and Japanese governments help the Korean government to suppress the revolting masses, this becomes a kind of Holy Alliance of the Orient. Such a measure might be kind to the Korean government, but it would not be kind to the Korean people." June 14, 1894; cited in Shinobu, *Mutsu* . . ., pp. 41-42.

[19] See note 15 above.

[20] Shinobu, *Mutsu* . . ., pp. 79-82.

many ministers opposed it, saying these are good people who riot against oppressive local officials. Therefore [merely] tame them. This caused Min to feel that he could not rely on the Ministers and he began to confer secretly with Yüan Shih-k'ai. Yüan thought that since Korea is very weak, there may be no hope for success [in putting down the riots] and if the Korean army is defeated and the rioters come to Seoul ... there will be more trouble with foreign countries. Therefore, Yüan wished to get it settled (the writer heard this from Yüan, himself). Also he wanted to make a great success [for himself] and at one time he wished to command Chinese police and merchants himself, marching [into the riot areas]. ... In order to help the Korean troops he loaned them a Chinese warship. On the 9th, General Hong and 800 Korean troops went aboard a Chinese warship and two Korean ships and sailed to Kunsan harbor. At that time I heard a rumor that there were Chinese troops aboard the warship who were joined by the Koreans. ... I tried but could not get the essential [information on this].

The Chinese warship did not return for several days so I asked our Foreign Office to dispatch a Japanese warship to investigate. The warship *Ōshima* was approved on the 16th, but the Chinese ship returned to Inchon that day and seemed ready to sail again. Our warship *Ōshima*, however, had to return to Japan, and I tried to get another Japanese ship through talking to the captain of another ship at Inchon. A cable was sent to Japan and the *Tsukushi* sailed to Inchon. The *Yamato* was there also. The Seoul troops met the Tonghak forces and were defeated. It was rumored that over half the Seoul troops fled before the encounter. Therefore 400 more troops were sent from Inchon aboard a [Korean] ship on the 23rd. But no one expected them to succeed; the tendency was to rely on the Chinese. However, I told the [Korean] Foreign Minister that it was not a good idea to rely on foreigners to settle an internal riot. This was told to the King and almost everyone at court, except various ministers, seemed in agreement with my opinion.

But on the 31st at the news of the fall of Zenshu [Chonju] castle the Korean Court was astonished and decided to ask help from China; and on June 1st an official request was written to Yüan Shih-k'ai for military assistance. (Because of contrary opinion the dispatch of the letter was postponed, but it was sent on the evening of June 3, I heard.) Already on June 2 I had sent Mr. Tei [a Korean] to the Chinese to ask if such a request had been received. Yüan said there was no official letter, but that a decision had been made informally and the Chinese would dispatch troops. On June 3rd I personally talked to Yüan for three hours, and I was informed of various particulars. The main theme was that if one wants to preserve peace in the Far East, it is wise to stop the Korean riots in an early stage. The reason for the riots is maladministration of the Korean government and local officials. "But," Yüan said, "if we remain bystanders the government will be overturned, foreign intervention will come, and Korea will be a battleground of foreign countries. Therefore I want to ignore the merits or demerits of the present Korean government and settle the riots to avoid a cause for foreign intervention."

However, though Mr. Yüan expressed this fair sounding opinion, in reality he had ambitions. Because in recent years Japan lacked the power of competition in Korea, secretly he undervalued Japan and wished to use this juncture to make clear [Chinese] suzerainty over Korea. And he wanted to establish his own merit. I could perceive this, and I said in a somewhat joking manner, "This talk annoys me very much. If you really dispatch your troops, then I'm afraid Japan will have to send troops also." Then Mr. Yüan changed color. "For what reason?" he asked. I replied, "In order to protect our legation and our people." Yüan said, "There is no need. There is no danger to foreigners." I said, "If the Korean government is not capable of affording protection, there is no need for us to rely on your troops." Yüan said, "If your country sends troops, other foreign countries will send troops." I said, "Fantastic. . . ."

On June 4 Yüan sent his secretary to say that he had received the official request [from the Korean government for troops]. I therefore cabled this to our government saying, "Told Yüan's secretary that we hoped they would observe the Tientsin Treaty. . . . My guess is 1500 troops from Weihaiwei. Will Japan send troops or not?" The next day I sent my secretary, Tei, to Mr. Yüan, who said that 1200 Chinese troops would be dispatched from Shanhaikuan. I cabled Tokyo and waited anxiously to receive an answer. On June 6 at 11:30 P.M. I received the answer, "Ōtori sails on warship with 300 sailors and 20 police as his guards, but do not make public the dispatch of Japanese sailors." Therefore I kept this secret. On June 7 our Foreign Minister told the Chinese government of this and I was instructed to tell the Korean government that Japan was dispatching troops in line with the Tientsin Treaty, but I kept the number secret. This was my cabled instruction. (I could sense from the cable that other forces than the 300 sailors would be sent). . . .[21]

So Sugimura wrote at Seoul. The diary seems candid enough, and if its testimony on the troop dispatching issue is counted, it must surely be adjudged to contradict the idea that Sugimura invited Chinese intervention. Quite the opposite: it shows him to have urged the Korean government not to ask for Chinese aid and to have warned Yüan that a call for Chinese troops might bring Japanese troops too. His putting the warning "in a somewhat joking manner" was consistent with his own uncertainty as to what the Japanese Foreign Office would do.

Thus while Japanese did participate in the Tonghak Rebellion and while Sugimura did confer with Yüan Shih-k'ai concerning the dispatch of Chinese troops to Korea, it should by no means be presumed that the Japanese government was behind either of those activities. What then was the pattern of Japanese intervention? To get at this we shall follow documents and deeds as closely as possible, observing the process by which the sending of troops to Korea led into the Sino-Japanese War and then dividing into two categories: first, and more important to this study, Japanese moves to "reform" Korea during and immediately after the war, and secondly, negotiations with China and the powers to terminate hostilities and re-establish "peace" in the Far East.

According to Mutsu's memoirs, even in late May, 1894, he did not consider the Tonghak matter acute. "From reports of Acting Minister Sugimura during May, I cannot think the Tonghak have the power to overthrow the government. It is too early for us to discuss the matter of dispatching troops . . . but we must watch the movements of the Tonghak, the measures of the Korean

[21] Sugimura Fukashi, "Zaikan Kushin Roku" (Memoir of Troubles while Living in Korea): Archives, PVM 3, pp. 285-301. Hereafter cited as Sugimura Diary.

government, and relations between the Korean palace and the Chinese."[22]

However, on June 2 he recommended tentatively to the cabinet that troops be dispatched. Tabohashi discusses the process by which he arrived at this. At first, says Tabohashi, the Foreign Office attitude reflected the opinion of Sugimura that there was no need yet for troops to be dispatched, and that, even if the situation developed so as to require a dispatch of troops, a small force would be enough. But to the Japanese government came various other information in addition to reports from the legation at Seoul. Some of these reports, whether intentionally or not, enlarged upon the facts and led to some mistakes in judgment of the situation. Thus Foreign Minister Mutsu maintained a calm and cold attitude, relying on Sugimura's reports during May, but at the end of May he began to become excited, especially after he received the information that the Chinese might dispatch troops. On May twenty-ninth he sent a telegram to Sugimura referring to the rumor that the Korean government was asking military assistance from China, and instructing Sugimura to investigate. Sugimura replied that Min had urged that the Chinese be asked to send troops, but that other ministers disagreed, so it was not yet certain. While Sugimura and Mutsu were not (yet) in favor of dispatching Japanese troops, military men, especially Deputy Chief of Staff Lieutenant General Kawakami Soroku, were urging such a move. Meanwhile the second Itō cabinet was in severe conflict with the Diet, and Itō, deciding to dissolve the Diet, called a cabinet meeting June 2. Shortly before the meeting a telegram from Sugimura arrived at the Foreign Office, saying that the Korean government had unofficially requested China to dispatch troops. "Mutsu attended the Cabinet meeting with this telegram in his hand. He said that if China sends an army to Korea without any justification, we must also send our army to prevent unforseen happenings and to maintain an equilibrium of power between Japan and China

[22] Shinobu, *Mutsu . . .*, p. 47, citing *Ken Ken Roku* (Mutsu's memoirs).

toward Korea." The army minister said it would be necessary to establish a general headquarters to control army and navy units sent to Korea.[23]

Actually, as far as putting down the Tonghaks was concerned, it was apparent by the time Chinese and Japanese troops arrived that there was no need for either of them, for the rebels had no further successes after May 31 and Korean government troops soon had the situation in south Korea under control. However, with the June 2 cabinet decision Mutsu entered upon what Shinobu calls a policy of "balance of power," whereby Japanese forces to match the Chinese would be sent, and, from an even footing, Mutsu would then negotiate a joint evacuation. The legal basis of this was the Tientsin Treaty which, by its "equality" provisions that neither Japan nor China would keep troops in Korea but that in the event of disturbances either could intervene upon giving notification to the other, implied that what one did the other would do also. Such a policy would merely restore the status quo ante, leaving the relative positions of Japan and China in Korea, as well as general conditions there, as they had been prior to June, 1894. But the dissatisfaction with which Japanese policy makers had come to view Japan's standing in Korea before the rebellion made this a result to be avoided rather than achieved. "Balance of power" was thus a working minimum, and the question of whether additional risks should be undertaken in pursuit of a "better" result was by no means foreclosed.[24]

The establishment of the General Headquarters organization, which was approved by the emperor on June 5, opened the way to pressure from the military toward the largest possible military commitment consistent with the immediate policy of "balance." This does not mean that all military men were looking for big trouble. A navy vice-admiral urged in late June that far too many

[23] Tabohashi (1940), II, 291-94, 304. Cf. Shinobu, *Mutsu* . . ., pp. 83-84.

[24] Shinobu, *Mutsu* . . ., pp. 125-26. Shinobu says Mutsu followed the "balance" policy until June 14, when the Japanese government decided to demand reform as the price of evacuation—*ibid.*, pp. 5-6.

Japanese ships had arrived at Inchon. "It seems like an actual war. As a result I am afraid of the effect on our treaty situation; the sentiment of foreign countries toward our country will not be good. It would be regrettable if this would cause trouble for our future policies. The Russians want conflict between China and Japan and they may plan some scheme. Our government should give attention to this."[25] However, General Headquarters largely reflected the view of army commander Kawakami, which was to match the Chinese with plenty to spare. He had sent two army majors to Korea and China on an inspection trip during April and May, and their observations had convinced him that even in the event of war Japan could win. Nor was he above hoodwinking his prime minister. The night after the June 2 cabinet meeting Kawakami discussed the matter of the number of troops to be dispatched with Mutsu. He reminded Mutsu that in 1882 and 1884 Chinese troops had taken the initiative in Seoul, and he said that this time Japan must take the initiative. He had reports, he said, that the Chinese were dispatching 5000 men; and he predicted that Li Hung-chang would dispatch 20,000 or 30,000 more if these were defeated. Mutsu said that to think in terms of sending 7000 or 8000 men was impossible, for Prime Minister Itō would not agree to so large a number. Kawakami then pointed out that all that was needed was approval to dispatch one brigade at first. "Since the Prime Minister knows that one brigade is about 2000 men, he will not oppose. However, if we dispatch a combined brigade, it will really number 7000 to 8000 men; this will be sufficient." Apparently Mutsu agreed to this and the next day obtained cabinet approval. After this, with General Headquarters established, it played a decisive role in determining numbers of troops to be dispatched and whether any should be withdrawn.[26]

[25] Tabohashi (1940), II, 312-13.

[26] Kokuryūkai, *Nisshi* . . ., I, 225-27. Shinobu, *Mutsu* . . ., pp. 169-70, 214-15. Tabohashi (1940). II, 304. The idea that Itō was deceived on the "combined brigade" appears in many Japanese books, but one is naturally skeptical, since they all seem to rely on the Kokuryūkai (Black Dragon Society) account. However, the following

Mutsu's position then became anomalous, for, notwithstanding his agreement with (or perhaps merely acquiescence in) the military logic of the desirability of a large force, he framed his instructions to Ōtori in a way that gave Ōtori to interpret his purpose as "balance" and negotiation toward joint evacuation. Mutsu's announcement to Western diplomats that Japan's sole purpose in sending troops was to protect her legation, consulates, and nationals in Korea[27] is, of course, no proof that he began with that limited objective, but Ōtori's reactions indicate that the Japanese minister himself was puzzled and dismayed at the large number of Japanese troops which began to arrive at Inchon. Sugimura's diary tells us that upon his arrival at Seoul (which he entered with 420 sailors and four cannons), Ōtori saw Yüan Shih-k'ai and came to a tentative agreement that matters should be settled peacefully and that a future conference should be had to arrange evacuation of forces. Then on June 10 he received word from Tokyo that one brigade of infantry with an engineering squad had sailed for Korea. Subsequently on the eleventh and twelfth he received cables from Tokyo that more troops were coming. Each time he cabled back to Mutsu "the landing of too many troops will cause trouble. Therefore until there is an order from me [the Minister] the landing of troops beyond a certain number should be prohibited. . . ."

Sugimura continues:

I [Sugimura] at this time thought there might be a hidden reason for our government's dispatching a large number of troops. If so the Minister

---

additional piece of evidence came to the author's attention. The diary, "Nisshi" (June 1894), of Imperial Grand Chamberlain Tokudaiji Sanenori says that he reported to the emperor on June 6 that approximately 3000 men were being dispatched to Korea. Then, under date of June 13, he says he had that day reported to the emperor that 8000 troops had arrived at Inchon. He says nothing on this subject in his entries between June 6 and 13. If the emperor was in the dark, perhaps Itō was also. See Tokudaiji, "Nishi" (unpub.), June, 1894.

[27] Treat, *op. cit.*, II, 449. Hitrovo (Tokyo) to Russ. Min. For. Affairs, June 8, 1894. No. 31: Krasny Archiv. "Russian Documents . . .," p. 490.

should consider this, and I was afraid the Minister's refusal to allow the troops to land would not be a suitable action. Therefore I expressed my personal interpretation to the Minister. He [Ōtori] replied that it would never be the intention of the Japanese government to cause trouble by landing too many troops and that he would not allow it. On the same day, the 12th, the Minister sent Captain Watanabe to Inchon to stop the entrance into the capital of large numbers of troops; Watanabe carried a letter to Brigade Commander [General] Ōshima regarding this. The main theme of the letter was that the situation in Korea was calm; therefore the entrance of a large number of troops into Seoul would be harmful to security. In addition, on the 13th, I [Sugimura] was sent to Inchon to await the arrival of Ōshima. . . . He landed at Inchon on the 16th. I saw him and told him of Minister Ōtori's order. He did not give me a definite reply, but he kept the soldiers at Inchon. However, I felt, seeing the newly arriving Japanese soldiers in high morale, that the aim of Minister Ōtori could not be realized and I felt that future planning should be on that basis. I returned to Seoul with an army major and a navy lieutenant commander. . . .[28]

Shinobu says that Mutsu actually agreed with Ōtori, but, General Headquarters being in command of the troops, it was impossible for him to arrange the evacuation of those already dispatched or to prevent the landing of additional ones. Under the circumstances he had to "break up his own policy, based on his own instructions." Mutsu himself described the situation as follows: "The tiger is very fast and so is an explosive situation. It is impossible to change the number of troops decided upon midway [in the operation] and if we look at the diplomacy of the Chinese government, they might take up any conceivable tactics and cheat us. According to telegrams from Tientsin and Peking, China was sending large bodies of troops and preparing for war. So on the one hand I considered Ōtori's request right, but on the other hand there might be incidents at any time. Trouble developing from poor military power on our side could lead to a dangerous situation.

[28] Sugimura Diary, Archives, PVM 3, pp. 307-14. Cf. Shinobu, *Mutsu Gaikō*, pp. 209-10.

So at this time I thought it only safe to send the combined brigade."[29]

On June 25 the Russian minister in Tokyo reported to St. Petersburg; "My personal conviction is, the present Cabinet having gone too far on the Korean problem, which is much heated in Japan, cannot recede without some plausible pretext or even a pretended success. But it seems, nobody wants a war, and it may be that it will be avoided without any foreign mediation."[30] By that time the Japanese government had indeed come to a decision that mere joint evacuation was not a sufficient result for Japan. The nature of this change of ground was expressed officially in notes exchanged between Japan and China. On June 7, duly under the terms of the Tientsin Treaty, each side had notified the other of the intention to send troops to Korea. The Chinese notification defined their purpose as "to restore the peace of our tributary state, and to dispel the anxiety of every nation residing in Korea for commercial purposes." The Japanese, while accepting the Chinese notification, registered objection to the definition of Korea as a tributary state of China and defined her own intervention as pursuant to the Chemulpo (Inchon) Convention of 1882 in accordance with "the procedure laid down by the Treaty of Tientsin."[31] However, Japan's determination not to withdraw her troops was not expressed as deriving from the tributary state issue, but as a proposal to China that before troops were withdrawn, "in order to cut the evil root" of future disturbances, a "mixed commission" (Sino-Japanese) should make a "serious investigation" and take "serious measures" to "guarantee" that the "maladministration" of the Korean government should be reformed. The Chinese government turned down this proposal on June 22, Li Hung-chang calling it a proposal that China "seize jointly the ruling of Korea."[32]

[29] Shinobu, *Mutsu . . .*, pp. 214-15, citing *Ken Ken Roku* (Mutsu's memoirs).

[30] Hitrovo (Tokyo) to Russ. Min. For. Affairs, June 25, 1894: Krasny Archiv, "Russian Documents . . .", p. 498.

[31] Treat, *op. cit.*, II, 450-51. Komura (Peking) to Mutsu, June 8, 9, 10, 1894: Archives, MT 1.6.1.5, pp. 23-39.

[32] Archives, SP 5, p. 81. Hitrovo to Russ. Min. For. Aff., June 25, 1894 and Cassini (Peking) to same, June 24, 1894: Krasny Archiv, *op. cit.*, pp. 496-97.

Tabohashi adjudges that Mutsu posed the issue in this way for "political reasons," namely that "a reform program approach, even if it failed, would make a good impression on European and American countries," whereas the tributary state issue would not seem a good reason to them, "who little understood the political situation in Korea." Mutsu, he says, was following a "delicate policy" which neither Ōtori nor Sugimura had the ability to carry out.[33]

Perhaps Mutsu's policy was too delicate for anyone to carry out, but the reactions of Japan's representatives at Seoul show up its vagaries very well. We have observed that Sugimura, who in April and May had told Mutsu frankly that the Tonghaks were nothing to worry about, saw in the oversize Japanese contingent landing in Korea a "hidden reason." He presumed, though he was not told, that it meant the Japanese government had decided on a big action to "sweep out Yüan, the Min clan, and the Chinese" from their dominant position in Korea. He and his assistant, Matsui Keishiro, tried repeatedly to impress this idea on Ōtori, as did others of the legation staff and Okamoto Ryunosuke, who arrived from Japan about this time. But, according to Sugimura, "He [Ōtori] was more than sixty years old and too careful in everything." Clearly the minister was irritated at the yes-and-no situation in which he found himself. He wanted clear-cut instructions from the foreign minister. On June 14, after no one had paid attention to his complaints about the large number of Japanese troops arriving, he wired Mutsu, stating bluntly that Japan should begin evacuation of troops unless she was prepared to break negotiations with China.[34]

Mutsu, however, was busy developing the joint reform proposal for submission to the Chinese, and he did not give Ōtori any precise indication of policy direction until the eighteenth when he aston-

[33] Tabohashi (1940), II, 355-56.

[34] Sugimura Diary, Archives, PVM 3, p. 504, also p. 311. Tabohashi (1940), II, 323-26, 328. Shinobu, *Mutsu* . . ., p. 229.

ished the minister with the following instruction: "With reference to our proposals relative to Korea . . . the Chinese government does not seem inclined to entertain our suggestions. If it turns out to be so the Japanese government cannot withdraw from its attitude now taken unless something should be accomplished to satisfy ourselves as well as the feeling of the public. . . . So we may take advantage of this opportunity to demand cessions of telegraph lines between Pusan and Seoul, abolition of taxes on Japanese in the interior . . . and the like." He concluded by telling Ōtori to be "prepared" to take "proper action."[35]

Ōtori's response was as close to rudeness as diplomats on the same side get. "Carefully considered your telegram of June 18, which was received June 20, 7 p.m. But I cannot take the steps mentioned in that telegram because we have no grounds whatever to make such demands against Korea. . . . I expect your prompt answer. It appears that some Powers entertain suspicion of our attitude toward Korea in sending such powerful forces. Hope you will take best possible means to explain our object. . . ."[36] Along with this he sent a vivid description of the reaction being created by the arrival of so many Japanese troops in the form of a "secret report from a Korean official on the atmosphere of a Korean cabinet meeting held June 18." It spoke of a "state of crisis" and "turmoil in the palace" due to the arrival of "ten Japanese warships each with 500 soldiers and in addition thirty merchant ships." It was feared that "the Japanese have some cunning plan." One minister ventured the opinion that "Russia and Japan were combining to attack China and Korea."[37]

Ōtori's voice to this point was a voice of warning against too many troops and too many demands lest the objectives of Japanese policy as he understood them, balance, negotiation, joint evacuation, peaceful settlement, be imperilled. This is a significant point,

[35] Mutsu to Ōtori, June 18, 1894, telegram No. 218: Archives, MT 1.6.1.5, pp. 20-21.
[36] Ōtori to Mutsu, June 20, 1894, telegram No. 291: Archives, MT 1.6.1.5, pp. 49-50.
[37] Letter, *ibid.*, pp. 115-25.

especially in view of the fact that he had been in Tokyo and received his instructions straight from Itō and Mutsu in early June. His evident mystification at the subsequent turn of events in Korea, unexpectedly large troop arrivals and the increasingly belligerent tone of Mutsu's instructions, indicates that balance and peaceful settlement had actually been the policy objective assigned to him and that policy was changing on a step by step twenty-four-hour basis rather than according to preconceived plan. Ōtori, a literal man, would not admit the change until it was spelled out for him, and Mutsu would not spell it out because he was not sure himself where he was going. The last of Ōtori's communications which could be classified as a warning was his wire to Mutsu of June 25 in which he said: "Telegraph for my information disposition of Treaty Powers, especially Great Britain, Russia, France, about the attitude of Japan toward Korea, and also telegraph from time to time every change of the disposition." This is a curious sort of communication. Had it gone from Mutsu to Ōtori, it would seem more normal, the foreign minister's imperative to be informed on every aspect of a tense diplomatic situation. But from Ōtori to Mutsu, it has a look of admonition about it, as though Ōtori were telling his superior that he had better pay more attention to the attitude of the treaty powers.[38]

However, by that time, Mutsu was spelling out his new policy —"reforms or else. . . ." On the twenty-second he had sent the first clear statement of policy change:

> The Chinese appear to be sending more troops and thus a clash seems inevitable. If Japanese troops stay in Inchon they will get in trouble with other countries' nationals. If this occurs it will be injurious to our national interest. Therefore it is the decision of a meeting attended by the Emperor that even though it causes some trouble between Japan and Korea, our troops should enter Seoul. They should enter as a combined brigade. This is a grave decision. As instructed before, have the Korean

[38] Ōtori to Mutsu, June 25, 1894, No. 308: Archives, MT 1.6.1.5, p. 53.

government repair the telegraph lines to Pusan; if they delay, have Japanese troops do it. Katō is coming with other instructions.[39]

On the twenty-third he clarified this in terms of overall policy with two more messages, the first of which said: "In consequence of failure of negotiations with Chinese government, Japanese soldiers cannot now be withdrawn from Korea on sole condition of withdrawal of Chinese troops, even if Tonghak party disturbance is quelled and even if collision with China should thereby become unavoidable sooner or later. We are bound now to do single-handed what we proposed to Chinese government. Detailed instructions to be brought by Katō; await his arrival. Concentrate all troops to Keijo [Seoul] immediately." The second, which Mutsu gave to Katō for transmission to Ōtori, was as follows: "To Ōtori 10. You are hereby instructed to strongly press upon Corean Government in the form of recommendation actual and effective reform . . . so as to guarantee against future misgovernment. You may support your argument with the reasons given in my reply to Chinese Minister which Katō brings to you. You may judiciously disclose the above to foreign representatives so as to justify act of Japanese government before the world."[40]

These instructions convinced Ōtori that a policy change had indeed been worked in Tokyo. And an interesting *volte-face* then occurred. Ōtori, in a manner of if-that's-what-you-wanted-why-didn't-you-say-so, began to frighten his superiors in Tokyo with bold propositions. Under date of June 26 he told Mutsu that, though Katō had not yet arrived, he had gathered much information and had come to the conclusion that "it is absolutely necessary at this moment to decide the question of Chinese suzerainty." He said

[39] Mutsu to Ōtori, June 22, 1894: Archives, MT 1.6.1.5, pp. 41-43. Katō was Katō Masao, not to be confused with Katō Komei (Takaaki), who, as a rising young man at the Japanese Foreign Office, was also becoming important at this time, soon (July, 1894) to become chief of the Political Affairs Bureau. Itō Seitoku (ed.), *Katō Kōmei* (Tokyo: Katō Kōmei Haku Denki Hensan Iinkai, 1929), I, 235.

[40] Mutsu to Ōtori, telegram No. 343 and to Katō for Ōtori, cipher telegram, no number, both dated June 23, 1894: Archives, MT 1.6.1.5, pp. 46, 50.

that the Chinese general had proclaimed that he was in Korea to aid the "dependent country" and asked, "Shall I force him to withdraw that proclamation?" On the twenty-eighth he reported that "the situation in Seoul is becoming dangerous. Old and young Japanese should be evacuated to Jinsen." And on the twenty-ninth he sent a long telegram to Mutsu explaining what had to be done to accomplish the new objective:

> Katō arrived . . . and I have been [sic] reported fully your instructions; being firmly convinced that no effectual reform could be made unless China trampled down and Corea put under our influence. . . . I have June 28 sent official letter to the Corean government demanding explanations in a day whether they recognize suzerainty of China. . . . If they answer they do not recognize it, I shall press Yüan Shih-k'ai . . . to withdraw soldiers immediately [as] prejudicial to independence of Corea and [press] Corean government to drive out Chinese soldiers; [and say that] if they are unable, we have to take matters into our hands. If they answer that they recognize Chinese [suzerainty] we shall immediately besiege Royal Palace and demand explanation and apology of [for] their grave violation of Article I of Kanghwa Treaty; if Korean government reply equivocal. . . . I shall resort to same measure as in first case. . . .[41]

Mutsu approved Ōtori's demanding that the words "dependent country" be withdrawn from the offending proclamation, but *he* now warned against the use of force toward either Chinese soldiers or the Korean palace. His answer to Ōtori's wire of June 29 is particularly interesting because it appears in the Foreign Office file both in draft form and in final, corrected form. Mutsu's first inclination was to say: "I approve your telegram #12 demanding explanations from Corean government, but before resorting to violent measures wait for further instructions." However, he crossed out the "I approve," substituting "Received," and crossed

[41] Ōtori to Mutsu, June 26, 29, 1894, Nos. 317, 327: Archives, MT 1.6.1.5, pp. 56-57, 102-5. No. 327 is also numbered 12.

out entirely "demanding explanations from Corean government but." Thus the telegram, as he sent it, read, "Received your telegram #12. Before resorting to violent measures wait for further instructions."[42] The Korean government staved off Ōtori's ultimatum by responding at noon on June 30 that it "confirmed" Article I of the Kanghwa Treaty. Ōtori reported this to Mutsu, but he added his objection to Mutsu's injunction against "violent measures." He argued that "nothing can be done without resorting to such measures" and asked for "full authority for that purpose."[43] And when such authority was not immediately forthcoming he dispatched two members of his Seoul legation to Japan to persuade the foreign minister.[44]

Meanwhile, on June 27, the Japanese cabinet approved a basic document on Korean reform. This document seems to have been drawn by Mutsu, presented to Itō, and, after its approval by the cabinet, transmitted as instructions on objectives to Ōtori. It began by pointing to bad administration and corruption in Korea which had turned popular sentiment against the government and resulted in insecurity. "As a result Japan is influenced by Korean affairs. If we cannot bring about relief measures at this time and take up active planning the situation will be hopeless. Not only will this affect the foundations of our independence, but the trouble will expand to the whole of Eastern Asia. This is why the Japanese government has decided to recommend domestic reform in Korea." It then listed the reforms to be undertaken: Korea must respect foreign representatives; she must establish a competent judicial system; she must have a strictly supervised system of government accounting and expenditure; a modern police system must be established; the army must be improved; Western-style teaching

[42] Mutsu to Ōtori, June 30, 1894, No. 266 (also numbered 20): Archives, MT 1.6.1.5, p. 111. Cf. Mutsu to Ōtori, June 28, 1894, No. 259: *ibid.*, p. 112 and Tabohashi (1940), II, 365.

[43] Ōtori to Mutsu, June 30, 1894, No. 343 (also numbered 15): Archives, MT 1.6.1.5, p. 112. Cf. Sill to Sec. State, July 2, 1894, No. 23: Dipl. Desp., Korea.

[44] Tabohashi (1940), II, 366.

must be introduced into schools; an adequate currency system must be established; transportation must be improved; amnesty must be accorded political prisoners; Koreans must be sent abroad for study; Japanese representatives in Seoul must have equal status with Chinese representatives; Japanese subjects in Korea must have the same treatment as Chinese; the harbor at Inchon must be improved.[45]

Ōtori presented these "recommendations" to the Korean government, but on July 10 and 11 in several dispatches to Mutsu he reported diplomacy at a dead end on every count. He said that Yüan was spreading the word that the influence of Japanese troops would not last long, and that, even though the Korean king might be inclined to accept Japanese advice to undertake reforms, pressure from the Chinese and their Korean supporters would prevent it. Even on the matter of repairing the Seoul-Pusan telegraph he could get no satisfaction. The Korean government, he said, not only refused to repair it, but would not allow "any foreign country" to repair it for them because repairing (or not repairing) the line was Korea's "sovereign right." The Korean government had appointed a three-man committee to talk about reforms with him, but "in my opinion they will do nothing, because within the Korean government there is no desire for reform and the pro-Chinese party is more and more influential." He said he was going to order Japanese troops to repair the telegraph.[46]

Diplomacy was also reaching a dead end in Sino-Japanese negotiations. The Chinese, having made their refusal to participate in a joint reform program with the Japanese, sought third-party mediation of the dispute, first Russian, then American, and British, on the basis of joint evacuation of forces first, discussion of reforms afterwards. The Japanese "politely but decidedly" declined

[45] Mutsu to Itō, presented at cabinet meeting and adopted, June 27, 1894: Archives, MT 1.6.1.5, pp. 58-75; put in form of instructions to Ōtori, June 28, and taken to Seoul by Kurino: *ibid.*, p. 78.

[46] Ōtori to Mutsu, July 10, 1894 (four dispatches) and July 11 (telegram No. 401 and unnumbered dispatch): Archives, MT 1.6.1.5, pp. 191-97, 252-55, 265-74.

Russian advice.[47] The United States refused to intervene beyond making good offices available to both sides, and ended by being accorded the singular honor of being made custodian of Chinese interests in Japan and Japanese interests in China while the war was fought.[48] British mediation probably had the best prospect of success. Mutsu himself seems to have been preparing for the possibility that it might require Japan to accept a compromise settlement when he wired Ōtori on July 8, "British good offices at Peking may have effect before long resulting in negotiations with Chinese government. In anticipation . . . you should secure in the meantime every possible material advantage. . . . Notwithstanding above prospect of negotiations, you need not avoid conflict in case of actual provocation."[49] This telegram, taken with Mutsu's next one on the subject of British mediation, which was sent to Ōtori on July 12, enables us to date rather precisely the point at which the Japanese cabinet decided to preclude further mediation and negotiation, whether under British auspices or another or several powers, and force China to the point of two alternatives; back out of Korea or war. This was to be accomplished by taking decisive unilateral action in Seoul. Although the author was unable to locate the precise document recording this cabinet decision, the evidence points clearly to its having been accomplished in meetings held July 10 and 11, the final decision having been made July 11. Mutsu gave Ōtori conditional approval for the use of force on July 10, but advised him to await instructions to be supplied "after the Cabinet decisions of July 11."[50] On July 12 Mutsu sent a decisive instruction: "38. British mediation in Peking having failed, it is now necessary to take decisive steps; consequently you will commence active

[47] Cassini (Peking) to Russ. Min. For. Affairs, July 7, 1894: Krasny Archiv, *op. cit.*, p. 511.

[48] Treat, *op. cit.*, II, 455-56, 468, 472-74. Sill to Sec. State, Aug. 7, 1894, No. 39: Dipl. Desp., Korea.

[49] Mutsu to Ōtori, July 8, 1894, No. 307 (also No. 33): Archives, MT 1.6.1.5, p. 181.

[50] Mutsu to Ōtori, July 10, 1894, No. 313 (also No. 34) and Ōtori to Mutsu, July 18, 1894, No. 451: Archives, MT 1.6.1.5, pp. 194, 291-92.

movement on some pretext, taking care to do what is least liable to criticism in the eyes of the world."[51]

It is clear from these two dispatches that between July 8 and July 12 the Japanese cabinet had decided that it would not allow British mediation to develop any possibility of success. The progression from "you need not avoid conflict in case of actual provocation" to "commence active movement on some pretext" represents the difference between a final stage of indecision, wherein the question of war or peace remains to some degree dependent on the doings of others, and the initial stage of decision, purposefully to pursue war. This is further illustrated in the bland pronouncement of the latter dispatch that British mediation had "failed," when in fact a final British effort, which had Russian support, to bring about the separating of rival forces in Korea by having Japanese troops move south and Chinese north, was in the making.[52] It stands in contrast to Mutsu's admission four days earlier of the possibility that British efforts might succeed.

At this point a conclusion may be drawn as to when the Japanese government made the decision to oust Chinese influence from Korea by force. It was not in 1876 or 1882 or 1884 or 1885 or 1893 or even in the spring of 1894 at the time of the murder of Kim and the Tonghak risings. It was taken only two weeks before the sinking of the *Kowshing* (July 25, 1894), which event marked the opening of hostilities. Of course, a climate conducive to this decision was produced by a number of background factors, the success of China in asserting the dependent state relationship since 1885,

[51] Mutsu to Ōtori, July 12, 1894, No. 338 (also No. 38): Archives, MT 1.6.1.5, p. 202. The Foreign Office file contains, in addition to the Japanese text, a somewhat clumsy English translation of this instruction. The key phrase is *aru kōjitsu* which I have translated as "some pretext." The translation in the file renders this as "any pretext," which seems rather too strong, especially considering the modifying phrase at the end of the sentence. *Aru kōjitsu* might also be rendered "a pretext" or "an excuse." Cf. Tabohashi (1940), II, 418.

[52] The final flurries of the mediation effort may be traced in "Russian Documents...," Krazny Archiv, in *Chinese Soc. and Pol. Sci. Rev.*, XVII, 638-57. See also Archives, SP 5, pp. 223-26 (relations with Britain) and 250-53 (relations with Russia).

the pressure for intervention by anti-government groups in Japan, increasing military preparedness and confidence in military circles in Japan,[53] awareness of a developing security problem versus Russia, as well as the more immediate causes of tension (the Kim and Tonghak affairs). However, caution died hard in the oligarchs, especially Itō, and, even as they arrived at the conclusion that realism now called for bold action, Itō sent Ōtori a special direct wire urging him not to be rash.[54]

The Sino-Japanese War was for Japan a short, glorious, and popular war. At its declaration all segments of the Japanese political scene immediately closed ranks behind the oligarchs to support the war effort. People's rights advocates were especially enthusiastic, for they saw it as a war for progress and civilization. Fukuzawa's *Jiji* newspaper hailed the opening of hostilities:

> War has begun between Japan and China, but if we trace its origins it is a war between a country which is trying to develop civilization and a country which disturbs the development of civilization. . . . From the beginning Japanese have had no hatred of the Chinese, no enmity. We regard the Chinese as a nation of the world and want to establish ordinary intercourse with them, but they are ignorant of proper international methods and they do not want the progress of civilization. . . . We only intend to develop world civilization and only intend to defeat the people who disturb it. Therefore this is not a war between people and people and country and country, but it is a kind of religious war.[55]

When the Seventh Diet convened in October, all the fiery opposition to the cabinet which had characterized the earlier diets had disappeared. In four days it passed all government measures presented to it, voted a huge war appropriation, and adjourned.

[53] Yamagata tells how he evaluated China's military potential in Stead, *Japan by the Japanese*, pp. 107-8.

[54] Tabohashi (1940), II, 419.

[55] *Jiji Shimpō*, July 29, 1894. See also Oka Yoshitake, "Nisshin Sensō to Tōji ni okeru Taigai Ishiki" (The Sino-Japanese War and Contemporary Japanese Public Opinion), *Kokka Gakkai Zasshi*, LXVIII (Dec. 1954, Feb. 1955), 101-30, 223-54.

Thus, from the viewpoint of the oligarchs, the move into war was politically astute, for it tamed the opposition parties. Also, it became quickly a military success, with Japanese forces piling up victories on land and sea. With this the case, and since we have observed that the viewpoint of the oligarchy after the affair of 1873 was that of realism par excellence in politics and diplomacy, the question that needs to be asked is perhaps not so much why did Itō and fellow policy makers undertake the war as why the degree of hesitation and trepidation which their records reveal. There is every evidence that their idea of war was that which "realists" in nation state diplomacy have generally accepted, that it is an unfortunate, but sometimes necessary, extension of diplomacy. If any of them felt moral or religious compunctions about it, they did not allow these feelings to enter their policy deliberations. However, they did have a "fear" of war, the same sort which Kennan voices in his argument for greater realism in American diplomacy, a concern lest its limited realistic objectives become obscured in emotion and anger, with people at large, or "public opinion," becoming involved in unreal emotional issues, delusions, and impractical idealisms.[56] Theirs was a fear of those uncontrollable factors which a war situation might unleash. And this would seem to qualify them as realists in Kennan's best sense of the word—sober professionals in foreign policy,[57] working in the interest of (Japanese) national security. They were as wary as they could be, given the exigencies, of merely short-term opportunism, and for this reason it is not sufficient to say that they decided for war in order to quiet the political opposition in Japan, or to give Japan's military machine a chance to show its muscles, or to make a territorial grab. These were background considerations, temptations to war, but they were secondary. The main point was the Korean problem, as, in the eyes of the oligarchs, it related to Japanese security. And though they became convinced that China must be ousted from

[56] Kennan, *American Diplomacy* . . ., pp. 19-20, 37, 52-54, 65-73, 91-103.
[57] *Ibid.*, p. 93.

the affairs of the peninsula before a solution to that problem satisfactory to Japan could be found, they were aware that this alone would not necessarily assure a "good outcome." The post-China era might bring other complications in Korea, particularly in the area of relations with Western powers. Hence the hesitation. Hence also the care to go to war in "Christian style," with Red Cross units and lawyers versed in international law accompanying the military forces,[58] and to avoid affronts to Westerners in Korea. Mutsu instructed Ōtori as follows, on the occasion of an incident in which the British consul at Seoul had an altercation with Japanese troops: "Regarding the British Consul, while his conduct is very strange and blamable, it is desirable that you will try to befriend him and not to show any antagonistic feeling, because England has been very friendly to us in connection with treaty revision, and since the Russian intervention she has shown us good will in every way. Moreover our object is to contend against China and Korea, and it is deemed highly important that we should maintain good terms as far as possible with other powers . . . [General] Ōshima has been instructed in the same sense."[59]

The hesitancy of the oligarchs in making the war decision may thus be attributed specifically to two related worries: (1) that public opinion in Japan, molded by impractical "idealists" (whether of the backward-looking reactionary variety or the forward-looking liberal variety, the sort who had advocated war for the Tonghaks

[58] Griffis, *Corea, the Hermit Nation*, p. 477.

[59] Mutsu to Ōtori, July 18, 1894, No. 372: Archives, MT 1.6.1.5, p. 290. Mr. N. Hagihara, who is making a detailed study of the process of formulation of the Anglo-Japanese Alliance, told the author that the smoothing over of this incident involving the British consul "may be a good place to start the story of that process." The Japanese had pressed the delicate negotiations for a new (equal) treaty with Britain almost to the point of signing when news of the fracas in Korea reached London. Earl Kimberley for Britain refused to sign as scheduled on July 14 and the Japanese had a few more moments of great consternation. However, upon receiving reassurances from Japan via Aoki, the Japanese negotiator in London, he signed on the sixteenth. The Russian intervention, which Mutsu mentions in this dispatch, seems to refer to the Russian attempt at mediation which originated with Cassini in Peking. Cassini, Min. in Peking, to Russ. Min. For. Aff., June 22, July 7: Krasny Archiv, *op. cit.*, pp. 494-95, 511-12.

or for Kim, might develop too much enthusiasm for the righteousness of Japan's cause and make an eventual "realistic" compromise settlement difficult; (2) that serious embroilment with Western powers might develop. There were safeguards against these, however, a centralized police directed by the Home Ministry, under whose censorship the press was placed by emergency ordinance immediately after the declaration of war, and a Foreign Office establishment well schooled in Western-style diplomacy. The oligarchs could be reasonably confident that these would see to the carrying out of their directives and prevent the development of untoward situations and happenings. In these areas, as in the field of military operations against China, events proved their hesitantly arrived confidence to be almost a perfect mirror of the situation. There were difficulties: accusations that atrocities were committed by Japanese troops at Port Arthur; the attempted assassination of Li Hung-chang at the Shimonoseki peace conference by a fanatical former Keio University student (one Koyama) who claimed that Li and the Chinese "annoyed the Emperor's mind," tried to annex "poor isolated" Korea, and caused Japanese to be killed in the Formosa expedition, Saga and Satsuma rebellions, and Seoul incidents, etc.; the Triple Intervention, and the outburst of indignation by the Japanese public at the retrocession of the Liaotung peninsula in conformance to the demands of Russia, France, and Germany; Diet antagonism to the Treaty of Shimonoseki.[60] But they were not insurmountable difficulties. The oligarchy was able to hold an even keel through them all, with the Home Ministry, police, and press censorship being employed to keep domestic seethings in check and the Foreign Office assuaging the powers. Sometimes all these had to go into gear at once, as in the case of the attempted assassination of Li, when the assailant was arrested, the best possible medical assistance procured for the victim, a popular campaign of sympathy for Li promoted, a degree

[60] On these several problems see Takeuchi, *War and Diplomacy . . .*, pp. 112, 116-20. Treat, *Dipl. Rel. . . .*, II, 433-35. Tabohashi (1951), pp. 487-90.

of magnanimity inserted into the negotiations—notably the granting of an armistice which Li had sought—and various other efforts made to assure foreign governments around the world of Japan's sincere regret at the incident. Emperor Meiji's armistice message began: "His Majesty the Emperor of Japan, having in view the untoward event which temporarily interrupted the negotiations for peace, has commanded his plenipotentiaries to consent to a temporary armistice."[61]

From the several vantage points considered above, the Japanese excursion into war with China seems to deserve to be called not only realistic diplomacy, but most successful realistic diplomacy: a victorious war, fought not inhumanely, without anger, or at least with domestic passions kept in check, and with international balances carefully respected. However, recognition of these as successful aspects of a war that was short, glorious, and, in addition, realistic does not necessarily mean that the whole adventure, even when judged solely within that frame of reference which holds nation-state politics and quests for national security to be the stark reality of modern times, added up to success. In fact, the core is still missing. The successes referred to above all fall in the category of peripheral arrangements necessary to opening up the main "problem" to correction. The problem, to Japanese policy makers, was Korea. To open up Korea to corrective action it was necessary to oust and defeat the Chinese, to check over-effervescence in Japan, and to soothe the powers into minimal interference. These were accomplished to the extent that by and large Korea was open to Japanese "correction" from the moment hostilities began (July 25, 1894) until the flight of the Korean king to the Russian legation in February, 1896. Practitioners of the art of diplomacy could hardly expect international and domestic conditions to fall into a setting more propitious for the unimpeded application of cool-

[61] The armistice agreement appears as Doc. No. 1071 in NGB, XXVIII, 324-27. Cf. correspondence on reactions abroad, *ibid.*, pp. 327-29. Also Tabohashi (1951), pp. 487-88, 491-93.

headed professional measures to a presumably well-understood situation, for surely by 1894 the Japanese knew Korean politics and affairs intimately.

The story of how Japanese professionals sought to take in hand the opportunity which "various unexpected happenings" opened to them in Korea in 1894 makes an interesting study in frustration and failure, the implications of which loom large. Indeed, the Japanese experience, if considered in broad compass, may be accounted to suggest that the realistic approach to international affairs, which disdains ideals but presumably advances the national interest, in fact does no more than pile complication on complication, with the result that realism descends step by step from enlightened self-interest to unadulterated expediency to cynical brutality. The question whether this is not, at least, less hypocritical than the self-righteous crusades to which idealism leads could logically be interposed here, but leaving it aside for the present we shall proceed to observe the descent of realism in specific terms as the Japanese attempted to "reform" Korea, beginning in July, 1894.

VI

Realism Frustrated (I): The Failure of Inoue, 1894-95

Once the Japanese cabinet had made its war decision, which, as we have seen, was taken on July 10 or 11, 1894, its agents in Korea could proceed with the business of remodeling the Korean government. Since Japanese forces were already in a position to control Seoul and its approaches, there was no need even to wait for the opening of hostilities. However, events of the next two or three weeks indicate that the Japanese had no already decided plan of procedure for the remodeling operation. For a few days the Foreign Office, at Ōtori's suggestion, considered trying to work through Min Yong-ik to develop the reforms they had been insisting were necessary in Korea. He was in Hongkong where Mutsu had the Japanese consul, Nakagawa, contact him with a proposition. Nakagawa reported that though he had used "all my persuasive power," he found that Min preferred to wait and see what happened, and he warned that Ōtori ought to be very careful in thinking Yong-ik would take a position as rival to other Min leaders in Seoul.[1] Next, Ōtori and his assistants at the Japanese legation in Seoul decided to bring forward, of all people, the entirely reactionary Taewongun, to lead the country to reform. Sugimura seems to have been the chief advocate of this idea and he has left a detailed account of its

[1] Ōtori to Mutsu, July 13; Mutsu to Nakagawa (Hongkong), July 14; Nakagawa to Mutsu, July 15, 1894, Nos. 24, 2, 5: Archives, MT 1.6.1.5, pp. 218, 220-21, 224-25.

development. He had established an indirect contact with the Taewongun early in July to sound out his attitude toward possible co-operation with Japan. The Taewongun had given no definite answer as late as July 20 despite an indirect invitation from Minister Ōtori, himself, two or three days earlier. Finally, on July 22, a message was received at the Japanese legation to the effect that a certain follower of the Taewongun, who was under house arrest at the order of the king, might be the one to persuade his master.

Ōtori decided to act quickly. He had ten Japanese guards "liberate" the man from house arrest and bring him to the Japanese legation where Sugimura explained the situation to him; then while he and a group of Japanese, led by Okamoto, went off to persuade the Taewongun to come forward, orders were given out for a Japanese contingent to surround the king's palace in the early morning of July 23. There was a brief encounter with Korean soldiers at the palace, but the sun rose to find the Japanese in control. There was almost a fiasco, however, as the Taewongun proved quite as able to argue all night as his Japanese persuaders. He refused to be hurried. At one point in the discussion Okamoto threatened to commit hara-kiri "to save the face of my minister," but still he was unmoved. Some of the Japanese prepared a *kago* in which to kidnap the Taewongun, but Okamoto refused to allow them to do it, and this set off a heated dispute among the Japanese. A messenger ran back to the Japanese legation to ask what to do. Ōtori sent Sugimura over to talk to the Taewongun. Sugimura made a long and persuasive speech on the chaos that threatened and pointed to the Taewongun as the man needed to take charge. The Taewongun then asked Sugimura whether he would promise "in the name of your Emperor" that "if the action succeeds, Japan will not demand a single piece of Korean territory." Sugimura said he was merely a low-class secretary and could not promise for the emperor, but "I represent Minister Ōtori who represents the Japanese government," and in that capacity he would promise.

The Taewongun had paper and brush brought out, and told Sugimura to sign the promise in the name of Ōtori, which Sugimura did.[2]

The Taewongun then agreed to go to the palace. He and Ōtori arrived there at approximately the same time, 11:00 A.M. on July 23, and "the Min advisers having run away," they went in immediately to see the king. The Taewongun reproached the king for the "bad government situation" and announced that he would take over the government and carry out the necessary reforms, discussion of the details of the reforms to be undertaken later. Beginning July 24 Sugimura met with the Taewongun "every day" and on July 25 Ōtori himself met him to demand that he "abolish" the dependency relationship with China and order the ousting of the Chinese army. After some delay he did declare the abolition of the preferential trade arrangement which China enjoyed, but it soon seemed to Sugimura that he was interested "only in grasping power and purging his opponents and did not see the need for a reform policy." Meanwhile the Japanese army, having disarmed all Korean troops in the Seoul Area, was proceeding southward to join combat with Chinese troops in south Korea.[3]

Ōtori had indeed acted with dispatch and, after a few misgivings, the Japanese Foreign Office urged him on in the line he was taking. On July 28 Mutsu wired Ōtori: "I am gratified of your success. Seize this opportunity to effect the most radical reforms in Corean Government in shortest time possible and give Tai Won Kun every assistance in your power and do your utmost to solidify his ascendancy so that it will last. If possible induce Tai Won Kun to employ capable Japanese in Corean Government service. These persons may be selected from those either in or out of Japanese Government or we may nominate and send them if so desired and you will take great care that Corean Government does not dismiss

[2] Tabohashi (1940), II, 436-41.

[3] *Ibid.*, pp. 442-49. See also Kim (Pres. of Korean Foreign Office) to Sill, American Min., Aug. 15, 1894—enclosure in Sill to Sec. State, Aug. 17, 1894, No. 43: Dipl. Desp., Korea.

Europeans and Americans already in their services." Also he promised "pecuniary assistance" to the Taewongun regime.[4]

But Mutsu was distressed at the on-the-spot decision in Seoul to deprive Koreans of their arms. The fact that he was aware of the broader implications of this is clear from his note to Prime Minister Itō dated August 7, in which he argues as follows:

> The aim of Japan when we dispatched troops to Korea lay not in the infringement of Korean independence but in reform of maladministration. This was decided at the highest meetings and this aim has been explicitly explained to other governments. However, since July 23, for expediency, the arms of Korean troops have been taken from them and Korean police powers limited. In reality the independence of the nation is thus infringed upon. If this situation continues long, we will invite the suspicion of other Powers, especially Russia. This may induce intervention. Therefore we should state clearly that Korea is our ally and we should return arms to the Korean government. We can provide Japanese officers to train and lead them to prepare for their independence, thus showing impartial and selfless intentions toward the Korean people and make our actions defensible before the other Powers. Of course, at present we are at war with China and because of this we cannot do the same as if we were at peace. However, to sustain the pride of Korean independence and to get the support of the Koreans is an emergency matter. Please decide on this at the supreme meeting, and I will instruct Ōtori.[5]

The Japanese cabinet approved Mutsu's proposals, including the return of arms to Korean soldiers and police, the following day.[6] In subsequent communications Mutsu emphasized to Itō that Korea was to be "treated as an ally not as an occupied country." The Korean government must be "consulted on all things." Japan should not interfere with Korean independence or hurt Korean pride, should pay for goods needed by the Japanese military; "there must be no looting." And he cautioned Ōtori, "Do not act

[4] Mutsu to Ōtori, July 28, 1894, No. 446: Archives, MT 1.6.1.5, pp. 416-18.
[5] Mutsu to Itō, Aug. 7, 1894: Archives, MT. 1.6.1.5, pp. 488-94.
[6] Cabinet decision, Aug. 8, 1894: Archives, MT 1.6.1.5, p. 495.

outside international law . . . Korea is an ally not an enemy. . . . The movement of Japanese troops should be approved by the Korean government." Korea, he said, must be treated with consideration, otherwise Koreans would "make accusations against Japan to other European powers," and there would be intervention, especially by "that government of the Power that always seeks to intervene [Russia]." "Already," he warned, "the Russian government is seeking to meddle and if given an excuse they will deliberately influence the Korean government."[7]

While such specific problems as the bearing of arms by Koreans were being considered, Mutsu also sought a definition of Japan's "fundamental policy" toward Korea. He drew up a long memorandum to Itō, for presentation to the cabinet, in which he pointed out that the cabinet had been handling Korean policy by "day to day" measures, that "the Japanese government went to war for the sake of Korean administrative reform and Korean independence, and we are now fighting China; though it is not yet certain whether Japan or China will win, by deciding on a fundamental principle [toward Korea] we can then relate diplomatic and military policies to it." And he set down four alternative principles "by other than which the problem of our future position toward Korea will not be solved." (A) Korea should be treated as an independent nation. (B) Though the independence of Korea be recognized, Japan for a long time or perpetually should directly or indirectly support her independence and defend her, checking the penetration of others. (C) Joint guarantee of the preservation of Korean territorial integrity should be made by Japan and China. (D) Japan should invite other powers, Europe, America, China, to guarantee the neutrality of Korea as with Switzerland and Belgium. In commenting on these Mutsu seems to have favored the second (B), though he pointed out the difficulties inherent in each. He said that if plan A were taken he would "expect reform to fail" and Chinese

[7] Mutsu to Itō, Aug. 15 and Mutsu to Ōtori, Aug. 21, 1894; Archives, MT 1.6.1.5, pp. 528-38, 559-70.

influence and the war to be repeated. Plan B would mean a "protectorate policy" and probably Russia and China and perhaps other powers would try to interfere. "If that happens is Japan capable of defending Korean independence by her own power?" Plan C was "once suggested by the British government." But this, he feared, would "mean the re-emergence of the dependent state theory." And even if no dependency problem were raised, "Japanese and Chinese interests in Korea are always contradictory and the principles of statesmen of the two countries are different and will clash." Plan D ignored the fact that "this war was caused by a clash of interests of Japan and China which should not involve third Powers." And also by it "Japan would lose much and the Japanese people would not be satisfied, for Japan dispatched a large number of troops and spent much money."[8]

In a later memo Mutsu referred to the cabinet decision as follows: "Last August 17 I submitted four plans. The Cabinet selected Plan B for the time being and decided to make a definite plan after the war was over. Since then I have based policy on that decision."[9]

Policy "for the time being" was formalized in a Treaty of Alliance between Japan and Korea, signed at Seoul by Ōtori and Korean Foreign Minister Kim on August 26, 1894. It consisted of three short articles:

Article I. The object of the alliance is to maintain the independence of Korea on a firm footing and to promote the respective interests of both Japan and Korea by expelling Chinese soldiers from Korean territory.

Article II Japan will undertake all warlike operations against China, both offensive and defensive, while Korea will undertake to give every

[8] Mutsu to Itō, Aug. 16, 1894: Archives, MT 1.6.1.5, pp. 539-57. Cf. Draft Proposal for Cabinet Conference by Mutsu, Aug. 17, 1894, in Itō, *Chōsen Kōshō Shiryō*, III, 599-604.

[9] Mutsu to Itō, June 3, 1895, No. 298: NGB, XVIII:1, p. 440. This document also appears (undated) in Itō, *Chōsen Kōshō Shiryō*, III, 597-98.

possible facility to Japanese soldiers regarding their movement and supply of provisions.

Article III. This treaty shall cease and determine at the conclusion of a Treaty of Peace with China.[10]

Behind it lay the simple facts of power, the Japanese seizure of the palace on July 23 and promises extracted by Ōtori from the king on July 25. But its broad application would presumably be conditioned by the concerns voiced by Foreign Minister Mutsu: Japan would induce reforms in Korea in ways that would "sustain the pride of Korean independence," obtain Korean co-operation and be considerate of Korea's position as an ally; she would be careful "not to act outside international law," but she would try to block "meddling" by third parties, especially Russia, trusting herself alone to handle a problem as close to Japan's security as Korea.

How should such policy be evaluated? Wanton aggression? Surely this is too harsh a description. Would "enlightened self-interest" be appropriate? Or perhaps "realism" of the sort which conscientious diplomatists employ and international relations experts of the realist persuasion advocate, that realism which allows itself to be tempered to an extent by consideration for the underdog but which must of necessity remain hard-fisted and practical "in the national interest." The words and the thinking would seem to bear the latter stamp, whether the action to follow would do so or not.

The active effort of the Japanese government to establish a stable and mutually acceptable Japan-Korea relationship within a framework of realistic "enlightened self-interest" may be divided into two stages. The first stage, which will be considered in this chapter, was relatively short, lasting by outside measurement no more than eighteen months. It may be dated from Ōtori's seizure of the

[10] William W. Rockhill (ed.), *Treaties and Conventions with or concerning China and Korea 1894–1904* (Washington: Government Prtg. Off., 1904), p. 429. See also Sill to Sec. State, Jan. 15, 1895, No. 83: Dipl. Desp., Korea.

palace on July 23, 1894, to the king's flight to the Russian legation in February, 1896—though after the murder of Queen Min on October 8, 1895, there was, as the Japanese say, *shikata ga nai* (nothing to be done). It was characterized perhaps by haste, over-optimism, and insufficient awareness of the depth of the problems involved. The second stage, which will be considered in the following chapter, lasted much longer, from approximately 1898 until August 22, 1910, annexation of Korea by Japan, and was characterized by great care, caution, attention to international arrangements to forestall foreign interference, and the personal supervision through much of the period of Itō Hirobumi, the Japanese epitome of realistic statesmanship. The shortcomings of Japan's effort in the first stage could certainly not be applied to the second. Yet in both cases the effort ended in frustration, failure, and brutality. Bald suppression was the last resort and end result of the Japanese application of enlightened self interest to Korea, in the long range as in the short.

One may be tempted to say, as many have, that there is nothing strange in this, that the Japanese planned it that way all along, merely biding time and awaiting opportunity to smash down the iron fist. However, unfortunately for simplicity of explication, the weight of the evidence seems to indicate that the Japanese government did not plan or desire brutality and suppression, rather fell into it in the face of unforeseen difficulties encountered in their Operation Korea. But let us follow the course of events.

Ōtori entered into the reform program with enthusiasm. He induced the king to appoint a council of seventeen members empowered to pass reform measures, and this body issued forth during the late summer and fall of 1894 a series of remarkable reform decrees, called in toto the Kabo Reform, after the year name. These were so sweeping as to call to mind the famous Hundred Days Reform undertaken by the Chinese government under K'ang Yu-wei in 1898. It should be noted that they were by no means merely a narrow imperialistic device. This was most clearly indicated in the new regulations regarding social classes, regulations which were certainly not necessary to the establishment of Japanese control and might in the long run jeopardize it, but which were in tune with the general idea of eliminating outmoded and backward institutions in Korea. "Men shall be employed for office without regard to origin," said one regulation. "Slavery both public and private is abolished in its entirety; the sale of human beings is forbidden; all are eligible for military and governmental service," said another. Others sought to establish the fundamental equality of classes, to place restrictions on concubinage, to legalize remarriage for widows, to eliminate eunuchs from politics, to deal with problems of unemployment, to forbid punishing the family of a criminal, to forbid arrests and punishments by other than duly constituted authorities, to eliminate the practice of "squeeze" and misuse of seals by officials. All of these, which are quite aside from the sinews of power, police, army, finance, and perhaps the educational system, were long overdue in Korea; and they pointed in the direction of a vast improvement in the social and political structure.[11]

In late September, American Minister Sill observed, however, that the reforms had little effect outside of Seoul, where magistrates disregarded the orders of the king, saying he was a helpless prisoner.[12] And from Ōtori's correspondence with Mutsu it is clear that he soon considered his program bogged down. He had built his tactical machinery for putting through the reforms around the Taewongun, but by September 21 he was convinced that the Taewongun was "not to be trusted. He is interested in power and the Confucian way.

[11] The reform measures are listed and discussed in Sill to Sec. State, Sept. 24, 1894, No. 55: Dipl. Desp., Korea. Cf. a list by Mutsu for the Russian minister in Tokyo: Archives, MT 1.6.1.5, pp. 343-34 (reverse pagination). A detailed contemporary study is W. H. Wilkinson, *The Corean Government: Constitutional Changes, July 1894–October 1895* (Shanghai: Statistical Dept. of the Inspectorate General of Customs, 1897). There is a good brief account in Hatada, *Chōsen Shi*, pp. 185-89. And on reform measures affecting social discrimination, see Herbert Passim, "The Paekchŏng of Korea: A Brief Social History," *Monumenta Nipponica*, XII, Nos. 3-4 (1956), pp. 57-60.

[12] Sill to Sec. State, Sept. 24, 1894, No. 55: Dipl. Desp., Korea.

Others are interested in personal profit and opportunism." Ōtori was also disturbed by growing rivalry between the Taewongun and the Min (queen's) party. He had thought that perhaps in the Taewongun's twenty-five-year-old grandson he had found a "progressive young man, favorable to Japan," but, Ōtori lamented, he too had changed, and was working mainly to cause the abdication of the queen because he wanted the throne himself. And he was "intriguing with the Russian and British Ministers." Then Pak Young-hyo, who had been in a "conspiracy" to reform the Korean government, had come to the Japanese legation to seek Japanese assistance, but Consul Sugimura had refused him and since then there had been no more talk with him.[13] Ōtori's gloom was heightened in early October by the presentation of a memorial by "a man supposed to be under the instigation of the Taewongun" urging the king to impeach several members of the reform council on the grounds that they had invited the Japanese army into Korea and involved the country in difficulties. The accused had tendered their resignations, which, however, "are not yet accepted by the King. Memorialist is under arrest. I am trying to restore [the council members] to their former position."[14]

Amidst Ōtori's complaints, Mutsu, at one point, "wondered" in a dispatch to the minister "if it would not be wise to use force against whichever group does not listen to your dissuasion." He thought it better "not to remain aloof" but advised "great caution to prevent any part in the Corean government from entertaining the idea of asking support of European or American diplomats." Ōtori rejected this, saying that he would try to reconcile the various groups "by assisting . . . progressives in the Cabinet on one side" and "supporting the Taewongun, yet restraining his despotism on the other side."[15]

[13] Ōtori to Mutsu, Sept. 21, 1894: Archives, MT 1.6.1.5, pp. 617-25.

[14] Same to same, undated (but internal evidence indicates Oct., 1894), No. 870: Archives, MT 1.6.1.5, p. 117.

[15] Mutsu to Ōtori, Sept. 30 and Ōtori to Mutsu, Oct. 1, 1894: Archives, MT 1.6.1.5, pp. 613-12 (reverse pagination), 616.

At any rate, by early October it was becoming clear that the plan to use the Taewongun as a vehicle for the reform program had misfired. Visiting messengers from the Japanese Foreign Office, Saionji and one Suematsu, seem to have reported unfavorably on Ōtori's management of affairs at Seoul, and on October 11 Ōtori was recalled to Tokyo. Mutsu had become convinced, as he recommended to Itō, that "a man of great stature and tested ability," namely Inoue Kaoru, should be sent to Korea. Ōtori was not pleased at his recall, and in fact did not immediately respond to what Sugimura says was "an indirect order of dismissal," but, upon receipt of a telegram announcing Inoue's appointment to his post, he gave up and left Seoul for Tokyo on October 19. Inoue arrived in Korea six days later, with Korea experts Okamoto and Saito and the Liberal party leader, Hoshi Toru, following him.[16] American Minister Sill evaluated the change as follows: "Mr. Ōtori made the mistake of ignoring and humiliating their Majesties and of depending too much on the Tai Won Kun who at once began his old practice of double dealing." Inoue, he noted, "is apparently determined to pursue a course quite different from that of his predecessor."[17] Mutsu explained the switch to his ministers in London, Berlin, St. Petersburg, and elsewhere as follows: ". . . for the reforms in Corea need the moral cooperation of a person of great ability and experience; besides the presence in Corea of our military commander of highest rank necessitates the residence as Minister of a personage of exalted rank." They were to "reply in the above sense" if asked about the matter by the governments to which they were accredited.[18]

Inoue moved into Seoul with an air of aplomb, a self-confident diplomat who knew how to handle people, especially Koreans. He

[16] Sugimura Diary, Archives, PVM 3, pp. 498-507. Ōtori recall, Oct. 11, 1894: Archives, MT 1.6.1.5, p. 672. Mutsu to Nabeshima (for Inoue Kaoru), Oct. 9, 1894: *ibid.*, pp. 683-84.

[17] Sill to Sec. State, Nov. 2, 1894, No. 65: Dipl. Desp., Korea.

[18] Mutsu to Uchida (London), Aoki (Berlin), Nishi (St. Petersburg), etc., Oct. 15, 1894: Archives, MT 1.6.1.5, pp. 689-88 (reverse pagination).

had a conference with British Consul Hillier in which, after diplomatic salutations and small talk about the weather, he told the Britisher, "My character is simple and direct; our policy toward Korea is long unchanged, it is simply to maintain Korean independence." He recollected his experiences in 1876 when he negotiated with the Korean government, the 1884 affair, and the subsequent years of "attempted cooperation" with China, troubles, the war, and cliques in the Korean government. "Korea is a sick man," he said. "The question is how to diagnose the disease, give medicine and bring about bodily recovery. Often the patient does not like the taste of the medicine, but it is for the recovery of the patient, nothing more."[19] According to Sugimura, who remained as first secretary of the Japanese legation and hence became the new minister's chief assistant, Inoue looked over the situation and decided on three fundamentals of policy: a clear separation of the royal household from the government, a clear definition of the position of the king, queen, and other leading families, and a clear definition of the responsibilities of each organ of government. He noted immediately that the principal anomaly was the position of the Taewongun, who, without political title, had such great power that it was "like two kings in one country." His first step was thus "to reject the Taewongun." To that end he called on the Taewongun, criticized his activities, explained Japanese policies, and refused a counter proposal put forth by some of the Taewongun's followers that Tonghak leaders be invited into Seoul. Instead, he had two Tonghak people jailed, and pressed the Taewongun to announce his retirement. "You always stand in the way," he accused the Taewongun. Finally the Taewongun promised to abstain from interference in political affairs, and "wrote it down."[20]

In his reports to Mutsu, Inoue discussed some of his arguments with Koreans in detail. He tells how Korean Prime Minister Kim

[19] Memorandum of conference between Inoue and Hillier, Seoul, Oct. 29, 1894: Archives, MT 1.6.1.5, pp. 745-56.

[20] Sugimura Diary, Archives, PVM 3, pp. 511-27.

(Hong-chip) had argued that "serving the King is like serving one's parents," but "I [Inoue] told him that a loyal son should not remain silent when the parents violate the domestic administration. . . . The parents of the country should be advised; this is the righteous way of a subject." And upon presenting a twenty-point reform program to the king, he reminded him that "if the King's ministers merely obey without discussing the right and wrong of your orders, that will lead to evil happenings." He spent an afternoon explaining the reform proposals to the king and his ministers, "finishing only half of them before dark." During the explanations the queen and the Taewongun were allowed to listen, but only from the next room.[21] Symptomatic of Inoue's task for the future was a request he made to Mutsu to locate and send to him a document signed by Pak Young-hyo in 1882 requesting the loan of Japanese troops to aid in establishing Korean independence. Mutsu replied that there was no such document in the Japanese Foreign Office.[22] But Inoue, having caught the inconsistency in Ōtori's efforts to produce reform through the Taewongun's reactionaries, began to turn to Pak, the reformer, as the man of the hour, despite his own earlier aversion to the Korean Reform party and the fact that Kim Ok-kiun's activities had completely discredited it in the king's eyes.

He did not immediately throw his whole support behind Pak, however, but sought first to make him acceptable to the various court factions. Observation of this may have been behind Sill's report in early December that Inoue was "disappointing," that he was still listening to the Taewongun group and had done nothing to secure the confidence of the king.[23] Actually, Inoue's main effort in the direction of the Taewongun party was on the old man's grandson, upon whom he urged the idea that "you must not let your wisdom be spoiled by old customs. I have called three people educated in Europe and Japan to study with you such subjects as

[21] Inoue to Mutsu, Nov. 4, 16, 20, 21, 1894: Archives, MT 1.6.1.5, pp. 974-75, 1055, 1056-57, 1130-1229.

[22] Mutsu to Inoue, Nov. 22, 1894: Archives, MT 1.6.1.5, pp. 846-47.

[23] Sill to Sec. State, Dec. 4, 1894, No. 68: Dipl. Desp., Korea.

European and American history. This will be a chance for you to change direction."[24] The grandson disappointed him, however, and by the end of December was under accusation for treasonable connections with the Tonghaks. This blossomed in February, 1895, into an accusation by Min Yong-ik that the Taewongun was plotting to murder the king to make way for his grandson's enthronement; and in May the young man was arrested for treason. According to Inoue's report to Mutsu, the Korean Ministry of Justice was determined to execute him, but "I [Inoue] advised them not to execute him because Japan is endeavouring to unite this country and this old custom of severe punishment is based on revenge. Minister Residents here are watching this case, and I advised no more than exile for ten years. Finally his life was spared and he was exiled to an island [off the Korean coast]."[25]

Despite this failure Inoue made excellent progress with the restitution of Pak to the good graces of the king and court. At a private audience with the king (queen in the next room) on December 8 (1894), he heard the king's complaints about intrigues to dethrone him and promised to support him, the queen, and the crown prince "if they would heed my advice . . . and the Queen would stay out of politics." Then "I having dispelled their doubts about the Pak Young-hyo matter," it was agreed that Pak should be restored to his former position. Accordingly, on December 17, the cabinet was reconstituted with Pak Young-hyo assuming a prominent position as home minister. Pak's friend and former fellow exile in Japan, So Kwang-pom, became minister of law (justice). Other "progressives" were Pak Chung-yang, Horace Allen's favorite "imbecile", as minister of education, and Yi Wan-yong, Chung Kyung-won, and Yi Cha-yun, vice-ministers of foreign affairs, justice, and agriculture and commerce respectively. American Minister Sill sized up the new cabinet as follows: Pak

[24] Inoue to Mutsu, Nov. 24, 1894: Archives, MT 1.6.1.5, pp. 1125-27.

[25] Inoue to Mutsu, Dec. 28, 1894, Feb. 12, May 23, 1895: Archives, MT 1.6.1.5, pp. 1279-1301, 1480-86, 1568-81. Mutsu to Itō, May 22, 1895: *ibid.*, p. 1566.

and the two Yi's were representatives of the "American Party"; Pak Young-hyo and So were the "Japan party," the vice-home minister was of the "Chinese party." And since the palace household minister was the king's brother and a son of the Taewongun, he concluded that all parties were represented. Kim Hong-chip, whose general conservatism had probably been the largest factor in his weathering the various political storms since 1884, though known earlier as pro-Chinese, remained prime minister. Japanese legation secretary Sugimura described the cabinet as being comprised of two groups, "the old group" headed by Kim Hong-chip and the "young group" headed by Pak Young-hyo.[26]

Within three weeks of the formation of the new cabinet Inoue was quite confident that he had matters well at hand at Seoul. He was "relying on Mr. Pak" and he felt he had succeeded in bringing Pak into very close relations with the king and queen. "The intimacy of Pak Young-hyo with the King and Queen cannot now be doubted, notwithstanding Taewongun who is secretly trying to influence King. He is firmly relied on by them and every thing that pass [*sic*] in the palace is reported to me always."[27] In addition, the international situation was encouraging. Mutsu reported that he had heard that "Russia is favorably disposed toward Japan as long as we do not injure Corean independence.... It is essential that our Corean policy should be managed in such a manner as to excite no suspicion whatever of other Powers especially Russia, although we are well aware that you are always careful on this point." And Inoue could reply happily that the Russian attitude had "also changed here," from "evading answers" to "admiration for my doings." "I frankly tell that my sole object is Corean independence and to do that requires more or less interference with the

[26] Sill's list and comments are in Sill to Sec. State, Dec. 18, 1894, No. 74: Dipl. Desp., Korea. For Inoue's list, see Archives, MT 1.6.1.5, p. 1248. On Kim Hong-chip, see enclosure by Foulk in Foote to Sec. State, Dec. 17, 1884, No. 128: Dipl. Desp., Korea. Sugimura's comments are in Sugimura Diary, Archives, PVM 3, pp. 590-91.

[27] Inoue to Mutsu, Jan. 7, 1895, No. 255: NGB, XXVIII:1, p. 377. Cf. Inoue to Mutsu, Dec. 25, 28, 1894: Archives, MT 1.6.1.5, pp. 1242, 1349.

King and Queen"[28]—for the time being, one would suppose.

On January 7 Inoue brought off an elaborate ceremonial testament to his success in setting the course of the Korean government toward progress. Within earshot of his ancestors at the royal tombs the Korean king, attended by the queen, the crown prince, the Taewongun, ministers of state, and various and sundry members of the royal household, made a solemn fourteen-article declaration whose main points were that the old subjection to China was ended forthwith, and His Majesty would labor to make firm the independence of Korea; that various departments and activities of the government, including the palace, would be put in order; that youths would be sent abroad to study; and that the laws would be clarified and ameliorated. On January 11 King's Orders in Council were issued to begin to put the reforms outlined in the oath into practice.[29] The whole procedure is reminiscent of the Meiji Emperor's Charter Oath, which very likely was in the back of Inoue's mind. At any rate, by January Inoue felt that he had the Koreans in line and he turned to the next big problem, money, the financial wherewithal to finance the reform operation.

In the same communication in which he reported the king's "charter oath" he told Mutsu,

> I have succeeded in establishing Corean independence in name, but for realizing the fact I cannot move a step without money. The army formerly divided into four independent bodies has, for example, been collected and brought under the control of War Department. We must now draw up new organization for it and improve men and materials; that is we must dismiss unfitted and pick up better fellow[s], must settle the unpaid salaries of five months, but how can this be effected without money. To make arrangements for the 300,000 and 5,000,000 [yen] . . . it may be difficult now to raise a public loan of Corean Government or to let the bankers invest in it. Under these circumstances I think the

[28] Mutsu to Inoue, Dec. 23 and Inoue to Mutsu, Dec. 25, 1894, Nos. 1166, 1189: Archives, MT 1.6.1.5, pp. 1238-36, 1245-42 (reverse pagination).

[29] Sill sent translations of the declaration and Orders in Council to Washington as enclosures in Sill to Sec. State, Jan. 17, 18, 1895, Nos. 84, 85: Dipl. Desp., Korea.

Japanese Government may loan 5,000,000 and pay it out of military budget. I strongly recommend this measure. With reference to the Diet I think it sufficient to obtain post facto approval.[30]

Mutsu, however, could only reply, "Matter of Corean loan is at present under consultation with some principal banks, not without hope of success. Prime Minister and Finance Minister are also greatly exerting themselves. Therefore until result of this effort becomes known it is impossible to inform you of determination of the Government regarding your telegram 161. The above sent after consultation with Prime Minister."[31]

This putting off by Tokyo elicited from Inoue a remarkable series of protests, which taken together must be accounted very good evidence that Inoue, at least, regarded his mission in Korea as something more enlightened than merely the subjection of that country to Japan. He answered Mutsu immediately in a tone of severity and disapproval.

Your telegram 195 received. Hurry the settlement of the 300,000 question; most strongly urge Shibusawa together with Finance Minister to accept the proposal and make immediate disposition of it; otherwise it is impossible for the Corean Government to cross over [get through] this year. I made the agent of Dai Ichi Branch Bank telegraph directly to Shibusawa in above sense. Bring at once before the Cabinet meeting the measure recommended in my telegram 161; as the result of your negotiation with bankers is yet [being already] started the reorganization of the army [is proceeding] according to my advice and now it is they (?) who [are] constantly pressing me for the speedy realization. I do not know what to do under the circumstances. I am at bay, I want an answer (?) certain whether yes or no. It is impossible for me to stay here any longer without having decided answer. If my last recommendation is approved by the Cabinet before the conclusion of negotiation with bankers, let us adopt it; it affects me little where the money comes [from];

[30] Inoue to Mutsu, Jan. 8, 1895, No. 9 (also No. 161): Archives, MT 1.6.1.5, pp. 1262-60 (reverse pagination); same document in NGB, XXVIII:1, pp. 315-16, here numbered No. 191.

[31] Mutsu to Inoue, Jan. 10, 1895, No. 193: NGB, XXVIII:1, p. 316.

what I want is speedy settlement, so while you are carrying on the negotiations with bankers, urge at the same time the Cabinet to adopt my recommendation and tell me at once yes or no.[32]

Mutsu responded from Hiroshima where he had gone to meet the Chinese delegation to discuss peace terms: "Negotiations with bankers almost certain to be settled successfully, but as they want certain conditions for loan, somebody will be sent to you with particulars. Diet being in session in Tokyo, Chinese Mission on the way, our forces are being dispatched, [and] Prime Minister and others are so much engaged just as the present moment and such being the case, I hope you will wait for a little while as I am doing my utmost."[33]

This reply, along with private information he received from Japanese financial circles, sent Inoue into a lengthy review of the whole situation in terms which may best be described as accusing his own government and the whole Tokyo financial apparatus of blindness and greed, and ending on a note of warning and command. Yes, he understood that they were "busily occupied at the present moment." But

knowing all that I cannot refrain from pressing the matter upon you. [With the Korean government] just roused to life by my own treatment, where can I go. I have just received private letter from Yasuda Takashi in which he speaks about loan overture made to Mitsui Bank, Iwasaki, etc. by you and Finance Minister and mentions refusal of Iwasaki. He speaks [says] that although this refusal is not without a considerable influence upon the rest of capitalists yet if they refuse at all [definitely] Mitsui Bank and Shibusawa alone will meet whole demand. He speaks besides that at the present moment when hostile feeling toward China is roused to such a degree it will be easy to sell loan for 5,000,000 or so provided Corean Government promise the interest of 8 percent and sell at 80 yen per share. That means the interest of 10 percent on capital. It is unreasonable and you will remember that as long as I remain at my present

[32] Inoue to Mutsu, Jan. 11, 1895, No. 194: NGB, XXVIII:1, p. 317. Question marks apparently inserted by Japanese editor, words in brackets by me.

[33] Mutsu to Inoue, Jan. 15, 1895, No. 196: NGB, XXVIII:1, p. 318.

post I cannot morally allow them to contract loan on such unfavorable terms. I insist that the interest should be less than 8 percent. Reason being that even loan made this country from Chinese Government or firm as [in] the period we styled practical anarchy or the loan contracted with Rothchild [sic] at the instance of British Consul-General never bear such high interest. Just think how inconsistent we are to charge such high interest considering that this Government is now practically in our hand, that we are dealing with reforming Corea and above all that we are helping their independence.

His warning was couched in the following terms: "Besides it is my object as well as yours, I suppose, to take whole financial power into our hands. We should not overlook their British bankers . . . [if] this last and most useful help come from some other quarter and in consequence the whole financial power fall into their hands, where shall we stand?" And he closed with what sounded like a command: "Send here more than one representative of the principal bankers such as Iwasaki, Mitsui Bank, and Shōkin [Yokohama Specie] Bank at the earliest possible date."[34]

Mutsu was nettled at this, especially at Inoue's "direct communication" with individual bankers. He called this "not only useless but very likely to create bad feeling" and emphasized the need to get "all bankers to assist us in combination." He thought there would be a "satisfactory settlement," and hoped to have a definite answer in "about ten days time." And, he warned, "I send this telegram after consultation with the Prime Minister."[35] Inoue stopped direct negotiations with bankers, sulked a few days, and then sent off another strong complaint:

My future in Corea is entirely hinged upon this question [loan] so let me know yes or no about the question before every other thing. Newspapers speak of loan as if it was undertaking to make Corean Government issue their loan at the general Japanese market. Were it so it may be paid in paper currency. Is it not? I remind you again that I will take

[34] Inoue to Mutsu, Jan. 16, 1895, No. 197: NGB, XXVIII:1, pp. 318-19.
[35] Inoue to Mutsu, Jan. 19, 26, 1895, Nos. 199, 200: NGB, XXVIII:1, pp. 320-21.

nothing but bar silver or coin for the payment. Corean Government experienced very great difficulties in crossing over [the] year. Hardships and discontent of official classes and soldiers whose salaries remained unpaid for about 3 months have reached such degree that they almost assumed form of riot. To save Corean Government from this crisis I made branch manager of Jinsen office of Dai Ichi National Bank loan them 130,000 yen taking customs revenue for security.[36]

This argument between Inoue and Mutsu over principal, interest and urgency of the projected Korean loan might have become increasingly bitter but for Inoue's suddenly becoming aware that Mutsu was ill with tuberculosis, which was soon to incapacitate him and then claim his life. Inoue wired Mutsu on January 31, "Feel very uneasy in learning from Japan Daily Mail that you are suffering from lung. Take great care of yourself." And he inquired directly of Prime Minister Itō, "Is not Foreign Minister sick at present?" and added, "I must now actually begin works of reform, that I must. I am forced by them to do so. I have been urging you to hurry up the settlement of the loan question but you have not yet given me any definite answer; can you not do so very soon. If not, tell me so." He followed this up with a detailed statement of Korea's debts and obligations and a plan by which Japan might loan Korea five or six million yen by taking the taxes of three or four provinces as security, having a Japanese official in the Korean Finance Ministry and Japanese officials on local tax teams to assure repayment. He included a twenty-year loan and payment schedule, setting the principal at 6,365,638 yen and interest at *9* per cent, immorally high by his own standards.[37]

The home office did not accept this either, and finally on March 3 Itō sent his frothing envoy something of a policy statement in which he reviewed the whole course of events.

[36] Inoue to Mutsu, Jan. 31, 1895, No. 201: NGB, XXVIII:1, p. 321.

[37] Inoue to Itō, Feb. 1, 1895, No. 203 and to Mutsu, Feb. 17, 1895, and encl. No. 222: NGB, XXVIII:1, pp. 322, 334-42.

Last June 7 the Tong Hak revolt occurred and because of it our government decided to send troops, and suddenly we sent a battalion to Seoul. Then the Korean reform problem came in . . . and the Sino-Japanese War developed. Nearly a year has passed and we have won almost every battle and now we have achieved final victory. . . . But now we must establish a definite policy regarding Korea. As a result of the war two or three big countries now have closer relations with Korea. China can no longer interfere, but for Britain and Russia it is easier to interfere, and only Japan can oppose their interference. If we actually protect Korean independence then no country will interfere, but if we fail in our policy in Korea then all these big countries will criticize us and the Korean problem will become very serious. Since you assumed your position you have carried out a proper policy and set definite principles of reform. This is very good, but one thing I fear is that after the war the financial situation will be difficult to balance. . . . It can become bad if reform is too costly. So don't get into a vicious circle. Of course, I don't attempt to forecast fifty years into the future, but other foreign countries seem to watch our policy, and in lending money we should follow international law, and make clear the conditions. Other details I explained to Suematsu, so please ask him.[38]

During the next two months, while Shimonoseki Treaty discussion and settlement and the Triple Intervention occupied the centre of attention in Japan, Inoue's midwinter enthusiasm that big things could be accomplished in Korea, with money, declined almost to the vanishing point. On May 19, he wired a tale of woe to Mutsu. He had, he said, succeeded in attaching Japanese advisers to all Korean government departments, except the royal household and foreign affairs, "which were purposely left off." However, he was encountering "foreign jealousy" and "plots and counterplots" in the Korean government. Reconciliation between Korean parties seemed "absolutely impossible." "A crisis may pass but another will follow." He did not know "what could be done," but thought it necessary to determine "degrees of interference, that is general line of policy," and "in order to consult of our future

[38] Itō to Inoue, Mar. 3, 1895 in Itō, *Chōsen Kōshō Shiryō*, III, 556-57.

policy" he wished to return to Tokyo on leave of absence. "Besides I am still suffering from rheumatism."[39]

Inoue returned to Japan in June, but meanwhile on May 25 cabinet members meeting in Tokyo without Itō, who was absent in Kyoto, discussed Korean policy and made a decision which envisaged a considerable narrowing of the range of Japanese activity and responsibility in Operation Korea from that set by the wartime policy "for the time being" (Mutsu's Plan B) of the preceding August. They now planned the following announcement:

> In taking up arms against China, Japan was actuated by the desire to withdraw Corea from what was regarded as the injurious influence of China. That desire was fully realized by the celebration of the Treaty of Shimonoseki.
>
> The perpetuation of the independence of Corea is a matter of common concern. Consequently the Imperial Government do not deem it necessary for them alone to assume the duty and responsibility of maintaining such independence. Accordingly, while expressing their readiness to cooperate with the other interested Powers in any measure having for its object the amelioration of the condition of the Peninsular Kingdom, the Imperial Government announce it to be their intention to rest their future relations with Corea upon their conventional rights.[40]

A month in Japan apparently improved Inoue's rheumatism, and rebuilt his enthusiasm to some extent. Though he had to accept curtailment of the program he had been advocating, he was sufficiently encouraged at the prospect of obtaining "between 2,000,000 and 3,000,000 yen" (via Diet approval) that he returned to Korea to institute a project best described as "conservative reform". In this he would work through the king, not the "liberal" ministers. The largest part of the money would be used for the construction of a Seoul-Jinsen railway and for the construction of a grand palace for the king (which would presumably build his

[39] Inoue to Mutsu, May 19, 1895, No. 279: NGB, XXVIII:1, pp. 420-21.

[40] Cabinet decision, May 25, 1895, No. 288: NGB, XXVIII:1, pp. 434-35; also in Itō, *Chōsen Kōshō Shiryō*, III, 596. However, the announcement was never made. See below, pp. 297–99.

prestige and guarantee his co-operation), with lesser amounts set aside to meet government deficits and to establish a reserve fund for the king's personal support. The railway, costing about a million yen, would be self liquidating via a special bank which could issue bills. He really needed 3,000,000 yen rather than 2,000,000, Inoue argued from Seoul, lest "a foreign country" (Russia) interfere. As late as August 29 he expected the money, for on that date he wired Acting Foreign Minister Saionji, who had replaced the ailing Mutsu, to remind him: "3,000,000 should be given under the name suggested [as per suggestion] in my secret dispatch number 79. Respecting money I have your instructions and my talk with the King and Government have been strictly on that understanding. On the occasion of change of Minister of Finance it is worthwhile to call attention to the fact that arrangements about the matter are too far advanced to admit change so that whatever changes may take place in the Government they must abide by your instructions and this [number 185] and my telegram 184."[41] Sugimura says "Inoue had promised the King that the Japanese government would send him 3,000,000 yen secretly. The King was much pleased. Inoue visited the Palace often and . . . his office was crowded with visitors from the Palace."[42]

However, within a week, the bubble which Inoue had been so carefully blowing up had burst. Miura Gorō arrived from Japan accredited as minister to Korea. Inoue seems at first to have taken this to mean merely that he himself, remaining envoy extraordinary, would break Miura in to the post and put him to carrying out policies he had already set in motion. He introduced Miura to the king and implied as much. But such was not to be the case. On September 4, Saionji addressed a telegram to Miura as minister, with instructions to deliver it to "Minister" Inoue. It informed Inoue definitely that there could not be two ministers in Korea,

[41] Inoue to Saionji, Aug. 6, 1895, No. 248 (also numbered 79, secret) and Aug. 29, 1895, No. 249 (also numbered 185): NGB, XXVIII:1, pp. 369-74. 374-75.

[42] Sugimura Diary, Archives, PVM 3, pp. 684-85.

that he should return to Japan, and that "regarding your telegram 185" it had been decided "not to convene an emergency Diet [to obtain the money]." The above was sent "upon consultation with the Prime Minister."[43] Inoue was very angry at this turn of events. He wired Saionji that he now had to stop conversations with the Korean king "in embarrassment" and Miura would be placed in the position of "not having one word to say on domestic policies." Furthermore, regarding the "two ministers" problem, he would come home. "I handed over my credentials to the King so I am no longer Minister to Korea. I am just a civilian. I had expected to stay here awhile to explain conditions to the new Minister . . . but now you order me to stop everything and return. So I stop and I shall leave tomorrow."[44]

Saionji responded with a conciliatory message, again addressed to *Minister* Miura for transmittal to *Count* Inoue. He said he would explain about the Diet session when Inoue returned . . . they would wait for the regular session. And though he had said to stop everything and return, he had not meant immediately. He hoped Inoue would explain conditions, etc., to the new minister, then come home as soon as possible. Inoue fired off another telegram warning Saionji that the cabinet had better prepare the way for the Diet to pass the appropriation or "Miura will have no place to stand," "we shall have to abandon Korea," "we shall lose our dignity," etc. He stayed on until September 17, but his efforts had ended in "embarrassment and dismay."[45]

The failure of Inoue and his reform program to refashion Korea to Japanese liking would seem, from Inoue's dispatches, to have been due mainly to lack of money. This may seem plausible. Certainly money spent "realistically" can handle many things, especially in "backward" states. But before accepting such a simple explanation

[43] Saionji to Miura, Sept. 4, 1895, No. 250: NGB, XXVIII:1, p. 375.

[44] Inoue to Saionji, Sept. 4, 1895, No. 251: *ibid.* Cf. Sugimura Diary, pp. 692-95.

[45] Saionji to Miura, Sept. 5 and Inoue to Saionji, Sept. 5, 1895, Nos. 253, 254: NGB, XXVIII:1, pp. 376-77. Sugimura Diary, pp. 692-95. Allen to Sec. State, Sept. 18, 1885, No. 146 gives the date of Inoue's departure.

it is necessary to ask two questions. First, why did the stay-at-home oligarchs feel it was necessary to keep up a go-slow sign on Inoue? And secondly, were the go-slow sign and the dearth (by Inoue's standards) of funds which resulted from it really the crucial factors in spoiling his efforts?

In answering the first question it should be said immediately that there was no lack of trust of Inoue or confidence in his abilities, as there might have been in the case of Ōtori. He was one of the oligarchs, in experience and in spirit. Also there could be no question of his being less knowledgeable of or concerned about Japan's overall financial position than the oligarchs at home, nor of his being less intimate than they with banking circles and the difficulties to be encountered in dealing with them. His main career in home affairs was in finance and his connections in the financial world were of the most intimate variety. Also, it cannot be argued that the Diet presented stumbling blocks of which Inoue was unaware. It is true that the Diet might have put a final veto on the three million yen appropriation had it met in emergency session in September. It had become obstreperous on non-money matters in May, following the Treaty of Shimonoseki and the Triple Intervention, on which it criticized the government severely. But it was notably supine in voting whatever the government asked through the whole course of the war, especially on money matters, and even in the heat of its post-Shimonoseki-Triple Intervention, anti-government sentiment, it voted approval of the government's post-bellum tax increase program.[46] One cannot escape the conclusion that, until the very end of Inoue's tour of duty in Korea, the Diet was not a serious obstacle to obtaining whatever funds the government desired.

Why then the go-slow sign? Why did not the stay-at-homes go all out in backing Inoue? The reason is to be found in their anxiety to keep the Korean venture in tune with Japan's overall relationships with the powers. As long as they could say, with a reasonably

[46] Takeuchi, *War and Diplomacy* . . ., pp. 113-14, 119-20.

straight face, that Korean independence was being accomplished they knew they would face no intervention, but to apply too much pressure too rapidly was dangerous. Of course, Inoue was as aware of this as the stay-at-homes. However, he was not so aware as they of the increasing delicacy of Japan's international position during the closing months of the war, February to May, 1895. When he formulated his plans and initiated his program in Korea he had relatively clear sailing. And though he was certainly aware of the accumulation of tensions surrounding the Shimonoseki negotiations, no doubt his absorption with problems in Korea led him to worry less about them than did the home government. The diplomatic developments leading into the Triple Intervention seem to have been principally responsible for their increasing gingerliness toward Korea, and, although we have said that the oligarchy was able to maintain "an even keel" through the Triple Intervention and the closely related Shimonoseki negotiations,[47] it is necessary here to examine these matters more closely, with a view to seeing better their relation to the Korean problem.

The thinking of the Japanese cabinet on these matters is conveniently summarized in a Special Study Number 5 entitled "Triple Intervention," compiled by the Japanese Foreign Office shortly after the events in question and kept in the Foreign Office archives. This document is permeated with realism: careful, cautious seeking after national advantage. The intervention by Russia, France, and Germany, it begins, was "not necessarily unexpected." As early as June, 1894, Russia and other nations had urged upon Japan the idea of simultaneous evacuation (with China) of Korea. The Russian minister had made a declaration favoring this on June 30. Also the British representative in Tokyo told Mutsu that China would accede to a declaration of Korean independence if there was no reference to Korea's position as a dependent state. Mutsu replied that such a declaration "would be inconsistent in itself." Russia remained in the background "am-

[47] See above chap. V, p. 258.

bitious for an opportunity to intervene." After Japanese victories various European powers began to urge an early end to the war. On October 8 the British minister in Tokyo asked Mutsu to stop the war on condition that the powers guarantee Korean independence and China pay an indemnity. He said the Russian minister was agreeable to this. Mutsu felt that Russian-British interests in the Far East had not been the same, but knew also that if Japan "distressed China too much" Russia and Britain might oppose it. Therefore Mutsu wished to divide Britain and Russia. A (London) *Times* editorial on October 10 opposed (British) intervention. Mutsu wrote to Itō, who was in Hiroshima, setting forth two plans for peace with China, asking his approval of one. Plan A set forth the following points: (1) In order to secure the independence of Korea and guarantee that there will be no new interference in Korean internal affairs, China should cede the Dairen area to Japan; (2) China should pay military expenses and reparations to Japan; (3) China should conclude a treaty with Japan on the same basis as with European powers (i.e., unequal); (4) China should fully guarantee the above three. Plan B was as follows: (1) The powers should guarantee Korean independence; (2) China should cede Formosa to Japan; (3) China should pay military expenses and reparations to Japan; (4) China should conclude a treaty with Japan on the same basis as with European powers.

"Itō agreed with Plan A." But he said that the terms should not be made public. Therefore, Japan's reply to Britain on October 23 omitted any mention of the plans, saying merely that "The Japanese government is not prepared to publish our conditions for ending the war." Then the American minister asked about the possibilities of mediation on November 6, but Mutsu replied, "We cannot negotiate until China gives direct notice of her desire to do so." The powers feared that Japanese armies would bring about the dissolution of China and in various ways they indicated that they could not see Japan's getting territorial cessions on the Chinese mainland. But their advice did not seem too strong. Although it seemed that some powers might not accept an Asiatic mainland cession, no power said this would impair its own interests. Therefore they had not openly protested.

Then the Chinese government sent its mission to Hiroshima. Mutsu drew up the basis for the treaty and brought it to Hiroshima, and a supreme meeting in the imperial presence adopted it. At the meeting Itō spoke, warning of the possibility of intervention. Mutsu suggested that, if intervention was inevitable, then prior to the negotiations an outline of the conditions of the peace treaty should be made known to European powers, especially Britain and Russia, so as to obtain their prior approval. Itō replied: "Though it seems intervention is inevitable, if we inform the Powers of the conditions, we invite intervention beforehand. They will criticize our conditions. This would place us in the position of demanding some conditions from China which have already been objected to. Therefore we should make such demands on China as we wish; let China receive the whole outcome of the war and, if other Powers object, then reconsider the matter." However, when the credentials of the Chinese envoys were examined, it was found that they had no plenipotentiary power, so the peace terms were not even shown to the Chinese representatives at Hiroshima. While waiting for a second Chinese delegation to appear, Mutsu became worried lest continued concealing of the peace terms excite the animosity of the powers, especially Russia. He discussed the matter with Itō, then journeyed to Tokyo where on February 14 he saw the Russian minister. Mutsu told him that he thought Japan was entitled to demand something as the outcome of the war against China and thus a cession of territory was "indispensable." He said he realized, however, that this concerned Russian interests, that he wished to avoid what would hurt Russian interests, and he asked the minister to speak frankly. The Russian minister told Mutsu that "Russia does not disagree with a territorial cession, but she wishes to have free passage to the Pacific. If your intention is Korean independence, we have no interest other than that." Also he "whispered" that the cession of Formosa would "not be disagreeable." However, he said that "a Japanese intervention to get territory on the mainland would not be advantageous to Japan." Mutsu replied that his consultation was for the purpose of ascertaining Russian interests, that "as for the interests and disinterests of Japan we shall consider them ourselves." But he "refrained from offending the Russian Minister." Mutsu concluded from the conversation that Russia would be definitely against the cession of Liaotung.

The Japanese government on February 16, having learned that the Chinese government wished to send new peace envoys, issued a statement that the dispatch of such envoys was "wholly useless" unless they would be prepared to negotiate on a basis of payment of reparations, the admission of the independence of Korea, cession of territory, a definite commercial treaty like those China had made with European nations, and possibly other matters. Mutsu had Vice-Minister Hayashi see the Russian minister in Tokyo and inform him of the four conditions mentioned above. On February 24 the Russian minister replied that the Russian government would not object to these items if the Japanese government would not interfere formally or materially with Korean independence. If the Japanese government would make a guarantee to this effect, Russia would advise China to enter negotiations and would advise other powers to follow suit. On February 27 Mutsu replied that he was "pleased to hear that if Japan recognized Korean independence, which was desired by Russia, Russia would recommend that China accept the peace terms and that the Powers approve." And he stated: "The Japanese government also does not hesitate to declare herewith that it recognizes Korean independence in name and in fact in line with its unchanging policy toward Korea."

On March 12 the Russian minister asked assurances that the Russian trade in the Tientsin area should not be hampered if Japanese troops marched into Chihli province. Mutsu gave assurances. "Russia's real intentions were unclear, but superficially she wanted nothing but Korean independence." Meanwhile

Minister Katō in London cabled that Russia, France, Britain, and even the United States seemed inclined to intervene in the settlement of the Far Eastern war, not apparently from the motive of private interest, but to insist that Chinese ports be open to foreign trade. They would probably propose to Japan that although a cession of territory on the mainland could not be accepted, occupation of other territories would not necessarily be opposed. Mutsu thought that, although the tendency to intervene might be in the embryo stage, there had been no definite decision among the powers concerned. Then as the negotiations with Li Hung-chang were about to open, on March 24, Mutsu received a telegram from Kurino, minister to the United States, saying that the secretary of state had revealed to him confidentially the outline of a cable from the American minister in Russia, to wit: The Russian ambition is very "high and large"; she will take advantage of troubled circumstances to inject her influence into China; she wants to occupy northern China and Manchuria; she will not recognize Japanese occupation of territory in these areas or allow Japan to become protector of Korea. The secretary feared that the outcome might not be in the "true interest" of Russia and Japan. Mutsu felt that he should be careful of Russia so he sought information from Nishi [at St. Petersburg]. Nishi had no real information, but he thought that if Japanese demands for territory were restricted to Formosa and the Chin-chou district of the Liaotung peninsula Russia would not object. Anyway, in line with the decision of the supreme meeting in Hiroshima on January 27, the Japanese government "wished to obtain the fullest possible result from the war, and so refrained from omitting the cession of the Liaotung peninsula from the treaty draft." The treaty was concluded on April 17 at Shimonoseki.

On April 20 Aoki reported from Berlin that the attitude of the German foreign minister had changed and that he now said Japan should be prevented from occupying southern Manchuria. Aoki argued that it was necessary for the independence of Korea, that the place had been taken by Japanese blood, and he urged that the wartime German-Japanese friendship should be continued. But the German said that the treaty as it stood would make Japan an "irresistible competitor" and he added that "the world would never accede to the Japanese desire [regarding Liaotung]." Mutsu felt the intervention was being organized by Russia, with the intention of using France and Germany. Germany wished to join it so as not to let Russia and France "be together in everything." Ministers Takahira in Italy and Katō in London supported this idea. Takahira thought that if Italy, England, and the United States would support Japan on the issue the intervention could be neutralized; but Japan would have to ask for this support. Mutsu cabled Katō (London) and Kurino (Washington) to discover to what extent Britain and the United States would assist Japan. The British government expressed "cordial sympathy," but said it would remain neutral; Kurino cabled that the United States would not contradict its neutrality. On April 23, Japan received the intervention notices. On April 29, Nishi reported that he had talked to the Russian foreign minister and expressed hope that the Russian government would not insist on too much lest the Japanese government have to follow military and popular sentiment and decline the recommendation. The foreign minister "expressed deep concern" but said Russia would not abandon the intervention. On April 30, Mutsu proposed to Russia, France, and Germany that Japan would abandon the cession of the Liaotung peninsula, except the Chin-chou district, and would occupy Liaotung only until reparations were paid. The Russian reply was "no." It was apparent that Russia would not accept any Japanese occupation of Liaotung, presumably for the sake of the independence of Korea, but "actually to prepare for her own aggressions in the future." "Unless Japan could challenge a new enemy, she must accept the recommendation."

Already on April 24 the cabinet had considered the situation. They did not know whether the three powers would resort to military intervention, but they considered that "since our overseas troops were concentrated in Liaotung and our fleet at the Pescadores Islands and our domestic armed forces were nearly zero, we might not be able to defend ourselves. We might have relied on diplomatic tactics until our fleet returned from the Pescadores, but how could it fight even Russia alone after ten months of war." Thus on April 24 the cabinet had decided to accept the triple recommendation wholly or in part. The question was also considered whether Japan should then rely on the three powers to get compensation from China or place the matter of reparations before a conference of powers generally. It was decided that, since May 8 had been set as the date of ratification of the treaty, any delay would give China the opportunity not to ratify. Also, there was the fear that a precedent might be established whereby future relations between Japan and China would always go to a conference of the powers. And it would have been "unbearable to the Japanese government and people to have had to express gratitude to the Triple Powers for having obtained compensation." Therefore it was decided to give up completely to the three powers, but not to give up at all to the Chinese. On May 5 Japan informed the three powers that she accepted the recommendation and renounced definitively the possession of the Liaotung peninsula, and on May 9 she received the congratulations of the three powers for acting in the interest of the general peace.[48]

This Japanese Foreign Office résumé was compiled from Japanese government documents which have since World War II been published in the *Nihon Gaikō Bunsho* (Japanese Foreign Affairs Documents) series.[49] Perusal of these documents indicates that the résumé portrays the course of events and the thinking of Japanese government leaders quite accurately, frequently employ-

[48] Archives, SP 5, pp. 446-504.

[49] Individual documents relating to the Triple Intervention may be found in NGB, XXVIII:1, under the heading "Concerning mediation by the Powers in the Sino-Japanese War," pp. 685-767 and in *ibid.*, XXVIII:2, under "The affair of the Three Power intervention," pp. 1-223.

ing the exact words of the documents. However, several additional points of information, which are of concern to this study, should be called to attention. First, the notorious assassination attempt on Li Hung-chang, which occurred at Shimonoseki on March 24, seriously embarrassed the Japanese government and placed its leaders on the defensive concerning Japan's reputation as a "civilized and progressive" nation. Although Japan's ministers abroad all reported no official condemnation of Japan for the incident, some press notices transmitted to Foreign Minister Mutsu were disturbing, such as one from Austria which said that Japan was "not yet a truly civilized nation. Japanese do not know the inviolability of hospitality as is proved by the attempts against the Russian Crown Prince and Li Hung-chang." And Aoki from Berlin reported all Europe to be "indignant at this barbarous outrage" and looking "with disdain on Japan's superficial civilization." He recommended that "full satisfaction be given immediately." Itō and Mutsu, feeling that definite evidence of Japan's sincerity in the negotiations must be given, beyond apologies and arranging the best possible medical treatment for Li, proposed to the cabinet that an armistice agreement, which Li had sought but which to that point Japan had refused, should be entered into. Military leaders were opposed, but Itō succeeded in convincing Yamagata, war minister, and Saigō Tsugumichi, navy minister, of the necessity of making this overture, and a formal armistice was concluded on March 30. It was to last until April 20, unless the peace negotiations were broken off in the meanwhile, and it included all fighting fronts except Formosa, which by omission was excepted. The news of the armistice was received abroad, Japan's representatives reported, "with genuine satisfaction."[50]

[50] Mutsu to Nishi (St. Petersburg), Aoki (Berlin), Sone (Paris), Ōyama (Vienna), Kurino (Washington), Katō (London), etc., Mar. 24, 1895, No. 1027: NGB, XXVIII: 2, pp. 292-93. Ōyama to Mutsu, Mar. 27: Aoki to Mutsu, Mar. 25; Nishi to Mutsu, Mar. 31, 1895, Nos. 1041, 1032, 1076: NGB, XXVIII:2, pp. 302, 295, 329. Sino-Japanese armistice, Mar. 30, 1895, No. 1071: *ibid.*, pp. 324-27. Tabohashi (1951), pp. 474-78. Kokuryūkai, *Nisshi* . . ., I, 324-28. The Russian crown prince assassination attempt had occurred at Ōtsu in 1891.

Secondly, a few additional remarks should be made about the Triple Intervention itself. The Foreign Office résumé, being more or less smoothly written, probably makes Japanese heads seem somewhat cooler than they were. The dispatches themselves abound with signs of alarm, worry, and indecisiveness, and sometimes show Japanese diplomats in rather comical aspect as they tried desperately to fathom changes in tone, conspicuous silences, and conflicting pieces of unofficial information. (For example, Katō in London tried to get the British foreign secretary to tell him whether the three powers were in earnest with their remonstrance. The latter responded, with a straight face presumably, that "some of his informants say yes and others no," which "fact" Katō duly reported.)[51] However, they seem to have gauged the situation rather accurately. Their idea that Germany had made a *volte-face* in backing up the Russian position is borne out by the Russian record of a basic policy meeting on the intervention.

At this meeting, Russian policy makers talked about the German "sudden change of views" and attributed this to commercial interests and the influence of Mr. Brandt, who had recently arrived at Berlin from Peking. (They did not, however, suggest the possibility that Germany was coming in to minimize the incidence of Franco-Russian co-operation.) Also, the Japanese estimate that there was a real possibility of Russian attack on the home islands unless the demands of the intervention were met is shown by this document to be correct. The Russians argued among themselves as to whether they would press the demand, with Grand Duke Admiral-General Alexis urging that "in no case" should hostilities be opened against Japan and Adjutant-General Obrucheff complaining that Russia was "secure neither in the West nor in Caucusus" and war would be "a great calamity for us." Privy Councillor Serge Witte, however, foresaw the day, if Japan were allowed to occupy southern Manchuria, "when the Mikado might become the Chinese Emperor and Russia would need hundreds of

[51] Katō to Mutsu, Apr. 25, 1895, No. 704: NGB, XXVIII:2, pp. 35-36.

thousands of troops and a considerable increase of her fleet for defense of her possessions and Siberian Railway." He insisted Russia must "decidedly declare" that she would not allow occupation of south Manchuria by Japan and that "in case of failure to realize our aim we should be compelled to take appropriate measures." He explained "appropriate measures" as "if Japan should not, contrary to our expectations, listen to our diplomatic insistence, our squadron must be ordered to open hostilities against the Japanese fleet and to bombard Japanese ports without occupying any points."

The conclusions of the conference indicate that Witte's thinking dominated the occasion: "... in the case of a determined refusal of Japan to follow our advice, to declare to the Japanese Government that we reserved for ourselves freedom of action and would act in conformity with our interests." Foreign Minister Lobanoff was so sure that this meant war that he hesitated four days in presenting the minute book to Tsar Nicholas. Then Nicholas, who, like Lobanoff, had been thinking in terms of letting the Japanese seizure of Liaotung go unchallenged and then seeking an east coast Korean port, called a palace meeting of Witte, Lobanoff, War Minister Vannovsky, and Grand Duke Alexis to discuss these conclusions. Witte "reiterated his opinion, the others raised very feeble objections or none at all, and in the last analysis Nicholas accepted Witte's proposal and then and there approved the minutes." Russia "faced war with Japan over Manchuria."[52] This determination of Russia to open hostilities if Japan did not assure full compliance with the intervention notices would seem to be further indicated by her refusal to give the slightest consideration to the

[52] Minutes on Meeting of Special Committee (Russian), April 11, 1895: Krazny Archiv, "First Steps of Russian Imperialism in Far East, 1888-1903," *Chinese Social and Political Science Review*, XVIII (1934–35), pp. 265-72. Lobanoff to Tsar, Apr. 15, 1895: *ibid.*, p. 265. B. A. Romanov, *Russia in Manchuria, 1892–1906* (trans. from the Russian by Susan Wilbur Jones) (Ann Arbor: J. W. Edwards, 1952), pp. 52-60, esp. pp. 57, 59. Miss Jones's translation is of the A. S. Enukidze Oriental Institute, Leningrad, 1928 edition, entitled *Rossiya v Manchzhurii.*

first—the "Chin-chou only"—Japanese reply, which preceded the final capitulation.[53]

Thirdly, what was Inoue's role relative to the Triple Intervention? Busy in Korea, he seems not to have had an active part as regards either the Shimonoseki negotiations or the pre-intervention plans of the Japanese cabinet. However, Mutsu informed him of the receipt of the intervention notices by telegraph shortly after they were received (April 23) and Inoue sent back his advice within forty-eight hours:

> Received your telegram regarding memorandum presented by Ministers of Russia, France, Germany. I fully conceive difficulty of your position. It need not be said that this is a moment which requires most mature counsel of our Government. I, for one, am of opinion that it would be better and after all more advantageous to confine our claims in [to] Formosa and indemnity, which must be increased. The result of the Berlin Congress on the Russian claim in Servia gives us sufficient warning in the present case. I can clearly see that such opinion will meet great opposition from military men, but I believe sincerely that such is to the interest of the country. I express my opinion to you. What is attitude of British government?[54]

After it was all over Mutsu informed him on May 15: "On May 9th the Ministers of Russia, France and Germany officially de-

[53] The actual Intervention notices are printed in the Japanese Foreign Office collection: NGB, XXVIII:2, pp. 14-17. As given there they are not quite identical, though all were received in Tokyo the same day, April 23. Hayashi, who received them at the Foreign Office, immediately transmitted an English translation of the Russian and French notices to Hiroshima, where the wartime government was sitting, and to Maiko, near Kobe, where Foreign Minister Mutsu lay ill. Hayashi added that the Russian minister, in delivering the note, had put a "special emphasis" on the word "definitive" in advising Japan to renounce possession of the peninsula of Liaotung. The abortive effort of the Japanese to obtain triple consent to their retaining the Chin-chou district (about one eighth of the total area) only is elaborated in several documents: e.g., Mutsu to Hayashi Nos. 748, 753: *ibid.*, pp. 63-65, 67. Japan's note of full compliance dated May 5, is to be found as No. 786: *ibid.*, pp. 81-82. The three powers' "congratulations," dated May 9, are Nos. 806, 807, 808: *ibid.*, pp. 98-99. Again these are not quite identical, but all pay tribute to the "wisdom" (Russia's the "high wisdom") of the Japanese government.

[54] Inoue to Mutsu, Apr. 25, 1895, No. 705: NGB, XXVIII:2, pp. 36-37.

clared that by renouncing definite possession of Feng Tien [Liaotung] Peninsula Japan has given new proof of her wisdom and expressed congratulations in interests of general peace."[55] It cannot be maintained that Inoue had a say in the decision of the Japanese cabinet to capitulate to the intervention if necessary, for his telegram of advice did not reach Mutsu until April 26, two days after the cabinet decision. But it is clear that his thinking coincided with theirs, and, that once he realized the problem of the larger frame of reference he became as concerned as they. Inoue's despair and "rheumatism" in May must therefore be placed in the setting that he now understood the necessity for and approved of the accent on caution.

Clearly Japan's leaders, including Inoue, became keenly alive to the fact that the eyes of the powers were upon them during the course of the Shimonoseki negotiations and they were genuinely frightened by the Triple Intervention. Was this fear of the powers then the basic factor in Inoue's inability to carry through his remodeling of Korea. The climate of conservatism it engendered was no doubt quite important in the reluctance of Tokyo to supply funds in sufficient amount to permit a maximum application of pressure in Korea. But was this really critical to the whole operation? Upon rereading the "cabinet declaration" of May 25, one would be tempted to say immediately that it was. According to that "decision" Japan abandoned completely the lone-hand approach to the sponsorship of Korean "independence and reform," which was an expression of "their readiness to co-operate with the other interested Powers in any measure having for its object the amelioration of the condition of the Peninsular Kingdom," and resting "their future relations with Corea upon their conventional rights."[56] It can certainly be said that the Japanese cabinet was sufficiently

[55] Mutsu to Inoue, May 15, 1895, No. 822: *ibid.*, p. 114.

[56] See above, note 40. A week before this "declaration" was drawn up, Foreign Minister Mutsu asked Katō in London whether he thought Britain would support a proposal for a joint guarantee by the powers of Korean independence. If such a guarantee were obtained, he said, Japan would at once withdraw her forces stationed there.

shaken by the Triple Intervention to *write down* a pronouncement of abandonment of Inoue's (and their) whole Korean remodeling effort.

However, this pronouncement was never issued. Mutsu comments on this in his general memorandum on Korean policy dated June 3:

> Last month on the 25th the Cabinet members who were in Tokyo met and drew up the attached declaration to send to various countries. I sent a telegram about this to Prime Minister Itō at Kyoto asking him to consult other Cabinet members in Kyoto and obtain the Emperor's approval. But Itō said the Emperor was coming home soon and we should wait until his arrival. But after that the French Minister suggested to me that we should coordinate everything regarding Korea with Russia. This suggestion of the French Minister's did not represent his Government's. He said he made it on behalf of the Russian Minister. Because of this we lost our opportunity to make the declaration. Also the Three Powers intervened regarding Liaotung. Now they are intervening about free passage around Taiwan. They bring up one problem after another. Certainly they will ask about Korean policy, so before another problem comes up we should decide whether to continue our policy without change [aforementioned Plan B of preceding August] or, leaving off interference, to return to a condition of ordinary treaty relations, conducted actively or passively. At any rate it is urgent that we decide on our objectives, so please obtain an Imperial decision.

An addenda to this document indicates that the policy decision Mutsu asked for was made the following day. But it was not so clear-cut as he had suggested it should be. The cabinet did not admit, even to itself, that the past year had represented any qualitative change in Japan's Korea policy. It decided that

> Japan's policy in the past has been to recognize Korean independence and to break down China's dependent country claim, making their

Katō expressed doubt that Britain would support this. Mutsu to Nabeshima (for Itō), draft instruction for Min. to England, May 18, 1895, No. 272: NGB, XXVIII:1, pp. 414-15. Mutsu to Katō, May 18, 1895, No. 277: *ibid.*, p. 419. Katō to Mutsu, May 19, 1895, No. 278: *ibid.*, pp. 419-20.

independence real. As a result of the war we caused China to recognize that Korea is completely independent and we also urged Russia to recognize their independence to us in name and in fact. Regarding this and based on our past policy we have made numerous pronouncements. Therefore our future Korean policy will have the objective of leaving off interference insofar as possible and causing Korea to stand up by herself. Thus it is decided to take up passive objectives. As a result of the above we shall not interfere strongly in Korean railroad and telegraph matters.[57]

This was the policy which Inoue came home to on his leave in June. Clearly the accent was on caution, but the oligarchs never strayed very far from that, and it is noteworthy that the idea of announcing to the world that Japan was retreating to ordinary treaty relationships was abandoned. Also the words "insofar as possible" could have a good deal of elasticity about them, if the situation in Korea seemed to promise results for more than "passive" measures. And the fact remains that there was no intervention on Korea, no Russian demand for half the country or even for a Korean port, no demand that Japan publicly and "definitively" renounce her occupation and control, as had been the case with Liaotung. Indeed the intervention on Liaotung, by bringing that area to the center of the diplomatic stage, very probably worked to leave Japan freer of interference by the powers in her Korean policy than she might otherwise have been. She could not, of course, annex Korea, but there is nothing to show that her policy makers had this in mind. Inoue's whole mission was predicated on the presumption that, if the Chinese hold were broken and Japan might have a reasonably free hand for a year or so, he could persuade the Korean government to move in a direction consonant with Japanese enlightened self-interest. There would be progress and improvement in it for Korea, as well as security for Japan. Undoubtedly, the climate of the Triple Intervention made Japan's policy makers feel inhibited about Korea to a certain extent, but not sufficiently to disrupt the program if Inoue had been able to sell it to the Koreans. Perhaps

[57] Mutsu to Itō, June 3, 1895, and addenda, No. 298: NGB, XXVIII:1, pp. 440-41.

the "petty" political shiftings at Seoul, which Inoue was so sure he could handle, were more fundamental to his failure than even the high tensions of international politics. It may be well, therefore, to review these from viewpoints other than Inoue's.

Sugimura's diary gives an interesting inside, and rather critical, account of Inoue's efforts to manipulate the political strings at Seoul. He says that the cabinet which Inoue sponsored, composed of the "old" Kim group and the "new" Pak group soon lost harmony. Pak did succeed in getting very close to the king and queen, for the king tried to use him as his messenger to Inoue and the queen tried to use him to curtail the power of the "old" group. Also, Japanese advisers, Saito as consultant to Pak himself and Hoshi Tōru as consultant to Minister of Justice So, worked to secure the ascendancy of their advisees and to defeat the "old" groups. They even circulated a rumor that the "old" group ministers would resign and that Pak would be the new prime minister. At one point the "old" group did resign, and Pak expected Inoue to have the king appoint him prime minister. However, Inoue urged the king not to accept the resignations, but to try to compose the friction. Pak began to feel less and less at ease. He told Sugimura that he actually owed his position to Inoue's power and the Japanese army. This was not good. "Inoue will be here only a few years and the army will leave. Then what will I depend on. Therefore I must increase my power, not only to keep my position but also to accomplish the reform of our country." Pak began increasing his power. He quarreled with his friend So, and when Inoue protected So he went to the king, obtained So's ouster and the appointment of a follower of his own as minister of justice. Inoue let this pass. Then Pak began to obtain the ouster of the "old" cabinet members one by one. Behind the scenes Saito and Hoshi were helping Pak. Finally when Prime Minister Kim resigned, Inoue became worried. He complained that everything "went too far" and that "no one listened to him." Saito and Hoshi urged that he might best go back to Japan before there was an explosion of some kind.

Inoue then decided to give full support to Pak's new cabinet and picked one Takana Kendō as his intermediary, instructing him to keep everything running smoothly. When Inoue left Seoul for Japan on June 7, Pak's position was very strong. He was "in charge." He told Sugimura that he liked Japanese business enterprise and Japanese help in improving the government administration but "I do not like to be interfered with on such matters as [appointments of] officials." He complained that there were getting to be too many Japanese advisers. "If this continues how will we be independent? Especially if other countries do the same. . . . The ex-Prime Minister had no backbone and bowed to foreign envoys [meaning Inoue, inserts Sugimura] so we must push out such boneless ministers." Thus Pak's attitude to the Japanese was becoming unfavorable. Meanwhile, the Pak group was dividing into two sections, one of which, good at the English language and having visited in the United States, was pro-American. This included Yi Wan-yong, now minister of education. However, Pak did not go along with these. He had been on good terms with Inoue when the latter left on his trip to Japan, seeing to the organization of a huge garden party honoring Inoue and "the first anniversary of Korean independence" on June 6, the day before Inoue's departure from Seoul, and he remained friendly with Saito and Hoshi. His relations with other Japanese (such as Sugimura?) was bad, but a Korean society to promote Japanese-Korean friendship was launched on June 23 and, though the pro-American group opposed this, Pak came "nearer and nearer Japanese ideas." Then an issue developed concerning court guards which estranged Pak and the king. There were some 700 or 800 such guards who had been trained "by American teachers" and another two battalions (about 800 men) called *Kunrentai* who had been drilled by Japanese. Pak recommended to the king that Kunrentai take over the entire court guard. At first the king made no objection, but then he refused, became angry at Pak, and decided to oust him. The underlying reason, Sugimura avers, was that the king had expected to use Pak to regain his own power, which had dwindled since the preceding summer, but that Pak had become very powerful, "like a dictator." Matters came to a climax in the early morning of July 7. To the Japanese legation came a message from the king carried by the foreign minister. Pak had been ousted the night before and ordered arrested.

I [Sugimura] was asked to order the Japanese not to help Pak. I was surprised at this quick turn of events. I said, "I am much surprised, but, of course, it concerns your internal affairs and I can't interfere. I'll do my best to notify Japanese not to help Pak, but it is so sudden. . . ." The King's messenger (Foreign Minister) said all right and was about to leave when suddenly there was a noise at the door and someone rushed in. It was Pak. The Foreign Minister left. Pak came in and I asked, "What are you going to do?" Pak said, "I must go to Japan." I said, "All right," and hid him upstairs. Then I sent for Saito and Hoshi, but they did not come. Okamoto came. It was already 6:00 A.M. and fifty or sixty policemen came into my office. The chief asked for Pak. I refused. They sat down to wait. About 7:00 we prepared to guard Pak, but neither Saito nor Hoshi came. I sent Okamoto to get them. Finally they came. We could think of no good plan so we decided to send Pak to Inchon. We had some plain clothed Japanese policemen and about ten of our legation guards take Pak out the back gate and taking a side road . . . to Inchon. Passing Seoul gate there were placards of the King ordering Pak's arrest. People threw stones but the party passed safely.

After Pak's departure, Sugimura went to the palace several times, exchanging "polite words," but the king issued a message saying "it is regrettable that the Japanese legation helped Pak." Then came word of Inoue's return. The king said he was glad, but really he was afraid. There was a rumor that Inoue would lead a three-thousand-man army to punish those responsible for the Pak affair. "But, contrary to the Koreans' expectation, Inoue led no Japanese army. He led only his wife. Some Japanese thought that Inoue would go to court and shake the King's neck, but, on the contrary, he was calm. . . ." Inoue had found that his first plan had been too radical. Before he left for Japan he talked to the king for a long while. The king told him that the Taewongun was always anti-foreign, but the Min were not. The Min were friendly to Japan, but Japan had refused them. This was "upside down." While in Japan, Inoue thought this over . . . "when he returned he caressed the King." He promised the king that the Japanese government would send him 3,000,000 yen secretly, and became friendly with many of the king's and queen's followers. "His office was crowded with visitors from the Palace." After his return from Japan Inoue decided not to talk about politics with Korean ministers, except one who was very close to the king and queen. This alienated the reformers. The friends of Pak were angry. "Yesterday Inoue was the friend of the reform party, but today he is the friend of the king." Seeking favor from the court, he alienated his friends and they became his enemies. His main business was now transmitting money to the king, and sending his relatives to Japan for study. Twenty Mins, aged 20 to 35, were sent to Japan for study. But the cabinet was ignored. Then Miura came. He told Inoue that no money was coming. Inoue was "dismayed."[58] It seems clear from this résumé of his comments that Sugimura was not impressed with Inoue's handling of affairs.

American Minister Sill's observations on some of these events help to round out the story of Inoue's difficulties. On March 1, 1895, he reported "political deadlock" in the cabinet. Pak Young-hyo was the "chief villain." He had been raised up to minister of home affairs by the Japanese, but the queen "who is very clever" had made him "quite her tool." He was refusing to accede to "certain great concessions for railways proposed by Count Inouye." The anti-Japanese hated him; now the Japanese might desert him. The Taewongun party was plotting, becoming stronger. The king was insisting confidentially that Russia intended soon to come to his assistance. On April 3, Sill reported a projected Japanese loan to

[58] The above is the author's résumé of pp. 589-694 of Sugimura's Diary, Archives, PVM 3.

Korea, three million yen which Korea needed with "great urgency." But the Japanese were trying to compel Koreans to take paper yen, "useless here." The Korean government objected so strongly that "the Japanese gave them 1,500,000 yen in silver." Later that month he described "Japanese methods." The Japanese were very "petty" regarding the king's finances, allowing him only $5000 salary (silver) and $500,000 for the whole royal household. They were demanding concessions in return for loans: "railroads for fifty years, telegraphs for twenty-five years, postal services for five years." But Pak, the "ex-refugee" who was now home minister, was giving the Japanese much trouble. He had become "virtual dictator," and he seemed "to have a sincere regard for his own country" and to "resent Japan's attempts to take everything to herself."

In his next report Sill discussed the arrest of the grandson of the Taewongun for treasonable plots, and observed that the plots were probably the Taewongun's own, but that the government was "afraid to arrest the old man because he has what the Japanese party sadly lack, viz. a strong Korean following." The king and his government were "mere tools or toys" of the Japanese. But shortly thereafter Sill sent in a list of eighty-eight reforms which Home Minister Pak had ordered instituted through Korea. Some were very impressive. Number 87 said, "Particulars of the assistance rendered by Japan in securing our independence should be circulated among the people." On May 25 he reported the resignation of Prime Minister Kim, leaving Pak acting Prime minister as well as home minister. However, Inoue "once all for the progressives" was now "backing the conservatives," for the progressives were "resisting Japanese demands."

Shortly thereafter Sill joined with the representatives of other Western nations in Seoul to send a joint note to the Korean minister of foreign affairs "aimed against the attempts of the Japanese to get control of everything of value in this country." (The State Department reprimanded him for this and for a reference he made to encouraging Korea "to resist the onerous demands of her oppressors".) On June 7, following the garden party, Sill reported that though Pak Chung-yang, former minister to the United States, was the new prime minister, Pak Young-hyo was the "virtual dictator." The party, planned by Young-hyo to honor Inoue and the first anniversary of "independence," had been something of a "mixup" because foreign representatives, including Sill, refused to admit that Korea had become "independent" as recently as a year ago. (Acting Secretary of State Adee approved his stand on this, noting that the United States had accepted Korean independence "as a fact" since 1882.) Also Sill had heard that Inoue had denounced Pak Young-hyo to the king as a "dangerous person," which, if such a denunciation occurred, must have produced some tension between party host and honored guest. "Pak," concluded Sill, was "really a Korean at heart." Horace N. Allen, Sill's secretary of legation, summed up a year's Japanese politicking at Seoul in a dispatch to the secretary of state, dated September 18, 1895, the day after Inoue, having been relieved by Miura, departed Korea. At first, Allen observed, Ōtori had humiliated the king by calling in the Taewongun and making him "practically dictator of public affairs." The Taewongun "repaid this favour by intriguing against Japan." Then Inoue had rejected the Taewongun, forced the queen aside and "forced upon the King the exiled Pak Young-hyo." At first Inoue had been friendly with this (the American) legation, but then was persuaded by Pak Young-hyo's group to a "different course." Kim Hong-chip, the prime minister, was of the Taewongun's party but Pak won supremacy. Then came "chaos." Inoue began to favor the Taewongun party again and denounced Pak. Then he went to Japan. When he returned, he tried to be "very conciliatory to all."[59]

[59] Résumé of information in the following documents: Sill to Sec. State, Mar. 1, Apr. 3, Apr. 17, Apr. 29, May 10, May 11, May 25, June 7, 1895, Nos. 94, 103, 107, 108, 110, 111, 115, 120; Allen to Sec. State, Sept. 18, 1895, No. 146; Olney to Sill June 21 and Adee to Sill, July 9, 1895, Nos. 83, 87, Instructions: Dipl. Desp., Korea. Also in George McCune Document Collection on Korea (microfilm).

Reading between the lines of these analyses, one may conclude that Inoue's difficulties in the Seoul political arena came from the fact that, however forward looking some of the reforms he sought to introduce, and however able, enthusiastic, and friendly to Japan his reform leader, Pak, might be, the whole program was after all more concerned with Japanese advantage than with Korean. And Pak, in common with king, queen, Taewongun, and all the others, was "really a Korean at heart." The dilemma inherent in this situation was undoubtedly more fundamental than the political twistings which showed on the surface. That the Japanese were not fully aware of this at this stage is clear. Very likely, the home oligarchs, and even Inoue himself, would have considered interference or the threat of interference by the powers the greater problem at the time. But a decade later, we shall see, though the powers ceased to interfere, the Koreans still could not be persuaded. This phenomenon will be discussed presently, but before closing the chapter on Japan's effort to remodel Korea during the Sino-Japanese War it is necessary to discuss the last act, which we may entitle "descent of realism"—to Miura, murder, and fiasco.

In the early morning hours of October 8, 1895, hardly a month after Miura assumed the post of minister to Korea and only three weeks after Inoue left the country, Japanese and Korean cutthroats entered the palace in darkness, cut down Queen Min and several of her attendants, and burned the queen's body in the courtyard outside after saturating it with oil. This was murder of the most heinous kind, planned in advance, perpetrated against a defenseless woman in her own apartments, and climaxed by the hideous body's burning on the lawn. Such an act must be adjudged utterly indefensible by even the minimum standards of civilized society. Even the most loosely constructed laws of war, the direst necessities of diplomatic intrigue, the most insistent demands of national security cannot excuse such murder most foul. Even primitive people recoil from such deeds, and neither the Japanese nor the Korean perpetrators can be excused on the ground of being primitives. However, the undeniable guilt of those individuals who were involved in the plot should not blind us to its broader implications. The fact that the duly accredited Japanese minister to Korea, Viscount Miura Gorō, and the first secretary of the Japanese Legation in Seoul, Sugimura Fukashi, were indisputably among those involved raises (or lowers) this to the level of national crime. But beyond that, considered against the background of the policies, attitudes, and concerns of the highest officials of the Japanese government, which have been defined, we think with good reason, as careful, cautious, reasonably enlightened, "realistic" nation state diplomacy, based upon a perfectly understandable quest for national security, the question must be asked whether such villainy is not a natural and almost automatic result of this practice of "realism" in international relations.

Of course, the case of the murder of the Korean queen could not be held to support an affirmative answer to this question if those high officials of the Japanese government who planned Korean policy could be shown to have been in fact a gang of conspirators and murderers, who having seized the machinery of government in Japan, used it to promote acts of criminal intent such as self-enrichment, enslavement, and aggression. Nor could it support an affirmative answer if the responsibility could be shown to have lain wholly with Miura and the others directly involved, if they had willfully and deliberately disobeyed the instructions of their government or engaged in acts utterly reprehensible to it. Then they would be the conspirators and murderers, and the government which they represented, by clearly disowning and disavowing them, would relieve itself and its policy of responsibility for the dastardly deed. In either of these cases the conspiracy could be fixed on individuals operating outside the law and custom of civilized society, and no question of national crime or "automatic result" from a type of approach to the conduct of international relations could be deduced. However, if no conspiracy can be clearly discerned, if, on the contrary, Japan's ordinary diplomatic business-as-usual led directly and naturally into such criminality, then the element of national crime would seem to be present. And if Japan's "ordinary diplomatic business-as-usual" is found to have been based upon attitudes and objectives common to nations at large, including "good" nations, like the United States, then these attitudes and objectives would seem to deserve the sharpest critical scrutiny.

In this latter regard it is interesting and ironic that a precedent for ousting an obstreperous queen was set two years previously in another small and backward monarchy, namely the Kingdom of Hawaii. There in January, 1893, Liliuokalani was ousted from her throne by a coup d'état in which the minister of the neighboring power, anxious presumably to promote progress and modernization in the kingdom and the security of his own nation, figured prominently. This was American Minister John L. Stevens. In many respects the cases are strikingly similar, even to the personalities of the two queens involved—Liliuokalani, author of the beautiful and plaintive song "Aloha Oe," a well-educated and talented woman "in the full vigor of mature womanhood," and Queen Min, "a striking figure and even at fifty four positively beautiful when her dark eyes flashed and a smile appeared on her pale thin face" and yet "the only man in the [Korean] royal family." Both were weighed down with political and family problems to which they applied backward-looking rather than progressive measures.[60] As to the ministers involved in these respective cases, Stevens and Miura, both were recalled and their deeds disavowed by their home governments, though both kingdoms were later annexed by the respective powers. However, in one respect the two cases are strikingly different. Liliuokalani was not murdered and her body burned on an oil-soaked pyre. The worst that happened to her was house arrest, and her supporters, though convicted of treason by a military commission manned by the

[60] See Ralph S. Kuykendall and A. Grove Day, *Hawaii: A History* (New York: Prentice-Hall, 1948), pp. 174-79 and Harrington, *God, Mammon . . .*, pp. 264-71.

conspirators and given heavy sentences, including death, were all pardoned. Why? Were these American conspirators gentler by nature than their Japanese counterparts; did something in their tradition and training stay their hands? Or was it merely that Liliuokalani gave up more easily than Queen Min, or that Hawaii at that stage was not so vital to American security as was Korea to Japan?[61] These are extremely difficult questions. Perhaps they can be further explored in the conclusions to this study. However, our immediate task is to probe the question of responsibility for the murder of Queen Min and its implications.

First, was there a conspiracy at high policy levels, involving the Japanese cabinet? Factors of past policy and continuity of personnel would seem to say no. The dominant cabinet ministers, Itō, Matsukata, Mutsu, Yamagata, Saigō Tsugumichi, and Inoue, who should be included with these, had long since established patterns of caution in international affairs and in Korean relations. Mutsu and Saigō, it is true, had favored the elder Saigō's adventurous ideas in the 1870's, but the price of their admission to the inner circle of the oligarchy had been cautious policy, and the others were firmly grounded in the tradition of Ōkubo and Iwakura. Their record of years of attention to the Korean problem said that they would not gamble everything, including Japan's international reputation, on the murder of a queen. Of course, Mutsu as foreign minister was relatively inactive because of his illness. His place had been taken by Saionji, a young blue blood with foreign experience who was in fact becoming Ito's protégé and who would not be likely to rock the boat. Gotō Shōjirō, lately an anti-government leader of the Liberal party, who was now a member of the cabinet as minister of agriculture, would seem to be the most likely suspect. He had been involved in the background of the 1884 Incident. He was more expansionist minded than the others and was critical of the capitulation to the Triple Intervention, but he had been

[61] Cf. the "stage of civilization" question, p. 152 above. On the "treason" trials in Hawaii, see Kuykendall and Day, *op. cit.*, pp. 185-86.

tempered by government service. He seems to have had little influence regarding Korean policy, perhaps because of his earlier foolishness, and there is nothing to indicate that he urged this plot on the other cabinet ministers or organized it behind their backs.

The cabinet had reset Korean policy in the cautious mode as recently as June 4, 1895, and this author has found no evidence that the decisions on that occasion were reversed at the cabinet level in the interval before the murder took place on October 8. It may be asked why then, if a relatively passive policy was to be kept in effect, should a man who turned out to be so much an activist as Miura have been put in charge of the Seoul legation? There is no clear answer to this, although certain bits of evidence may be pieced together. Inoue's efforts to manipulate the various groups at Seoul into a significant reorganization of the political and financial structure of the Korean government had bogged down in frustration. Japanese influence was still large, but its most promising area of advancement lay in the further development of the Kunrentai, the Japanese-trained body of Korean troops. Miura, a military man, might supervise this. Otherwise, there was little to be done and a holding operation was the most the Japanese could hope for. There was no need to waste Inoue's time on this. The significant diplomacy was being done in Tokyo, and a man of stern countenance, like Miura, by glowering at the Koreans, could presumably keep them relatively cowed. Miura outlined his ideas on Korea to the cabinet before proceeding to take up his post. He said there were three possible policies. (1) Japan, having brought about the independence of Korea by the victory over China, might protect and reform Korea "by our own power." This was the best policy, but it was very difficult, would require money and manpower. However, if Japan were patient, the world might "after several years" accept the idea of Korea's being under Japanese protection. (2) Japan might protect Korea in concert with the "impartial Powers of Europe and America," but in such a case must be careful to avoid the breakup of Korea into parts, and safeguard the interests of Japanese people versus foreigners. (3) Japan might share the occupation of Korea with one strong country (Russia) in which case everything should wait upon making agreement with her after which there could be strong action. He said he did not care which policy was followed, but he wished to be instructed because otherwise, since he was not so talented or such a good diplomat as Inoue, he could only "drift with the wind."[62]

The author could find no definite instruction in answer to this. However, Saionji afterwards, in explaining the situation surrounding Miura's appointment to Japan's overseas ministers resident, says that before sending Miura to Korea he "warned" him that relations with the powers relative to the Liaotung intervention and Formosa were unsettled and it would be very bad to complicate matters by arousing suspicious about Japan's handling of the Korean problem. "In spite of this Minister Miura went against our Government's intention and did the things I have discussed. I am so surprised that I cannot stop being surprised. The reasons for his doing these things are set forth in the attached document (D), but since he acted contrary to Government instructions, we have no alternative but to punish him according to law. . . . Concerning the Incident, of course our Government had no connection with it and Minister Miura acted in complete disobedience to his instructions. . . ." While this is an after-the-event protestation by the acting foreign minister, there would seem to be no reason for doubting its sincerity. The communication was clearly for purposes of explication to Japan's overseas diplomats, not propaganda for the outside world. It bears the classification "secret" and it discusses the process by which the involvement of Miura and other Japanese legation officials in the murder came to light, along with the quoted comments about the minister's violation of his government's "intention" and "instructions."[63] In addition, other

[62] Miura Gorō, statement of opinion regarding Korean policy, Aug. 7, 1895, No. 350: NGB, XXVIII:1, pp. 482-84. Cf. McKenzie, *The Tragedy of Korea*, p. 58.

[63] Saionji to Overseas Ministers, Nov. 8, 1895, No. 430: NGB, XXVIII:1, pp. 566-68.

documents from Tokyo demanding information and explanations, particularly one from Inoue to Sugimura, indicate that the home government was genuinely surprised at the turn of events.[64] It can therefore be said with fair certainty that there was no conspiracy at high policy levels whereby Miura was secretly instructed to take such violent measures.

Then the second question, was there conspiracy on the local level at the Japanese legation in Seoul? We shall answer immediately that there was and we shall trace its development from inside Japanese sources. In doing so, however, we shall leave open for the moment the question of whether the existence of this local conspiracy against the intention and instructions of the Japanese government thereby absolves that government and its long-range policy from blame. Our best source on the development of the conspiracy is again Sugimura's diary. The Japanese legation secretary was involved in it up to his ears and, notwithstanding, he has left a perfectly frank account of its development. The following is a summary of his account.

After Inoue left Korea the friendship between the Korean court and the Japanese legation "totally cooled." Court officials who formerly came to the legation ceased to come and at the same time the court began to destroy the new regime and the new army. First they destroyed the financial structure. At the time of the compilation of 1895 finance measures they had followed the advice of the Japanese adviser, Nio, but now they declared many taxes as court assets, tried to control the mint, etc. Secondly, they destroyed the legal procedures regarding appointment of officials. The court "grasped power even down to small officials." They issued rescripts under the signature of the minister of the imperial household. Thirdly, they began to destroy the cabinet system, making changes by court order in early October, and, fourthly, they began to destroy the new military structure, wherein Korean troops had been trained by Japanese officers. A new commander of these

[64] Inoue to Sugimura, Oct. 8, 1895, No. 356: *ibid.*, p. 492.

troops was appointed, a favorite of the court, but he was unable to get more than nominal control of the troops. Then there was a rumor that the troops would be ordered to disperse.

The reason the court became so arrogant has already been related. (Checking back on this to an earlier part of the diary, we find the following:) The queen had succeeded in completely breaking the power of the Taewongun in April and May, 1895, and had proceeded to use the reformer Pak for a time. But Pak and her Min family came to odds and Pak was forced to flee. She and the Min then turned against Japan and began to rely on Russian and American groups. The American palace adviser LeGendre and the Russian Waeber became her friends. The Russian minister had tried for ten years to get into collaboration with the court. The American minister said that if Korea suffered America would help her, but "actually his only intention was to protect Americans." However, American missionaries were close to the court and got the American minister to help. Thus the court got secret advice from the American and Russian ministers. Russian prestige went up as a result of the Triple Intervention. The queen was superficially friendly to Japan during Inoue's second stay.

(Then Sugimura resumes the story:) Both Japanese and Koreans feared the arrogant attitude of the Korean court and wondered how it would end. "It seemed to me" that there existed a deep connection between the court and the Russian minister. According to the investigation of a detective it seems that in early July, 1895, when the court decided to dispose of Pak, there was a confidential promise between the court and the Russian minister. The queen's ministers talked confidentially to him and he replied through the American LeGendre:

> The Queen and the Min are one and they are incompatible with the Japanese. Though Japan and Korea are neighbors they are divided by sea. On the contrary Russia and Korea are real neighbors, joined by land. Russia is the most powerful nation in the world and Japan cannot be compared with her. This fact is shown by Japan's having to return

the Liaotung Peninsula this spring. Russia will never impair Korean independence, so if Korea would rely on Russia, it would become very safe. Also Russia is an absolute monarchy and so, with their example, can protect the Korean sovereign.

The above information came from a "secret report from Korean sources." Later the queen often said such things as the Japanese and the Min are incompatible, there must be revenge against Japan, Russia is the strongest country in the world, and we must rely on Russia. "Thus the account of the Russian minister's secret words would seem to be true." However, the second coming of Inoue postponed her plans a little while. Then Inoue returned to Japan. Meanwhile, the number of Koreans who deplored the situation and foresaw the danger of national ruin gradually increased. Almost all said that the real intention of the court was first of all to dissolve the Kunrentai, then assassinate members of the cabinet and restore the dictatorship of the Min family. It was said that the court had already made a secret pact with the Russian minister to lease a northern port to Russia. Koreans who opposed these things began to gather around the Taewongun and seek his participation in the court. Those Koreans who wanted the Taewongun back in the court could be divided into three groups: the cabinet group, the Pak group, and the Taewongun group. A Japanese, Asayama Kenzō, who had connections with Pak and honestly wished to bring forth the Taewongun, formed a secret connection with the latter.

(Sugimura continues:)

In late September one of the Koreans Yi Shu-kai called on me late at night three different times. He was indignant and angry and said there was no other way to get relief than to push up the Taewongun. I [Sugimura] said the Taewongun's character was changeable. He said that the Taewongun would never bother Japan again. However, I gave no hint as to whether he could expect help or not. Another Korean, Cho, came and talked the same way. Meanwhile there were rumors of an impending coup by the Taewongun. After consultation with Okamoto

[Ryunosuke] I secretly dispatched Suzuki Junken to the home of the Taewongun to explore the latter's ideas. He reported that the Taewongun was indignant at the state of affairs in Korea but did not seem so indignant as to be planning a coup. . . . Various Japanese advisers in the Government reported that reforms were failing because of interference by the Court and they asked Minister Miura's help. He saw the King twice, but without result. At that time I said to Nio and the other advisers that we were in a desperate situation, which required the utmost determination. At the end of September Deputy Consul Horiguchi saw the Taewongun and brought a message from him. I took Horiguchi into Miura's office where we both heard the words of the Taewongun as entrusted to Horiguchi. In brief the message was that the present situation was ominous, that the Taewongun bitterly criticized Former Minister Inoue, considering his policies responsible, and wished to see Mr. Miura personally to discuss ways to save the situation.

Miura did not answer, but after Horiguchi left the room he said to me [Sugimura] that when he left Tokyo he had expected no incident until at least January or February but now an incident "is right before my eyes . . ." On October 1 or 2 Mr. Miura said that he thought he should reply to the message from the Taewongun brought by Horiguchi the other day. If the Taewongun were really big enough to stand up, how would it be to assist him. I replied that the Taewongun was very power hungry and very changeable, therefore not to be relied on in important things. We had bitter experience in that last year. Mr. Miura then asked if there was any other means than assisting him. I replied that there was none. The Minister said that if things go on as they are we will have to watch sitting down while Russia takes Korea. The demerits of the Taewongun could be controlled later. I replied that in an emergency it might be all right to assist the Taewongun, but that first we should get a severe promise from him, and drew up an agreement as follows: the Taewongun should assist the King only in Court affairs, not political matters and should not interfere with promotions etc. of government officials; reformist people should be allowed to take the lead in political affairs and, listening to Japanese advisers, should reform the administration and make the independence of Korea firm; the eldest grandson of the Taewongun should become Minister of the King's Household; the Taewongun's youngest grandson should study in Japan for three years. . . . Then Mr. Miura asked whether he should dispatch Horiguchi with this plan in his pocket and have him conspire with the Taewongun. I replied that Horiguchi was too young, that the Taewongun would never reveal his mind to him. Rather the most dependable person was Okamoto Ryunosuke. Miura said, "Well then, invite Okamoto and I'll confer with him. . . ."

At a meeting at the Legation three days later the matter was explained to Okamoto and he was asked to go and see the Taewongun. He accepted, and, after reading the four points, he urged small amendments. . . . Okamoto returned from the Taewongun and reported that he had had a long conversation with him and his grandsons, that he had been glad to agree with the secret promises and had so written with a brush. Okamoto had told him to wait until the time comes. Now we conferred at the Japanese legation as to how to assist the Taewongun. It was outlined that we should stimulate the Kunrentai and Korean adventurers to form a connection with the Taewongun and that we should direct them from behind the scenes. I said that formerly Pak had tried to exchange the Kunrentai and the Court guards but had failed due to the Court's taking the initiative. Now if we waited, the Court would dissolve the Kunrentai. . . . Therefore it was necessary to determine the date of the uprising and prepare for it. We conferred and set the date as October 10, and as for its preparation I daresay I planned it myself. It was decided that Okamoto, under pretense of going back to Japan, would go to Inchon and await a telegram to return. He left Seoul on the 6th. Also on the 6th Minister Miura conferred with Lt. Colonel Kususe, adviser to the Kunrentai, and told him to go to Inchon, under guise of returning to Japan, and await orders. There were rumors of quarrels between Korean police and Kunrentai, rumors which were actually circulated by the Court in order to obtain a reason for dissolving the Kunrentai. Japanese officers visited their barracks and found them calm. . . . At 11:00 A.M. on the 7th the Korean War Minister came to the Legation and said that as the Kunrentai had shown signs of unrest and attacked the police, the King wished to dissolve the corps. Minister Miura said that our officers had investigated the police affair and found it to be a false rumor, probably a pretext of the Court, and that our officers had trained the Kunrentai very well. . . . After leaving Miura the War Minister told me that the King's instructions included also a second point which he had not dared to mention to Miura, namely that the King intended to invite Min Yong-ik to take control of affairs at the Court, which had recently been in turmoil. Then I said I would convey the information, then at 12:20 noon talked to Mayahara, commander of Japanese troops in Seoul. I said, "The situation is imminent and we had better not wait until the 10th. Is your preparation good?" He said, "Good."

After lunch I discussed matters with Miura. He said we should temporarily approve the appointment of Min, "But the time is imminent. If we lose an hour the Court may take the initiative. We had better do it tomorrow as you advise. . . ." Three telegrams were sent to Okamoto at Inchon before a reply was finally received about 4:00 P.M. Then plans were begun. Okamoto was to be back in Seoul by 12:00 midnight or 1:00 A.M. and meet the Taewongun. Meanwhile Mayahara would have Japanese officers manipulate the Kunrentai. At about 2:00 A.M. the 2nd Battalion of the Kunrentai would be dispatched to welcome the Taewongun. Other Kunrentai troops would wait at the Palace grounds to protect his entrance to the Palace. The 1st Battalion, under pretence of protecting the Court would enter the Palace with him. Asayama Kenzō would manage Koreans under Yi Shu-kai, go to the Taewongun's house and facilitate the entrance of Okamoto there, avoiding any Korean guards. . . .

Before this time we occasionally cabled the Foreign Minister in Tokyo that the situation was gradually coming to a head, but received no reply. Inoue cabled Miura that he should go to the Palace and see the King and Queen and have them control the arrogance of the Court, but his advice seemed ineffective. Therefore we cabled Inoue that we were not sure whether an incident could be avoided.

During the evening [of October 7] Minister Miura became worried as to whether the Koreans could get into the Palace under their own power and decided to ask Kunitomo [Shigeakira] and Adachi [Kenzo] to bring about ten Japanese adventurers to assist the Koreans. I talked to Adachi and said that if Japanese adventurers join the Taewongun they should be attired in Korean costumes and preferably they should not enter the Palace; or if they do enter the Palace, they should be out by dawn so that foreigners would remain unaware of our connection with the affair. Adachi agreed. That night Miura was invited to dinner by Consul Uchida and I went to my residence. During the night Okamoto returned from Inchon, met the Taewongun, and at 3:00 A.M. on October 8 left the latter's residence for the Palace, protected by Kunrentai men. At dawn they entered the Palace.

Postscript. The Incident was inevitable under the stress of the situation and I cannot say that I was not one of the planners. No, I was really at the center of the planning. By my first plan Japanese were not to be used in the uprising, reliance on the Kunrentai being preferred. Only Okamoto, Asayama and an interpreter with each battalion were to be involved. Also my plan sought to guard against the Taewongun's intrusion into political affairs and expected to obtain the satisfaction of the Queen and Crown Prince by keeping out the grandson of the Taewongun. But the outcome was different from my first purpose . . . Japanese and Koreans became unrestrained and did things on their own. Thus some fifty or sixty participated. This was unexpected. And the Japanese connection could not be hidden. Though the situation was unavoidable I rather regret what happened myself.[65]

Other documents add little to this. The record of the trial of Miura, Sugimura, Okamoto, and forty-five other Japanese involved in the murder, which was held at Hiroshima in January, 1896, brings out these same circumstances in less detail. The Japanese newspaper *Jiji Shimpō* in reporting the trial gave a detailed recapitulation of the incident, adding one point which Sugimura does not quite make clear, namely that Miura and Okamoto specifically suggested the murder of the queen as an object of the coup. "To cut the evil root of twenty years," said Miura, "the Queen should be disposed of when you enter the Palace." And Okamoto, as director of the entering party, gave orders that the "fox be disposed of."[66]

[65] Sugimura Diary, Archives, PVM 3, pp. 709-57.

[66] Jan. 23, 1896. An official account of the trial appears in the Foreign Office archives materials as an attached document to Sugimura's Diary, PVM 3, pp. 758-98. A full text in English is printed as an appendix to McKenzie's *The Tragedy of Korea*, pp. 263-68. A report from Inoue Kaoru given to the American minister at Tokyo, Dun, is reproduced in Treat, *Dipl. Rel. . . .*, *1895–1905*, pp. 9-10. H. N. Allen reported in Allen to Sec. State, Oct. 10, 1895, No. 156: Dipl. Desp., Korea (also in McCune Document Collection). Cf. Harrington, *op. cit.*, pp. 268-74.

To their superiors in Tokyo, Miura and Sugimura acknowledged their complicity by stages after the incident. Their first reports, sent from Seoul and received in Tokyo on the eighth, tried to pretend innocence without actually lying. Sugimura wired Inoue that there was "no evidence of Japanese troops urging the Kunrentai," that "among the counselors Okamoto might have had some slight connection with the Taewongun," that "secret envoys came [to the legation] from the Taewongun but the Minister rejected them," and that the queen was "probably" murdered. Miura reported the incident to Saionji as if it were exclusively the work of the Korean "training troops" (Kunrentai) and the Taewongun. "Our guard troops" were only "trying to calm things down." There was a "small clash" between them and Korean training troops. "Only two shots" were fired. "Both the King and the Crown Prince" were "safe." The queen's whereabouts "only" was "not clear." The "reason" for the incident was that the "training troops" heard that "their arms would be taken away," their force "dissolved," and their chief "punished."

However, late that night, Miura dispatched two more telegrams in response to pointed demands from Saionji and Inoue for information on the extent of Japanese participation in the incident, whether "secretly or openly." In one, he summed up the events of the day in terms of his conversations with foreign envoys in Seoul. The Russian minister had called and said "over thirty people were seen in Japanese civilian clothes with swords," some of whom "were seen to enter the Queen's palace, bring out a woman, drag her into the garden and murder her with swords." But "I [Miura] said that no Japanese troops guarded the Taewongun and there is nothing about the murder of the Queen in the report of the leader of our guard troops who went out to calm things. Regarding Japanese civilians with swords, I have no idea. Perhaps there were some rebels." The Russian minister said, "There are witnesses. . . ." In the other telegram, Miura said that he was answering specifically the "telegraphic order" of Saionji "to investigate whether or not Japanese participated in the morning's incident." They had, he admitted. "This incident was made by Koreans on the surface, but in the background Japanese participated more or less. And in fact I [Miura] winked at it." He explained his reason as follows:

> The Kunrentai, trained by us, was going to be dissolved. If this situation were left untouched, Korea would move away from Japan and all the works done by our country during the last year would end in failure, so I believed. Therefore . . . a crisis . . . Kunrentai angry. It became clear that they had the desire to use the Taewongun to advantage. . . . The Queen has always had a tendency to rely on other countries. Thus even if we assist her, she is a bag without a bottom. But the Taewongun is different. There need be no fear that he will be dependent on Russia or America. He is a bag with a bottom. Through him a solid foundation of government may be made and Korean independence accomplished. This is why I winked and let them go ahead. But our troops went out truly for the purpose of calming the Incident and did not once assist them. However, by request through private channels, some Japanese were enrolled as guards for the Taewongun on his way to the Palace. Even these merely guarded, did not do violence.[67]

On October 14 Miura explained his "winking" directly to Prime Minister Itō in a long dispatch in which he reviewed the course of the queen's seizure of power after Inoue's return to Japan. He said she had been "planning to murder members of pro-Japanese parties," and admitting that the "action taken by me was unskillful," suggested that "if it caused any inconvenience in diplomacy, you may change the personnel of the Legation beginning with me." But he expressed "the profound desire" that the "objective" not be changed. And on November 5 Consul Uchida Sadatsuchi at Seoul sent a detailed account of the whole episode to Saionji in which he said very definitely that "the Incident derived from a joint plan by the Taewongun and Minister Miura . . .

[67] Sugimura to Inoue, Miura to Saionji, Inoue to Sugimura, Saionji to Miura, Miura to Saionji, all dated Oct. 8, 1895, numbered respectively 357, 354, 356, 353, 359: NGB, XXVIII:1, pp. 491-92, 494-95. Miura to Saionji, Oct. 9, 1895, No. 358: *ibid.*, pp. 493-94.

Japanese were induced to participate directly or indirectly by Miura, and Sugimura worked to make the arrangements."[68]

So much for the admissions of guilt from the Japanese legation at Seoul. Clearly Minister Miura and his subordinates were at the heart of a local conspiracy. Does this, taken together with the absence of conspiracy on the upper, cabinet, echelon, mean that Japan's policy in the large is thereby exonerated? The answer must be "no." True, Japanese policy makers did not plan murder, nor even a seizure of power by violent coup. True also, Miura and his subordinates were recalled to Japan, and "by order of the Emperor" arrested upon arrival and made to stand trial in Hiroshima District Court.[69] And true, the Japanese government sent a trusted Foreign Office official, Komura Jutaro, to Korea to make a thorough and honest investigation of the affair, "getting opinions not only of Japanese legation personnel and important Japanese residents but also those of Korean government officials, foreign legations and important foreign residents," and they sent Count Inoue back to Seoul as imperial representative to "comfort Korea and say that it was regrettable that Japanese had participated in the Incident."[70]

Miura, Sugimura, *et al* were not convicted, however. Perhaps the judge surrendered his judgment to narrow nationalism, but perhaps not. It may have been a sense of poetic justice that caused him to make no distinction between the "good" policies of the government and the "bad" actions of Miura. After all, had not Miura merely plunged unafraid into the sewer that lay at the end of policy's highroad? In this connection it is most interesting that Komura, who was appointed minister to succeed the discredited Miura on October 17, advised Acting Foreign Minister Saionji on the eve of the one-month anniversary of the queen's murder that

[68] Miura to Itō, Oct. 14, 1895, No. 378: NGB, XXVIII:1, pp. 512-14. Uchida to Saionji, Nov. 5, 1895, No. 424: *ibid.*, pp. 552-62.

[69] *Tōkyō Asahi* (newspaper), October 27, 1895 and *Meiji Hennenshi*, IX, 314.

[70] Saionji to Komura, Oct. 10, 27, 1895, Nos. 367, 406: NGB, XXVIII:1, pp. 499-500, 532.

he thought it "necessary to have Japanese troops enter the Palace to prevent the King from running to the Russian legation." He thought "it will not cause trouble." This from the man who had been sent to restore dignity and respectability to Japan's handling of the Korean problem. Saionji replied with an unequivocable "no." Such was not permissible, and the Foreign Office, Inoue, and also Komura went ahead to make every effort to prevent such an untoward happening by peaceful and diplomatic means, emphasizing consultations with the representatives of the powers in Korea, assurances of amicability to Russia, and quietude.[71] It was to no avail. Inoue decided by mid-November that the views of the Seoul representatives of the "three Powers" (Russia, France, and Germany?) were "very divergent" from Japan's and that his staying was "no longer useful." He returned to Japan shortly, bowing out of the Korean problem for the last time.[72] Komura

[71] Komura to Saionji, Nov. 7 and Saionji to Komura, Oct. 17, Nov. 8, 1895, Nos. 427, 384, 428: NGB, XXVIII:1, pp. 565, 517, 566. Komura was probably right in that Japanese troops could have entered the palace without trouble, for foreigners in Seoul a few days later suggested the need for such a measure to stabilize the situation—Treat, *Dipl. Rel. . . . 1895–1905*, pp. 11-12.

Mutsu from his sickbed had emphasized the desirability of "watching the situation and not doing anything," and Saionji stressed the idea of consulting with the representatives of other countries in his instructions to Inoue, Komura, and others in the Japanese diplomatic establishment. E.g., Mutsu to Saionji, Oct. 9; Saionji to Komura, Oct. 18, 26; Saionji to Inoue (secret), Oct. 23, 1895, Nos. 362, 388, 402, 395: NGB, XXVIII:1, pp. 469, 519, 536, 523. Cf. Inoue conversation with Allen, Harrington, *op. cit.*, pp. 277-88.

Quietude was made difficult by Kunrentai leaders who "camped" in the palace and demanded protection from Japanese troops (Lt. Col. Tamura to Lt. Gen. Kawakami, Nov. 3, 1895, No. 417: NGB, XXVIII:1, p. 537) and by the king, who took for himself the title of emperor and began a project of sending envoys abroad to announce the fact. Allen thought this was engineered by the Japanese (Allen to Sec. State, Oct. 19, 1895, No. 161: Dipl. Desp., Korea), but Japanese documents show them to be very distressed by it (Saionji to Miura, Oct. 14; Miura to Saionji, Oct. 14; Komura to Saionji, Oct. 26, 1895, Nos. 373, 375, 403: NGB, XXVIII:1, pp. 510, 511, 530).

[72] Inoue to Saionji, Nov. 13, 1895, No. 441: *ibid.*, p. 578. In later years Inoue, as an Elder Statesman, was consulted on Korean affairs but seems not to have taken an active or forceful role, save once, in 1907, when he helped stimulate the organization of the Oriental Development Company (see below, chap. IX). He devoted himself mainly to business and the Nishi Hongwanji Buddhist organization. Inoue Kaoru Denki Hensankai (comp.), *Segai Inoue Kōden* (Life of Marquis Inoue) (Tokyo: Naigai Shoseki Kabushiki Kaisha, 1934), IV, V (esp. V, pp. 39-48).

stayed on as minister at Seoul, amidst rumors that plans were afoot for the king to place himself under the aegis of the Russian legation. He could not stop him by peaceful means, and could only report the final dénoument of Japan's grand effort to remodel Korea along lines which Inoue had called "promoting the interests of Japan and Korea in parallel fashion": the king and crown prince had gone to the Russian legation in the early morning of February 11, Japan's Korean friends were in hiding.[73]

He might have used troops, Komura said, but he wished to avoid clashing with Russia. On May 14 at Seoul and on June 9 at Moscow Japanese representatives signed agreements with Russia which officially ended Japan's unilateral effort to "solve" the Korean problem. The accent was on friendly advice and mutual financial assistance to Korea, if necessary, and careful limitation of the number of Japanese guards allowed in Korea—200 to guard the Seoul-Pusan telegraph and 800 distributed among the several Japanese settlements, which number would be matched by Russia. Korean police and armed forces would be matters of mutual concern as would "other points" which might arise. These agreements were respectively entitled the Waeber-Komura memorandum and the Lobanoff-Yamagata arrangement, after the signers.[74]

The Sino-Japanese War years, 1894–95, were years of opportunity for Japan's diplomatic realists in their search for a solution to the Korean problem. In contrast to the 1885–94 period, during which their cool heads saw with painful clarity that prudence demanded passivity and even retreat in Korean affairs, the rapid fire sequence of events in the summer of 1894—which brought the elimination of Chinese and the augmentation of Japanese power and prestige in

[73] Komura to Saionji, Feb. 11, 1896, No. 352: NGB, XXIX, p. 682. Same to same, Feb. 13, 1895, No. 353: *ibid.*, pp. 683-84. Inoue quotation from lecture by Oka Yoshitake at Tokyo University, May 28, 1954, citing Inoue's letter to Mutsu, dated Feb. 17, 1895.

Horace Allen helped Russian Minister Waeber arrange the flight of the king to the Russian legation, in a coolie disguise to avoid Kunrentai palace guards. Harrington, *op. cit.*, pp. 288-90.

[74] Texts in Rockhill, *Treaties . . .*, pp. 430-32.

the peninsula, the quieting of anti-government criticism at home, and the acquiescence of the powers—set a remarkably favorable climate for activity. And Japanese policy makers had moved with all the skill and speed they could muster. Yet they failed. By the fall of 1895 their diplomacy was at that dead end where only naked force and brutality, murder, could retrieve their program of "progress." From this, to their credit, they recoiled in horror. Why had they failed? Inoue's biography gives an answer which, taking future policy as an indicator, seems to be the one which Japan's leaders accepted. "Inoue succeeded Ōtori and made every effort to improve the Korean situation. For six months he was successful. But unfortunately the Triple Intervention ruined his plans and then the Min murder made Japan's international position very critical. After that, as a result of the Russo-Japanese agreements, Inoue's policies were completely nullified. Except for these happenings there would have been wonderful fruits to his policy."[75] So it was now Russia, as it had once been China. If only Russia could be eliminated from Korean affairs, those "wonderful fruits" might still be realized.

[75] Inoue, *Segai* . . ., IV, 538.

VII

Realism Frustrated (II): The Failure of Itō, 1905-9

Although 1896 saw Japan's Korea policy again in disarray and her policy makers in gloom at the prospect of an indefinite prolongation and intensification of the sense of insecurity about Korea, "a dagger pointed at the home islands," the next decade was kind to Japan. By the end of 1905 a series of fortuitous events and a mighty Japanese military effort had eliminated Russia from Korean affairs and even given Japan control of the south Manchurian area, which constituted precisely the double guarantee of freedom of action in the peninsular kingdom which her policy makers had wanted in 1895. In addition, other powers with interests there, especially Britain and the United States, had sworn off "meddling" in Korea, being content to leave it to Japan to do the "world's work" of remedying her condition as a "derelict state" and confer on her the "benefits of modern civilization."[1]

It is not the concern of this study to trace in detail the course of events during the decade 1896–1905. The diplomacy of the period is reminiscent of the 1885–94 years, with Russia in the old Chinese saddle, Japan trying to hang on to the stirrup, and intrigue rife in Seoul. There were differences, of course. Russia was not a

[1] Choice of words after Frederick Wells Williams' Introduction to K. Asakawa, *The Russo-Japanese Conflict* (Cambridge: Riverside Press, 1904), p. vi and George Trumbull Ladd, "The Annexation of Korea: An Essay in Benevolent Assimilation," *Yale Review*, N.S. I (1911–12), 639.

Confucian "elder brother," which fact made her influence less elusive and less penetrating than the Chinese had been. And Russia's Far Eastern policy was actually more interested in Manchuria than Korea. But she could thwart anything Japan wanted to do in Korea, which, from the Japanese point of view, made the situation as unsatisfactory as had been the earlier arrangement with China under the Tientsin Treaty. Under these conditions, Japan's oligarchs, realists to the core, held their tempers and negotiated carefully and painstakingly for eight years trying to find a way out, then deciding that this was to no avail, plunged into war—again with many misgivings. The events of these years, the whole background of the Russo-Japanese War, make a fascinating story in themselves, but since, as regards the Japanese relationship to Korea, they present no radically new situation, we shall here present only a brief review of the highlights and refer the reader to other studies for fuller details.[2] It was only after the war that Japanese policy makers found a really radically altered situation vis à vis Korea, when the powers, all of them, were suddenly gone—no more to complicate the Korean scene. Free of all foreign encumbrances Japan could proceed with the long-delayed remodeling operation, dealing with Koreans alone. Realistic diplomacy could not ask for a more advantageous situation. "Wonderful fruits" would surely result. The main purpose of this chapter will be to discuss the planting of the fruit trees, 1905–10, but first follows a brief review of the diplomacy of the 1896–1905 period.

After the aforementioned Russo-Japanese agreements of May-June, 1896, Japan was almost completely quiescent for two years.

[2] See Asakawa, *op. cit.*, pp. 267-372. Takeuchi, *War and Diplomacy . . .*, pp. 121-59. A. M. Pooley (ed.), *The Secret Memoirs of Count Tadasu Hayashi* (New York: G. P. Putnam, 1915), pp. 61-211, for discussions based on Japanese sources.

Romanov, *Russia in Manchuria . . .*, pp. 102-387, and Andrew Malozemoff, *Russian Far Eastern Policy*, 1881-1904 (Berkeley, 1958); on Russian sources.

Treat, *Dipl. Rel. . . ., 1895–1905*, pp. 167-259 and Harrington, *God, Mammon . . .*, pp. 283-335, on American sources.

William L. Langer, *The Diplomacy of Imperialism* (2nd ed.; New York: Alfred A. Knopf, 1951), esp. pp. 460-73, 690-92, 720-27, 747-84, on European sources.

During that time Waeber, a mild and sympathetic man friendly to Korean progress, was replaced by Alexis N. de Speyer as Russian minister at Seoul. De Speyer was a militant, forward-policy man who conspicuously threw his weight around. The agreements with Japan were violated with impunity as numerous Russian military and financial advisers were brought in in a very un-mutual way. Witte seems to have backed these measures at first, but then entertained "fear of [financial] losses" and in April, 1898, de Speyer was relieved of his post in favor of a "somewhat less aggressive" minister. Undoubtedly, the tense Russo-British rivalry over Port Arthur and Weihaiwei was the main cause of this easing up.[3] At any rate, shortly thereafter, Russia favored Japan slightly with the Nishi-Rosen Agreement, which was signed in Tokyo on April 25. By this, the 1896 agreements were reaffirmed with renewed pledges that neither Russia nor Japan would appoint military instructors or financial advisers to Korea without beforehand arriving at a mutual agreement on the subject. This was no gain for Japan, but the last article admitted Japan to have large industrial and commercial enterprises in Korea and said that Russia would "not hinder the development of commercial and industrial relations between Japan and Korea."[4] The importance of Japanese economic activity in Korea will be considered in a subsequent chapter. Suffice it to say here that the opportunity to invest money in Korea without being able to influence the direction of political affairs did not spell "security" to Japanese oligarchs, particularly inasmuch as Russian economic activity seemed to the Japanese to be bent on tying Korea into the fast developing Siberian-Manchurian railway system. Itō and Yamagata discussed the overall question of policy with Nishi, Komura, Hayashi Gonsuke (Komura's successor in Korea), and Katō and decided that what the Japanese called *Man Kan Kōkan* (exchanging Korea for Manchuria) might in the

[3] Harrington, *op. cit.*, pp. 296-301. Romanov, *op. cit.*, pp. 108-17. Clarence N. Weems, Jr., "The Korean Reform and Independence Movement," pp. 277-99, 360-462.

[4] Rockhill, *Treaties . . .*, p. 433.

future serve as the goal of negotiations with Russia. That is, all agreed, except Katō who "opposed with anger," pointing out that there was little use negotiating with Russia, who insisted on absolute freedom of action in Manchuria while relegating Japan to equal status with her in Korea. Katō, as minister to London, preferred to work for close ties with England. Anyway, Japan had no leverage for negotiations with Russia until 1902 when a combination of European political rivalries and some astute diplomacy by Katō, now foreign minister, and Hayashi, who took over his London post, set the British alliance in the lap of the Japanese government.[5] The Elder Statesmen, Itō especially, had mixed feelings about this, hoping to heal the breach with Russia rather than see it widened by a definitive lining up of Japan with Britain.

However, they decided to use the alliance to bring pressure on Russia for a settlement along Man Kan Kōkan lines. In June, 1903, Elder Statesmen Itō, Yamagata, Matsukata, Inoue, and Ōyama met with Katsura, premier; Komura, now foreign minister; Terauchi, army minister; and Yamamoto, navy minister, to draw up a basic policy position for instituting serious negotiations with Russia. In it they emphasized that "Korea is an important outpost of Japan's line of defense and Japan consequently considers her independence absolutely essential to her own repose and safety. Moreover, the political as well as commercial and industrial interests and influence which Japan possesses in Korea are paramount over those of other powers. These interests and influence, Japan, having regard to her own security, cannot consent to surrender to, or share with, another Power." From this policy base Foreign Minister Komura authorized Kurino, who had been appointed to Nishi's old post at St. Petersburg, to propose the following points as a basis for Japanese-Russian understanding: (1) a mutual engagement to respect the independence of China and Korea and to maintain the principle of equal opportunity for the commerce and industry of all nations in those countries; (2) a

[5] Itō, *Katō Kōmei*, I, 274. Takeuchi, *op. cit.*, pp. 124-28.

reciprocal recognition of Japan's preponderating interests in Korea and Russia's special interests in railway enterprises in Manchuria, and of the right of Japan to take in Korea, and of Russia to take in Manchuria, such measures as might be necessary for the protection of those respective interests, subject to article 1; (3) a reciprocal undertaking not to impede the development of industrial and commercial activities, Japan in Korea, Russia in Manchuria, not inconsistent with article 1; (4) a reciprocal engagement that, in case it should be found necessary to send troops by Japan to Korea or Russia to Manchuria for the purpose either of protecting interests per article 2 or of suppressing insurrection or disorder liable to create international complications, the troops sent would in no case exceed the actual number required, and would be recalled forthwith as soon as their missions were accomplished; (5) the recognition on the part of Russia of the exclusive right of Japan to give advice and assistance in the interest of reform and good government in Korea, including military assistance; (6) this agreement to supersede all previous arrangements between Japan and Russia respecting Korea.[6]

This was clearly Man Kan Kōkan, with the Japanese allowing themselves some slight bargaining area by defining Russian interests in Manchuria ("special" and "railway") more narrowly than Japan's in Korea (simply "preponderating"). Several months of negotiation after this proposal revealed that Russia would do no more than meet Japan halfway on Korea while maintaining Manchuria "and its littoral" as "in all respects outside Japan's sphere of interest." On this the negotiations broke down and Japan opened hostilities. After the war Russia agreed to leave Korea to Japan, by the Portsmouth Treaty, September 1905. Meanwhile President Theodore Roosevelt had made up his mind that "we cannot possibly interfere for the Koreans against Japan" and his approval of the Taft-Katsura memorandum in July had given Japan an American go-ahead sign on Korea even before the Portsmouth

[6] Asakawa, *op. cit.*, pp. 296-305.

conference convened. England had done the same in the August, 1905, renewal of the Anglo-Japanese alliance.[7]

Thus it was that by the fall of 1905 the diplomatic stage was in almost perfect order for Japan's realist statesmen par excellence to solve their nation's basic security problem. All the necessary papers were signed for Japanese doctors of civilization to proceed on Operation Korea, with only the wrigglings of the patient and such professional ethics as seemed applicable to the doctors to constitute inhibiting factors. It may be objected immediately that this metaphor is not appropriate for the Japanese because they were aggressors, not doctors of civilization, and by no stretch of the imagination could they be presumed to have professional ethics. This poses very interesting questions. We recall Inoue's use of the "giving medicine to a sick man" expression to describe what Japan was trying to do in Korea during his heyday there, and the phraseology employed by Yale Professors F. W. Williams and George Trumbull Ladd, a sample of which was given at the beginning of this chapter. Of course, Williams' opinion might be dismissed under the heading, "China specialist trying to write a pleasant introduction to a book done by a bright Japanese student at Yale." And Ladd, having been for several months of the year 1907 a guest and sort of unofficial adviser to Itō in Korea, may be presumed to have viewed Japanese motives through rose-tinted glasses. But the more serious historical work of W. E. Griffis and Payson J. Treat, as observed earlier in this study, points in the direction of acceptance of the idea, though the equally serious work of Nelson, Sunoo, Harrington, and others would reject it entirely. Bearing all this in mind, we shall adopt a middle course; let the metaphor stand, but only in a carefully defined and restricted sense. The thought and action patterns of Japanese oligarchs as we have observed them to this point would

[7] Asakawa, *op. cit.*, pp. 305-62, esp. pp. 308-9. Romanov, *op. cit.*, p. 291. A. Whitney Griswold, *The Far Eastern Policy of the United States* (New York: Harcourt, Brace & Co., 1938), pp. 125, 115-16. J. V. A. MacMurray (comp. and ed.), *Treaties and Agreements With and Concerning China, 1894–1919* (New York: Oxford University Press, 1921), I, 522 ff.

seem to indicate clearly enough that, despite Inoue's flirtation with the medical metaphor, they were too hard-headed to indulge themselves in such idealistic balderdash as descriptive of their main objective which was, namely, Japanese security. (Whether this might also be balderdash, we shall leave aside for the present.) However, admitting security to be their objective says nothing of means. The oligarchs were also concerned about means, and this is where the metaphor—in restricted usage—becomes applicable.

In our modern world "good" governments do not apologize for pursuing national security. In fact a citizen living under a "good" government is not considered a "good" citizen unless he has some concern in this regard, and certainly a public official must have great concern. Otherwise he becomes a "security risk." Of course, it is recognized that the position of a "good" citizen under a "bad" government is anomalous, for a "bad" government will deliberately go beyond the legitimate pursuit of national security into the illegitimate pursuit of aggression. However, inasmuch as both of these pursuits take a nation outside its own borders and involve it in efforts to influence other states, the boundary between them is difficult to ascertain in terms of extent of interference alone. This difficulty is heightened by the natural tendency of any given nation to set its own security requirements higher than another nation would consider necessary.

In the case of Japan versus Korea, it could be argued that, since the powers came around to approving Japan's interference there during the Russo-Japanese War, such would constitute a sufficient admission that the Korean problem was legitimately a security problem for Japan. But this neglects the possibility that aggression was being acquiesced to for reasons of impotence or disinterest. Hence the question of means becomes important as a yardstick for measuring the guilt of Japan, for ascertaining whether her actions in Korea could be classified as those of a "good" government pursuing legitimate security interests or those of a "bad" government bent on aggression. The outcome, annexation in 1910, of course, immediately suggests the latter, aggression. But lest our judgment be too hasty, we should recall that though the United States annexed both Hawaii and the Philippines in 1898, we would be reluctant to call these simply instances of aggression. And, in fact, when we examine the documents which reveal the thinking of those leaders of the Japanese government who organized the Korean program from 1905 to 1910, we find that, even though free of interference by other nations, they *were* anxious to be benevolent, to develop the Japanese-Korean relationship in ways that would be acceptable and helpful to Koreans while meeting their own security requirements. Thus within that restricted framework which required that Japanese security must come first they may be called doctors of civilization, seeking to bring enlightenment and reform to Korea, not with idealistic balderdash but with realism of the best enlightened-self-interest variety. At least, they seem to have begun that way.

The Japanese government set its own statute of limitations on the Korean operation in a "protocol concluded between Japan and Korea on February 23, 1904, regarding the situation in Korea." By Article I they took unto themselves very wide powers: "For the purposes of maintaining a permanent and solid friendship between Japan and Korea and firmly establishing peace in the Far East, the Imperial Government of Korea shall place full confidence in the Imperial Government of Japan and adopt the advice of the latter in regard to improvements in administration." But by Articles II and III they imposed certain limitations on themselves. In carrying out these "improvements" they would at the same time "ensure the safety and repose of the Imperial House of Korea" and they would "definitively guarantee the independence and territorial integrity of the Korean Empire."[18] Why did Japan's

[8] Henry Chung (comp.), *Treaties and Conventions between Corea and Other Powers* (New York: H. S. Nichols, Inc., 1919), p. 213. Cf. Asakawa, *op. cit.*, p. 367.

leaders write down these limitations at all? Korea was powerless, the war was on, Japanese troops were occupying the country. Of course, the inclusion of these articles would make Japan's action more justifiable in the eyes of the world, but, on the other hand, they could prove very embarrassing later, when Japan would wish to put aside the Imperial House of Korea and completely extinguish Korean independence.

In September, 1905, Hayashi, who had been Japanese minister at Seoul (distinguish from Count Hayashi at London), was sent to Korea as imperial plenipotentiary to do the spadework for the establishment of a Japanese "Residency-General" there and to make recommendations. His lengthy report to then Foreign Minister Katsura, dated September 25, is rather revealing of attitudes and intentions. He concentrated on the Korean court, describing the emperor as being pro-Russian-anti-Japanese in the Russo-Japanese War and as having made attempts to contact the Russians. His "fundamental policy" was to "use one big country against another" and within the court to have "various groups oppose each other to his profit." His "dream" was to be "Emperor-dictator." The Japanese financial adviser, says Hayashi, made a good effort, but ran into the emperor's opposition. "Therefore it is very difficult to clean up the Court, but very important to do this if the evil roots in Korean politics are to be cut. If we can clean up the Court and then cut off the weeds from the root, we can achieve success in improving government administration in Korea as a whole. Even though it necessitates the use of some pressure, we must get some Japanese officials into high places to watch the Emperor and reform the order of the Court. Thus we can check a willful sovereign and ambitious persons . . . and can manage Korea peacefully." Regarding anti-Japanese political currents, he pointed to the "Junenkai" and "rioters" called "Righteous Army." The Junenkai, he says, "was encouraged by American missionaries several years ago and at first I myself was sympathetic," but gradually it had "changed" into an anti-Japanese political group.

"I can't judge yet whether the Emperor's court directs the Righteous Army and the Junenkai, but I am suspicious."[9]

It can be said that in general the leaders of the Japanese government, as of the fall of 1905, intended to have their "improvements" without annexing Korea and without resort to brutality. And at that point they turned over direction of the whole Korean operation to the one of their number, Itō Hirobumi, who was most insistent that this should be the case, that Korea should and could be corrected in a way that respected Korean sensibilities and employed only civilized methods. Internationally, the way was cleared for Itō to take a very strong hand in Korea's affairs by an agreement between Japan and Korea, signed on November 17, 1905, and a "declaration of the Japanese government" relating to Korea issued on November 22. The first empowered Japan through "a Resident General who shall reside at Seoul" to take charge "primarily" of diplomatic matters. This was an open invitation for all other countries to close their legations and leave Korea. The "declaration" of November 22 explained why:

> The relations of propinquity have made it necessary for Japan to take and exercise, for reasons closely connected with her own safety and repose, a paramount interest and influence in the political and military affairs of Korea. The measures hitherto taken have been purely advisory, but the experience of recent years has demonstrated the insufficiency of measures of guidance alone. The unwise and improvident action of Korea, more especially in the domain of her international concerns, has in the past been the most fruitful source of complications. . . .[10]

The aforementioned prior agreements with the United States, Britain, and Russia guaranteed that there would be no objections from these governments, which forthwith recalled their ministers

[9] Hayashi to Katsura, Sept. 25, 1905, No. 2498: Archives, MT 1.6.1.24 (Documents relating to the improvement of the Korean court), pp. 2-11.

[10] Chung, *Treaties . . .*, pp. 221-23.

resident in Korea, and other countries one by one "acknowledged" the Japanese intention to establish a Residency General.[11] The wording of Japan's final communication concerning this to foreign governments makes an interesting study in verbal vacillation, which underscores the Japanese determination to avoid this time the sort of clumsiness that had wrecked their Kabo reform attempt. Under date of January 19, 1906, Foreign Minister Katō sent the following note to all ambassadors and ministers abroad for transmission to the governments to which they were respectively accredited: "After date referred to [February 1] all local affairs appertaining to the functions of foreign consuls on account of which communications have hitherto been made at Seoul directly to the Korean government are to be communicated to the Residency General, while such matters as have hitherto been communicated by them to the Korean local authorities are to be referred to the Residencies." Crossed out was a harsher version wherein instead of "be communicated to" the wording had been "come under the jurisdiction of" and instead of "are to be referred to" had been "shall be dealt with by."[12]

Meanwhile Itō was intent upon setting up the residency generalship in such a way that it (and he, as resident general) would be as free as possible from interference from other agencies of his own Japanese government, especially the army. The author has been able to locate only a few documents on this subject, but these are extremely interesting. A triangular exchange of communications between Deputy Foreign Minister Chinda, Komura, who was now ambassador to Peking and apparently a close friend of Chinda, and Katsura, the prime minister, illustrates one aspect of the issue, that involving the relationship of the Residency General and

[11] The United States legation was closed on Nov. 24—Treat, *Dipl. Rel. . . ., 1895–1905*, pp. 254-56. For "acknowledgments" from many other countries, see Archives, MT 1.1.2.40 (Documents relating to the establishment of the Residency General), pp. 330-90.

[12] Katō to all ambassadors and ministers, Jan. 19, 1906: MT 1.1.2.40, pp. 312-10 (reverse pagination).

the Japanese Foreign Office. Chinda wrote to Komura on December 12:

> As for the administrative organization of the Residency General, our Government is now discussing that matter. There are two opinions among the Genro and the Cabinet Ministers. One opinion is to make the Residency General a completely civilian organization. The other is to make it a military organization [word used here is *bukan soshiki*; *gunji seifu* (military government) was first used, then crossed out]. But the general tendency is to separate the Residency General completely from the Foreign Office and put it under the direct control of the Emperor. If this is done, it becomes fundamentally different from what you expected. Also this means that Japanese foreign policy may lose its consistency and this would be very bad for us. Therefore if you have an opinion, please tell Katsura directly. Express your opinion.

(Chinda had originally made the last sentence read: "Ask the Minister first, then after you get an explanation express your opinion." But he crossed out the first part of the sentence, leaving only the words "express your opinion.")[13]

Komura did express his opinion to Katsura:

> You told me that the Resident General would previously report to the Foreign Minister before doing important business, but now [I understand] he will be able to take initiative. I am afraid this will mean conflicting orders. Formerly we decided that all foreign affairs regarding Korea would be handled by the Foreign Office in Tokyo and only local matters would be handled by the Resident General; with this foreigners would gradually withdraw their officials from Korea. But if the Resident General has real power regarding these matters all foreign ministers resident in Korea will stay and this will be embarrassing. Please consider this, and I reserve my opinion on other points.[14]

Katsura replied:

> I received your communication. Truly the defect in the Residency General system is that your point is not considered. The regulation is

[13] Chinda to Komura (Peking), Dec. 12, 1905, No. 135: MT 1.1.2.40, pp. 72-73.
[14] Komura to Katsura, Dec. 19, 1905, No. 77: MT 1.1.2.40, pp. 86-87.

that the Resident General should be under the direct control of the Emperor and as for foreign matters they go through the Foreign Minister to the Prime Minister and are decided. The Resident General represents Japan in Korea and controls foreign matters there, including matters regarding foreigners. In case of important foreign matters it is decided that he should previously consult with the Foreign Minister. Therefore regarding foreign affairs we may interpret the regulation to mean that foreign affairs powers exist both in the Resident General and the Foreign Minister. I think there will not be any trouble.

If this sounds like double talk, it may be well to quote also a final paragraph which Katsura wrote in this letter, then crossed out: "Generally speaking we can consider there will be no trouble. We decided on this understanding so I agreed with it. But since I received your suggestion I wanted to get your point over as clearly as possible, so yesterday I brought it up immediately. But that regulation was already decided and ordered for printing today. I am sorry but there is no way to change or improve it. However, please don't worry."[15]

Further evidence that the resident general designate was determined to hold interference from Tokyo to a minimum is to be found in Itō's insistence that he, as resident general, should be the supreme military commander as well as civilian head of the Japanese entourage in Korea. General Ōshima Kenichi has left a pointed commentary on this:

When taking this new position [Resident General] Itō demanded huge powers . . . the military equivalent of Field Marshall. So we [the army] complained very much. I wired Assistant Chief of Staff Kodama about it and he agreed with me. I then met with Itō and explained that the army opposed. Itō said that in this case [without the powers he demanded] he would not take the position. This defeated me, for at that time the very rise or fall of the Japanese government depended on the handling of this big job of Resident General of Korea, and only Itō would do. Thus when Itō demanded the field marshall position it caused

[15] Katsura to Komura, Dec. 21, 1905: MT 1.1.2.40, pp. 239-43.

a big argument. Yamagata was opposed, but because he wanted Itō to be the first Resident-General, there was no way out. Thus reluctantly Yamagata gave in to Itō's demand. Kodama also was reluctant. He approved on the surface, but he told me by telephone to oppose publicly, which I did. Afterwards I also reluctantly gave in. In the end the army accepted Itō's demand as a special case for Itō, but felt that it would set a bad precedent for a civilian to have military powers. When Itō was about to leave for Korea as Resident General, we had a party. . . . He said to me in a jovial way, "Though you opposed me, I am in command of the soldiers. . . ."[16]

The reason for Itō's insistence on this may be deduced from orders which he issued to govern the conduct of Japanese troops in Korea. He reminded them that "our occupation army is watched very closely by foreigners and Koreans." Therefore the soldiers "must be very careful." Especially they "must not behave in a rough manner, especially toward women . . . do not forget you are a civilized people." He defined our "responsibility toward Koreans" as "not only to protect them but to suggest improvements in their administration." All Japanese in Korea, soldiers and civilians alike, bore a responsibility in this, he said, and the fact that the "Korean people do not generally speaking understand the situation" made the task difficult and patience all the more necessary.[17] On the

[16] Hiratsuka Atsushi (ed.), *Itō Hakubun Hiroku* (Private Papers of Itō) (Tokyo: Shunjūsha, 1929), I, 314-15. Further evidence that Itō got what he wanted in setting up the Residency General may be found in Katsura to Hayashi, Nov. 19, 20, 22, 1905: Archives, MT 1.1.2.40, pp. 17, 18-19, 26-29 and Hayashi to Katsura, Dec. 4, 1905: *ibid.*, pp. 62-71.

In his Nov. 22 letter Katsura says, "Based on Itō's opinion, we decided to promulgate the Imperial decree as follows. . . ." The imperial ordinances defining the position of the resident general can best be understood in terms of these background arguments. He was to be directly under the Japanese emperor, hence not subject to the cabinet, and he was to be in command of all Japanese personnel in Korea, including those employed by the Korean government. However, he would leave purely diplomatic matters to the Foreign Office in Tokyo, which obviated any excuse for foreign governments to keep diplomatic representatives in Korea. The basic ordinance is printed in the Residency General's *Annual Report for 1907*, pp. 111-15. See also *ibid.*, pp. 6-7. Cf. *Papers Relating to the Diplomatic Relations of the United States* (1906), II, 1025.

[17] Hiratsuka, *op. cit.*, I, No. 77, pp. 313-14.

eve of his departure for Korea Itō discussed his "fundamental policy toward Korea" at a meeting to which newsmen were invited. The basic relationships, he said, had been set by treaty, but these must be applied in detail. He pointed to the existence of corruption and poverty in Korea. He wished to improve these and he wished to "build Korean faith in us." "Unfortunately," he admitted, "many Japanese have bad attitudes toward Koreans, but Korea is now under our protection. . . . We must watch ourselves and get rid of these bad attitudes."[18]

This last comment, made in the presence of representatives of the press, must, of course, be tentatively labeled "press release" or "propaganda" rather than seriously considered as representing Itō's real attitude. However, many pieces of evidence point to the conclusion that his desire to be as free as possible from army and Foreign Office pressures was indeed motivated by a determination to make the Residency General mild, benevolent, and helpful to Koreans—so far as possible within the requirements of Japanese security.

With regard to these requirements Itō was the very epitome of the sort of realism—"enlightened self-interest"—which this study has found to have been generally characteristic of the oligarchs after 1873. He was the ablest and the coolest of them all. He could balance all the factors. Ōtori might be slow-witted; Mutsu might come down with tuberculosis in the crisis; Katō might get hot-headed at Russia; Miura might fall into intrigue and murder; Yamagata and other military men might be overly inclined to put their confidence in troops and force alone; even Inoue might get out of focus, overestimating the power of money and underestimating the potentiality for obstruction of a decadent court. But one rarely meets in the pages of history a more perfect manifestation of professional realistic statesmanship than that embodied in Itō. A capacity to view enemies and diplomatic antagonists without

[18] Remarks, Jan. 30, 1906, Hiratsuka, *op. cit.*, II (*Zoku*), speech section, No. 37, pp. 220-23.

anger, to expunge excesses of enthusiasm from himself and his colleagues, to remain supremely cool and cautious even in moments of extreme tension distinguished his career from beginning to end. Perhaps the best illustration of this is to be found in the conduct he demanded of his fellow oligarchs and the emperor at the close of the Sino-Japanese War, as the vainglory of victory swelled through Japan. "Think cautiously, grasp opportunities and be flexible," he told them. And in line with this he called for maximum demands on China, consonant with accepted international practice, but insisted on "surrender" to the three powers when the Triple Intervention was registered. This intervention, he observed, was Russian organized "to weaken our position in Korea." France and Germany joined "only because of the political situation in Europe. They had no special interest in Korea . . . Russia invited them. Russia has not yet shown her ambition in the Far East, but she is like an underground bamboo. Her ambition will come out. We must watch the future. . . ."[19]

Yet watching the future he had, in the next decade, sought Man Kan Kōkan exchange as a basis of settlement with Russia, then failing that he approved the war, then worked for the compromise peace which allowed Japan to begin to exercise a free hand in Korea while enjoying international approval. Through years of muddling through, Itō, above all, had kept the balances which enabled Japan to stand as of February 1, 1906, poised and ready for Operation Korea, rich in experience, well equipped with men and money, and with an international carte blanche. And in addition, as he took command of the Residency General himself, Itō gave evidence of his awareness of the need to incorporate one further balance wheel into the solution of the problem, namely consideration for the Koreans, which his predecessors had been clumsy about, but which he was so sufficiently determined to pur-

[19] Komatsu Midori (ed.), *Itō Kō Zenshū* (Complete Works of Prince Itō) (Toyko: Itō Kō Zenshū Han Kōkai, 1927), I, *Bunshu* section, pp. 203-5, 211. Hiratsuka, *op. cit.*, I, No. 13, pp. 63-64 and Hiratsuka, II (*Zoku*), speeches, pp. 7-9.

sue that he took pains to insulate his administration from the pressures of his own countrymen. Of course, this need not mean sincere, heart-felt concern for Koreans. But it does mean that he knew there were delicate human equations involved in the Korean-Japanese relationship. He needed and wanted Korean support, and he expected to pursue policies enlightened enough to win it for his administration.

The importance of this has been largely lost sight of amidst the tendency of both scholarly and popular opinion since the 1930's to regard the process of Japanese annexation of Korea as a simple case of aggression. The author recalls a discussion with an able young Korean of the present generation, who vouched for the fact that Koreans—none of them—make any distinction between good and bad or gentle and harsh Japanese administrators. All were tyrants, the "gentle" perhaps most villainous of all because they were deceitful as well as tyrannical. And as for Itō specifically, he pointed out that all that needs to be said is that the Korean who assassinated him (at Harbin in 1909) has been a hero to his countrymen ever since. We do not question the accuracy of this description of Korean sentiment. Indeed, the author found verification of it in Korea in the spring of 1959 at a showing of the very popular, recently produced Korean motion picture, *King Kojong and the Martyr, An Joong-gun* (the man who killed Itō). Behind the Korean audience's obvious emotional involvement, the cheers and tears for An, the hisses for Itō, lay decades of oppression of Korea by Japan. Nevertheless, it should be remembered that at the time responsible and practical people around the world, as distinguished from foolish idealists and special pleaders, considered Japanese guardianship of Korea to be necessary and Itō's administration to be praiseworthy. A particularly good example of this is a large book on the subject by the aforementioned George Trumbull Ladd, written after he had visited Korea for several months in 1907 and published by Charles Scribner's Company, New York, the following year. He concluded that "if Marquis Ito, and his sympathetic, effective supporters, at home and in the Residency-General, can be sustained for five years, and can be succeeded for a generation by those of like purpose and character, then the problem of the relations of Japan and Korea will have been solved." And further, he thought that by this Japan would "secure and maintain a well merited place among the foremost nations of the civilized world—thus enjoying prosperity at home and contributing her full share toward the blessing of mankind."[20]

Ladd's book has been noted in passing by numerous studies of Korea, and dismissed as being of little or no consequence. The recent evaluation of Korean scholar, Chon Dong, summarizes the opinions succinctly; "Ladd fails to grasp the real ambition of Japan in Korea."[21] It has been said that Ladd visited Korea at the invitation of Resident General Itō, which would naturally establish a presumption that his views are suspect, either as propaganda or poppycock. However, closer inspection of Ladd suggests that he should not be dismissed so easily, indeed that he was a penetrating student of human behavior and that his evaluation of Itō's regime was entirely consistent with the conclusions he derived from years of scholarly inquiry into that general subject. Ladd was a distinguished American philosopher and psychologist. He began his professional career as a Congregationalist pastor, but formal religion was too narrow for him and he went on to become professor of philosophy at Yale, while spending also much effort, in collaboration with William James and others, in developing the study of psychology. He helped found and was the second president of the American Psychological Association, and he was the author of some twenty books and numerous articles in the fields of philosophy and psychology.

He was not an adherent of any single philosophical school, preferring to stand apart and criticise them all, but it is clear that even

[20] George Trumbull Ladd, *In Korea with Marquis Ito* (New York: Charles Scribner's Sons, 1908), pp. 462-63.

[21] Chon Dong, "Japanese Annexation of Korea," (Unpub. Ph.D. diss., University of Colorado, 1955; University Microfilms, Ann Arbor, T'55,D717j), p. 374.

while criticising its more extreme aspects he was much influenced by the pragmatism of William James. He did not accept entirely the argument that the worth of an idea or an ethic lay in its practical consequences, but he found that "the realities of life have done more for the successful solution of concrete problems of duty than have the abstract classifications and the debates in casuistry of the moralists." He admitted that it was "out of dreams and aspirations of the lofty moral sort" that "heroes and martyrs and men who are prophets and forerunners of great moral and spiritual uplifts are made," but that nevertheless practicality was the best guide. "Midst fairly settled law and custom a calculated obligation of duty might be made." And what any man might do bore "a limitation suggested by the word can." One should be optimistic on this and work "to the extremest limits of one's resources," but there was no use expecting to overturn "fairly settled law and custom."[22]

These general contours of Laddian thought help to explain why he and practical people everywhere favored Itō's regime in Korea and explained away examples of Japanese cruelty or oppression. Ladd was not intellectually dishonest, nor was he merely taken in by Itō's hospitality. Nor can it be said that he suffered from myopia because of writing too soon, before the more brutal aspects of Itō's administration began to show themselves. Indeed, he reiterated his favorable evaluation of it after the bitter Korean antagonism to the Japanese had been made manifest in Itō's assassination and the Japanese had used extreme, repressive measures in effecting the annexation. In his article entitled "The Annexation of Korea: An Essay in 'Benevolent Assimilation,'" which was published in July, 1912, Ladd wrote: "The frankly and consistently avowed

[22] George Trumbull Ladd, *What Ought I To Do? An Inquiry into the Nature and Kinds of Virtue and into the Sanctions, Aims, and Values of the Moral Life* (New York: Longmans, Green & Co., 1915), especially pp. 102-3, 162-63, 188, 210-12, 234, 276, 301-6. For the main events of Ladd's life and listings of his works, see Dumas Malone (ed.), *Dictionary of American Biography* (New York: Scribner's, 1933), X, 525-26 and Library of Congress Catalogue.

attempt of the first Resident-General, the late Prince Ito, was to establish a protectorate in Korea which should at the same time relieve the people of the oppressions of their own government, confer upon them the benefits of modern civilization, and also render them grateful, sympathetic, and friendly allies of Japan . . . [Japan's] protectorate made no pretence of disinterestedness of the purely missionary order; but neither can its claim to benevolence be charged with hypocrisy. . . . The welfare of Japan as well as Korea required enforcing reforms in Korea."[23]

In his book, *In Korea with Marquis Ito*, Ladd refutes at length those "over-credulous" missionaries, who, led by Homer B. Hulbert, were denouncing Japanese actions and motives, and he found the anti-Japanese *Korea Daily News* simply determined "to oppose and traduce everything remotely connected with Japan."[24] Hulbert, an American missionary teacher and sometime adviser to the Korean government, whose experience in Korea dated back to 1886, had generally approved of Japanese efforts to reform Korea up to 1904. But the events of 1905, particularly the tactics employed by the Japanese to induce the Korean government to accept the Residency-General under the aforementioned agreement of November 17, 1905, convinced him that Japan was Korea's worst enemy. He had appeared at Washington shortly after the signing of the November agreement as unofficial representative of the Korean emperor to plead for American aid in resisting the Japanese, bearing a letter to this effect from the emperor himself. Also H. N. Allen, the former medical missionary who had recently been retired from the American legation at Seoul, partly because his friendship for Korea and Koreans had sometimes led him into insubordination vis à vis the State Department, had received $10,000 and a

[23] *Yale Review*, N.S. I (July 1912), 639, 645.

[24] Ladd, *In Korea* . . ., pp. 44, 47-54, 94-98. The *Korea Daily News* was edited by Mr. E. T. Bethell, a young English journalist who had settled in Seoul in 1904. It had both English and Korean editions. It was suppressed by order of the British Consular Court in Seoul, after the Japanese had complained to the British. See McKenzie, *The Tragedy of Korea*, pp. 212-40.

strong plea from the Korean monarch to help arouse American help against the Japanese.[25] Hulbert and Allen had tried to get hearings in Washington but the State Department and President Theodore Roosevelt would not listen. However, subsequently Hulbert and an English writer, McKenzie, published accounts showing the Japanese to have used tactics of terror and brute force in obtaining Korean agreement to the establishment of the Residency-General. Specifically, they said, Japanese Minister Hayashi, General Hasegawa, and Itō himself had kept Korean ministers in session far into the night, with Japanese troops in the courtyard and palace, and Hasegawa, at one point, even pulling his sword and dragging the Korean prime minister, Han Kyu-sul, from the room when the latter refused to sign.[26]

Ladd argues that there were only a few bodyguards with the Japanese, that there were no sword pullings and draggings, and that Prime Minister Han, finding the other ministers in favor of signing, himself ran from the room in tears, stumbled into the women's quarters, and, but for Itō's intercession in his behalf, would have been punished for *that*. Of course, concludes Ladd, Korea did not enter into the treaty "with a willing heart" or in a "jubilant spirit" since she was "under a sort of compulsion," but "if all treaties made under such conditions may be repudiated . . . the peace of the world cannot be secured or even promoted by any number of treaties."[27]

Similarly, Ladd refutes the charges levelled at the Japanese by the Korean mission to the Hague Conference of 1907, which incident occurred shortly after his departure from Korea and which rather severely embarrassed the conference as well as the Japanese. As a result of this mission, which was dispatched secretly by the

[25] Harrington, *God, Mammon . . .*, pp. 48, 200, 332-35.

[26] Hulbert, *The Passing of Korea*, pp. 208-24. McKenzie, *The Tragedy of Korea*, pp. 130-41. See also Eleanor Tupper and George E. McReynolds, *Japan in American Public Opinion* (New York: Macmillan, 1937), pp. 92-93. Nelson, *Korea and the Old Orders . . .*, pp. 263-67. Clarence N. Weems, Jr., "Korean Reforms . . .," pp. 118-19.

[27] Ladd, *In Korea . . .*, pp. 252-79, esp. pp. 253-54, 261-62, 266-67, 277-78.

Korean emperor to protest Japanese domination of his country, the emperor was forced to abdicate, the Japanese then installing his feeble-minded son in his stead and instituting a new "convention" which put all substantial powers, domestic as well as foreign, in the hands of the Residency-General.[28] Ladd calls the sending of this mission a "last act of insane treachery on the part of the Emperor and his Court" and argues that it was the emperor's own cabinet which initiated the demand for his abdication. Concerning the anti-Japanese riots which broke out in the Seoul area and elsewhere when the news of the abdication became known, he explains that these were stimulated by Korean soldiers who did not really deserve the name soldiers at all. They were "intrinsically worthless for the legitimate purposes of an army, and dangerous in the extreme as a force to provoke and intensify all manner of lawlessness." They were "undisciplined troops," "rowdies," who having "deserted" their barracks became "centres of all the forces of sedition, arson, and murder." After General Yi, the Korean minister of war, read (from the residence of Japanese Commanding General Hasegawa) a rescript of disbandment of the Korean army to its superior officers "the mutiny" spread. In reducing it, Ladd explains, the Japanese military authorities "made a mistake" in accepting the services of "some thirty civilians to assist the police and soldiers in searching for the fugitive mutineers . . . in the spirit of vengeance, therefore, there was no doubt considerable return of excesses on the part of irresponsible individuals among the Japanese civilian volunteers." However, "otherwise the very trying situation in which these revolts of the Korean military forces placed the Japanese Government in Seoul was apparently met with commendable moderation and skill."[29]

This moderation and skill cited by Ladd is described in some detail by McKenzie, who toured around the Korean countryside

[28] Chung, *Treaties* . . ., pp. 223-24.

[29] Ladd, *In Korea* . . ., chapter entitled "July, 1907 and Afterward," esp. pp. 424-25, 427, 435, 437-38.

at this time. He gives eyewitness testimony to the burning of scores of Korean villages by Japanese soldiers in their search for "rebels" and the desperate heroism of the tattered "Righteous Army" of Koreans who thought it better "to die a free man than to live as the slave of Japan."[30] That McKenzie told the substantial truth about the application of "the strong hand of Japan" (one of his chapter titles) after the Hague episode cannot be doubted. Even Japanese government documents speak of the riots and their suppression, including burning of villages.[31]

How could Ladd have been so blind? The answer would seem to be that he was not blind, he was merely being realistic. "Midst fairly settled" practices of international relations a weak and troubled country like Korea, strategically located in the world political arena, had to be controlled by a stable power, benevolently if possible, but firmly, if necessary. Not only Professor Ladd, but other sensible, and influential, foreigners reached the same conclusion. Hulbert and his group of Korean special pleaders pricked a few consciences and asked some embarrassing questions, but it proved to be a tempest in a teapot, unable to stir the lethargy of world opinion.

Japanese documents register this and also the fact that Japanese government leaders were at first worried, then reassured on the matter. Itō's office had drawn up a report on Hulbert at the time he "sold his possessions" and left Korea in May, 1907, prior to the Hague affair in July. It said that he had "lived in Korea twenty years." He had "entered Korea with no property" but through "activities in real estate he made 160,000 yen." His business connections were chiefly with "Bostwick and Collbran" and "when their business began to decline after the Russo-Japanese War,

[30] McKenzie, *The Tragedy of Korea*, pp. 185-208, esp. pp. 191. 203. McKenzie, *Korea's Fight for Freedom*, pp. 132-70.

[31] Mr. Chong-Ik Kim is preparing a detailed analysis of these Korean rebel activities and Japanese efforts to suppress them in his thesis entitled "The Techniques of Political Power: Japan in Korea, 1905–1910" (Stanford University). The riots will be discussed further, later in this chapter.

Hulbert had a connection with the Korean court and, under secret orders from Mr. Bostwick, he began to concentrate on attacking Japan." The report anticipated that he would "act in ways hostile to Japan."[32] From the Hague, Japanese representative Tsuzuki (Tsudzuki) reported the arrival and activities of Hulbert and the Korean emissaries, vouchsafing that "it is Hulbert who is pulling string."[33] Tsuzuki further advised Foreign Minister Hayashi that, since "the Conference here consist of overwhelming majority of small nations," the affair might become "a foyer of sympathy for weaker nations" which might have "comparatively lasting effects on the opinion of the world in general." He thought "a move directed against the personality or status of the [Korean] Emperor, such as deposition or abdication, more likely to awaken pro-Korean sympathy than a purely political move such as veiled or open annexation."[34]

Hayashi ordered his diplomatic establishment to follow the moves of Hulbert closely, which they did for many months, with Hayashi himself sometimes writing refutations to his accusations. For example, he heard from the Japanese consul in San Francisco that Hulbert told the San Francisco Chamber of Commerce the steps Japan was taking in Korea "would mean the destruction of American influence not only in Korea but in China. U.S. goods now paying seven percent duty would be obliged to pay 40% to 50%." Also "Japan will cultivate cotton and wheat in Korea to compete with American industries." Hayashi instructed the consul to say that "all the Treaty rights of Americans are most scrupulously respected" and that the cotton-wheat competition charges

[32] Tsuruhara, General Affairs Dept. Chief, Residency General, to Chinda, Deputy For. Min., May 9, 1907: Archives, MT 2.4.1.9 (Documents relating to dispatch of secret Korean mission . . .), pp. 22-26. On the activities of Bostwick and Collbran see Harrington, *God, Mammon* . . ., pp. 186-89, 198-200.

[33] Tzudzuki to Hayashi, For. Min., July 3, 1907, No. 2704: Archives, MT 2.4.1.9, p. 73. See also same to same, June 29, 30, July 2, 3, 4, 5, 7, 9, 16, 18, 19: MT 2.4.1.9, pp. 47, 51-52, 55, 72-73, 81, 100, 103, 105, 196, 211, 247.

[34] Same to same, July 16, 1907, No. 2938: MT 2.4.1.9, p. 196.

were absurd, for Korea had only 17,000 square miles of arable land, mostly in rice.[35]

However, the anxiety of the Japanese Foreign Office as to Hulbert's effectiveness was relieved by reports from overseas and from queries of foreign residents in Japan which showed that Westerners were not inclined to accept his accusations at face value. Aoki in Washington reported that, although Hulbert was denouncing Japan, when he discussed this with the acting secretary of state, the latter had said, "We are familiar with the method of those agitators. We shall know exactly how to deal with them."[36] Inoue Katsunosuke, adopted son of Inoue Kaoru, reported newspaper sentiments in Berlin favorable to Japan, such as "The Corean delegate at the Hague seems to have forgotten that on November 17, 1905 an agreement was signed in Seoul by which Corea was made a vassal state of Japan . . ." and describing Itō as "a real benefactor to a depraved country."[37] From St. Petersburg Japanese Minister Motono reported that Izvolsky had "scolded" the Koreans and "no paper assailed Japan."[38] The Italian public and press were "indifferent", reported Takahira from Rome.[39] Komura from London quoted the *London Times* as suggesting that if Japan used a "judicious mixture of firmness, of tact and of patience" in Korea she would achieve "what we have achieved in Egypt," the reconciliation "of a discontented nationality with foreign administration for their good."[40] Even the press of Glasgow, Scotland,

[35] Hayashi to Itō, July 6, 1905, No. 1835: MT 2.4.1.9, p. 80. Matsubara (San Francisco) to For. Min., Nov. 18, 21, 1907, Nos. 4861, 4929 and Hayashi to Matsubara, Nov. 21, 22, 1907, Nos. 3240, 3223; Hayashi memo (ca. Nov. 25): *ibid.*, pp. 797-98, 802-7, 825.

[36] Aoki to Hayashi, July 24, 1907, No. 3094: MT 2.4.1.9, pp. 371-70 (reverse pagination). Cf. Aoki to Hayashi, July 23, 27, 1907, Nos. 3081, 3155: *ibid.*, pp. 353, 532-31 (rev. pag.).

[37] Inoue to Hayashi, July 18, 27, 1907, Nos. 2966, 3170: MT 2.4.1.9, pp. 208-7 (rev. pag.), 353. Cf. same to same, July 21, 22, Nos. 3050, 3062: *ibid.*, pp. 312-11, 339-37 (rev. pag.).

[38] Motono to Hayashi, July 19, 22, 1907, Nos. 2419, 3052: *ibid.*, pp. 245-47, 332-35.

[39] Takahira to For. Min., July 22, 27, 1907, Nos. 3068, 3174: *ibid.*, pp. 340, 355.

[40] Komura to Hayashi, July 30, 1907, No. 3201: *ibid.*, pp. 586-85 (rev. pag.).

favored Japan.[41] And the governor of Kanagawa (Yokohama) prefecture reported that Westerners resident in Japan were "ridiculing the foolishness of Korea."[42]

Perhaps the best statements of responsible world opinion were contained in *New York Tribune* editorials of July 20 and 26, 1907, which were reported to the Japanese Foreign Office by Minister Aoki. "Corea," said the *Tribune*, had been "saved by Japan from Russian conquest and agreed to conduct its foreign affairs through the Japanese government . . .," an "arrangement recognized by all the world." Hence "the gravity of the offense of the Emperor of Corea in sending a delegation to La Hague unknown to Japan may be estimated if we imagine the Emir of Bokhara sending one to ask intervention between him and the Czar or the Annamese King against France or some Indian Maharajah asking La Hague to expel the British from Hindustan. The title of Japan to deal with Corea, as she has, is at least as good as that of Russia, France, England or any other Power to deal as they have with subject nations . . . Korea has been a source of irritation . . . menace to peace . . . well to have the menace removed. The peace and progress of the world are more important." And to put it in scientific terms, "the Law of survival of the fittest prevails among states as well as plants and animals. Corea has been conspicuously unfit. . . . Had Corea manifested one tenth of Japan's energy and ability, she would have established and maintained her sovereignty. Instead she was cruel, corrupt and ignorant, and displayed none of the essential elements of sovereign nationality."[43]

If Itō and other Japanese government leaders were distressed, conscience-wise, at finding it "necessary" to use force to thwart Korean "foolishness," they certainly could find comfort in such

[41] Brown (Glasgow) to Hayashi, July 30, 1907, No. 3658: *ibid.*, pp. 682-81 (rev. pag.).

[42] Gov. Kanagawa to For. Min., July 24, 27, 1907, Nos. 1929, 1972: *ibid.*, pp. 381-83, 536-38.

[43] Aoki to Hayashi, July 21, 27, 1907, Nos. 3035, 3155: *ibid.*, pp. 285-84, 532-31 (rev. pag.).

expressions of understanding. Were they distressed, did they feel guilty? poses an interesting question over which we might pause a moment. It was said early in this study that perhaps the most distinguishing characteristic of the circle of Meiji oligarchs, forged by Ōkubo and Iwakura and inherited by Itō, was the ability to put personal feelings aside, whether anger or shame or fear, in order to move forward the interests of the modern state they were creating. They had no time to measure matters in an eternal scale of values. It would certainly please them that a professor of philosophy who tried to do so might praise their work, and they were by no means disinterested in the advance of civilization. But the vehicle within which they worked, namely the Japanese state, consumed their whole energies. Without it, as far as they could see, there would be no advance of civilization; hence its protection and its interests must first be secured. Personal feelings, guilt or other, could not be allowed to stand in the way. However, they were not bludgeoning patriotic fools. They were *enlightened* servants of the state, fully sensitive to the fact that the long-range interests of Japan would not be served by the sort of international brigandage and piracy which would inflame world opinion against her. In this sense they were distressed, if they did not feel guilty, that force came into play before the Hague mission affair was resolved.

Japanese documents concerning the abdication of the emperor illustrate this in their insistence that it was not the resident general, but the Korean cabinet ministers who forced the abdication. As observed above, Ladd made a big point of this. Of course, his argument only registers his conviction that the distinction was important. And as for the Japanese, their use of the argument for foreign consumption deserves the connotation, propaganda. However, the intramural correspondence of Itō, Prime Minister Saionji, and Foreign Minister Hayashi indicates that, quite aside from the propaganda value of the distinction, they thought it to be a true one. Immediately after news of the Hague affair reached Tokyo, it was decided that Hayashi would go to Seoul to consult with Itō and bring him the views of the home government. While waiting for Hayashi, Itō sent the following report on the situation to Deputy Foreign Minister Chinda with instructions that it be conveyed to Saionji:

> The Korean ministers of state, hearing that the Hague mission had excited public opinion in Japan and the coming here of the Foreign Minister, decided there was need for some decisive action. They have been meeting every day and they have decided to have the Emperor retire. They are avoiding assistance from me and are trying to arrange it themselves. Prime Minister Yi saw the Emperor and advised abdication, but the Emperor refused. The whole cabinet recommended abdication yesterday, but the Emperor became angry and they retired. The Emperor then asked me to visit him. I wanted to wait to hear the opinion of our home government from Hayashi, but I went to see the Emperor and he asked me my opinion. I said I could make no reply. Then the Korean ministers pressed the Emperor to abdicate simultaneously with the arrival of the Foreign Minister at Seoul. Nine of their senior statesmen went into consultation with him at 1:00 A.M. today. They got his abdication and promulgated it at 3:00 A.M.[44]

A few days later, Itō wrote that "the old Emperor, after being forced to abdicate by his Ministers," was trying to "regain sovereignty by various underhand measures." He had "ordered his guard into readiness to kill the Ministers" but had failed "due to the arrival of Japanese soldiers thirty minutes before [the attempt]."[45]

Hayashi's version was expressed in communications to his Foreign Office subordinates. Before going to Korea he cabled Komura in London: "It seems to be an act of betrayal that the Korean Emperor dispatched mission to Hague to criticize Japanese activities and our government deeply regrets it. Our government wishes to protect its honour and interests. Therefore in order to confer with Resident General Itō, I, myself, shall go to Seoul."

[44] Itō to Chinda, July 19, 1907, No. 2993: *ibid.*, pp. 226-30.

[45] Itō to Saionji, July 22, 1907, No. 3054: *ibid.*, pp. 318-23.

Seikan Ron: Japan's Council of State, as yet ill at ease on chairs, arguing over whether to conquer Korea (1873) (Iwakura is at the table, center; Saigō standing, foreground)

The Japanese prints are reproduced by courtesy of Mr. Yoshiyuki Sakurai, from his collection.

Hanabusa, Japanese Minister, fleeing Seoul to the British frigate, *Flying Fish*, after antiforeign riot (July, 1882) (Hanabusa, hair flying, is standing in center of the small boat)

Hanabusa returning to Inchon with Japanese warships (August, 1882)

Hanabusa, after his return, admonishing the Korean King and Taewongun for the 1882 Incident

Assassination of Kim Ok-kiun in Shanghai (1894)

Ascent of Kim's ghost, with eulogy

Burning of the Japanese Legation, December, 1884, as Koreans and Chinese watch

Itō Hirobumi, Resident General

Uchida Ryōhei,
Black Dragon Chieftain

General Terauchi,
Annexer of Korea

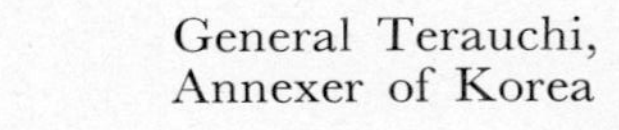

From Seoul he informed Chinda: "The enmity of Seoul citizens against Ministers grew violent, especially among Emperor's guards. On July 19 there was an attempt to go into the Palace and kill all the Ministers. They fled and were barely able to arrive at the Resident General's residence at 11:30 P.M., asking protection. Therefore Hasegawa was ordered to march and our soldiers took up positions at 11:58." To Motono in St. Petersburg he explained that the abdication had taken place, then, "I add for your information that the abdication was in no way the result of any insinuation or suggestion made by the Japanese government, and that it apparently originated out of the sole desire of the Corean government to mitigate the demands of Japan which they had anticipated to be heavy."[46]

When one analyzes the balance of Japanese-Korean relationships which Itō constructed during his first year and a half as resident general against the background of certain related activities in Japan, it becomes apparent that the Hague affair and the abdication were indeed distressing to Itō and to the Saionji-Hayashi leadership in Japan, which bore his stamp and was much more congenial to his delicacy of operation than the Yamagata-oriented Katsura government had been. It will be remembered that Itō was very careful to insulate the Residency General against the latter at the time of its organization. It is the author's opinion that probably too much has been made by many writers of the civilian (Itō-Saionji) versus military (Yamagata-Katsura) cleavage in the oligarchy in the late Meiji period. It should be remembered that oligarchs and protégés in both groups were steeped in the realistic tradition of Ōkubo and were never so far out of step that their differences could not be composed at the slightest hint of threat to their political supremacy from outside forces. (The most conspicuous example of this being their defeat of the liberal parties.)

[46] Hayashi to Komura (London), July 13; to Chinda (Tokyo), July 20; to Motono (St. Petersburg), July 20, 1907, Nos. 1913, 30-0, 1974: *ibid*, pp. 142-43, 248-49, 259-61.

However, this is not to deny that there was a considerable area of difference between the two groups, especially on the issue of how much force should be applied in backing up Japanese overseas ventures. Itō's awareness of this was clearly expressed in his determination to keep the military command to himself in Korea, so as to keep the use of force to a minimum. But, of course, the use of force on any large scale would give the more military minded renewed opportunity.

Also Itō's administration was dependent in no small way on the Korean emperor, or rather on the maintenance of a rather precarious balance between His Majesty and "progressive" ministers grouped around him. In this, Itō improved upon Inoue's earlier effort to have Pak Young-hyo push his reform program on an unwilling court. Inoue had failed, but Itō had many advantages—superior talents, a treaty structure legalizing his commanding position at Seoul, no Queen Min or Taewongun to complicate things, no foreign interference, and full knowledge of Inoue's previous experience.

Itō's approach to the problem of building a Korean reform ministry which would be responsive to his bidding yet have the confidence of their emperor was to avoid using Pak, while keeping him near at hand, and to rely on such members of Philip Jaisohn's Independence Club as could be induced to collaborate. Pak was definitely available again, but Itō was suspicious of him because of the anti-Japanese tendencies he had exhibited during his several months in power in 1895, and anyway, he was *persona non grata* to his emperor, most recently for his supposed involvement in a plot to force the latter's abdication engineered by one General An Kyong-su in 1898. General An had been executed in 1900.[47] Pak, of course, was in Japan through all this. After the establishment of the Residency General, he seems to have expected to be called to Seoul, but no call came, and finally he began to make arrangements to return to Korea on his own. Japanese authorities watched and

[47] C. N. Weems, "Korean Reform . . .," pp. 175-76, 497.

reported his every move. Meanwhile Itō, in March, 1906, had taken up the matter of the "return of high Koreans in Japan," including Pak, with the Korean emperor. The emperor approved the return of some fifteen, but rejected fourteen others. Pak was on the rejected list. Itō told Saionji that it would be difficult to get the emperor's permission for the return of these fourteen, but perhaps it could be done "later." Then on April 17, a minor official of the Residency General informed the vice-foreign minister in Japan that "the Korean emperor has removed all titles from the fourteen returnees, and in that condition will allow them to return." He advised that this information be passed on to Koreans in Japan, among whom there were apparently some discussion and consternation on the issue of whether to return or not. A report by Japanese authorities, seemingly for the Home Ministry, speaks of one Korean who talked with his "friends and neighbors," urging that "the situation is changing in Korea so it might not be a good time to go back. Even if I return I could not get an official position, but would have to go into business."[48]

Pak himself made no move to return until the following year, when Tokyo authorities began to report various rumors about his plans, and then suddenly, according to a report dated June 10, 1907,

> Pak Young-hyo left secretly on June 6 and arrived in Korea [Pusan] on June 8, informing his secretary by telegram. His secretary was quite surprised. We cannot understand his intention in going to Korea so secretly. . . . It may be that he returned on special invitation of the Korean Emperor. There is a rumor that a special messenger visited him in Tokyo a few days ago. . . . One Japanese, named Nakamura,

[48] Itō to Saionji, Mar. 26, 1906, No. 668 (confidential): Archives, MT 1.1.2.41. (Documents relating to exiled Koreans), pp. 23-32. Seoul Residency to Vice For. Min., Apr. 17, 1906: *ibid.*, pp. 51-52. No sender or addressee (Home Ministry report), Mar. 31, 1906: *ibid.*, pp. 42-43.

Cf. other such reports on Koreans: Yamaguchi Prefecture Internal Affairs Office to Home Min., Mar. 29, 1906 (secret, urgent): *ibid.*, pp. 39-41; Tokyo Metro. Police and various prefectural governors to For. Office, many reports, 1906-7: *ibid.*, pp. 53-170. Even an "American prostitute" named "Miss Dare," who had been employed by a Korean, was reported on. Gov. Kanagawa Pref. to For. Min., May 1, 1906, No. 1106 (secret): *ibid.*, pp. 83-84.

accompanied Pak to Korea. This Nakamura seems to be a gambler. He is a member of Tōa Dōbunkai. P.S. A member of the youth group of Tōa Dōbunkai and reporter on the Mainichi newspaper told us that he carried a secret message from Pak to Resident General Itō saying that Pak and a friend wished to return to Korea. According to him Itō had approved the return of the friend, but said that some Koreans objected to Pak. "However, later I'll arrange it and make him Prime Minister," said Itō.

The above document contains an interesting notation alongside the "P.S." section. It says, "Omit this" (before transmission to Itō?). Also with it is an "attached document" on Pak's companion, Nakamura, describing him as "Nakamura Tahachiro, born 1868 in Nagano prefecture, member Kokka Shakai Tō [National Socialist party], no occupation, ability as a speaker, gambler, organized Tōa Seinenkai [East Asia Young Men's Society] in 1904. a branch of Tōa Dōbunkai. Its aim is China-Korea progress, development and leadership." Nakamura had also organized a movement to help outcasts in Japan.

Another report, which suggests, incidentally, that Japanese police were very up to date in reading the mail of Pak's secretary in Tokyo, says: "Pak's secretary received a letter yesterday from Pak. In it Pak said, 'I have gone to Pusan to obtain special permission to return to Korea. Until I get this permission I will not return to Japan. I am working on this. When I get permission I will send you money. Prepare to leave Japan.' " Another report concerned Pak's finances. "According to rumor," it said, he had received 1000 yen from Pyongyang in February and another 700 yen in April. Apparently the Foreign Ministry forwarded all these reports (with or without the untactful "P.S.") to Itō with a notification from Deputy Foreign Minister Chinda, "Pak Young-hyo has left Japan, landed in Pusan on the 8th. Please ask Japanese agency in Pusan to protect him and to inquire as to his plans."[49]

[49] Dep. For. Min. to Res. General, June 13, 1907: *ibid.*, p. 90. Investigation reports dated June 10, 12, 13, 17, 1907: *ibid.*, pp. 91-100, 110-11.

On June 22 Ito sent a commentary on Pak's activities to Hayashi:

Pak wrote urgently from Pusan on June 8, apologizing for his return and asking my protection. I ordered the agent in Pusan to let him stay there and to await further orders. -My reason was to limit Pak's contact with other Koreans and prevent rumors. I also ordered the Agency to find out Pak's reason for returning to Korea. Possible reasons are as follows: at the Emperor's secret order, invited by other Koreans, his own personal wishes. Or did he make some special agreement with the Japanese government before he left Japan? [Mutual suspicion? *Viz.*, "P.S." above.] Pak has for a long time wanted to return to Korea and from his speech and action it seems that his personal wishes constitute the reason for his return, not an order from the Emperor or an invitation from other Koreans. Thinking he would not be punished, he came. In Pusan Pak has been staying with an American missionary, named Irving. I showed Pak's telegram to the Emperor and next day I instructed Pak to remain quietly in Pusan until official permission to come to Seoul was forthcoming. I also arranged for Attorney General Cho to call on Pak secretly. The people around Pak seem reliable, and I do not think he has political intentions. Accordingly on the 11th I asked the Emperor's permission for Pak to enter, and the Emperor approved it immediately. I sent word to Pak that it was all right for him to come to Seoul. Pak then sent a letter of apology to the Emperor, saying he deserved punishment, and he informed me that he would not leave Pusan until he received an answer from the Emperor. I urged the Emperor to answer, and he did. Pak came to Seoul and is staying at a Japanese hotel.[50]

These documents concerning the return of Korean exiles are quoted in some detail for the light they shed, not only on the attitude of the Residency General toward the return and possible employment of Pak, but also on two other points: namely, Itō's emphasis on deference to the will of the Korean emperor[51] concerning the returnees, a matter in which the emperor was

[50] Itō to Hayashi, June 22, 1907, No. 1640: MT 1.1.2.41, pp. 119-26.

[51] Other indications of such deference appear in the formality of official visits, care in seating arrangements, attention to titles, etc. See Itō memo, No. 179, June 14, 1906, and No. 186, Nov. 12, 1906: Kensei Shiryō Shitsu.

particularly sensitive, and the way in which Koreans in Japan were watched and reported on. Clearly, Itō was being guarded against surprises from this quarter, although, as Pak's case indicates, the surveillants were sometimes mystified.

With Pak Young-hyo on the sidelines and pains taken to reassure the emperor that he was more than a figurehead, Itō undertook to build a "reform" administration around former members of the Independence Club, who, under Jaisohn's (So Che-pil) inspired leadership, had made a remarkable effort to set Korea on the road to progress in 1896–97. The principal figures in this were Yi Wan-yong, who became prime minister under the Residency General, and Pak Che-sun. These and others of the Independence Club who collaborated with the Japanese can be and usually are set off as traitors in contrast to those like Jaisohn and Syngman Rhee who denounced the Japanese from abroad, and Han Kyu-sul and Yi Ch'ae-yon who, remaining in Korea, refused to collaborate and paid for it with loss of office, rank, and even, as seems to have been the case with Yi Ch'ae-won, life as well. However, Clarence Weems, in his very penetrating study of the Independence Club, cautions against too harsh a judgment on the "traitors." He observes that Jaisohn himself and the entire Independence group had to depend on "good relations with the dominant Russians" to launch their program in 1896, and that the Korean emperor, whose abdication the "traitors" helped to bring about in 1907, had himself played a major role in the ruination of the club's valiant effort to promote reforms which were clearly necessary if Korea was to have even a small chance to survive as an independent state. The emperor ignored Jaisohn's recommendations, favored reactionaries at court, sponsored the vigorously anti-reform "Peddlers' Guild" movement, and ended by decreeing the dissolution of the Independence Club and the arrest of its leaders. These activities brought the Independence movement to such a point of desperation that its members fell into such things as the aforementioned plot by General An to dethrone the emperor and the voting of a resolution to invite

Pak Young-hyo, already under cloud as a traitor, from Japan to take over leadership of the government. These doings were the Koreans' own, not the result of Japanese pressure, for the Japanese were incapable of pressure at the time of their occurrence in 1898.

Weems takes a tolerant view of General An, puppet Prime Minister Yi Wan-yong, Pak Che-sun, who signed the key documents for the Residency General in 1905 and 1907, and even Pak Young-hyo himself. He does not find their devotion to their country's welfare to be significantly less than that of their fellow reformers who refused to deal with Japan. The difficult conditions in which they worked pressed them all toward compromises with foreigners whose interests were by no means identical with Korea's, and the fact that some of them trusted the Japanese is not surprising. The writer is inclined to agree with Weems in this, while pointing out that however good the motives and trying the situation of the collaborators, and admitting that as of 1905 or 1907 they, like many Western observers, could not be sure whether a period of Japanese guidance might not benefit their country, their collaboration in the end contributed to the subjection of their countrymen to long and harsh colonial rule. In his final assessment of Korea's independence and reform movement Weems puts much less blame for its failure on the factor of collaboration with the Japanese than on the inability of its Western-minded and oriented leaders, particularly Jaisohn, to appreciate the potential contribution of the conservative nativist reform movement embodied in the Tonghaks and to co-operate with it. For a "positive design for reform" to have developed successfully in Korea, he says, it was necessary to have within it "an element of conservatism." But Jaisohn and his Independence Club associates tried to "stand in a cultural vacuum while preaching change."[52] Again, this writer feels, Weems has made a very astute observation, but we shall reserve further

[52] C. N. Weems, "Korean Reform . . .," pp. 136-525, esp. pp. 149-50, 165-66, 174-78, 243-44, 254, 277, 298, 476-77, 486, 495, 497-502, 514.

mention of the Tonghaks and our estimate of their role, especially as related to the Japanese, for the next chapter.

It should be observed here that Itō was sagacious enough to include an element of conservatism in establishing *his* "design for reform," not in the sense of favoring Tonghak elements (though his relationship with these especially after 1907 poses interesting questions), but in his coddling of emperor and court while at the same time utilizing reformist ministers to effect drastic changes in the direction of modernization in all branches of the Korean government. Itō knew very well that a circumspect handling of the emperor was necessary if his reform program was to develop smoothly, without violence, and he wished and hoped to keep the emperor happy, while minimizing his opportunities to disturb the progress of reform. In this Itō failed, despite all the advantages of his situation and all the astuteness he could command. His own Residency General's report for 1907 deals rather plaintively with this. A basic trouble, he says, was that the ministers of state were constituted as a "deliberative board" (*Wi-jong-bu*) rather than as a true cabinet. The Japanese, in the reforms of 1895, had tried to make it a true cabinet, in which the minister of the imperial household was not included, "the object being to draw a clear line of demarcation between the Court and the State." However, thereafter, the old system had been reverted to, even to the point of restoring the imperial household minister to the "board," which occurred in June, 1898. In 1905 this official was again removed from the "board" and with his duties confined to the imperial household, the separation of state and court was again "attempted." However, the Imperial Palace was frequented by diviners, fortune tellers and other persons, men and women, of obscure origin and questionable character, their sole object being to cheat and to extract money from the Imperial purse. In the face of these perilous conditions the resident general could not remain silent. Hence, as stated in the report for 1906, the residency general, having obtained the Imperial consent, caused, in 1906, the police adviser to station constables at each gate of the Palace, in order to keep off persons of questionable character, and at the same time the "Palace Precincts Ordinance" was promulgated, by which passes were to be issued only to known persons who had legitimate business with the Court.

"Thus the Resident General used his best exertions to purify the chronic state of corruption which had become so deeply rooted in the Imperial Household, and to improve the management of Court affairs through the intervention of advisers and councillors. But inasmuch as the Court was free to accept or reject this advice at will, the reforms in the Imperial Household were not satisfactorily carried into effect. . . ."[53] So complains the report.

The Hague mission affair very probably convinced Itō that he could no longer tolerate the old emperor. The emperor, vacillating and weak though he may have been over his long years of rule, was stubborn when it came to intrusions on his royal powers, especially by reformers—whether of the native or foreign variety—and his years of experience in intrigue-ridden Seoul had given him not only countless subterranean connections but a real capacity to find ways to embarrass if not defeat his captors of the moment. He was not happy with the new regime, and even guards and checkers at the palace gates could not prevent his telling the world about it. Itō had to find a new formula. A circumspect Residency General working through reformist Korean ministers, atop a ballast of royal conservatism, was "not enough." But, Itō thought, co-operation could be re-established if one leg of the triangle, the Residency General, assumed a more active role and another, the court, became more pliable. The ministers, at this point, were no problem, in fact were a help. Fortunately for Itō *they* pushed for the abdication of the emperor, which was obtained July 19, thus allowing him to make the fine distinction that it was a move demanded by Korean leaders themselves. Also, they signed the new seven-article agreement of July 24, 1907, which spelled out vast new powers for the resident general, including veto power over all laws, ordinances,

[53] Residency General, *Annual Report for 1907*, pp. 12-17.

and regulations and the appointment of officials, and, most important, the right to appoint Japanese subjects as officials of the Korean government. Surely this, plus the fact that the new emperor was a very dull boy, would be sufficient. Itō hoped it would be, but he expected some trouble. On July 19 he informed the Foreign Office that he had ordered General Hasegawa "to take reasonable measures to preserve peace in Seoul." On July 21, he wired Prime Minister Saionji: "Situation in Seoul complicated. . . . Perhaps another brigade should be dispatched from Japan. Local areas calm as they have little news from Seoul, but expect some unrest in a few days." Saionji assured him the troops were coming.[54]

The abdication signed on July 19 was promulgated in formal ceremony on July 22. These were accompanied by some unrest in Seoul, during which Premier Yi Wan-yong's house was burned, attacks were made on other pro-Japanese Koreans, and a plot on Itō's life was thwarted. Japanese soldiers silenced these outbreaks in the capital, however, and "every Japanese camp was put on watch" with Japanese officers in the Korean army beginning to put ammunition and weapons into warehouses and "keep the key." In general things were "calm".[55]

There was for the moment more trouble in Tokyo, where Korean students, to the consternation of Japanese authorities, began to hold meetings and denounce Japan. According to Japanese police reports, "One Korean student brought a pistol and said he would kill his Japanese teacher, but his elder brother took the pistol from him." Others said they would leave Japan for the United States or France. A group gathered at the former Korean legation in Tokyo and said they would die rather than accept the abdication. However, some of their fellows, like an "elder brother," counselled patience. The chief of Korean students in Tokyo stressed the need

[54] Itō to Chinda, Dep. For. Min., July 19, 1907: Archives, MT 2.4.1.9, p. 242; to Saionji, July 21, 1907: *ibid.*, p. 305. Saionji to Itō, July 24, 1907: *ibid.*, p. 372.

[55] Chief. Gen. Staff to For. Min., July 22, 1907, No. 477: Archives, MT 2.4.1.9, pp. 925-26. Dong, "Japanese Annexation . . .," p. 521.

for friendship between China, Japan, and Korea and expressed the feeling that Koreans would not revolt if it were clear that Japan was only cleaning up the Korean court, "which had been corrupt for fifty years." Japanese friends of Pak Young-hyo hastily organized a Japan-Korean Friendship Society and came out in favor of a new Korean regime headed by Pak.[56] In Seoul, however, the first serious omen that the abdication had wounded Korean sensibilities beyond repair came from Pak himself. He accepted a call from the now abdicated emperor to become "Minister of the Imperial Household" and very briefly became the center of a movement to undo the abdication. Itō informed Saionji that "even Mr. Pak Young-hyo agrees with the old Emperor's intention to recover sovereignty in the future." At this "treachery" Itō did not equivocate. He had Pak arrested and banished to Quelpart Island, the news of which rather disconcerted the "Pak for Premier" movement in Tokyo.[57]

Far more ominous from Itō's point of view was the problem of the Korean army. It will be recalled that once before, in 1894, Ōtori had begun to take their weapons away from them, but had been stopped by Mutsu's caustic reminder that they were Japan's "allies." Itō had certainly stood behind Mutsu on this. With the establishment of the Residency General Japanese military advisers had undertaken to introduce "improvements" into the Korean army, which was, for all the Chinese, Japanese, Russian, and other instructions accorded it in the past, still a nondescript collection of mercenaries. Itō seems to have intended developing a fairly coherent Korean military organization, however, for as late as July 2, 1907, at Japanese suggestion, a conscription law was enacted making all Korean males aged seventeen to forty liable for military

[56] Tokyo Metro. Police reports to For. Min., July 19, 24, 26, 29, Aug. 14, 1907, Nos. 1878, 1944, 1968, 2010, 2164: Archives, MT 2.4.1.9, pp. 275, 490-97, 523-25, 587-90, 653-55. Other reports: *ibid.*, pp. 189-91, 198-201 *et seq.*

[57] Itō to Saionji, July 22, 1907, No. 3054: Archives, MT 2.4.1.9, pp. 318-19. Chief General Staff to Cmd. Gen. in Korea, July 24, 1907, No. 1932: *ibid.*, p. 431. Metro. Police to For. Min., Aug. 14, 1907, No. 2164: *ibid.*, p. 655. Ladd, *In Korea . . .*, p. 429. Dong, "Japanese Annexation . . . " p. 322.

service.[58] Evidently he expected they could be fit (loyally) into his balance of Japanese-Korean administration. However, Itō was also aware that the most difficult aspects of the problem of gaining support for his regime were not necessarily confined to the upper echelons of government, court, ministers, and the like. In various memoranda which he wrote down, perhaps for himself, during the year preceding the Hague affair, he mentions the general anti-Japanese feeling among Koreans and admits it to have been increasing, for example: "Recently a faithful attitude can be seen in the Korean Emperor but the anti-Japanese arguments increase day by day." And again, "When Hideyoshi attacked Korea, his followers murdered many Koreans and today Koreans remember this. Propagandists of anti-Japanese feeling argue, 'Though the Japanese say their purpose is to help Koreans, their real purpose is to annihilate them.' " Another, "Even now the Koreans have not awakened. The Emperor just talks, but has no honesty, and I know that anti-Japanese feeling is increasing."[59] Such comments indicate that, for all his savoir faire, Itō was uneasy. Instead of responding to treatment, Korean hostility, he could feel, was increasing. Then the abdication crisis unquestionably made him edgy, as the quick arrest of Pak Young-hyo testifies. He had been treating Pak with easy tolerance and might have found him useful at that juncture. But suddenly, his whole administration had been shaken by a "stubborn, stupid and weak little man," the foreign minister was coming to see him, there would be criticism at home. He had to put things in order in a hurry, with no chances taken.

While mending political fences through the collaborationist ministers, he turned a suspicious eye on the Korean military. One of his earliest dispatches on the crisis, sent July 19, makes particular mention that "about 4:00 o'clock some Korean soldiers attacked our policemen" and adds even the street location of the place in

[58] Res. Gen., *Annual Report for 1907*, pp. 34-35.

[59] Itō memo, Nos. 95, 108, no day, 1906: Kensei Shiryō Shitsu.; Hiratsuka, *Itō Hakubun . . .*, I, 321 (Doc. No. 79).

Seoul where the attack took place.[60] If the weapons of the Korean army became spread about the countryside through defection of the soldiers, there could be much trouble, and Itō was determined to stop that. Hence the quiet campaign to lock up the weapons and "keep the key." But maintaining an army with its weapons locked up could hardly go on for long, and, therefore, as one of the first acts of the new emperor, he demanded through the Korean ministry and obtained an imperial rescript disbanding the army. The excuse was that, since a new conscription system was being inaugurated anyway, time was necessary to plan it. Also, "every effort should be made to practise economy with the view of devoting funds to the prosecution of useful enterprises. . . . We therefore hereby order Our officials to select men necessary for guarding the Imperial Family, and temporarily disband all the rest." The rescript was promulgated on August 1, 1907.[61]

This inaugurated a new phase for Itō's administration, best described as the "controlling riots" phase, from which it never really emerged. Despite special precautions taken by the Japanese to prevent untoward incidents during the carrying out of the army disbandment order, the dramatic suicide of a patriotic battalion commander in Seoul provided a spark that set off a chain reaction of revolts which swept far beyond the capital, into remote country districts, from the far south to the Yalu River. For example, the captain of a Japanese warship at Genzan (Wonsan) reported that several hundred rioters in that district abducted a Japanese mailman, held a meeting at which they planned a march on Seoul, and chased eleven Japanese policemen to the safety of the warship. An army company was requested to restore order. On September 3, General Hasegawa took time out from his direction of the riot suppressing activities to write a general report on the situation. He noted that several Korean societies and groups incited the riots with "violent speeches" claiming that "they had lost the Empress,

[60] Itō to Chinda (for Saionji), July 19, 1907: Archives, MT 2.4.1.9, p. 240.
[61] Res. Gen., *Annual Report for 1907*, p. 35.

now the Emperor," and urging "kill Korean traitors." He predicted, however, that only a few would resist to the death and "after six months or so it will be calm." He analyzed Korea by classes as follows: "The upper class is very shocked that Japanese can now be officials; the middle class is not so shocked and feels that the new convention recognizes the defacto situation. It is about 50/50 pro and con the new convention. The lower class has been oppressed by officials and the upper class and will come to see Japanese officials as protectors of the people." As for the disbanding of the army, it had been successfully accomplished "except along the Yalu River." Koreans generally did not regret the disbanding, he thought, for they knew the soldiers to be "arrogant, expensive, weak, and do-nothing."[62]

Hasegawa's report proved over-sanguine. In late November, Itō admitted confidentially to Foreign Minister Hayashi that very harsh measures had been employed in trying to put down the riots. Mr. Bethell's newspaper, before its suppression in October, treated Seoul citizens to unvarnished accounts of Japanese brutality, which McKenzie after his inspection trip largely endorsed. And although British policy was pro-Japanese, and it was the British consular court that silenced Bethell,[63] the accusations of these two Englishmen apparently stirred British officialdom to make an investigation, or at least Itō thought it had. He informed Hayashi that "according to a confidential report," the British government had heard rumors that "in local districts" Japanese troops had been "too severe" and was investigating. Japanese troops had, he ad-

[62] Maruyama, police investigator, to Gen. Staff to For. Off., Aug. 2, 1907, No. 2045 (confidential, re: suicide); Army Cmdr. (Seoul) to Chief Gen. Staff to For. Min., July 31, 1907; Sasebo Naval Dist. Cmdr. to Dep. Navy Min., Aug. 11, 1907 (re: Genzan); Archives, MT 2.4.1.9, pp. 982-83, 980, 1020-21. Hasegawa to For. Min. via Itō, Sept. 3, 1907, No. 2422: *ibid.*, pp. 1120-44.

[63] Cf. above, note 24. Bethell's articles are reprinted in McKenzie, *The Tragedy of Korea*, pp. 224-37.

Hayashi in a report from Seoul, dated Sept. 25, 1905, spoke of Bethell as follows: "The Emperor gives money out of his pocket to Bethell, who controls the Korean English language newspaper, to get him to write anti-Japanese propaganda." Hayashi to Katsura, For. Min., No. 2498: MT 1.6.1.24, p. 3.

mitted, "sometimes resorted to burning a whole village because a few citizens were letting the rioters stay in their houses." This was deplorable and he would stop it; he said: "I found that during my absence the military measures against riotous people had been too severe and I have ordered the military to change them. Japanese soldiers were burning stones and gems without distinguishing. Recently, however, our troops have been paying attention to my order."[64]

One does not know whether the Japanese riot suppressors became more gentle, but they were assuredly very active for many months. Itō's deputy chief of general affairs at Seoul, Tsuruhara, filed a very gloomy report to the Foreign Office in mid-December:

> The disbandment of Korean troops caused the first riot in the 1st battalion at Seoul, then they spread . . . everywhere except along the Seoul-Pusan Railway and the North-east Railway fell into a totally riotous condition. It would be peaceful by day, riotous by night, with farmers hiding weapons and attacking Japanese soldiers and civilians if they appeared weak. Still there is unrest everywhere except in the coastal areas. The leaders are disbanded soldiers and obstinate local Confucianists. Pro Japanese Koreans have been killed without reason, even Koreans who merely wear Western clothing or have short hair are killed. The anti Japanese feeling is deep rooted. . . . The rioters are different from thieves and robbers. However, the traditional thieves and robbers are also being assimilated into the rioting groups. Ordinary people cannot live on doing their daily work. Some are fleeing with their families, some have been killed, some have lost their homes, Now there is cold and starvation. It is a calamitous situation. Japanese residents and business people are all retreating from the interior. Riot taming missions have been sent into every district. The Korean government has ordered control measures on arms and powder. . . .[65]

The Japanese army chief of staff reported to the Foreign Office that

[64] Itō to Hayashi, Nov. 29, 1907 (two letters): Archives, MT 2.4.1.9, pp. 1286-89. The absence referred to was Itō's going to Tokyo where he had been elevated to the rank of prince.

[65] Dec. 13, 1907, No. 3224: Archives, MT 2.4.1.9, pp. 1309-15.

between July, 1907, and July 4, 1908, some 11,962 Korean "rioters" had been killed and 4,961 had "surrendered."[66] Other reports give somewhat different figures, but a general tabulation of the number of Koreans in arms against the Japanese, which Chon Dong accepts, is very likely close to the truth. It shows 50,000 Koreans fighting 324 engagements with the Japanese in 1907; 70,000 in 1450 engagements in 1908; 28,000 in 950 engagements in 1909; and 1,900 in 147 engagements in 1910.[67]

Itō tried to be "peaceful and calm"[68] but "riot controlling" remained a constant feature of his administration until his resignation in June, 1909. The best he could do, beyond issuing occasional reminders to his troops that gentleness was to be preferred, was to try to set geographical limits at the Korean border. Even this was difficult. The question of how far, geographically, the "taming missions" should go came to something of a head in August, 1908, while Itō was in Tokyo and his deputy resident general, Sone, whom Itō had carefully schooled in the art of mildness, was left in charge at Seoul. Many Korean "rioters" had crossed the Tumen and Yalu Rivers into Manchuria, and Sone became very excited about the possibility of their grouping there to re-enter Korea. He wired Itō for permission to send Japanese troops into Manchuria to break up the rebel bands, urging that negotiations be undertaken with the Chinese government to permit this. Itō replied firmly in the negative, but Sone thought the matter so urgent that he sent messages to Terauchi and Komura advising them of the problem and asking that the matter be reconsidered. He specifically asked instructions of Komura, who was then foreign minister. Komura replied, "The opinion of our government is that we cannot dispatch troops across the river, even if there are Korean

[66] Aug. 18, 1907, No. 1933: *ibid.*, p. 1946.

[67] Res. Gen., Controlling Riots Section report, 1908: Archives, MT 1.1.2.55 (Res. Gen. administrative matters), p. 46. Dong, "Japanese Annexation . . ." pp. 328-29, citing Kuzū, *Nikkan Gappō* . . ., I, 366.

[68] Note his words of caution to Japanese judges in Korea—Itō memo, Nos. 8, 9, June 13, 1908: Kensei Shiryō Shitsu.

rioters in the area. The Resident General will instruct you."[69]

Consideration of the abdication affair, the disbandment of the Korean army, and the controlling riots campaign brings up, quite naturally, the question, was not Itō, after all, pleased with these, since he was planning annexation anyway and they gave him additional pretexts for fastening a tight Japanese grip on Korea? As had been pointed out earlier, many studies assume that "from the beginning" the Japanese government's "scheme" for Korea was annexation, and on this basis the Residency General constituted merely a semifinal step in that direction, with Itō cynically seeking annexation while pretending otherwise. Among careful scholarly studies, the most recent to argue this way is Chon Dong's, a doctoral dissertation completed at the University of Colorado in 1955. Dong takes pains to emphasize Itō's duplicity and hypocrisy. He says Itō's actions were "the studied tactics of scheming imperialists" and describes his argument that the protectorate was inevitable in order to "secure the safety of the independence of Japan" as "absolutely nonsense."[70]

One of Dong's key proofs of this is a speech to officials in the Residency General which Itō gave at the time of the signing of the Seven-Article Treaty of July, 1907. He quotes this as follows, punctuation his: ". . . today there is a discussion of the annexation of Korea. . . . All necessary steps have been taken. . . . There is no use to repeat such a discussion here. Of course, if Korea rejects our proposal [for the annexation] there is no question about our resort to forceful means. . . . If such disagreement should occur in Korea I am determined to call the troops from home and take steps

[69] Sone to Itō, Aug. 7, 1908, unnumbered: Archives, MT 2.4.1.9, pp. 1912-14. Itō to Sone, Aug. 8: *ibid.*, pp. 1919-20. Sone to Terauchi, Aug. 12: *ibid.*, pp. 1926-27: to Komura, Aug. 30: *ibid.*, pp. 1963-65. Komura to Sone, Aug. 31: *ibid.*, pp. 1966-68. Cf. Sone to Hayashi, For. Min., Mar. 2, 1908, No. 587: MT 2.4.1.9, pp. 1470-74, for a general description of the border situation.

[70] Dong, *op. cit.*, pp. 230, 304, 335. A very recent study by another Korean scholar gives a much more dispassionate analysis of Ito's role. See Bibliography, page 515, under Kim, Chong-Ik, Japan in Korea (1905–1910): The Techniques of Political Power.

for complete suppression." And he notes the hypocrisy in Itō's telling newspaper editors the same day that "there is no necessity for Japan to annex Korea." For this speech to Residency General officials, Dong relies on the Amur River or Black Dragon Society (Kokuryūkai) publication, *Nikkan Gappō Hishi* (Secret History of the Merger of Japan and Korea), on which, he tells us, his discussion of the 1905–10 period is "based almost wholly." He regards this as a reliable source "because it was compiled by an official of the Kokuryūkai, and Japanese annexationists were either members of that society or closely connected with it." The present writer agrees with Dong that this "Secret History" is a most important source for Japanese-Korean relations of the 1905–10 period and that the documents quoted therein are extremely revealing and probably accurate, though, for reasons which will be more thoroughly considered later, it must be used with great care. Dong has, in fact, indicated the key problem in using the work, namely, that it was composed by Japanese annexationists. However, he fails to point out specifically the very important fact that the tone of the whole work is *anti*-Itō and his administration, that these ardent advocates of annexation considered Itō an obstacle to their cause. The overall relationship of Itō and these Black Dragon annexationists is very complex, and is better left aside for the moment, but let us reread the quotation from Itō's speech to the Residency General officials in the context that there had been advocacy and even demands for immediate and definite annexation of Korea from annexationist groups and that Itō knew some of his subordinates in the Residency General to harbor those sentiments. The speech then becomes an admonition, "We are not going to entertain any arguments for annexation here. . . . Of course, if Korea rejects our proposal," not "for the annexation," as Dong inserts, but "for the Seven Article Treaty we have drawn up . . ." then "I am determined to call troops from home. . . ." It can readily be seen that this would put Itō in a totally different light, resisting extremists among his own countrymen, yet trying to avoid the accusation, which they often made, that he was "weak-kneed." And his statement to newspaper editors becomes, not hypocrisy, but a clear statement of his own view on the subject.[71]

Does this mean that we must reject the "scheming imperialist" interpretation of Itō? Without thereby absolving Itō of blame for acts of brutality committed by agencies under his direction—or detracting an iota of sympathy for the Korean nation or people—in the interest of understanding the forces at work in the situation we are compelled to say yes, we must reject that interpretation, at least in any ordinary and obvious meaning of the term. Indeed Chon Dong, whom we have singled out as the most recent, and who is probably the best informed, advocate of the "scheming imperialist" thesis, in his careful recitation of the "Secret History" material brings out evidence which, had he not already settled on the thesis, he would surely have admitted to be contradictory to it. This evidence again and again shows Itō, between 1907 and 1909, and his alter ego Sone, thereafter, to be resisting demands for annexation. Dong explains this in such terms as the following. "Tokyo" regarded annexation as unavoidable. Itō's object was "the same," but he was more "cautious," and "Itō was neither a liberal nor the champion of Korea's independence, but a shrewd and cautious diplomat and administrator for all that was to the advantage of the Japanese empire." Regarding Sone he says, "The appointment of Sone to the resident generalship was for the purpose of an immediate annexation of Korea. Before Sone was appointed to the position, Sugiyama told Song and Uchida [annexationists, of whom more will be said later], 'If Sone is not sufficiently committed to the final plot, we will just dismiss him.' " But he does not see any problem in the fact that Sone *was* dismissed and that in going ahead with annexation Premier Katsura violated a "secret pledge" which, according to Dong, relying on the "Secret History," he made to Itō and Sone at the time of Itō's resignation. The pledge was that

[71] *Ibid.*, p. 324; see also Dong's comments on Kuzū, *Nikkan Gappō Hishi*, in his abstract of dissertation. The quotation in question is from *Nikkan Gappō Hishi*, I, 333.

there should be no annexation of Korea at least for another seven or eight years.[72]

The possibility that Dong's material should be interpreted in a different way is not, of itself, sufficient proof that Itō's opposition to annexation was more than a façade. But there are additional pieces of evidence. In the communication, dated July 29, 1907, in which he informed Prime Minister Saionji that the Korean army was being disbanded, Itō said, quite unnecessarily for the purpose at hand, that later on "under the conscription law" a "reorganized powerful army" should be built up in Korea.[73] He seems to be telling himself he is not suppressing the Koreans permanently. A Tokyo Metropolitan Police report to Foreign Minister Hayashi, dated September 6, 1907, says the following: "According to a member of the Yamagata group, Marquis Itō's attitude is too peaceful and calm. He is the most weak kneed among the weak kneed party. This is shown by the fact that he wants Japan to back Korean finance, let them adhere to the Convention, and have them gradually repay the money. But the Yamagata circle feels that if Korea in ten or twenty years becomes independent in finance, the Korean government will revolt. Therefore it urges strong policy. Korea should be kept perpetually dependent and the Koreans should be taxed."[74] Tokutomi, in his collection of Katsura's papers, quotes the following concerning Itō, written by Katsura to Yamagata. It is dated April 17, 1909, at which time Katsura was prime minister: "The sooner the day of his replacement the better for the next step in our policy. An influential person is not necessary. I recommend Mr. Sone as our next resident general, because it will be easy to move him as we wish. If this is not done, progress in all things will be difficult. Now is the best time. Terauchi and Komura agree with me."[75]

[72] Dong, *op. cit.*, pp. 335-48, esp. pp. 335-36, 345-46.

[73] Itō to Saionji, July 29, 1907, No. 105 (confidential): Archives, MT 2.1.4.9, pp. 562-63.

[74] No. 2374: *ibid.*, pp. 685-87.

[75] Tokutomi Iichirō (ed.), *Kōshaku Katsura Tarō Den* (Tokyo, 1917), II, 454.

These latter communications indicate that by 1909, and perhaps as early as 1907, the Yamagata-Katsura military faction of the oligarchy *did* have in mind annexation as the ultimate solution for the Korean problem, but also indicated therein is the fact that Itō was still opposed to annexation as late as April, 1909, and, in their opinion, might make a fight against it. If he did, they well knew they would have to compromise, as had been done time after time in intra-oligarchy squabbles, and with Itō as resident general he would set the terms, as he had so often done in the past. However, Itō offered his resignation as resident general shortly after Katsura had so ardently wished it, to return to Japan as president of the Privy Council. It was accepted by the emperor on June 14, 1909, at which time he assumed the new post. Sone, his vice-resident general at Seoul, was named resident general, officially taking up his new position on June 26.[76]

Does this mean that Itō capitulated to the Yamagata faction and gave his support thereafter to plans for annexation, that he made a compromise, that he exacted a guarantee of no annexation, or what? The evidence is conflicting, and perhaps it can never be perfectly resolved for Itō died too soon, unfortunately or fortunately, ironically or naturally, at the hands of a Korean patriot who shot him to death in the railway station at Harbin, Manchuria, October 26, 1909. At the time of his death annexationists were still very dissatisfied with the state of affairs in Korea; it took some months for the annexation machinery to move into high gear. But had Itō been laying plans to help this? To oppose it? Or no plans at all? Despite the fact that the evidence may not permit a positive answer to these specific questions, some of it is interesting and suggestive. Already mentioned is the idea that at the time of Itō's resignation he exacted a "secret pledge" from Katsura, to which Sone was party, guaranteeing no annexation for seven or eight

[76] Itō's resignation as resident general, handwritten, no day, 1909 is Doc. No. 188 in the Itō collection at Kensei Shiryō Shitsu. His appointment as Privy Council president is announced in Imperial Household Minister to Komura, June 14, 1909: Archives, MT 1.1.2.40, pp. 423-25. See also Sone to Komura, June 26, 1909. *ibid.*, p. 429.

years. Katsura "deliberately forgot" this pledge after Itō's death.[77] If accepted as true, the pledge affair might be construed to mean that Itō was now in favor of annexation, but wanted to plan it carefully and accomplish it thoroughly; or it might be taken to mean the opposite, that he was trying to avoid annexation altogether, perhaps buying time for the Residency General to get in better functioning order along principles of his own, including the maintenance of Korea's separate identity. Either interpretation is possible, but remembering that the "Secret History" is the source of information about the pledge, one must judge it quite likely that in the Black Dragon compilers' minds, at least, the latter "avoid annexation" interpretation was correct. As a patriotic society devoted to the furtherance of Japanese leadership in Greater East Asia, their compilations on the Meiji era were for the basic purpose of separating "true patriots" from the "weak kneed." As has been said, their "Secret History" is anti-Itō. They regarded the evidence of Itō's and Sone's opposition to annexation of Korea as shocking proof of high-placed betrayal of Japan's patriotic ideals. Katsura retrieved his reputation (with them) by reneging on the pledge.

It is interesting that another basic source disputes the "Secret History" account in a way that produces the curious effect of showing Itō to have been strongly, even emotionally, concerned for the defense of Korean individuality, and then to have changed suddenly to support a definite annexation plan in July, 1909. This paradox is contained in a statement of Itō's former private secretary, who later became chief of the Foreign Office political affairs bureau, Kurachi Tetsukichi. It was made and recorded at the Japanese Foreign Office in November, 1939, because, says Kurachi, "Everybody who knew the true facts concerning the annexation of Korea is already dead and today I am the only one left. What is called the inside story of Korean annexation is sometimes far from the truth, so I should like to put down the facts for future historians."

[77] Dong, *op. cit.*, pp. 345-46. Kuzū, *Nikkan Gappō* . . ., II, 617-18.

The statement is a long one, but the following paraphrase should bring out the essential points.

In the spring of 1909 when Itō was about to resign from his position as Resident General, there was some argument as to his successor, and finally vice-Resident General Sone was chosen unofficially. Up to that time matters concerning Korea had been assigned to the Resident General and the Tokyo government made it a policy not to interfere very much. This was good as long as the Resident General was Itō but with Sone it might not be so good. There was the argument that if Sone became Resident General, he should carry out policies according to the instructions of the Government. Sone should be told this, and if he agreed, then he might be appointed. Also at that time there were criticisms from some that Itō's was a do-nothing policy. Therefore it was important to establish the Government's main policy line toward Korea and it was necessary to put it in writing. I [Kurachi] as chief of political affairs bureau [of the Foreign Office] was ordered by Foreign Minister Komura to make a draft. He stated his opinion, I made a first draft, he corrected it, and the final draft was made. This draft was very simple, consisting of only two articles and a preface as follows: "The policy of Japan toward Korea is to establish our power in the peninsula and strictly hold this power. Since the Russo-Japanese war our power in Korea has been increasing, especially since the year before last when the Japanese-Korean treaty was made. The situation has greatly improved but our power is still not enough and our relationship with Korean officials not satisfactory. Therefore from now on it is necessary to try to increase our actual power and make a deeper foundation to establish incomparable power. In order to accomplish this purpose the Japanese government deems it necessary at this time to establish the following main policy and to carry out various plans in accordance. Article 1. At a suitable time carry out Korean annexation [*heigō* is the word used here for annexation]. This is the surest means to establish our power in Korea, to annex the peninsula and make it one part of our territory. It is our long-term policy that, considering the external and internal situation, at a suitable opportunity, we should carry out annexation, put the peninsula under our rule nominally and actually and end all treaty relationships. Article 2. Until the time comes for annexation, based on a policy of annexation, we should preserve our actual power as protector and increase that power in Korea."

This original draft was kept secret. It was shown to Premier Katsura on March 30, but to no one else, not even to the Genrō or to other Cabinet members. The reason was first of all that Itō's opinion concerning the matter was not clear. Itō did not say anything about the Korean future and it was difficult to estimate his true intention. I was, in fact, his private secretary whenever he came back to Tokyo. I met him every day so I was in a position to learn his movements and opinions very well, but even I could not understand what his opinion about Korea was. Regarding this there occurred the following episode. One day quite some time before his resignation, in 1908, I was treated to supper at his home in Ōmori and after the meal we talked. Itō was listening to me while lying on the *tatami* and when I said something to the effect that it was necessary to strengthen the present Residency General system, he jumped up and asked me why. So I stated as reasons such things as, though Japan had taken over the power of foreign affairs and defense there, as far as the economic aspect is concerned nothing is in our hands, for example, customs, currency, banks are all like a foreign country. Then Itō became very excited and he made rebuttal of my arguments one after the other. "We have power in foreign and military affairs and legal rights. There is no need for others. You say customs, currencies, banks, etc. are all different. But there are such differences even in one country and in colonies. Even Formosa is different from Japan. These are no trouble at all. Why is it necessary to strengthen these?" I said I would study further and stopped the argument.

Thus when Itō talked about Korea he did not express his true intention. And regarding this policy draft, not even Katsura and Komura knew Itō's true intention. If he opposed, it would make a very bad situation, so Katsura and Komura took an extremely cautious approach and undertook to sound him out unofficially. Accordingly in early April [1909] at a garden party at Mr. Mori's in Takanawa [Meguro district in Tokyo] Katsura and Komura requested a meeting with him in a few days. On April 10 they visited him at his official [Tokyo] residence and said frankly, "We must annex Korea and we should like to follow this policy," and showed him the aforementioned articles.

Then Itō said clearly that he completely agreed with them. The two ministers were rather taken aback, as they had expected the opposite and were prepared to argue with him. After that Katsura and Komura showed the draft to Sone. He also agreed and suggested they show it to Yamagata. The draft was then kept secret until July 6, when it was presented at a Cabinet meeting and approved.

Kurachi then devotes a section to "the literal meaning of the word *heigō* [annexation]" which seems more appropriately discussed in the chapter to follow. After that he makes a few remarks on how annexation was to proceed. "Basic policy was established . . . but at that time we did not expect to carry out annexation so quickly . . . expected to take a long time, study, etc." He drew up a long draft plan of details for Komura, which he "thought" was also shown to Itō for, "When I asked Itō about it just before he left for Manchuria, he said, 'I guess that's about it (*Maa, daitai anna mono darō*).' "

Kurachi entitles the next section of his statement, "Uchida Ryōhei's Memory." Uchida was the chief of the Black Dragon Society, its principal activist in Korea in the 1905–10 period, and his recollections and writings constitute the main source from which the society's "Secret History" was compiled. To correct statements left by Uchida was undoubtedly the main reason for Kurachi's making his statement at all. Concerning Uchida he says,

The late Mr. Uchida Ryōhei was one who contributed greatly to Korean annexation. While he was alive he spoke to me as follows: "In the book by Komatsu Midori there is a memorandum from you [Kurachi] to Komatsu, the contents of which are at variance with the facts. According to your memorandum the basic annexation policy was established in early April, 1909, with Katsura, Komura, Itō and Sone all in agreement. But the fact is that at that time our Government had no certain policy toward Korea. Therefore naturally Sone, as the new resident general, did not know of any basic policy toward Korea. That is why he suppressed our [Uchida's and friends'] annexation movement. It was due to our movement that annexation was finally realized." Also Mr.

Uchida says in his memoir on Korean annexation published in the Secret History, "... regarding the Foreign Office statement that [Korean] policy was decided in July . . . it is a mistake fashioned for the interests of private individuals. . . . Actually there were two parties. The Yamagata-Terauchi military group supported annexation, the Itō, Inoue, Komura civilian group supported a leave-as-is policy, and Katsura belonged to the latter group but stood in between. In February, 1909 Yamagata said that the Japanese emperor should become the Korean emperor too. Itō opposed this. In June when Itō resigned he conferred secretly with Katursa and Sone. They decided to maintain the present situation in Korea and await the result. So who could believe that annexation was decided at a Cabinet meeting in July? The fact that the three big heads, Itō, Katsura and Sone, had made this secret agreement was told [to me] by Sone."

Kurachi corrects this as follows: "There seems on the surface to be a discrepancy between Uchida's explanation and mine. However, the point is that the big heads who made the decision in the Imperial meeting in July kept it secret. Even Sone said nothing about it. Uchida did not know this and Uchida thought that his version was right. But for this our opinions are not contrary. Rather we agree."

In the last two sections of his statement Kurachi explains that since the final steps in treaty revision for Japan were being negotiated, "some felt annexation should be postponed beyond treaty revision." But suddenly, on October 26, Itō was assassinated at Harbin.

> I [Kurachi] was sent to Manchuria to investigate. . . . I found it was not a large scale plan, but small, planned in Vladivostok by Koreans, so I suggested to our Government that the incident be minimized. But in Korea Japanese felt that the assassination had been sponsored by the Korean emperor and that annexation should be accomplished quickly. . . . The situation in Korea became worse and worse, and the situation inside and outside Japan changed. It was seen that annexation would cause no hinderance to treaty revision, and in January, 1910 a policy of

immediate annexation was established. In May General Terauchi was appointed resident general to carry it out. . . ."[78]

Making allowance for Kurachi's being at pains to show that the government leaders, including Itō, deserved substantial "credit" for the annexation, and for Uchida's being at pains to show that many of them, especially Itō, dragged their feet, how shall we apportion—not the credit—but the blame? In the first place, we shall not attempt to make what would probably be a specious differentiation between the two or several possible groupings of Japanese government leaders. We know that Yamagata's military element was more inclined toward forceful measures than Itō's civilian element, and that some (Katsura? Komura?) may have stood in between. But they constituted essentially a single oligarchy of statesmen whose decisions were essentially collective, whether each member was in full agreement or not. Thus in 1905, at the time the Residency General was set up, it was the collective opinion that the handling of the Korean problem should be left to Itō and the sort of civilian measures he would devise. Yamagata may have had misgivings, but he was sufficiently impressed with the arguments in favor of this that he even gave in on Itō's having the military command in Korea, which was clearly, from Japanese government perspective, a danger zone. This is the sort of concession the war department in any government would be reluctant to make. The collective Japanese government decision then, at the time of the establishment of the Residency General, was to go along with Itō's plan.[79]

What was Itō's plan? It was *not* annexation and not brutal tyranny. It was to establish a sort of triangular balance, Residency General, Korean court, and Korean reform ministry, through

[78] Kurachi Tetsukichi, "Kankoku Heigō no Ikisatsu" (Particulars on the Annexation of Korea), statement made in Nov., 1939, at Japanese Foreign Office, printed "for office reference," April, 1950, Tokyo. See Preface, pp. 1-5, 6-13. Cf. Kaneko Kentarō (ed.), *Itō Hakubun Den* (Life of Ito Hirobumi) (Tokyo, 1940), III, 838, concerning the April 10 meeting.

[79] "Complete agreement," Kaneko, *op. cit.*, III, 682.

which Japanese-Korean co-operation could obtain to produce reform and modernization of Korea and which would render Japan secure from any possible threat launched via Korea. Of the two objectives, the second, Japanese security, was the overriding one, but Itō was confident that both could be obtained, and within the limits set by security he strove hard for co-operation.[80] George Trumbull Ladd could approve this and so could responsible government officials around the world. It was decent and it was realistic. "It made no pretense of disinterestedness of the purely missionary order" but no practical man, not even one whose professional interest was morals and ethics, could expect or wish that. "The realities of life" and of nations and peoples had to be considered. It is "midst fairly settled law and custom" that the "calculated obligation of duty" must be made.[81] Surely in the affairs of nations, the security of one's own country must come first.

However, by July, 1909, we can say with confidence that the collective opinion of the Japanese oligarchy was that Itō's system was not enough to meet the requirements of Japanese security. Power, power, power is the word repeated over and over again in Kurachi's draft statement on Korean policy. Things had not worked out well. The Korean court had caused trouble, the disbanded army had caused trouble, there seemed to be no end of riots and unrest. More Japanese power in Korea was an obvious remedy. Itō himself was disappointed[82] and there is little doubt that, whether he sought a longer trial period for his system or not, before his death he gave his acquiescence to the proposition that if things did not improve annexation would be "necessary." Itō's assassination took the heart out of those who wished to try restraint a little longer

[80] Even McKenzie, one of the severest critics of the Japanese regime, admits this, *Korea's Fight for Freedom*, p. 104.

[81] Ladd, "The Annexation of Korea," p. 645 and *What Ought I to Do?*, p. 103.

[82] There is a clear expression of this in a letter Itō sent to Katsura to request more troops. He says, "Observing the situation here and considering the future, I am very worried. If you have a good idea, please tell it to me." Itō's letters to Katsura, No. 33, May 6, 1908: Kensei Shiryō Shitsu.

and, though Sone made an effort to hold out, he broke literally and physically as the annexation band wagon began to roll.[83]

In July, 1910, General Terauchi settled in Seoul and "it was as though a chill had passed over the city. He said little in public but . . . things began to happen. Four newspapers were suspended in a night. An item in their columns was objectionable. Let others be careful. . . . every day brought its tale of arrests," as "the hardest and most relentless form of Imperial administration" was fastened on Korea.[84]

So once again Japan's realistic diplomacy left the high road of enlightened self-interest and went down the low road of suppression, brutality, and murder. Inoue's Kabo reforms of 1894–95 had ended in Miura, and now Itō had led to Terauchi. It was almost as if the two roads were interconnected. Of course, Inoue had had a very short time and had been beset by many difficulties—foreign interference, lack of funds, Taewongun, Queen's party. But Itō also, the most astute, the ablest, had failed, with no foreign interference, no lack of funds, and no really well-organized Korean opposition. What defeated him? Was it merely Hulbert and the bizarre sequence of events he may have set in motion: Hague appeal, abdication, troop disbandment, riots? Certainly this had fanned into flame smoldering coals of opposition among the Korean people and, while the riots went on, Korea could not perhaps be labeled "secure". But gradually they were being controlled. They could hardly be called a serious physical threat to the Residency General, and once they were over Itō's balances might work out. From an outside view, they do not seem to make annexation so urgent or necessary as Japanese leaders seemed to think it had become by late 1909. Was there some other factor in their inside view?

We have seen above a statement by Uchida Ryōhei to the effect that "it was due to our movement that annexation was finally

[83] *Tōkyō Mainichi* (newspaper), Dec. 5, 1909. Sone gave his resignation from his sick-bed. See Dong, "Japanese Annexation . . .," pp. 347, 351.

[84] McKenzie, *Korea's Fight for Freedom*, pp. 176, 182.

realized." What was "our movement" and how does it fit into the picture? Consideration of this will remind us that we have spent the last two chapters almost entirely within the Japanese oligarchy, with the realists. We need not apologize for this. To an unusual degree in a modern state, the structure of the Japanese government insulated its top policy makers from the influences of Japanese society at large and made their closed door decisions decisive. This, we suggested, made them an excellent example, perhaps the best possible, of a foreign policy elite which could work at foreign relations problems intelligently and realistically without being pushed off balance by the pressure of popular moods of the moment. However, even Japanese statesmen of the oligarchic Meiji era were not entirely insulated. Earlier, we separated their antagonists on the Korean problem into liberals and reactionaries. To these we shall now return.

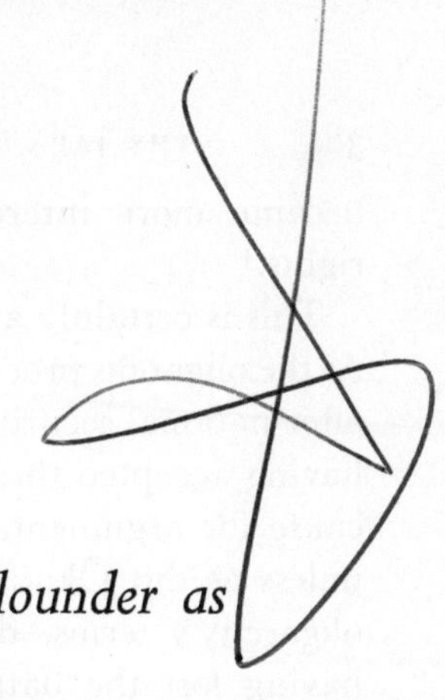

VIII

Reverse Idealism: Liberals Flounder as Reactionaries Rise

When last the anti-oligarchy forces were considered the liberals held the limelight, but, it was suggested, they were losing focus. During the Sino-Japanese War period, as they lost the struggle for Diet supremacy to the oligarchs, they became bedfellows with reactionaries on the Korean issue. This was the beginning of the end for Japanese liberalism, and the dawn of a new day for reaction.

Japanese historian Oka Yoshitake, much of whose postwar research and writing has been concerned with the political forces of the Meiji period, has emphasized as a main trend among Japanese liberals that their nationalism became stronger, their liberalism weaker as the period wore on. This, he says, was true of Ōi, of Fukuzawa, and of many others. Their schemes for promoting popular rights in Korea certainly contributed to this, for, though Ōi had argued that "excitement" about such mainland activities would "create opportunities" for the realization of popular rights in Japan, the opposite proved to be the case. The sense of international rivalry and crisis, added to the conviction that "China and Korea had no prospect of establishing democracy themselves," turned the liberals into advocates of Japanese leadership or hegemony in eastern Asia (*Tōa no meishu*). And in fact they became more interested in national strength than in popular rights.[1]

This is certainly an important part of the story of their demise. As the oligarchs proceeded to develop national strength and to look after national security with great assiduousness, Japanese liberals, having accepted these as their principal objectives also, had little cause for argument. They had no real voice in policy making, unless as did Ōkuma and Gotō, they accepted office under the oligarchy's terms, divorced from their party connections. And having lost the battle of cabinet responsibility, they could not embarrass the Genrō by ousting its hand-picked ministers. In the Diet they could enjoy some prestige, have an opportunity to give patriotic speeches, be obstreperous on minor matters, and, if they became sufficiently cynical, make money by bribe taking. But by 1900 the energy and idealism of the Meiji liberals were gone and most of them did not know where or how they had lost them. Even Fukuzawa could only say, shortly before his death in 1901, "I am very satisfied with the development of Japan up to now."[2] One of Fukuzawa's students, Ozaki Yukio, lived long enough (beyond ninety) to see that the national strength and strong foreign policy he and his friends had so warmly advocated during the Sino-Russo-Japanese war period was not turning out so well. At least, during and after World War I he began to oppose continental expansion and in the 1930's took a courageous stand against ultra-

[1] Oka, "Jiyūtō Saha to Nashiyonarizumu," pp. 9-14; "Nisshin Sensō to Tōji ni okeru Taigai Ishiki" (Contemporary Public Opinion and the Sino-Japanese War), *Kokka Gakkai Zasshi* (Dec. 1954, Feb. 1955), pp. 101-29, 223-54; "Jōyaku Kaisei Rongi ni Arawareta Tōji no Taigai Ishiki," (Contemporary Sentiment on Foreign Powers appearing in the Treaty Revision Argument), *Kokka Gakkai Zasshi*, LXVII (Aug., Sept. 1953), pp. 1-24, 183-206.

In the last article see especially Part 4, pp. 195-206, where some liberals argue that the government must become one "based on popular opinion" in order to bring maximum national strength to bear on the treaty revision issue, and Fukuzawa argues rather cynically that it must also compete in power politics with Western nations.

[2] Maruyama Masao, "Meiji Kokka no Shisō" (The Thought of the Meiji State) in Rekishigaku Keknkyūkai (ed.), *Nihon Shakai no Shiteki Kyūmei* (Historical Studies of Japanese Society) (Tokyo: Iwanami, 1949), p. 211.

nationalism.[3] But others like Inoue Kakugorō, Ōi, and the fiery founder of the Liberal party, Itagaki Taisuke, did not live so long, and during the last years of Meiji could find less and less about which to quarrel with the oligarchy's management of affairs.

With specific regard to the Korean problem the Foreign Office, through the Tokyo Metropolitan Police, kept close tabs on the latter-day descendants of the liberal opposition during the 1905–10 period. In contrast to the denunciations of government policy for its neglect of both Japanese and Korean rights and progress, with which Fukuzawa, Ōi, Kakugorō and others had enlivened the 1880–94 period (perhaps Kakugorō's "Memory of Seoul," reprinted with prefatorial remarks by Kim Ok-kiun and Pak Young-hyo and many illustrations in a Tokyo magazine in January, 1895, was the last of these),[4] the police reports show them to be generally in support of Itō and government policy. For example, the Hague affair and abdication crisis of July, 1907, gave rise to considerable discussion of the situation in Korea among these groups, concerning which the police reported as follows. The Kenseihontō (True Constitution party), which had been organized under Ōkuma's leadership to keep up the fight against the Itō-Yamagata oligarchy and numbered Etō Shinsaku, son of Etō Shimpei among its prominent members, sent a delegation to see Prime Minister Saionji to find out what government policy would be in the crisis. Having learned from him something of the nature of the "new convention" (signed July 24), they held a meeting to discuss it. Some of their members said it was "weak kneed" but they decided

[3] Mendel, "Ozaki Yukio: The Political Conscience of Modern Japan," pp. 343-56, esp. pp. 348-49.

[4] Inoue Kakugorō, "Kanjo no Zammu," *Fūzoku Gahō* (Jan. 1895), entire issue, 32 pages. Illustrations include: (cover) burning Japanese legation at Seoul; Takezoe's flight; Seoul residents being murdered by Chinese soldiers; photographer Honda Bokunosuke's wife and family "being outraged by Chinese soldiers"; Capt. Isobayashi being killed at Inchon; Korean king and queen accepting Inoue's proposal to begin reform; king taking oath at the tomb of his royal ancestors. The last two illustrations, inappropriate to the earlier edition, may be thought of as marking a transition; with the Japanese government now "taking up its duties" re Korea, the liberals could rest the subject.

not to oppose it, rather to "watch carefully to see how it would work out."[5]

The Yukōkai, of which Ozaki Yukio was a prominent member, talked about a "total purge of Korea," delegated two members to see the prime minister and foreign minister, and talked about sending a mission to Korea to investigate matters there. However, the opinion that "Korean policy is in the brain of Resident General Itō" and "we should not become too agitated" prevailed. They too approved the new convention. The Japan-Korea Friendship Society, which was organized by Japanese friends of Pak Young-hyo, heard one Nakamura Yaroku, a friend and perhaps relative of Pak's erstwhile traveling companion, the aforementioned Nakamura Tahachiro, argue that "the Japanese people are silent but the Government should not feel they can dispose of the [Korean] matter carelessly." The "main thing" was to obtain "thoroughgoing reform in Korea." Resident General Itō "should be accused of negligence . . . Japanese police in Korea have been rough and lacking in kindness. . . . their attitude should change." The critical attitude of this group, however, melted away in "disappointment" when their candidate for the Korean premiership, Pak, was arrested in Seoul.[6]

So-called Shimpotō (Progressive party) followers of Ōkuma were reported as approving the new convention and Itō's handling of the abdication affair, although "they do not wish to approve it openly in an assembly lest it exalt Itō and the Seiyūkai party."[7]

[5] Metro. Police to For. Min., July 18, 30, 1907, Nos. 1858, 2020: Archives, MT 2.4.1.9, pp. 223-25, 599. Re Kenseihonto see Scalapino, *Democracy and the Party Movement . . .*, pp. 177-79.

[6] Metro. Police to For. Min., July 13, 19, 26 and Aug. 14, 1907, Nos. 1806, 1811, 1875, 1983, 2104: Archives, MT 2.4.1.9, pp. 172-74, 178-79, 270-73, 548, 653-55.

[7] Metro. Police to For. Min., July 26, 28, 1907, Nos. 1978, 1992: *ibid.*, pp. 541-42, 578-80. Actually, the name Shimpotō was an anachronism at this time. Ōkuma's party had worn the name for a time, then amalgamated with the Jiyūtō to form the Kenseitō, which later split into the Seiyūkai and various remnants which refused to accept Itō's terms for the organization of the Seiyūkai. One of these remnants is no doubt referred to here. See Scalapino, *op. cit.*, pp. 170, 173, 179.

The later famous Inukai Ki was among these. (The Seiyūkai, of course, as the party founded, or captured, by Itō in 1900, and still largely responsive to Saionji, gave no trouble.) Also a rather large group of Diet members called the Daidō (Like Thinkers) Club, which stood between the majority Seiyūkai and minority Kenseihontō parties in the Diet, passed a resolution approving the convention. They called it "a step forward . . . toward the fulfillment of our national objectives."[8] The governor of Chiba prefecture reported that an assemblage of journalists there had voted approval of the convention, and one Kubata Yoshiro, who seems to have been important enough to have a police report all his own, said, "The Convention is good. It is preferable to formal annexation for that would make the Koreans angry. Korea is an uncivilized country and we need smart officials there. Japanese officials of the half-modern variety should be retired."[9] The great liberal newspapers, which in times past had often bitterly denounced the oligarchs' doings, were only mildly critical. Fukuzawa's *Jiji Shimpō* said that "if the [Japanese] government does not know about such things [as the Hague mission], its responsibility is great. . . ." However, the paper "does not ask what opinion Resident General Itō has in his mind." It only "hopes that he will take suitable measures as soon as possible. If no measures are taken, our prestige will be damaged."[10]

The picture of liberals following the oligarchy's cue on Korea continued on to the end of the annexation story. In December, 1909, when Itō's successor, Sone, was confronted with a direct "petition" for annexation by the extremist Ilchin Society and tried to back

[8] Metro. Police to For. Min., July 26, 1907, No. 1962: Archives, MT 2.4.1.9, pp. 515-16. Scalapino says this Daido Club was controlled by Katsura through some of his supporters—*op. cit.*, p. 188, note 106. Re Seiyūkai see Scalapino, pp. 179, 183, 186, 189.

[9] Chiba gov. to For. Min., July 27, 1907, No. 1988 and Metro. Police to For. Min., July 26, 1907, unnumbered: Archives, MT 2.4.1.9, pp. 565-67, 546-47.

[10] *Jiji Shimpō*, July 7, 8, 1907. *Tōkyō Asahi* was somewhat more critical, but only in a very legalistic way and without proposing Itō's ouster or anything so drastic as that (July 11, 1907).

away from the issue, *Jiji Shimpō* supported him. It warned, "We can understand why the Ilchin Society made such a proposal, but its opinion is not the opinion of the majority of Koreans. Therefore we must take care not to overestimate the opinion of the Ilchin Society and neglect the majority's opinion. We cannot know the future, but for the time being we hope there will be no change in present conditions." *Tōkyō Mainichi*, which had its beginnings as an opinion outlet for Ōkuma's progressive party, editorialized: "Whether annexation should be realized immediately or not is questionable. It would mean an economic burden for Japan and even more important it is uncertain whether other Powers would recognize it." *Tōkyō Asahi* said: "Japan at present is not in the position to be able to annex Korea. The material and spiritual situation is not right for this. Economically speaking Japan cannot endure the burden." The *Asahi* interviewed Ōkuma and found that he agreed this was "not a suitable time."[11]

The following August, however, as the cabinet pushed through the annexation, and General Terauchi settled in Seoul, liberal press and liberal leaders literally wept happy tears of endorsement. *Jiji Shimpō* fairly outdid itself in enthusiasm. It published a special annexation commemorative edition, August 27, 1910, probably its grandest technical accomplishment of the whole Meiji era. Inside an extravagant border of pretty flowers, birds, and chickens were oversize portraits of Yamagata, Itō, Terauchi, Katsura, Komura, Sone, and Korean puppet premier, Yi Wan-yong, and smaller pictures of Itagaki, Ōkuma, Hanabusa, Moriyama and, others. And on its pages those who had figured prominently in the Korean problem through the years spoke their sentiments. It is interesting to see how liberals are mingled with bureaucratic servants of the oligarchy, under its leaders' very eyes. Itagaki reminisced on the great Conquer Korea (Seikan) argument of 1873 and contributed a dewey-eyed Chinese poem:

[11] *Jiji Shimpō*, editorial, Dec. 8, 1909. *Tōkyō Mainichi*, editorial, Dec. 8, 1909. *Tōkyō Asahi*, editorial, Dec. 7, 1909. Ōkuma on annexation, *Asahi, ibid.*

Regarding annexation, our Japan does not necessarily like it and does not covet it
But if Korea observes our sovereignty and helps us in developing the culture and stabilizing the society, what more can I ask?
If Korean public opinion becomes one and they wish to remove their national boundaries,
Then I agree with annexation.

Ōkuma, too, recalled Seikan days, and he spoke particularly of LeGendre's role.

When Foreign Minister Soejima went to Peking he met an American named LeGendre, and from their first meeting Soejima agreed completely with his ideas. Later upon Soejima's recommendation LeGendre entered our Foreign Office. LeGendre's opinion was that Japan should annex Korea, Formosa, and Manchuria, thus to make a semicircle around China, threaten Russia in Siberia and take the leadership in Asia. In those days many samurai visited the Foreign Office to hear LeGendre talk, forming a long line. LeGendre's ideas surely had some influence in exciting Saigō and his dissatisfied samurai followers. . . . However, Seikan was not carried out and our country lost many important people because of this. The Southwestern affair [Satsuma Rebellion] arose, but on the other hand the effort of the people was concentrated in internal affairs, which brought about the opening of the Diet. For many years we have tried to handle Korea, even at the cost of blood, and now we have accomplished peaceful annexation. It is like a dream.

Inoue Kakugorō, who, it was explained, was "now a Diet member and a business man," contributed a piece entitled, "Before and After the Seoul Incident." His purpose in going to Korea, he said, was "in a word to make Korea move toward civilization." He recalled his association with Fukuzawa, and ended with quotations from his "Memory of Seoul."

Alongside these were accounts of their experiences by various men who had held official positions in Korea. Moriyama Shigeru, now a member of the House of Peers, wrote about "The Beginning of Negotiations between Japan and Korea." He recalled that he had gone to Korea seven times between 1869 and 1876. The Koreans had been so "obstinate" that he had once said, "if my next attempt at negotiation fails, we should dispatch 500,000 samurai to the Peninsula." Hanabusa, who had resigned from diplomacy and entered the service of the imperial court after the 1882 incident, recalled his adventure in connection with that incident. Ōtori, now a baron, recalled the hectic days preceding the outbreak of the Sino-Japanese War. "When the Chinese dispatched troops to Korea, I was in Japan due to illness. When I left Japan for Korea from Yokohama Foreign Minister Mutsu came to see me off. I said, 'I can't say now whether I shall return alive.' Mutsu, with tears in his eyes, said, 'If you die in Korea, I will collect your bones. Please do your best.' . . . I acted only on the orders of our Government [in Korea] but in those days there were many foreign diplomats who disturbed us, many Chinese officials who were full of tricks and many obstinate Koreans."[12]

The only hints of criticism of the government's handling of the Korean problem printed in *Jiji Shimpō* appeared in a memoir of Fukuzawa which was advertised in the August 27 commemorative edition and published serially, beginning August 30. Billed as "dealing with many secret matters" and "not revealed during Fukuzawa's lifetime," it was entitled, "The Seoul Incident from Beginning to End." In it Fukuzawa speaks disparagingly of Japanese government policy as "retreat and guard," of the government's failure to extend aid to Kim and Pak, and of Takezoe's failure to live up to his "pledge to be true."[13] But its reference was to 1884 and, set amidst stories of the happy developments of 1910, there was no bitterness in it, merely a tale of tribulation mellowed by subsequent success. *Tōkyō Mainichi* was not so elaborate as *Jiji* in its coverage of annexation, but it was equally enthusiastic. Its tone was set in an editorial published on August 23, entitled, "The Happiness of the World." It was sure that the Japanese people

[12] All of these articles are in *Jiji Shimpō*, Aug. 27, 1910.
[13] *Jiji Shimpō*, Aug. 30 through Sept. 8, 1910.

would approve and that foreigners would not oppose annexation for, "The world can enjoy peace only when all countries reach the same level of civilization. . . . It cannot permit such a thing as low civilization countries." Interestingly, but not uncharacteristically, the only word of caution against over-enthusiasm came, not from the liberal press, but from the government mouthpiece, *Tōkyō Nichi Nichi*. It urged in an editorial: "Korean annexation should be celebrated. But there should not be excessive celebration, for there have been bad floods in the Kantō area and the sufferers will not be pleased at so much happiness. . . ."[14]

In consideration of the record of the Japanese liberals' struggle for popular rights in Japan and their often voiced concerns in this regard for other Asiatic countries, the author made a special search for expressions of interest that the Koreans have rights of representation and voting now that Japan and Korea were "one." Significantly, there is almost complete silence on this matter. In fact the one statement from an avowed liberal which could be found was *opposed* to Korean political participation. Inukai Ki, product of Fukuzawa's Keio school, leader of the Kenseihontō party faction which demanded that the party refuse all bureaucratic enticements, organizer (in 1912) of a society to protect constitutional government and eradicate clan oligarchy, had the following to say in a signed article in *Jiji Shimpō*: "Koreans are basically suspicious and accustomed to bribery in politics. To grant them the right of political participation would be to spread infection in the Diet."[15] The only expression favorable to Korean political participation from a party man was that of Ōishi Masami, who was probably better classified as a bureaucrat. He had been minister to Korea briefly in 1892–93 and was later leader of the Kenseihontō faction which favored co-operation with the bureaucrats (1907) and then accepted Katsura's leadership (1913). He said in some "chatter"

[14] *Tōkyō Nichi Nichi*, editorial, Aug. 25, 1910.

[15] *Jiji Shimpō*, Aug. 25, 1910. On Inukai see Scalapino, *op. cit.*, pp. 78, 190, 192-93; also Jansen, *The Japanese and Sun Yat-sen*, pp. 29 ff.

reported in *Tayō Magazine* in October, 1910, that "the purpose of annexation must be assimilation." But, "in both the central and local Korean governments we should employ able Koreans as soon as possible," and "as civilization in Korea progresses we should complete a system of self governing. Ultimately we should try to send representatives of Korea to our Diet. When self governing is realized on the one hand and the duty of military service is accepted on the other, we shall be able to say that assimilation is complete."[16]

A Professor Tomizu of the law faculty of Tokyo Imperial university said that "after a complete assimilation we should give political rights to the Korean people" but noted that there was no obligation to do so: "When our constitution was written it did not anticipate the annexation [of Korea]. Therefore it is not correct to assert that our constitution applies to such new territory."[17] Hasebe Junkō, speaker of the lower house of the Diet, reiterated this latter point: "The Japanese constitution does not apply to territory and people which were not part of Japanese territory and people when it was promulgated. The day when we could give such rights to Koreans is far away for many reasons." (He does not explain the reasons.)[18] A person who signed himself by the pen name Kanigambo (Crab Seeing Priest) summed the matter up very well in a "private opinion" which he wrote for the *Ōsaka Asahi* newspaper: "The purpose for which a country has a colony is not for the interests of the inhabitants of the colony but for the interest of the mother country. Seeing this it is natural that the rights of the inhabitants of the colony should not be equal to those of the mother country."[19] So went the "does the constitution follow the flag" argument in Japan. Really no argument, for practically nothing was said about it. It seems not even to have occurred to Japanese liberals to raise the issue.

[16] *Tayō* (magazine), Oct., 1910, p. 89. On Ōishi see Scalapino, *op. cit.*, pp. 191-94.
[17] *Tōkyō Nichi Nichi*, Aug. 31, 1910.
[18] *Ibid.*, Sept. 6, 1910.
[19] Oct. 12, 1910.

However, before burying Japanese liberalism in the graveyard of Korean annexation, one or two additional spadesful of information should be turned up. Japanese historian Maruyama, after tracing the process by which popular rights advocates became supporters of Japanese imperialism (he uses Kuga Katsunan, Tokutomi Sohō, and Fukuzawa as principal examples), points to two developments of the post Sino-Japanese War era which are important in this connection, namely, nonpolitical individualism and socialism. These deserve our consideration, for they are a part of the heritage of the liberal movement. The latter-day liberals discussed above, those who accommodated themselves so well to Korean annexation on the oligarchy's terms, had by 1910 also accommodated themselves to a constitutional system which lacked civil liberties and cabinet responsibility. What of those who did not accommodate? Maruyama notes that as the demand for popular rights disappeared from the main political stage, as freedom of speech and learning came to be neglected at the universities, "non political individualism spread among Japanese intellectuals. For example, suicide became prevalent among students . . . and, quoting the journalist Yamagi Aizan, 'Though the Government intended to make loyalists through the educational institutions, students thought of love and stars and violets and decided that their purpose lay in the fulfillment of their own desires. Thus they indulged in extreme individualism, without considering the future of the state.' " After quoting the poet Kunikida to the effect that "there is freedom in the mountains and forests," Maruyama says: "But outside the mountains and forests there was no freedom in the Meiji 30's [1897–1907]."[20]

Regarding the socialists, Maruyama says, "the Socialists of the Meiji 30's were the real successors to the popular rights advocates of the Meiji 20's." The fact that the government vigorously suppressed them, he feels, is a testimonial to their "strength of feeling." But, "considering their overall situation their movement was

[20] Maruyama, "Meiji Kokka . . .," pp. 204-12, 216, 218, 220, 227-28.

premature. They could not obtain a large following or bear any weight in Japanese politics [at that time]."[21] Maruyama, as a supporter of the present-day Japanese socialist party, might be expected to credit these early socialists with greater rightness of perspective than they actually had. Brief mention of four of their leaders will indicate the degree to which their paths diverged in action and in thought, though it can be said that they had a common outlook in advocating the uplift of the common man and in opposing the imperialism of the day. Abe Isō, a Waseda University professor, who had studied the ideas of Ralph Bellamy while in the United States, was an early and insistent advocate of labor's right to organize and later in the 1920's he took the lead in efforts to build a social democratic party in Japan. Though defeated in both by government opposition and persecution he remained the true social democrat, never wavering from an insistence on peaceful change through parliamentary procedures. On the other hand, Kōtoku Denjirō, who had been closely associated with the Liberal party intellectual, Nakae Chōmin, in his early days and had later visited America, became an advocate of terroristic methods to achieve an ideal anarchist society. He read Kropotkin, but doubtlessly government suppression of the socialist movement contributed as much to his decision for "direct action." He was hanged in 1911 for a plot against the Meiji emperor in which he seems not to have participated. One of his last writings was a "Refutation of Christianity." Uchimura Kanzō was a Christian (though of the churchless and sectless variety), socialist, and a pacifist. He had studied under Dr. William Clark, president of Massachusetts Agricultural College who had come to Japan in 1875 to become head of the Sapporo Agricultural College. Uchimura had many followers, among them the recent president of Tokyo University, Yanaibara Tadao. Lastly, among the early Japanese socialists was Katayama Sen who, of the group, was probably the most frequent visitor to America. He, like Kōtoku, came to advocate violent

[21] *Ibid.*, pp. 219-20.

overthrow of the old order, but by communist revolution rather than sporadic violence. He is said to have been one of the original members of the American Communist party and spent his last years in Moscow, where he died in 1933 and was buried in Red Square.

A short quotation from Kōtoku and Uchimura respectively will illustrate the general approach of the Japanese socialists to international relations, which singled out imperialism as the great evil. Said Kōtoku:

> How prevalent imperialism has become. It spreads like wildfire. All the countries of the world are awed into obedience and there is no country which does not praise, admire and sustain it. Look! The whole English nation believes in it, a warlike Emperor of Germany advocates it ardently, and needless to say it is the traditional policy of Russia. Furthermore France, Austria and Italy give it cordial welcome. Even America seems recently to be beginning to follow it. And turning to our own country, Japan, ever since the Sino-Japanese war victory the whole country, inside the government and out, has been embracing it with wild enthusiasm.

The following is from Uchimura:

> Although there is no philosopher who lectures on the harmony of the universe, there are many divisions of soldiers on the land, and we can hear weapons clashing everywhere. Although there is no poet who consoles the people in their sorrow and grief, there are warships of thousands of tons on the sea, and they make the waves rage. Inside the country families are in great disorder, fathers and sons feel bitter against one another, children are in conflict and mother-in-law and daughter-in-law eye each other with contempt. But toward the outside Japan is proud, calling herself the land of cherry blossoms in the Eastern Sea, and the land of gentlemen. This is what imperialism really is.[22]

Although their paths were to diverge later, Japanese socialists, from the groups represented by these several leaders, came together briefly to produce a weekly newspaper, *Heimin Shimbun* (The

[22] *Ibid.*, pp. 212-13.

Common People's Newspaper) which maintained publication for slightly more than a year—November, 1903 to January, 1905—when it was finally suppressed by the government.[23] Though only incidentally concerned with Korean affairs, most of its issues, in fact, making no specific mention of Korea at all, its pages do contain some references which make it possible to state with fair clarity the socialist stand on the Korean problem at that time. On April 3, 1904, appeared an editorial entitled, "Selling Civilization by Force," which argued as follows:

> Looking at present day diplomacy in the Orient, in contrast to the Russian government's violent attitude toward Korea, one is supposed to see Japan as raising an army of righteousness in her behalf. Korea's timid newspapers do not report what they should report and timid politicians do not argue as they should argue, so here are the facts. A Japan-Korea alliance was first proposed to the Korean court by our envoy Hayashi on January 20 . . . then as a result of the shooting in Inchon on February 9, the Korean Emperor was forced to accept. There was some disagreement among Korean ministers but our envoy by strong measures obtained agreement. After that opposition arose from pro-Russian groups, some of whom threw a bomb at the home of the Foreign Minister, and there was a loud anti-Japanese voice. At this Hayashi suppressed the pro Russian groups and had those who tried to obstruct the Japanese-Korean agreement executed under military order. But still there is much opposition, and even the Emperor does not seem to trust us. This is what newspapers report. . . . undoubtedly some Koreans are pro Russian and some pro Japanese, but this is not the feeling of most of the Korean people. These are only high officials of the

[23] Nishida Nagatoshi (comp.), *Heimin Shimbun* (Osaka and Tokyo: Sōgensha, 1953), Introduction and list of people connected with paper, pp. 1-22. Cf. Chitoshi Yanaga, *Japan Since Perry* (New York: McGraw-Hill, 1949), p. 236. Yanaga mentions Kōtoku, Sakai (Tōshihiko), Nishikawa Kōjirō (who like Sakai was close to Katayama Sen), and Ishikawa (Sanshirō, who was close to Uchimura)—*op. cit.*, pp. 236, 239 and *Heimin Shimbun*, p. 19. Katayama Sen lists Kōtoku, Sakai, Abe, and Kinoshita Naoe (Christian Socialist) as original editors, and Ishikawa and Nishikawa as subsequently taking over the editorship. Katayama Sen, *Nihon no Rōdō Undo* (The Japanese Labor Movement) (Tokyo: Iwanami, 1952), pp. 341-42. Cf. *Seijigaku Jiten*, p. 1227. Anyway, it is clear that all these socialist groups participated.

Court and Government and is the result of their looking out for their own name and interests, so they are not trustworthy. As a result of the war they have had pain and suffering, but it is their own doing. If the Korean common people, like the Indian people mentioned before, do not have self ambition or greed, they will not flatter Japanese or Russians or any other country. And if they are satisfied with the nature of that small peninsula and want to spend their lives there peacefully, there is no excuse or right for Japanese moral imperialists to shed blood on their soil. We daresay it is definitely unjust and unrighteous to sell civilization by force. If our national policy is expansion and penetration and simply to win wars, there is no need to talk about it, but if our policy is based on righteousness and humanity it should be reiterated that it is impossible to sell civilization by force.[24]

On June 19 *Heimin* devoted another long article to Korea. Its topic was that Korea should be respected and its argument was as follows:

How is Korea to be saved? Politicians say we dared to risk the Sino-Japanese war for Korean independence. Now the Russo-Japanese war has begun and they say proudly that we will rescue Korea politically. However, it is hard to see how that which they call political rescue will protect Korean independence. The Sino-Japanese war was able to drive out Chinese power from Korea and the Russo-Japanese war intends to drive out Russian power from Korea. Thus Japanese politicians call them wars of righteousness. However, it is necessary to have criticism from our side as to whether the Japanese attitude is based on righteousness as they say. For instance, we should consider the standpoint of the Korean people. Is it not true that Chinese, Russian and Japanese political ambitions have been competing in Korea. Korea always lies at the feet of the victor. They don't know which is right and which is wrong. Korea at the present time is nothing but a sacrifice to the barbarian international morality which says victory is righteousness. Japanese, despising the Korean people, are always saying that Koreans have no idea of nation, no idea of patriotism. We think it natural that Koreans should have no nationalistic feelings, as their happiness and

[24] *Heimin Shimbun*, editorial, Apr. 3, 1904, No. 21, II, 119-21.

peace have been spoiled by the nation's leaders. Historically Korea has been the contributor of literature, science, technical knowledge, religion and morals to Japan, bringing these from China and India. But as a reward Japan has given Korea only invasion. From the viewpoint of the Korean people there is no difference between China, Russia and Japan. They are all invaders. The political rescue of Korea is planned with its government as the core, but the worst troubles in Korea arise there . . . [it is] a poisonous worm which sucks blood from the people. The Emperor's court is rich, the nobles are rich but the people poor. . . . Some say the Korean people are idle and cunning, with no ability to be anything but slaves. They are not so by nature. In fact they are diligent and patient. The history of invasion by other countries has brought them to the situation of today.

We feel sympathy for the Korean past and we regret the present situation. But it is doubtful if we can lead them by any nationalistic pattern. Politicians in Japan speak of "Korean independence." However, foreign powers might not admit Korean independence, and even the Japanese politicians who talk of Korean independence do not desire it really in their hearts. Is there not a single [able] person in all Korea? We see from world history that the only way for people to get out of trouble is to know themselves. This means "rejection of the nationalist idea." That is it! Do not be surprised at rejecting the idea of nation. This may sound like a devil's saying for people with national pride and ambition. But it will sound good to the ears of Koreans. For instance, consider the Sino-Japanese war. Japan on the surface declares Korea to be independent, but underneath she always insists on her own privileges and honor. So it is always Korea which suffers from trouble and damage. But the international morality which approves the right of the strong pays no attention to this. Therefore unless Korea can break down this idea of international morality she cannot avoid great trouble as the scene of international conflicts. Perhaps some Korean intellectuals already know this.

You may have hope regarding the nature of the Korean people. They are very practical, and never pessimistic under any sort of suppression. Their desire is happiness in this world, not in the next. They are already tired of the class system and the bad effects of the invasion policy. Therefore if you lead them with a great policy beyond nationalism and with great human sympathy, you may expect peace in that peninsula someday. It is beyond our knowledge whether it is possible to lead the Korean court and government into good policies. The idea of politicians who want to make reforms with that government as the center is very hard to understand. Let the politician wave his arms, but be hesitant in his recommendations to the Korean people. It is natural that there should be some difference between what we expect and what Japanese politicians expect. They love their policy and we socialists love Korea! That is the reason.[25]

In 1907, during the abdication affair, the Tokyo Metropolitan Police reported to the foreign minister a "Resolution of Socialists regarding the Korean Affair," as follows: "We esteem the freedom of the Korean people and their right to self government. We recognize that it is against the interest of common people to invade them with an imperialistic policy. We therefore urge the Japanese government to be faithful to its former guarantee of Korean independence. Dated July 21, 1907, signed Socialist leaders." A second police report commented that socialists opposed the government's Korea policy on humanitarian grounds and that they were against the new convention, but "the formal resolution was not really passed by an assembly. It was simply drawn up by one Ichikawa and approved by Kōtoku Denjirō."[26]

Thus nonpolitical individualists and socialists may be counted as offshoots of the liberal movement, who would have protested the annexation in 1910, but by then the former were entirely engrossed in stars and violets (or had committed suicide) and the latter were enroute to jail (or, with Kōtoku, execution). In short, liberal idealism, which had espoused humanitarian principles, international mindedness, progressive institutions, parliamentarianism and democratic rights, had compromised away its essence, at least insofar as the Korean problem was concerned. In

[25] *Heimin Shimbun*, June 19, 1904, II, 349-51.

[26] Chief, Metrol Police to For. Min., July 23, 26, 1907, Nos. 1923, 1959: Archives, MT 2.4.1.9, pp. 362-63, 513-14.

the end, it deferred with hardly a murmur to the oligarchs' "realistic" handling of the situation, whether Itō's patient balancing or Terauchi's abrupt suppression.

Although the liberals can be said to have had no appreciable effect on Japan's course toward solution of the Korean problem in its final stages, except as they reinforced the realists, the opposite is true of that second group of idealists who stemmed from the same Conquer Korea (Seikan) beginnings, the reactionaries. We shall continue to refer to them by that name, although as admitted earlier when they were introduced in this study, finding a precise name for them is a difficult proposition.[27] E. Herbert Norman, who did the pioneer work in those Japanese sources which tell of their activities and brought them to the attention of Western scholarship in an article published in 1944, gave some consideration to this problem. He noted various appellations which might be thought appropriate, then found something wrong with each. For example, "secret societies" seems to lend itself to their description, until one remembers that, though many of their plots and activities were planned in secret, their leaders were well-known, even famous individuals, and they maintained publishing associations to publicize their "secret" doings. The term "reactionary" Norman discards as "too negative." They were dynamic, positive, vigorous, never satisfied. "Loyalist," "nationalist," or "ultranationalist" might be appropriate, if one remembers that they were quite capable of *disloyalty* to their own government, or even the emperor, if they felt that these were engaging in what, according to their standards, were "bad" policies. In placing them in the Japanese political scene Norman calls special attention to their close personal and emotional relationship to Saigō Takamori, their early leaders serving under him in the Satsuma Rebellion, and their later glorifying of his name. It is "quite fitting," he says, that one of their first official publications should be "an elaborate heavily documented six volume history of the Satsuma Revolt with rich bio-

[27] See above, pp. 215–17.

graphical material on Saigo, his lieutenants and most casual associates. Had he survived, Saigo would have inspired if not organized the type of society which sprang up after his death."[28] In this "patriotic" history, incidentally, the Satsuma Rebellion is referred to as *Seinan no Eki*, the War of the Southwest, which reminds one of that American euphemism, War Between the States, and suggests that our strange pairing of Saigō and John C. Calhoun may not be entirely inappropriate.

Norman concludes that, whatever they might be called, these people were bad, attributing to them a principal share of responsibility for Japanese aggression. "It is these societies rather than any political parties which have molded public opinion in favor of aggression. . . ." Their role after 1931 was to "throw into high gear the intricate machinery of their various organizations. The flood of propaganda which then poured forth from this source played upon the basest emotions of greed and chauvinism in order to gain public approval for the army's venture."[29] Norman's indictment is measured and precise, and though written during World War II is far above the standard polemic on Japanese aggression which filled so many international affairs journals during that period. It is as if today, or rather in a period of hot war between the West and the Soviet, an American (or Canadian) scholar would try to discover which group within the communist conspiracy had misled other, less guilty, elements into aggression against us. This is criticism of a much higher order than most are capable of, certainly in wartime. Yet it is still part of a searching for villains in order to explain villainies, an approach which has long been with us in historical writing and which seems to be especially enticing to students of international problems.

In this study we are more interested in explaining than blaming, though we shall not flinch from blaming if, in conclusion, it seems warranted. In fact, as a matter of blaming, we shall be quite

[28] Norman, "The Genyosha . . .," *Pac. Affairs* (Sept. 1944), pp. 261-65.
[29] *Ibid.*, p. 283.

prepared to say, as many have said, that villainous things were done in Korea and later through all east Asia under Japanese authority. Hence "Japan" was to blame, including all Japanese, except those who expatriated themselves, since their government acted in their name and they did nothing or too little to alter its course. But such blanket blaming does not satisfy more sensitive minds who know from the study of history and society that people are pretty much alike everywhere and who reason that when a whole nation goes on a rampage it must be because iniquitous elements in the society of that nation got the upper hand and led it astray. In the case of Japan the most obvious candidates for this sort of differentiated blame have been the militarists, from Yamagata through Terauchi and Tanaka to Tōjō, and most early studies attributed Japan's aggressive moves to the "military clique." Others, however, refused to exonerate the civilian oligarchs and, finding Itō, Saionji, and Konoe two-faced, argued that the militarists merely provided the strong arm for carrying out policies for which both sides were responsible. During and immediately after World War II, other groups were singled out for blame, the *Zaibatsu* (financial clique),[30] the emperor institution,[31] and the reactionary-ultranationalist-patriotic societies which Norman discovered.[32]

However, when one adds all these groups together, he finds that they comprised almost the entire active leadership of prewar Japan, except for thwarted "democratic elements," which, according to

[30] E.g., T. A. Bisson, *Japan's War Economy* (New York: Institute of Pacific Relations, 1945). Pauley Commission (*Report on Japanese Reparations to the President of the United States*, Washington, 1946).

[31] E.g., Owen Lattimore, *Solution in Asia* (Boston: Little, Brown & Co., 1945) and "The Sacred Cow of Japan," *The Atlantic*, CLXXV (Jan. 1945), 45-51. Andrew Roth, *Dilemma in Japan* (Boston: Little, Brown & Co., 1945). Kate L. Mitchell, "The Political Function of the Japanese Emperor," *Amerasia*, VI (Oct. 1952), 382-90.

[32] Assisted by A. Morgan Young, *Imperial Japan, 1926–1938* (New York: Morrow, 1938). Hugh Byas, *Government by Assassination* (New York: Knopf, 1942). See also R. T. Pollard, "Dynamics of Japanese Imperialism." *Pacific Historical Review*, VIII, 1 (Mar. 1939), pp. 5-36. The author has emphasized the role of these groups, especially after 1931, in an article, "Government versus 'Patriot': The Background of Japan's Asiatic Expansion," *Pacific Historical Review*, XX, 1 (Feb. 1951), pp. 31-42.

the Occupation's premise, once released from bondage would set Japan on a course of international respectability. The Occupation turned tail on this premise in 1947–48, having discovered that communists and fellow travelers were threatening to play the leading role among democratic elements, and helped to rebuild the position of old line party men and their big business affiliates. These are safe, conservative "liberal-democrats," descendants of the Itagaki-Ōkuma-Hara-Shidehara tradition, advocates and practitioners of parliamentary government, but distrustful of popular sovereignty, which today they are trying to strike from the new postwar constitution. It does not improve one's confidence in them to recall that their lineal predecessors applauded the seizure of Korea and subsequently surrendered to totalitarian government.[33] Dissatisfied here, one looks to the left of these tired-out liberals, to the present-day socialists (or social democrats), the second largest party in the Diet, and one may feel a surge of hope. Here are vigor and idealism, determined support of popular sovereignty—with enough votes to prevent its being taken out of the constitution by amendment—advocacy of improved living standards for common people, opposition to weapons and warfare, and a fierce pride in Japan's potential role as neutralist leader toward a new and better world. But then one stops and wonders—the fierce pride, the denunciation of America as reactionary. Is this Fukuzawa and Ōi Kentaro denouncing China in the 1880's? Are these the lineal descendants of the most energetic liberals of that day, who, with marvelous idealism, nerve, and verve, finding themselves frustrated in Japan tried to "kill themselves for righteousness" in Korea, only to go down the road to chauvinism. We do not suggest that there is a parallel, only that one might develop, for neutralism could become nationalism and it is not inconceivable that a Hiroshima peace shrine could be

[33] Scalapino's is a blow by blow description of their abandonment of liberal principles, as his title indicates: *Democracy and the Party Movement in Prewar Japan: the Failure of the First Attempt.*

turned into a new version of *Yasukuni Jinja.* Marius Jansen has made uncomfortably explicit the fact that these most active liberals of the Meiji era were perfectly sincere in their democratic aspirations, but that they ended in very close co-operation with reactionary-ultranationalist-patriotic societies in seeking ways to bring not only Korea but all the rest of eastern Asia under Japanese dominion.[34] And when we add the liberals, both "tired-out" and "energetic" to our list of responsible parties, we are indeed back again to an indictment of "Japan" as a whole.

These musings beyond the Korean problem are introduced here to indicate why we should be wary of replacing a general scheming Japan explanation of the Japanese seizure of Korea, which we have found to be untenable, with a differentiated scheming reactionary-ultranationalist-patriotic societies explanation. One feels a strong temptation to do this. Upon first delving into the documents set forth in their various "secret histories,"[35] the author felt as Norman also must have felt, that here indeed was the key, the revelation of the motive force behind not only the seizure of Korea but the whole course of modern Japanese expansion. One is shocked at the barefaced boasting, at the utter lack of apology for the advocacy of crimes of aggression, at the smug assumption that Japan *should* rule Korea and China and the rest of Asia, perhaps the whole world, as though this were a virtuous course. Here are the villains, a lying, scheming bunch of cutthroats and assassins. The oligarchs were, at least, concerned about breaches of civilized international practice and the censure of world opinion for practical reasons, if not for reasons of conscience, but the compatriots have no concern whatever. With them treaties are nothing, laws are nothing; nothing is important save the great goal of spreading what they consider virtue around the world. But reading accounts

[34] Jansen, "Ōi . . .," pp. 305-6, 316 and *The Japanese and Sun Yat-sen*, pp. 28-31, 41-58, 217-22. Delmer Brown touches on the rise of postwar nationalism in his *Nationalism in Japan* (Berkeley: Univ. of California Press, 1955), pp. 251-78.

[35] Kokuryūkai (and Kuzū), *Tōa Senkaku . . ., Nikkan Gappō . . ., Nisshi Kōsho . . .*, etc.

of dangerous journeys into hostile areas, of personal self-sacrifice, and lifelong devotion to the cause, one gradually realizes that they are sincerely, grimly in earnest and admits reluctantly that they may not be hypocrites at all but, perhaps, madmen. Yet they are not mad enough to be madmen. They know what they are doing.

Tōyama Mitsuru, the unquestioned leader of the societies, though characteristically he did not hold an office in them, apparently exuded qualities of sincerity, dignity, inscrutable wisdom, and unimpeachable honesty to a degree that even a man who met him casually on a train "could never forget him." One of his disciples, Sugiyama Shigemaru, who figures prominently in the Korea story, attributed his finding a purpose in life to the happenstance of a meeting with Tōyama. Tōyama's principal disciple, and the most important of all in the Korea story, Uchida Ryōhei, was an incredibly active and, in his way, brilliant person. Before 1900 he had traveled widely in Siberia, as well as Korea and China, and made himself extremely well versed in the geography and customs, as well as the languages, of those areas.[36] Tōyama, Uchida, and Sugiyama were all dead long before this study was undertaken, but the author has had an unusual opportunity to become acquainted with the virtues, and they are real virtues, of a Japanese family steeped in the reactionary-ultranationalist tradition. This is the Masaki (or Mazaki) family, whose most famous member was General Masaki Jinzaburō, inspector general of military education in the 1930's, who along with General Araki Sadao, was the idol of the super-loyalist "Young Officer" element. General Masaki died, at age 81, on August 31, 1956, but before his last illness set in, in the summer of 1954, the author had the opportunity to interview him at his home in Tokyo,and through this and numerous discussions with his nephew and exponent, Mr. Masaki Masaru, to appreciate the

[36] On Tōyama, Uchida, and Sugiyama see Jansen, *The Japanese . . .*, pp. 34-39, 180-81, 217. See also Taketora Ogata, "Mitsuru Toyama," *Contemporary Japan*, IX (July 1940), 818-29 and Seizo Kimase, *Mitsuru Toyama Kämpft für Grossasien* (Munich, 1941).

insufficiency of merely denouncing and accusing the reactionaries, whether of the Meiji era or later.

Prior to his discussions with the Masakis the author, though he had never met anyone prominently associated with the Young Officers, was nevertheless quite well informed about the movement from his own research and from careful reading of Royal Wald's "The Young Officer Movement,"[37] the best study of it available at the time. Knowing well the large contribution the movement had made to the development of totalitarianism in Japan, he entered into the discussions in a reproving frame of mind. This was not dissipated by young Mr. Masaki's careful explanation that his uncle had played no part in the Pacific War. This, the author observed, was only because he had been kept out by the Tōjō clique for conspiracy to set up a premature military dictatorship, the attempted coup of February 26, 1936. Mr. Masaki argued that in this case too his uncle had been falsely accused, for he had not been a party to this Young Officer plot, in fact had been surprised by the uprising. This is like saying that Saigō bore no responsibility for the Satsuma Rebellion because his followers, incited by his teachings, began it without his express permission.

Though our discussions of uncle's responsibility ended in deadlock, the author's interest in and respect for the younger Mr. Masaki grew. The loyalty implicit in his effort to defend his uncle's honor was touching, and the author found himself thinking of the samurai code. Along with loyalty there were also honesty and sincerity. We translated documents together, and though there were many places where a softening of the translation might have made Japan and her ultranationalists look more creditable, Mr. Masaki never softened a translation.

The interview with General Masaki was like a lesson in samurai virtues. The General had no excuses to offer. He was simple and

[37] Ph.D. diss., University of California, Berkeley, 1949. Cf. Richard Storry, *The Double Patriots* (London: Chatto & Windus, 1957). For an example of a direct father-son link between the old Kokuryūkai and the Young Officers, see Kuzū, *Tōa Senkaku* . . ., III, 41-42.

direct in speech, avoiding the circumlocutions with which the Japanese language abounds. He dressed simply, lived unostentatiously, was obviously unconcerned about material possessions. He was interested, he said, in truth, in justice, and in duty, and he would answer any questions. He looked very frail, but he brushed aside the suggestion that he might rest on a nearby couch during the interview. He said he was sorry that he could speak only in Japanese, but that his nephew, who knew his mind very well, could clarify any points which did not seem understandable.

From his discussion and the later clarifications there emerged several points which seem pertinent to our effort to understand the reactionaries. First, to General Masaki, Japanese history was to be explained largely in terms of family and clan connections and rivalries. Especially important was the dominance and tyranny of the Chōshū clan from Meiji times onward. From his lifetime of experience in the Japanese army he could say that the "Chōshū clique" had "oppressed Saga men terribly." (The Masaki family is from Saga, which we recall was the home country of Etō Shimpei, who was executed in 1874.) The Young Officers had represented a climactic effort to break through the Chōshū stranglehold, which had been perpetuated not only by Chōshū men themselves, but by the military training schools which they had founded and continued to dominate. It failed and Masaki, though he had played no part in the actual attempted coup, went to jail. That was "no great matter," but the Control Group, whose leader came to be Tōjō, had taken charge of the government and led Japan to ruin. Tōjō was a "turtle" who had betrayed the higher aspirations and deeper loyalties and suppressed the "individualism" of the younger officers, especially Saga men.

The Masaki knowledge of clan and family connections in Japan was remarkable, and certainly a history of Japan by genealogy needs to be written, but it is suggestive of their preoccupation with clan rivalries that even the younger Mr. Masaki, in his memoir of his experiences in the United States, makes American politics revolve around "the Eisenhower brothers and the Dulles brothers."[38]

General Masaki had little confidence that the wrongs done in Japan by Chōshū leadership could be righted by parliamentary means. He expressed the feeling that, in Japan at least, even political assassination was sometimes necessary. Why? Because a statesman should be prepared to die for his principles, and, because Japan's being small, social and political pressures became very intense there. Sometimes there was no other way for able men to break through the system and rise to leadership. Did this mean that thoroughgoing social and political revolution was necessary? By no means, for one of the tragedies of recent years is that "low class people" have been able to come to the top. Reflecting on this paradox, the author remembered Saigō and Etō and their efforts on behalf of discontented samurai.

While General Masaki found Chōshū oppression to have been the main source of Japan's domestic troubles, a deep-seated Russophobia characterized his international outlook. This was not simply anti-communist, but carried far back into the tsarist period. The Russians had always been supreme villains, evil in themselves and menacing to Japan. Hearing this, the author recalled that Uchida Ryōhei's first important tract, written after his Siberian Travels, was entitled, in translation, "Great Blemishes on the Seamy Side of Russia." And he wondered whether General Masaki's preoccupation with Russia and secret plots might be reflected in the large amount of space which his nephew's memoir of America devotes to the Rosenberg spy case, the death of Stalin, and curiously (to an American) the bizarre slaying of Serge Rubenstein.[39]

To General Masaki, the present condition of Japan and the world was so bad as almost to bring tears to his eyes. People were running wild after money, gewgaws, and pleasure. Everything was

[38] Masaki Masaru, *Hokengaku Angya* (Insurance Pilgrimage) (Tokyo: Hoken Kenkyūsho, 1956), pp. 235-38.

[39] *Ibid.*, pp. 239-51, 259-66.

deteriorating and there seemed to be no stopping it. There was no one to take heroic measures. He wished he could "get up and do something," but it was no use (*shikata ga nai*), he was too weak, his life was almost over. He closed with a warning to beware of Russia. America should guard even if Japanese politicians could not see the need.

The author came away from the interview, not angry as he had expected he might be, but with a profound feeling of sadness. Here was an old man of courage, dignity, chivalry, and honesty, spending his last years in bitterness, frustration, and regret because the world had passed him by. He had spent his whole life fighting to restore a set of samurai values that had gone down in the 1870's with the rebellions of Etō and Saigō, values which once had a great deal of virtue in them perhaps, but which were so restricted by the horizontal barriers of class and the vertical barriers of section that in the wider world of social mobility and international contact they had lost all validity. He blamed Chōshū and Russia mostly, the former (Itō, Yamagata, etc.) for breaking down the samurai system, and the latter as the most conspicuous example of the Western pressure which had forced Japan into a new world of Western-dominated states and practices. What he needed most in his education, the author reflected later, he had obviously never had. Weaned on chivalry, he had never learned the lesson of Don Quixote.

Having met General Masaki, we may now understand better why Tōyama Mitsuru was a respected and even venerated man in Japan, and also why we have called his followers "reactionaries" and defined the motivation for their actions in Korea and elsewhere as "reverse idealism." Their great duty, as they saw it, was to hold the line against the breakdown of the old samurai values and Asian heritage and to roll back the Western wave which had all but engulfed eastern Asia. So overwhelming had been their defeat in the 1870's that they were for a time without a coherent program, and they resorted mainly to the "good" samurai remedy of personal vengeance. The treaty revision issue and the Sino-Japanese War provided some opportunity for the exercise of their talents, though in general they followed the lead of the liberals on the war. A progressive war against reactionary China for Western-style independence and reform in Korea was not, however, really congenial to their basic attitudes, and it was only after 1900 that they began to find a consistent focus. This was on two objectives, war with Russia and "merger" with Korea, each of which was part of a larger whole, war with Russia being expandable to war with the whole Western world and merger with Korea being capable of extension to include China and other areas of eastern Asia. Surrounded with samurai ethics, emperor adulation, and the idea that peoples unschooled in Confucian culture were barbarians, these ideas were connected to deep roots in the soil of traditional Japan. It should not be thought that all these connections were made, even in the 1900–10 period. It remained for "philosophers of the right" like Ōkawa Shūmei, Kita Ikki, Tachibana Kōzaburo, Fujisawa Chikao, and the authors of the Kokuryūkai publications in the 1920's and 1930's to fit the pieces together into a polished ideological pattern.[40] But the feeling that they were "rooted in oriental tradition" enabled the reactionaries, despite their lack of coherence and consistency, to touch the sensibilities of millions of Japanese, who were after all so recently emerged from the old Asiatic past that even leaders of the march forward had moments of uncertainty, and felt shame when reminded that they were violating their own traditions.

In addition, there was a factor of strength in the reactionaries beyond the appeal to tradition, something more basic perhaps and

[40] John O. Gauntlett (trans.), *Kokutai no Hongi: Cardinal Principles of the National Polity of Japan* (Cambridge: Harvard University Press, 1949), is a convenient example of this. See Ōkawa Shūmei, *Nihon Nisenroppyaku Nenshi* (2600 Years of Japanese History) (Tokyo: Dai Ichi Shoten, 1939), for an explanation of the whole course of Japanese history in these terms. Ōkawa's book went through eighteen printings between July and December, 1939. Cf. Fujisawa Chikao, "The Reassertion of Japanese State Philosophy," *Cultural Nippon*, II (Mar. 1934), 35-49.

more positive. Actually, by 1900, the best minds of eastern Asia were tired of the old traditions, of the false class structure, and general stagnation, and those who could be called liberals or realists in any of the countries of eastern Asia, whether Japan, China, Korea, even southeast Asia and the Philippines, were invigorated by and welcomed the new winds of progress from the modern West. They might be ashamed at times of violating old traditions but they did not wish to return to them. Thus on appeal to tradition alone, the reactionaries could not have done much to influence the course of affairs once determined advocates of progress got the helm, as they did in Japan. However, to learn progress Asians had to accept, temporarily at least, a position of inferiority to Westerners, study *their* languages, observe *their* institutions, and accept their insolence. Unfortunately there was a great deal of the last. Viewed in the context of the whole wide world, eastern Asia was a region, a section, and sectional pride was a factor which contributed to the rise of the Japanese reactionaries. They said that east Asians were as good as, if not better than, anybody else, especially Westerners, said it over and over again all around eastern Asia. On this subject they could find rapport, not only with traditionalists but also with Asian reformers. Jansen has shown how, on this basis, they entered the confidence not only of Japanese liberals, but of the Chinese reform groups of Liang Ch'i-ch'ao and Sun Yat-sen, and the Filipinos of Aguinaldo.[41] Connections with other southeast Asians, Indians, and even Arabs have not been studied, but they existed.[42]

Against this background of attitudes and ideology, let us now turn to the activities of the reactionaries with regard to their two specific goals of the late Meiji era, war with Russia and merger with Korea. The first can be dismissed quickly since it is only indirectly pertinent to our main theme. After Uchida Ryōhei returned from his Siberian travels he organized in 1901 the Kokuryūkai, Black Dragon Society, or, more meaningfully in this connection, Amur

[41] Jansen, *The Japanese and Sun Yat-sen*, pp. 59-81.
[42] Mentioned in Kuzū, *Tōa Senkaku . . .*, III, 261-64, 361-62.

River Society. By a curious coincidence the characters for Amur River also mean Black Dragon. The society's major objective at the time was to mold Japanese public opinion and bring pressure on the government to make war on Russia. In 1903 members of the Kokūryukai and its parent organization, the Genyōsha, Black Ocean Society, spawned the Tai-ro Dōshikai, Anti-Russian League, and toward the end of the Russo-Japanese War they organized the Konwa Mondai Dōshi Rengokai, or Federated Societies Concerning the Peace Problem. The purpose of the latter was to oppose the compromise Portsmouth peace, and to this end it sponsored a mass meeting at Hibiya Park in Tokyo to demand prolongation of the war until "complete" victory had been achieved.[43] There is no doubt that the reactionaries pushed the Japanese government toward war with Russia by every means at their command and also tried to prevent the Portsmouth peace. However, the question of how much actual influence they had is difficult to answer. Their own compilations give a great deal of credit to themselves, and there is no doubt that they sent letters and even threats to the oligarchs, especially to Itō because of his efforts to negotiate with Russia. For example, one, which the author saw among Itō's papers and hence could be sure it was delivered, promised "immediate Heaven-sent punishment" for Itō if he did not take a "strong policy."[44] Also there is a story that Tōyama himself, impertinently attired in informal *yukata*, visited Itō and threatened him with dire consequences if he persisted in his "weak" ways.[45] And there is no doubt that the mass gathering in Hibiya Park occurred. Still it is difficult to estimate whether the oligarchs were moved by all this or whether they simply began the war and made the peace in accordance with their own realistic analysis of the situation. Even if it could be argued that they responded to threats

[43] *Ibid.*, I, chaps. 47, 49, 60, and pp. 871-81 deal with these matters. The mass meeting is also described in *Meiji Hennenshi*, XII, 492.

[44] Letters to Itō No. 110, June 10, 1903, Kensei Shiryō Shitsu Collection. Also No. 20, no date, may be another example.

[45] Norman, "The Genyosha . . .," pp. 271-72.

and pressures to begin the war, they certainly did not respond to demands to prolong it beyond Portsmouth, which makes the other argument dubious also. In measuring the total influence of the reactionaries many things must be considered: the already discussed complex of attitudes involving tradition, progress, and Asian sensitivity; more specific matters like threatening letters and public demonstrations; and most specific of all, personal links between reactionaries and organs of government, the army, the bureaucracy, the Diet. For example, many of them were close to or a part of the army intelligence network, their knowledge of the geography, inner politics, and customs of eastern Asia being most useful.

With regard to the Russo-Japanese War the author will not attempt a precise estimate of the influence of the reactionaries. Suffice it to say that they were a part of the general situation which the oligarchs took into view in deciding whether, when, and how long to make war. However, with the Russian war behind them, whether they were satisfied or not with its outcome, the reactionaries turned their main attention to the Korean problem. In their activities on this we are most interested, and we shall try to evaluate their effect as precisely as we can. Once again we must beware of braggadocio, for our principal source for their doings is their own compilation, *Nikkan Gappō Hishi* (The Secret History of the Merger of Japan and Korea). But it is a rich source, two large volumes, specifically devoted to the subject, replete with quotations from letters, notes on interviews, and reminiscences which reveal a most intimate knowledge of affairs in Korea, 1905–10. These are mainly those of Uchida Ryōhei, chief of the Kokuryūkai and on-the-spot co-ordinator of reactionary enterprises in Korea during these years. The chief difficulty for the evaluator is the braggadocio, for the reactionaries want the lion's share of credit for the merging. One notices, for example, that, though the compilation includes numerous letters *from* Uchida and his friends *to* high government officials such as Itō and Katsura, there are few coming in the other direction. Then how much attention did they receive? Perhaps actions rather than words will be our best indicator, although the testimony of Itō's secretary Kurachi, already cited, plus certain references to Uchida and his friends in Itō's papers and other government files and the press, with which we can supplement the "Secret History" material, constitute sufficient proof that the role they played was an important one.

One of the things that may surprise us, in view of their ultimate effect on Korea, is that the Japanese reactionaries had many Korean friends. They claim a million members in their Korean organization,[46] which is certainly an exaggeration, but they seem to have had no difficulty in finding friendly circles of Korean society in which to move. The basic relationship developed out of the participation of the Japanese Ten Yu Kyō (Saving Chivalry under Heaven) contingent in the Tonghak Rebellion of 1894. Clarence Weems, arguing that the Tonghak movement was truly Korean and devoted to the best interests of the country, albeit conservative and anti-foreign in its outlook, discounts the idea, presented in many books, that they collaborated with the Japanese at this time. He thinks that Japan "may have been abetting the Tonghak Ch'ondokyo as early as 1904 . . . but did not do so in any way before that date." He bases this partly on the revulsion at the Korean court's acceptance of the Japanese alliance and control (July–August, 1894) which was "deeply felt by Tonghak membership generally and many of its leaders, whatever may be the truth of the assertion that the Society received Japanese aid at some stage of its history."[47]

However, when one remembers the anti-government, tradition-minded approach of the Japanese reactionaries, the idea of their finding a welcome in Tonghak ranks does not seem so improbable. It does not in any way detract from the sincerity of the Tonghaks, though it might detract from their intelligence, to suggest that

[46] Kuzū, *Nikkan Gappō* . . ., I, 31-32 and II, 220.
[47] Weems, "Korean Reform . . .," pp. 83, 101 and note 12, chap. V.

they accepted some Japanese adventurers who agreed with the proposition that things were rotten at Seoul. Anyway, Japanese sources, which Weems did not use, say very clearly that some such contact was established in 1894. Uchida is specifically mentioned, along with Adachi Kenzō, who became a leading ultranationalist of the 1930's, as members of the Ten Yu Kyō group.[48] Exactly how this relationship developed is not clear, but the "Secret History" tells us that the Ilchin Hoe (Japanese Isshin Kai), the society which linked the Japanese reactionaries with their Korean comrades during the 1905–10 period, was "a changed form of the Tonghak party."[49] One of the main changes seems to have occurred during the Russo-Japanese War when the Japanese army in Korea began to subsidize the society to encourage its pro-Japanese proclivities.[50] However, as will be shown, this does not mean that its members became merely minions of the Residency General afterwards.

During the era of the Residency General, the Korean leaders of the Ilchin Society were Yi Yong-koo and Song Pyong-chun and its Japanese adviser was Uchida Ryōhei. Later, it developed close relationships with two other groups, the Suh Book Hak (Northwest Educational) Society and the Tai Han (Great Korea) Society. These last two societies were "usually anti Japanese" but Yi Yong-koo and Uchida worked to get them to co-operate with the Ilchin Society for the Japan-Korea merger movement.[51]

The ideological basis of the partnership between Japanese reactionaries and their Korean friends may best be explained by discussing our use of the word, merger, in defining their goal for Korea. The Japanese word is *gappō*, which appears in the title of their "Secret History" and which they use insistently. It is a curious

[48] Kokuryūkai, *Nisshi . . .*, I, 220. Kuzū, *Nikkan Gappō . . .*, I, Preface. Hatada, *Chōsen Shi*, p. 183. Jiji Shimpō, Jan. 23, 1896. Cf. Sunoo, "Technique of Japanese Imperialism," *Korean Rev.*, I, 1, p. 47, note 70. Also Russian sources indicate Japanese participation in the movement: chap. V above, note 16 and Nihon Nōshōmusho, *Rokoku . . .*, p. 473.

[49] Kuzū, *Nikkan Gappō . . .*, I, 41.

[50] *Ibid.*, I, 28, 166, 168-69, 562.

[51] *Ibid.*, II, 104-5, 112-15.

word which, the author was told, sounds more Chinese than Japanese to a Japanese ear. It is not even given in the large Kenkyūsha Japanese dictionary which sits at the author's elbow, but it is not in his Chinese dictionary either. The two characters which compose the word mean respectively "to agree with or to unite with" and "country," which, to the Japanese means also "Japan." Hence *Nikkan Gappō* is "Japan-Korea uniting countries," or "Japan-Korea uniting Japan," which is redundant but rather ironically plausible in view of the long-range outcome. The usual Japanese words for annexation are *gappei*, *heigō*, and *heidon*, all of which appear in Kenkyūsha's dictionary. It seems that the word *gappō* was the special "reactionaries' word" for the Korean problem, just as, interestingly enough, there was a special "government word" also, namely *heigō*. The fact that the one is in the dictionary and the other not may be in itself a sort of minute commentary on which group, in the end, ran the annexation show.

At any rate, Itō's sometime secretary, Kurachi, has left us an interesting discourse on this very subject, which he entitled, "The Literal Meaning of *Heigō*." He says that in the policy documents on Korea which he drew up for Foreign Minister Komura in 1909 "the word *heigō* was utilized for the first time and considerable care was taken about that," because "at that time, though there were arguments about that Korea was to be annexed (*gappei*), the meaning was not clearly understood." Then he explains that the words *gappei*, frequently applied to "business combinations," and *gappō*, which might imply "a form of federation like Austria-Hungary," were used by some but were unsuitable because—

according to Foreign Minister Komura, Korea was to come completely to Japan and there would be no treaties between Korea and other foreign countries. [However] the word *heidon* [annex, devour, swallow up] was too aggressive to use, so after various considerations I [Kurachi] thought out a new wording, heigō, which until that time had not been used. This was stronger than *gappei*, meaning that the other's territory should become part of Japan's territory. Since then the term *heigō* has been used widely in public documents, but in these Korean policy documents it was used for the first time. Having newly invented the word *heigō*, I did not stress it too much, knowing there would be argument about it. So even Prime Minister Katsura, when he read the policy documents, sometimes read *heigō* as *gappei* without noticing it himself.[52]

Mr. Kurachi undoubtedly had the inside story on heigō, since he composed it himself, but he was perhaps too well educated to appreciate the meaning of gappō, at least as the reactionaries used it. The Western-minded secretary thought it might mean a "federation like Austria-Hungary" but that is too legalistic a description. To Uchida and his friends it was a more romantic affair, a federation perhaps but one whose institutional lines were indistinct, a sort of Asian brotherhood in search of an ideal, *Dai Tō Gappō* (Great Oriental Federation), the first step toward which was a "federating," or better, "merging" of Korea and Japan. The relationship would be a very intimate one, like "lips and teeth." (This is a Chinese expression formerly used to describe the relationship between China and her dependent states.)[53] The precise form of the relationship was not spelled out, which undoubtedly was a factor in maintaining the enthusiasm of its Korean supporters, but the term, Great Oriental Federation, certainly brings to mind the East Asia co-prosperity ideas which figured so prominently in the Japan-dominated Far East of the World War II period. Also, like the co-prosperity theme, it contained strong anti-Western overtones, as evidenced in Yi Yong-koo's analysis of the root of Korea's troubles expressed to a Japanese friend: "I know it is Christianity which misleads the Korean people and if one goes more deeply, it is the American people who penetrated the Korean brain through Christianity."[54]

Though the ultimate meaning of gappō was vague, certain

[52] Kurachi, "Kankoku Heigō . . .," p. 5.

[53] Kuzū, *Nikkan Gappō* . . ., I, 41, 44. Cf. Nelson, *Korea and the Old Orders* . . ., p. 87, note 2.

[54] Kuzū, *Nikkan Gappō* . . ., II, p. 627. Same theme, *ibid.*, I, 292-93, 453-54.

specific objectives showed through. Since "without a basic reformation Korea's twenty million people could not be saved," halfway measures were not enough. The Korean emperorship should be abolished, the cabinet of Yi Wan-yong broken up, the currency, tax, and local administration system of the Residency General abolished. These had "caused the Korean people to lose 20 million yuan [dollars]" and won their enmity. Gradualism, indecisiveness were bad for Japan and bad for Korea. The solution was gappō, immediate, decisive.[55]

It will be observed that such demands as these constituted an implicit attack on Itō's administration, which observation brings us to consideration of the relationship between the reactionaries and Japanese policy makers, especially the resident general, on the Korean issue. As has been shown, there is substantial evidence to indicate that Itō, pursuing enlightened self-interest for Japan, tried to make of the Residency General a joint Japanese-Korean enterprise. Until at least the spring or summer of 1909 he was a determined opponent of annexation. Yet there is also evidence that Uchida Ryōhei was off and on in the pay of the Residency General and that the Ilchin Society received money from Japanese government officials, perhaps from Itō himself. Does this bring us back to the conclusion that Itō was a complete hypocrite, secretly supporting annexation while officially taking a stand against it? Outwardly it would seem so. However, since the "Secret History," from which the evidence for this is drawn, takes the view that Itō was guilty of exactly the opposite, what to its compilers was betrayal of the annexation cause, it would seem wise to analyze the matter as carefully as possible.

According to the "Secret History" Uchida was recommended to Itō by his "senior clansman," Sugiyama Shigemaru, in words of high praise: "Sugiyama said, 'There is no comparable good horse in the world, but no one can control this good horse. Even you

[55] *Ibid.*, I, 66-95, 545-47 and II, pp. 104-5, 112, 257, 651. Cf. Tōyama Mitsuru et al to For. Min., July 14, 1907, Archives, MT 2.4.1.9, pp. 163-64.

Mr. Itō might fail.' Itō asked, 'Who is he?' Sugiyama answered, 'Uchida Ryōhei.' "[56] This recommending seems to have taken place in late 1905 or early 1906, and Itō seems to have accepted the challenge, for soon thereafter Uchida was in Korea, presumably in the employ of the Residency General. The braggadocio in the episode is interesting, the more so because the ultimate source for the tale is probably Uchida himself. But in view of it, perhaps the most interesting point is the unwitting admission that to that time Itō had probably never heard of Uchida. This makes it entirely possible that Uchida got the job, not as a noted annexationist but as an adventurous young man who had been to Korea before. The "Secret History" does not tell us what Uchida's position was, but one suspects that Itō did not pay very much attention to him, at least, not at first.

As for Sugiyama, there is evidence, other than that in the "Secret History," that he was fairly well acquainted with Itō. Born in Fukuoka in 1864, the son of a teacher of Confucian precepts, he, unlike most members of the Genyōsha-Kokuryūkai circle, held various official positions which brought him into contact with Yamagata, Katsura, Terauchi, and others, as well as Itō. Jansen concludes that "he was an intimate friend and associate of outstanding Japanese military and political leaders."[57] The "Secret History" shows him having dinner at Itō's Tokyo residence, calling on Katsura at his home, arranging interviews for Uchida with Yamagata, Katsura, and Terauchi, receiving memos from them to pass on to Uchida (this, in 1909).[58] While there is no reason to doubt that Sugiyama moved among the top leaders of the Japanese government, one gets a very definite impression that he, rather than they, pushed the association. For example, the author was able to locate among Itō's papers a considerable number of letters which could be classed as rather personal in nature from Sugiyama

[56] Kuzū, *Nikkan Gappō* . . ., I, 11.
[57] Kuzū, *Tōa Senkaku* . . ., III, 758-63. Jansen, *The Japanese* . . ., p. 40.
[58] Kuzū, *Nikkan Gappō* . . ., I, 149-51 and II, 153, 156, 203, 501.

to Itō, but none from Itō to Sugiyama. Thus, November 29, 1898: "I hear that you have returned from a long trip. I should like to see you, but due to illness I cannot present myself before you. However, I hear from Arahina that you are well and I am glad." Again, October 19, 1900: "I hear that you have organized a new cabinet. I hope you will take care of your health and be able to work for our country." And on May 20, 1901: "When I left Japan I received your many kindnesses. As I have just arrived in the United States I have no adequate information on economic affairs yet. . . ."[59] Perhaps it can be said that Sugiyama had been "buttering up" Itō for a number of years before the great Korean venture began.

It is clear from correspondence between Uchida and Sugiyama that by January, 1907, they were very critical of Itō's administration. General Hasegawa had "fallen into the tactics of the Korean Emperor," police adviser Maruyama was "obstructing the Ilchin society," the Residency General's reform program was a "complete failure," and Uchida advised Sugiyama to "let higher officials [in Tokyo] know the true face of the Korean situation" and seek a fundamental change in policy. "Gappō should be accomplished immediately."[60] However, though Uchida was certainly working hard to develop the Ilchin Society as a vehicle for gappō, and put in words of praise for it at the Residency General whenever he could,[61] he remained quite circumspect in his relationship with Itō. He did not tell the resident's office that he was adviser to the society, then technically resigned the post when he learned that Itō knew and was angry about it,[62] and, in a set of recommendations on policy which he sent to Itō in February, 1907, he showed none of the hostility to the Residency General which the letters to Sugiyama a month earlier reveal. He urged that the Korean

[59] These three letters and others from Sugiyama to Itō are in Letters to Itō (folder), No. 24: Kensei Shiryō Shitsu.

[60] Uchida to Sugiyama, Jan. 1, 14, 1907: *Nikkan Gappō* . . ., I, 66-95.

[61] *Nikkan Gappō* . . ., I, 29, is an example.

[62] *Ibid.*, pp. 42, 56.

emperor should be replaced for he was "too idle and too clever," but the overall import of his recommendations was that the Residency General should do more, take more power, engage in a wider range of activities. He closed with an urging that the Ilchin Society should "be rewarded for its good work" and the observation that it was a religious rather than a political organization.[63]

In the spring of 1907, according to the "Secret History," Uchida returned on a visit to Japan, accompanied by Song Pyong-chun of the Ilchin Society. There, Sugiyama arranged for them to see Terauchi and Yamagata. To each of these in turn Uchida described the merits of the Ilchin Society and asked for an expression of good will. Terauchi said: "I promised Sugiyama to hear your opinion, so I'll just listen." Yamagata said: "The problems of Korea are the responsibility of the Resident General and I don't know about them. But as for your opinion I might give you friendly advice . . . many difficulties . . . language difficulty. Therefore we must develop our program gradually. Then the Koreans will not be angry and we can succeed in our administration. . . . Also the Korean Emperor is very clever, so if it were I instead of Itō, I might not be able to stand up for three days under him. Itō is Japan's best politician, so if we trust him everything will be all right. Please be patient." On this the "Secret History" comments, "Song was thankfully excited by this encouragement."[64]

The chief sort of "encouragement" which Uchida wanted at this point was money. Apparently the society's wartime subsidy from the Japanese army in Korea had dried up or was in danger of drying up. (Hasegawa had been "violently angry" at Song.)[65] At any rate, the financial condition of the society was "bad," and Uchida hoped to get money directly from the Residency General to remedy this. After his return to Seoul from Japan he made direct application to Itō on behalf of the society. After some discussion,

[63] Uchida to Itō, no day, Feb., 1907: *Nikkan Gappō* . . ., I, 113-31.
[64] *Nikkan Gappō* . . ., I, 149-52.
[65] *Ibid.*, pp. 55, 61.

in which Itō seems to have quizzed Uchida rather sharply on whether the Ilchin Society was against Japan (which Itō would surely not differentiate from the Residency General) and Uchida gave assurances that it was not, Itō agreed "to help the Ilchin society pay their debts." On May 15 (1907), according to the "Secret History," at the order of General Hasegawa, the Japanese army paid 100,000 yen to the Ilchin Society. Uchida promised "great care" in its expenditure, concerning which he gave an accounting to Hasegawa. This showed that 50,000 yen was to be used to pay off a bank loan, 4700 yen for speechmaking around the country, 6300 yen to help businesses get into operation, 2500 yen to help a friendly society, and the balance to be deposited as capital.[66]

Meanwhile the Ilchin Society had also presented Itō with a letter of condemnation of the Korean cabinet as constituted (Pak Che-sun, Yi Wan-yong, etc.) and Itō seems to have talked about this with Uchida also. Uchida advocated a new Ilchin Society cabinet, which Itō rejected, but he seems to have been impressed with the possibility of integrating a new element, and a pro-Japanese one, into the old cabinet. Late in May he suggested the idea of co-operation with the Ilchin Society to Pak Che-sun who was prime minister at the time. The thought made Pak so angry that he resigned. This is interesting in view of the fact that Pak was already collaborating with the Japanese, and suggests that his antagonism to the Ilchin group may have had more to do with their Tonghak background than their Japanese connections. However, Yi Wan-yong, who succeeded to the premiership, "though reluctant at first," took Song Pyong-chun into his cabinet as minister of agriculture, commerce, and industry.[67] If the Korean emperor thought of Song as a Tonghak, his admission to the cabinet could have been a principal reason for the emperor's dispatching the Hague mission. Song, it should be noted, took the

[66] *Ibid.*, 32, 198, 200-1, 240-46.
[67] *Ibid.*, pp. 201, 239, 247-48.

lead in denouncing the emperor and demanding his abdication in July after the mission episode.

Though Itō thus helped the Ilchin Society settle its debts and brought one of its members into the cabinet, the Hague mission-abdication affair and its aftermath roused his suspicions that its objectives were not the same as his, and conversely it soured Uchida and his friends on Itō. The Japanese reactionaries, both in Japan and Korea, took advantage of these events to begin making demands rather than requests. In Japan, Tōyama and his associates sent a strongly worded memorandum to Foreign Minister Hayashi "asserting and confirming" that the sovereignty of the Korean emperor should be "delegated to our nation" and warning against any attempt to "act in a compromising and expedient way." Adachi Kenzō and others visited Katsura personally.[68]

In Seoul, Uchida, at first news of the Hague mission, rushed to Itō to urge "definitive measures," but Itō said there was no hurry, to await details. Disappointed, Uchida went into conference with his Ilchin associates, Yi Yong-koo and Song Pyong-chun. They decided, "Now is the time. We must force the abdication of the Korean Emperor." However, they could not depend on Yi Wan-yong, the prime minister. Song suggested that if Yi felt that the resident general had already approved the abdication, he would agree to it. Uchida warned that the resident general could not be counted on for the abdication problem. Song said, "Of course not, but we will only *say* that we have his approval in order to get Yi Wan-yong's agreement."[69] Thus, according to the "Secret History," it was settled that Song would make the spectacular demand for the emperor's abdication. At the height of the abdication crisis, while the ministers were holding sessions with the emperor, Uchida wired Sugiyama: "Last night Ministers pressed for abdication but were rejected. I do not know Resident General's

[68] Tōyama *et al* to For. Min., July 14, 1907: Archives, MT 2.4.1.9, pp. 163-64. Chief Metro. Police to For. Min., July 11, 1907: *ibid.*, pp. 158-59.

[69] *Nikkan Gappō . . .*, I, 282-83.

intentions. The appointment of Pak Young-hyo as Imperial Household Minister is very strange. I, Uchida, will take action in cooperation with Ilchin society. Therefore I rather hesitate to ask Resident General for expense money. If you have any money to spare, please send me any amount."[70]

Thus we have a curious phenomenon, Uchida and the Ilchin Society concocting a *pro*-Japanese plot *against* the resident general, from whom they had received money. But is this merely pushing fine distinctions to absurdity? Itō was in charge. Why not put the blame squarely on him and be done with it? Or simply call it a Japanese plot? Perhaps it should be reiterated that such fine distinctions are introduced not for purposes of justifying or blaming, but because they may help to explain the mechanics of international villainy. Even so we should reject the one instance as unimportant, except that it fits into the pattern of relationships between the Ilchin Society and the resident general which developed after July, 1907.

Uchida was very disappointed at the outcome of the July affair. Abdication of the emperor was secured, but to him the new treaty was "only a small enlargement of the Treaty of November 17, 1905" and "still a long way from the final purpose."[71] Hence he set to work with redoubled energy to mount pressure on Itō for the realization of gappō. The Ilchin Society volunteered its services to Itō in helping to calm the rioting which developed out of the disbanding of the Korean army. Yi Yong-koo made speeches urging Korean villages to establish "self-defense corps" to fend off "rebels," and Uchida undertook an "unofficial mission" to investigate conditions in north Korea, which gave him an opportunity to stress gappō ideas in a number of reports to Itō.[72] However, Itō continued to "disappoint" him. He urged upon Itō a plan for giving money to Ilchin Society people so that they could establish

[70] *Ibid.*, p. 311.
[71] *Ibid.*, pp. 342, 545.
[72] *Ibid.*, pp. 394-408, 444-76.

themselves in "industries" just as after the Meiji Restoration the Japanese government "gave bonds to samurai families . . . and recommended they go into industries." It can be seen that this was well calculated to please Itō, who, according to the "Secret History," actually "promised" 500,000 yen for the project. Also Uchida thought the Ilchin Society should be rewarded for its "services in the abdication," not only financially, but by having more of its members appointed to the cabinet. However, Itō broke his promise regarding the money and refused to change the cabinet.[73] Also he warned Uchida that it "would not be good for your future to go too deeply into the Ilchin society." Uchida replied, "Even if I cut off my hand I could not cut my relationship with them now."[74]

In the words of the "Secret History": "These tactics toward the Ilchin society as well as toward Uchida made Uchida very doubtful of Itō's inner mind, and he became sure that Itō had no intention of carrying out the final solution of the Korean problem." Hence "he decided to take up drastic means immediately."[75] Drastic measures consisted first of an exchange of communications with Sugiyama in which they decided it was necessary to force Itō to resign. Then Uchida saw Song Pyong-chun, the Ilchin cabinet minister, and urged him to resign in order to discomfort Itō. Accordingly, Song submitted his resignation, accusing Prime Minister Yi Wan-yong of various failures. However, says the "Secret History," Itō was clever. He had Yi apologize to Song, then said to Song, "Since Yi has apologized, there is no need for you to resign." Song said, "It is already decided." Itō then changed the subject and said, "It is a very difficult task to operate basic policies and keep people reassured at this time of the restoration of the nation. Surely you do not object to this." And then Song, "without realizing that he was being led along by Itō," spoke out about his long-time plan to revise the local administration to stop the selling of offices. Itō then

[73] *Ibid.*, pp. 342-43, 553-54, 614-15.
[74] *Ibid.*, pp. 562-63.
[75] *Ibid.*, p. 566.

"tapped his knee and praised Song's excellent ideas." Itō said, "We must have a proper person to handle this. Will you take the position of Minister of Internal Affairs and carry it out?" And he "winked" at Yi Wan-yong, who then also supported the idea. By these tactics, Song was "befuddled," and he took the post.[76]

At this, the Ilchin Society members were furious at Song and wanted to attack the cabinet anyway, but Uchida tried to calm them and on June 20, 1908, wrote to Sugiyama asking advice.[77]

Through the summer and fall of 1908, Uchida and Sugiyama conducted a vigorous letter writing campaign to undermine Itō, and to get Song to resign from the cabinet. The fact that Song did not resign they attributed to Itō's holding him a prisoner in his post, though gradually there was some "breach of feeling" between Uchida and Song.[78] Also Uchida began sending bitter denunciations of Itō to Katsura and Terauchi. To Katsura he wrote that officials of the Residency General were forgetting their "great mission." Itō had given rights to Korea's only copper mine to the America firm, Collbran; he did not understand the class system in Korea, especially that the emperor was only the emperor of the upper class and all other Koreans were resentful, hence "conflict in the country." His currency reforms had failed, there were many bankruptcies. Itō was "not a great statesman" and he had caused "great unhappiness to this nation." It was "regrettable that he had been appointed" to the residency generalship.[79]

In September, Uchida, apparently in Tokyo, wrote to Terauchi: "Yi Yong-koo has come to Tokyo, but has been surrounded by newspaper reporters so I have had no chance to talk with him. . . . However, the situation in Korea is dangerous. Anti Japanese groups are becoming powerful. The conflict within the Ilchin society is increasing. Yi apparently has come to Tokyo to report this. I cannot explain it all in a letter, but I would like to meet you

[76] *Ibid.*, pp. 580-81; see also pp. 573-74.
[77] *Ibid.*, pp. 585-86, 590.
[78] *Nikkan Gappō* . . ., I, 611–12, 631 and II, 54, 63.
[79] Uchida to Katsura, June 28, 1908: *Nikkan Gappō* . . ., I, 596–610.

personally and explain in detail."[80] Uchida, by this time, was probably *persona non grata* to Itō, and evidently he did not return to Korea, but carried on his campaign from Japan. He wrote to Itō in November, purporting to quote Yi Yong-koo, "If there were a good policy, I would come back to Seoul, but I do not like the recent attitude of Song and I urge him to resign. This is not my opinion only but that of all the nameless members. . . ."[81]

Itō himself came to Tokyo in February, 1909, and the "Secret History" reports it as follows: "When Itō returned to Tokyo in February he had in his mind a satisfied feeling because the Korean Emperor had had a successful tour around Korea. Itō expected a welcome in Japan. But no voices, either high or low, praised his success. He was disappointed."[82] In May, Itō, again in Tokyo, summoned Uchida to his residence. The "Secret History" records the interview as follows: "When Uchida arrived Itō's attitude was unusually stern. He said sternly, 'You have been expressing opposition to the Residency General and I have heard that you delivered such in writing. If this is true, I should like to hear your motive.' Uchida knew he was angry, but felt it necessary to break down his argument. He said, 'I have not expressed opposition to the administration of the Resident General except as his policy is against our national policy of Japan. I criticize this . . . ' Itō at a loss and his lip trembling, suddenly changed the subject. He brought out treasured swords and showed them to Uchida."[83]

Afterwards, Uchida called on Sugiyama, Katsura, and Yamagata and told them about this, and, the "Secret History" explains, "Itō's big speech at Seiyoken [April, 1909, in which he defended his Korean policies] together with his accusation of Uchida made them feel that even such a tactful statesman as Itō had lost his temper. Shortly thereafter an unofficial decision that he should

[80] Uchida to Terauchi, Sept. 15, 1908: *ibid.*, pp. 615–17. Yi had arrived on Sept. 13: *ibid.*, p. 613.

[81] Uchida to Itō, Nov. 10, 1908: *ibid.*, p. 631.

[82] *Nikkan Gappō . . .*, II, 70.

[83] *Ibid.*, p. 74.

resign was made." After this, "Katsura made Itō the object of a power conflict in which even the gappō issue was utilized." Perhaps because of this, Itō seems in the early fall of 1909 to have restrained his enmity of Uchida, and he even, according to the "Secret History," privately gave Uchida 10,000 yen for his "troubled work." However, though Katsura had agreed (to annexation), Sugiyama was afraid that "when Itō returned from Manchuria he might raise opposition." But "fortunately" he was invited to Itō's residence for dinner and there "he obtained Itō's approval." Thus "it was decided."[84]

Most of the information on the last several pages is taken, as indicated, from the "Secret History," which, though very revealing of the attitudes of the reactionaries, may not be entirely reliable in its analysis of "Itō's mind." Some additional light is thrown on that, as well as on the financial transactions between the residency general and the Ilchin Society, by two letters from Itō to Katsura, contained not in the "Secret History" but in Katsura's papers. One, dated October 5, 1908, enclosed an application for money on behalf of the Ilchin Society which Song had sent to the resident general. In it Song apologized for the "impolite" behavior of Yi Yong-koo and referred to the "food and clothing problem of the Ilchin society." He asked Itō to "please give this some understanding. Otherwise the Ilchin society will be driven to desperation and the so-called pro Japanese party will be exterminated." Itō added a comment to Katsura, "Please read carefully."[85]

The second letter, dated December 6, 1908, suggests that he was trying to avoid their pecuniary demands. Itō says: "The other day vice-Resident Sone and I had a discussion about the Ilchin society. Since it is important, I report it to you and I should like to have your agreement. On the matter of how to deal with them I decided to follow the line which you and the other ministers agreed on, and I

[84] *Ibid.*, pp. 77, 87-88, 102, 110, 152.

[85] Itō to Katsura, Oct. 5, 1908 and enclosure, Song to Itō, Oct. 1, 1908, No. 46: Letters to Katsura, Kensei Shiryō Shitsu.

told Sone the same. We shall give final benefits to the Ilchin society and in doing so try to make them understand our intentions, persuading them to take jobs in various places and cease relying so much on us."[86]

Uchida and his friends seem to have thought that once Itó's resignation had been secured, they would have clear sailing toward the great goal of gappō. However, they were soon embroiled with the presumably pliable Sone. An expression of Sone's attitude appears in a report he made to Katsura in September (1909). Here he argued that "it is best to take a very cool attitude toward the Ilchin society. . . . We have already given much support to them and recently I told their members to devote themselves strictly to business. If we give more support it will make them too dependent on us. Then they will ask more support and it will be a trouble to our country."[87] By October, Uchida's confederates were expressing the idea that Sone should resign, fearing that he "might make mistakes."[88]

The assassination of Itō in Harbin on October 26 brought matters to a head. According to the "Secret History", many Japanese newspapers were angry at the assassination, but almost none said that gappō should be carried out. Most said that the Korean problem "should not be taken up carelessly because of this and pretended to show generosity." Also "Katsura held off Uchida," which caused Uchida to surmise that Katsura had been interested mainly in the "power struggle with Itō" and now thought "there was no need to hurry."[89] However, many of the Ilchin leaders took the opportunity of Itō's funeral to gather in Tokyo, where a "Korean Problem Friends" group was formed and, at the direction of Uchida and Song, a proposal for gappō was drafted

[86] Itō to Katsura, Dec. 6, 1908, No. 37: *ibid.*

[87] Sone to Katsura, Sept. 14, 1909, unnumbered: Letters to Katsura, Kensei Shiryō Shitsu.

[88] Takeda Niriyuki to Uchida, Oct. 8, 1900: *Nikkan Gappō* . . ., II, 171 and Kikuchi Chuzaburō to Sugiyama, Oct. 20, 1909: *ibid.*, pp. 174-75.

[89] *Ibid.*, p. 182. A check of the newspapers indicates this was generally the case.

by one Takeda Noriyuki. Sugiyama arranged to present this to Katsura, Yamagata, and Terauchi. And though Terauchi asked several critical questions about it, "in Japan the preparations of Uchida and others were progressing." However, in Seoul Resident General Sone became very "unfavorable" to Uchida who sent letters to Yamagata complaining about him. On November 28 Uchida left Japan for Seoul.[90]

In Seoul the Ilchin Society was engaged in argument with its co-operating parties, the Northwest Educational and Great Korea Societies, which seem to have been willing to co-operate to the extent of ousting the cabinet of Yi Wan-yong, but unwilling to go further in endorsing gappō. The Ilchin Society decided to proceed without them. December 3 (1909) was "the most significant day in the history of Korean gappō." On that day the Ilchin Society broke with the others and adopted a revised form of Takeda's proposal. And on December 4 Yi Yong-Koo "at the head of one million members" presented petitions for gappō to the Korean emperor, to Resident General Sone, and to Prime Minister Yi Wan-yong.[91]

To the emperor, Yi Yong-koo and his "one million members" spoke on behalf of "twenty million Korean people." They greeted him with "one hundred bows" as the "father of our twenty million people and the sky above our land" but reminded him that "our country has had troubles beyond description . . . the political and economic situation is horrible." There might be "hot talk in foreign countries," but really it was a matter of "our rebirth." Looking at history, "we cannot divide Japan and Korea," and though there had been "anti-Japanese feeling" now the Japanese emperor was "going to offer us his mercy." To reject it would be like "spitting at the sky." To Resident General Sone they argued that the world situation was critical, "the countries like wolves." In the twentieth century "the small country of Korea must depend on a big country. Therefore Korea should depend on the Japanese

[90] *Ibid.*, pp. 197, 202-5, 214.
[91] *Ibid.*, pp. 215-20; see also pp. 115, 143-144, 167-68.

emperor's righteousness." And to Prime Minister Yi Wan-yong, "In this world the strong country will defeat the weak; for example, India, Burma and Indo-China have all been defeated. If Japan had not helped us at the time of the Kapsin incident we would have been wiped out. The reason our country of Korea exists now is because of Japanese protection. So even if we give military, diplomatic and judicial power to Japan, it is only to maintain our existence. If we stand alone we cannot exist, so the only way to maintain the peace of our people and country is to realize the merger [gappō] of Japan and Korea."[92]

In general, says the "Secret History," Korean society did not understand what gappō meant, but "all those who did understand agreed with it." The situation was "peaceful." But Japanese reporters and correspondents in Seoul "showed an unfavorable attitude." This was because "Sone did not like Uchida's movement and bribed the reporters with Government money." They sent "false telegrams" to Japan and "led the Japanese public to misunderstand." And, on Sone's advice, Prime Minister Yi Wan-yong rejected the proposal, once on December 7, again on December 9, and again on December 16. However, when the proposal was presented a fourth time it was "not finally rejected because the Resident General had received an order from Katsura that the proposal should be accepted." Sone, not able to reject it, merely "kept it under his hand."[93]

The author was unable to verify this "Secret History" information from other sources except to the following extent. He located two letters from Army Minister Terauchi to Katsura, dated December 9 and 16 (1909) respectively. In the first Terauchi says,

> The time has come when we can no longer neglect the riots of the Korean people, but having no power to suppress them I can only worry. I have not received a formal report since [the latest] riots. As I have

[92] Archives, SP 9 (Reference Materials *re* Korean Independence Movement), pp. 13-26. Cf. *Nikkan Gappō* . . ., II, 221-33.

[93] *Nikkan Gappō* . . ., II, 278-80, 284-85.

delivered the telegrams of Uchida to you from time to time, you already know their contents. We have tried to stop the Ilchin society from making trouble. Resident General Sone did not intervene in the activities of the Yi Cabinet, and as a result the Yi Cabinet held discussions and arranged bribes, and the old members specially attended a discussion meeting which was anti-Japanese. These activities are considered as resistance to our Empire and they will obstruct the policy of our Empire. We have tried to act as carefully as possible, but if this situation continues it will be bad for the members of the pro-Japanese group and they will begin to complain. We should consider this. One of these days I hope to see you. Until then. . . .[94]

The second of these letters from Terauchi enclosed a telegram he had received from one Ōkubo [son of Toshimichi?], who was apparently in Seoul. Ōkubo's telegram says,

Yesterday I invited Messrs. Usagawa, Sakakibara and Akashi to talk, and we came to the conclusion that we should consider the relief of the Ilchin society regarding annexation measures. The first point is that newspaper and political circles in Seoul have attacked the Ilchin society and taken a cool attitude toward annexation, and such differences of opinion among the Japanese are good for the anti Japanese propagandist. Therefore we should try to harmonize the opinion of the newspapers and come closer to the Ilchin society. For this we should give some money. The second point is that the anti annexation and anti Ilchin society arguments which are propagated by Yi Wan-yong's group should be suppressed. If we take these two measures we can completely defeat the anti Japanese argument. Therefore this morning I had Mr. Usagawa try to persuade the Resident General and then I tried. The Resident General understood and approved. In order to consider the method of attaining the goal, I sent Mr. Akashi and Mr. Ishizuka to talk with him. Mr. Ishizuka feels it will not cost too much money to reverse opinions in Seoul with regard to annexation or to weaken the anti Ilchin society arguments. Mr. Ishizuka said he understands the Government's purpose and will help. Therefore I shall avoid

[94] Terauchi to Katsura, Dec. 8, 1909 (urgent), No. 11: Letters to Katsura, Kensei Shiryō Shitsu.

any close connection with the doings of the Resident General and watch developments for a while. However, as I have orders from you, until I finish my task, I shall continue to help the Resident General.

Terauchi's comment on this was, "Last night I received this telegram from Ōkubo, which I forward. If you find any important point, please say so and I will send it to Ōkubo."[95]

Also in December the reactionary societies organized several gappō meetings in Tokyo and the Kokuryūkai issued a "Letter to Intellectuals" which discussed the "big mistakes" of the residency general, the "true face of Itō's administration," and Sone's failures. The system of extraterritoriality which "separated Japanese from Koreans," this letter argued, had been bad because it prevented a "fusing with Japan feeling" among the Koreans. Koreans had had "a harsh time under Itō's administration." Sone had taken a "gradual policy" like Itō but liked to call it an "industrial policy." The name might sound "beautiful" but it had not helped Korea. Gappō was the "medicine of recovery" and the request for it came "from the side of the Korean people." It represented their "earnest desire." Japanese opinion had been cool to the idea because of "Sone's oppression" and "false reports" but the Kokuryūkai had "studied the problem for ten years" and urged "your intellectual judgment."[96]

However, according to the "Secret History," Sone called Uchida the "chief troublemaker" in Seoul and tried to send him back to Tokyo. Also there being rumors that assassins were seeking Yi Yong-koo, Terauchi had ordered Seoul military police to protect Yi. "Sone knew this and thought that Terauchi had supported Uchida in making the Ilchin proposal. He accused Terauchi and his hate for Uchida grew stronger." At any rate "even though more than twenty days had passed since the gappō proposal," nothing was done, and the "comrades in Korea" were "disappointed."[97] On

[95] Terauchi to Katsura, Dec. 16, 1909 and enclosure, and Ōkubo to Terauchi, Dec. 15, 1909, No. 12: *ibid.*

[96] *Nikkan Gappō* . . ., II, 306, 333-42, 345-51, 359, 360-96 (the letter to intellectuals).

[97] *Ibid.*, pp. 408-9, 418, 421.

December 26 Uchida returned to Tokyo to press for Sone's dismissal. He did not see Yamagata, Katsura, and Terauchi directly, but through Sugiyama got word to them of "Sone's ignorance." Finally, Katsura ordered Sone to Japan. Returning in January (1910), he "saw Katsura, said nothing of gappō and went to his villa." Uchida then "strongly urged" Sone's removal. Yamagata and Katsura were reluctant because "they had approved Sone and had not yet reported his failures to the Emperor." On February 2 Katsura gave Sugiyama a memorandum saying that "gappō shall be accepted in due course and all contrary views will be rejected" but "how long is taken for gappō is a matter of Japanese government policy and Koreans are not permitted to make suggestions." After that, Katsura, not wanting to fire Sone, suggested that he resign because of illness, but Sone "pretended not to understand and merely stayed in his sick bed." At this Sugiyama got a friend of Sone's to take him a gift of a beautiful knife and fork "from Sugiyama" and ask directly about his intentions. Sone "immediately complained of a stomach ache and lay down."[98]

The "Secret History" does not say exactly when Sone's dismissal from his post was finally decided. It says only that the Genro and the cabinet finally met and appointed Terauchi as his successor, to hold the position of resident general concurrently with that of army minister. Then "Terauchi called on Sone at his sick bed, asked for his resignation and finally Sone resigned."[99] Uchida's confederate, Takeda, compiled a long report on various injustices in Korea, arguing that, after gappō, "rights and obligations" should be shared "equally" by all Korean people. And as soon as Terauchi took up his new position Uchida presented him with a long letter urging that gappō be carried out, that the Yi Wan-yong cabinet could "not be trusted," and that an Ilchin Society cabinet should be formed.[100]

[98] *Ibid.*, pp. 462, 466-67, 501, 616-17.
[99] *Ibid.*, pp. 623-24.
[100] *Ibid.*, pp. 631-49, 651-70.

Though it is difficult to measure the influence of the reactionaries' gappō campaign on the total annexation process, we may be sure that it was considerable. Perhaps it can be summed up by saying that reactionaries jostled the elbows of realists, like Itō, to such an extent that they could not perform a mild and benevolent Operation Korea, forcing them instead to carve the patient so mercilessly that they could never hope to release him from the hospital.

Was this the intention of the reactionaries? Perhaps it was, and yet the strange idealism, "reverse idealism" we have called it, which surrounded the gappō concept does not permit an easy answer. Two things disturb us. First, Japanese reactionaries spent their whole lives on projects of this sort, relatively unrewarded financially, daring all sorts of dangers. Why? Secondly, a few Koreans, at least, co-operated with them, trusted them, and apparently believed that the gappō mission held a promise of good things for Korea. How could they be so foolish?

Certain last-stage developments in the relationship between the Japanese and Korean leadership of the Ilchin Society throw an interesting light on these questions. The fact is that during the summer of 1910 as the Japanese government effected the annexation, *heigō* rather than *gappō*, Uchida Ryōhei and Yi Yong-koo, the respective Japanese and Korean leaders of the Ilchin Society, came to a parting of the ways, a cleavage which undoubtedly cut through the rank and file also. This was on the question whether, with annexation, the objectives of the society had been sufficiently attained. It will be recalled that one of Uchida's major objectives over several years had been the establishment of a cabinet composed entirely of members of the Ilchin Society. This he had urged very strongly upon Itō and Sone, both directly and in terms of attacks on the cabinet of Yi Wan-yong. But, though as related, Song Pyong-chun had become a cabinet minister, Itō and Sone would not proceed further in this direction. When Terauchi became resident general, Uchida pressed him also to set up an Ilchin cabinet. But somehow he seems a little less adamant about it. In the aforementioned letter of advice to Terauchi, which he probably wrote in early June, 1910, Uchida employs an interesting contradiction. While advocating an Ilchin cabinet and denouncing that of Yi Wan-yong, he also tells Terauchi at one point: "Yi Wan-yong is a suspicious person, but he is not a self-acting person. He is mostly a puppet moved by others, so he could be utilized without harm."[101]

In addition, Uchida began to prepare his Korean friends in the Ilchin Society for the possibility that Terauchi might develop the great gappō objective, not through them, but through their long-time target of criticism, Yi Wan-yong. He told the Ilchin Society chief, Yi Yong-koo, that, with Terauchi's coming to Seoul, it might be best for the society to "take the attitude of doing nothing at this time." He was afraid, he said, that for it to propose an Ilchin cabinet "might have an unfavorable result," and he urged Yi Yong-koo not to take action "outside my leadership."[102] When Terauchi reached Seoul in July, he did indeed deal with Yi Wan-yong, largely ignoring the Ilchin Society. The "Secret History" explains that as soon as Terauchi entered Seoul "such fellows as Oka, Matsui and Kikuchi who under Sone had obstructed the big policy of Japan were fired from the Residency General." And the Yi Wan-yong group which had "also acted as puppets under Sone" was "at a loss." But Terauchi, "though he bent the bow to the limit, did not let the arrow fly [at them]." Instead he invited Yi Wan-yong to a conference, told him "for the first time" that annexation (heigō) was "unavoidable," and handed him a draft of an annexation treaty. Yi's cabinet adopted this on August 22, thus clearing the way for annexation, and it is Yi Wan-yong's signature which appears on the final annexation treaty, dated August 29.[103]

Obviously, this called for some explanations to his Korean con-

[101] *Ibid.*, p. 661.
[102] *Ibid.*, p. 670.
[103] *Ibid.*, pp. 678-79, 682, 689. Chung, *Treaties and Conventions . . .*, pp. 225-26.

federates from Uchida. In a letter addressed to Yi Yong-koo and Song Pyong-chun, dated August 29, he attempted to salve their wounded feelings. He explained that Sugiyama Shigemaru had visited Prince Yamagata on August 23, and been told of the Prince's audience with the Japanese emperor at which the circumstances of the annexation were discussed. Yamagata had said that it was through Yi Wan-yong that the Korean emperor's approval of annexation had been obtained. "Perhaps no one but Yi Wan-yong could have endured doing such a thing." And the emperor had said, "Yi Wan-yong should be regarded as an *erai* [great, monstrous] person, who because he has in the past punished his political opponents with great cruelty, could bear to do this today." This meant, Uchida emphasized, that the Japanese emperor knew about the "unfaithfulness" of Yi Wan-yong. And, he continued, "the next day Sugiyama saw Katsura and expressed his gratitude that our two friends Yi [Yong-koo] and Song had not been placed in the position of having to spoil their lives." Sugiyama had been worried that he might have "seen my two friends, Yi and Song, for the last time" but now their situation was "good," while that of Yi Wan-yong was "bad." And, according to Sugiyama, all they should do was "keep quiet for awhile."[104]

"Actually," the "Secret History" avers, "it was due to the contributions of the Ilchin Society that the Japanese government had the opportunity to realize gappō." And in recognition of this it was decided to offer titles of honor to Yi Yong-koo and Song Pyong-chun. Song accepted. But Yi Yong-koo declined, saying, "Although gappō is established it is my future responsibility to look after the happiness of the twenty million Korean people and the peaceful repose of the Korean royal family." On September 12, 1910, Terauchi ordered the dissolution of the Ilchin Society and offered it 50,000 yen for "dissolution expenses." Yi Yong-koo replied: "We are friendly to Japan and we support the Residency

[104] Uchida to Yi Yong-koo and Song Pyong-chun, Aug. 29, 1910, *Nikkan Gappō* . . ., II, 705-6.

General through fire and water carrying out its orders, but circumstances today make it impossible for us to dissolve. Therefore please allow us to wait for some time." However, the society was ordered dissolved. Uchida talked to Sugiyama about the matter in Tokyo and then sent a letter to Yi and Song explaining: "The dissolution of the Ilchin society is unavoidable. Only the Jitenkyo (Serving Heaven) association can be maintained, but through this religious group the mutual fusion of Japan and Korea will be done." Yi Yong-koo had worked so hard he had become "too tired." He "became ill. . . ."[105]

One could dwell at length on this treachery compounded, Japanese reactionaries double-crossing Korean traitors. But to put them in their best light, let us say that the reactionaries believed in their "reverse ideal," that they really expected by the magic of gappō to see the "Asian races revived," according to time-honoured traditions. (In defense of this assumption one could point to the continuing efforts of Uchida and his Kokuryūkai compatriots to merge Asian peoples and exalt Eastern traditions, efforts which gathered adherents as the years passed and formed the ideological basis of the Greater Asia crusade of the 1930's and '40's.)[106] Granted this, their role in the Korean annexation story becomes strikingly like that of the liberals. Beginning with an ideal, albeit a "reverse" one, in the end they compromised with realism. Just as the large majority of Japanese liberals gave up their promotion of progress and freedom for Korea and simply supported the efforts of realist oligarchs to stabilize conditions there, assuming perhaps that eventually these liberal goals would be realized if Japanese rule became secure, so the reactionaries accepted realistic heigō in lieu of romantic gappō, assuming on their part that Asian merger and revival would come eventually, again after Japanese rule became secure. It is noteworthy that in making these compromises Japanese

[105] *Nikkan Gappō* . . ., II, 708-12.

[106] Conroy, "Government versus 'Patriot,' " *op. cit.*, and "Japan's War in China: An Ideological Somersault," *Pacific Historical Review*, XXI, 4 (Nov. 1952), pp. 367-79, considers some of these later developments.

liberals and reactionaries alike lost their Korean friends. There was no room in the final compromise either for a Pak Young-hyo who sought to co-operate with Japan in the interest of the freedom and progress of his country or for a Yi Yong-koo who sought to do so to revive its Eastern heritage. The "solution" to the Korean problem, annexation, heigō, to which Japanese liberals and reactionaries alike subscribed in the end, eliminated the cross-currents and the friendships, drawing a sharp line of distinction between Japanese and Koreans, Japanese ruling, Koreans ruled.

Should it be said then that the reactionary cause was as bankrupt as the liberal and that annexation, as performed on its purely national, self-interest-for Japan Koreans-be-damned basis, represented the triumph of realistic diplomacy? Our answer to this is "no." Both compromised with realism, it is true, but the compromises were very different in nature. Liberalism was bankrupt certainly. This is made clear by the fact that the liberals tended more and more to leave the Korean problem to the oligarchy's handling, until after 1905 they could endorse Itō's residency generalship, whether mild (1905–7) or firm (after 1907), or Sone's, or Terauchi's. They had compromised away *jiyū minken* (people's rights) for Koreans and in so doing took long and irretrievable steps away from them in Japan. But the reactionary compromise was much less concessive. It was no carte blanche to the oligarchs to handle Korea as they saw fit. It would not accept Itō, whether mild or firm, or Sone, only Terauchi. Thus with realistic policy in its more delicate form, that which, though based squarely on Japan's national security interests, tried to obtain these within a framework of enlightened concern for international opinion in general and the progress of Korea in particular, they would not compromise. Only with the brutal and arrogant brand of Terauchi would they concur. This, it should be noted, contained several of the elements of their reverse idealism—samurai pride in Eastern traditions, violence, disdain for progress, implications of Confucian hierarchy among nations and peoples. Terauchi himself was too much a product of the oligarchy's realistic approach to shout these things openly, and indeed his reports as governor-general of Korea, published annually in English, constitute model mouthings of benevolent reform leadership.[107] But the reactionaries could be sure, from his connections, actions, and attitudes, that of all the realists he was one of those who stood closest to the old traditions, and that when the Greater Asia band wagon began to roll he and his sort would be on it. In short, while the liberal endorsement of heigō compromised away the very soul of liberalism, the reactionaries could endorse it as a step in their direction. In performing heigō, realism was coming close to reaction.

This movement of realism toward reaction is a most interesting phenomenon. Speaking in the specific terms of the Korean issue, we would ask why, in the last analysis, was it Terauchi and not Itō? Was not Itō's brand of realism sufficient for Japan's security interests? Certainly it would seem so to an outsider. Is the pull from Itō to Terauchi, then, to be explained simply as the result of the machinations of the reverse idealists, Uchida and company. The story of their activities told above indicates clearly enough that they exerted themselves to undo Itō's efforts to practise enlightened realism. But do they deserve the full credit, which they so boastfully claim, for this. One suspects not. They could plot and scheme, persuade and threaten, but they were after all only on the fringes not in the seats of government power. And Japan's Meiji oligarchs, who did occupy those seats, were by no means inept at thwarting opposition groups, even those which were well organized and had much popular backing. On the Korean issue, they were utterly impervious to the arguments of their socialist critics, as expressed in *Heimin Shimbun*, yet even Itō could not bring himself to squelch Uchida and company, not even when he knew that they were undermining his own position. Why? The evidence discussed above does not, we think, admit the easy answer of personal

[107] E.g., Korea Government General, *Annual Report of Reforms and Progress in Chosen (Korea), 1910-1911* (Seoul: Govt. Gen., Dec., 1911).

hypocrisy on the part of Itō and others. Rather, it would seem, a more complex phenomenon was at work. This may be stated in general terms as "the susceptibility of Realism to Reaction in international affairs." Here, we would suggest, lies the key to the waning of liberalism and the waxing of reaction in a climate of realist diplomacy. And here is the rock on which Kennan and Morgenthau and Niebuhr and all the other advocates of cold and careful realism in international politics founder.[108] They expect Itō and enlightened realism, but it is Terauchi's stage they set.

This may seem too large a conclusion to be drawn from our single Japan-Korea case, but there are good reasons for thinking it is not. These revolve around the proposition that the basic force at work in Japan's descent from enlightened realism to brutality in the treatment of Korea is the keystone in the arch of all realistic diplomacy, national security. But before elaborating this theme it is necessary to dispose of an alternative hypothesis, which, if true, would perhaps limit the application of the Japan-Korea case to a smaller circle of nations, those generally described as being of the "have-not" variety. This hypothesis, briefly stated, is as follows. The underlying force which propelled Japan toward the Korean annexation was economic; markets, raw materials, and profits.

[108] Clinton Rossiter is very perceptive in grouping these together on the basis of their common assumption that human fallibility is so deep-rooted (original sin?) that in conservative, realistic "national interest" diplomacy lies the only hope to avoid disaster. But the above-noted phenomenon induces us to lay aside his seeming endorsement of this idea and to suggest that there may be more hope in the "liberal perfectionism" which his article decries. Rossiter, "The Old Conservatism and the New Diplomacy," *Virginia Quarterly Review*, XXXII, 1 (Winter 1956), pp. 28-49.

IX

Some Economic Matters

Alongside the tendency in Western works to explain the annexation of Korea as a Japanese plot, there has developed in Japanese historical writing a tendency to explain it in the terminology of economic determinism, as the seemingly inevitable result of Japanese capitalism's reaching the "stage" of imperialism. One's first impulse might be to apply the label, Marxist, to this and dismiss it as a stereotype. However, consideration of the intellectual milieu out of which this interpretation emerged makes it clear that such an easy dismissal is unfair, for the argument has come, not merely out of Communist party line propaganda, but also out of dignified, scholarly, and sometimes heroic searching for explanations beyond the cheap jingoism that passed for scholarship in pre-World War II Japan.

The basic work was done by historians of the so-called Rōnō (Labor-Farmer) and Kōza (Lecturers on Capitalism)[1] schools of the 1930's. Leaders of the Rōnō school were Tsuchiya Takao of Tokyo University, Ouchi Hyoe of Tokyo and later Hosei University, Inomata Tsunao, and Sakisaka Itsuro, and the Kōza included among its principals Hattori Shisō, Hani Gorō, Shinobu Seizaburō, and Hirano Yoshitarō. Although the Rōnō had no connection with organized communism and the Kōza, while it had connections was by no means responsible to its discipline,[2]

[1] The name Kōza came from the title of a collective work published by Iwanami Shōten in 1933, entitled *Nihon Shihon Shugi Hattatsu Shi Kōza* (Lectures on the History of the Development of Japanese Capitalism).

[2] Noro Eitaro, a Communist leader and editor of the Japanese Communist news-

both groups applied to the interpretation of modern Japanese history Marxist theories which emphasized the role of economic forces and found the causes of Japanese imperialism in feudal origins and capitalist development. In saying this it should not be assumed that Rōnō and Kōza were in agreement. Quite the opposite. They engaged in vigorous controversy. Nor should it be assumed that they laid out in specific terms the application of their theories to such specific matters as the Korean annexation. Their main interest was to determine the nature of the Meiji Restoration, upon which problem their major efforts and arguments were concentrated and from which their rather far-reaching generalization about the later Meiji and subsequent eras was merely a projection. But the projection pointed clearly in the direction of economic or Marxist interpretation. Furthermore, their work was so impressive especially in comparison with the unobjective nationalistic writings of *goyō gakusha* (pseudo-scholars), who populated the prewar Japanese horizon, that it set a sort of frame of reference from which postwar Japanese scholarship, freed from nationalist pressures, took its cue.[3]

An example of this, with special reference to the Korean problem, is Hatada Takeshi's *Chōsen Shi* (History of Korea), published in

---

paper *Akahata* (Red Flag), who died in prison in 1934, was something of a hero to members of the group, but the postwar Japanese *Dictionary of Political Science* thinks it "improbable" that they answered the party dictates. Heibonsha (publ.), *Seijigaku Jiten* (Tokyo, 1954), pp. 1063–64, 1119–20. Also, writings of some of the school, e.g., Shinobu, have received "savage" treatment in reviews by party spokesmen. Cf. Marius Jansen, "From Hatoyama to Hatoyama," *Far Eastern Quarterly*, XIV, 1, (Nov. 1954) pp. 69-70.

[3] This is not to imply that there were only two types of historians, nationalistic and economic-Marxist, in prewar Japan. There was a third type, of which Tabohashi Kiyoshi is an excellent example. These were painstaking collectors of data who ventured few, if any, interpretations. Their work is of huge importance to scholarship, but, since it did not provide the sort of spectacular "scientific" challenge to Japan *uber alles* apologists which the Rōnō and Kōza groups put forth, it was relatively uninspiring to those younger scholars who needed a set of historical "principles" to cling to in their intellectual fight against ultranationalist totalitarianism. Hence, postwar historical theory, rejecting the nationalist hypothesis with vehemence, has tended to embrace the only well-developed alternative, the economic-Marxist hypothesis. See John K. Fairbank and Masataka Banno, *Japanese Studies on Modern China* (Rutland, Vt.: Charles Tuttle, 1955), Intro., pp. xiii-xvi.

1951, which, although it covers the whole course of the Meiji period Japan-Korea relationship in a brief forty pages, gives considerable space to economic matters and makes some very strong statements in this regard. According to Hatada, as early as the 1880's Korea was becoming "bound in as a market for Japanese capitalism." Soon great quantities of Japanese textiles and other manufactures were being sent to Korea and "almost all" Korean foodstuff exports were being sent to Japan. "Japanese capitalism penetrated Korea and made it a market for its merchandise and a source of foodstuffs. Korea was an indispensable market for the growth of Japanese capitalism. . . . Thus the growth of Japanese capitalism had to retrieve political defeats and further promote economic penetration," which led into the Sino-Japanese War, etc.[4] This is not to say that Hatada neglects all other factors to stress the economic. We have noted earlier that his words are sometimes suggestive of the Japanese government plot approach[5] and he gives much space to diplomatic and political developments. But when he speaks of economic matters he uses the language of economic determinism, capitalism "grows, binds in, penetrates," markets are "indispensable."

In this, Hatada reflects the best interpretative prewar Japanese scholarship, that which disdained jingoism and, seeking more satisfactory explanations, found them in the ponderous working of economic forces. His references to sources show his indebtedness to the economic historians of the 1930's. Who were these and to what extent do their sources justify the sweeping conclusions they passed on to Hatada? Among Hatada's references Shinobu Seizaburō, Kitagawa Osamu, and Shikata Hiroshi loom largest as the appliers of economic interpretation to the Korean problem. Shinobu was, of course, a leading light of the Kōza Marxist school. Kitagawa, though not so prominent, was certainly of that persuasion also, as shown by the fact that he presents his findings in a

[4] Hatada, *Chōsen Shi*, pp. 168, 177-78.

[5] See above, p. 82.

favorite Kōza organ, *Rekishi Kagaku.*[6] Shikata is more difficult to classify. As a professor at Keijō University he was somewhat removed from the schools of argument in Japan. Also, perhaps because of his location, his central interest was Korea and, of course, he had the records of the residency and governor generalships close at hand. Among the economic historians, his documentation is fullest and his knowledge of Korea most impressive, but, as the title of his major work, "Chōsen ni okeru Kindai Shihonshugi no Seiritsu Katei" (The Process of Formation of Modern Capitalism in Korea) suggests, he also sees capitalism working as a sort of automatic force.[7]

But let us examine in some detail the arguments and sources of these and one or two others of the Japanese scholars who discovered in the 1930's that economic forces lay behind the Japanese penetration of Korea. Shinobu's basic work is his *Mutsu Gaikō* (Mutsu's Diplomacy) (1935), subtitled "A Study of the Diplomatic History of the Sino-Japanese War." It is an imposing work, replete with details, events, conversations, diplomatic exchanges, etc. Its sources include the memoirs of Mutsu, Sugimura, and Hayashi, biographies of Inoue Kaoru and other prominent Japanese leaders, studies by Western writers, especially Americans, a wide coverage of contemporary newspapers, and, perhaps for theoretical bolstering, works of Hattori Shisō. The author seeks to balance the factors that led to war, and, in general, it must be said, he does a good job of it. His exploration of diplomatic, political, and military motivations is quite thorough, considering the material available to him at the time, and his findings on these have been utilized in the appropriate place in the study. However, one of the factors in the balance is economic, concerning which Shinobu early in his study makes the flat statement that Korea was "already [by the spring of 1894] an indispensable market for Japanese capitalism."

[6] Kitagawa Osamu, "Nisshin Sensō made no Nissen Bōeki" (Japanese-Korean Trade to the Sino-Japanese War), *Rekishi Kagaku*, No. 1 (1932), pp. 64-79.

[7] Shikata in *Chōsen Shakai Keizai Shi Kenkyū* (Researches into Korean Social and Economic History) (Tokyo: Tōkōshoin, 1933), pp. 1-226.

To this he attributes a "strong interest" for war in Japan.[8]

Perhaps the best support he gives for his economic component consists of two quotations from the businessmen's journal, *Tōkyō Keizai Zasshi*. One, dated June 16, 1894, argues that "If the Chinese government helps the Korean government suppress the Tonghaks, the whole country of Korea will be owned by China. . . . [Thus] great damage to Japan. At present the trade of the whole country is ruled by Japanese, but if China intervenes and suppresses the revolting masses the benefits of foreign trade will gradually go to China. That is clear." The other, dated August 4, 1894, is very expansive: "We have already begun the war with China so we should not only expel Chinese influence from Korea but we should advance into China and insofar as possible increase the benefits of the war. What are the benefits of the war? There may be many but among them one would be to prevent Chinese trade and shipping and turn the profits of their markets to us. . . . This is the main objective of the war with China."[9]

But other than this Shinobu gives little evidence to support the idea of Korea's indispensability to Japanese capitalism. Indeed, that which he presents is contradictory. He speaks of the importance of the developing Japanese cotton industry, but quotes contemporary newspaper articles which express worry about the need for imports of raw cotton from China, which in the event of war, would likely be cut off.[10] He shows how the government's conscription of merchant ships in June, 1894, "greatly damaged business."[11] He quotes a *Jiji Shimpō* newspaper editorial to the effect that the war was "not a war of chivalry but a war for our profit" (the words "our profit" being deleted from his book by censors in

[8] Shinobu, *Mutsu Gaikō*, pp. 37-38.

[9] *Ibid.*, pp. 52, 551. Shinobu's dating of the second article seems to be incorrect. He gives Sept. 22, 1894, whereas an item in the August 4 issue appears to fit his reference, though there is a story on this theme in the Sept. 22 issue also. This is the only "mistake" the author could discover in Shinobu's numerous quotations from contemporary sources, though he checked many of them.

[10] *Ibid.*, pp. 90-97.

[11] *Ibid.*, pp. 113-16.

prewar printings). But he also quotes an editorial from the same newspaper which contradicts this, saying that the war was for "civilization," a "sort of religious war."[12]

In short, there is nothing in Shinobu's close-up, specialized study to justify the heavy overcast of economic determinism which pervades his more general interpretative studies, *Kindai Nihon Gaikōshi* (Modern Japanese Diplomatic History) and *Kindai Nihon Sangyōshi Josetsu* (Introduction to the History of Modern Japanese Industry), both published in 1942, and his postwar works. One may speculate how far the government censor's deletion of his citation on profit motive contributed to his becoming convinced that the real secret of modern Japan lies in the capitalism-imperialism complex.

Kitagawa speaks of the "monopolistic position of Japan in the Korean market" during the years 1875–84, and regards Japan's progress toward the Sino-Japanese War as based essentially on her efforts to hold and expand this market in the face of competition from China, 1885–94. He gives import-export statistics and particularly emphasizes the development of Japanese capitalism by showing that whereas in 1878 only 22 per cent of Japanese exports to Korea were made in Japan, the rest being European in origin and merely processed through Japanese brokers, by 1897 this figure stood at 90 per cent.[13] For source material he relies heavily on two works which loom prominently in all later studies of economic factors in the Japanese-Korean relationship, *Chōsen Tsūshō Jijō* (The Condition of Korean Commerce), 1895, by one Shiokawa Ichitarō, and the so-called Russian Finance Ministry report, translated into Japanese as *Rokoku Ōkurashō Kankoku Shi* (The Situation in Korea), 1905.[14] The role of these as basic sources will be discussed subsequently.

[12] *Ibid.*, pp. 554, 549-50. The "our profit" editorial without deletions may be seen in *Jiji Shimpō*, Mar. 12, 1895. It is entitled "Not Chivalry But Self Interest," and it does make a strong point of the Korean market as an object of the war.

[13] Kitagawa, *op. cit.*, p. 69.

[14] Shiokawa Ichitarō, *Chōsen Tsūshō Jijō* (The Condition of Korean Commerce) (Tokyo: Yao Shoten, 1895). Nihon Nōshōmushō, *Rokoku Ōkurashō Kankoku Shi.*

Shikata Hiroshi in his "The Process of Formation of Modern Capitalism in Korea" sets out to explain how Korea, which at the time of its opening had "no capital, no machines, no techniques, no enterprising minds and not even an interest or desire" for economic development, was "infiltrated" by capitalism. "Foreign capital and technicians contributed to the development and Korea was in fact absorbed by Japan both economically and politically."[15] He begins by focusing on the change from land to money economy. Before the opening of the ports land was the only form of capital. It passed automatically from father to son and the government taxed it but "there was no need to regard land as a commodity." However, under capitalism "everything must be expressed in terms of money value, so the first requirement of capitalism in Korea was land reform." The first official step toward this was taken in 1898 when a land measurement office was set up. It was soon abolished due to inefficiency and the hostility of the people, but was re-established in 1905 with Japanese advisers.[16]

In the meantime, Shikata continues, concepts and practices regarding land ownership had been changing in accord with the activities of foreigners in the treaty ports. There the question was posed whether foreigners could purchase land and buildings and make them their own property. Legally, according to the treaties, they could not. However, they found ways to do so, extending out into the countryside beyond the foreign settlement. The development is difficult to trace because it was illegal, but various means were employed, such as obtaining land in the name of a Korean and bribing officials for their approval, or by paying the land tax to Korean officials (who were glad to collect) and getting them to record the holding in their names. He cites instances of this last being done by Japanese from the records of the Ministry of Agriculture and Commerce. In 1902 the first Japanese agricultural association in Korea was established in the Moppo district. This

[15] Shikata, *op. cit.*, pp. 7-8.
[16] *Ibid.*, pp. 9, 15-19.

began to purchase sizeable tracts of land. Another land purchasing company, the Chōsen Kogyō Kabushiki Kaisha, was formed in September, 1904, and soon had some 22,000 acres. Up to the Russo-Japanese War, more land was held by other foreigners than by Japanese, but after that Japanese buying activities increased to such a point that the price of land in south Korea increased sharply. In October, 1906, on the advice of the Residency General, the Korean government issued a "proclamation regarding regulations about land and buildings" by which it recognized the right of alien ownership. This, says Shikata, "adjusted the legal system to reality." Land now became "movable [exchangeable] property." This "quick land reform" was required by "the needs of foreign capitalism." A slower process would have been sufficient for domestic needs. And because of the "hasty issuance of the new regulations they failed," but "in another sense they succeeded by establishing a legal basis where there had been none."[17]

Next, Shikata takes up the process by which a sound monetary system was established in Korea, the sort which, he says, "the development of capitalism required." In the latter years of the Yi dynasty when the ports were being opened the Korean currency system was very confused. There were many types of coins, whose value was uncertain. Only one, a copper coin, whose value was about one Japanese *mon* (penny), was fairly stable and popular. The confused monetary situation posed many problems to foreigners in the open ports. Just before the outbreak of the Sino-Japanese War Ōtori urged currency reform on the Korean government with the result that it tried to establish four types of coins, silver, nickel, copper, and brass, at set values. However, the minting of coins was relatively uncontrolled, there being, in addition to official government minting, various private mintings under special palace permission and also private mintings without permission. "Foreign merchants could not endure the confused currency situation and in 1902 foreign consuls gathered at the Japanese consulate to

[17] *Ibid.*, pp. 21-40.

discuss the matter and decided to advise the Korean government to stabilize the currency system." But nothing was accomplished.[18]

However, before this, Japanese coins and currency had begun to circulate in Korea. These consisted mainly of one-yen silver coins and Bank of Japan paper notes. By 1897 there were about three-million-yen worth of these and, because they were stable in value, they were playing the role of standard currency. Then with the adoption of the gold standard in Japan the silver coins were withdrawn from Korea, leaving foreign merchants "confused". To retrieve the situation, the Japanese Dai Ichi Bank, which had branches in Korea, issued a specially stamped one-yen silver coin for use only in Korea. As this coin became standard in Korea the Dai Ichi Bank assumed the role of central bank in Korea. These things were done with the approval of the Korean government, whose financial adviser, "a Britisher named Brown [McLeavy Brown] agreed with these measures." Russian efforts to oust Brown in 1898 and again in 1901, in the midst of which a Russian bank was established, disturbed this situation, with the Korean government in 1901 prohibiting the circulation of the stamped coin. But the Russian bank closed its doors shortly, and in the fall of 1901 the Dai Ichi Bank began to establish "financial hegemony" by beginning to issue bank notes directly.[19]

Gradually "not only Japanese but Koreans also" began to keep accounts at the Dai Ichi Bank and its note issue grew, some sixteen million yen being issued in 1902. And despite some obstruction by the Korean government, "probably arranged by Russia," and the appearance of forged notes from Vladivostok, the position of the bank grew stronger. Then in August, 1904, Mekata Tanetaro became financial adviser to the Korean government. He arranged for the withdrawal from circulation of the old Korean coins and the minting of new ones, along the lines of the Japanese currency system. Thus "Japanese financial hegemony over Korea was established

[18] *Ibid.*, pp. 44-65.
[19] *Ibid.*, pp. 70-79.

and a step toward Japanese-Korean economic unity taken."[20]

Next, Shikata discusses "the development of foreign trade and commercial capital" in Korea. For statistics he relies mainly on Shiokawa and the Russian Finance Ministry report. From a position of "respecting agriculture and despising commercial activities" Koreans were gradually drawn into trade with the foreigners. From 1876 to 1881 Japanese merchants held a virtually "monopolistic position" in the Korean trade, hampered only by the Korean anti-foreign attitude, and their own tendency to pawn off shoddy goods for a quick profit. Then from 1881 to 1904 there was fierce competition between Chinese and Japanese traders, with other foreigners playing a minor role as missionaries and concession seekers. During this period the Chinese generally had the best of things, being far superior to the Japanese at peddling operations. But after the Russo-Japanese War the victory of Japanese merchants over Chinese was "completely secured."[21]

The introduction of foreign goods to Korea had a large effect on the Korean economy and society, says Shikata. The Korean farmer sold his crops for money to pay for them and became more and more enmeshed in the money economy. After 1894 he was required to pay his taxes in money. Often he sold his whole crop to Japanese merchants even before the harvest. This was at the root of such things as the rice export prohibition, by which the Korean government had sought to prevent the shipment of needed foodstuffs out of Korea.[22]

Having emphasized economic matters through the whole course of his study and used to a considerable degree the language of economic determinism, Shikata then proceeds to his general conclusions, which are most interesting in view of our present effort to establish the importance of the economic factor in the Korean annexation story. He says that he has treated the subjects of land,

[20] *Ibid.*, pp. 86-87, 95, 99-101.
[21] *Ibid.*, pp. 136, 161-63, 171-75.
[22] *Ibid.*, pp. 186-93.

currency, and trade in order to show "how capitalism flowed into Korea like water, from the outside; it came floating in on commerce." But "requiring a basis inside the country" it had brought about the development of a currency and finance system by making land a commodity. Japan was the main base from which capitalism came to Korea, but it was noteworthy that Japan played this role at the same time that she was suffering from unequal treaties and receiving foreign investment at home, while establishing her own capitalistic industry. Thus "what we see is capitalism without capital and the capitalist who lacks capital" as the purveyors of capitalism to Korea. "The country which reorganized Korea along the road to capitalism was the most backward of the world powers knocking at Korea's door. Bearers of Japan's advance to Korea were people with only small capital. . . . The advent of the big business man did not occur until after annexation." Hence it may be said that "the political led the economic."[23]

Concerning these three advocates of economic interpretation, who specifically studied the Korean problem, we shall say, tentatively, that their findings in themselves seem an insufficient basis for Hatada's strong economic leanings. However, other writers, not cited by him, contributed to the prewar climate of economic interpretation out of knowledge of which he wrote. For example, Hosokawa Karoku in 1941 published an important study on Korea as part of a History of Colonization (*Shokuminshi*), in which he chronicled into four periods the process by which Japan secured economic dominion over Korea, besting first China and then Russia. He shows that there were 210 Japanese commercial houses in Korea as of 1896 compared with 42 Chinese and only 6 run by other foreigners, and also that by 1898 the number of Japanese residents in Korea totalled 15,062 as against 2530 Chinese and 220 of all other nationalities. He gives import-export statistics showing a vast superiority of Japan over all other foreigners, roughly 70 per cent Japanese for the years 1902–10, although,

[23] *Ibid.*, pp. 204-11.

curiously, this percentage was slightly higher in 1902 than it was in 1910 (reverse capitalism?). Hosokawa does not cite his sources for his post-1900 figures, but for earlier material he relies heavily on Shiokawa.[24]

In 1944 Miyamoto Mataji, a historian trained in European economic history, published the results of long and painstaking researches into "The Ups and Downs of Korean Trade and the Sino-Japanese War" (Taisen Bōeki no Shōchō to Nisshin Sensō). He used the secondary studies of Shikata and Kitagawa and one on the opening of Korea by Okudaira Takehiko,[25] which was also used by Hatada in his postwar study. In addition, he used the old "data books," Shiokawa and the Russian Finance Ministry report, some Japanese Foreign Office documents, reports of a Japan-Korea commercial association, Meiji period newspapers, and the businessmen's magazine, *Tōkyō Keizai Zasshi.*

Miyamoto begins by describing the foreign trade conditions of "closed Korea," noting that Japan during the period sent mainly copper to Korea in exchange for such items as raw cotton, pepper, medicinal "carrots," and tiger skins. But about the time of the Meiji Restoration the components of this trade changed and the volume increased. Japan began sending cotton goods, which she had imported from England, and Korea began to send rice, beans, sea products, and cow hides. Gradually Japan relied less on English-made cotton goods and more on those of Japanese manufacture. The value of the trade by 1876 was 163,946 yen. Then, Miyamoto explains the Kanghwa Treaty "from the economic point of view" and the developments resulting from it, the first being that Japan assumed and held from 1877 to 1884 "an exclusive position in the Korean market." From 1884 to 1894 the essence of the story is "Chinese penetration of the Korean market" and "struggle between Japanese and Chinese merchants." Other foreigners were

[24] Hosokawa Karoku, "Chōsen," in *Shokumin Shi* (Gendai Bunmeishi, No. 10, Tokyo: Tōyō Keizai Shimpōsha, 1941), esp. pp. 233-34.

[25] Okudaira Takehiko, *Chōsen Kaikoku Kōshō Shimatsu* (Negotiations on the Opening of Korea from Beginning to End) (Tokyo: Tōkōshoin, 1935).

engaged in missionary enterprises and concession seeking, and, though some of their doings were famous, their importance was small. The main theme was the effort of the Japanese to advance from Pusan, Inchon, and Wonsan toward Seoul versus the effort of the Chinese to advance from Seoul outward toward Pusan and the other Japanese treaty port centres. In the competition the "Chinese merchants were superior." Their way of life and customs were more similar to those of the Koreans and, because they brought British cotton cloth directly from Hongkong or Shanghai, they could undersell the Japanese, who relayed it to Korea through Japanese middlemen in Nagasaki and Kobe. Also, the Japanese government's practice of collecting export taxes hampered the Japanese.

However, in 1894, with the "change from commercial to industrial capitalism in Japan," the Japanese began to regain the advantage. In 1894 "1000 Japanese per month went to Korea" and such opinions as that of a Mr. Sakatani, who urged the Japanese government to sponsor fishing, mining, and railroad companies in Korea, began to be heard.[26]

In this study, Miyamoto makes no clear-cut statement that the causes of the Sino-Japanese War were economic, though his reliance on Kitagawa for important arguments and his general emphasis would seem to indicate that he thought this to be the case. And in another article, on the grain export prohibition and the Sino-Japanese war, he stresses the idea that these controversies over economic matters "made Japanese public opinion hostile to Korea and formed the psychological background for the Sino-Japanese war."[27] But, of course, this is very different from proving that Japanese capitalism was moving in some inexorable way toward the engulfment of Korea. In short, to sum up this excursion into

[26] Miyamoto Mataji, "Taisen Bōeki no Shōchō to Nisshin Sensō" (The Ups and Downs of Korean Trade and the Sino-Japanese War), *Keizaishi Kenkyū*, XXXI, No. 7-8 (1944), pp. 47-77.

[27] Miyamoto Mataji, "Bōkokurei Jiken to Nisshin Sensō" (The Grain Export Prohibition Affair and the Sino-Japanese War), *Keizaigaku Kenkyū*, XIII, 1 (1945), pp. 89-106.

the writings of the economic historians of the 1930's it may be said that, when they came to grips with the specifics of the Japan-Korea relationship, even though they looked very hard for the economic factor, they could not conclusively prove that it was decisive.

Now, leaving aside matters of interpretation and evaluation, let us go behind these secondary works and see what facts, figures, and opinions are contained in the main contemporary sources. First of all, it should be said that the official statistical records published or compiled by various departments and agents of the Japanese government are so voluminous, yet so scattered, that to make a thorough search of them for information pertinent to the Korean problem would probably take a team of specialists many years. Since the author's purpose is merely to assess the degree of importance of the economic as compared with other factors in the Japanese course toward annexation of Korea, comprehensive study of these has not seemed necessary, even if it were possible. Consequently, the author will limit the present discussion to certain more generalized contemporary compilations of the facts, figures, and opinions of the pre-annexation period, while remembering that below these lies a vast subsoil of particulars to which cross-checks have been made in order to estimate the accuracy of a more general work, but which has not been explored in a systematic way.[28]

[28] The sort of materials which constitute this subsoil is as follows: Gaimushō Kirokukyoku (Japanese Foreign Office Records Division), *Tsūshō Ihen* (Consular Reports), series continued as *Tsūshō Isan, Tsūshō Hōkoku,* and again *Tsūshō Ihen*, 1881–1910, most of which are deposited at the Ueno Branch of the Diet Library, some at Tokyo University, though there seems to be no continuous set.

Nōshōmushō (Japanese Ministry of Agriculture and Commerce), *Kankoku Bōeki Nempyō* (Korean Foreign Trade Yearbook, 1901–7), *Kankoku Bōeki Yōran* (Korean Foreign Trade Survey, 1907–10 *et seq*), *Kankoku Kōgyō Chōsa Hōkoku* (Reports on Investigations of Korean Mining), *Kankoku ni okeru Nōgyō Chōsa* (Investigation of Agriculture in Korea), *Kankoku ni okeru Mensaku Chōsa* (Investigation of Cotton Production in Korea), *Taishikan Bōeki Chōsa Hokoku* (Report of Investigations regarding Chinese and Korean Foreign Trade), *Kankoku Jijō Chōsa Shiryō* (Data Pertaining to Investigations of Conditions in Korea).

Ōkurashō (Japanese Ministry of Finance), *Gaikoku Bōeki Gairan* (General survey of Foreign Trade, 1891–1910).

For information on the economic aspect of Japanese-Korean relations before 1900 the best compendia of collected and organized, though uninterpreted, data are the aforementioned study of "The Condition of Korean Commerce" of Shiokawa (1895) and the Russian Finance Ministry report (1905). Almost all later Japanese students of the subject rely heavily on these for basic facts and figures. There would seem to be no reason to question the reliability of these sources. Shiokawa was a Japanese consular clerk at Seoul and a careful and conscientious compiler of data from first-hand records which he knew intimately. He seems to have had no ax to grind other than to show the ups and downs and changing composition of the trade, from 1876 to 1894.[29] The Russian Finance Ministry report might at first be approached with suspicion, since it was very likely compiled as a source of background information on the developing Russo-Japanese rivalry in Korea. The original Russian text was very probably published in St. Petersburg, about

---

Tōkanfu (Residency General), *Tōkanfu Tōkei Nempyō* (Statistical Yearbook of the Residency General, 1907–10, *Annual Reports on Reforms and Progress in Korea* (1906–10), *Kankoku Tsūran* (Handbook on Korea, 1906-10), *Kyoryū Mindan Jijō Yoran* (Handbook of Conditions of Residents' Organizations), *Kankoku Kakuhō Bōeki Gaikyō* (Conditions of Trade in Various Korean Ports), *Zaikankoku Nihonjin Sangyō Dantai Ichiran* (Survey of Japanese Business Organizations in Korea).

Chōsen Sōtokufu (Government General of Korea), *Chōsen Tetsudōshi* (History of Korean Railroads), *Table of Trade and Shipping for the year 1911*, *Annual Report on Reforms and Progress in Chosen, 1910–11*, and *Chōsen Tetsudō Ensen Shijō Ippan* (Survey of Markets along Korean Railroads).

Dai Ichi Bank, *Kankoku ni okeru Dai Ichi Ginkō* (The Dai Ichi Bank in Korea), *Kankoku Kakushiten Shutsuchōjo Kaigyō Irai Eigyō Jōkyō* (Conditions of Business at the Various Branches in Korea since their Opening).

Genzan Shōkōkaigisho (Genzan Chamber of Commerce), *60 Nenshi* (60-Year History of the Genzan Chamber of Commerce, [1942]), illustrative of many chambers of commerce histories of their activities in Korean port cities.

Tōyōtakushoku Kabushiki Kaisha (Oriental Development Co.), *Shokumin Tōkei* (Statistics on Colonization, 1911 *et seq.*), 10 Nenshi (10-Year History of Oriental Development Co., [1918],) 20-Nenshi (20-Year History).

Nikkan Tsūshō Kyōkai (Japan-Korea Trade Society), *Hōkoku* (Report, monthly 1895–98, 39 vols.).

[29] Itō mentions Shiokawa as the translator at the Japanese legation at Seoul in 1904. Journal of Itō, Mar. 13–Apr. 1, 1904, No. 184: Kensei Shiryō Shitsu.

1900, since all information contained in the book is pre-1900, but the exact date is not given in the Japanese translation which was available to the author. One's suspicions are allayed, however, by the circumstances of the translation. It was done under the auspices of the Japanese Ministry of Agriculture and Commerce, whose conclusion that the book was sufficiently valuable and reliable to be worth translating was, of course, based on inside knowledge of the subject. Certainly, the book's objectivity and detachment are remarkable, considering the developing rivalry between Japan and Russia. Perhaps there is a hint of anti-Japanism in the treatment of post-1895 material, but otherwise its impartiality is complete. The Japanese editor pays tribute to this in the preface by saying, "This book is very correct." In short, the Russian Finance Ministry report, approved as accurate by opposing sides in a diplomatic rivalry, must be highly accredited.

The report contains some very detailed information for the early years of Japanese relationships with Korea, 1872–82, as shown in the following tables:[30]

VALUE OF EXPORTS AND IMPORTS 1872–1882 (no figures for 1876)

Year	*Exports, Korea to Japan*	*Imports, Korea from Japan*	*Total*
1872	Yen 52,382	Yen 59,664	
1873	55,935	57,522	
1874	59,787	68,930	
1875	82,572	81,374	
July 1, 1877 to June 30, 1878	119,538	228,554	348,092
July 1 to Dec. 31, 1878	154,707	142,618	297,325
1879	677,061	566,953	1,244,014
1880	1,373,671	978,013	2,351,684
1881	1,882,657	1,944,731	3,827,394 [*sic*]
Jan. 1, 1882 to June 30, 1882	897,225	742,562	1,639,787

[30] Nihon Nōshōmushō, *Rokoku Ōkurashō* . . ., pp. 110, 112, 113-14.

SOURCE OF IMPORTS TO KOREA FROM JAPAN

Year		*Made in Japan*	*Made in a Foreign Country*
July 1, 1877 to June 30, 1878	Yen	81,149	141,405
July 1, 1878 to Dec. 31, 1878		19,332	113,286
1879		55,647	511,306
1880		116,130	861,883
1881		202,069	1,742,668
Jan. 1, 1882 to June 30, 1882		47,519	695,043
Total	Yen	537,846 [*sic*]	4,065,591

This last table is further broken into its component product parts as follows:[31]

IMPORTS TO KOREA FROM JAPAN, JULY 1, 1877 TO JUNE 30, 1882

Japan Made		*Foreign Made*	
Product	*Value in Yen*	*Product*	*Value in Yen*
rice	22,692	shirting	2,305,990
sake (rice wine)	22,755	linen	907,446
copper	197,909	cotton cloth marked T	151,457
tin	6,666	other cotton cloth	145,470
ironware	7,862	cotton thread	38,403
lasting? (*rasutoringu*)	75,935	raw cotton	20,703
silk manufactures	29,717	feathers	38,819
muslin	2,980	silk cloth	13,337
linen	9,983	dyes	180,889
umbrellas	4,921	tin	67,644
mirrors	6,528	nickel	27,775
lacquer ware	8,067	zinc	10,596
mosquito netting	2,761	copper coin	37,681
matches	22,262	guns	8,604
miscellaneous	109,405	glassware	9,595
		medicines	18,272
Total	537,846 [*sic*]		
		miscellaneous	82,910
		Total	4,065,591

[31] *Ibid.*, pp. 114-15.

Another table breaks down exports from Korea to Japan into specific products. Figures cover the five-year period, July 1, 1877 to June 30, 1882.[32]

Product	*Value in Yen*
beans	557,057
leather	829,131
bone	67,131
bean cake	9,395
rice	1,529,636
bronze	7,356
gold	972,242
silver	87,056
sea ear	19,298
hair	4,432
kaijin [sea product?]	171,382
dried fish	86,620
seaweed	178,016
blankets	67,175
flax	43,342
raw silk	174,019
rope	62,463
carrots	60,202
medicine	48,805
miscellaneous	130,098
Total	5,104,859 [*sic*]

Thus the total value of the Japan-Korea trade through the years of Japan's monopolistic position, 1877–82, was of the order of ten million yen, about equally divided between imports and exports. This represented an increase of approximately twenty times over the total for the pre-Kanghwa Treaty years, 1872–75, but the ratio of imports to exports remained almost the same. A further fact which emerges clearly is that only about one-eighth of the Japanese imports into Korea during the 1877–82 years were Japanese made,

[32] *Ibid.*, pp. 115-16.

the great bulk being made in other foreign countries and merely processed through Japan to Korea. The information contained in the tables came chiefly, according to the Russian Finance Ministry report, from Japanese custom house figures, which the Japanese translators of the report do not deny.

For information on the later 1880's and early 1890's Shiokawa's compilations are fuller. He is especially interested in comparing Japanese with Chinese trade in Korea and his tables comparing Chinese and Japanese imports to Korea during the years 1885–92 have been given earlier in this study.[33] These show an import ratio of 19 per cent for China and 81 per cent for Japan in 1885, changing to 45 per cent China, 55 per cent Japan by 1892. During these ten years, as the value of Japanese imports approximately doubled, the value of Chinese imports increased nearly sevenfold. The following table on exports helps to round out the picture for those years.[34] It should be noted that Shiokawa's values are expressed in dollars, whose ratio to the Japanese yen was about four to five.

TOTAL AMOUNT OF EXPORTS FROM JINSEN, GENZAN, AND PUSAN

Year	*Total*	*To China*	*To Japan*	*China*	*Japan*
1885	$388,023	$9,479	$377,775	3%	97%
1886	504,225	15,977	488,041	4%	96%
1887	804,996	18,873	783,752	2%	98%
1888	867,058	71,946	785,238	8%	92%
1889	1,233,841	109,796	1,122,276	9%	91%
1890	3,550,478	70,922	3,475,098	2%	98%
1891	3,366,344	136,464	3,219,887	4%	96%
1892	2,443,739	149,861	2,271,928	6%	94%

The Russian Finance Ministry report again brings out the matter of the origin (country of manufacture) of the various imports to Korea in a table based on records of the custom house at Inchon, 1890–91, as follows:[35]

[33] See above chap. IV, pp. 194-96.

[34] Shiokawa, *Chōsen Tsūshō Jijō*, p. 64.

[35] *Rokoku Ōkurashō . . .*, p. 137.

Country of manufacture	*Per cent*
England	54
Japan	24
China	13
Germany	6
America	2
Russia and France	1

About 1890, explains the report, cotton goods manufactured in Japan first appeared in Korea. "After a very short time" they began to "challenge successfully the position of English manufactures." The reasons "are said to be" as follows. "Compared to Manchester goods the Japanese is inferior in quality, but the price is lower. This is because Japanese wages are low and transportation costs are low." The following price comparison "is according to reports of the British consulate for 1898."[36]

Price per *tan* in dollars

	England	*Japan*
Shirting	$3.20 to 5.10	$3.00 to 4.00
Sheeting (grey)	$4.50 to 4.60	$4.30 to 4.50
Sheeting (red)	$1.90 to 3.30	$2.60 to 3.40
Gray rough cloth	$4.70 to 4.90	$4.20 to 4.30
T marked cotton cloth	$2.60 to 2.70	$2.40 to 2.50

The Russian Finance Ministry report sums up its consideration of the 1884–94 period as follows: "These ten years were the years during which Japan established her economic position in Korea by peaceful means, but this economic position inevitably became the basis of political influence and made it easy."[37]

Among various odds and ends concerning the period 1895–99, the report cites figures supplied by the Russian financial agent, Alexieff, on the number of Japanese merchants in Korea in 1899.

[36] *Ibid.*, p. 157.
[37] *Ibid.*, p. 472.

Number of Japanese Merchants in Korea, July 1, 1899[38]

Place	*Total*	*Type*		
		Brokers & Import-Export	*Wholesale*	*Retail*
Pusan	949	294	18	637
Jinsen (Inchon)	800	24	25	751
Genzan (Wonsan)	133	54	22	57

Perhaps the most significant points to be drawn from the Russian Finance Ministry report are these: imports from Japan to Korea in the unexceptional year 1892 were up more than 50 per cent over 1881, totalling $2,555,675 (approx. yen 2,940,000)—yen 1,944,731 for 1881—and a large percentage of these, perhaps 30 per cent to 40 per cent,[39] were made in Japan, as compared with no more than 12 per cent in 1881. However, the Chinese had been steadily whittling away at the import market, percentagewise, until by 1892 they had 45 percent of it, $2,055,555 (approx. yen 2,370,000) worth. In receiving Korean exports Japan had likewise ascended more than 50 per cent, $2,271,928 (approx. yen 2,505,000) in 1892 from yen 1,882,657 in 1881, and here, in contrast to imports, she remained far ahead of the Chinese, 94 per cent to 6 per cent. Certainly, it is correct to say of this period, as the economic interpretationists do, that Japanese economic activity in Korea was increasing, that it was at the same time meeting severe Chinese competition in imports, and that more goods in the Japanese trade were being made in Japan. But this does not necessarily make Japanese capitalism the cause of the Sino-Japanese War.

[38] *Ibid.*, pp. 134-35.

[39] Perhaps this figure should be higher. A Japanese Foreign Office publication, which presumably utilized first-hand statistics, puts the figure at 82 per cent Japan made. But this work, published in 1952, speaks of the "development of Japanese industrial capitalism after 1884" and its efforts to push into Korea, which suggests that it too had imbibed the economic hypothesis. *Shinsei Nihon Gaikō Hyakunen Shi* (100-Year History of Diplomacy of the New-Born Japan) (Tokyo: Gaimushō, 1952), pp. 44-45. My figure of 30 to 40 per cent is merely an estimate based on the tables in the Russian Finance Ministry report.

True, one can find rather strong talk of economic purposefulness, even beyond that which Shinobu cited, in the business magazine *Tōkyō Keizai Zasshi.* For example, an article claiming that the "first objective" of the Sino-Japanese War "must be to monopolize Korean trade," and presenting statistical "proof" that the influence of the opening of the war was "not so bad" even in the area of Japan-China trade. Exports from Japan to China even after war had begun are shown to have been at a higher level than a year before, though imports to Japan from China had dropped. Also, this journal strongly advocated that a proposed railroad from Seoul to Inchon "must adopt narrow gauge track because it is this way in Japan. Then we can use Japanese trains. . . . Some say that Korean railways should have a wide gauge because China has wide gauge. . . . We disagree." And at year's end, it spoke "Farewell to Meiji 27 (1894)" in these terms: "Before the outbreak of the Sino-Japanese war the public was fearful of its economic implications, but foreign trade this year has increased both in imports and exports and war bonds to the extent of 80,000,000 yen have been sold . . . Business has quickened. . . . Thus Meiji 27 has been the year in which our Japanese empire has entered the community of world powers, in which we have taken our first step to world power. . . ."[40]

But against this, *Jiji Shimpō* was harping mainly on the "war for civilization" theme, *Tōkyō Nichi Nichi* thought the war simply "unavoidable" because of the "attitude of China," and *Kokumin Shimbun* saw it as Japan's bid to "stand on the stage of world politics."[41] The evidence may be somewhat conflicting, but it certainly does not, to this writer, justify an interpretation of the Sino-Japanese War which finds its principal cause in Japanese capitalism's penetration of the Korean market. Despite its increase

[40] *Tōkyō Keizai Zasshi,* Sept. 22, Oct. 20, Nov. 24, Dec. 29, 1894, pp. 434, 580-82, 761, 960-61.

[41] *Jiji Shimpō,* July 29, Aug. 5, 1894, editorials. *Tōkyō Nichi Nichi,* July 20, 1894. *Kokumin Shimbun,* Aug. 31, 1894, editorial.

in volume and value the Korean trade remained small and it is doubtful if its advocates were in a position to make a very large impression on policy decisions of the Japanese government. It is interesting to note in this regard that very recently second thoughts have been raised among Japanese scholars, even among those who favor an economic interpretation, which indicate an awareness of the weakness of the economic argument. On this point, more will be said at the end of this chapter.

Proceeding to the contemporary sources of information on economic matters for the post-Sino-Japanese War period (to 1910) one finds, unhappily, no such sturdy statistical works as Shiokawa and the Russian Finance Ministry report. However, there are a number of items which, taken together, give a fairly clear picture of major developments. Probably the best for breadth of compass are *Kan Hantō* (The Korean Peninsula) by Shinobu Jumpei, father of Shinobu Seizaburo (1901), and *Chōsen Nōgyō Imin Ron* (Discussion of Agricultural Immigration to Korea) by Kanbe Masao (1910). The elder Shinobu, unlike his son, is no theorist. He was on the staff of the Japanese consulate at Seoul from 1897 to 1901, during which time he compiled the materials for his book. The following is a résumé of information he gives on the activities and the position of Japanese residents in Korea.

In 1892, Japanese residents of Pusan, Seoul, and Inchon organized themselves into "settlement corporations" through which they handled public affairs. They elected representatives empowered to "maintain their common interests and make decisions." Though the ultimate authority rested with the Japanese consul in each port, these representatives of the settlers did many things, such as establishing a hospital and a water service in Pusan and reclaiming tideland areas in Inchon. In Pusan, Inchon, and Seoul (and surely Wonsan also, which Shinobu does not mention) the settlement corporations were very active in establishing schools. In Pusan 7000 yen out of a total budget of 28,000 yen were expended on education in 1897. In Inchon, this figure was 4700 yen out of a total budget of 18,000 yen. Most of the Japanese in Korea came from Nagasaki and Yamaguchi prefectures, after which ranked Ōita, Hiroshima, and Hyōgō prefectures and Ōsaka city. The most active merchants were from Ōsaka, while Nagasaki and Yamaguchi supplied mostly small merchants and laborers.[42] Ōsaka and Kobe were the main Japanese centers for Korean trade, as indicated in the following table, which also shows the total volume of trade for the years 1896–99. Shinobu got his figures from "reports of Japanese custom houses compiled by the author."[43]

Year	*Total Imports (All countries to Korea)*	*Total Imports (Japan to Korea)*	*Total Imports (Osaka and Kobe to Korea)*
1899	Yen 10,279,474	6,658,200	5,149,785
1898	11,921,296	5,844,331	3,866,640
1897	10,179,196	5,196,572	3,469,272
1896	6,669,612	3,367,693	1,352,397
	Total Exports (Korea to all countries)	*Total Exports (Korea to Japan)*	*Total Exports (Korea to Osaka and Kobe)*
1899	Yen 4,997,845	4,205,382	3,004,556
1898	5,709,489	4,796,032	1.995,166
1897	8,973,895	8,864,359	5,774,082
1896	4,728,700	4,528,925	3,559,880

Shinobu discusses "the comparative merits and demerits" of Japanese and Chinese merchants in order to answer the question, "Why do Chinese merchants become more successful than Japanese?" The Chinese, he says, are "rich in commercial capital." They "do not suffer from high interest." They are "superior to the Japanese in commercial morality." Their customers include "not only Chinese but Koreans and other foreigners, while the customers

[42] Shinobu Jumpei, *Kan Hantō* (The Korean Peninsula) (Tokyo: Tōkyōdo, 1901), pp. 5-7, 11-12.
[43] *Ibid.*, pp. 12-13.

of Japanese merchants are mainly Japanese." As a rule, the Chinese merchant's goods are "cheaper than the Japanese merchant's in wholesale price." Japanese merchants tend to "speculate" but the Chinese do not. Chinese merchants have "good relations with each other." The Chinese merchant's character "is plain and patient." The Chinese do not indulge in "unproductive consumption." These he explains in some detail. Regarding the high Japanese wholesale prices, he says they are partly the result of "high import taxes in Japan" and the presence of Ōsaka and Kobe middlemen. The Chinese pay no tax or a very small one in Hongkong and Shanghai. The problem regarding speculation is that the Chinese merchant goes to Korea to stay, but the Japanese goes for only three to five years to make money and return to Japan. Regarding unproductive consumption, the 6000 Japanese settlers of Seoul and Inchon maintain some 200 geisha girls, prostitutes, and singing girls, and many other nonproducers. The Chinese are "very thrifty."[44]

Concerning the number of foreign residents in Seoul in 1899, Shinobu presents the following table.

Nationality	*No. of Houses*	*No. of People*	*Men*	*Women*
Japanese	512	1764	997	767
Chinese	181	989	931	58
American	32	62	33	29
English	15	42	18	24
French	6	17	10	7
German	4	9	6	3
Russian	2	9	8	1
Total	757[sic]	2054[sic]	1165[sic]	889

To this, he adds a footnote that the number of Chinese is actually much larger than these figures indicate, because, in December and

[44] *Ibid.*, pp. 17-31.

January when the figures were taken, many Chinese go to visit "their native place." "Last year [1898] an official of the Chinese consulate said there were about 1500 Chinese in Seoul in February or March." Regarding the ownership of lands and buildings by foreigners, Shinobu says there are "no clear regulations," and Japanese "with modern concepts of property" face many problems.[45]

Shinobu devotes a section to the good (or bad) old capitalistic practice of lending money, especially as it pertained to small-scale operators. In Seoul, he says, there were about forty Japanese pawnshops, whose customers were mainly Koreans. When a Japanese made a loan to a Japanese, if land or a building were put up as security, the interest rate would be only 2½ per cent per month (lower perhaps because titles to land and buildings were never clear?). If no security were given, the going rate was 4 per cent to 5 per cent per month. When a Japanese loaned money to a Korean, if the latter's security were below seven yen in value, the interest rate would be 10 per cent per month; if the security were worth thirty-five yen, the rate would be 7 per cent; if it were more than thirty-five yen, the rate would be 5 per cent per month. Among Koreans, with each other, these rates were 8 per cent, 6 per cent, and 5 per cent respectively. Interest on small bank loans was generally five sen per day (one and one-half yen per month).[46]

As an example of conditions at a place outside the three original treaty ports, Shinobu discusses Pyongyang. Here, there were 42 Japanese houses and 119 Japanese people as of December, 1899. Also in Pyongyang were twenty American missionaries. The Japanese residents were mainly engaged in foreign trade, although there were also a Japanese-run candy shop and a Japanese drug store.[47] Such tidbits of first-hand information fill the 694 pages of *Kan Hantō*, with references to Korean history, a description of the

[45] *Ibid.*, pp. 39-41.
[46] *Ibid.*, pp. 48-49.
[47] *Ibid.*, pp. 199-200.

Korean palace, and a section on an old Korean battlefield included amidst facts and figures the author knew at first hand. It points to no special conclusion unless it be that the Japanese in Korea were small in number and rather blundering, yet the Japanese were bringing more than half their total imports to Korea and taking almost all her exports.

Kanbe Masao's study contains a dedication to "Learning and the Motherland,"[48] which may be said to sum up rather well its general character. Kanbe, who was a professor on the law faculty of Kyoto Imperial University and a specialist in economics and finance, does a careful job of presenting facts and figures on various aspects of Japanese economic activity in Korea, not just the agricultural, though he stresses that. He is aware of the problem of conflicting statistics, and there is evidence that he tried to verify his figures from various sources. For example, on the matter of population he cites the Residency General's agriculture, commerce, and industry section figures for the end of the year 1909: 12,484,621 Koreans, 144,735 Japanese, and 13,109 other foreigners resident in Korea. But then he notes that the internal affairs section of the Residency General came out with slightly different figures for the same time, year's end 1909: Koreans—12,363,400, Japanese—143,045, other foreigners—11,791.[49] Certainly, his facts and figures can be trusted, even though the critical reader will become aware that "for the Motherland" he is all the while urging, sometimes unconsciously, Japanese immigration to Korea, which he considers to be sluggish and much in need of agricultural immigrants.

In his first chapter he surveys those "general conditions" which affected the Japanese farmer in Korea. He gives the following table of occupations of Japanese in Korea, as of December, 1908.[50]

[48] Kanbe Masao, *Chōsen Nōgyō Imin Ron* (Discussion of Agricultural Immigration to Korea) (Tokyo: Yūhikaku, 1910), Frontispiece.

[49] *Ibid.*, pp. 1, 2, 7.

[50] *Ibid.*, pp. 5-6.

Occupation	Number of Japanese engaged therein
Merchant	47,398
Miscellaneous business	16,815
Official	15,584
Laborer	15,237
Industry	11,763
Agriculture	4,889
No occupation	4,424
Geisha entertainer or prostitute	4,253
Fishing	2,956
Doctor or midwife	1,166
Teacher	918
Journalist	379
Priest or missionary	278
Lawyer	108

The reason for the large proportion of merchants, says Kanbe (with an air of lamentation), is that this is the easiest occupation for foreigners in a foreign land to follow. Other foreigners, though not so numerous as the Japanese, have a similarly large proportion of merchants. He gives a table of imports and exports to show the amount of trade these merchants were handling, the figures being taken from Residency General reports for 1908.[51]

	Exports from Korea		
(to all countries)	Yen 16,248,888	(to Japan)	Yen 12,157,885
	Imports to Korea		
(from all countries)	36,648,770	(from Japan)	21,814,091
Total (exports and imports)	Yen 52,897,658		33,971,976

Then Kanbe discusses other economic activities which were in competition with agriculture for the Japanese resident's attention.

[51] *Ibid.*, p. 7.

Money lending, while occasionally a full-time occupation, was more often a sideline, and since interest charges were very high many Japanese engaged in it. On the other hand, it was clear that ordinary laboring jobs did not attract Japanese in Korea and while a fair number worked at them, "Korean laborers are better than Japanese," and, "in contrast to Japanese immigrants in America and Hawaii, the Japanese in Korea do not like to work as laborers." In the field of industry Japanese immigrants had "good prospects" for managerial and entrepreneurial positions though as of 1909 there were only 78 factories with a total capital of 1,910,000 yen. High interest rates, high wages for labor, high price of coal and poor transportation facilities were some of the impediments to advancement in this field. Some Japanese were playing the role of landlord in Korea. By 1908 some 8472 Japanese owned 228,090,529 *tsubo* of land (about 186,000 acres), which was valued at 135,032,353 yen. Also 7580 Japanese owned houses valued at 12,088,450 yen. Since the value of this Japanese-owned property tended to rise, especially near cities, the rentals did likewise, and, from increased profits made in renting land and houses, Japanese landlords often became money lenders also. As for fishing, Kanbe points out that his figure of 2956 people engaged in the trade included only those Japanese who were living in Korea, not those who fished in Korean waters out of Japan. Prospects for fishermen, he thought, were rather good. In mining "the Korean is better than the Japanese" but there "are good prospects for Japanese capital in mining." Kanbe is "very sorry" to find that "the number of Japanese missionaries is small." He presents a table to show that out of 464 Americans in Korea 338 were missionaries, a figure absolutely higher than its Japanese counterpart, and in relation to total number of residents simply beyond compare.[52]

Having run the gamut of occupations, Kanbe returns to agriculture, making the point that while the number of Japanese "great landowners" is large, the number of Japanese "small

[52] *Ibid.*, pp. 8-45.

farmers" is small. This, he says, is "not good." The chief body of Japanese immigrants, he avers, should be "small independent farmers." This is because the economic development of Korea will be "chiefly by agriculture," and Japanese small farmers "strong in physique," "diligent," and living close to the Korean people "all over the country" could lead the way. Such "small independent farmers" are much to be preferred to landlords, who, living a "playboy" type existence in the cities, "have no direct relationship to the Korean people and land."[53] Kanbe asks whether there is room for Japanese agricultural immigrants in Korea and gives some eighty-three pages of facts and figures showing that the answer is "yes"—there is plenty of room; 1,200,397 *chōbu* (almost three million acres) of uncultivated land, about two-thirds of the total amount then under cultivation, lay awaiting development. And in addition there was much room for increasing the productivity of land already under cultivation. For example, in Japan 1.78 *koku* of rice was obtained per *tan* of land under rice cultivation compared with only .91 *koku* in Korea. Even if Korea should become crowded, such Japanese immigration should continue, and to make room for it some Koreans might immigrate to "cold parts" of Japan, where the climate was similar to Korea's. "Japanese people should emigrate to Korea and conversely we should bring Korean people to Japan. Only in this way can we secure our national defense and promote our national wealth."[54]

Despite the fact that Japanese immigration to Korea, particularly of the agricultural variety, was a desirable thing, Kanbe admits that it did not seem to be developing. And he devotes a chapter to explaining why Japanese people do not want to immigrate to Korea. First the typical Japanese loves his homeland. He is unwilling to live and die in Korea. An exception might be Pusan, which some Japanese residents consider almost as a part of Nagasaki prefecture. As of March, 1907, there were 2700 Japanese

[53] *Ibid.*, p. 49.
[54] *Ibid.*, pp. 54-137, esp. pp. 77, 136.

graves at Pusan, but "in Seoul, Inchon and Wonsan there are no Japanese graves at all." In addition "life and fortune" in Korea "are insecure, especially in the countryside." Korea "lacks educational, amusement and medical facilities." The Korean land system "is very complicated." Japanese "cannot understand" this and other conditions, which often "causes them to fail in their enterprises." Floods and droughts and other natural causes damage crops with the result that "farming is difficult." Most Japanese, when they get to Korea, "do not wish to be farmers but gentlemen." Yet they may not be able to make much money because "interest rates are high." These problems might be overcome, but, Kanbe finds, "there is a lack of organizations to encourage immigration to Korea." The few that existed, he shows, had very little money to spend on immigration ventures. Thus Ōita prefecture had an association to promote such immigration but even in 1910 it had only 600 yen to spend. Okayama prefecture did better, spending 6000 yen per year after 1908, Ishikawa spent 1,500 yen per year after 1908, Shimane 4,000 yen per year (from 1907), Kagawa 1000 yen, and Nagano 1000 yen. Thus only six prefectures gave any money at all and their contributions were very small.[55]

Kanbe then discusses how to promote Japanese migration to Korea. He advocates the establishment of more associations or institutions dedicated to such promotion, especially, he suggests, of the type established in Okayama prefecture, the Kankoku Nōgyō Shōrei Kumiai (Society to Encourage Korean Agriculture). Also such an organization as the Tōyō-takushoku Kabushiki Kaisha (Oriental Development Company), which was established under government auspices in 1908, he considers to be much needed for it "can buy land in Korea and sell it to Japanese immigrants on easy terms." However, "a private association or institution is better than an official one, because, if an official enterprise fails the Government would lose face, but for a private one it does not matter." He concludes on a note of advice for

[55] *Ibid.*, pp. 138-59, esp. p. 151.

immigrants. The best kind are working farmers, strong of body and will. It is well if they take their families, but to do so they should have some money, a friend or relative in Korea, and "some religion." Those who have had the experience of military service have an advantage, for "one old military uniform which the immigrant possesses is enough to scare the Koreans." January is the best time to immigrate to Korea, because Korean landowners want money badly at that time and the price of land is low. A Korean tenant needs money just before the autumn harvest, but the landowner wants it in January . . . the Korean New Year is in February. He hopes that many Japanese will go to Korea.[56]

Kanbe's book provides a close-up view of the contribution of grass roots economic forces to the Japanese penetration of Korea, the lure of land and a new start for the depressed agricultural masses of Japan. But the evidence he presents is by no means suggestive of the idea that this provided an important pull or push to the annexation process. Quite the opposite. In the very year annexation was being accomplished he is complaining of the lack of Japanese interest in Korea as a land and population frontier. Compared with Hawaii, for example, which Japan did not annex or try to annex, the grass roots pressure from the frontier must be said to have been almost entirely lacking.[57]

But what of upper echelon economic activity? Concerning this, information on Japanese banks and railroads in Korea and the aforementioned Oriental Development Company is instructive. The activities of the Dai Ichi Bank have already been discussed to some extent. This bank, with its several branches in Seoul and the open port cities, was the focal point of Japanese economic activity in Korea until November, 1909, when its functions were all transferred to the newly organized Bank of Chōsen. Just prior to its closing this bank published a sort of official history of its Korean

[56] *Ibid.*, pp. 160-82, esp. pp. 168, 176.
[57] See Conroy, *The Japanese Frontier in Hawaii*, Chaps. IX-XII.

operations which is useful for perspective on its course of development.[58] The Dai Ichi Bank in Korea, which had its beginning with the establishment of a branch at Pusan in June, 1878, was originally for the purpose of aiding commercial intercourse between Japan and Korea, circulating (and converting) Japanese currency in Korea and buying gold produced in Korea. It took on other functions as time went on, including customs administration, currency administration, the making of loans to the Korean government, issuance of bank notes, handling of the Korean national budget, and acting as a Korean central bank. Its branches at the several open ports became agents for the collection of Korean customs as a result of an agreement drawn between the chief of the bank's Pusan branch and von Möllendorff, then of the Korean Finance Ministry, in February, 1884. About that same time Japan undertook to build a specie reserve for which 300,000 yen were loaned to the bank by the Japanese government that it might purchase gold and silver.[59]

These remained the principal activities of the Dai Ichi Bank until 1897, though, as we have seen from Shikata's discussion, Japanese currency was by then circulating in Korea to an amount of about three million yen. In November of that year Alexieff was installed as financial adviser to the Korean government, whereupon he established a Russo-Korean bank and got the Korean government to prohibit the circulation of Japanese currency. This setback was retrieved in 1905 when the Korean government (under duress) turned over the currency administration to the Dai Ichi Bank, recognized its bank notes, and reorganized Korean currencies according to Japanese models. Also at that time, in accordance with the advice of financial adviser Mekata, the bank became the depository for the Korean national treasury and budget watch-

[58] Dai Ichi Ginkō, *Kankoku ni okeru Dai Ichi Ginkō* (The Dai Ichi Bank in Korea) (Tokyo: Dai Ichi Ginkō, 1908); *Kankoku Kakushiten Shutsu Chōjo Kaigyō Irai Eigyō Jōkyō* (Conditions of Business at the Various Branches in Korea since their opening) (Tokyo: Dai Ichi Ginkō, 1908).

[59] Dai Ichi Ginkō, *Kankoku ni okeru . . .*, pp. 73-76.

dog. The Dai Ichi Bank thus became the central bank of Korea. As for its lending operations, it seven times funneled loans from Japan to the Korean government, in 1884, 1895, 1899, 1900, 1901, 1902, and 1905.[60]

This official banking story is continued in a book published in English in 1921 under the auspices of Dai Ichi's successor as central bank of Korea, the Bank of Chōsen. This is not, strictly speaking, a contemporary account, but, since it was published well before the intellectual warfare over economic interpretation broke out, it may be admitted as near-contemporary evidence—especially so inasmuch as its compiler, Hoshino Tokuji, manager of the bank's research department, gives an account of his sentiments at the time of the annexation. Hoshino discusses the development of a money economy in Korea, emphasizing the role of restaurants. Traders at the fairs could exchange most goods by barter, he says, but all of them being away from home had to patronize the restaurants for food and the restaurant keepers needed an easy medium of exchange. Coins were used in these transactions and "often the government established restaurants to teach the people the use of money." He tells of the vicissitudes of Korean coinage through the early Meiji period, of the activities of the Dai Ichi Bank and its taking over the duties of central bank in 1905. The Dai Ichi, he says, was "a private joint-stock bank in Japan" but in Korea it became a "central bank ad interim." Its handling of customs duties, he reiterates, was based on the agreement with von Mollendorf. Alongside the Dai Ichi Bank there were established under the Residency General some eight agricultural and industrial banks, with eleven branches, having a total capital of one million yen in 1906. These were associated with local credit associations in 1907, and though they were small they gave some help to agriculture. On October 30, 1909, the Bank of Chōsen, first called Bank of Korea, was established to take over the central bank operations of the Dai Ichi Bank. This was first conceived by Itō and was endorsed by leading

[60] *Ibid.*, pp. 82-98.

financiers, including President Shibusawa of the Dai Ichi Bank.[61]

Itō, says Hoshino, "seems to have been well disposed toward foreign investment in mines in the country." Thus at the end of the protectorate four American corporations and four American individuals had concessions, as did two British corporations and one British individual, two French individuals, one Russian individual, and one Italian individual. As to railroads, Japan built them, the first being the Seoul-Inchon line, a concession which was purchased by a Japanese syndicate from the American, James R. Morse, in 1898. Construction was completed in 1900. A Seoul-Pusan railroad was completed in 1905 by another Japanese syndicate and a Seoul-Wiju line was built by the Japanese army in 1906.[62]

Perhaps Hoshino's most interesting comments are in his introductory pages, where he discusses his interpretation of the overall course of events and own feelings at the time of annexation. He had felt sorry for Korea. "From a political point of view" her position had been "most unfortunate." She had suffered many foreign invasions. But the peninsula "as an American writer termed it" pointed like a dagger at the very heart of Japan, so Japan "could not leave it with safety in the hands of any nation showing an aggressive taint." Yet "whatever may have been the cause of the wars fought on her soil it was all the same to her inhabitants—to them it simply meant dire misery." However, "the time seems to be drawing near [1921] when a position so unfortunate will be converted into a very fortunate [one] at least from the economic viewpoint . . . easy access to markets . . . population increase, etc. The author [Hoshino] wrote in the Seoul press as follows on the morning following annexation: '. . . though an apparently cruel act, Japan has done only what a good surgeon would have done to a patient in order to save his life. . . . [The Korean] people will exist, thrive and prosper . . . but we sympathize with that temporary feeling of humiliation. . . . A Briton is proud of his being a Briton whether he

[61] T. Hoshino, *Economic History of Chosen* (Seoul, 1921), pp. 44-67.
[62] *Ibid.*, pp. 87-88, 102.

be a descendant of a Norman or a Saxon. Time performs meracles, [sic!]. It is not at all unlikely that we Japanese of two different origins may be holding with one accord a great festival in commemoration of this memorable event."[63]

It is interesting that Hoshino, writing an admittedly superficial "Economic History of Chosen"—though from his position he must have known that history well—even in 1921 considers economic development a thing of the future, not a cause of annexation.

Concerning the building of Korean railroads, another official history, the Korean Government-General railroad bureau's *Chōsen Tetsudōshi* (History of Korean Railroads), is perhaps our best source of factual information. It tells us that although the Korean government in August, 1894, assented to Japanese construction of Seoul-Inchon and Seoul-Pusan railway lines, it was actually the American, Morse, who got the first concession, for the Seoul-Inchon line, in March, 1896. "Foreign Minister Komura registered a protest with the Korean government, but in vain." According to the agreement Morse was supposed to begin construction within twelve months, but because of lack of capital he was unable to do so, and he offered to sell the concession to a Japanese syndicate. This syndicate consisted of sixteen members, including Iwasaki, Shibusawa, Mitsui, and Yasuda. While the negotiations were going on Morse received an offer from a representative of a French syndicate. He reported this to the Japanese syndicate and raised his price. Shibusawa called on Prime Minister Itō and asked for government help "because this railroad is very important." Itō agreed and the syndicate "paid 1,702,452 yen on December 31, 1898 for the concession." The syndicate became a limited partnership in May, 1899, and construction was begun. The road was completed on July 8, 1900, the track width being 4 feet 8 inches.[64] (Japanese standard gauge was 3 feet 6 inches.)

[63] *Ibid.*, pp. 4-6, 27-29.

[64] Chōsen Sōtokufu, *Chōsen Tetsudōshi* (History of Korean Railroads) (Seoul, 1915), pp. 7, 10, 21-22, 25, 44-45, 48-50, 53.

The Seoul-Pusan project also encountered vicissitudes. Japan was unable to act on the agreement of 1894 until February, 1896, when she sent an agent to Korea to further the project. However, "about this time the Korean King fled to the Russian legation and anti-Japanese feeling was prevalent." The agent was "not successful." However, in 1898, after the Russo-Japanese agreement (the Nishi-Rosen agreement which specified that "the Russian government will not hinder the development of commercial and industrial relations between Japan and Korea"),[65] the attitude of European powers became more friendly and Japanese Minister to Korea Katō renewed negotiations with the Korean government. He argued that the Korea government had already given its permission for the construction of the line in 1894 and "if you put off our request again we will begin construction of the line anyway." In August, 1898, Itō visited Korea, and the Korean government "in order to welcome Itō" decided to reopen the negotiations. A contract empowering the Japanese to go ahead with construction of the road was signed on September 8, 1898. According to the contract work had to be begun within three years, but, since economic conditions in Japan were "not very good," almost the full time passed without the work's being started. Finally on June 25, 1901, a Seoul-Pusan Railroad Company was established and under its direction work on the road was begun in August of that year. In 1903 the Seoul-Pusan Railroad Company was combined with the Seoul-Inchon Company. The Seoul-Pusan line was completed on January 1, 1905.[66]

A concession for what was to become the Seoul-Wiju (Gishu) railroad, running between the Korean capital and the Yalu river boundary, was first obtained by a French company in July, 1896. But the company failed to begin construction and in February, 1899, offered to sell the concession to the Russian government. The Russian government was "busy with the Manchurian rail-

[65] Rockhill, *Treaties . . .*, p. 433.
[66] *Chōsen Tetsudōshi*, pp. 68-69, 76, 90, 106, 116, Appendix p. 5.

road" at the time and turned them down. Then they offered to sell the concession to the Japanese government, but "the negotiations were not successful" and eventually the concession lapsed. Meanwhile, the Korean government gave permission to a Korean company to build the road and "construction was progressing very slowly" when "suddenly on February 16, 1903 the Russian Minister at Seoul asked permission to finish the railroad." Japanese Minister Hayashi, under instruction from Foreign Minister Komura, tried to ascertain from the Russian minister whether the "rumor" about this was true or not and received from him the answer, "I doubt that we can attain the goal," whereupon Hayashi urged the Korean government not to give the concession to Russia. On February 20 the Korean foreign ministry officially refused the Russian request and on February 21 the Russian minister visited the Japanese legation at Seoul to say that he would not pursue the concession further. In February, 1904, immediately after the outbreak of the Russo-Japanese War, the Japanese government decided to begin construction of a military railroad and construction was soon begun. The road was completed in April, 1906.[67]

A Seoul-Wonsan (Genzan) railroad concession was also sought first by a French company in 1896, but the Korean government refused to approve it, and the following year issued a statement that such a concession would not be granted to any foreigners. In 1898 Russians, Germans, and Americans approached the Korean government seeking a concession "but in vain," and in June, 1899, the Japanese government made inquiries and was likewise refused. There the matter rested until August, 1904, when the Japanese government decided to build a military railroad from Seoul to Wonsan, concerning which notice was served on the Korean government in September. Construction was delayed, however, and the road was not completed until 1914.[68]

In addition to banks and railroads, a third upper echelon

[67] *Ibid.*, pp. 130-33, 137-40, 151-52, Appendix p. 6.
[68] *Ibid.*, pp. 153-54, 156, Appendix p. 12.

Japanese economic activity in Korea remains to be considered, the Tōyō Takushoku Kabushiki Kaisha (Oriental Development Company). This seems to have been proposed originally by Inoue Kaoru, who in his later years was a business tycoon as well as an Elder Statesman. According to his biographer, Inoue brought the matter of Korean economic development to the attention of Itō and Katsura in August, 1907, and arranged consultations with business leaders, especially of the Mitsui firm.[69] The problem to be dealt with was defined by the Residency General in its official report in these terms: "The country [Korea] will never be developed unless a well organized company initiate the exploitation of agriculture and industry with adequate capital and skilled labor. This method has often proved previously the pioneer of material civilization in underdeveloped countries."[70]

Official descriptions of the organizing of the Oriental Development Company and its early operations are contained in the annual report of the Residency General for 1908–9 and that of the Government-General for 1910–11 and in the ten-year history of the company, published in 1918. These do not mention Inoue's earlier activity, but date the inception of the idea of such a company to a visit of Katsura to Korea in October, 1907, at which time he met with Itō and discussed the need for economic development of Korea. After his return to Japan Katsura appointed a "committee composed of statesmen, business-men, bankers, economists and others" to look into the matter. This committee outlined a plan for such a company, which considered methods of raising capital, what the company's functions would be, and pointed to the need for a government subsidy. "A formal application for sanction" was then made by Katsura to the minister of finance on December 22, 1907. The application was approved at a cabinet meeting and a draft of a law concerning the proposed company was submitted to the Diet by the government on March 18, 1908. The bill had

[69] *Segai Inoue Kō Den,* V, 171-72.
[70] Residency General, *Annual Report for 1908–1909,* p. 16.

passed both houses by the twenty-sixth of March. The law was promulgated by the Japanese government on August 26 and the following day approved by the Korean government "as Law No. 22." "Thus the company came into existence under the name of the 'Oriental Development Company,' in accordance with the laws of both the Japanese and the Korean governments."

The company began operations formally on December 28, 1908, as a joint-stock company with a total capital of ten million yen, derived from the issuance of 200,000 shares valued at fifty yen each. Of these, the Korean government received 60,000 shares for which it gave over to the company 5700 *chō* (13,960 acres) of rice land and an equal amount of upland fields, the total value of this land being figured at three million yen. Of the remaining 140,000 shares, 8400 shares were "set aside as preferential for the Imperial Households of both Japan and Korea" and 1000 shares were taken by the directors of the company. The rest, 130,600 shares, was offered for sale to the public. In the end, of the whole 200,000 shares, 136,138 were taken by 6590 Japanese and 63,862 by 499 Koreans. The president of the company, in accordance with the organization law, was to be the appointee of the Japanese government, and to this post General Baron Usagawa Kazumasa was named. Vice-presidents, directors, and auditors included five Japanese and three Koreans. In addition to the capital raised by sale of shares, the Japanese government supplied a subsidy of 300,000 yen per year, beginning in 1908 and scheduled to continue for eight years, with the proviso that, when the annual dividend earned by the company should exceed eight per cent, the amount of such excess should be deducted from the subsidy. The main purpose of the company was to encourage the exploitation of Korean agricultural land by helping both Japanese and Korean farmers to settle and develop it, but it could also "engage in fishing or other undertakings deemed necessary to exploitation as accessory to the main business."

The company had an auspicious beginning. When company shares were offered for sale "the public" sought to subscribe some

35 or 36 times the amount offered. And when the land which the Korean government gave over for its shares was surveyed exactly, "it was found" to comprise almost twice as much acreage as that which was required. Nevertheless, the company soon found it necessary to give up the fishing operations it had embarked upon and to seek land other than that which the Korean government had designated for it, the upland areas especially seeming to be unsuitable. Therefore, the company purchased or rented additional land to the extent of 7485 chō (18,336 acres) rented and 8599 chō (21,067 acres) purchased by the end of the year 1910. The dividends for the first three years of operation being only 6 per cent each year, no part of the subsidy could be returned As for the number of Japanese immigrants brought to Korea under Oriental Development Company auspices, the total as of the end of the year 1910 was 160 families, of whom 45 did not stay. The company had received applications from 1235 families, but was "rather conservative" in its selections so as "not to bring to the Peninsula any kind of *mauvais sujets*."[71]

Although only 160 Japanese families were brought to Korea by the Oriental Development Company to the end of 1910, the subsequent development of its immigration program may be of some use to our effort to gauge the importance of economic factors in the annexation. The table on the following page gives the figures for the years 1910–18.[72]

These figures are not very imposing, especially when one remembers the proximity of Korea to Japan and the fact that the opportunity of taking up Oriental Development Company land was well advertised in Japan.[73] They compare very unfavorably with the figures for Japanese agricultural immigration to Hawaii,

[71] *Ibid.*, pp. 16-20. Govt. General, *Annual Report for 1910–1911*, pp. 187-88. Tōyōtakushoku Kabushiki Kaisha, *10 Nenshi*, pp. 123-48 (basic statutes and regulations). Cf. Tōkanfu, Outline of Main Works: Archives, MT 1.1.2.55, p. 50.

[72] Tōyōtakushoku, *10 Nenshi*, p. 90.

[73] E.g., Tōyōtakushoku Kabushiki Kaisha, *Chōsen Ijū Tebikigusa* (Guide for Immigrants to Korea) (Seoul, 1911; rev. ed., 1915).

Year	*Recruits desired (No. of Families)*	*Applicants (No. of Families)*	*Accepted (No. of Families)*
1910	—	1,235	160
1911	1,000	1,714	720
1912	1,045	2,086	1,167
1913	1,200	3,472	1,330
1914	1,500	1,964	1,108
1915	1,560	1,284	774
1916	1,530	1,101	542
1917	1,050	1,553	650
1918	1,060	1,282	—

which received almost no impetus from the Japanese government, and little in its later stages from the Hawaiian government.[74] At any rate, the 160 families, less 45, who went to Korea in 1910 cannot be considered an "economic pressure" for annexation. Perhaps the most imposing thing about the Oriental Development Company was its huge office building in Seoul,[75] which may be indicative of the fact that the company was a rather artificial thing, trying not very successfully to stimulate economic activity where none existed.

One further point about the organization of the Oriental Development Company may be mentioned in passing. Early in March, 1908, as the Tokyo government was preparing to submit the bills establishing the company to the Japanese Diet, Itō sent a rather strongly worded letter to Katsura criticising the plan on three points: "1. It does not take the Korean government and people into account. 2. Thus it does not consider the interests of the Korean government. 3. The political relationship between Japan and Korea is different from normal relationships between other countries, but regarding land ownership there is no difference. If the plan provides only for Japanese to obtain land, what

[74] Conroy, *The Japanese Frontier* . . ., pp. 65-138, 154.

[75] See photograph in Govt. Gen., *Annual Report for 1910–1911*, opposite p. 188.

do we do if people of other countries demand the same right?"[76] This may be an indication that a hint of Tokyo (Katsura) interference in Itō's Residency General was implicit in the Oriental Development Company project. Itō does not seem to have become a direct antagonist of the company, but the following three points should be noted. (1) The final regulations provided that Korean as well as Japanese settlers should be eligible to take up company land. (2) The company was placed "under the strict control of the Governments of both Japan and Korea"[77] (giving Itō a double influence?). (3) The company did practically nothing until after Itō's departure from the scene.

Let us now attempt to draw a conclusion on the importance of economic factors in the annexation process. In order to be as precise as possible it seems wise to make a chronological division and speak first of the pre-1900 Sino-Japanese War period. Here, the conclusion is clear and unequivocal: economic factors were negligible, insufficient, unimportant. The Sino-Japanese War, though it was Japan's first big step toward annexation of Korea, was not an economic war, caused neither by Sino-Japanese trade rivalry in Korea nor by the penetration of the peninsula by Japanese capitalism. This conclusion is suggested by the fact that during this period the economic stakes in Korea were small, involved only a few Japanese, and the Japanese government accepted ups and downs in regard to them with equanimity. Moreover, it is strongly reinforced by a most interesting recent trend among Japanese historians of the economic determinist persuasion.

The work of the prewar Rōnō and Kōza schools has already been alluded to and the fact that they established a frame of reference for postwar Japanese scholarship noted. A veritable flood of postwar writing on various aspects of Meiji history has been directed toward supporting, elaborating, and refining their arguments, and Hatada's *Chōsen Shi* has been considered as an example of their

[76] Itō to Katsura, Mar. 10, 1908, No. 32: Letters to Katsura, Kensei Shiryō Shitsu.
[77] Resident General, *Annual Report for 1908–1909*, p. 18.

influence on an analysis of the Korean problem. However, and this must be constituted a tribute to the independence and perspicacity of postwar Japanese scholarship, although the feudalism-capitalism-imperialism motif has remained central, greater knowledge of facts and reassessment of causes have led to an important modification of interpretation which has been generally accepted by all historians, even those noted for being most adamantly Marxist. This concerns specifically the problem of the Sino-Japanese War. It is now generally accepted that the causes of the Sino-Japanese War were *not* economic, to be found neither in the search for markets on the mainland of an expanding Japanese capitalism nor in economic-based class struggle in Japan. This is admitted even by Inoue Kiyoshi, the leading exponent of pure Marxist historicizing. Inoue, in his study of "The Formation of Japanese Imperialism," says specifically that the Sino-Japanese War did not grow out of Japanese capitalism. Rather "in actuality as well as on the surface" it was "planned, prepared for and carried out" by the "absolutist Emperor regime."[78] It is interesting to observe in this connection that here we have the phenomenon of a Japanese Marxist coming very close to the plot theory which so many American writers have favored and which has been discussed and dismissed as inadequate earlier in this study. At any rate, with support even from Inoue, we can confidently bury the economic hypothesis—for the period through the Sino-Japanese War.

However, thereafter, Inoue parts company with those Americans who presume that the plotting continued right on to World War II, and with any other sort of political or diplomatic explanation. Such, for him, is invalidated by the emergence of more automatic forces, namely capitalism and its offshoot, imperialism. After the Sino-Japanese War, says Inoue, Japanese capitalism, helped along by the war indemnity, moved into the industrial stage from which

[78] Inoue Kiyoshi, "Nihon Teikokushugi no Keisei" (The Formation of Japanese Imperialism) in Rekishigaku Kenkyūkai (ed.,) *Kindai Nihon no Keisei* (The Formation of Modern Japan) (Tokyo: Iwanami Shōten, 1953), p. 53.

imperialism began. He asks the specific question, "when did Japanese imperialism begin?" and answers it by suggesting that the turning point was about 1900. It is "not important" he says whether one argues for 1900 or 1904-5 but "I [Inoue] consider 1900 as the turning point." In that year "Japan participated actively in an imperialist war [Peking expedition]" and inside the country with the appearance of Itō Hirobumi's Seiyūkai party the alliance between the bourgeoisie and the absolutist Emperor regime developed. Of course, this did not mean that the bourgeoisie had taken over political power, which happening did not occur until "the defeat in war [World War II]" but the Russo-Japanese War was "very different from the war of a decade before." The intervening development of industrial capitalism and the bourgeoisie made it truly a capitalist-imperialist war.[79]

However, it should be noted that Inoue does not carry his argument beyond the Russo-Japanese War to the specifics of Korean annexation, which must certainly be considered the first territorial fruit of this developing imperialism. He does not show precisely how Japanese industrial capitalism and the bourgeoisie contributed to that annexation. And in fact, when he discusses Korea, which discussion is brief and limited to the period before the Russian war, the evidence he submits would seem to negate rather than support his hypothesis. He notes that at the time of the Sino-Japanese War Japan had insufficient money and power to carry out the reforms she contemplated in Korea, which implies that by the time of the Russo-Japanese War she had plenty of both. Yet he admits that to 1904 there was no significant Japanese investment, either public or private, in Korea. The only "productive capital investment" was the Seoul-Inchon railway which "was built more for military than for economic reasons."[80] Hence, the idea that economic factors operating during the post-Sino-Japanese War period brought about the annexation of Korea, though

[79] *Ibid.*, pp. 122-23, 127.
[80] *Ibid.*, pp. 110-13.

implied by Inoue in his theoretical construction, is by no means proven by him.

In considering specific information on the period from the late 1890's to 1910, we have already discussed the contemporary works of Shinobu Jumpei (1901) and Kanbe Masao (1910), the records of Japanese banking, railroad building, and agricultural development (Oriental Development Company) in Korea. This evidence is not conclusive as to pressure toward annexation generated by economic forces, but the slowness and weakness of the railroad and agriculture programs indicate clearly that there was no great impetus from Japanese capitalism in *them.* With regard to trade and its offshoot, banking, there is room for argument that in these areas the tentacles of Japanese capitalism were stretching forth without regard to political and diplomatic requirements or in such a way as to pull these along behind.

Here, in addition to the material already cited, one could point to the pleadings of certain Japanese businessmen who thought there existed large economic opportunities in Korea. For example, Ōta Seizo, head of the Hakata (Kyushu) Chamber of Commerce, sent in proposals which the governor of Fukuoka transmitted to Foreign Minister Komura, under date of December 14, 1904. Japan, he argued, was "winning a complete victory" over Russia and it was time to plan postwar policy "so as to obtain a better place in the world market." Capital must be encouraged to move from "the inside [Japan]" to "the outside [Korea and Manchuria]." To do this, improvements were necessary "in a hurry." An "Oriental bank," improvement of the currency system, freeing of trade, mining, manufacturing, and "free going and coming" of Japanese to the mainland were necessary.[81] The Japanese consul at Pusan, the chamber of commerce there, and the head of a Japanese farmers' group of Kunsan were among others, who in 1904 addressed to the Foreign Office or the Ministry of Agriculture

[81] Ōta Seizo to For. Min. Komura, Dec. 14: 1904, Archives, MT 1.1.2.33, pp. 54-60. Same to same, Dec. 5, 1904, *ibid.*, pp. 61-62.

and Commerce similar urgings to pay heed to larger economic prospects in Korea.[82]

Also K. Asakawa, whose contemporary study (1904) of the background of the Russo-Japanese War might be judged pro-Japanese, but certainly not Marxist, says in his introductory remarks that, "For Japan, the issues appear to be only partly political, but mainly economical. . . . Among the most remarkable tendencies of Japan's economic life of recent years has been the enormous growth of her population, along with an immense growth of her trade and industries." He puts the number of Japanese in Korea at "nearly 30,000" and, quoting Finance Ministry figures, he shows the total foreign trade of Japan to have grown from 49,742,831 yen in 1873 to 606,637,959 yen in 1903, of which the Korean trade amounted to 20,676,000 yen in 1903. This last figure represented an increase of some six and one-half million yen over the Japan-Korea trade total for 1897. Asakawa is at pains to emphasize the importance of this trade and also the importance of Japanese immigration to Korean agriculture in building a foundation for his argument that "community of interest" demanded that Japan assume an active role of "assistance" to Korean "sovereignty."[83] But he does not consider negative aspects of this, such as the fact that few of the Japanese immigrants took up agriculture in Korea and almost none thought in terms of a long stay, or the value of the trade compared with the cost of protecting it. And again with Asakawa, as with the other contemporary accounts which stress economic themes, there is a strong tendency to emphasize the future. The future would presumably bring the realization of economic prospects hitherto only dimly seen.

However, the future, to annexation at least, remained dim. Figures for five years of Japanese "protection" (1905–9) show

[82] E.g., Ariyoshi Akira, Consul at Pusan, to For. Min., May, no day, 1904: Archives, MT 1.1.2.33, pp. 16-22. Pusan Chamber of Commerce to For. Min. Komura, May 18, 1904: *ibid.*, pp. 30-37. Nakanishi Jōichi, Kunsan, to Min. of Agr. and Com., Dec. no day, 1904: *ibid.*, pp. 69-76.

[83] Asakawa, *The Russo-Japanese Conflict*, pp. 1-2, 19-21, 26-30.

three years of rapid increase, but then sharp decline. Annexation (1910) can hardly be called the outgrowth of an expanding trade. Rather it seems to have rescued the trade from decline.

Korean-Japanese trade figures (in yen)[84]

	1905	1906	1907	1908	1909	1910
Exports	5,611,925	7,234,934	12,948,247	10,963,353	12,081,738	15,378,643
Imports	24,041,216	23,266,234	28,293,381	24,040,465	21,852,245	25,348,085
Total	29,653,141	30,501,168	41,241,628	35,003,818	33,933,983	40,726,728

Certainly Japanese businessmen were disappointed with the course of affairs. Mr. Ōta of the Hakata Chamber of Commerce appealed again to the Foreign Ministry in 1906, arguing that "Government regulations" and "poor equipment" were preventing the realization of economic opportunities in Korea and also Manchuria.[85] But by 1910, even with annexation, the businessmen could not refrain from expressing dissatisfaction. *Tōkyō Keizai Zasshi* "on reading the explanation of Korean annexation" had the following complaint: "We agree with the political aspects but we are disappointed in the economic. For ten years, says the Government, the rate of tariff between Japan and Korea will be preserved. Thus exports and imports must pay duty. . . . This is not good. Foreign Minister Komura gives as the main reason for annexation political necessity, and he says we must not affect the interests of foreign powers adversely in Korea. . . . We oppose. We say remove the tariff and do not worry about the interests of other foreigners."[86]

This evidence may not be sufficient to defeat the thesis that Japanese capitalism, accelerating rapidly after 1900, was the motive force behind the Korean annexation, but it would seem to throw it into serious question. And on the level of scholarly interpretation one further piece of evidence remains to be introduced. A very recent development in Japanese scholarship seems to indicate that even among those of Marxist inclination doubts of the

[84] Govt. Gen., *Annual Report for 1910–1911*, p. 262.
[85] Ōta Seizo to For. Min. Katō, Feb. 5, 1906: Archives, MT 1.1.2.33, pp. 64-66.
[86] *Tōkyō Keizai Zasshi*, Sept. 3, 1910, pp. 4-5.

importance of the economic factor *post*-1900 also are beginning to appear. This is clearly indicated in a "review and criticism" of writings on "the formation of Japanese imperialism" by Furuya Tetsuo, which appeared in December, 1956. Furuya is anxious to support the thesis that the Russo-Japanese War was an imperialist war from the Japanese side, the outgrowth of an imperialism that had its beginnings in Japanese participation among European powers in the Boxer affair—"the first imperialist step for Japan." But he is troubled at the lack of economic factors in it. He finds that two (non-Marxist) Japanese historians, Shimomura Fujio and Fujimura Michio, have gone so far as to say that "the Russo-Japanese war was not done by the Japanese bourgeoisie nor did it originate in the demands of the bourgeoisie toward the Manchurian market." However, Furuya argues, these gentlemen "have made a mistake. Their definition of imperialism is not correct." He agrees that the Russo-Japanese War was not the result of the Japanese bourgeois' seeking mainland markets, but "whether a war is imperialist or not does not depend entirely on the internal economic development of capitalism." Rather "in a later developing country" such as Japan "the international political situation may exert more influence on decision making than the internal economic structure." Thus, he concludes that the formation of Japanese imperialism and its external advance *can* be seen in the period between the Boxer Rebellion and the Russo-Japanese War.[87]

Since we are concerned here with the assessment of economic matters in their relation to the Korean annexation, we need not argue whether non-economic imperialism is in fact imperialism. If it is, if there is such a thing as purely political imperialism, then

[87] Furuya Tetsuo, "Nihon Teikoku Shugi no Seiritsu wo Megutte" (Concerning the Formation of Japanese Imperialism), *Rekishigaku Kenkyū* (Dec. 1956), pp. 40-46. The articles which Furuya refers to are the following: Shimomura Fujio, Nichiro Sensō to Manshū Shijō" (The Russo-Japanese War and the Manchurian Market) (Nagoya University Studies, Literature Dept.), XIV and Fujimura Michio, "Nichiro Sensō no Seikaku ni Yosete" (On the Character of the Russo-Japanese War), *Rekishigaku Kenkyū*, No. 195 (May 1956), pp. 1-13.

we would point to the preceding several chapters of this study as an effort to unravel its component parts. But Furuya's sense of the need to eliminate the economic factor, even as he defends the idea that Japan was propelled into Korea and Manchuria by imperialist urges developing around 1900, would seem to be highly significant, indeed, in pointing to the probability that economic reasons for the Russo-Japanese War, and hence for the Korean annexation, were nonexistent or very minor. Certainly he would have pointed them out if he could have found them, for with them he could have demolished the arguments of Shimomura and Fujimura and supported his own imperialism argument much more effectively. As it is, we must come to the conclusion that even those scholars who are most anxious to follow the projection of Rōnō and Kōza scholarship into a capitalism-imperialism explanation of the development of Japanese expansion on the Asian mainland are unable to do so, not only for the pre-Sino-Japanese War period but also for the Russo-Japanese War period.

We therefore arrive at our conclusion for this chapter: Economic matters had no important effect in determining the Japanese course toward annexation of Korea.

X

Conclusion

Close-up study of an historical problem is a chastening experience. One finds many surprises: likeable, or at least understandable, qualities in individuals or groups he expected to detest, curious disparities between intention and execution, comparisons where contrasts were anticipated. This was certainly true of the present study. The author began it in fair certainty that the Japanese annexation of Korea was essentially a question of timing, with Japanese leaders biding their time and waiting for a favorable opportunity. But instead of finding proof of this, he realized more and more how strong is the American disposition to see Japanese expansion (or that of another power) in terms of long-range, nefarious design, without being aware that our own not inconsiderable extraterritorial activities could appear quite as sinister, viewed from the outside with little attention to internal arguments, contradictions, and pressures. Utilization of a sort of slide rule on American expansion for the scaling of Japanese plots was a considerable help in avoiding this pitfall. After all, does the fact that Theodore Roosevelt plotted to send Dewey to Manila Bay mean that the United States had schemed for thirty-five years to take the Philippines? No, it does not, and neither is the Japanese seizure of Korea to be explained by any such simple plot hypothesis.

This is our first conclusion, rejection of the plot idea.[1] The

[1] One other piece of evidence, in addition to that already discussed, may be given in

documents do not reveal it and the American expansion comparison, which proves to be much more of a comparison than a contrast, renders any attempt to establish it on the basis of circumstantial evidence a mere (ludicrous) contrivance.

Instead, emerges a picture of rival Japanese groups, which, for want of better labels, we have called liberals, realists, and reactionaries, addressing themselves to the Korea problem for reasons associated with their respective socio-political-philosophic attitudes. To see each group in its best light, which, of course, is the way they saw themselves (and the way in which similar groupings in our own society see themselves), the liberals were large-minded, enthusiastic, and optimistic seekers after freedom and progress for all men, in Japan, in Korea, and everywhere else, and, since the most recent impulses in this right direction had come from the West, they were to a large degree admirers and advocates of "Western-style," though occasionally embarrassed and irritated by the arrogance of Westerners. The realists were practical, cautiously progressive, but concerned above all else with Japanese security and national interest, thoughtful, careful players in the chess game of international politics. The reactionaries were proud. Attached to old traditions which were being undercut by new and alien currents, they were pessimistic and resentful, yet determined to defend that way of life, that heritage which dignified civilized Easterners over barbarian Westerners. The Japanese course

---

support of our rejection of the idea that the Japanese oligarchs were developing a long-range expansionist "plot," involving Korea, Manchuria, etc. It is well known that the American railroad magnate, E. H. Harriman, in 1905 proposed the idea of joint development of Manchurian railroads to the Japanese government and was rejected, which would seem to indicate that the Japanese leaders had their own scheme. However, Japanese documents show that they were quite indecisive on the matter. Prime Minister Katsura and the Council of Elder Statesmen were very much inclined to accept it. Only Foreign Minister Komura registered a vigorous objection and, while he no doubt represented the emerging of a more expansive concept of Japan's national interest, it is interesting that the argument with which he won over the others was in the opposite vein—namely, that Japan, not being sovereign in Manchuria, had no right to enter into such an agreement. See Gaimushō, *Komura Gaikōshi* (History of the Diplomacy of Komura) (Tokyo, 1953), II, 204-15.

toward annexation of Korea was not one stream, one clear-cut national approach, but three streams, whose origins were ideologically and philosophically far apart, like three different springs in the mountains, and which only gradually merged into the flood that engulfed Korea.

This merging process, the compromising of aims by which Japanese decision on Korea was reached and Japan at large determined upon annexation, or seizure, of Korea (gappō, gappei, heigō, heidon, etc., becoming indistinguishable), as the solution to the Korean problem, was not, however, a simple blending of three equal parts. Realists held the helm and managed the operation continually after 1873, and though they were jostled by liberals in the eighties and nineties and by reactionaries later, they never lost control. However, their aims underwent a subtle shift, from an original determination to maintain Korea as a separate political entity only partially controlled and directed by Japan (enlightened national interest) to a decision to subject the peninsula entirely to Japanese rule. Why?

Realists in international politics and their advocates generally pride themselves above all on the possession of a cold and calculating eye, which can see a situation dispassionately and enable them to act with tactical flexibility "in the national interest," intelligently considered over a long range. Yet here, in the case of the Korean annexation, it would seem that Japan's long-range national interest was not served by clamping down the iron fist. Twenty million Koreans, next-door neighbors, were so completely alienated that a century may not repair the damage, and Japanese reactionaries, whose reverse idealism was to bring Japan to national disaster in the 1930's, tasted a first confidence-inspiring success. Does this mean that Japan's realists, after wrestling carefully and cautiously with the Korean problem for thirty-five years, suddenly lost their heads at the end, and became victims of a phobia of some kind? Were they maddened by the assassination of Itō, frightened by the Korean riots, convinced by Uchida Ryōhei and the Ilchin Society, suddenly subjected to furious popular pressure, confronted with a tense international situation?

The psychological effect of Itō's assassination is difficult to estimate, but the even more critical assassination of Ōkubo and the untimely deaths of Kido, Iwakura, and Mutsu had not upset the equanimity of the others, and, anyway, Itō seems to have agreed to annexation before his assassination. As for riots, which were the expression of Korean discontent at the toughening up of the Residency General after the dramatic Hague protest, they unquestionably distressed Itō and perhaps caused him to lose confidence in his own ability to effect a compromise regime. Suppression was the easiest way to dispose of them, but he certainly knew well that it would make a compromise regime all the more impossible. Uchida's gappō movement added to the sense of immediate crisis, which the riots generated, a sense of long-range ideological and institutional crisis. The trouble with the Residency General, said Uchida, was that it was not built upon that foundation of Asian tradition and Confucian relationships which it was imperial Japan's sacred duty to revive and defend against the alien influences of the modern era. Itō did not believe this, but Uchida and his Ilchin confederates constituted a living example of Japanese-Korean collaboration, albeit on a dead (or, viewing the future, deadly?) issue. They could, on occasion, when he gave them money,[2] perform riot quieting duties, and he could hardly cuff off the one area of ardent "loyalty" to Japanese-Korean solidarity merely because it was for the wrong reasons. Hence, the Ilchin-ers were able to wax stronger, until they could gain attention for their great-crisis, need-for-drastic-action idea in the highest

[2] Specific instances of Itō's giving money or promising it to the Ilchin Society have been considered in chapter VIII, pp. 422, 428. That there were further transactions seems to be implied in a list of folders of "Documents Destroyed by Fire" compiled by the Japanese Foreign Office. One of these has the title, "Secret money handled by Mr. Kurachi in the Resident General's office, Nov., 1908." However, the other side of the government's ambivalent attitude toward this group may be represented in another title therein: "Secret money expenditure for the investigation of bad Japanese in Korea, 1896–1904." Gaimushō, *Shōshitsu Mokuroku* (1947), p. 344.

echelons of the Tokyo government. They hammered away. But, of course, the great crisis they were talking about was that of Eastern culture, the old order, whose inadequacies were being revealed by the electric lights of the modern age. And government realists were not interested in shutting off the electric lights, in manning Confucian guardposts with samurai swords; all that had been put aside in 1868, definitively in 1873.

On the other points, too, the answer is quite clearly negative. There was no special popular pressure and there was no great international crisis, Japan being in every way more secure than she had been in a hundred years and there being no meddling in Korea by other powers. Yet suddenly Itō gave up, Sone became "ill," and the oligarchs, apparently with no serious dissension, decided to abandon the experiment in collaborative government, the Residency General, and clamp down the iron fist, Heigō.

The fact that there was no special compulsion for Korean annexation in 1909–10 would seem to lift the problem out of its local setting and to suggest that more deeply laid forces were at work. The capitalism-imperialism thesis has been examined with a view to ascertaining whether a strong economic undercurrent brought Japan to the definitive annexation action (Chapter IX). But this has been rejected because, to put it oversimply, there was no money in the Korean venture and nobody wanted to go to Korea. We must find our explanation, it seems, not in the underground of Marxian economics, but on the drawing room chessboard of international politics, where nation-states are graded according to rank and power is queen.

Here, according to the realist school of experts in international relations, the game can be played calmly and relatively peacefully, if it is done by sober professionals equipped with a good knowledge of the facts and implications of geography, resources, and military strength, and a certain detachment concerning social conditions, cultural patterns, and, indeed, right and wrong. Nothing will change very much or very fast, for balances will be kept among the powerful, and the weak will be fit in as buffers, satellites, neutral zones, and the like. There will be some shifting around, of course. Some states, under skillful management will wax somewhat, others will wane, but a pawn cannot expect to become a knight, nor can its spokesman expect to have the voice of a knight at the bargaining tables. The internal structures of states are their own affair, at least for the powerful, and the weak will find it wise to follow the pattern of a powerful neighbor. A world balance of this sort might have been reached in the first quarter of this century had the United States helped to work it out, instead of indulging in foolish and disruptive idealism, Wilsonian variety. And it might still be worked out if Americans (and Communists?) will cease deluding themselves that they can or should remake the world. Particularly alarming is the recent MacArthurian version of idealism (reverse idealism?) which would make Americans out of the Chinese Communists if we have to bomb their cities to do it. In a world so thoroughly equipped with human fallibility, let us be rational, careful, cautious, measure our strength and the enemy's, negotiate the buffers, speak softly, and carry a big stick. The alternative is global war.

Mr. Kennan, who is perhaps the most brilliant and perceptive advocate of this realism in international politics, is aware, in addition, that it is not feasible for the balancers of power to try to set up laws and rules of international conduct, ignoring change and flux, because some peoples are too dissatisfied "to accept the rules of the game." It is a "task for diplomacy" to ease changes.[3] And he knows that there can be illusions about security (the watchword of realism), if it is thought of in absolute terms, as if "there could or should be such a thing as total military security for the United States."[4]

[3] Kennan, *American Diplomacy*, pp. 96-98. See also Hans J. Morgenthau, *Politics Among Nations* (2nd ed.; New York; Alfred A. Knopf, 1954) and Edward H. Carr, *The Twenty Years' Crisis, 1919–1939* (London: Macmillan, 1951), for other excellent presentations of the argument for realism.

[4] George F. Kennan, "The Illusion of Security," *The Atlantic*, CVIC, 2 (Aug. 1954), pp. 31-34, esp. p. 32.

History's sorry list of wars to establish kingdoms of righteousness, to rout out evil, and even to end war permits no gainsaying this argument. Certainly, such an imperfect stability, if it could be established, would be better than the chaos engendered by crusading and counter crusading, out of which planetary self-destruction is now clearly a possibility. However, Kennan himself, though he works and argues in its behalf, has misgivings that it may not be possible of achievement, even (or perhaps especially) where the processes of democracy allow popular enthusiasms to exercise great influence on the formation of foreign policy. He hopes that a greater professionalism in the conduct of foreign affairs might remedy this, but, writing amidst irrational McCarthyist hysteria in his own country, he admits that the view of those professionals, who, like himself, advocated a postwar policy toward Russia that assumed power rivalry rather than co-operation, "was not fully rounded."

He says:

> We were right about the nature of Soviet power; but we were wrong about the ability of American democracy at this stage of its history to bear for long a situation full of instability, inconvenience, and military danger. Perhaps Harry Hopkins and F.D.R. had more reason than we then supposed to believe that everything depended on the possibility of changing the attitude of the Soviet regime. But, if so, this is then only an indication that the dilemma was crueler than any of us really appreciated, and the crisis of our time one of such profundity that even the vast dislocations of World War II were only a partial symptom of it.[5]

The lesson of Japan's seizure of Korea, while only one vignette of modern history, points to the frightening possibility that the dilemma is indeed crueler than Mr. Kennan has thought. It seems to indicate that the sort of realistic balance (or semi-balance) he advocates is simply impossible to obtain in practice, even though in its theoretical construction it seems logical and workable. This

[5] Kennan, *Am. Dipl.*, p. 87.

is because the case of Korea exhibits striking failure *amidst almost perfect conditions.* It may not qualify as a laboratory test of realist diplomacy, but it is probably as close to that as an historical situation can bring us. Here, during the 1905–9 period, one of the truly great professionals of diplomacy, Itō Hirobumi,[6] operating at the height of his powers against a background of long and intimate acquaintanceship with both the broad and narrow, long-range and short-range problems involved, untroubled by popular pressure or acute international crisis, was nevertheless unable to maintain the restraint he himself thought to be necessary for the long-range national interest of Japan. Why? Mr. Kennan's formula would suggest that wayward idealism was at work, spoiling the good sober work of the professional. And indeed, examination of the details of the situation shows a company of idealists, Uchida's reactionaries, hard at work to influence policy and seemingly, if one judges by the outcome, enjoying success. So far so good for Kennan's idea.

However, the fact that it is the *reverse* idealists who are in at the finish is a most interesting phenomenon. Why not the liberals, who in the early stages were much more troublesome with their vigorous pursuit of freedom and progress? Giving in to the oligarchy in

[6] In addition to the already discussed examples of the intelligence and restraint which characterized Itō's approach to Japan's national interests, two more may be cited, which serve also to remind us of the tremendous weight Itō's opinions had in Japanese policy decisions. Both concern relations with the United States. (a) At the time of the American decision to annex Hawaii the Japanese Minister at Washington, Hoshi, and Foreign Minister Ōkuma both favored and indeed transmitted a strong protest to the United States government. However, as soon as Itō, who was in London, heard of it, he sent urgent advice to Tokyo not to persist in this move, which resulted in the swift withdrawal of the protest. See Itō to Ōkuma, July 2, 1897: Letters of Itō, Kensei Shiryō Shitsu, printed in NGB, XXX, 1007; Ōkuma to Itō, July 8, 1897: NGB, XXX, 1010-11; Conroy, *Japanese Frontier* . . ., pp. 137-38. (b) In November, 1907, from Seoul, Itō sent a long letter to the cabinet concerning his "uneasiness" at signs of developing antagonism between Japan and the United States resulting from "indiscretions on both sides." Particularly, he called attention to the "impolite behavior" of the then Japanese minister to Washington, Aoki, in criticising President Roosevelt, and suggested that Aoki be recalled, which he was. Gaimushō, *Nihon Gaikō Nempyō narabi ni Shuyō Bunsho* (Japanese Foreign Affairs Chronology and Important Documents) (Tokyo, 1955), I, 282-84.

Japan and backing its policies in Korea (whatever they were) or withdrawing from political life, they had faded away, except for the small group who tried to protest via socialism and were blotted out. Itō and his fellow realists could subdue these, yet could not (or would not?) subdue the reactionaries. And this brings us to consideration of what would seem to be the fallacy in the approach of the realist school, which we have defined as "the susceptibility of realism to reaction in international affairs."

The realist school, and Kennan makes this very explicit, deplores the "perfectionism" of "idealists," whether, considering American types, they be of the Wilsonian-Rooseveltian variety or the MacArthur-McCarthy variety, because in their seeking to remake the world according to one ideal or another they disrupt the normal "realistic" practice of nation state diplomacy. Since the following through of either type of idealism is a grand crusade of one sort or another, there would seem to be no need to distinguish between them. However, dividing them may lead us closer to an understanding of the problems involved. In the terminology of our study, Wilsonian-Rooseveltian idealism is clearly of the liberal variety and finds its Japanese counterpart in the idealism of the Japanese liberals, Fukuzawa and company. Broad-visioned and progressive, it looks out on the wider world with interest, sympathy, and hope that men the world over can come to mutual appreciation and understanding. But, it should be added, the American version of this had been tarnished, no less than the Japanese, by samurai heritage (preserved in popular art form by the Wild West and samurai movie respectively—exact counterparts). Indeed, it has been the supreme delusion of liberals everywhere that the fight for freedom and progress can sometimes be aided by resort to violence, though the fact that to fall into violence is to fall into quicksand may be illustrated on many levels of action, of which the Seoul uprising of 1884 and the American entry into World War I may serve as examples in widely divergent areas and points of time. However, it should be emphasized that the liberal delusion has been on means, not on ends (except as their vision has been obscured by racial, social, creedal, and national boundaries which they inherit but from which they consistently strive to escape, even at the difficult price of diminution of pride).[7]

The idealism of MacArthur and McCarthy is of a different stamp. Its Japanese counterpart is the idealism of Saigō, Tōyama Mitsuru, Uchida Ryōhei, and friends. It bases itself firmly on past practices and ideas and looks out on the wider world with suspicion, antagonism, and worry that intruders may disturb its goodly heritage. It is generally defensive—Senator Taft, Japanese Jōi (Expel the Barbarians)—but in a crisis situation it seeks to extend the defense perimeter as far as possible, in which process isolationists became war mongers.[8] Thus, reactionary idealism will resort to violence in its fight to protect our heritage even more willingly and certainly more desperately than the liberal sallies "to build a better world." (Examples are the desperate fight by the American South in the Civil War, and its counterpart, the Satsuma Rebellion in Japan.) However, this brings us to the essential delusion of reactionary idealism, which is the exact opposite of that of the liberal variety. It is a delusion of ends, not means. Reactionaries, by force, try to shore up a structure which has become anachronistic, which cannot stand the test of fair competition in the wider world, which may have had some validity as a "peculiar institution"[9] in a limited spacial and temporal setting, but which needs the cross-currents of fresh ideas and the opportunity to change more than anything else. The technique of force is right for shoring up such a structure, in

[7] In Levenson's terms they seek "value" above "history," even though it is painful to give up history (traditions). See Joseph R. Levenson, " 'History' and 'Value': The Tensions of Intellectual Choice in Modern China," in Arthur F. Wright (ed.), *Studies in Chinese Thought* (Chicago: University of Chicago Press), pp. 146-94.

[8] It is interesting in this regard that Saigō in 1876, in a sort of final plea for *Jōi*, advocated bringing not only Korea, but Manchuria and Eastern Siberia under Japanese control, Sekai Genba's memo of conversation with Saigō, Jan. 9, 1876: *Dai Saigō Zenshū* (Tokyo, 1927), II, 776-80.

[9] See Kenneth M. Stampp, *The Peculiar Institution: Slavery in the Ante Bellum South* (New York: Alfred A. Knopf, 1956).

the sense that it is the only way it can be preserved, but, in Fukuzawa's words, this becomes "indulgence" in the "ostentatious character of institutions." Fukuzawa applied this to Japanese feudalism. But it would apply equally in the present day to American capitalism (old variety), which may have accomplished great things in the nineteenth century but which, in a world crying for a more equitable distribution of goods, hardly deserves to be defended at the Yangtze river—or anywhere, and to Russian communism (hammer and sickle variety) which may have given the Russian people a new lease on life, but which, insofar as it must defend the purity of the dialectic with a million troops and an army of secret police, is merely another example of shoring up a peculiar institution.

Now the trouble with the seemingly sensible realistic formula for balance and, hopefully, peace in a world of too many tensions is that, without perhaps intending to do so, it works to shore up these peculiar institutions by sharply prescribing the range of argument and by allowing them to gain identification with the national interest. Quite aside from the proposition that the whole nation-state system may be approaching outdatedness, the fact that institutions and attitudes which are indefensible from a world perspective, because of their historical association with a nation or a region, not only find protection under the practice of realistic diplomacy, but wax large like cancers, unscrutinized and unattended. Thus in the case of Korea, the illusion that all of eastern Asia should live under the benevolence of a Japanese imperial system rooted in the gods and Confucian virtue was fostered by an annexation that was indulged in by realistic Japanese leaders only because it seemed better to be safe than sorry in Korea, and was accepted by "sensible" leaders of other nations because they were not inclined to inquire into the sphere of interest of another power. The ultimate result of the waxing of Japanese reaction is well known. But our Korean example would seem to indicate that it is impossible to expect any statesman, no matter how professional and no matter how impervious to popular notions of the moment, if his frame of reference is national interest, even enlightened national interest, to act otherwise than according to the better-safe-than-sorry postulate. This automatically veers his policy toward reaction, and the descent of realism toward brutality follows. Instead of balance and restraint, there results indulgence, which, if persisted in in the present state of armament, must sooner or later trigger the mechanism of global destruction.

Is there another alternative? There may be, but it presents challenges of the dimension suggested in the idea that nations must become good rather than merely intelligently self interested in their international conduct, and policy formulation must be concerned more, not less, with questions of abstract justice and morality. The challenge runs to the very roots of the state system, to its philosophy and its assumptions as well as its conduct. It is like saying that a game of chess should change into a game of giveaway. Impossible, and yet a game of giveaway can be strangely refreshing, and curiously contagious, especially after long hours of serious play have produced no champion. International politics is no parlor game, but it might be worthwhile, since so much else has failed, to attempt to formulate an approach consonant with the higher aspirations of man, on the assumption that the many could learn to operate on that higher plane which a few have attained. Since this would surely involve idealism, where those aspirations have been expressed, the pitfalls into which idealism has fallen in the past must be understood and avoided. With this in mind we might employ another clumsy term and call this "better" approach "steady idealism." Its ingredients would be something of the following, to which, curiously, liberal idealism, realism, and reactionary idealism would each have something to contribute.

Its basic assumptions and its goals would be unashamedly and optimistically liberal, starting with the proposition that the world and all its people are as beautiful and good as technicolor makes them appear, and seeking freedom, material comfort, enlightenment, and happiness for all men (and women). It would insist that every human institution must be evaluated and eventually modified according to this frame of reference and every act of diplomacy considered in this light. However, steady idealism would recognize that the crusade and the coup d'état, with their overtones of vehemence and violence, are not only unfruitful but self defeating. It would have the patience of Job along with the gentleness of Gandhi. Perhaps from realism it can acquire the methodology of patience and circumspection, without betraying its higher aspirations. And from reaction it can learn about pride, that men cling to outmoded attitudes and institutions because they are proud, which is not merely sinful because the inside kernel of pride is self-respect. Steady idealism would turn the wheels of progress without mashing self-respect into the roadbed.

Returning to the specifics of the Korean problem, how might this be applied? It is interesting that Frank Williston ("Reflections on American-Korean Relations," 1948), in observing that American policy failed to concern itself with what was "basically right and decent for the Korean people" during the pre-annexation period because it looked first to the broader concerns of international politics, attributes a share of the responsibility for this to that generation's George Kennan. (This was the uncle of the present Mr. Kennan, whose articles and arguments certainly helped bolster Theodore Roosevelt's determination to be coldly realistic about Korea.) Williston seems to estimate that the new George Kennan might represent history's repeating itself.[10] One wonders whether he would consider the Korean War, which broke out two years after his article was published, as proof that this was or was not the case.

Regardless of later implications, it is easy to say that TR should have "saved" Korea, but how? Alternatives to his looking the other way because the Koreans "could not strike one blow in their own

[10] Frank Williston, "Reflections on American-Korean Relations," *Korean Review*, I, 1 (March 1948), pp. 7-10.

defense" do not seem promising. The United States might have teamed with Russia to force Japan to accept a division of Korea (at the 38th parallel?), or gone to war with Japan (and Russia? and Britain?) to "preserve Korean independence." We can hardly question Roosevelt's wisdom in avoiding these alternatives, but were there no others? What would steady idealism have to say? It might begin with Williston's prescription of that which is "basically right and decent for the Korean people."

What would have been basically right and decent for the Korean people? To have left them alone, under China's Confucian wing, as a backward but neutralized state? The sorry results of interference by "advanced" nations compel respectful consideration of this, and Nelson's *Korea and the Old Orders in Eastern Asia* certainly gives that. But, even a sympathetic view of Korea's political and social structure in the late nineteenth century admits its inadequacy and even depravity. Clarence Weems observes that its officialdom, basking in the security of isolation, had "made a mockery of the Confucian principle of political control through moral example. . . . Pseudo scholars . . . ingrained vices . . . general enervation . . . extortion, bribery, sale of offices, and the most maddening injustices. . . ."[11]

Since our present study has focused its attention on Japan and the process of formulation of Japanese policy toward Korea, it has been only incidentally concerned with the question of how badly Korea needed reform. But we have no reason for not accepting the conclusion of Weems and many others that conditions in Korea were very bad. Of course, it is possible to argue from the proposition that "self government is better than good government,"[12] that no form of outside interference is tolerable in the internal affairs of another nation. Certainly the Korean case illustrates the way in which meddling by outsiders leads to misrule by outsiders, a condition which by any measure of steady idealism would be

[11] C. N. Weems, "The Korean Reform and Independence Movement," pp. 14-17, 75.
[12] Williston, *op. cit.*, p. 8.

far worse than self-misrule. And yet the study of history does not admit the conclusion that progress is entirely an illusion. The techniques and the institutions of man have clearly shown improvement over the centuries and, though the very nature of discovery makes it unreasonable to expect that every part of the world should be at exactly the same level at all times, the sort of isolation and egocentricity which refuses to permit even the communication of new ideas from the outside would seem to run counter not only to the basic interests of men but even to their basic instincts.

Therefore, we must conclude that quite within the frame of reference of what was basically right and decent for the Korean people Korea did need fresh currents of ideas from the outside. And in that light the activities of Allen, Foulk, Hanabusa, Inoue Kakugorō, Waeber, and other "meddlers" cannot be viewed merely cynically. They were in a real sense bearers of civilization to Korea, particularly insofar as they were able to inspire young Koreans to take an interest in new ideas. The phenomenon of Korean progressivism was perhaps the healthiest thing that had developed in Korea in two hundred years. But, as Weems so well points out, the progressives tended to go overboard, to alienate themselves from their own heritage and from conservative reformers who might have helped them. Their attempted coup of 1884 cast a shadow of distrust over their whole future. Takezoe, and Foulk also, bear a heavy responsibility in this for not talking them out of the resort to violence.

Over the long range, it is possible to see where Japan and the United States, by the application of steady idealism, might have helped Korea and themselves a great deal more than they did by basing policy on their national interests. A little more sense of involvement by the American State Department would have lessened the Japanese sense of urgency that Korea had to be made secure. Not only might Takezoe and Foulk have dissuaded the coupists of 1884, but their successors might have effected a pleasant all-around surprise by persuading the king to accept the Tonghak petition. And in 1898 the Independence Club could no doubt have used both funds and sage advice. Even after America and Japan became Pacific rivals after the turn of the century, since there was a certain ideological kinship in their respective civilizing missions in the Philippines and Korea, they might have exchanged inspection teams to verify the same, instead of delimiting spheres of influence. And when the Korean secret mission appeared at The Hague, the United States might have volunteered to allow the Hague Court to investigate American management of the Philippines if the Japanese would allow the same for Korea.

A final word might suggest that the problem areas of the world, those strategically located corridors, peninsulas, and islands, should be redefined as opportunity areas, where under the floodlights of international opinion powers can come down to earth with people, and locate their real interests.

Bibliography

I. PRIMARY SOURCES

Unpublished

Japanese Ministry of Foreign Affairs, Archives (Library of Congress microfilm). The following sections of this vast collection of over two million pages were the most useful to this study:
SP 5, History of Japanese-Korean Relations, etc.
SP 9, Reference Materials re Korean Independence Movement.
PVM 3, Documents relating to Korea, including Sugimura Diary
MT 1.1.2.40, Documents relating to the establishment of the Residency General
MT 1.6.1.5, Documents relating to the internal reorganization of Korea, 1894–95
MT 1.6.1.24, Documents relating to the improvement of the Korean court
MT 1.1.2.41, Documents relating to exiled Koreans
MT 1.1.2.33, Miscellaneous proposals re China-Korea administration
MT 1.1.2.55, Residency General Administrative matters
MT 2.4.1.9, Documents relating to the secret Korean mission to The Hague
It should be emphasized that the above-mentioned groups of documents, though running to hundreds of papers, represent only a fraction of the total amount of material pertinent to the Korean problem contained in this collection, but these provided the author with a microscopic view of certain key aspects, 1894-1909, as well as a general view from the inside, to 1894 (SP 5), which he was able to check with published Foreign Office documents (see below Gaimushō, *Nihon Gaikō Bunsho*). A guide to the entire Archives has been published: Cecil H. Uyehara (comp.), *Checklist of Archives in the Japanese Ministry of Foreign Affairs, Tokyo, Japan, 1868–1945* (Washington: Library of Congress, 1954). Actually there are very few documents for the pre-1894 period in the collection, but a vast number for the 1894-1910 and, of course, later periods.

Kensei Shiryō Shitsu Collection. "Materials relating to Constitutional Government," Diet Building, Tokyo. Papers of leading statesmen of the Meiji period. Those of Itō, Katsura, Inoue Kaoru, and part of Mutsu's are indexed. Many of these documents have appeared in printed collections and, since cross-checking indicates that these were very carefully done, it is advisable for foreign scholars to use them, as problems of paleography and style are almost insurmountable, even after a specific document is located. Most useful to this study were a number of documents from the Itō and Katsura collections.

Ōkuma Kenkyū Shitsu Collection. This Ōkuma Research Room, located at Waseda University, Tokyo, contains mainly letters *to* Ōkuma. There is an excellent index to individual items: *Ōkuma Bunsho Mokuroku* (Waseda, 1952).

Gaimushō (Japanese Foreign Office), Tokyo. Here the author found a number of pertinent items not included in the microfilmed Archives collection. There is a "Gaimushō Genzon Kiroku Mokuroku" (Index to Records Kept at the Foreign Office at the Present Time), compiled in 1947, 8 vols. and a "Shōshitsu Mokuroku" (Index to Documents Destroyed by Fire), also compiled in 1947, 1 vol. Especially valuable for this study were the statement of Mr. Kurachi Tetsukichi entitled "Kankoku Heigō no Iki Satsu" (Particulars regarding the Annexation of Korea), recorded in November, 1939, and reproduced "for office reference" in a thirteen-page pamphlet in April, 1950, and a record of conversations between Inoue Kaoru and the Korean king and his cabinet, 1894–95.

Itō Ke Bunsho (Itō Family Papers). In typescript, about 90 vols. Papers which were in Itō's possession, hence mainly letters to Itō. There are several volumes of this set at Meiji Shimbun Bunko (Library of Meiji Newspapers) at Tokyo University and many more at the Kensei Shiryō Shitsu in the Diet Building. Especially useful to this study was Volume LXVII which contains letters from Vice-Resident General Sone to Itō.

United States Department of State, Diplomatic Despatches, Korea, 1883–1905; Instructions, Korea, 1883–1905. Some use was also made of Despatches and Instructions, Japan and China. These documents, which are housed in the National Archives in Washington and are in large part available also on microfilm, have, of course, been carefully combed by other scholars, notably Treat, Nelson, Harrington, and Griswold, and the author used them to supplement rather than repeat their work and to check difficult points. He also used papers of the U.S. Consul, Nagasaki, 1883–87, and Yokohama, 1888–94 and some Miscellaneous Letters, Post Records and Consular Despatches, Seoul.

George McCune Document Collection (microfilm). This collection was generously loaned to the author by the owner, Mrs. Evelyn B. McCune. It contains hundreds of documents from the U.S. legation at Seoul from the 1880's to 1905, many of which are duplicated in the above State Department collection. Some of these documents have been published, see McCune and Harrison below.

Tokudaiji Sanenori, Grand Chamberlain to Meiji Emperor. "Nisshi" (Daily Record). Reports the chamberlain carried to the emperor during 1894. Copy loaned to author by Mr. N. Hagihara.

Published

Government document collections, reports, and other official compilations

Chōsen Sōtokufu (Government General of Korea).

Annual Report on Reforms and Progress in Chosen (Korea), 1910–11. Seoul, 1911.

Chōsen Tetsudōshi (History of Korean Railroads). Keijō (Seoul): Chōsen Sōtokufu Tetsudōkyoku, 1915.

Chōsen Tetsudō Ensen Shijō Ippan (Survey of Markets along Korean Railroads). Keijō (Seoul): Chōsen Sōtokufu Tetsudōkyoku, 1912.

Table of Trade and Shipping for the Year 1911. Keijō (Seoul), 1912.

Gaimushō (Japanese Foreign Office).

Dai Nihon Gaikō Bunsho (continued as *Nihon Gaikō Bunsho*) (Japanese Foreign Affairs Documents). Tokyo: 1936–56. Vols. I-XXXIII. This series is the Japanese equivalent of *Papers Relating to the Foreign Relations of the United States.* Very valuable for this study, especially those volumes relating to the period before 1896 (Vols. I-XXVIII) for which there are few manuscript documents in the Archives collection.

Jōyaku Kaisei Keika Gaiyō (Outline of Progress toward Treaty Revision). Tokyo, 1950.

Komura Gaikōshi (History of the Diplomacy of Komura). Tokyo, 1953. 2 vols. Because the editing schedule of the above Foreign Affairs Documents indicated that the documents of the Komura period (post–1900) would not be published for some years, the Japanese Foreign Office put out this summary study, based on documents in the process of being edited and an old work by Shinobu Jumpei entitled *Kōshaku Komura Jutarō* (Marquis Komura Jutarō).

Nihon Gaikō Nempyō narabi ni Shuyō Bunsho (Japanese Foreign Affairs Chronology and Important Documents). Tokyo, 1955. 2 vols.

Shinsei Nihon Gaikō Hyakunen Shi (100-Year History of the Diplomacy of New-Born Japan). Tokyo, 1952.

Tsūshō Ihen (continued as *Tsūshō Hōkoku* and *Tsūshō Isan*) (Japanese Consular Reports). There are scattered volumes from 1881–94 and a continuous series thereafter, in the Ueno branch of the Diet Library.

Kankoku Jijō (Conditions in Korea, based on records of Japanese consulates in Korea). Tokyo: Gaimushō Tsūshōkyoku, 1904.

Genzan Shōkōkaigisho (Wonsan Chamber of Commerce) (ed.).

Genzan Shōkōkaigisho 60 Nenshi (60-year History of the Wonsan Chamber of Commerce). Genzan (Wonsan), 1942.

Hanabusa Diary. Contained in Vol X of Gaimushō, *Nihon Gaikō Bunsho* (Japanese Foreign Affairs Documents).

Kaburagi Yosao. *Chōsenkoku Genzan Shuchō Fukumeisho* (Report of Investigations at Wonsan, Korea). Tokyo: Gaimushō Tsūshōkyoku, 1895.

Keijō Kyoryū Mindan Yakusho (Seoul Residents' Corporation Office).

Keijō Hattatsu Shi (History of the Development of Seoul). Keijō (Seoul), 1912.

Keijō Shōkōkaigisho (Seoul Chamber of Commerce and Industry) (ed.).

Keijō Shōkōkaigisho 25 Nenshi (25-Year History of the Seoul Chamber of Commerce and Industry). Keijō (Seoul), 1941.

Krasny Archiv. (The following are collections of Russian tsarist documents pertaining to the Far East released by the Soviet government.)

"Russian Documents Relating to the Sino-Japanese War, 1894–1895"; "First Steps of Russian Imperialism in the Far East, 1888–1903"; "On the Eve of the Russo-Japanese War," *Chinese Social and Political Science Review*, XVII (1933–34), 480-515, 632-670; XVIII (1934–35), 236-81, 572-94; XIX (1935–36), 125-39, 234-67.

Naikaku Tōkeikyoku (Japanese Cabinet, Bureau of Statistics).

Nihon Teikoku Tōkei Nenkan (Statistical Yearbook of Imperial Japan). Vols. III, VI, XVI. This set, which begins with 1882, may be found in the Library of the Faculty of Economics at Tokyo University.

Nōshōmushō (Japanese Ministry of Agriculture and Commerce).
Kankoku Bōeki Nempyō (Korean Foreign Trade Yearbook). Tokyo: Nōshōmushō Kanzeikyoku, 1901–7.
Kankoku Bōeki Yōran (Korean Foreign Trade Survey). Seoul: Nōshōmushō Kanzeikyoku Doshibu, 1907–10.
Kankoku Jijō Chōsa Shiryō (Data Pertaining to Investigations of Conditions in Korea). Tokyo: Nōshōmushō Shōkōkyoku, 1905.
Kankoku Kōgyō Chōsa Hōkoku (Reports on Investigations of Korean Mining). Tokyo, 1906. 6 vols.
Kankoku ni okeru Mensaku Chōsa (Investigation of Cotton Production in Korea). Tokyo: Nōshōmushō Nōjishikenjō, 1905.
Kankoku ni okeru Nōgyō Chōsa (Investigation of Agriculture in Korea). Tokyo: Nōshōmushō Nōjishikenjō, 1906.
Taishikan Bōeki Chōsa Hōkoku (Report of Investigations regarding Chinese and Korean Foreign Trade). Tokyo, 1904–5. 4 Vols.
(trans.). *Rokoku Ōkurashō Kankoku Shi* (The Russian Finance Ministry's Situation in Korea), Tokyo, 1905.

Ōkurashō (Japanese Finance Ministry).
Gaikoku Bōeki Gairan (General Survey of Foreign Trade). Tokyo, 1891 *et seq.* Yearly, set at Ueno branch of Diet Library.

Pauley Commission. *Report on Japanese Reparations to the President of the United States.* Washington, 1946.

Russian Finance Ministry. *Situation in Korea.* See above Nōshōmushō (trans.). *Rokoku Ōkurashō . . .*

Teikoku Shugiin Giin (Japanese Imperial Diet).
Dai Nihon Teikoku Gikai Shi (History of the Japanese Imperial Diet). Tokyo, 1890–1905.

Tōkanfu (Residency General) of Korea.
Annual Report for 1907 on Reforms and Progress in Korea. Seoul, 1908.
Annual Report on Reforms and Progress in Korea (1908–9). Seoul, 1909.
Kankoku Kakuho Bōeki Gaikyō (Conditions of Trade in Various Korean Ports). Seoul, 1907.
Kankoku Tsūran (Handbook on Korea). Seoul: Nōshōkōbu, 1910.
Kyoryū Mindan Jijō Yōran (Handbook of Conditions of Residents' Organizations). Seoul: Tōkanfu Chihōbu, 1909.
Tōkanfu Tōkei Nempyō (Statistical Yearbook of the Residency General). Seoul, 1906-10.
Zaikankoku Nihonjin Sangyō Dantai Ichiran (Survey of Japanese Business Organizations in Korea). Seoul, 1907.

U.S. Congress. *Congressional Record,* 66th Cong., 1st Sess., Sept. 19, 1919. Statement by Fred A. Dolph.

U.S. Department of State. *Papers Relating to the Foreign Relations of the United States.*

Other collections of documents, contemporary newspapers and periodicals, and writings of participants in the events of the period, including those Japanese-style biographic compilations which are built around quotations from such.

Beasley, W. G. *Select Documents on Japanese Foreign Policy, 1853–1868.* London: Oxford University Press, 1955.

Blacker, Carmen (trans.). "Kyūhanjō (Conditions in an Old Feudal Clan) by Fukuzawa Yukichi," *Monumenta Nipponica*, IX, 1-2 (1953), pp. 304-29.

Chōsen Kyōkai (Korea Society). *Chōsen Kyōkai Kaihō* (Reports of the Korea Society), Nos. 1-10 (1902–5).

Chung, Henry (comp.). *Treaties and Conventions between Corea and Other Powers.* New York: H. S. Nichols Inc., 1919.

Dai Ichi Ginkō (Dai Ichi Bank). *Kankoku ni okeru Daiichi Ginkō* (The Dai Ichi Bank in Korea). Tokyo, 1908.

Dai Ichi Ginkō. *Kankoku Kakushiten Shutsuchōjo Kaigyō Irai Eigyō Jōkyō* (Conditions of business at the Various Branches in Korea since their Opening). Tokyo, 1908.

Dai Saigō Zenshū Kankōkai (Great Saigō Collection Publishing Association) (ed.). *Dai Saigō Zenshū* (Great Saigō Collection). Tokyo: Heibonsha, 1926–27. 3 vols.

de Bary, William Theodore, ed. *Sources of the Japanese Tradition.* New York: Columbia University Press, 1958.

Heard, Augustine. "China and Japan in Korea," *North American Review*, CLIX (1894), 300-8.

Hirano Yoshitarō (ed.). *Bajō Ōi Kentarō Den* (Biography of Ōi Kentarō). Tokyo: Ōi Bajō Den Hensanbu, 1938. Contains numerous writings and quotations of Ōi, as well as a running account of his activities.

Hiratsuka Atsushi (ed.). *Itō Hakubun Hiroku* (Private Papers of Itō). Tokyo: Shunjūsha, 1929. 2 vols. Selected documents from Itō family collection, with comments by persons associated with particular documents.

Hulbert, Homer. *The Passing of Korea.* New York: Doubleday, Page & Co., 1906. Lament by a long-time resident and friend of Korea.

Inoue Kakugorō. *Kanjo no Zammu* (Memory of Seoul). Tokyo: Shunyōdō, 1891. Reprinted in *Fūzoku Gahō* (journal) (Jan. 1895), entire issue. Inoue was Fukuzawa Yukichi's "action man" in Korea.

Inoue Kaoru Denki Hensankai (Inoue Kaoru Biographical Compilation Society (comp.). *Segai Inoue Kō Den* (life of Marquis Inoue). Tokyo: Naigai Shoseki Kabushiki Kaisha, 1933–34. 5 vols.

Ishikawa Mikiakira. *Fukuzawa Yukichi Den* (Life of Fukuzawa Yukichi). Tokyo: Iwanami Shōten, 1932-33. 4 vols. Volume III contains much material on Korea, quotations from Fukuzawa's writings on the subject, etc.

Itagaki Taisuke. *Jiyūtō Shi* (History of the Liberal Party). Tokyo, 1913, 2 vols.

Itō Hirobumi (ed.). *Chōsen Kōshō Shiryō* (Materials on Negotiations with Korea). Tokyo: Hisho Ruisan Kankōkai, 1936. 3 Vols. These volumes are part of Itō's 26-volume *Hisho Ruisan* (Collection of Private Papers) set, revised by Kaneko Kentarō and others, 1934–36.

Itō Hakubun Den. See below, Kaneko.

Itō Seitoku (ed.). *Katō Kōmei.* Tokyo: Katō Kōmei Haku Denki Hensan Iinkai, 1929. 2 vols.

Iwakura Tomomi Kankei Bunsho. See below, Ōtsuka.

Iwakura Kō Kyūseki Hozonkai (comp.). *Iwakura Kō Jikki* (Authentic Records of Prince Iwakura). Tokyo, 1927. 3 vols.

Jiji Shimpō (newspaper), 1882–1910. Files of this newspaper, which was edited by Fukuzawa Yukichi during his lifetime, are in Tokyo University's Meiji Bunko.

Kaneko Kentarō (ed.). *Itō Hakubun Den* (Life of Itō Hirobumi). Tokyo, 1940. 3 vols.

Kanjō Shūhō (Seoul Weekly). Newspaper published in Seoul by Inoue Kakurorō, Feb. 1–April 5, 1886. Professor Yoshiyuki Sakurai of Tokyo Metropolitan University has copies of issues Number 2 through 10 of this very rare item.

Katayama Sen. *Nihon no Rōdō Undō* (The Japanese Labor Movement). Tokyo: Iwanami Shōten, 1952.

Kokumin Shimbun (newspaper), 1890–1910. Files in Tokyo University's Meiji Bunko.

Kokuryūkai (ed.). *Seinan Kiden* (Records of the Southwest; i.e., Satsuma Rebellion). Tokyo, 1908–12. 3 vols.

Komatsu Midori (ed.). *Itō Kō Zenshū* (Complete Works of Prince Itō). Tokyo: Itō Kō Zenshū Han Kōkai, 1927. 3 vols. Not really "complete," of course, but contains many items on the Korean problem.

Kondō Yoshio (ed.). *Inoue Kakugorō Sensei Den* (Life of Teacher Inoue Kakugorō). Tokyo: Denki Hensankai, 1943. Based on Inoue's memoirs, according to editor. Very detailed, many quotations, though no precise documentation.

Kurachi Tetsukichi. *Kankoku Heigō no Ikisatsu* (Particulars on the Annexation of Korea). Printed by Gaimushō "for office reference," Tokyo, 1950. See above Gaimushō, in "unpublished" list.

Kuroda Kashihiko (ed.). *Gensui Terauchi Hakushaku Den* (Life of Field Marshal Count Terauchi). Tokyo, 1920.

Kuzū Yoshihisa. *Nikkan Gappō Hishi* (Secret History of the Merger of Japan and Korea). Tokyo: Kokuryūkai, 1936. 2 vols. Based on unpublished letters and memoirs of Uchida Ryōhei.

Ladd, George Trumbull. *In Korea with Marquis Itō*. New York: Charles Scribner's Sons, 1908. Professor of Philosophy Ladd was a contemporary observer of the Residency General.

———. "The Annexation of Korea: An Essay in 'Benevolent Assimilation,' " *The Yale Review*, N.S., 1 (1911–12), 639-56.

———. *What Ought I to Do? An Inquiry into the Nature and Kinds of Virtue and into the Sanctions, Aims, and Values of the Moral Life*. New York: Longmans, Green & Co., 1915.

———. *What Should I Believe? An Inquiry into the Nature, Grounds and Value of the Faiths of Science, Society, Morals, and Religion*. New York: Longmans, Green & Co., 1915.

LeGendre, General [Charles]. *Progressive Japan: A Study of the Political and Social Needs of the Empire*. New York & Yokohama: C. Levy, 1878.

McCune, George M. and John A. Harrison (eds.). *Korean-American Relations: Documents Pertaining to the Far Eastern Diplomacy of the United States*. Some of the documents from the McCune Collection (see above), covering the years 1883–86.

McKenzie, F. A. *The Tragedy of Korea*. New York: E. P. Dutton & Co., 1908. On-the-spot observer of the Residency General.

———. *Korea's Fight for Freedom*. New York: Fleming H. Revell Co., 1920.

MacMurray, John V. A. (comp. and ed.). *Treaties and Documents with and concerning China, 1894–1919*. New York: Oxford University Press, 1921. 2 vols.

Mainichi (newspaper). From 1885; at first *Tōkyō–Yokohama Mainichi*, then simply *Tōkyō Mainichi*. Generally reflected views of Ōkuma's Kaishintō. File at Tokyo University, Meiji Bunko.

Meiji Hennenshi. See below, Nakayama.

Miyazaka Kuro (ed.). *Meiji, Taishō, Shōwa Rekishi Shiryō Zenshū* (Collection of Historical Materials of the Meiji, Taishō, and Shōwa Periods). Tokyo- Yugosha, 1932–33. 17 Vols. Volume VI, "Gaikō" (Diplomacy) was pertinent to this study.

Nakayama Yasumasa (comp.). *Shimbun Shūsei Meiji Hennenshi* (Newspaper Collection, Meiji Period). Tokyo: Zaisei Keizai Gakkai, 1934–36. 15 vols. Reprints articles from all leading Japanese newspapers of the period, 1868–1912.

Nishida Nagatoshi (comp.). *Heimin Shimbun* (The Common People's Newspaper). Osaka and Tokyo: Sōgensha, 1953. 2 vols. Reproduces the articles which appeared in this "Socialist" newspaper during its brief existence, Nov., 1903–Jan. 1905.

Nikkan Tsūshō Kyōkai (Japan-Korea Commercial Association). *Nikkan Tsūshō Kyōkai Hōkoku* (Bulletin of the Association). 39 vols. At Ueno branch of Diet Library; set runs monthly from Sept., 1895–Nov., 1898.

Ōishi Masami. "Danwa" (Chatter), *Taiyō*, XVI, 13 (1910), pp. 89–90.

Ōkubo Toshikazu (ed.). *Ōkubo Toshimichi Bunsho* (Ōkubo Toshimichi Documents). Tokyo: Nihon Shiseki Kyōkai, 1927–31. 10 vols. Reference was made to Vol. V in this study. Sets of these may be found at the Gaimushō and at the Kensei Shiryō Shitsu.

Ōkubo Toshimichi. *Ōkubo Toshimichi Nikki* (Diaries of Ōkubo Toshimichi). Tokyo: Nihon Shiseki Kyōkai, 1927. 2 vols.

Ōtsuka Takematsu (ed.). *Iwakura Tomomi Kankei Bunsho* (Documents relating to Iwakura Tomomi). Tokyo: Nihon Shiseki Kyōkai, 1927–35. 8 vols.

Ozaki Yukio. *Gakudō Kaikoroku* (Memoirs of Ozaki). Tokyo: Yūkeisha, 1951. 2 vols.

Pooley, A. M. (ed.). *The Secret Memoirs of Count Tadasu Hayashi*. New York: G. P. Putnam, 1915. This widely quoted work should be used with the greatest circumspection for, insofar as the author could discover, there is no Japanese counterpart of these "memoirs." Furthermore, there would seem to be contradictions between the Hayashi who emerges from these and the one who appears in authentic Japanese Foreign Office documents. A careful study of this is needed.

Presseisen, Ernest L. "Roots of Japanese Imperialism: A Memorandum of General LeGendre," *Journal of Modern History*, XXIX, 2 (1957), pp. 108–11.

Rockhill, William W. (ed.). *Treaties and Conventions with or concerning China and Korea, 1894–1904*. Washington: Government Printing Office, 1904.

Sada Kakubo. "Seikan Hyōron" (Conquer Korea Critique) in *Meiji Bunka Zenshū*, VI. See below, Yoshino.

Sands, William F. "Korea and the Korean Emperor," *Century*, LXIX (1905), 577–84. Sands was Horace Allen's U.S. legation secretary and later adviser to the Korean government.

———. *Undiplomatic Memories*. New York: Whittlesley House, 1930.

Shimbun Zasshi (newspaper), irregular, 1871–74. This newspaper, which seems at first to have had backing from Kido Kōin, may be found in Tokyo University's Meiji Bunko. It became the *Akebono*, a daily from 1875 to 1882, and took an increasingly anti-government tone, often presenting the ideas of Ōi Kentarō.

Shiokawa Ichitarō. *Chōsen Tsūshō Jijō* (The Condition of Korean Commerce). Tokyo: Yao Shōten, 1895. Basic and reliable source on Japanese-Korean trade to 1895, written by a Japanese consular official at Seoul.

Sugimura Fukashi. "Zaikan Kushin Roku" (Memoir of Troubles While Living in Korea). There may be a published version of this, for some Japanese sources cite it, but for this study the Library of Congress microfilm of the handwritten original was used. It is contained in pages 283–798 of Japanese Ministry of Foreign Affairs, Archives, PVM 3. Sugimura was Japanese legation secretary at Seoul during 1894–95.

Tōkyō Keizai Zasshi (Tokyo Economic Magazine). A journal reflecting business views, file at Tokyo University's Meiji Bunko.

Tōkyō Nichi Nichi Shimbun (newspaper). The Japanese government mouthpiece during the Meiji era, began publication in 1872. File at Meiji Bunko.

Tōyōtakushoku Kabushiki Kaisha (Oriental Development Co.). *Chōsen Ijū Tebikigusa* (Guide for Immigrants to Korea). Keijō (Seoul), 1911. Rev. ed. 1915.

———. Shokumin Tōkei (Statistics on Colonization). Keijō (Seoul), 1911 and yearly thereafter.

———. *10 Nenshi* (10-year History of Oriental Developent Co.). Keijō (Seoul), 1918.

———. *20 Nenshi* (20-year History, of same). Keijō (Seoul), 1928.

United States, Dept. of State. *Register* (corrected to Jan. 1, 1895). Washington: Government Printing Office, 1895.

Yoshino Sakuzō (ed.). *Meiji Bunka Zenshū* (Collected Materials on Meiji Culture). Tokyo, 1928–30. 24 vols. Volume VI, "Gaikō" (Diplomacy) was useful to this study.

Yubin Hochi (Newspaper). June, 1872–Dec., 1894, then continued as *Hochi Shimbun* through the rest of the Meiji era. An early editor, Fujita Mokichi, was a disciple of Fukuzawa Yukichi. Later (1880's) the paper tended to express the opinions of Ōkuma's Kaishintō party. File at Meiji Bunko.

II. SECONDARY SOURCES

Unpublished

Bartz, Carl F., Jr. "The Korean Seclusion Policy, 1860–1876." PhD. diss., University of California, Berkeley, 1952.

Corrigan, Francis P. "The Early Years of Chinese Intervention in Korea, 1882–87." Thesis for certificate of East Asian Institute, Columbia University, New York, 1956.

Dong, Chon. "Japanese Annexation of Korea: A Study of Korean-Japanese Relations to 1910." PhD diss., University of Colorado, Boulder, 1955. (University microfilms, Ann Arbor, T'55,D717j.)

Kim, Chong-Ik. "Japan in Korea (1905–1910): The Techniques of Political Power." Ph.D diss. in Political Science. Stanford University, Sept., 1958. This work parallels the latter part of the present study and makes a useful comparison, since it was done independently, and was not seen by the author until the present study was in press. Its main archival base is the Hoover library collection of Seoul Residency General documents, which in many cases duplicate materials used in this study, but give added information on some points, particularly on Japanese suppression of Korean "rebels". Mr. Kim, fully aware of the weakness of past emotional interpretations, emphasizes that his work "is not concerned with the question of whether power must have a moral basis nor does it deal with the problem of whether techniques of debatable ethical values should be used in political relationships" (p. 3). He credits Ito with "sincerity in his early promise to Korea" (p. 54), but, though he recognizes "the ambivalence of Japanese policy execution in Korea" (p. 264–5), he does not sufficiently explore the relationships of Japanese political and ideological groups to explain it.

McCune, George M. "Korean Relations with China and Japan, 1800–1864." PhD diss., University of California, Berkeley, 1941.

Oka Yoshitake. Lecture on early Meiji politics and diplomacy, May 28, 1954, at Tokyo University.

Weems, Clarence N., Jr. "The Korean Reform and Independence Movement (1881–1898)." PhD diss., Columbia University, New York, 1954. (University microfilms, Ann Arbor, No. 8859.)

Weems, Benjamin B. "Grass Roots Nationalism in Nineteenth Century Korea: The Tonghak Movement, 1860–1905." Paper presented at Far Eastern Association Meeting, Philadelphia, April, 1956.

Published

Anesaki, Masaharu. *History of Japanese Religion with Special Reference to the Social and Moral Life of the Nation*. London: Kegan Paul, 1930.

Asakawa, K. *The Russo-Japanese Conflict: Its Causes and Effects*. Cambridge: Riverside Press, 1904.

Battistini, Lawrence H. "The Korean Problem in the Nineteenth Century," *Monumenta Nipponica*, VIII, 1-2 (1952), pp. 47-66.

Beckmann, George M. "The Meiji Restoration and Constitutional Development of Japan, 1868–1871," *Hōgaku Kenkyū* (Journal of Law), XXVI, 6 (no year), pp. 468-458 (reverse pagination).

———. "Political Crises and the Crystallization of Japanese Constitutional Thought, 1871–1881," *Pacific Historical Review*, XXIII, 3 (1954), pp. 259–70.

———. *The Making of the Meiji Constitution: The Oligarchs and the Constitutional Development of Japan 1861-1891*. Lawrence: University of Kansas Press, 1957.

Bisson, T. A. *Japan's War Economy*. New York: Institute of Pacific Relations, 1945.

Black, John R. *Young Japan: Yokohama and Yedo*. London: Trubner & Co., 1881, 2 vols.

Borton, Hugh. *Japan's Modern Century*. New York: Ronald Press Co., 1955.

Brown, Delmer M. *Nationalism in Japan: An Introductory Historical Analysis*. Berkeley: University of California Press, 1955.

Brown, Sidney D. "Kido Takayoshi (1833–1877): Meiji Japan's Cautious Revolutionary," *Pacific Historical Review*, XXV, 2 (1956), pp. 151–62.

Byas, Hugh. *Government by Assassination*. New York: Alfred A. Knopf, 1942.

Carr, Edward H. *The Twenty Year Crisis, 1919–1939*. London: Macmillan, 1951.

Chung, Henry. *The Case of Korea*, New York: Fleming H. Revell, 1921.

Conroy, Hilary. "Government versus 'Patriot': The Background of Japan's Asiatic Expansion," *Pacific Historical Review*, XX, 1 (1951), pp. 31-42.

———. "*Chōsen Mondai*: The Korean Problem in Meiji Japan," *Proceedings of the American Philosophical Society*, C, 5 (1956), pp. 443–54.

———. "Japan's War in China," *Pacific Historical Review*, XXI, 4 (Nov. 1952), 367–79.

———. "Japanese Nationalism and Expansionism," *American Historical Review*, LX, 4 (1955), pp. 818–29.

———. *The Japanese Frontier in Hawaii, 1868–1898*. Berkeley: University of California Press, 1953.

Croly, Herbert. *Willard Straight*. New York: Macmillan, 1924.

Dolph, Fred A. "Briefs for Korea." Presented to U.S. Congress, 1919.
———. *Japanese Stewardship of Korea, Economic and Financial*. Washington, 1920.
Eckel, Paul. *The Far East Since 1500*. New York: Harcourt, Brace & Co., 1948.
Funaoka Seigo. *Japan im Sternbild Ostasiens*. Tokyo: Tōhō Shōten, 1942. 2 vols.
Fujimoto Shōsaku. *Kyojin Tōyama Mitsuru Ō* (Grand Old Tōyama Mitsuru). Tokyo, 1922.
Fujimura Michio. "Nichiro Sensō no Seikaku ni Yosete" (On the Character of the Russo-Japanese War), *Rekishigaku Kenkyū* (Journal of Historical Studies), No. 195 (May 1956), pp. 1-13.
Fujisawa, Chikao. "The Reassertion of Japanese State Philosophy," *Cultural Nippon*, II (March 1943), 35-49.
Furuya Tetsuo. "Nihon Teikoku Shugi no Seiritsu wo Megutte," (Concerning the Formation of Japanese Imperialism), *Rekishigaku Kenkyū* (Journal of Historical Science) (Dec. 1956), pp. 41-46.
Gauntlett, John O. (trans.). *Kokutai no Hongi* (Cardinal Principles of the National Polity of Japan). Cambridge: Harvard University Press, 1949.
Grajdanzev, Andrew J. *Modern Korea*. New York: Institute of Pacific Relations, 1944.
Griffis, William E. "Japan's Absorption of Korea," *North American Review*, CXCII (Oct. 1910), 516-26.
———. *Corea: The Hermit Nation*. New York: Charles Scribner's Sons, 1907. Eighth edition.
Hamada, Kengi. *Prince Ito*. London: Geo. Allen & Unwin, Ltd., 1936.
Hamilton, Angus. *Korea*. New York: Charles Scribner's Sons, 1904.
Harrington, Fred Harvey. *God, Mammon, and the Japanese: Dr. Horace N. Allen and Korean-American Relations, 1884–1905*. Madison: University of Wisconsin Press, 1944.
Hasei Chiyomatsu (ed.). *Daiichi Ginkō Gojūnen Shōshi* (50-year Brief History of the Dai Ichi Bank). Tokyo, 1925.
Hashima Hanjiro. "Kōka Jōyaku Teiketsu Tōji no Tsuioku" (Review of the Signing of the Treaty of Kanghwa), *Seikyū Gakusō* (Korean Historical Society Review), V. (Aug. 1931), 171-79.
Hatada Takeshi. *Chōsen Shi* (History of Korea). Tokyo: Iwanami Shōten, 1951. Best short history of Korea.
Hidaka Setsu. *Meiji Hisshi: Saigō Takamori Ansatsu Jiken* (The Saigō Takamori Assassination Incident, [an episode in] the Secret History of the Meiji Period). Tokyo: Shōyōsha, 1938. Not very reliable; Preface is best part.
Hishida, Seiji G. *The International Position of Japan as a Great Power*. New York: Columbia University Press, 1905.
Hori Makoto. "Beijin LeGendre Kengensho ni tsuite" (Concerning the Proposals of the American LeGendre), *Kokka Gakkai Zasshi* (Journal of the Association of Political and Social Sciences), LI, 5 (1937), pp. 114–31.
Hoshino, T. *Economic History of Chosen*. Seoul, 1921.
Hosokawa Karoku. "Chōsen" (Korea) in *Shokuminshi* (History of Colonization), No. 10 of *Gendai Bunmeishi* (History of Modern Civilization series), pp. 213–369. Tokyo: Tōyō Keizai Shimpōsha, 1941.
House, Edward H. *The Japanese Expedition to Formosa*. Tokyo, 1875.
Idditti, Smimasa. *The Life of Marquis Shigenobu Okuma: A Maker of New Japan*. Tokyo: Hokuseido, 1940.
Ike, Nobutaka. *The Beginnings of Political Democracy in Japan*. Baltimore: Johns Hopkins University Press, 1950.

Ike, Nobutaka. "Triumph of the Peace Party in Japan in 1873," *Far Eastern Quarterly*, II, 3 (1943), pp. 286–95.

Inoue Kiyoshi. "Nihon Teikokushugi no Keisei" (The Formation of Japanese Imperialism) in Rekishigakū Kenkyūkai (Historical Science Assoc. (ed.)), *Kindai Nihon no Keisei* (The Formation of Modern Japan), pp. 51-130. Tokyo: Iwanami Shōten, 1953.

Ishikawa Ryoichi (ed.). *Jiyūtō Ōsaka Jiken* (The Liberal Party's Osaka Incident). Tokyo: Jiyūtō Ōsaka Jiken Shuppan Kyoku, 1933. Revealing, though wandering, story of this "save Korea" incident of 1885.

Jansen, Marius. "From Hatoyama to Hatoyama," *Far Eastern Quarterly*, XIV, 1 (1954), pp. 65-79.

———. "Ōi Kentarō: Radicalism and Chauvinism," *Far Eastern Quarterly*, XI, 3 (1952), pp. 305-16.

———. *The Japanese and Sun Yat-sen*. Cambridge: Harvard University Press, 1954.

Jones, G. H. "His Majesty the King of Korea," *Korean Repository*, III (1891), 426-27.

———. "The Japanese Invasion," *Korean Repository*, I (1892), 308-11.

———. "The Taiwon Kun," Korean Repository, V (1898), 243-50.

Junkin, W. M. "The King's Oath at the Ancestral Temple," *Korean Repository*, II (1895), 76-77.

———. "The Tong Hak," *Korean Repository*, II (1895), 56-60.

———. "Among the Tong Haks," *Korean Repository*, II (1895), 201-8.

Kanbe Masao. *Chōsen Nōgyō Imin Ron* (Discussion of Agricultural Immigration to Korea). Tokyo: Yūhikaku, 1910.

Kang, Younghill. *The Grass Roof*. New York: Scribner's, 1932. Beautifully written expression of a sensitive young Korean's feelings versus Japan.

Kennan, George F. *American Diplomacy, 1900–1950*. Chicago: University of Chicago Press, 1951.

———. "The Illusion of Security," *The Atlantic*, CVIC, 2 (Aug. 1954).

———. *Russia, The Atom and the West*. New York: Harper & Bros., 1957.

Kimase, Seizo. *Mitsuru Toyama Kämpft für Grossasien*. Munich, 1941.

Kitagawa Osamu. "Nisshin Sensō made no Nissen Bōeki" (Japanese-Korean Trade to the Sino-Japanese War), *Rekishi Kagaku* (Historical Science), No. 1 (1932), pp. 64-79. "Kōza" approach.

Kiyozawa Kiyoshi. *Gaiseika to shite no Ōkubo Toshimichi* (Ōkubo Toshimichi as a Statesman). Tokyo: Chūō Kōron Sha, 1942. An excellent study.

———. *Nihon Gaikōshi* (History of Japanese Diplomacy). Tokyo: *Tōyō Keizai Shimpō Sha*, 1942. 2 vols. Carefully done by a private scholar of moderate views.

Kublin, Hyman. "The Attitude of China during the Liu-ch'iu Controversy, 1871–1881," *Pacific Historical Review*, XVIII, 2 (1949), pp. 213-31.

———. "The Origins of Japanese Socialist Tradition," *Journal of Politics*, XIV, 2 (1952), pp. 257-80.

Kuykendall, Ralph S. and A. Grove Day. *Hawaii: A History*. New York: Prentice-Hall, 1948.

Kuzū Yoshihisa. *Nisshi Kōshō Gaishi* (History of Sino-Japanese Negotiations). Tokyo: Kokuryūkai, 1938–39. 2 Vols. Official "Black Dragon" Society long-range interpretation of Japan's continental diplomacy based on materials compiled in such works as *Seinan Kiden* and *Nikkan Gappō Hishi* (see primary published list, above and *Tōa Senkaku Shishi Kiden*, below). First volume, covering years 1868–1905, gives heavy emphasis to Korean problem.

Kuzū Yoshihisa. *Tōa Senkaku Shishi Kiden* (Records of Pioneer East Asia Adventurers). Tokyo: Kokuryūkai, 1933–36. 3 vols. Contains some 2600 pages of biographical sketches.

Langer, William L. *The Diplomacy of Imperialism, 1890–1902*. New York: Alfred A. Knopf, 1951. 2 vols., second edition.

Lattimore, Owen. *Solution in Asia*. Boston: Little, Brown & Co., 1945.

———. "The Sacred Cow of Japan," *The Atlantic*, CLXXV (Jan. 1945), 45-51.

Lay, A. H. "A brief Sketch of the History of Political Parties in Japan," *Transactions of the Asiatic Society of Japan*, XXX (1902), 363-462.

Levenson, J. R. "'History' and 'Value': The Tensions of Intellectual Choice in Modern China" in Arthur F. Wright (ed.), *Studies in Chinese Thought*. Chicago: University of Chicago Press, 1953.

Liem, Channing. *America's Finest Gift to Korea: The Life of Philip Jaisohn*. New York: William Frederick Press, 1952.

Lin, T. C. "Li Hung-chang: His Korea Policies, 1870–1885," *Chinese Social and Political Science Review*, XIX, 2 (1935), pp. 202-33.

McCune, George M. (with Arthur L. Grey, Jr.). *Korea Today*. Cambridge: Harvard University Press, 1950.

———. "The Exchange of Envoys between Korea and Japan during the Tokugawa Period," *Far Eastern Quarterly*, V, 3 (1946), pp. 308-25.

———. "The Japanese Trading Post at Pusan," *Korean Review*, I, 1 (1948), pp. 11-15.

Malozemoff, Andrew. *Russian Far Eastern Policy, 1881–1904*. Berkeley: University of California Press, 1958. Thorough study using Russian sources.

Maruyama Masao. "Fukuzawa Yukichi no Tetsugaku" (The Philosophy of Fukuzawa Yukichi), *Kokka Gakkai Zasshi* (Journal of the Association of Political and Social Sciences), LXI, 3 (1947), pp. 129-63. A brilliant analysis.

———. "Meiji Kokka no Shisō" (The Thought of the Meiji State) in Rekishigaku Kenkyū Kai (ed.), *Nihon Shakai no Shiteki Kyūmei* (Historical Studies of Japanese Society). Tokyo: Iwanami, 1949.

Masaki Masaru. *Hokengaku Angya* (Insurance Pilgrimage). Tokyo: Hoken Kenkyūsho, 1956.

Matono Hansuke. *Etō Nampaku* (Biography of Etō Shimpei). Tokyo: Nampaku Kenshokai, 1928. 2 vols.

Meinecke, Friedrich. "Das Wesen der Staatsräson," in *Die Idee der Staatsräson in der neueren Geschichte*. Munich and Berlin: Verlag von R. Oldenbourg, 1925. 2nd ed.

Mendel, Douglas H., Jr. "Ozaki Yukio: Political Conscience of Modern Japan," *Far Eastern Quarterly*, XV, 3 (1956), pp. 343–56.

Mitchell, Kate L. "The Political Function of the Japanese Emperor," *Amerasia*, VI (Oct. 1942), 382-90.

Miyakawa Tōru. "Fukuzawa Yukichi ni okeru 'Keimō Seishin' no Kōzō" (The Structure of the "Spirit of Enlightenment" in Fukuzawa Yukichi). *Tōyō Bunka Kenkyūjo*, VI (Nov. 1954), 241-64.

Miyamoto Mataji. "Bōkokurei Jiken to Nisshin Sensō" (The Grain Export Prohibition Affair and the Sino-Japanese War), *Keizaigaku Kenkyū* (Economic Studies), XIII, 1 (1945), pp. 89-106.

———. "Nisshin Sensō no Sengo Keiei to Bōeki Kakuchōsaku" (Foreign Trade Expansion Policy and Post Sino-Japanese War Programs), *Keizaigaku Kenkyū* (Economic Studies), XIII, 2, XIV, 1 (1947-48).

———. "Taisen Bōeki no Shōchō to Nisshin Sensō" (The Ups and Downs of Korean

Trade and the Sino-Japanese War), *Keizaishi Kenkyū*, XXXI, No. 7-8 (1944), pp. 47-77. Careful studies. Miyamoto leans toward the Rōnō school.

Moore, S. F. "The Butchers of Korea," *Korean Repository*, V (1898), 127-32. Information on effects of Kabo reform.

Morgenthau, Hans J. *Politics Among Nations*. New York: Alfred A. Knopf, 1954. 2nd ed.

Morrison, John W. "Japan and the West: The Career of Fukuzawa Yukichi," *The Western Humanities Review*, VII, 3 (1953), pp. 233-44.

Mörsel, F. W. "The Emeute of 1884," *Korean Repository*, IV (1897), 95-98, 135-40, 212-19.

Mounsey, Augustus H. *The Satsuma Rebellion*. London: John Murray, 1879.

Nelson, M. Frederick. *Korea and the Old Orders in Eastern Asia*. Baton Rouge: Louisiana State University Press, 1946. Brilliant and sympathetic appraisal of the Chinese-Korean Confucian relationship.

Noble, Harold J. "The United States and Sino-Korean Relations, 1885–1887," *Pacific Historical Review*, II (1933), 292-304.

Nock, Elizabeth T. "The Satsuma Rebellion of 1877: Letters of John Capen Hubbard," *Far Eastern Quarterly*, VII, 4. (1948), pp. 368-75.

Norman, E. Herbert. "The Genyosha: A Study in the Origins of Japanese Imperialism," *Pacific Affairs*, XVII, 3 (1944), pp. 261-84.

Ogata, Taketora. "Mitsuru Toyama," *Contemporary Japan*, IX (July 1940), 818-29.

Oka Yoshitake. "Jiyūtō Saha to Nashironarizumu: Ōi Kentarō no Baai" (The Left Wing of the Liberal Party and Nationalism: Case of Ōi Kentarō), *Shakai Gaku Hyōron* (Social Science Review), May, 1951, pp. 9-14.

———. "Jōyaku Kaisei Rongi ni Arawareta Tōji no Taigai Ishiki" (Contemporary Sentiment on Foreign Powers appearing in the Treaty Revision Argument), *Kokka Gakkai Zasshi* (Journal of the Association of Political and Social Sciences), LXVII (Aug., Sept. 1953), 1-24, 183-206.

———. "Nisshin Sensō to Tōji ni okeru Taigai Ishiki" (The Sino-Japanese War and Contemporary Japanese Public Opinion), *Kokka Gakkai Zasshi*, LXVIII (Dec. 1954; Feb. 1955), 101-29, 223-54.

Ōkawa Shūmei. *Nihon Nisenroppyaku Nenshi* (2600 Years of Japanese History). Tokyo: Dai Ichi Shōten, 1939.

Ōkubo Toshiaki. *Mori Arinori* (Biography of Mori Arinori) Tokyo: Bunkyō Shoin, 1944.

Okudaira Takehiko. *Chōsen Kaikoku Kōshō Shimatsu* (Negotiations on the Opening of Korea from Beginning to End). Tokyo: Tōkōshoin, 1935.

Oliver, Robert T. *Korea: Forgotten Nation*. Washington: Public Affairs Press, 1944.

———. *Syngman Rhee: The Man Behind the Myth*. New York: Dodd, Mead, 1955.

Osgood, Cornelius. *The Koreans and their Culture*. New York: Ronald Press Co., 1951.

Parker, E. H. "The Manchu Relations with Korea," *Transactions of the Asiatic Society of Japan*, XV (1887), 96-102.

Passim, Herbert. "The Paekchéng of Korea: A Brief Social History," *Monumenta Nipponica*, XII, No. 3-4 (1956), pp. 27-72.

Pollard, R. T. "American Relations with Korea, 1882-1895," *Chinese Social and Political Science Review*, XVI (1932-33), 425-71.

———. "Dynamics of Japanese Imperialism," *Pacific Historical Review*, VIII, 1 (1939), pp. 5-36.

Powell, E. A. "Japan's Policy in Korea," *Atlantic Monthly*, CXXIX (March 1922), 395-412.

Roggendorf, Joseph. Review of Ike's *The Beginnings of Political Democracy in Japan* in *Monumenta Nipponica*, VIII, No. 1-2 (1952), pp. 440-43.

Romanov, B. A. (Susan Wilbur Jones, trans.). *Russia in Manchuria (1892–1906)*. Ann Arbor: J. W. Edwards, 1953. Detailed, thoroughly documented study based on Russian archives. From 1928 Leningrad edition.

Ross, Frank E. "The American Naval Attack on Shimonoseki in 1863," *Chinese Social and Political Science Review*, XVIII (1934-35), 146-55.

Rossiter, Clinton. "The Old Conservatism and the New Diplomacy," *Virginia Quarterly Review*, XXXII, 1 (1956), pp. 28-49.

Roth, Andrew. *Dilemma in Japan*. Little, Brown & Co., 1945.

Sakai, Robert K. "Feudal Society and Modern Leadership in Satsuma-han," *Journal of Asian Studies*, XVI, 3 (May 1957), pp. 365-76.

Sakurai Yoshiyuki. "Meiji Ki ni okeru Taikan Ishiki no Ichi Kosatsu" (A Consideration of Consciousness of Korea in Meiji Times), *Chōsen Gakkai Hō* (Report of Korean Studies Association), XXI, 1 (1954), pp. 4-5.

Samura Hachirō. *Tokan no Susume* (Let us Go to Korea). Tokyo: Rakuseisha, 1909.

Sanematsu Takamori (adapted by Moriaki Sakamoto). *Great Saigō: The Life of Saigō Takamori*. Tokyo: Kaitakusha, 1942. Undocumented, but seems to have an intimate knowledge of details.

Scalapino, Robert A. *Democracy and the Party Movement in Prewar Japan*. Berkeley: University of California Press, 1953.

Shikata Hiroshi. "Chosen ni okeru Kindai Shihonshugi no Seiritsu Katei" (The Process of Formation of Modern Capitalism in Korea) in *Chōsen Shakai, Keizai Shi Kenkyū* (Studies in Korean Economic and Social History). Tokyo: Tōkōshoin, 1933. Solid, book length study.

Shimomura Fujio. "Nichiro Sensō to Manshū Shijō" (The Russo-Japanese War and the Manchurian Market), *Nagoya University Studies*, Literature Department, XIV.

Shinobu Jumpei. *Kan Hantō* (The Korean Peninsula). Tokyo: Tōkyōdo, 1901. Full of facts and figures.

Shinobu Seizaburō. *Kindai Nihon Gaikoshi* (Modern Japanese Diplomatic History). Tokyo: Chūō Kōron Sha, 1942. A basic work of the Kōza school.

———. *Mutsu Gaikō* (Mutsu's Diplomacy). Tokyo: Sōbunkaku, 1935. Detailed study of events leading up to the Sino-Japanese War, based on primary sources. "Kōza" interpretation not evident.

Smith, Thomas C. *Political Change and Industrial Development in Japan: Government Enterprise, 1868–1880*. Stanford: Stanford University Press, 1955.

Stampp, Kenneth M. *The Peculiar Institution: Slavery in the Ante Bellum South*. New York: Alfred A. Knopf, 1956.

Stead, Alfred (ed.). *Japan by the Japanese*. New York: Dodd, Mead, & Co., 1904. Section on Japanese Diplomacy by N. Ariga especially valuable.

Stoetzel, Jean. *Without the Chrysanthemum and the Sword: A Study of the Attitudes of Youth in Postwar Japan*. New York: Columbia University Press, 1955.

Storry, Richard. *The Double Patriots: A Study of Japanese Nationalism*. London, Chatto & Windus, 1957.

Sunoo Hag-wo'n. "A study of the Development and the Technique of Japanese Imperialism in Korea, 1904–1910," *Korean Review*, I, 1 (1948), pp. 27-51.

Tabohashi Kiyoshi. *Kindai Nissen Kankei no Kenkyū* (A Study of Modern Japanese-Korean Relations). Keijō (Seoul): Chōsen Sōtokufu Chūsūin, 1940. 2 vols.

Detailed and scholarly study of Japanese-Korean relations to the outbreak of the Sino-Japanese War.

———. *Nisshin Seneki Gaikōshi no Kenkyū* (A Study of the Diplomatic History of the Sino-Japanese War). Tokyo: Tokoshoin & Co., 1951. Sequel to the above two-volume work of Tabohashi, this is a detailed study of the events of 1894–95 and contains as well a summary of earlier Japanese-Korean relations which adds a few points not covered in the above volumes. Tabohashi's scholarship is meticulous, his interpretations guarded, and his source material rich. His works were extremely valuable to our present study.

———. *Meiji Gaikōshi* (Diplomatic History of the Meiji Era). Tokyo: Iwanami Shōten, 1934.

———. "Kindai Chōsen ni okeru Kaikō no Kenkyū" (Study of the Opening of Ports in Modern Korea) in *Oda Sensei Shōju Kinen Chōsen Ronshū* (Essays on Korea in Memory of Professor Oda). Keijō (Seoul), 1934.

Takeuchi, Tatsuji. *War and Diplomacy in the Japanese Empire*. Chicago: University of Chicago Press, 1935.

Tanaka Sōgorō. *Seikan Ron Seinan Sensō* (The Conquer Korea Argument and the War of the Southwest). Tokyo: Hakuyōsha, 1939.

Thompson, Kenneth W. "Theories and Problems of Foreign Policy" in Roy C. Macridis (ed.), *Foreign Policy in World Politics*. Englewood Cliffs, N.J.: Prentice-Hall, 1958.

Tōhōykōkai (East Asia Cooperation Association). *Chōsen Ihō* (Report on Korea). Tokyo: Yao Shōten, 1893, This association was organized in 1891 to study Asian problems. Former Foreign Minister Soejima was a prominent member.

Tokutomi Ichirō (ed.). *Kōshaku Katsura Tarō Den* (Life of Katsura). Tokyo, 1917.

Tōyama Shigeki. *Meiji Ishin* (The Meiji Restoration). Tokyo: Iwanami Shōten, 1951. "Kōza" type interpretation; brilliantly argued.

———. "Seikan Ron, Jiyūminken Ron, Hōken Ron" (The Conquer Korea, People's Rights, and Feudalism Arguments), *Rekishigaku Kenkyū*, No. 143 (Jan. 1950), pp. 1-12. Contains keen insights into the relationships between these arguments.

Tōyama Shigeki and Sato Shinichi (eds.). *Nihonshi Kenkyū Nyūmon* (Guide to Japanese Historical Research). Tokyo: Tōkyō Daigaku Shuppan Kai, 1954. Valuable discussion of the state of historical research on Meiji Japan, including Sino-Russo wars and Korean problem.

Treat, Payson J. *Diplomatic Relations between Japan and the United States, 1853–1895*. Stanford: Stanford University Press, 1932. 2 vols.

———. *Diplomatic Relations between Japan and the United States, 1895–1905*. Stanford: Stanford University Press, 1938.

———. "China and Korea, 1885–1895," *Political Science Quarterly*, XLIX (1934), 506-43.

———. "The Cause of the Sino-Japanese War, 1894," *Pacific Historical Review*, VIII, 2 (1939), pp. 149-57.

Tsiang, T. F. "Sino-Japanese Diplomatic Relations, 1870–1894," *Chinese Social and Political Science Review*, XVII (1933–34), 1-106. Used all available Chinese documents; thorough study.

Tsuchiya Takao. *Ishin Keizaishi* (Economic History of the Restoration), Tokyo: Chūō Kōron Sha, 1942. Rōnō interpretation of the Meiji Restoration; brilliantly argued.

Tsuda Saōkichi. "Saigō Takamori Ron" (The Argument about Saigō Takamori), *Chūō Kōron* (Oct. 1957), pp. 280-87.
Tupper, Eleanor and McReynolds, George E. *Japan in American Public Opinion.* New York: Macmillan, 1937.
Uyehara, G. E. *The Political Development of Japan, 1867–1909.* New York, 1910.
Watanabe Ikujirō. *Meijishi Kenkyū* (Study of Meiji History). Tokyo: Kyōritsu Shuppan, 1944. Most thorough treatment of the conquer Korea argument of 1873.
Wilkinson, W. H. *The Corean Government: Constitutional Changes, July 1894–October 1895.* Shanghai: Statistical Department of the Inspectorate General of Customs, 1897.
Williston, Frank G. "Reflections on American-Korean Relations," *Korean Review,* I, 1 (1948), pp. 3-10.
Wright, Mary C. "The Adaptability of Ch'ing Diplomacy: The Case of Korea." *Journal of Asian Studies,* XVII, 3 (May 1958), pp. 363-81.
Yamamoto Yūzō. *Saigō* to *Ōkubo* (Saigō and Ōkubo). Tokyo: Kadokawa Bunko edition, 1954.
Yanaga, Chitoshi. *Japan Since Perry.* New York: McGraw-Hill, 1949.
Yanaibara Tadao. *Nihon Shokumin Seisaku no Kaiko* (Review of Japanese Colonization Policies). Tokyo: Tokyō Daigaku, no date. Chapter 7 discusses Korea.
Yoshino Sakuzō. "Nihon Gaikō no Onjin Shōgun LeGendre" (General LeGendre, Benefactor of Japanese Diplomacy), *Meiji Bunka Kenkyū* (Studies in Meiji Culture) (July, August 1927).
Young, A. Morgan. *Imperial Japan.* New York: Morrow, 1938.

BIBLIOGRAPHIES AND REFERENCE WORKS

Unpublished

Gaimushō (Japanese Foreign Office). "Gaimushō Genzon Kiroku Mokuroku" (Index to Records kept at the Foreign Office at the Present Time). 1947. 8 vols.
———. "Shōshitsu Mokuroku" (Documents Destroyed by Fire). 1947.
Kensei Shiryō Shitsu (Research Room for Materials relating to Constitutional Government). "Kensei Shiryō Shizō Mokuroku" (Catalogue of Treasures in the Kensei Shiryō Collection). 1954. A list of the various subdivisions of this collection, at the Diet Building, Tokyo.
Kindaishi Kondankai (Conference on Modern History). "Tōkyō Nichi Nichi Shimbun Shasetsu Mokuroku" (Index to Editorials in the Tokyo Nichi Nichi Newspaper). 1954. This conference occasionally compiles specialized bibliographical lists, such as this, which may be found at Tokyo University's Meiji Bunko.
"Yoshino Bunko Shomei Mokuroku" (Index to works in the library of Prof. Yoshino Sakuzō). 3 vols. At Tokyo University Law Faculty Library.

Published

Fairbank, John K. and Masataka Banno. *Japanese Studies of Modern China*. Rutland, Vt.: Charles Tuttle, 1955. This work only incidentally touches on studies of Korea, but its notations on the methodology and approaches of Japanese scholars and its introductory comments on the place of Marxism in the thought of Japanese historians were very useful to the present study.

Far Eastern Quarterly bibliographies. Since 1940, usually published in August, continued as *Journal of Asian Studies*.

Honjo Eijiro. *Nihon Keizaishi Daisan Bunken* (Third Bibliography of Japanese Economic History). Tokyo: Nihon Hyōronsha, 1953. 3 vols. Standard bibliography of Japanese history.

Malone, Dumas (ed.). *Dictionary of American Biography*, Vol. X. New York: Scribner's, 1933.

Marcus, Richard (ed.). *Korean Studies Guide*. Berkeley: University of California Press, 1954.

Nachod, Oscar. *Bibliographie von Japan* (continued by Hans Praesent and Wolf Haenisch). Leipzig: Hiersemann, 1926–37. 5 vols.

Nakamura Tetsu *et al* (eds.). *Seijigaku Jiten* (Dictionary of Political Science). Tokyo: Heibonsha, 1954.

Pritchard, Earl H. (ed.). *Bulletin of Far Eastern Bibliography*. Washington: American Council of Learned Societies, 1936–39. 4 vols.

Sakurai Yoshiyuki. *Meiji Nenkan Chōsen Kenkyū Bunkenshi* (Bibliography of Meiji Period Studies of Korea). Keijō (Seoul): Shomotsudōkōkai, 1941. A very careful compilation, which proved extremely useful for the present study.

Tokyo University, Faculty of Law. *Meiji Shimbun Zasshi Bunko Shozō Mokuroku* (Catalogue of Newspapers and Magazines in the Meiji Bunko). Tokyo, 1930–41. 3 vols.

U.S. Library of Congress Reference Dept. (Comp.). *Korea: An Annotated Bibliography of Publications in Far Eastern Languages*. Washington, 1950.

———. *Korea: An Annotated Bibliography of Publications in Western Languages*. Washington, 1950.

Uyehara, Cecil H. (comp.). *Checklist of Archives in the Japanese Ministry of Foreign Affairs, Tokyo, Japan, 1868–1945*, Microfilmed for the Library of Congress, 1949–51. Washington, 1954.

Waseda University, Ōkuma Research Rooms (ed.). *Ōkuma Bunsho Mokuroku* (Catalogue of Ōkuma Documents). Tokyo: Waseda University, 1952.

Wenckstern, Friedrich von. *Bibliography of Japan* (to 1893). Leiden: Brill, 1895.

———. *Bibliography of the Japanese Empire* (1894–1906). Tokyo: Maruzen, 1907.

Romanized titles in characters follow in order of listing above.

Errata: p. 525, character for *ryō* omitted in Kensei Shiryō Shitsu; p. 526, Kaburagi item out of order; Teikoku . . . *Gikai Shi* omitted; p. 527, *Dai Saigō* . . . omitted, now on p. 530; p. 528, Itō Seitoku omitted, for Kuroda title read *Gensui Terauchi* . . .; p. 530, for Yoshino title read *Meiji Bunka Zenshū*; p. 531, Miyakawa omitted; p. 534, Tokutomi omitted.

憲政資料室

大隈研究室

外務省

伊藤家文書

徳大寺実則　　日誌

朝鮮総督府　　朝鮮鉄道史

朝鮮鉄道沿線市場一般

外務省　　日本外交文書

小村外交史

日本外交年表及び主要文書

新生日本外交百年史

通商彙編，通商報告

通商彙纂

韓国事情

鏑木余三男	朝鮮国元山出張復命書
元山商工会議所(編)	元山商工会議所六十年史
花房質義日記	日本外交文書 の 第十巻
京城居留民団役所	京城発達史
京城商工会議所	京城商工会議所二十五年史
内閣統計局	日本帝国統計年鑑
農商務省	韓国貿易年表
	韓国貿易要覧
	韓国事情調査資料
	韓国鉱業調査報告
	韓国に於ける綿産調査
	韓国に於ける農業調査
	対清韓貿易調査報告
	露国大蔵省韓国誌
大蔵省	外国貿易概覧

統監府　韓国各港貿易概況
韓国通覧
居留民団事情要覧
統監府統計年表
在韓国日本人産業団体一覧
朝鮮協会　朝鮮協会会報
第一銀行　韓国に於ける第一銀行
韓国各支店出張所開業依頼
営業情況
平野義太郎　馬城大井憲太郎伝
平塚篤　伊藤博文秘録
井上角五郎　京城の残夢
井上馨伝記編纂会　世外井上侯伝
石河幹明　福沢諭吉伝
板垣退助　自由党史
伊藤博文　朝鮮交渉資料

金子堅太郎　秘書類纂

岩倉公旧蹟保存会　岩倉具視関係文書

福沢諭吉,編者,時事新報

金子堅太郎　伊藤博文伝

漢城週報

片山潜　日本の労働運動

黒龍会　西南紀伝

小松緑　伊藤公全集

近藤吉雄　井上角五郎先生伝

倉知鉄吉　韓国併合の経緯

黒田謙一　日本殖民思想史

葛生能久　日韓合邦秘史

毎日

明治変年史　(新聞集成明治変年史)

宮坂九郎　明治大正昭和歴史資料全集

中山安政　新聞集成明治編年史
西田長寿　平民新聞
日韓通商協会　日韓通商協会報告
大石正巳　談話
大久保利謙　大久保利通文書
大久保利通　大久保利通日記
大塚武松　岩倉具視関係文書
尾崎行雄　学堂懐古録
佐田白芳　征韓評論
新聞雑誌
塩川一太郎　朝鮮通商事情
杉村濬　在韓苦心録
東京経済雑誌
東京日日新聞
東洋拓殖株式会社　朝鮮移住手引草
殖民統計
十年史
二十年史

吉野作造　日本外交の恩人將軍李仙得
郵便報知
藤本庄作　巨人頭山滿翁
古屋哲夫　日本帝国主義の成立をめぐって
大西郷全集
藤村道生　日露戦争の性格に寄せて
長谷川千代松　第一銀行五十年小史
羽島半次郎　江華條約締結当時の追憶
旗田巍　朝鮮史
日高節　明治秘史西郷隆盛暗殺事件
堀誠　米人李仙得建言書について
細川嘉六　現代文明史 #10
井上清　日本帝国主義の形成
石川諒一　自由党大阪事件
神戸正雄　朝鮮農業移民論

北川 修	日清戦争までの日鮮貿易
	歴史科学
清沢 洌	外政家としての大久保利通
	日本外交史
葛生能久	日支交渉外史
	東亜先覚志士記伝
丸山真男	福沢諭吉の哲学
	「国家学会雑誌」
	明治国家の思想
	「日本社会の史的究明」
真崎 勝	保険学行脚
的野半介	江藤南白
宮本又次	防穀令事件と日清戦争
	日清戦争の戦後経　と
	貿易拡張策「経済学研究」

岡 義武　自由党左派とナショナリズム
「社会学評論」
條約改正論議に現はれた当時の対外意識
日清戦争と当時に於ける対外意識

大川周明　日本二千六百年史

大久保利謙　森 有礼

奥平武彦　朝鮮開国交渉始末

櫻井義之　明治期に於ける対韓意識の一考察「朝鮮学会報」

佐村八郎　渡韓のすすめ

四方博　朝鮮に於ける近代資本主義の成立過程
「朝鮮社会経済史研究」

下村富士男　日露戦争と満洲市場

信夫淳平　韓半島

信夫清三郎　近代日本外交史
陸奥外交

田保橋潔　近代日鮮関係の研究
日清戦役外交史の研究
明治外交史
近代朝鮮に於ける開港の研究　小田先生論集

田中惣五郎　征韓論西南戦争

東邦協会　朝鮮彙報

遠山茂樹　明治維新

征韓論・自由民権論

封建論

遠山茂樹

佐藤進一　日本史研究入門

土屋喬雄　維新経済史

津田左右吉　西郷隆盛論

渡辺幾治郎　明治史研究

山本有三　西郷と大久保

矢内原忠雄　日本植民政策の回顧

吉野作造　日本外交の恩人将軍李仙得,

明治文化研究

外務省　外務省現存記録目録
焼失目録
憲政資料所蔵目録
近代史懇談会　東京日日新聞社説目録
吉野文庫名目録
本庄栄治郎　日本経済史第三文献
中村哲　政治学事典
櫻井義之　明治年間朝鮮研究文献誌
東京大学　明治新聞雑誌文庫所蔵目録
早稲田大学　大隈文庫目録

Index

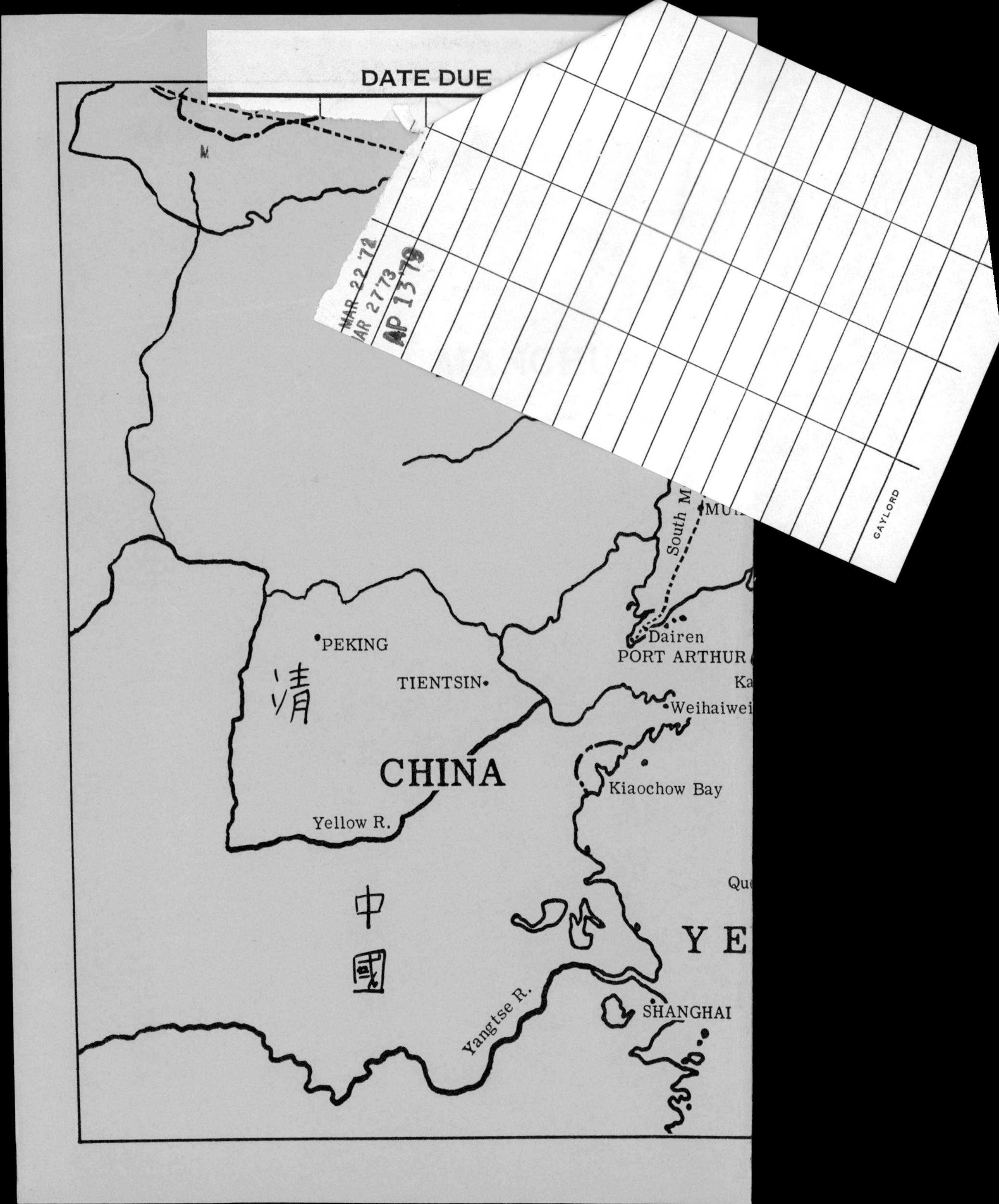
DATE DUE
MAR 22 '72
MAR 27 '73
AP 13 '79
GAYLORD
PEKING
TIENTSIN
清
CHINA
Yellow R.
中
國
Yangtse R.
SHANGHAI
Dairen
PORT ARTHUR
Weihaiwei
Kiaochow Bay
South M
YE